THE ROUTLEDGE COMPANION TO GENDER AND JAPANESE CULTURE

This *Companion* is a comprehensive examination of the varied ways in which gender issues manifest throughout culture in Japan, using a range of international perspectives to examine private and public constructions of identity, as well as gender- and sexuality-inflected cultural production.

The Routledge Companion to Gender and Japanese Culture features both new work and updated accounts of classic scholarship, providing a go-to reference work for contemporary scholarship on gender in Japanese culture. The volume is interdisciplinary in scope, with chapters drawing from a range of perspectives, fields, and disciplines, including anthropology, art history, history, law, linguistics, literature, media and cultural studies, politics, and sociology. This reflects the fundamentally interdisciplinary nature of the dual focal points of this volume—gender and culture—and the ways in which these themes infuse a range of disciplines and subfields.

In this volume, Jennifer Coates, Lucy Fraser, and Mark Pendleton have brought together an essential guide to experiences of gender in Japanese culture today—perfect for students, scholars, and anyone else interested in Japan, culture, gender studies, and beyond.

Jennifer Coates is Senior Lecturer in Japanese Studies at the School of East Asian Studies, University of Sheffield. She is the author of *Making Icons: Repetition and the Female Image in Japanese Cinema, 1945–1964* (2016), as well as a number of journal articles and book chapters on cinema and audiences in postwar and contemporary Japan. Her current ethnographic research project focuses on early postwar film audiences in Japan.

Lucy Fraser is Lecturer in Japanese at The University of Queensland, where she teaches Japanese literature, popular culture, and language. She researches fairy tale studies in Japanese and English, with particular interests in ideas of gender and animals in retellings of folktales and traditional stories. She is the author of *The Pleasures of Metamorphosis: Japanese and English Fairy Tale Transformations of "The Little Mermaid"* (2017). She has translated short stories by writers such as Kawakami Hiromi and Hoshino Tomoyuki and literary and cultural studies criticism by scholars such as Kan Satoko, Fujimoto Yukari, and Honda Masuko.

Mark Pendleton is Lecturer in Japanese Studies at the University of Sheffield. A cultural and social historian by training, his research interests lie in modern and contemporary Japan, East Asian memory studies, and transnational histories of gender and sexuality. He has published in a number of academic journals including *Japanese Studies* and *Asian Studies Review*, and has contributed book chapters on topics related to historical justice and memory, transnational sexual politics in East Asia, and Japanese dark tourism. He is a member of the editorial committee of leading history journal *History Workshop Journal*.

"*The Routledge Companion to Gender and Japanese Culture* is an unprecedented collection of new and updated accounts of original texts which constitutes the most comprehensive overview of both classic and contemporary scholarship in the field of gender and culture. This interdisciplinary-based volume analyzes the distribution of power across genders from all aspects of life in Japan and challenges us to re-examine the crossroads of culture and gender."

Hideko Abe, *Chair and Professor, East Asian Studies, Colby College*

"At last, a handbook on Japanese gender. And one which is both comprehensive and up-to-date in terms of coverage, methodology and theory. This should rightly go straight on to the reading lists of anyone teaching courses on contemporary Japan."

Roger Goodman, *Nissan Professor of Japanese Studies, University of Oxford*

"*The Routledge Companion to Gender and Japanese Culture* offers a wide range of refreshing and critical perspectives on genders and Japanese culture. Particularly impressive is how this volume tackles the complex intersecting issues of gender, race, ethnicity, class, and others. It is informative, accessible, essential reading for anyone who wishes to have a comprehensive understanding of genders in Japan."

Kazue Harada, *Assistant Professor of Japanese, Japanese Language and Culture, Miami University, Ohio*

"*The Routledge Companion to Gender and Japanese Culture* is an important and useful resource with a broad scope of essays from accomplished scholars. This vital collection faithfully reflects the history of the field and paves the way for future research and pedagogy on gender and society in Japan."

Kathryn Hemmann, *Assistant Professor, Japanese Literature and Popular Culture, George Mason University*

THE ROUTLEDGE COMPANION TO GENDER AND JAPANESE CULTURE

Edited by
Jennifer Coates, Lucy Fraser, and Mark Pendleton

LONDON AND NEW YORK

First published 2020
by Routledge
2 Park Square, Milton Park, Abingdon, Oxon OX14 4RN

and by Routledge
52 Vanderbilt Avenue, New York, NY 10017

Routledge is an imprint of the Taylor & Francis Group, an informa business

© 2020 selection and editorial matter, Jennifer Coates, Lucy Fraser, and Mark Pendleton; individual chapters, the contributors

The right of Jennifer Coates, Lucy Fraser, and Mark Pendleton to be identified as the authors of the editorial material, and of the authors for their individual chapters, has been asserted in accordance with sections 77 and 78 of the Copyright, Designs and Patents Act 1988.

All rights reserved. No part of this book may be reprinted or reproduced or utilised in any form or by any electronic, mechanical, or other means, now known or hereafter invented, including photocopying and recording, or in any information storage or retrieval system, without permission in writing from the publishers.

Trademark notice: Product or corporate names may be trademarks or registered trademarks, and are used only for identification and explanation without intent to infringe.

British Library Cataloguing-in-Publication Data
A catalogue record for this book is available from the British Library

Library of Congress Cataloging-in-Publication Data
A catalog record for this book has been requested

ISBN: 978-1-138-89520-1 (hbk)
ISBN: 978-1-315-17958-2 (ebk)

Typeset in Bembo
by Apex CoVantage, LLC

Printed in the United Kingdom
by Henry Ling Limited

CONTENTS

List of figures ix
List of tables x
Acknowledgements xi
Contributor biographies xii
Note on the romanization of Japanese xx

    Introduction: gender and culture in Japan today 1
    Jennifer Coates, Lucy Fraser, and Mark Pendleton

PART I
Theorizing and historicizing gender and Japanese culture 9

  1 Gendering modern Japanese history: a historiographical update 11
     Barbara Molony

  2 Gender in pre-modern Japan 22
     Rajyashree Pandey

  3 Debates in Japanese feminism 31
     Ayako Kano

  4 Gender and language 40
     Miyako Inoue

  5 Masculinity studies in Japan 50
     Emma E. Cook

6	Transgender, non-binary genders, and intersex in Japan S. P. F. Dale	60
7	Gender and ethnicity in urban Japan Jamie Coates	69

PART II
Home, family, and the "private sphere" — 81

8	Gender and the *Koseki* David Chapman	83
9	Attitudes to marriage and childbearing Ekaterina Hertog	92
10	Family, inequality, and the work-family balance in contemporary Japan Aya Ezawa	106
11	Intimacy in and beyond the family Allison Alexy	115
12	Rural gender construction and decline: negotiating risks through nostalgia Anna Vainio	125
13	Changing folk cultures of pregnancy and childbirth Manami Yasui Translated by Lucy Fraser and Madelein Shimizu	135
14	Religion and gender in Japan Yumi Murayama and Erica Baffelli	146

PART III
Work, politics, and the "public sphere" — 155

15	Gender and the law: progress and remaining problems Stephanie Assmann	157
16	Gender and the workplace Helen Macnaughtan	168
17	Sex Work Toru Takeoka	179

18	Gender, labour, and migration in Japan *Helena Hof and Gracia Liu-Farrer*	189
19	Women in electoral politics *Emma Dalton*	199
20	Demanding publics: women and activism *Chelsea Szendi Schieder*	210
21	Lesbians and queer women in Japan *Jane Wallace*	219

PART IV
Cultures of play: leisure, music, and performance — 229

22	Gender and musical subcultures in Japan *Rosemary Overell*	231
23	Gender in digital technologies and cultures *Jennifer Coates and Laura Haapio-Kirk*	240
24	Women and physical culture in Japanese history *Keiko Ikeda*	251
25	Myths of masculinity in the martial arts *Oleg Benesch*	261
26	The continuum of male beauty in contemporary Japan *Masafumi Monden*	270
27	Performing gender: cosplay and otaku cultures and spaces *Emerald King*	279

PART V
Cultural production: literature, cinema, and popular culture — 289

28	Gender in Japanese literature and literary studies *Laura Clark and Lucy Fraser*	291
29	Gender and poetry *Andrew Campana*	302

30 Gender, manga, and anime *Grace En-Yi Ting*	311
31 Cuteness studies and Japan *Joshua Paul Dale*	320
32 Gender and visual culture *Gunhild Borggreen*	331
33 Gender, media, and misogyny in Japan *Sally McLaren*	340
34 Representing girls in cinema *Kate Taylor-Jones and Georgia Thomas-Parr*	351
35 Gendered desires: pornography and consumption *Alexandra Hambleton*	361

PART VI
Texts and contexts: case studies — **371**

36 Gendered high and low culture in Japan: the transgressing flesh in Kawabata's dance writing *Fusako Innami*	373
37 Genre and gender: romantic friendships and the homosocial imperative in the *ninkyō* (chivalrous) genre film *Isolde Standish*	382
38 Girls with arms and girls as arms in anime: the use of girls for "soft" militarism *Akiko Sugawa-Shimada*	391
39 Beyond the "parasite single" *Lynne Nakano*	399
40 Japanese gay men's experiences of gender: negotiating the hetero system *Thomas Baudinette*	408

Index — 418

FIGURES

9.1	Women's perceptions of ideal work-life balance arrangements after marriage	98
9.2	Work-life balance actually expected by women after marriage	99
9.3	Work-life balance desired by men after marriage	99
15.1	Shares of full-time and part-time employees	164
16.1	Male and female labour participation rate: 1960, 1985, 2015	171
16.2	Percentage of workers in non-regular employment by age and sex: 1985 and 2015	172
19.1	Women in upper house	201
19.2	Women in lower house	202
23.1	Stickers used in messaging app LINE	246
31.1	Nagasawa Rosetsu's late 18th c. depiction of a frolicking puppy	323
31.2	Nakahara Junichi's 1941 cover illustration for the magazine *The Shōjo's Friend*	324
31.3	The original Kewpie Mayonnaise jar from 1925	325
31.4	A small girl meets a yuru kyara at the 2018 Yuru Kyara Grand Prix in Osaka	328

TABLES

9.1	Marriage and childbearing trends	94
9.2	Trends in social and economic indicators in Japan	95
9.3	Attitudes to marriage and childbearing	97
9.4	Expectations of marriage	97

ACKNOWLEDGEMENTS

The editors would like to thank all contributing authors for their time, patience, and excellent work. We are also indebted to a senior advisory board who kindly provided feedback on individual chapters, as did some additional anonymous reviewers. Tomoko Aoyama, Andrea Germer, Janet Hunter, Mire Koikari, Vera Mackie, Mark McLelland, Laura Miller, and Hiroko Takeda all gave generously of their time and expertise to strengthen the volume and its contents. Any remaining errors are our responsibility. Our gratitude also goes to the artist Pyuupiru for allowing the use of her captivating self-portrait on the cover of this volume, and to Emily Wakeling for facilitating the relationship with Pyuupiru.

We are grateful to our friends and families for their constant support throughout the production of this volume, and to colleagues and co-workers who have encouraged the project throughout its development. A volume of this size requires a significant amount of time, and we are conscious that it has been possible to commit our own time to this project thanks to family members, friends, and colleagues stepping in to relieve us of other tasks, both at home and at work. We greatly appreciate the often-invisible labour performed by those allies both in and outside academia who have made our work on this volume possible.

CONTRIBUTOR BIOGRAPHIES

Allison Alexy is an assistant professor in the Departments of Asian Languages and Cultures, and Women's Studies at the University of Michigan. Trained as a cultural anthropologist, she holds a BA from the University of Chicago and a PhD from Yale University. Her research examines ideals and experiences of family lives, constructions of intimacy, and legal responses to family conflicts in Japan. She has co-edited two collections: *Home and Family in Japan* (Routledge 2011) and *Intimate Japan* (Hawai'i 2019). Her book *Intimate Disconnections: Divorce and the Romance of Independence* is forthcoming from the University of Chicago Press.

Stephanie Assmann is a professor in the School of Economics and Management at Hyogo University, Kobe, Japan. Her fields of interest are the social anthropology of gender and employment, consumption, and food. Recent publications on gender and employment include "Diversity in the Japanese Firm" (*Handbook of Japanese Management*, Routledge, 2016, edited by Parissa Haghirian) and "Gender Equality in Japan: The Equal Employment Opportunity Law Revisited" (*The Asia Pacific Journal Japan Focus* 44 (2) 2014).

Erica Baffelli is currently Senior Lecturer in Japanese Studies at The University of Manchester (UK). Before arriving at Manchester in 2013, she was Senior Lecturer in Asian Religions at the University of Otago (New Zealand 2007–2013). She is interested in religion in contemporary Japan, with a focus on groups founded from the 1970s onwards. Recent publications include: (with Ian Reader) *Dynamism and the Ageing of a Japanese "New" Religion* (2019); *Media and New Religions in Japan* (2016); Baffelli and Reader (eds), *Aftermath: the Impact and Ramifications of the Aum Affair* (special issue of the *Japanese Journal of Religious Studies* 39 (1) 2012).

Thomas Baudinette is Lecturer in Japanese Studies in the Department of International Studies at Macquarie University. Thomas's scholarly research focuses upon the Japanese gay media landscape and the circulation of Japanese queer pop culture in Southeast Asia. His work has appeared in *Japan Forum*, *East Asian Journal of Popular Culture*, *Language and Sexuality*, and *Continuum*. He was awarded the 2016 Ian Nish Prize by the British Association for Japanese Studies.

Contributor biographies

Oleg Benesch is Senior Lecturer in East Asian History at the University of York. He is the author of *Inventing the Way of the Samurai: Nationalism, Internationalism, and Bushido in Modern Japan* (Oxford University Press 2014) and, together with Ran Zwigenberg, *Japan's Castles: Citadels of Modernity in War and Peace* (Cambridge University Press 2019). For more information on Oleg and his research, please see www.olegbenesch.com

Gunhild Borggreen is an associate professor in art history and visual culture at the Department of Arts and Cultural Studies, University of Copenhagen. She has published in journals and anthologies on issues within Japanese contemporary art and visual culture that include gender, identity, and performance, as well as cultural dimensions of technology and robotics. Parts of her research include the reception of Japanese art in Denmark and Scandinavia. Recently, Gunhild has been engaged in field study research on Japanese art festivals and collaborative modes of artistic practice.

Andrew Campana is an assistant professor of Japanese literature and media in the Department of Asian Studies at Cornell University. He has performed and published widely in both English and Japanese as a multimedia poet and translator and is currently working on a book manuscript on poetry across multiple media forms in twentieth-century Japan.

David Chapman is Associate Professor of Japanese Studies in the School of Languages and Cultures at the University of Queensland in Australia. His research interests include history, identity, and citizenship. He is the author of *The Bonin Islanders 1830 to the Present: Narrating Japanese Nationality* (Lexington Books 2016), co-author of *Japan in Australia: Culture, Context and Connection* (Routledge forthcoming) and *Koseki, Identification and Documentation: Japan's Household Registration System and Citizenship* (Routledge 2014), and author of *Zainichi Korean Identity and Ethnicity* (Routledge 2007).

Laura Clark is an early career researcher specializing in contemporary Japanese fiction and gender issues, with a particular interest in connections between popular cultural products and social values. Her PhD research focused on the career of Murakami Haruki and Japanese discourses of gender and normalcy, and she has previously published on depictions of masculinity in Murakami's works. She teaches Japanese literature and language.

Jamie Coates is Lecturer in East Asian Studies at the University of Sheffield. Trained as an anthropologist, he researches how migration experiences, creative practices, and media consumption among young Chinese people in Japan and China afford new kinds of imaginaries and identities.

Jennifer Coates is Senior Lecturer in Japanese Studies at the School of East Asian Studies, University of Sheffield. She is the author of *Making Icons: Repetition and the Female Image in Japanese Cinema, 1945–1964* (Hong Kong University Press 2016), as well as a number of journal articles and book chapters on cinema and audiences in postwar and contemporary Japan. Her current ethnographic research project focuses on early postwar film audiences in Japan.

Emma E. Cook is a social anthropologist with interests ranging from gender, employment, family, and intimacy, to food, health, risk, emotion, and well-being. She is the co-editor of *Intimate Japan: Ethnographies of Closeness and Conflict* (University of Hawai'i Press 2019) and the author of *Reconstructing Adult Masculinities: Part-Time Work in Contemporary Japan* (Routledge

2016). She has published in *Cultural Anthropology's Theorizing the Contemporary, Fieldsights* series and in the *Japanese Review of Cultural Anthropology (JRCA), Japanese Studies, Asian Anthropology, Social Science Japan Journal*, and *Asian Journal of Social Science*.

Joshua Paul Dale founded the new academic field of cuteness studies. He is a co-editor of *The Aesthetics and Affects of Cuteness* (Routledge 2017) and the editor of "Cute Studies," a special issue of the *East Asian Journal of Popular Culture* (Intellect 2016). His book on the cute and kawaii aesthetics and the affective response that underlies them is forthcoming from Profile Books in 2021. Dale is a tenured faculty member (*gaikokujinkyōshi*) in the Department of Foreign Languages and Literatures at Tokyo Gakugei University. He holds a PhD in English from the University at Buffalo.

S. P. F. Dale is an independent researcher specializing in gender and sexuality studies, queer studies, sociology, and minority issues in Japan. Dale received a PhD in global studies from Sophia University and has formerly taught at Hitotsubashi University and Sophia University, as well as other institutions in Tokyo. Her research so far has focused on x-gender and non-binary identity in Japan.

Emma Dalton is Lecturer in Japanese in the School of Global, Urban and Social Studies at RMIT University. She has lectured at universities in Australia, New Zealand, and Japan for over a decade in the areas of Japanese language and Japanese and Asian studies. Her research interests include the relationship between women and the Japanese state, and especially the position of women in politics. She publishes widely for academic, student, and media audiences.

Aya Ezawa is University Lecturer in Japanese studies at Leiden University. Her research focuses, among others, on the gender and class dimensions of social policy. She is the author of *Single Mothers in Contemporary Japan: Motherhood, Class, and Reproductive Practice* (Lexington Books).

Lucy Fraser is Lecturer in Japanese at The University of Queensland, where she teaches Japanese literature, popular culture, and language. She researches fairy tale studies in Japanese and English, with particular interests in ideas of gender and animals in retellings of folktales and traditional stories. She is the author of *The Pleasures of Metamorphosis: Japanese and English Fairy Tale Transformations of "The Little Mermaid"* (Wayne State University Press 2017). She has translated short stories by writers such as Kawakami Hiromi and Hoshino Tomoyuki and literary and cultural studies criticism by scholars such as Kan Satoko, Fujimoto Yukari, and Honda Masuko.

Laura Haapio-Kirk is a PhD researcher on the ERC-funded Anthropology of Smartphones and Smart Ageing project at the Department of Anthropology, University College London. She was also a visiting researcher at the Graduate School of Human Sciences, Osaka University, conducting fieldwork in Kyoto, Japan. Prior to this, she was a research assistant and public engagement fellow on the ERC-funded Why We Post project and has published about digital education in anthropology. She has a masters in visual anthropology from the University of Oxford and is interested in drawing as both a research method and tool for dissemination.

Alexandra Hambleton is an assistant professor in the Department of English at Tsuda University. She received her PhD from The University of Tokyo's Graduate School of Interdisciplinary

Information Studies in 2017. Her work focuses on gender, sexuality, and media in contemporary Japan, and she is the author of "When Women Watch: The Subversive Potential of Female-Friendly Pornography in Japan" (*Porn Studies* 2015) and "Women and Sexual Desire in the Japanese Popular Media" (in *The Precarious Self: Women and the Media in Asia*, 2012).

Ekaterina Hertog works at the Department of Sociology at the University of Oxford. She analyses gender differences in time use in East Asia. Her current research focuses on the gender imbalances in the domestic division of labour. She has a number of papers on this topic available online, including "Domestic Division of Labour and Fertility Preference in China, Japan, South Korea, and Taiwan," in *Demographic Research*, and a working paper "Do Better-Educated Couples Share Domestic Work More Equitably in Japan? It Depends on the Day of the Week," looking at the link between education and gender equality in domestic work in Japan.

Helena Hof, PhD, is a research associate at the Institute of Asia-Pacific Studies and a member of the Institute of Asian Migrations, both at Waseda University, Japan. Her sociological research lies at the intersections of mobility studies, skilled migration, global cities, and diversity and gender at the workplace. Her most recent publications are "The Eurostars Going Global: Distinction and Alternative Lifepaths in Young Europeans' Migration to Asia," forthcoming in *Mobilities*, and "'Worklife Pathways' to Singapore and Japan: Gender and Racial Dynamics in Europeans' Mobility to Asia," *Social Science Japan Journal* 21 (1) 2018. Her ORCID is: 0000-0002-4131-3498.

Keiko Ikeda is a professor in the Faculty of Education at Hokkaido University, Sapporo, Japan. She researches and publishes in a wide area, including topics stemming from the history of sport (particularly British and Japanese), sport journalism, and feminism in sport. Her initial major monograph, emanating from her doctoral dissertation, focuses upon the pioneering British journalist Pierce Egan (1774–1849) and was published as *Pre-Victorian Sport: Pierce Egan's "Sporting World"* (Fumaido Publishing 1996). Professor Ikeda has been a visiting Fellow at both the Centre for the Study of Social History at University of Warwick and in the International Centre for Sport History at De Montfort University in the United Kingdom.

Fusako Innami is an assistant professor in Japanese and performance studies in the School of Modern Languages and Cultures, Durham University, UK. Her research interests include the body and the senses, love and intimacy, and translation, including inter-media translation of the body into language and the cross-cultural circulation of ideas, particularly phenomenological and psychoanalytic thoughts. Her publications include articles in *Culture, Theory and Critique* and *Contemporary Japan*; performing arts articles for Bunkamura, *Danceart*, and Glyndebourne Opera; and a book manuscript on touch (under review). She received her MA from New York University and a DPhil from the University of Oxford.

Miyako Inoue teaches linguistic anthropology and Japan studies at Stanford University. Her first book, titled *Vicarious Language: The Political Economy of Gender and Speech in Japan* (University of California Press), examines a phenomenon commonly called "women's language" in Japanese modern society in its critical linkage with Japan's national and capitalist modernity. She is currently working on a book-length project on a social history of "verbatim" in Japanese. She traces the historical development of the Japanese shorthand technique used in the Diet since the late nineteenth century and of the stenographic typewriter introduced to the Japanese court after Word War II.

Ayako Kano is Professor of Japanese Studies in the Department of East Asian Languages and Civilizations at the University of Pennsylvania. She is also Core Faculty Member in the Gender, Sexuality, and Women's Studies Program and Graduate Group Faculty Member in History and in Comparative Literature and Literary Theory. Her books include *Acting Like a Woman in Modern Japan: Theater, Gender, and Nationalism* (Palgrave 2001) and *Japanese Feminist Debates: A Century of Contention on Sex, Love, and Labor* (University of Hawai'i Press 2016). She also co-edited *Rethinking Japanese Feminisms* (University of Hawai'i Press 2018) with Julia Bullock and James Welker.

Emerald King is a lecturer in Japanese at La Trobe University, Australia. Her research is divided between women in Japanese literature from the late 1960s to the early 2000s and reading costumes as text. Her publications reflect this research divide: "*Sakura ga meijiru*: Unlocking the shōjo wardrobe—cosplay; manga; 2.5D space" (2019); "Women Who Don't Eat in Japanese Literature" (2018); "Absent Mothers, Constructed Families and Rabbit Babies" (2017); "Tailored Translations—Translating and Transporting Cosplay Costumes across Texts, Cultures, and Dimensions" (2016).

Gracia Liu-Farrer is Professor of Sociology at the Graduate School of Asia-Pacific Studies and Director of Institute of Asian Migrations, Waseda University, Japan. Her research investigates cross-border migration and social mobility in Asia and Europe. She is the co-editor of *Routledge Handbook of Asian Migration* (2018, with Brenda Yeoh) and the author of *Immigrant Japan: Mobility and Belonging in an Ethno-Nationalist Society* (Cornell University Press 2019).

Helen Macnaughtan is Chair of the Japan Research Centre and Senior Lecturer in International Business and Management for Japan at SOAS University of London. Her research interests focus on a broad range of topics relating to gender, employment, and sport in Japan. Her publications have focused on the history of women and work and the gendering of employment in Japan, the role of women as consumers of home appliances in postwar Japan, and the story of Japan's gold medal victory in women's volleyball at the Tokyo 1964 Olympics. Publications can be accessed at: http://soas.academia.edu/HelenMacnaughtan.

Sally McLaren was until recently based in Japan and held positions lecturing in Japanese popular culture, media, and gender studies at Kwansei Gakuin University, Doshisha University, and Doshisha Women's College of Liberal Arts. She currently tutors in Japanese language at The University of New South Wales and in media law and ethics at Western Sydney University. Her research takes an interdisciplinary approach, focusing on gender, media, and power in the Asia-Pacific region.

Barbara Molony, Professor of Japanese History at Santa Clara University, co-President of the Coordinating Council for Women in History, and past president of the American Historical Association Pacific Coast Branch, specializes in research on women's rights, transnational feminisms, and the construction and representation of gender in Japan and East Asia. She has published more than two dozen articles and chapters on these topics. She has also co-authored or co-edited *Women's Activism and "Second Wave" Feminism: Transnational Histories* (with Jennifer Nelson, 2017), *Gender in Modern East Asia* (with Janet Theiss and Hyaeweol Choi, 2016), *Modern East Asia: An Integrated History* (with Jonathan Lipman and Michael Robinson, 2010), *Asia's New Mothers: Crafting Gender Roles and Childcare Networks in East and Southeast Asian Societies* (with Ochiai Emiko, 2008), and *Gendering Modern Japanese History* (with Kathleen Uno, 2005). She is an associate editor of *Women and Social Movements in Modern Empires since 1820*. She is co-author of *Ichikawa Fusae: A Political Biography* (forthcoming).

Masafumi Monden is a lecturer in Japanese studies at the University of Western Australia, specializing in contemporary Japanese culture. He lectures and publishes widely in the areas of clothing, art, beauty, youth, and popular culture, and is the author of *Japanese Fashion Cultures: Dress and Gender in Contemporary Japan* (2015). He is currently conducting research on cultural imaginations of Japanese girlhood and boyhood and the cultural history of fashion and the body in Japan. Dr Monden is a recent recipient of the Japan Foundation Japanese Studies Fellowship (2016) and The National Library of Australia Fellowship in Japan Studies (2017).

Yumi Murayama received her PhD in theology from The University of St. Andrew, Scotland. She is currently Research Associate at the Nanzan Institute for Religion and Culture, Nanzan University, Nagoya. Her research focuses on gender and religion, and she is currently developing a project on gender and new religious movements in Japan. Recent publications include "Prophet in the Twilight: Yanaihara Tadao's Intellectual Resistance Against the Asia-Pacific War" in W. Brecher and M. Myers (eds) *Japan's Asia-Pacific War as Lived and Remembered: New Interpretations* (University of Hawaii Press 2019) and "The Samurai Christians: Uchimura, Ebina, and their Bible" in K. K. Yeo and Melanie Baffes (eds) *Text and Context: Vernacular Approaches to the Bible in Global Christianity* (Wipf and Stock 2018).

Lynne Nakano is Professor in the Department of Japanese Studies at The Chinese University of Hong Kong. Her research interests include volunteerism in Japan, and women, gender, and family in Hong Kong, Japan, and China. She is currently conducting research on special education in Japan. She is author of the book *Community Volunteers in Japan: Everyday Stories of Social Change* and numerous book chapters and articles.

Rosemary Overell is Lecturer at the University of Otago, New Zealand. She considers how gendered subjectivities are co-constituted by and through mediation, drawing particularly on Lacanian psychoanalysis to explore a variety of mediated sites. In particular, she considers the intersections between affect and signification and how these produce gender. She is the author of *Affective Intensities in Extreme Music Scenes* (Palgrave 2014) and editor of *Orienting Feminisms* (with Catherine Dale, Palgrave 2018). Rosemary is also a regular contributor to *un* magazine.

Rajyashree Pandey is Professor of Japanese Studies at the Politics department of Goldsmiths, University of London. She is the author of *Perfumed Sleeves and Tangled Hair: Body, Woman and Desire in Medieval Japanese Narratives* (University of Hawaii Press 2016) and *Writing and Renunciation in Medieval Japan: The Works of the Poet-Priest Kamo no Chōmei* (University of Michigan Press 1998). She has also published articles in a wide range of journals from *Monumenta Nipponica* to *Postcolonial Studies* on medieval Japanese literature and Buddhism, as well as on gender, sexuality, and Japanese popular culture.

Mark Pendleton is Lecturer in Japanese Studies at the University of Sheffield. A cultural and social historian by training, his research interests lie in modern and contemporary Japan, East Asian memory studies, and transnational histories of gender and sexuality. He has published in a number of academic journals, including *Japanese Studies* and *Asian Studies Review*, and has contributed book chapters on topics related to historical justice and memory, transnational sexual politics in East Asia, and Japanese dark tourism. He is a member of the editorial committee of leading history journal *History Workshop Journal*.

Chelsea Szendi Schieder is an associate professor in the School of Economics at Aoyama Gakuin University in Tokyo, Japan. She writes about protest, women, violence, and Japan for academic and general audiences. Her articles on women and activism have appeared in *Monthly Review*, *Dissent*, and *World Policy Journal*. Her book on the gendered politics of protest in the 1960s in Japan, entitled *Co-Ed Revolution: The Female Student in the Japanese New Left*, is forthcoming with Duke University Press. Her next project will consider the social impact of shifting energy policies in postwar Japan.

Madelein Shimizu is a member of the Japan Association of Translators, specializing in advertising, manufacturing, economics, family registers (*koseki*), and birth certificates. She holds a Master of Arts in Japanese Interpreting and Translation (MAJIT) from the University of Queensland.

Isolde Standish is a freelance writer and emeritus reader in film and media at SOAS, University of London. She has published extensively on Japanese cinema. Her main publications include *Myth and Masculinity in the Japanese Cinema: Towards a Political Reading of the Tragic Hero* (Routledge/Curzon 2000); *A New History of Japanese Cinema: A Century of Narrative Film* (Continuum 2005); and *Politics, Porn and Protest: Japanese Avant-Garde Cinema in the 1960s and 1970s* (Continuum 2011). She is currently working on a book-length study of Ōshima Nagisa for which she received a two-year Leverhulme Major Research Fellowship.

Akiko Sugawa-Shimada is Professor in the Graduate School of Urban Innovation at Yokohama National University, Japan. Dr Sugawa-Shimada is the author of a number of books and articles on anime, manga, and cultural studies, including *Girls and Magic: How Have Girl Heroes Been Accepted?* (2013), which won the 2014 Japan Society of Animation Studies Award, as well as chapters in *Japanese Animation: East Asian Perspectives* (2013), *Teaching Japanese Popular Culture* (2016), *Shojo Across Media* (2019), and *Women's Manga in Asia and Beyond* (2019), and, as co-author, *Contents Tourism in Japan* (2017). Her website is: akikosugawa.2-d.jp

Toru Takeoka is an associate professor in the Department of Sociology, Ritsumeikan University. His research interest lies in urban sociology, particularly the sociology of urban spaces and occupations, and is based on fieldwork conducted in Tokyo's Kabukicho red-light district. Currently, he is working on secondary analysis of original records of social surveys conducted around the 1950s to investigate the origins of urban sociology and the sociology of work. His dissertation on the Kabukicho district was published as *Ikinobiru toshi* (The city living on) (Shinyosha 2017), and the book was awarded the 2018 Prize for Young Scholars by the Japan Association for Urban Sociology.

Kate Taylor-Jones is Professor of East Asian Cinema at the University of Sheffield. She is the co-editor of *International Cinema and the Girl* (Palgrave Macmillan 2015) and *Prostitution and Sex Work in Global Cinema: New Takes on Fallen Women* (Palgrave Macmillan 2017) and has published widely in a variety of fields. Her latest monograph study, *Divine Work: Japanese Colonial Cinema and Its Legacy*, was published by Bloomsbury Press in 2017. Kate is editor-in-chief of *The East Asian Journal of Popular Culture*, and her forthcoming book, *Ninagawa Mika, Miyake Kyoko,*

Contributor biographies

and Ando Momoko: Shōjo Dreams and Unruly Idols, will be published with Edinburgh University Press in 2020.

Georgia Thomas-Parr is a PhD candidate at The University of Sheffield. Her ethnographic research observes the relation between anime fandom and feminine adolescence in the United Kingdom. She has a BA in film studies and English literature from Bangor University and makes visual essays under the title "Visions of Girlhood."

Grace En-Yi Ting is an assistant professor in gender studies at the University of Hong Kong. She specializes in queer and feminist approaches to Japanese literary and cultural studies, with an emphasis on women writers and girls' culture. She is currently working on a book manuscript titled *Minor Intimacies: Queerness, the Normative, and the Everyday in Contemporary Japan*, which theorizes the potential of "queer readings" for post-1980s representations of femininities and the everyday in Japan, seen against a broader context involving transnational flows of literary and popular cultural texts as well as queer theory.

Anna Vainio is a doctoral researcher at the School of East Asian Studies at the University of Sheffield. Working in the field of anthropology, her doctoral thesis looks at long-term developmental processes in rural Tohoku both before and after the 2011 disaster. Her overall research interests focus on community development in post-growth contexts, traditionalism and heritage in the construction of ideas of rural development, and the role of affect and imagination in understanding micro-level experiences of macro-level policies.

Jane Wallace was awarded her PhD from the University of Leeds in December 2018. Her doctoral research examined community practice among LGBTQ+ communities in the Kansai region of Japan. Jane spent an extended period in the region carrying out ethnographic research. Since graduating, Jane has established a career in research development in the United Kingdom. She currently works for a national women's sector organization managing the strategic, research, and impact elements of a national project. Jane is passionate about applying lessons from her doctoral research to effect genuine systems change within the UK third sector.

Manami Yasui is Professor at the International Research Center for Japanese Studies (Nichibunken), Kyoto, Japan. She received her degree in literature from Osaka University in 1997. Her research encompasses Japanese folklore studies and cultural anthropology. She continues to conduct fieldwork in Japan and Micronesia in order to shed light on folk customs and human relations as they relate to changes sin practices relating to pregnancy and childbirth, medical care, and more.

NOTE ON THE ROMANIZATION OF JAPANESE

Japanese names are given in the Japanese manner of family name first, followed by the given name. Where a Japanese academic publishes in English and uses the Anglophone convention of given name followed by family name, authors have given their names in the same order. For the romanization of Japanese words in the text, macrons indicate long vowels, but are not given in words commonly used in English (for example, Tokyo rather than Tōkyō).

Authors have used the standard English translations of the titles of books, magazines, television shows, and films; where a text has been distributed under an alternative English title, that title is cited as "a.k.a." Japanese titles are given in brackets at the first mention of each text, alongside the date of publication or release in Japan.

All translations are the author's own unless otherwise indicated.

INTRODUCTION
Gender and culture in Japan today

Jennifer Coates, Lucy Fraser, and Mark Pendleton

During the planning, writing, and editing of this volume, gender has become a primary focus of public discussion around the world. At the time of writing, we are in the middle of a dynamic global reconsideration of gender and its relation to many different aspects of culture: public and private, global and domestic, and popular and "high" culture. Though these debates have manifested in new and intensified forms, they reflect long-standing contestations over the cultural politics of gender. The chapters to follow draw from decades of rigorous scholarship, embedded fieldwork, and the collective expertise of the community that Barbara Molony's chapter describes emerging in 1975. In this short introduction, we will briefly sketch some developing concerns in the field that, we believe, will shape the scholarship still to come.

Aided by ever-evolving technologies of communication that carry news, updates, gossip, protest, and accusation around the world in seconds, popular understanding of the gendered behaviours, spaces, places, and identities that inform culture is at a moment of rapid expansion. In recent years, the "whisper networks" that once carried a large portion of what we know, and what we think we know, about others' gender identities, gendered behaviours, and modes of engagement have become very public indeed, and this has significant implications for how we study gender today. At the same time, more traditional modes of tracking the operations of gender in daily life such as the Gender Equality Bureau Cabinet Office and the World Equality Forum's annual Gender Gap Report show slower yet significant changes in gender-related circumstances at a population level and as global comparative statistics, respectively. This edited volume seeks to acknowledge the history of the field and begin to address seismic shifts in the wake of today's popular gender-related social movements, connecting these up with the macro trends emerging at a global level.

Shifts in the field: gender, culture, and #MeToo in Japan

Since October 2017, people around the world have been sharing their experiences of gender discrimination and abuses of power on the micro-blogging site Twitter, using the phrase #MeToo. Japan's own #MeToo movement, which uses both the English language phrase and the Japanese #私も, put the nation among the top ten users of the hashtag in the first weeks after Hollywood actress Alyssa Milano echoed activist Tarana Burke's 2006 use of the phrase, sparking the global movement (Pesek 2018). #MeToo-related tweets totalled around 60,000 over two months in Japan, the eighth largest by nation in the world according to an Asahi Shimbun study based on analysis by Crimson Hexagon (Mishima et al. 2017).

When a blogger using the name Ha-Chu accused a prominent Dentsu advertising employee of sexual harassment on 16 December 2017, the number of tweets increased by 10,000 from 17–18 December, pushing Japan to third place worldwide among nations using the hashtag. #MeToo surfaced again when opposition lawmakers held up papers bearing the slogan in the Diet before a joint hearing on allegations of sexual harassment against the Administrative Vice Finance Minister Fukuda Junichi on 20 April 2018 (Yamagishi 2018). Following the delivery of a formal letter of protest from TV Asahi News Corp to the Finance Ministry complaining about the alleged sexual harassment of a female reporter, Internal Affairs Minister and State Minister for Gender Equality Noda Seiko announced plans to hold hearings for women working in the media to discuss sexual harassment. As the initial response to the global #MeToo movement diversified in Japan into #WithYou, a hashtag acknowledging the reluctance of victims to speak up about sexual harassment and abuse, 86 female journalists formed the Women in Media Network in May 2018, organizing to build solidarity for victims and expose perpetrators.

While aspects of the ongoing conversation around #MeToo in Japan resemble the wider global discourse on the topic, certain issues and phrasing specific to Japan can shed light on the gender-related harassment issues that do not yet have a name in many other countries and languages. For example, alongside #WithYou, Japanese media coverage also includes discussion of the "black box," the term journalist Itō Shiori has used to describe the way allegations of gendered abuses of power are boxed up and concealed from view (Itō 2017). In this respect, Japanese media discourse was ahead of the global turn to examining gender-related abuse and harassment in popular culture and everyday life. Almost five months before #MeToo began trending globally in October 2017, Itō brought the issue to national attention. Itō held a public press conference at Tokyo District Court on 29 May 2017 to announce her intention to file a petition to re-open a case against Yamaguchi Noriyuki, then the Washington Bureau chief of the Tokyo Broadcasting System (TBS). Itō accused Yamaguchi of drugging and sexually assaulting her on 3 April 2015 (Watanabe 2017). After viewing security footage to confirm her recollection of the events that occurred at the Sheraton Miyako Hotel in Tokyo, Itō filed a criminal complaint with Takanawa police station on 30 April 2015 (McNeill 2017). On 8 June 2015, the case was transferred to the First Section of the Metropolitan Police Department in Tokyo and Itō was informed that a scheduled arrest warrant for Yamaguchi had been cancelled. Prosecutors dropped the charges against Yamaguchi on 22 July 2016.

When Tokyo prosecutors rejected Itō's petition to overturn the decision in 2016, she decided to go public with her case. In September 2017, the 28-year-old filed a civil lawsuit against Yamaguchi, a senior journalist with close ties to Prime Minister Abe Shinzō. Japanese and English language news outlets picked up the story almost immediately and followed Itō's case closely for a number of years (Otake and Osaki 2017; Watanabe 2017; Hernon 2018; Rich 2017). Yamaguchi responded to the allegations in an open letter to Itō published in the monthly magazine *Hanada* (Yamaguchi 2017), further fuelling media coverage. Japanese Twitter users' strong response to the #MeToo movement (Twitter 2018) and development of the original #WithYou response could be attributed in part to the ongoing discussion of Itō's case at the time the hashtag gained popular attention around the world.

Itō alleges that a "black box" has been placed over her case, hiding the original crime, the unwillingness of law enforcement to investigate, and the prosecutors' reluctance to bring Yamaguchi to trial (Itō 2017). She argues that Japan's bureaucratic approach to the prosecution of sex-related crimes discourages victims from reporting rape and assault, much less sexual harassment and "power harassment" (a Japanese term for harassment perpetrated by those with social or politicial power). Despite documentary evidence, victims often report widespread unwillingness to believe their stories. For example, the TV Asahi News Corp journalist mentioned previously gained the support of her employer only after circumventing internal resistance and taking her story, complete with taped records of the conversations in question, to rival news outlet Shūkan Shinchō (Asahi Shinbun 2018). In 2014, a survey on violence against women conducted by the Gender Equality Bureau Cabinet Office (*Naikakufu danjokyōdō sankaku kyoku*) found that of 117 female respondents with experience of forced sexual activity, only 4.3 percent had contacted police (2014). In the same year, only 37.2 percent of those prosecuted for sex-related assaults were indicted. As McLaren argues in this volume, Itō's experience brings to light an entrenched culture of sexism and misogyny across the media industry that reflects Japan's wider social, legal, and political cultures. Other chapters in this volume also address the media representation of those cultures (Baudinette; Dale; Coates and Haapio-Kirk; Taylor-Jones and Thomas-Parr).

Yet as Linda Hasunuma and Ki-Young Shin argue, "backlash" both online and in print journalism has slowed the progress of the Japanese #Me Too movement to the point that South Korean #MeToo discourse, initially lagging behind, has now overtaken Japan in terms of accusations made and investigative discourse sustained (2019, 102). This would seem an appropriate juncture to pick up the issue in scholarship on gender in Japan, exploring the roots of the online moment as well as its successes and failures.

More than a decade ago, *Gender and Power in the Japanese Visual Field* (Mostow et al. 2003) raised the question of how "the cultural constructions of gender and sexuality serve the purposes of power" (Mostow 2003, 1). Following Chino Kaori's groundbreaking essay "Gender in Japanese Art" (*Nihon bijutsu no jendā*, 1993), which demonstrated that an idea of the "feminine" has been historically appropriated by male elites, masking masculine power and its operations (2003), Joshua Mostow highlighted "the essentially gendered nature of power in Japanese cultural self-definition" (2003, 8). The events, reportage, and responses described previously underline the importance of continuing this investigation into the relations between gender and power, not only in the field of visual culture, but across public and private or domestic cultures, as well as in Japan's legal system, educational sphere, and leisure cultures.

Today, scholars and cultural commentators continue to debate the distribution of power across gendered demographics in everyday life. In 2018, for the first time, Japan rose rather than fell on the World Economic Forum's Gender Gap Report; however, Gill Steel argues that we must move "beyond the gender gap" (2019) to understand the distribution of power relative to gender in Japanese everyday life. While Japanese women are reporting increased levels of happiness (Steel 2019, 6), Japanese men are reportedly significantly less happy, and the population overall are "fairly unhappy" (Steel 2019, 6). In order to better understand the nuanced distribution of power, happiness, aspiration, and satisfaction across the genders, this volume seeks to avoid conflating "gender" with "women," "minority," or "disempowered." Instead we trace the operations of gendering across a broad range of positions, identifications, and daily life circumstances to better understand the role of gender in Japanese culture today.

In the first chapter of this volume, Molony praises the turn to studying masculinities in Japanese studies of gender across the last quarter century, noting that while men have been the subjects of a great quantity of scholarship, they had previously been "unmarked by gender considerations" (in relation to literary studies, see also Clark and Fraser). Also in this volume, Emma Cook argues for greater nuance to our understanding of Japanese masculinities, "also interrogating the complex ways in which women co-construct and reinforce norms and ideals of masculinities." In the organization of this volume, we have attempted to challenge any simplistic binary understandings or easy boundaries around ideas of "gender," "culture," and "Japan." For this reason, our opening section contextualizes overview survey chapters on gender in Japanese history with studies of groups and individuals often relegated to the sidelines of the field or considered other in relation to an imagined basic unit of subjectivity that is then gendered male or female. Encompassing studies on transgender rights and recognition in Japan (S. P. F. Dale), and gender and its operations in non-Japanese communities living in Japan (Jamie Coates), we have attempted to begin from a stance that acknowledges variation in experiences of gender and gendering. As we progress through the volume, ways of studying gender that account for the deeply intertwined nature of groups, individuals, and experiences often presented as separate issues are showcased in chapters such as Allison Alexy's chapter on intimacy and Aya Ezawa's study of the work-life balance. We hope that this volume will contribute to a field that continues to champion difference and nuance, producing even more varied approaches to the study of gender in Japan.

The Routledge Companion to Gender and Japanese Culture

The Routledge Companion to Gender and Japanese Culture sketches the contours of the field. The collection features both new work and updated accounts of classic scholarship, providing a go-to reference work for contemporary scholarship on gender in Japanese culture. The volume is interdisciplinary in scope, with chapters drawing from a range of perspectives, fields, and disciplines, including anthropology, art history, history, law, linguistics, literature, media and cultural studies, politics, and sociology. This reflects the fundamentally interdisciplinary nature of the dual focal points of this volume—gender and culture—and the ways in which these themes infuse a range of disciplines and subfields.

The volume brings together scholarship from Japan, Europe, Australia, New Zealand, North America, the United Kingdom, and across East Asia. From senior academics widely regarded as leaders in the field who reflect on decades of scholarship to emerging voices bringing fresh approaches and new case studies to research on gender in Japan, we have collected a diverse range of chapters that consider key issues relating to gender in Japanese culture from a variety of enlightening perspectives. Each chapter in this volume understands gender issues as pressing in our current circumstances and recognizes that these issues are beyond the capacity of one single scholar to fully address. We hope that this volume will become part of a wider conversation on the intersections of gender and culture in Japan that considers new angles while drawing from the path-breaking scholarship that has reshaped the field over the decades.

The Routledge Companion to Gender and Japanese Culture is divided into five sections, structured around key themes in the study of gender. "Theorizing and Historicising Gender and Japanese Culture" opens the volume with Barbara Molony's historiographical overview of the field of Japanese history, updating earlier accounts to include significant works published in recent years. This opening section focuses on various disciplinary and subdisciplinary approaches to gender in Japanese culture, including approaches from premodern and modern history (Pandey, Molony), cultural studies, sociology, anthropology, queer theory, and linguistics (Inoue). Individual chapters chart the emergence, recognition, and development of a range of gendered identities and positions, from feminist identities (Kano) to transgender experiences (Dale). We attempt to trouble easy boundaries, considering gender issues from a variety of embodied perspectives, from the domestic to the migrant gendered body (Jamie Coates) and from the historical to the contemporary (Cook).

The next three sections of the volume are structured around key themes that have been central to the field of gender studies over time. In "Home, Family, and the Private Sphere," contributors explore diverse family structures and intimate relationships. Though we have divided the volume into these sections, each section necessarily addresses the others; for example, the section devoted to the "private sphere" questions what might constitute a private realm, addressing issues of intimacy (Alexy), aging (Vainio), belief (Murayama and Baffelli), and reproduction (Hertog, Yasui). The private space of the home is nonetheless subject to publicly mandated legal imperatives, as demonstrated in David Chapman's chapter on "Gender and the *Koseki*" and Manami Yasui's study of the shift in childbirth practices from private to institutional spaces. Aya Ezawa's contribution assesses the work-life balance that determines much of family life in contemporary Japan, demonstrating the uneasy pull between the demands of the public and private spheres experienced by many working people.

From there we move into the more explicitly public realm of work and politics, exploring the relation of gender to law (Assmann), labour (Macnaughtan, Takeoka), and migration (Hof and Liu-Farrer). "Work, Politics, and the Public Sphere" includes chapters on political and social organizing, from the experiences of women in electoral politics (Dalton) to the history of gender-related activism (Schieder) and the organization of spaces and communities for lesbian and queer women (Wallace).

In "Cultures of Play: Leisure, Music, and Performance," contributors explore the ways in which gender informs cultures of recreation, including sport (Ikeda, Benesch), music (Overell), participation in digital cultures (Coates and Haapio-Kirk), and self-presentation (Monden, King). This section leads into the final two parts of the volume, which consider representations of gender in the culture industries and their products.

"Cultural Production: Literature, Cinema, and Popular Culture" charts gender representation behind the scenes, on the page or screen, and in the audience or readership of the popular culture industries and their outputs in Japan. From literature (Clark and Fraser), poetry (Campana), anime and manga (Ting), to magazines and fashion (Joshua Dale), visual cultures (Borggreen), cinema and media (McLaren, Taylor-Jones and Thomas-Parr), and pornography (Hambleton), this section takes a broad view of gender issues and representations in the field of cultural production.

Finally, "Texts and Contexts: Case Studies" presents a series of close readings of text and genre from the perspective of gender and its related issues. From the broad overview of the field and its history presented in Section 1, we narrow our focus to this final set of case studies, framed as a kind of "how-to" section, demonstrating the application of the knowledge presented earlier in the volume. From Fusako Innami's reading of the dance writing of Kawabata Yasunari against the mixture of high and low cultures characterizing the interwar period to Isolde Standish's reconsideration of her earlier study of gender and genre in the *ninkyō* or "chivalrous" genre of Japanese gangster film (*yakuza eiga*), this section demonstrates how textual analysis sensitive to gender and its operations can reveal nuance and complexity in a variety of areas of study. Individual chapters consider militarism in Japanese anime (Sugawa-Shimada), classic figures of gendered media discourse such as the "parasite single" (Nakano), and the experiences of gay men in Tokyo's vibrant Shinjuku Ni-chōme nightlife area (Baudinette). We hope that these examples of close analysis of texts, genres, and anthropological fieldsites will guide students and researchers towards applying the rich historical and theoretical traditions gathered together in this volume in their own work.

Nevertheless, we have not been able to include a number of important themes and approaches in gender studies in this volume. The popularity of Murata Sayaka's novel *Konbini ningen* (2016; translated into English by Ginny Tapley Takemori as *Convenience Store Woman* in 2018) highlighted to international audiences the intersections of gender and precarity in Japanese working cultures. These themes are touched upon in this volume (e.g. Coates; Hof and Liu-Farrer;

Vainio), but a greater range of scholarship exists in both English and Japanese. Similarly, while we cover a range of diverse communities, there is still a need for ongoing work to challenge Japanese discourses of homogeneity. Gendered responses to Japan's role as a settler colonial state in places like Okinawa and Hokkaido is also only touched upon in this volume. Other exciting takes on gender studies in the Japanese context include food and consumption, which are being explored from a range of disciplines, and environmental and animal studies.

As our understandings of gender and gender-related issues and behaviours are changing rapidly in today's fast-moving mediascape, new resources for the teaching of gender studies and Japanese studies become ever more necessary, as do new approaches to the topic. In many areas, including Japan, the recent online activism documented in the opening paragraphs of this introduction has chimed with pre-existing reporting on gendered and sexual violence at varying degrees of public exposure. This volume makes a timely contribution to the fields of gender studies and Japanese studies, as well as those disciplinary areas directly addressed in individual contributions. In the chapters that follow, we consider the changing landscape of gender and Japanese culture today. In doing so, we hope students, researchers, and other readers will join us in challenging existing conceptions of gender and imagining new futures for the study of gender and culture in Japan and beyond.

References

Asahi Shimbun. (2018) "TV Asahi Files Protest with Ministry Over Sex Advances Claim," *Asahi Shimbun* 20 April. www.asahi.com/ajw/articles/AJ201804200053.html.

Chino, K. (2003) "Gender in Japanese Art," in J. S. Mostow, N. Bryson and M. Graybill (eds) *Gender and Power in the Japanese Visual Field*, Honolulu: University of Hawaii Press, 17–34.

Gender Equality Bureau Cabinet Office. (2014) "Descriptions of Women's Active Participation in Reports on Corporate Governance." www.gender.go.jp/policy/mieruka/pdf/joukyou_2014_e_1.pdf.

Hasunuma, L. and Shin, K. Y. (2019) "#MeToo in Japan and South Korea: #WeToo, #WithYou," *Journal of Women, Politics & Policy* 40 (1) 97–111.

Hernon, M. (2018) "Shiori Ito, the Face of the #MeToo Movement in Japan, Speaks Out," *Tokyo Weekender* 2 February. www.tokyoweekender.com/2018/02/shiori-ito-face-metoo-movement-japan-speaks/.

Itō, S. (2017) *Burakku bokkusu* (Black Box), Tokyo: Bungei Shunju.

McNeill, D. (2017) "Murder of the Soul: Shiori and Rape in Japan," *The Asia-Pacific Journal: Japan Focus* 15 (3).

Mishima, A., Yamamoto, N. and Sudo, T. (2017) "#MeToo Say Victims of Sexual Harassment in Japan," *Asahi Shimbun* 22 December. www.asahi.com/ajw/articles/AJ201712220046.html.

Mostow, J. S. (2003) "Gender and Power in the Japanese Visual Field: Introduction," in J. S. Mostow, N. Bryson and M. Graybill (eds) *Gender and Power in the Japanese Visual Field*, Honolulu: University of Hawaii Press, 1–16.

Otake, T. and Osaki, T. (2017) "Rape Allegation Against High-Profile Journalist, Dropped by Prosecutors Last Year, Returns in Civil Suit," *Japan Times* 6 December. www.japantimes.co.jp/news/2017/12/06/national/crime-legal/rape-allegations-high-profile-journalist-dropped-prosecutors-last-year-return-civil-suit/#.WtC6Wcjaut8.

Pesek, W. (2018) "Japan's Quiet #MeToo Moment Says Everything," *The Japan Times* 12 January. www.japantimes.co.jp/opinion/2018/01/12/commentary/japan-commentary/japans-quiet-metoo-movement-says-everything/#.WnvwWUuYPMI.

Rich, M. (2017) "She Broke Japan's Silence on Rape," *New York Times* 12 December. www.nytimes.com/2017/12/29/world/asia/japan-rape.html.

Steel, G. (2019) *Beyond the Gender Gap in Japan*, Michigan Monograph Series in Japanese Studies, Ann Arbor: University of Michigan Press.

Twitter. (2018) "Itō Shiori san o sugoku ouensuru kai #MeToo #WeToo" (Group to Strongly Support Ms Itō Shiori). https://twitter.com/ouenshiori.

Watanabe, K. (2017) "Watashi mo reipusareta: chomei jānarisuto kara no higai o, josei ga jitsumei de kokuhaku" (I Was Also Raped: Woman Injured by Famous Journalist Reveals Her Real Name), *Buzzfeed*

Japan News 29 May. www.buzzfeed.com/jp/kazukiwatanabe/20170529?utm_term=.ptZk6K4Q66#.ldR0wqeDww.

Yamagishi, K. (2018) "#MeToo Takes Off as Opposition Lawmakers Raise Papers in Protest," *The Asahi Shimbun* 20 April. www.asahi.com/ajw/articles/AJ201804200027.html.

Yamaguchi, N. (2017) "Watashi o uttaeta: Itō Shiori e" (To Itō Shiori: I Was Sued), *Hanada* 12 (October) 254–256.

PART I

Theorizing and historicizing gender and Japanese culture

PART 1

1
GENDERING MODERN JAPANESE HISTORY
A historiographical update

Barbara Molony

The "Introduction" to *Gendering Modern Japanese History*, an edited collection of essays initially presented at a 1997 workshop at Santa Clara University, was crafted in 2005 by my co-editor, Kathleen Uno, and me. The collected essays and our description of the state of the field focused on two major issues—the imbrication of gender and modernity and the impact of "gendering" (by which we meant gendered analysis) on undermining dominant historical narratives, a major goal of feminist historiography frequently articulated at that time. The introduction noted important historical trends that addressed those issues from the late twentieth century through the first half-decade of the twenty-first. We were still able to write at that time, "While modern Japanese history has not yet been restructured by a foregrounding of gender, historians of Japan have, indeed, begun to embrace gender as an analytic category" (Molony and Uno 2005, 1). While the dominant narratives of modern Japanese history had not yet been sufficiently challenged by considerations of gender (our introduction's second major issue, as noted previously), the insertion of gender as an analytic category into existing narratives such as modernity was well underway.

Since then, historiographical directions in the field of gender/ed history have grown in exciting ways. This chapter focuses primarily on new scholarship since 2005; for a fine analysis of the historiography of gender and modernity until that point—and after—including extensive and helpful citations of works in the endnotes, see Vera Mackie's 2013 essay in the *Journal of Women's History* (2013). Our use of the gerund "gendering" in the book's title implied an ongoing or dynamic process, and indeed growth has been dynamic. Our two major foci in 2005, finding gender in analysis of modernity and tearing down—or at least challenging—dominant narratives by viewing history through a gendered frame, have continued to be addressed in works published after *Gendering Modern Japanese History* and have been joined by numerous other categories. Histories focusing on gendered modernities from the late nineteenth into the twentieth centuries have proliferated. These are primarily cultural in orientation, while also addressing political issues (see Sato 2003; Silverberg 2006; Freedman 2010; Germer et al. 2014; Freedman et al. 2013; and essays in Weinbaum et al. 2008). Marcia Yonemoto's innovative monograph on women in the early modern era overturns traditional discourses on women in that era and will cause those of us who focus on the modern era to reassess our thinking about the modern turn. That is, she shows that early modern women had considerable power to influence political practice and social structure, in contradiction to official patriarchal norms. The modern demand for rights was thus grounded in early modern practices (Yonemoto 2016).

The intersections of modernity with other categories have provided useful ways of undermining dominant narratives. These include a wide range of works focusing on the intersection of modernity and consumption (Yamashita 2016; Gordon 2007; Francks and Hunter 2012; Garon and Maclachlan 2006). The intersection of gendered modernity and material culture has been highlighted in scholarship on material objects, such as sewing machines, and on domestic space (Gordon 2011; Sand 2005). Modernity's linkage with sexualities and reproduction has produced a bourgeoning field of study, including new interpretations of the sex trades, control and manipulation of sexualities under colonialism, reproduction and contraception, and bodily liberation (Mihalopoulos 2011; Frühstück 2003; Takeda 2005; Takeuchi-Demirci 2018; Seaman 2017; Terazawa 2018; Bullock 2010). The relationship between gender, sexuality, and family structures, while itself a familiar topic, has also been readdressed in new ways in recent years (Holloway 2010; Ueno 2009; Ochiai and Molony 2008). An extraordinarily large collection of works on women's writing builds on a field that has long been framed as explicitly gendered. A small but representative sampling of the many works published since the appearance of *Gendering Modern Japanese History* by historians and non-historians that contribute to our understanding of the linkage of gendered modernity and print culture includes excellent studies by Sarah Frederick (2006), Ronald P. Loftus (2004), Michiko Suzuki (2010), and Anne Walthall (2010).

One of the most exciting developments in the last quarter century is the naming of masculinity studies. Men and their activities have long been the dominant feature in most historical works. Some fine monographs and articles that specifically note that they are about men have also been part of the canon of Japanese history, though they have tended to be unmarked by gender considerations. (To be fair, women's history in its infancy was not framed in terms of gender construction, either, but rather as compensation for women's inexcusable absence in historiography.) Masculinities are now part of a marked category; *Gendering Modern Japanese History* included only 4 of 16 essays on masculinities, a proportion representative of the field of gender history at that time. Recent works that subject masculinity to gender scrutiny are too numerous to mention in their entirety, but a few by the following authors give a taste of the growing field: historical monographs by Jason G. Karlin (2014) and Sabine Frühstück (2007); pathbreaking collections edited by Sabine Frühstück and Anne Walthall (2011) and by Kam Louie and Morris Low (2003); several studies that focus on changing masculinities in the contemporary era, including works by Romit Dasgupta (2012) and James E. Roberson and Nobue Suzuki's edited collection (2003); and Mire Koikari's recent work on re-masculinizing Japan in the wake of the tragic 3.11 disaster (2017).

LGBTQ history has become an extraordinarily fertile field. Several important collections of essays or documents cover a variety of historical aspects of LGBTQ as well as contemporary issues. These include collections edited by Mark McLelland and Vera Mackie (2014); Mark McLelland et al. (2015); Mark McLelland et al. (2007); Sharon Chalmers (2002); Fred Martin, Peter A. Jackson, Mark McLelland, and Audrey Yue (2008); and Mark McLelland and Romit Dasgupta (2015). Articles and monographs are numerous as well, including those by Claire Maree (2007) and Mark McLelland (2005). This listing does not do the field justice; numerous additional articles and monographs round out this field.

Economic history is one of the foundational "dominant narrative" areas of research that has also been shaken up in recent decades by framing it in terms of gender. Works on the intersection of modernity and the economy can no longer fail to be viewed through the lens of gender, especially when we consider labour and household issues. Scholars who have addressed these issues in recent years include Janet Hunter (2003), Sheldon Garon (2013), Christopher Gerteis (2010), Helen Macnaughtan (2005, 2015a, 2015b), Ayako Kano, and Vera Mackie (2012, 2013).

Gender has also deeply permeated migration studies. An important examination of gendered migration in the 1974 movie *Sandakan No. 8* (*Sandakan hachiban shōkan bōkyō*, Kumai Kei) based on Yamazaki Tomoko's historical recreation of Japanese women in the overseas sex trades (1975) was one of the first gendered works available to Anglophone audiences. Thus, we see that treatment of gendered diasporas and migrations has a 50-year history in women's studies. Recent works focus not only on Japanese overseas migration in the sex trades (Mihalopoulos 2011; Oharazeki 2016) but also on migrant Asian women trafficked in Japan today (Aoyama 2011; Parreñas 2011).

Another area that that been radically modified by its engendering is diplomatic history. Gender, diplomacy, and foreign relations, especially but not exclusively during the Occupation (1945–1952) and Cold War eras, have been addressed by Mire Koikari (2008, 2015), Sarah Kovner (2012), Naoko Shibusawa (2006), John Dower (1999), Jan Bardsley (2014), Akiko Takenaka (2016), and Mark McLelland (2012, 2017). And, finally, two other areas that have been long considered part of the dominant historical narrative, law and politics, have been greatly enhanced by seeing them through the lens of gender and modernity. Monographs by Harald Fuess (2004) and Robin LeBlanc (2010) and a collection edited by Susan L. Burns and Barbara J. Brooks (2014) are important additions to the study of law and politics. Scholarship on the creation of gendered law under pressure from women's movements and government self-interest has been cogently redefined in the past decade as state feminism, with new works by Miriam Murase (2006), Yoshie Kobayashi (2004), and Ayako Kano (2016).

Those cited previously are just the tip of the iceberg of works in the fields I have defined here, and most of these works easily fall into more than one of these categories. For example, Karlin's *Gender and Nation in Meiji Japan*, which I have included as a work that historicizes the linkage of masculinity and modernity, could also be placed in the cultural modernities section, as it takes the opposite track from *Gendering Modern Japanese History* in its insightful focus on the losers under modernity. My categories here all have permeable boundaries. For the most part, I have not included the extraordinary profusion of journal articles nor pulled out individual essays from excellent collections; only some of these many excellent works are mentioned here.

Gender/ed history has been vastly expanded by focus on paradigms we did not highlight in our "Introduction," though many of us employed them in our published works. One of the most important of those categories we left unmarked is the historical study of feminisms. We did not emphasize this as a primary category in the "Introduction," perhaps because it seemed to some critics at the time to represent an old-fashioned dominant narrative itself (albeit within the marginalized field of women's history). Moreover, a critical re-examination, beginning in the 1980s, of the activities of Japanese feminists during World War II somewhat diminished the attractiveness of the study of feminisms and feminists at that time. The questioning of the study of feminism initially arose because several Japanese historians strongly criticized feminists' support for their government during wartime, especially in light of the exposure during the 1970s and 1980s of the oppression of wartime "comfort women" (see Soh 2008; Molony et al. 2016). Since then, new directions in the study of feminisms have emerged. Some scholars have now merged studies of imperialism, feminism, and modernity. In a recent work, Mark Driscoll offers a particularly innovative way of addressing violence, gender, modernity in the metropole, and feminism (2010). Other scholars who worked on gendered colonial modernity are Donald Smith (2006), Barbara Molony (2017a), and Noriko J. Horiguchi (2012).

Historians like Suzuki Yūko (1986) and Kanō Mikiyo (1987) took to task both feminist leaders and average women—designating the latter as the "home front"—for not actively opposing a government that carried out gendered violence. Leading feminist scholar and sociologist Ueno Chizuko analyzed this late twentieth-century historiographical turn in her critique of nationalism and feminism, originally published in Japanese and translated as *Nationalism and Gender* in 2004. The bitterness of this issue has subsided in recent decades, not because the issue of war responsibility has disappeared but rather because Japanese feminists' wartime activities have become the widely accepted interpretation in works by feminist historians (see Germer 2006, 2013a, 2013b; Wilson 2006). Some historians have begun to disentangle the indisputable support for the war—or silent complicity—by most of the Japanese population, including feminists who sought inclusion in the state, from guilt associated with sexual violence against other Asian women under Japanese imperialism. I have begun, but by no means completed, an examination of the minds of Japanese feminists, many of whom likely knew about the comfort women but said little or nothing. Was their complicity a case of "inattentional blindness"—that is, did they casually observe but not truly see because they were blinded by other wartime issues that seemed at the moment more important, or because they held classist attitudes about women in sex work, whether voluntary or coerced (Molony 2017b)?

Ironically, the critical re-examination of feminism, rather than suppressing the field, has revitalized it, and the history of feminisms has reemerged as an exceptionally exciting field of analysis by both historians and historically oriented scholars trained in other fields. What is particularly exciting is that the analysis of feminism has expanded beyond the middle of the twentieth century and addresses very recent history as well. Vera Mackie's *Feminism in Modern Japan* (2003) remains the book of record in the field of feminist history, and her work has been joined by outstanding recent works by historians and historically oriented non-historians— (Mackie 1997), Julia Bullock, Ayako Kano, James Welker (2018), and Elyssa Faison (2007)—among others who have built powerful new tools for examining the architecture of historical feminisms. Works on historical feminisms before 1945 by Elizabeth Dorn Lublin (2010), Marnie Anderson (2010), Mara Patessio (2011), Hiroko Tomida (2004; Tomida and Daniels 2005), Jan Bardsley (2007), Teruko Craig (see Hiratsuka 2006), Dina Lowy (2007), and Mariko Tamanoi (2009) have given us a much deeper insight into the motivations and contexts of feminist movements during those years. Many of these were transnational feminist movements, a category that I will develop more fully subsequently. Breakthrough works on feminisms in the last two decades by Setsu Shigematsu (2012) and Laura Dales (2009) have also taken us in new directions.

Other paradigms that are central to feminist scholarship but have not always been explicitly designated as such in the Japan field are transnationalism and intersectionality. And yet both, especially transnationalism, have been central to Japanese feminist praxis for the past century. The identified categories of transnational and intersectional feminist studies have a more recent history and were first named in Western scholarship (see Molony and Nelson 2017). Discussions about the relationship between feminism, imperialism, nationalism, and transnationalism began to emerge globally in the late 1980s and 1990s and consolidate into a field of inquiry referred to as transnational feminist studies. This field was interdisciplinary, a trend that is now significant in the historiography of Japanese gender and feminism studies as well. In one of their foundational works, Inderpal Grewal and Karen Kaplan noted that transnational feminist studies are the "study [of] the relations between women from different cultures and nations" (2000). Transnational approaches differed from many earlier feminist studies in that gender inequality and relationships between gender and power came to be studied across national boundaries and among women operating in transnational feminist networks across those boundaries. The Japan field, as we will see subsequently, dealt with transnational history for several decades, as Japanese feminisms, more commonly than in the case of many Western feminist movements, crossed boundaries from their conception. In addition, the emphasis in transnational feminist history is not only on imbalances of power structured by gender but also on relationships of power structured by global economic and political relations that cross borders; these kinds of relationships include imperialism, the "legacies of imperialism" (Grewal and Kaplan 2000), and globalization, issues addressed in works on Japanese feminism.

Transnational feminist analysis became a central feature of global feminism about a decade after "Third World feminism" developed in "opposition to white second-wave feminists' single-pronged analyses of gender oppression that elided Third World women's multiple and complex oppressions in their various social locations" (Herr 2014, 1). Ranjoo Seodu Herr noted that transnational feminist analyses considered "nation-states and nationalism as detrimental to feminist causes, whereas Third World feminists [were] relatively neutral to, and at times even approving of, nation-states and nationalism" (2014, 2). Rather than focusing on the problems of the nation-state, as did transnational feminist analysis, Third World feminism focused more intently on local and national contexts. The study of feminism on the ground was precisely what one of the heroes of Japanese feminism, journalist and activist Yayori Matsui, called for. Her 1987 volume *Women's Asia* is a classic example of post-colonial Third World feminist analysis that highlighted community-oriented Asian feminisms. Matsui was a major force in Japanese anti-imperialist feminism that focused on cross-border sexual exploitation and domestic exploitation caused by global capitalism. Third World feminist analysis has lost its appeal as a field of scholarly inquiry in the past decade, partially due to the global reconfiguration that essentially erased the term "Third World" following the end of the Cold War. Nevertheless, Herr and others have argued for a reclamation of the content of that paradigm, even in the absence of the nomenclature itself, in order to bring greater attention to *people on the ground* rather than the *networks of organizations* highlighted in transnational feminist analysis. This kind of granular, on-the-ground study is not as common among historians of Japan writing in English, although local history societies of Japanese women who are not professional historians have continued to unearth details about their foremothers' lives and activities (though to call studying Japanese communities a Third World approach is a bit of a stretch).

Most of the work in English on transnational feminisms in Japan deals with interactions of women across national borders. Beginning in the late nineteenth century, religious feminist organizations, such as the Woman's Christian Temperance Union, the Young Women's Christian Association, and pacifist organizations that were nominally secular but whose members were often Christian, were linked transnationally to counterparts in the Americas, Europe, and Australia. Japanese secular organizations that worked for suffrage, consumer rights, birth control, and other goals also forged transnational bonds, such as networks with the Pan Pacific Women's Association, the International Woman Suffrage Alliance, the Women's International League of Peace and Freedom, Planned Parenthood, and other global organizations. Many of these women, absent a formal political voice as women were not able to vote until 1946, used these global links to gain some political power (see Shibahara 2014; Yasutake 2004, 2006, 2009; Ogawa 2004a, 2004b, 2007a, 2007b; Germer 2003; Molony 2010). As Grewal and Kaplan note, as opposed to internationalism focused on formal international alliances among nations, transnational feminists attended to "transnational circuits of information, capital, and labor, [to] critique a system founded on inequality and exploitation" (2000). These circuits have long been a staple of Japanese feminist history. And yet, as Ueno Chizuko notes, it is difficult in the modern world for "feminism [to] transcend nationalism," that is, to be truly transnational (Ueno 2004, 143–146).

The concept of intersectionality, first articulated by women of colour in the United States in the 1970s and 1980s and coined as a theoretical term in 1991 by Kimberlé Crenshaw, has been a powerful analytical tool in feminist and antiracist studies that allows for theorizing "the dynamics of difference and sameness," including along overlapping axes of gender, class, race, ethnicity, and sexuality (Cho et al. 2013, 787). An "intersectional frame of analysis" allows us to examine the historical identity categories that have produced complex relationships of power that defy simple dichotomous statements such as "men oppress women." In addition, activists may undertake "political interventions employing an intersectional lens" (Cho et al. 2013, 785).

Much of the recent scholarship on gender in Japan has employed intersectional analyses, and this is nowhere more evident than in the works that address gender in its colonial, imperialist, ethnic, queer, social class, and diasporic contexts. Many of these works are cited previously, but here I draw attention to a small number of works that particularly foreground intersectionality. The intersectional approaches of activists are analyzed in a number of studies, including those by Setsu Shigematsu (2012) and Vera Mackie (2017) and the queer and lesbian voices highlighted by Mark McLelland, Kazuhiko Suganuma, and James Welker (2007) and by Sharon Chalmers (2002). Intersectional historiographic approaches are even more visible in most contemporary scholarship on modernity and gender in Japan. Some good examples, among many others, are chapters by Setsu Shigematsu, Akwi Seo, and Ayako Kano in Bullock, Kano, and Welker's edited collection (Bullock, et. al. 2018). A significant edited collection that is centred on intersectionality is Kumiko Fujimura-Fanselow's *Transforming Japan* (2011).

The field of gender/ed history is still in the dynamic process of development—that is, we do have "miles to go before [we] sleep" (Frost 1969 [1923])—but tremendous strides have been made. In 1975, a group of Japanese, American, and Australian researchers in Tokyo, many of us very young graduate students, met twice a month to discuss our research. From this grew two additional scholarly meetings in the next few years. In 1978, a small group of US graduate students from that group, most of us in our 20s, presented the first panel on women's (not yet gender) studies at an Association for Asian Studies annual meeting (Merry White, sociology; Liza Crihfield Dalby, anthropology; Kathleen Molony, history; and Barbara Molony, history). We were met with mocking scepticism by some in the audience, excitement by others. A few months later, we took part in a meeting hosted by the International Group for the Study of Women, a group of Japanese women scholars—some from the 1975 group and others more established and senior than that group—at the recently opened National Women's Education Center near Tokyo (see White and Molony 1979). The field of Japanese women's studies was underway on both sides of the Pacific, but that did not prevent many of us from hearing comments from our disciplinary colleagues who focused on other parts of the world, especially the United States and Europe, that the Japan field was playing a game of "catch-up." In the last half century, numerous scholarly and professional organizations focusing on gender, sexuality, women's and men's studies, and feminism have sprung up in Japan. Websites for the Gender History Society (*Jendaashi gakkai*), Women's Studies Association of Japan (*Nihon josei gakkai*), and WINET—Women's Information Network (a very extensive database on women's issues and women's studies), among many others, are rich sources of materials on scholarship and activism. Even the venerable historical journal of record in Japan, *Shigaku zasshi* (Journal of historical studies), which first started publishing about a dozen articles per year on women in the 1970s and 1980s, expanded its coverage greatly, both thematically and in terms of number of articles. A search in the journal's archives in November 2018 for "gender" uncovered 478 hits. We can say with certainly that today, although we look forward to further growth in the areas of transnationalism, intersectionality, and other paradigms, the Japan field of gender/ed history has not only caught up but, in terms of theoretical and empirical sophistication, has taken a leading role in gender scholarship.

References

Anderson, M. S. (2010) *A Place in Public: Women's Rights in Meiji Japan*, Cambridge, MA: Harvard University Asia Center.

Aoyama, K. (2011) "Migrants and the Sex Industry," in K. Fujimura-Fanselow (ed) *Transforming Japan: How Feminism and Diversity Are Making a Difference*, New York: Feminist Press.

Bardsley, J. (2007) *The Bluestockings of Japan: New Woman Essays and Fiction from Seitō, 1911–16*, Ann Arbor: Center for Japanese Studies, University of Michigan.

Bardsley, J. (2014) *Women and Democracy in Cold War Japan*, London: Bloomsbury.

Bullock, J. (2010) *The Other Women's Lib: Gender and Body in Japanese Women's Fiction*, Honolulu: University of Hawai'i Press.

Bullock, J., Kano, A. and Welker, J. (eds) (2018) *Rethinking Japanese Feminisms*, Honolulu: University of Hawai'i Press.

Burns, S. L. and Brooks, B. J. (eds) (2014) *Gender and Law in the Japanese Imperium*, Honolulu: University of Hawaii Press.

Chalmers, S. (2002) *Emerging Lesbian Voices from Japan*, London: RoutledgeCurzon.

Cho, S., Crenshaw, K. W. and McCall, L. (eds) (2013) "Toward a Field of Intersectionality Studies: Theory, Application, and Praxis," *Signs* 38 (4) (Summer) 785–787.

Crenshaw, K. W. (1991) "Mapping the Margins: Intersectionality, Identity Politics, and Violence Against Women of Color," *Stanford Law Review* 1241–1299.

Dales, L. (2009) *Feminist Movements in Contemporary Japan*, Abingdon, Oxon: Routledge.

Dasgupta, R. (2012) *Re-Reading the Salaryman in Japan: Crafting Masculinities*, London: Routledge.

Dower, J. (1999) *Embracing Defeat: Japan in the Wake of World War II*, New York: W.W. Norton.

Driscoll, M. (2010) *Absolute Erotic, Absolute Grotesque: The Living, the Dead, and the Undead in Japan's Imperialism, 1895–1945*, Durham, NC: Duke University Press.

Faison, E. (2007) *Managing Women: Disciplining Labor in Modern Japan*, Berkeley: University of California Press.

Francks, P. and Hunter, J. (eds) (2012) *The Historical Consumer: Consumption and Everyday Life in Japan, 1850–2000*, Basingstoke: Palgrave Macmillan.

Frederick, S. (2006) *Turning Pages: Reading and Writing Women's Magazines in Interwar Japan*, Honolulu: University of Hawai'i Press.

Freedman, A. (2010) *Tokyo in Transit: Japanese Culture and the Rails and Roads*, Stanford, CA: Stanford University Press.

Freedman, A., Miller, L. and Yano, C. R. (eds) (2013) *Modern Girls on the Go: Gender, Mobility and Labor in Japan*, Stanford, CA: Stanford University Press.

Frost, R. (1969 [1923]) "Stopping by Woods on a Snowy Evening," in E. C. Lathem (ed) *The Poetry of Robert Frost*, New York and Chicago: Holt, Rhinehart, and Winston.

Frühstück, S. (2003) *Colonizing Sex: Sexology and Social Control in Modern Japan*, Berkeley: University of California Press.

Frühstück, S. (2007) *Uneasy Warriors: Gender, Memory, and Popular Culture in the Japanese Army*, Berkeley, CA: University of California Press.

Frühstück, S. and Walthall, A. (eds) (2011) *Recreating Japanese Men*, Berkeley: University of California Press.

Fuess, H. (2004) *Divorce in Japan*, Stanford, CA: Stanford University Press.

Fujimura-Fanselow, K. (2011) *Transforming Japan: How Feminism and Diversity Are Making a Difference*, New York: Feminist Press.

Garon, S. (2013) *Beyond Our Means: Why America Spends While the World Saves*, Princeton: Princeton University Press.

Garon, S. and Maclachlan, P. L. (eds) (2006) *The Ambivalent Consumer: Questioning Consumption in East and the West*, Ithaca, NY: Cornell University Press.

Germer, A. (2003) "Feminist History in Japan: National and International Perspectives," *Intersections: Gender, History and Culture in the Asian Context* 9.

Germer, A. (2006) "The Inner and Outer Domain: Sexuality and the Nation-State in Japanese Feminist Historiography," *Social Science Japan Journal* 9 (1) 51–72.

Germer, A. (2013a) "Japanese Feminists After Versailles: Between the State and the Ethnic Nation," *Journal of Women's History* 25 (3) 92–115.

Germer, A. (2013b) "Visible Cultures, Invisible Politics: Propaganda in the Magazine *Nippon Fujin*, 1942–1945," *Japan Forum* 25 (4) 505–539.

Germer, A., Mackie, V. and Wöhr, U. (eds) (2014) *Gender, Nation and State in Modern Japan*, Abingdon, Oxon: Routledge.

Gerteis, C. (2010) *Gender Struggles: Wage-Earning Women and Male-Dominated Unions in Postwar Japan*, Cambridge, MA: Harvard University Press.

Gordon, A. (2007) "Consumption, Leisure and the Middle Class in Transwar Japan," *Social Science Japan Journal* 10 (1).

Gordon, A. (2011) *Fabricating Consumers: The Sewing Machine in Modern Japan*, Berkeley: University of California Press.

Grewal, I. and Kaplan, C. (2000) "Postcolonial Studies and Transnational Feminist Practices," *Jouvert: Journal of Postcolonial Studies* 5 (1). https://legacy.chass.ncsu.edu/jouvert/v5i1/grewal.htm.

Herr, R. S. (2014) "Reclaiming Third World Feminism: Or Why Transnational Feminism Needs Third World Feminism," *Meridians* 12 (1) 1–30.

Hiratsuka, R. (2006) *In the Beginning, Woman Was the Sun: The Autobiography of a Japanese Feminist*, trans. Teruko Craig, New York: Columbia University Press.

Holloway, S. D. (2010) *Women and Family in Contemporary Japan*, Cambridge: Cambridge University Press.

Horiguchi, N. J. (2012) *Women Adrift: The Literature of Japan's Imperial Body*, Minneapolis: University of Minnesota Press.

Hunter, J. (2003) *Women and the Labour Market in Japan's Industrialising Economy*, London: Routledge Curzon.

Kano, A. (2016) *Japanese Feminist Debates: A Century of Contention on Sex, Love and Labor*, Honolulu: University of Hawai'i Press.

Kano, A. and Mackie, V. (2012) "Is Shinzo Abe Really a Feminist?" *East Asia Forum* 9.

Kano, A. and Mackie, V. (2013) "The Gender Fault-Line in Japan," *East Asia Forum* 3.

Kanō, M. (1987) *Onnatachi no jūgo* (Women and the Home Front), Tokyo: Chikuma Shobō.

Karlin, J. G. (2014) *Gender and Nation in Meiji Japan: Modernity, Loss, and the Doing of History*, Honolulu: University of Hawai'i Press.

Kobayashi, Y. (2004) *A Path Toward Gender Equality: State Feminism in Japan*, New York: Routledge.

Koikari, M. (2008) *Pedagogy of Democracy: Feminism and the Cold War in the United States Occupation of Japan, 1945–1952*, Philadelphia: Temple University Press.

Koikari, M. (2015) *Cold War Encounters in US-Occupied Okinawa: Women, Militarized Domesticity, and Transnationalism in East Asia*, Cambridge: Cambridge University Press.

Koikari, M. (2017) "Re-Masculinizing the Nation: Gender, Disaster, and the Politics of National Resilience in Post-3.11 Japan," *Japan Forum* 1–22.

Kovner, S. (2012) *Occupying Power: Sex Workers and Servicemen in Postwar Japan*, Stanford, CA: Stanford University Press.

LeBlanc, R. (2010) *The Art of the Gut: Manhood, Power and Ethics in Japanese Politics*, Berkeley: University of California Press.

Loftus, R. P. (2004) *Telling Lives: Women's Self-Writing in Modern Japan*, Honolulu: University of Hawaii Press.

Louie, K. and Low, M. (2003) *Asian Masculinities: The Meaning and Practice of Manhood in China and Japan*, London: RoutledgeCurzon.

Lowy, D. (2007) *The Japanese "New Woman": Images of Gender and Modernity*, New Brunswick, NJ: Rutgers University Press.

Lublin, E. D. (2010) *Reforming Japan: The Woman's Christian Temperance Union in the Meiji Period*, Honolulu: University of Hawaii Press.

Mackie, V. (1997) *Creating Socialist Women in Japan: Gender, Labour and Activism, 1900–1937*, Cambridge: Cambridge University Press.

Mackie, V. (2003) *Feminism in Modern Japan: Citizenship, Embodiment and Sexuality*, Cambridge: Cambridge University Press.

Mackie, V. (2013) "Gender and Modernity in Japan's 'Long Twentieth Century'," *Journal of Women's History* 25 (3).
Mackie, V. (2017) "Transnational Activism: One Thousand Wednesdays from Seoul to Glendale," in B. Molony and J. Nelson (eds) *Women's Activism and "Second Wave Feminism: Transnational Histories*, London: Bloomsbury Academic.
Macnaughtan, H. (2005) *Women, Work, and the Japanese Economic Miracle: The Case of the Cotton Textile Industry, 1945–1975*, London: RoutledgeCurzon.
Macnaughtan, H. (2015a) "Abe's Womenomics Needs to Include Men, Too," *East Asia Forum* 25.
Macnaughtan, H. (2015b) "Is Abe's Womenomics Working?" *East Asia Forum* 27.
Maree, C. (2007) "The Un/State of Lesbian Studies in Japan," *Journal of Lesbian Studies* 11 (3–4).
Martin, Fran P., Jackson, A., McLelland, M. and Yue, A. (eds) (2008) *AsiaPacificQueer: Rethinking Gender and Sexualities*, Urbana, IL: University of Illinois Press.
Matsui, Y. (1987) *Women's Asia*, London: Zed Books.
McLelland, M. (2005) *Queer Japan from the Pacific War to the Internet Age*, Lanham, MD: Rowman & Littlefield.
McLelland, M. (2012) *Love, Sex, and Democracy During the American Occupation of Japan*, New York: Palgrave Macmillan.
McLelland, M. (2017) *The End of Cool Japan: Ethical, Legal and Cultural Challenges to Japanese Popular Culture*, Abingdon, Oxon: Routledge.
McLelland, M. and Dasgupta, R. (eds) (2015) *Genders, Transgenders and Sexualities in Japan*, Abingdon, Oxon: Routledge.
McLelland, M. and Mackie, V. (eds) (2014) *Routledge Handbook of Sexuality Studies in East Asia*, Abingdon, Oxon: Routledge.
McLelland, M., Nagaike, K., Suganuma, K. and Welker, J. (eds) (2015) *Boys Love Manga and Beyond: History, Culture, and Community in Japan*, Jackson: University of Mississippi Press.
McLelland, M., Suganuma, K. and Welker, J. (eds) (2007) *Queer Voices from Japan: First Person Narratives from Japan's Sexual Minorities*, Lanham, MD: Rowman & Littlefield.
Mihalopoulos, B. (2011) *Sex in Japan's Globalization, 1870–1930*, London: Pickering and Chatto.
Molony, B. (2010) "Crossing Boundaries: Transnational Feminisms in Twentieth-Century Japan," in M. Roces and L. Edwards (eds) *Women's Movements in Asia*, Abingdon, Oxon: Routledge.
Molony, B., Theiss, J. and Choi, H. (2016) *Gender in Modern East Asia: An Integrated History*, Boulder, CO: Westview Press.
Molony, B. (2017a) "Engendering Modern Japanese History Through the Lens of Empire," in K. K. Sklar and T. Dublin (eds) *Women and Social Movements in Modern Empires Since 1820*, online, Alexander Street.
Molony, B. (2017b) "Japanese Feminists' Attitudes Toward Gendered Violence in World War II." Paper Presented at the Women in Asia Conference, University of Western Australia, Perth, WA.
Molony, B. and Nelson, J. (eds) (2017) "Introduction," in B. Molony and J. Nelson (eds) *Women's Activism and "Second Wave" Feminism: Transnational Histories*, London: Bloomsbury Academic.
Molony, B. and Uno, K. (eds) (2005) *Gendering Modern Japanese History*, Cambridge, MA: Harvard University Asia Center.
Murase, M. (2006) *Cooperation over Conflict: The Women's Movement and the State in Postwar Japan*, New York: Routledge.
Ochiai, E. and Molony, B. (eds) (2008) *Asia's New Mothers*, Folkestone, Kent: Global Oriental.
Ogawa, M. (2004a) "'Hull-House' in Downtown Tokyo: The Transplantation of a Settlement House from the United States into Japan and the North American Missionary Women, 1919–1945," *Journal of World History* 15 (3).
Ogawa, M. (2004b) "Rescue Work for Japanese Women: The Birth and Development of the Jiaikan Rescue Home and the Missionaries of the Woman's Christian Temperance Union, Japan, 1886–1921," *U.S.—Japan Women's Journal* 26.
Ogawa, M. (2007a) "Estranged Sisterhood: The Wartime Trans-Pacific Dialogue of the World's Woman's Christian Temperance Union, 1931–1945," *Japanese Journal of American Studies* 18.
Ogawa, M. (2007b) "The 'White Ribbon League of Nations' Meets Japan: The Trans-Pacific Activism of the Woman's Christian Temperance Union, 1906–1930," *Diplomatic History* 31 (1).
Oharazeki, K. (2016) *Japanese Prostitutes in the North American West, 1887–1920*, Seattle: University of Washington Press.

Parreñas, R. S. (2011) *Intimate Flirtations: Labor, Migration, and Sex Trafficking in Tokyo*, Stanford, CA: Stanford University Press.
Patessio, M. (2011) *Women and Public Life in Early Meiji Japan*, Ann Arbor: University of Michigan.
Roberson, J. E. and Suzuki, N. (2003) *Men and Masculinities in Contemporary Japan: Dislocating the Salaryman Doxa*, London: RoutledgeCurzon.
Sand, J. (2005) *House and Home in Modern Japan: Architecture, Domestic Space, and Bourgeois Culture, 1880–1930*, Cambridge, MA: Harvard East Asian Monographs.
Sato, B. (2003) *The New Japanese Woman: Modernity, Media, and Women in Interwar Japan*, Durham, NC: Duke University Press.
Seaman, A. C. (2017) *Writing Pregnancy in Low-Fertility Japan*, Honolulu: University of Hawai'i Press.
Shibahara, Taeko (2014) *Japanese Women and the Transnational Feminist Movement Before World War II*, Philadelphia: Temple University Press.
Shibusawa, N. (2006) *America's Geisha Ally: Reimaging the Japanese Enemy*, Cambridge, MA: Harvard University Press.
Shigematsu, S. (2012) *Scream from the Shadows: The Women's Liberation Movement in Japan*, Minneapolis: University of Minnesota Press.
Silverberg, M. (2006) *Erotic, Grotesque Nonsense: The Mass Culture of Japanese Modern Times*, Berkeley: University of California Press.
Smith, W. D. (2006) "Digging Through Layers of Class, Gender, and Ethnicity: Korean Women Miners in Prewar Japan," in K. Lahiri-Dutt and M. Macintyre (eds) *Women Miners in Developing Countries: Pit Women and Others*, Farnham: Ashgate Publishing.
Soh, C. S. (2008) *The Comfort Women: Sexual Violence and Postcolonial Memory in Korea and Japan*, Chicago: University of Chicago Press.
Suzuki, M. (2010) *Becoming Modern Women: Love and Female Identity in Prewar Japanese Literature and Culture*, Stanford, CA: Stanford University Press.
Suzuki, Y. (1986) *Feminizumo to sensō* (Feminism and War), Tokyo: Marujusha.
Takeda, H. (2005) *The Political Economy of Reproduction in Japan: Between Nation-State and Everyday Life*, Abingdon, Oxon: RoutledgeCurzon.
Takenaka, A. (2016) "Gender and Post-War Relief: Support for War-Widowed Mothers in Occupied Japan (1945–52)," *Gender & History* 28 (3) 775–793.
Takeuchi-Demirci, A. (2018) *Contraceptive Diplomacy: Reproductive Politics and Imperial Ambitions in the United States and Japan*, Stanford, CA: Stanford University Press.
Tamanoi, M. (2009) "Suffragist Women, Corrupt Officials, and Waste Control in Prewar Japan: Two Plays by Kaneko Shigeri," *Journal of Asian Studies* 68 (3) 805–834.
Terazawa, Y. (2018) *Knowledge, Power, and Women's Reproductive Health in Japan, 1690–1945*, Basingstoke: Palgrave Macmillan.
Tomida, H. (2004) *Hiratsuka Raichō and Early Japanese Feminism*, Leiden: Brill.
Tomida, H. and Daniels, G. (eds) (2005) *Japanese Women: Emerging from Subservience, 1868–1945*, Folkestone, Kent: Global Oriental.
Ueno, C. (2004) *Nationalism and Gender*, trans. Beverley Yamamoto, Melbourne, VIC: TransPacific Press.
Ueno, C. (2009) *The Modern Family in Japan: Its Rise and Fall*, Melbourne, VIC: TransPacific Press.
Walthall, A. (2010) "Women and Literacy from Edo to Meiji," in P. F. Kornicki, M. Patessio and G. G. Rowley (eds) *The Female as Subject: Reading and Writing in Early Modern Japan*, Ann Arbor: University of Michigan Press.
Weinbaum, A. E., Thomas, L. M., Ramamurthy, P., Poiger, U. G., Dong, M.Y. and Barlow, T. E. (eds) (2008) *The Modern Girl Around the World: Consumption, Modernity, and Globalization*, Durham, NC: Duke University Press.
White, M. I. and Molony, B. (eds) (1979) *Proceedings of the Tokyo Symposium on Women*, Tokyo: International Group for the Study of Women.
Wilson, S. (2006) "Family or State? Nation, War, and Gender in Japan, 1937–1945," *Critical Asian Studies* 38 (2) 209–238.
Yamashita, S. H. (2016) *Daily Life in Wartime Japan, 1940–1945*, Lawrence, KS: University Press of Kansas.
Yamazaki, T. (1975 [1972]) *Sandakan hachiban shōkan*, Tokyo: Bungei Shunju.

Yasutake, R. (2004) *Transnational Women's Activism: The United States, Japan, and Japanese Immigrant Communities in California, 1859–1920*, New York: New York University Press.

Yasutake, R. (2006) "Men, Women, and Temperance in Meiji Japan: Engendering WCTU Activism from a Transnational Perspective," *Japanese Journal of American Studies* 17.

Yasutake, R. (2009) "The First Wave of International Women's Movements from a Japanese Perspective: Western Outreach and Japanese Women Activists During the Interwar Years," *Women's Studies International Forum* 32.

Yonemoto, M. (2016) *The Problem of Women in Early Modern Japan*, Berkeley: University of California Press.

2
GENDER IN PRE-MODERN JAPAN

Rajyashree Pandey

There was a time when a courtly text such as the eleventh-century romance *The Tale of Genji* was appreciated purely for its aesthetic qualities and seen as an exemplar of the "rule of taste" (Morris 1964). Today this is no longer the case. Scholars have become increasingly attentive to the ideological underpinnings of even the most refined narratives and poetic compositions of pre-modern Japan. The operation of power and politics and the workings of gender are no longer seen as extrinsic to texts but as central to their very constitution.

As a conceptual category, widely deployed in feminist writing, from the outset, the term *gender* served a political function. There was an inherent paradox in the claim that emerged from the eighteenth century that equality and liberty were the "natural" state of man and the emphatic denial of it to women (or indeed to those of different "colours" or "races"). The rationale that was offered for the exclusion of women from what was purportedly a universal right was that sexual difference was something inscribed on the body, a fact of nature, that could not be changed, and that it was this difference that rendered women innately inferior to men. The radical difference that was seen to separate men from women now came to be grounded in a biology whose claims to truth could not be challenged.

For those who sought to contest this view, the chief argument became that sexual or biological difference did not determine intellectual and other differences. The category "gender" emerged precisely as a way of arguing that social roles were not necessarily bound to sex and that sexual or biological difference did not determine intellectual and other differences. Gender, it was argued, was "a social category imposed on a sexed body" (Scott 1986).

Gender is a category that allows for an analysis of how one comes to occupy one's place in the social world as a man or woman. However, it was "woman," the unprivileged and marked term of the man-woman binary that took centre stage in research on the workings of gender. Scholars sought to reveal how the sex/gender system operated in the production of knowledge across a wide range of disciplines and how it privileged the lives and activities of men and systematically neglected or denigrated women and their roles in society.

Medieval Japanese studies, for the most part, has taken its cue from the work undertaken by 1960s and 1970s feminism, making its primary task the reinstatement of women into the historical, religious, and literary narratives from which they have been systematically written out. In so doing, they radically questioned the androcentric biases of earlier scholarly writings in the field. It is in this context that what we might call "women's history" (*joseishi*) first emerged (see also Molony in this volume). Economic and social history, for example, took a new direction by focusing on the complex intersections between gender and class, allowing for new perspectives on a diverse range of interrelated themes such as family, marriage, household systems, property rights, and women's labour in medieval and early modern Japan (Tonomura et al. 1999; Wakita et al. 1999; Tonomura 2017). New approaches emerged, which sought to explore hitherto neglected fields such as sexuality and the social construction of motherhood, menstruation, childbirth, abortion, wet-nursing, and so on (Wakita 1985, 1992; Kimura 2009).

The project of writing women's histories reverberated across many other disciplines. A four-volume collection published in Japanese in 1989, under the title *Shīrizu: josei to bukkyō* (Women and Buddhism Series), and an edited volume in English, entitled *Engendering Faith: Women and Buddhism in Premodern Japan*, which followed in 2002, heralded a new departure from previous research that had focused exclusively on religious groups formed around male leaders or on sectarian histories and the doctrinal debates within particular schools of Buddhism (Pandey 2004, 223–244). These new works offered a critique of earlier studies on Buddhism on the grounds that both the sources that were investigated and the questions that were asked in such accounts inevitably focused on institutions in which men played a central role and from which women, for the most part, were excluded. The task for scholars became one of "retrieval," whereby women who were hidden from and silenced in the official religious and historical records could be reinstated by making them visible (Ruch 2002).

In recent decades, scholars have also revisited well-known Buddhist canonical works and popular literary/Buddhist tales to highlight the misogynistic nature of Buddhist ideology, institutions, and practices and to demonstrate how Buddhism sought to justify the claim that women were inferior to men by attributing to them various vices and failings (Marra 1993; Faure 2003; Kimbrough 2008). Academic writings on classical and medieval works in a wide range of genres from romance fiction (*monogatari*), poetic diaries (*nikki*), and *waka* poetry to popular tales (*setsuwa*, *otogizōshi*) have likewise sought to unveil the workings of gender and the operations of power that often lie behind the aesthetic, humorous, religious, or supernatural dimensions of courtly and popular texts (Tonomura 1994; Laffin 2013; Li 2009; Kawashima 2001; Sarra 1999; Goodwin 2007).

In the last few decades, for example, there has been a new orientation in the study of the Heian classic, *The Tale of Genji*, whereby it is no longer read simply as a tale about the romantic escapades of an idealized hero, but rather as a particularly powerful instantiation, by a female author, of the workings of unequal gender relations, which lie at the heart of sexual liaisons. This new approach is evident in the series of articles written for the journal *Genji kenkyū* (Genji research) from 1996–2005 (Mitamura, et. al. 1996–2005). Scholarly writings have sought to highlight not only women's suffering, but also their resistance to oppressive patriarchal norms. It is in this context that the term "female agency," defined as the capacity of women to resist male domination, or, at the very least, to express the desire to be liberated from it, has acquired critical purchase (Field 1987; Bargen 1997; Sarra 1999).

Questions of gender are now seen as central to any understanding of the literary/Buddhist texts of medieval Japan. This is therefore a propitious moment for a critical reappraisal of current approaches to the study of gender in the medieval Japanese textual tradition. As I hope to demonstrate, scholars, for the most part, have tended to take the methodological approach of the feminist projects of the 1960s and 1970s, which means that many of the core presumptions that have gone into the making of categories such as "body," "gender," "woman," and "agency," have remained, for the most part, unexamined. In this chapter, I would like to offer new perspectives for reading well-known classical and medieval texts of Japan by focusing on how these by now highly naturalized categories have been discursively produced and how they have come to acquire their status as ontologically given.

By highlighting the cultural and historical variability of these concepts, I also seek to demonstrate that a transposition of contemporary understandings of these terms to the Japanese past produces anachronistic readings of the worlds we seek to analyse. Curious as it may seem, the new insights I seek to offer on gender in medieval Japanese texts resonate with the claims of post-structural feminists who have addressed the problem of treating our core categories of analysis as ahistorical, universal, and foundational truths (Riley 1988; Scott 2005; Butler 1990). Bringing these feminist theoretical perspectives in conversation with medieval Japanese texts, I suggest, may help us better understand other worlds without domesticating them into mirrors of our own.

Body

The idea of the body as self-evident, a given with fixed meanings, is no longer tenable: like childhood, death, madness, sex and so on, the body is now seen as having a history. Michel Foucault, for example, challenged the commonly held assumption that the body "obeys the exclusive laws of physiology and that it escapes the influence of history." Through a reading of the multiplicity of regimes to which the body is subjected, he argued that, "nothing in man—not even his body—is sufficiently stable to serve as the basis for self-recognition or for understanding other men" (Foucault 1997, 153). Conceptions of the body in medieval Japanese narratives, as we shall see subsequently, do indeed amply demonstrate the historically and culturally contingent nature of the ways in which bodies are inhabited, imagined, and visualized.

First, debates over the extent to which the mind and body are distinct or connected, which lie at the heart of the Western philosophical tradition dating back at least to the seventeenth century and most famously the work of René Descartes, find no counterpart in East Asian religious traditions. Both Daoist and Buddhist writings work with the assumption that the body and mind are integrally connected. The body, far from being defined as pure materiality, is seen rather as a psychosomatic process, "something done, rather than something one has" (Ames 1993, 168). In medieval Japanese texts, "thought" does not function as the other of "feeling" or emotion: the verb *omou* encapsulates both feeling and thinking (Kasulis 1993, 303). Both material and mental/emotional processes are integrally linked and central to the constitution of a meaningful body/self. The word *mi* in the Japanese medieval lexicon that corresponds to the term "body" makes no distinction between the physical body and what we might call the psychic, social, or cultural body; hence, one of the most common usages of the term *mi* is to signify a person's status or standing in the world.

Second, the body is not the site of eroticism in the literary and pictorial traditions of medieval Japan. In a work such as *The Tale of Genji* for example, love and desire are not generated through descriptions of the lines or curves of the body. Both the physical and psychic attributes that go into the making of the body find expression in the robes within which the body is enveloped. Robes, which are metonymically linked to the body, are not mere embellishments that adorn, cover, and enhance the beauty of the body: they are part and parcel of embodied being, and it is the two together as an ensemble that have the power to generate erotic and affective desire in *Genji* (Pandey 2016, 34–42).

Third, neither the body nor nature in the medieval context is something set in stone, seen as inert and passive matter with immutable attributes. Medieval bodies are granted transformative powers that render the boundaries between gods, humans, men, women, and beasts porous and fluid. The popular tales of medieval Japan conjure up an altogether unfamiliar cosmology in which plants, animals, humans, and supernatural beings intermingle and make possible the strangest of boundary crossings. A man has sex with a turnip. A young girl eats the turnip, falls pregnant, and gives birth to a boy. A snake is aroused and has sex with a woman. A priest makes love to a young boy who falls pregnant and gives birth to a baby, who turns out to be a nugget of gold. A beautiful woman turns out to be a deceitful fox; a young boy reveals himself to be a bodhisattva. All bodies, even those of women, are conceptualized as active agents that can defy common expectations and perform miraculous transformations.

Sex/gender

As I have argued, feminist scholars of the 1960s and 1970s treated sex as a biological truth that could not be challenged or changed. Both the body and sex were seen as belonging to the domain of "nature," while gender was taken to be a social construct that pertained to the realm of "culture." In this way, the distinction between "nature" and "culture" came to be naturalized as an ontological fact. Women's sexual organs were seen as central to their womanhood, and this became the ground for assuming that "woman" as a category was stable and internally coherent. Even when scholars acknowledged the differences that separated women across class, race, and status and adopted the more capacious category "women," their analyses took as given that for all their diverse experiences, women recognised themselves as *women* and that this was a self-evident identity. These assumptions undergird much of the scholarship on the literary and Buddhist texts of medieval Japan.

However, as I have argued, the medieval Japanese imaginary was one in which man and woman were not defined primarily through their sexual organs, and their world was not organised through the distinctions of nature/culture and sex/gender. Women were undoubtedly the incomplete, lesser, inferior versions of men, but the body and sexual difference were not the grounds for affirming this preordained hierarchy. What it meant to be a woman was by no means grounded in the body, given that the body itself was unstable and imbued with transformational potential. The instability of the body and of woman as fixed categories has consequences for understanding what we mean by gender in the medieval Japanese textual tradition.

This may explain why Judith Butler's work, which challenges the binaries of sex/gender and nature/culture, can be fruitfully pressed into service for an analysis of gender in pre-modern Japanese texts. Judith Butler argues that gender "ought not to be conceived as a noun or a substantial thing or a static cultural marker," but rather as "an activity, a becoming," (1990, 112). The binaries of sex/gender, man/woman, and hetero/homosexuality are not facts or truths about the world that are made manifest through our actions. Rather, through the endless repetition of certain acts, we create the illusion of the stability of gender. This is why Butler refers to gender as "performative." In pre-modern Japanese literary texts, gender functions precisely like this, as a kind of script. It is the specificity of the gendered performance, that is to say, the particularity of the script that is enacted, rather than the sexual attributes and reproductive functions of the body, that gives substance to the categories male and female.

Gender and romance narratives (*monogatari*)

The anonymous twelfth-century fictional tale *Torikaebaya monogatari* (The Tale of "If Only I Could Change Them Back") exemplifies perfectly the idea of gender as something that is not a given but rather a matter of becoming through repeated performance. The daughter of the Minister of the Right, Himegimi, is raised as a boy and takes her place at the court as a man, while her brother Wakagimi, brought up as a girl, enters court as a lady. Through forms of rigorous self-fashioning, that is to say, through the cultivation of particular emotional dispositions and forms of bodily comportment appropriate to their respective genders, Himegimi and Wakagimi are able to transform themselves such that they can successfully take on their new gendered roles, regardless of their sexual attributes. In this tale "words designating 'man' or 'woman' often appear with verbs that imply the mutability or superficiality of that very status" (Pflugfelder 1992, 355). In the end, *Torikaebaya monogatari* returns the two siblings to their original gendered roles, but much of the text engages in playful inversions whose effect is to expose the fictive nature of the fixity of gender as the basis of a stable identity.

Gender difference in a work such as *The Tale of Genji* does not register overtly through the body, clothes, and ideals of beauty, but this does not mean that men and women in the text are indistinguishable one from the other or that their relationships are unmarked by the play of power. How gender comes to be coded depends on the context in which it is performed. Within the dense social world of the *Genji*, for example, gender, status, age, and highly aestheticized forms of erotics often crisscross, creating a multitude of possibilities. Gender is performative and not fixed and given, and thus how it is performed—what constitutes being a woman—is itself shaped by class, which again, far from being stable, functions as a dynamic and fluid category. The shifting contexts within which amorous encounters take place are always imbricated in a variety of asymmetries and hierarchies, which sometimes work together and at other times pull in different directions, thereby attesting to the inadequacy of treating either gender or class in isolation, outside of the setting or stage (*bamen*) upon which they are brought into play. It is the possibilities offered by different ways of "doing" gender that the text explores through the many romantic encounters that constitute the tale (Pandey 2016, 55–81).

Gender and *waka* poetry

The performative aspects of gender are most clearly discernible in *waka* poetry, where gender is disassociated from the body and sex and is principally a matter of certain prescribed stylizations of performative roles. *Waka* poetry's dominant themes are nature and love, both of which are expressed through a prescribed repertoire of images and vocabulary. The central figures of love poems are *otoko* (man) and *onna* (woman), who appear in the poems through terms such as *kimi* (you), *hito* (male or female lover), or *ware* (I). These terms are used for both men and women alike. They indicate nothing about the gender, identity, or social status of either the poet or the one who is being addressed. Furthermore, *ware* speaks to fluid, multiple selves that often blend into one another, inhabiting as they do the same experiential space (Miyake 1996, 63).

When a poem is described as being a woman's poem (*onna no uta*), what is at issue is not the sexual or personal identity of the composer of the poem (Vieillard-Baron 2013, 1–23) but rather the particular stylized role or persona to be adopted by the poet that is consonant with woman, not as a real, living being, but rather as a trope or an idea. Even when a poem is marked as anonymous or when there is no headnote explaining the circumstances under which it was composed, it is possible to infer which persona a poet has adopted.

This is because in the *waka* tradition, the woman is always positioned as the one who waits and pines for her male lover, while the man is the one who visits at night and departs before dawn. He is the one who initiates the affair and composes the morning-after poem to which his lady is expected to respond. A poet, regardless of his or her biological sex (a category that has no real meaning in this context), can slip seamlessly into the persona of the waiting female or the male who visits. It is through the performative stances adopted by poets that *otoko* and *onna* come into being, and only provisionally so, within the discursive space of *waka* poetry.

Buddhism and gender

Many of the observations I have made previously could be challenged by turning to Buddhist texts, which are undoubtedly gendered and treat woman as the marked category, both implicitly and explicitly defined as different from and inferior to man, the normative ideal. The fact that a woman must attain rebirth as a man before she can embark on her journey to become a Buddha has often been singled out as proof of Buddhism's fundamental misogyny. In the *Lotus Sutra*, for example, one of the Buddha's disciples, Śāriputra, expresses doubts about the eight-year-old daughter of the dragon king possessing the necessary requisites for attaining Buddhahood on the grounds that the female body is a "filthy" thing, subject to the five obstructions. The "five obstructions" (*itsutsu no sawari*) refer to the impossibility for women to attain rebirth as a Brahmā, Indra, Māra, Cakravartin, or Wheel-Turning King and, most significantly, Buddha. However, it is hard to distil from this text any sense of "woman" as an essentialist and abiding identity, for the text overturns Śāriputra's account of the innateness of women's failings by recounting the rapid transformation of the dragon girl into a man and her achievement of Buddhahood. It does so by pointing to the provisional and shifting boundaries between men, women, dragons, and Buddhas. The fact that the body in medieval Japanese texts is unstable and granted enormous potential necessarily makes the categories man and woman porous and unstable, defying any consolidation of them as unchanging or always fixed in the same way.

Indeed, the instability of man and woman as fixed and enduring entities is the subject of conscious thematization in the *Vimalakīrti Sutra*. As in the *Lotus Sutra*, Śāriputra challenges a goddess residing in the house of the lay bodhisattva Vimalakīrti by saying that if she were truly endowed with wisdom, she would be able to change herself into a male. The goddess promptly does so by changing herself into a man *and* turning Śāriputra into a woman. Drawing on the doctrine of nonduality, she claims that neither maleness nor femaleness are innate or stable characteristics, thereby attesting to the provisional nature of gendered identities (Thurman 1976, 56–63).

Gender and agency

Buddhist texts defy the stabilization of "man" and "woman" as fixed identities. This has implications for what we might mean when we use the term *agency* as a category for analyzing both women's oppression and their capacity to resist male domination. I would suggest that in scholarly writings on Japanese literary and Buddhist texts, the term itself is often left unexamined. Agency is implicitly understood to signify the capacity for action that inheres to all humans, defined as autonomous individuals with free will, whose natural inclination is to strive to resist the oppressive conditions of their lives (Johnson 2003, 115), and that this is universally the case regardless of temporal and cultural differences. This conception of agency is based on a number of presumptions that bear examination. First, agency is a specifically modern humanist idea born of liberal thought, which presupposes the supremacy of Man, who replaces the gods as the maker of meaning in the world. Agency in this understanding is something possessed by humans alone. And yet such an anthropocentric view of agency would have been unrecognizable to our forebears, both in Japan and elsewhere, for they inhabited worlds where humans were not the sole actors and makers of meaning: gods, buddhas, beasts, dreams, and material objects worked together with humans as active agents in a shared cosmological and worldly order.

Medieval texts consistently fail to attribute the events that take place in the world solely to human intentions and will; rather they present them as effects unfolding as a consequence of a concatenation of forces, in which a significant role is assigned to the power of the divine and to karma from past lives. The unlikely union of Genji with the Akashi Lady when Genji is in exile in Suma, for example, comes about not as a result of the personal agency of either of the protagonists but due to the intervention of a number of supernatural agents. The amorous entanglements in which women find themselves embroiled are viewed not through the prism of coercion or consent but rather through the Buddhist notion of *sukuse*, fate or karma, a recurrent term in the text (Genji monogatari 1993, 177).

Second, the moral charge of celebrating agency often takes the form of treating it as conceptually interchangeable with the idea of resistance against relations of power and domination. This means that acts, particularly religious ones, that work in consonance *with* social conventions rather than *against* them cannot be granted real agency. If personhood in medieval Japan is a social phenomenon, and if it is not imagined as an individual and secular identity, then agency in this context would have to be disentangled from nineteenth-century liberalism, which speaks an altogether different language of choice and self-determination.

Scholars have singled out nunhood as one of the sites upon which women's response to Buddhism's "misogyny" came to be played out in the medieval period. Some have seen the act of tonsure (the practice of shaving the head) as an act of resistance to unequal social arrangements: nunhood, in this reading, becomes the space of freedom that a woman actively chooses (Ruch 1990, 510). Others, working within the same conceptual framework of agency, have claimed precisely the opposite, arguing that the practice of tonsure was "a form of death in life" (Field 1987, 189). If we work within the framework of agency understood as either liberation or subjection, the particular reading that we favour becomes little more than an arbitrary choice. To do so produces anachronistic readings, which turn the *Genji* into a secular text where piety simply becomes a displacement or metaphor that obscures (when read through the lens of gender, agency, and resistance) the "truth" of the inequality and injustice of gender relations.

The starting point for our study of gender in medieval Japanese texts must involve historicizing Man, Woman, Body, and Agency—the analytic categories that are central to our readings of gender in the literary and Buddhist texts of medieval Japan and recognizing that these concepts do not travel seamlessly across different temporalities and cultural traditions. In our well-meaning concern and sympathy for women in pre-modern Japan, we often treat as entirely unproblematic key terms such as *gender, women, resistance, subjecthood,* and *agency*, which we deploy as if they were universally applicable rather than as contested categories that have been the subject of impassioned debates amongst serious scholars. By ignoring these debates, we fail to do justice to the very cause that we claim to have espoused. There is also a danger here that in our desire to speak on behalf our "sisters," we sometimes unwittingly reproduce the imperialising gestures of first-world feminism (Talpade Mohanty 1984, 333–358).

To conclude, gender difference was undoubtedly central to the hierarchical order of the world of pre-modern Japan, and women within it were without question positioned as inferior to men. However, difference was not constituted through "man" and "woman" understood as fixed and stable categories, defined through their bodies. Gender was inextricably tied to the performative aspects of the body. The performance of gender was by no means uniform, and it produced a multiplicity of ways of being "woman" or "man." The instability of the body and its potential for transformation made gender a materialization that was never fixed or complete: it was in the nature of a verb rather than a noun.

Further readings

Mostow, J., Bryson, N. and Graybill, M. (eds) (2003) *Gender and Power in the Japanese Visual Field*, Honolulu: University of Hawai'i Press.

Pflugfelder, G. (1999) *Cartographies of Desire: Male-Male Sexuality in Japanese Discourse 1600–1950*, Berkeley: University of California Press.
Yoda, T. (2004) *Gender and National Literature: Heian Texts in the Construction of Japanese Modernity*, Durham, NC: Duke University Press.

Related chapters

13 Changing Folk Cultures of Pregnancy and Childbirth
28 Gender in Japanese Literature and Literary Studies
33 Gender, Media, and Misogyny in Japan

References

Ames, R. (1993) "The Meaning of the Body in Classical Chinese Philosophy," in T. P. Kasulis et al. (eds) *Self as Body in Asian Theory and Practice*, New York: SUNY Press.
Bargen, D. (1997) *A Woman's Weapon: Spirit Possession in the Tale of Genji*, Honolulu: University of Hawaii Press.
Butler, J. (1990) *Gender Trouble: Feminism and the Subversion of Identity*, New York: Routledge.
Faure, B. (2003) *The Power of Denial: Buddhism, Purity, and Gender*, Princeton, NJ: Princeton University Press.
Field, N. (1987) *The Splendor of Longing in the Tale of Genji*, Princeton, NJ: Princeton University Press.
Foucault, M. (1997) "Nietzsche, Genealogy, History," in S. Simon et al. (eds) D. F. Bouchard (trans.) *Language, Counter-Memory, Practice: Selected Essays and Interviews by Michel Foucault*, Ithaca, NY: Cornell University Press.
Genji monogatari. (1993) *Shin nihon koten bungaku taikei*, Tokyo: Iwanami Shoten, 19.
Goodwin, J. (2007) *Selling Songs and Smiles: The Sex Trade in Heian and Kamakura Japan*, Honolulu: University of Hawai'i Press.
Johnson, W. (2003) "On Agency," *Journal of Social History* 37 (1) 113–124.
Kasulis, T. (1993) "The Body—Japanese Style," in T. P. Kasulis et al. (eds) *Self as Body in Asian Theory and Practice*, New York: SUNY Press.
Kawashima, T. (2001) *Writing Margins: The Textual Construction of Gender in Heian and Kamakura Japan*, Cambridge, MA: Harvard University Press.
Kimbrough, K. (2008) *Preachers, Poets, Women and the Way: Izumi Shikibu and the Buddhist Literature of Medieval Japan*, Ann Arbor: Center for Japanese Studies.
Kimura, S. (2009) *Chibusa wa dare no mono ka: Chūsei monogatari ni miru sei to kenryoku*. Tokyo: Shinyōsha.
Laffin, C. (2013) *Rewriting Medieval Japanese Women: Politics, Personality, and Literary Production in the Life of Nun Abutsu*, Honolulu: University of Hawaii Press.
Li, M. (2009) *Ambiguous Bodies: Reading the Grotesque in Japanese Setsuwa Tales*, Stanford: Stanford University Press.
Marra, M. (1993) "The Buddhist Mythmaking of Defilement: Sacred Courtesans of Medieval Japan," *Journal of Asian Studies* 52 (1) 49–65.
Mitamura, M., Kawazoe, F. and Matsui, K. (eds) (1996–2005) *Genji kenkyū*, 10 vols. Tokyo: Kanrin shobō.
Miyake, L. (1996) "The Tosa Diary: In the Interstices of Gender and Criticism," in P. Schalow and J. Hunter (eds) *The Woman's Hand: Gender and Theory in Japanese Women's Writing*, Stanford, CA: Stanford University Press, 41–74.
Morris, I. (1964) *The World of the Shining Prince: Court Life in Ancient Japan*, Oxford: Oxford University Press.
Pandey, R. (2004) "Medieval Experience, Modern Visions: Women in Buddhism," *Monumenta Nipponica* 59 (2) 223–244.
Pandey, R. (2016) *Perfumed Sleeves and Tangled Hair: Body, Woman, and Desire in Medieval Japanese Narratives*, Honolulu: University of Hawaii Press.
Pflugfelder, G. (1992) "Strange Fates: Sex, Gender, and Sexuality in *Torikaebaya Monogatari*," *Monumenta Nipponica* 47 (3) 347–368.
Riley, D. (1988) *"Am I That Name?": Feminism and the Category of "Women" in History*, Minneapolis: University of Minnesota Press.

Ruch, B. (ed) (2002) *Engendering Faith: Women and Buddhism in Premodern Japan*, Ann Arbor: Center for Japanese Studies.

Ruch, B. (1990) "The Other Side of Culture," in K. Yamamura (ed) *The Cambridge History of Japan: Medieval Japan*, vol. 3, Cambridge: Cambridge University Press.

Sarra, E. (1999) *Fictions of Femininity: Literary Inventions of Gender in Japanese Court Women's Memoirs*, Stanford, CA: Stanford University Press.

Scott, J. W. (1986) "Gender: A Useful Category of Historical Analysis," *The American Historical Review* 91 (5) 1053-1075.

Scott, J. W. (2005) "The Evidence of Experience,' in G. Spiegel (ed) *Practicing History: New Directions in Historical Writing after the Linguistic Turn*, New York: Routledge.

Talpade Mohanty, C. (1984). "Under Western Eyes: Feminist Scholarship and Colonial Discourses," *Boundary 2* 12 (3) 333-358.

Thurman, R. (trans) (1976) *The Holy Teaching of Vimalakirti: A Mahayana Scripture*, University Park and London: Pennsylvania State University Press.

Tonomura, H. (1994) "Black Hair and Red Trousers: Gendering the Flesh in Medieval Japan," *American Historical Review* 99 (1) 129–154.

Tonomura, H. (2017) "Family, Women and Gender in Medieval Society," in K. Friday (ed) *Routledge Handbook of Premodern Japanese History*, London: Routledge.

Tonomura, H., Walthall, A. and Wakita, H. (eds) (1999) *Women and Class in Japanese History*, Ann Arbor: Center for Japanese Studies Publications Program.

Vieillard-Baron, M. (2013) "Male? Female? Gender Confusion in Classical Poetry (*waka*)," *Cipango— French Journal of Japanese Studies* 2, English Selection, 1–23.

Wakita, H. (1985) *Bosei o tou: rekishiteki hensen*, Kyoto: Jinbun shoin.

Wakita, H. (1992) *Nihon chūsei joseishi no kenkyū: Seibetsu yakuwari buntan to bosei, kasei, seiai*, Tokyo: University of Tokyo Press.

Wakita, H., Bouchey, A. and Ueno, C. (eds) (1999) *Gender and Japanese History*, Osaka: Osaka University Press.

3
DEBATES IN JAPANESE FEMINISM

Ayako Kano

The space of debates

Japan presents a paradox: How can a nation that is so highly developed be so gender-unequal that it ranks 114th out of 144 nations (in 2017) on the World Economic Forum's Global Gender Gap Index? Could it be that lack of consensus about gender equality—how to define it, how to achieve it, whether it is desirable—has something to do with this paradox? This chapter examines debates in Japanese feminism. I begin with the role of debate in Japanese publishing culture in general and the sphere of feminist debate in particular, then describe a series of debates about abortion, motherhood, housework, and paid employment.

Debates might be a common feature of intellectual history in general, but the particular prominence of debate in modern Japan can be attributed to a few factors. At least since the late nineteenth century, an intellectual class and educated readership has supported the wide circulation of newspapers and journals, starting with the *Meiroku zasshi* (Meiji six journal 1874–75). This journal, for example, featured an early debate on the definition of equality between women and men (Yamaguchi 1989). Highly informed and motivated editors often stage-managed published conversations and contentions. In the 1920s and 1930s, as leftist intellectuals were forced out of academia along with the rise in militarism, they were recruited by the expanding journalistic world, and general interest magazines such as *Chūō kōron* (Central public debate 1899–) and *Bungei shunjū* (Literary seasons 1923–) became their chief venues of expressions. As these journals competed with one another, their editorial strategies evolved to include staged debates, along with interviews, dialogues (*taidan*), and round-table discussions (*zadankai*) that remain features of Japanese publishing to the present day (Ōsawa 2015).

From its inception, women were part of this world as editors, contributors, and readers. Activists like Kishida Toshiko and Fukuda Hideko aspired to political roles, and public speech making (*enzetsu*) became a new outlet for women's expression in the early Meiji period (Anderson 2010; Patessio 2011). Such roles would eventually become restricted as the government clamped down on women's political activities, yet women continued to publicize their views through writing and circulating petitions. The first journal to be edited by a woman was *Fujin no tomo* (Ladies' companion 1906–), founded by educator Hani Motoko, which sought to promote ideals of feminine education and cultivation. We see the clear emergence of a feminist discursive space in the early twentieth century, with the founding of the journal *Seitō*

(Blue-stocking 1911–1916). This was the first journal to defy existing social expectations about women, and although the publication lasted for only seven years, it launched the writing careers of such women as Hiratsuka Raichō and Itō Noe, who engaged in spirited debates about reproduction, motherhood, and sexuality. Prominent literary figures like the poet Yosano Akiko were also drawn into *Seitō's* ambit. The journal has thus received well-deserved attention and has benefited from sustained scholarly scrutiny (Bardsley 2007; Lowy 2007).

This was followed by another magazine with a long-lived presence in Japanese feminist debates. *Fujin kōron* (Ladies' public debate 1916–) touted the goal of enlightening women through high-quality materials and included a section titled "Public Debate" (*kōron*) in each issue (Frederick 2006). It became the dominant venue for writers on women's issues and helped establish the subject position of "women voicing their opinions in public." Although the publication became more commercialized in the late 1920s, it was intermittently the most important venue for feminist debate in Japan as one of the sites for the "motherhood protection debates," as well as the first wave of "housewife debates," discussed subsequently. The magazine also created a discursive space that guided readers into becoming thinkers and writers themselves. Its column "Free Discussion" (*jiyū rondan*) invited commentaries from readers, and groups of readers organized local discussion circles (Nakao 2009).

In the early twentieth century, a magazine culture focusing on women flourished due to the confluence of several factors: the high rate of literacy due to compulsory education, the rise in publishing technology, women's migration to the cities, and access to white-collar jobs. These contributed to what might be called a female public sphere in which feminist debates could take place. The women's suffrage movement, driven by activists like Ichikawa Fusae and Oku Mumeo, became a major locus of feminist discourse in the 1920s. Socialist and anarchist circles gave rise to intellectuals like Yamakawa Kikue and Takamure Itsue, who were also prominent participants in various debates in that era (Sievers 1983; Mackie 2003).

The expanding empire offered opportunities for some female writers and activists, and feminist support for government policies during this time has constituted an ambivalent legacy for postwar Japanese feminism (Garon 1997; Horiguchi 2012). In the postwar period, popular magazines exploded and new venues were established for discussion of social issues. The late 1960s to 1970s, known as the era of "women's lib," yielded a large number of small-scale mimeographed publications, called "mini-komi." These carried on the ethos of publications like *Seitō*, combining topical, activist, and artistic content, fostering a community of writers and readers that was crucial to the raising of women's consciousness (Shigematsu 2012).

The 1980s was a golden era of feminist debates. The decade saw a flourishing print culture enabled by the economic boom, a critical mass of women entering higher education, and the emergence of female and feminist voices in academia. Movements for gender equality policy gained momentum, and women's studies courses, conferences, and organizations began to lead to the publication of journals and books. The *feminizumu* (feminism, written in the katakana syllabary) boom in the 1980s was at once commercial, political, and academic in nature. The generation of scholars who came into prominence in this era led the feminist debates into the twenty-first century. Sociologist Ehara Yumiko orchestrated a series of five edited volumes of feminist debates on topic such as "commodification of sexuality," "reproductive technology," "nationalism," and "liberalism". She thus became one of the most important coordinators of feminist debate in 1980s and 1990s Japan (Ehara 1990, 1992, 1995, 1996, 1998, 2001). Ueno Chizuko became one of the most prolific and prominent feminist scholars and enlivened the discursive arena through her policy of never backing down from an intellectual fight (see foreword to Ueno 2009, xi–xx). The 1990s were not a "lost decade" for Japanese women, as the economic narrative would suggest. It was an era of significant advances for Japanese women.

But the backlash that followed these advances revealed significant divergence of public opinion about women's roles in society (Kano 2011).

By 2011, many important print journals had ceased publication, and much of the discussion had moved online. The landscape of digital feminist debate is still a little difficult to discern, but informal feminist and gender discussions have continued to take place online on electronic bulletin boards like *Hatsugen komachi* (http://komachi.yomiuri.co.jp).

Debates on abortion

Japan has been characterized as a nation where debates on reproductive choice have been low key and where a tacit consensus has prevailed about abortion as a necessary evil. But, in reality, a lively debate has existed for many decades, and feminists have not been unanimous on the issue. A number of factors make Japanese discussions about abortion unusual, if not unique, in the world (Morioka 2001). First, Japan was one of the earliest nations to decriminalize abortion (1948), and this happened as part of a program that explicitly touted eugenic goals. It was not achieved without controversy, but the circumstances under which decriminalization happened have meant that much less public debate surrounded this momentous change. Second, two decades later, just as the world's advanced industrialized democracies were turning toward liberalizing abortion in the 1960s and 1970s, Japanese public discussion shifted in favour of greater restriction. Although no drastic legal changes resulted, the debate was visible and emotionally charged. Third, while abortion remained accessible and was described as the most popular form of birth control in postwar Japan, access to the contraceptive pill was delayed by several decades and remained controversial for a long time (Norgren 2001). Fourth, Japanese feminist activists, rather than simply arguing for access to abortion as a woman's right, developed a more nuanced argument. This was partly due to the intervention from advocates of the rights of individuals living with congenital disabilities. In other words, the feminist argument about abortion has become deeply intertwined with arguments about eugenics, bioethics, and disability rights in post-1970s Japan.

The beginning of a feminist debate on abortion came in 1915, with the publication of Harada Satsuki's "From a Woman in Prison to a Man" in the pages of the journal *Seitō*. The text takes the form of a letter written by a woman charged with abortion, which was illegal at the time. Harada voices a strong statement in favour of the right to terminate, using the analogy of menstruation and amputation to argue that a woman should not be punished for deciding to get rid of parts of her own body. Also prominent was the depiction of dire poverty that would lead a woman to "bear total responsibility" for the potential life of the fetus by choosing to terminate it since "I do not have the right to force this kind of life on a child" (Harada 1915; for English translation, Bardsley 2007, 70–76). This text provoked the ire of censors but also sparked a lively debate involving prominent intellectuals, including members of the nascent feminist *rondan* (sphere of debate). Most interesting was the response of Itō Noe, who would eventually take over as editor of *Seitō*. This firebrand feminist was vehemently opposed to abortion, but her argument also reveals a deep anxiety about her economic situation. She explains that she was also impoverished when she was pregnant, but thought that "a child would not be born if it were not strong enough to survive this kind of life," and if it could not survive, then it would naturally die (Itō 1915). It is ambiguous whether this statement reflects the high infant mortality rate or persistent practices of child abandonment as alternative to economically motivated infanticide (Sawayama 1998; Drixler 2013). What is striking here is the model of minimalist definition of parental responsibility. Few would agree with Itō's drastic reliance on "nature" to take care of offspring—in the decades that followed, economic destitution would be one of the dominant reasons for arguing in favour of making abortion available. Later it became one of the primary justifications allowing abortion in the postwar period; the "economic reasons" clause has been used in 99 percent of abortion cases to the present day (Katō 2009).

While the economic argument would be used mostly by the side justifying abortion, with Itō a striking exception, a eugenic argument was used first by the proponents and then by the opponents of abortion. Hiratsuka Raichō was one of the earliest and most vocal proponents of eugenics, believing that some individuals were more qualified than others to reproduce. In a 1917 article, she deplored the fact that that people suffering from alcoholism, tuberculosis, leprosy, syphilis, and mental illnesses were bearing children. She called for restrictive qualifications for marriage in order to control the quality of reproduction (Hiratsuka 1917). It is important to remember that eugenics was understood in the early twentieth century to be a rational and even progressive response to social problems, in line with sanitation and hygiene (Otsubo and Bartholomew 1998). Contention existed between those who wanted eugenics to benefit the individual, the family, or the state, but access to reproductive control for women would come at the price of supporting eugenic arguments in the pre-1945 period, and most feminists were in favour.

In the 1960s, the fear of overpopulation that had driven the liberalization of abortion in the postwar period gave way to the era of high economic growth and the need for "high quality" workers. A campaign to prevent the birth of "unhappy children" provided low-cost prenatal testing, including amniocentesis, a recently developed testing technique. This was coupled with the wide accessibility of abortion, unlike elsewhere in the developed nations of the Western bloc. This is precisely why disability rights groups in Japan perceived it with great alarm and why this juncture of prenatal testing and selective abortion became a very contested issue in Japan, more so than in other countries (Kato 2009).

In response to criticism from disability rights advocates, who pointed to selective abortion as a form of eugenics, Japanese feminists have had to develop a more nuanced argument to defend the right to abortion. Unlike the binary of "fetal right to live" versus "woman's right to choose" that has driven the debates in the United States, for example, in Japan, there has been a feminist call for a "society in which women want to give birth." Yet the low birthrate since the 1980s points to a society in which many women do not feel they can or want to give birth. The aversion to eugenics has also led to a difficult position for women wishing to assert more control over reproduction. Prenatal testing and access to reproductive technologies continue to be restricted for various reasons, including the ideology of leaving things to nature, which we saw with Itō Noe in the 1910s (Kano 2016, 64–103).

Debates on motherhood and beyond

Debates on motherhood and employment have erupted at various intervals in modern Japanese history. The various strands can be distilled to a few basic questions: Is motherhood the most important role in women's lives, or is it just one of many? If motherhood is understood to be significant, how should the state or society support it? If it is only one of many roles, what is the role of paid employment in women's lives? How far should women pursue equality with men in paid employment, and what should be the balance between pursuit of career and family? Lack of consensus on these issues may be part of the reason Japan continues to rank low in global measures of "gender equality."

One of the earliest feminist debates is known as the "motherhood protection debate," which began in the 1910s, but the questions it raised persist today. At that point, women were excluded from formal political activity, as the 1890 Law on Associations and Meetings barred women from attending political meetings or joining political organizations (Nolte and Hastings 1991). The official state ideology was to educate women to become "good wives, wise mothers," yet young single women were recruited en masse into factory labour, especially in textile mills. "Motherhood protection" became a concept used by labour activists as well as by feminists associated with *Seitō* (Molony 1993).

The most fundamental concept raised at this historical juncture was whether the state should help mothers if they needed financial support. The poet Yosano Akiko argued that "women's professional independence must be the rule" and that only financially independent women with enough savings had the right to become mothers (Yosano 1918). As a prolific poet, financial supporter of her family, and mother of a large number of children, Yosano was unusual among women in her generation in having achieved a high degree of financial independence and in being able to claim that she had done so through her own labour rather than through inheritance (Rodd 1991; Horiguchi 2012). Yosano's position bears a striking resemblance to the libertarian position in contemporary society, which insists on seeing reproduction as a private matter that should be shielded from state interference, even if that means rejecting state assistance.

In contrast, founder of *Seitō* Hiratsuka Raichō insisted on state protection of motherhood, since "mothers are the wellspring of life" and emphasized the social significance of motherhood (1918). But in doing so, she ended up calling for the state's eugenic control of quality of reproduction, as we saw previously. Disentangling arguments for the social significance of motherhood from arguments for state control of motherhood proved difficult. Thus, Yosano argued against state intervention and posited reproduction as a personal matter, but she had little to say about women for whom financial independence was impossible. Hiratsuka, on the other hand, wanted to emphasize the importance of motherhood, but ended up arguing for its control and regulation by the state. The tension between the wish *not* to equate women with mothers on the one hand and the wish to argue for support for women *as* mothers on the other hand is one of the enduring dilemmas for feminist arguments (Kano 2016, 111–112).

Hiratsuka would go on to found the New Women's Society (Shin Fujin Kyōkai) in 1919 and would advocate not only motherhood protection, but also job training and better working conditions for women, as well as women's right to participate in politics (Sievers 1983). Yosano would assist in the founding of the private Bunka Gakuin school in 1921 and promoted the egalitarian education of female and male students. Education and teaching as a profession would remain a viable path toward financial independence for many women, and teachers were among the first to obtain paid maternity leave and childcare leave. Thus, for neither of these interlocutors did the idea of motherhood protection remain a merely intellectual topic.

In the following decades, the motherhood protection debate was extended into a debate about the political future. Socialist feminist Yamakawa Kikue proposed in 1918 that, "for a fundamental solution, we must seek change in the economic relations that created and exacerbated women's problems in the first place." Yamakawa criticized both Yosano's call for independence within the existing capitalist structure and Hiratsuka's call for state protection. For Yamakawa, only socialism could release women from economic dependence on men. Takamure Itsue entered the debate a few years later, advocating an alternative to both capitalism and socialism in the form of radical agrarian anarchism (1926). That women like Takamure and Yamakawa would debate the shape of a post-capitalism is remarkable, and, as described previously, the interwar *rondan* of the 1920s and early 1930s made such imagined futures seem palpable to these women.

Transnational references in the debates are also significant. Takamure identified Yosano's advocacy of women's independence with Anglo-American liberal feminist traditions, Hiratsuka's advocacy of motherhood protection with German and Scandinavian maternalist feminism, Yamakawa's position with Russian socialist feminism, and her own position as the new direction for Japanese feminism, within the global map of feminist ideologies.

The housewife debates which began in the 1950s and developed in several waves in the ensuing decades further extended motifs of the motherhood protection debates (Ueno 1982; Myōki 2009; Bardsley 2014). Isono Toshiko and others proposed an alternative to women's economic independence via employment by advocating payment for housework and reproductive labour. Those who opposed her argued from a traditional Marxist viewpoint, dismissing housework as not creating value because it does not produce commodities and thus was not deserving of pay. This debate exposed the disagreement between those who affirmed the existing capitalist system by demanding pay for housework and those who saw such demands as giving into the capitalist status quo. Japan in the 1950s and 1960s was a high-pressure laboratory of capitalist development, and these debates were at the forefront of global trends (Ueno 1999). What Isono had discovered, that is, women's "unpaid labor" in the home, later became part of the common terminology of international feminism as a concept that explains the continued economic gap between women and men.

Women continued to make further advances into the workforce, and arguments for women's economic independence and equality in the workplace began to be more forceful. In the 1970s, however, Takeda Kyōko suggested a radical transformation of values, claiming that, "the housewife alone is the figure of a liberated human being." Takeda lauded housewives as having chosen to place themselves in positions of weakness and rejecting economic independence via employment, "in order to coexist with and help out children, the elderly, and the disabled" who are even less capable of economic independence (Ueno 1982, 2, 134–149). The critique of capitalism was part of the countercultural atmosphere and the women's lib movement of the 1960s and 1970s, but ironically this was also the era in which the full-time housewife was the most hegemonic, due to postwar social policy. The postwar industrial and welfare policy in Japan had been designed to support a particular model of life, paying "family wage" to married male workers and providing low-cost company housing and other benefits in exchange for long hours of work and loyalty to the corporation. Married women were expected to support this system by shouldering all aspects of home life (Ōsawa 2011).

In the 1980s, the debate about the value of paid employment and workplace equality culminated in the Equal Employment Opportunity Law of 1985, but it also saw Kanō Mikiyo call for a "total withdrawal" from the workplace as a form of radical feminist protest (1985). The celebration and vilification of the full-time housewife would continue intermittently in the 1990s and 2000s, even as social reality changed so that the majority of married women would be working at least part-time (Myōki 2009). Even after the material basis for the full-time housewife evaporated, the ideology of the liberated housewife continued to persist.

Recent debates focus on how to address the declining birthrate (Takeda 2005) and work-life-balance, whether the state should support individuals or families with children, and how to evaluate paid and unpaid work (Kano 2016). The passing of the Basic Law for Gender Equal Society in 1999 resulted in a harsh backlash from conservatives and revealed the lack of social consensus about gender roles (Kano 2011). While most feminists were critical of the sexual division of labour that equated womanhood with housewife-hood and motherhood, they were divided in how much the government should support women who wished to focus on those roles rather than paid employment. And while most feminists valued economic independence for women, not all saw gender equality within a capitalist system as the ultimate goal (Kano 2018). In the meantime, the position of full-time housewife continues to be protected through insurance and pension provisions, and employment for women and men is far from truly equal (Miura 2016). Thus, the debates continue.

Further reading

Bullock, J., Kano, A. and Welker, J. (eds) (2018) *Rethinking Japanese Feminisms,* Honolulu: University of Hawai'i Press, is an edited anthology showcasing differing views on how to define Japanese feminism.
Kano, A. (2016) *Japanese Feminist Debates: A Century of Contention on Sex, Love, and Labor,* Honolulu: University of Hawai'i Press, is a study of debates on prostitution, abortion, motherhood, employment, and equality.
Mackie, V. (2003) *Feminism in Modern Japan: Citizenship, Embodiment and Sexuality,* Cambridge: Cambridge University Press, provides an excellent historical overview of Japanese feminism as a social movement.

Related chapters

1   *Gendering Modern Japanese History*: An Historiographical Update
9   Attitudes to Marriage and Childbearing
10 Family, Inequality, and the Work-Family Balance in Contemporary Japan
13 Changing Folk Cultures of Pregnancy and Childbirth
15 Gender and the Law: Progress and Remaining Problems
16 Gender and the Workplace
20 Demanding Publics: Women and Activism

References

Anderson, M. (2010) *A Place in Public: Women's Rights in Meiji Japan*, Cambridge, MA: Harvard University Asia Center.
Bardsley, J. (2007) *The Bluestockings of Japan: New Woman Essays and Fiction from Seitō, 1911–16*, Ann Arbor: Center for Japanese Studies, the University of Michigan.
Bardsley, J. (2014) *Women and Democracy in Cold War Japan*, New York: Bloomsbury.
Drixler, F. (2013) *Mabiki: Infanticide and Population Growth in Eastern Japan, 1660–1950*, Berkeley: University of California Press.
Ehara, Y. (ed) (1990) *Feminizumu ronsō: 70 nendai kara 90 nendai e* (Feminist Debates: From the 1970s to the 1990s), Tokyo: Keisō shobō.
Ehara, Y. (1992) *Feminizumu no shuchō* (The Claims of Feminism), Tokyo: Keisō shobō.
Ehara, Y. (1995) *Sei no shōhinka: Feminizumu no shuchō 2* (Commodification of Sex), Tokyo: Keisō shobō.
Ehara, Y. (1996) *Seishoku gijutsu to jendā: Feminizumu no shuchō 3* (Reproductive Technology and Gender), Tokyo: Keisō shobō.
Ehara, Y. (1998) *Sei, bōryoku nēshon: Feminizumu no shuchō 4* (Sex, Violence, Nation), Tokyo: Keisō shobō.
Ehara, Y. (2001) *Feminizumu to riberarizumu: Feminizumu no shuchō 5* (Feminism and Liberalism), Tokyo: Keisō shobō.
Frederick, S. (2006) *Turning Pages: Reading and Writing Women's Magazines in Interwar Japan*, Honolulu: University of Hawai'i Press.
Garon, S. (1997) *Molding Japanese Minds: The State in Everyday Life*, Princeton: Princeton University Press.
Harada, S. (1915) "Gokuchū no onna yori otoko ni" (From a Woman in Prison to a Man), *Seitō* 5 (6).
Hiratsuka, R. (1917) "Hinin no kahi o ronzu" (Debating Whether or Not to Allow Contraception), *Nihon Hyōron* 3 (9).
Hiratsuka, R. (1918) "Bosei hogo no shuchō wa irai shugi ka" (Is the Advocacy of Motherhood Protection Guilty of Dependence), *Fujin Kōron* 3 (5).

Horiguchi, N. J. (2012) *Women Adrift: The Literature of Japan's Imperial Body*, Minneapolis: University of Minnesota Press.
Itō, N. (1915) "Shishin: Nogami Yae sama e" (Private letter: To Ms. Nogami Yae), *Seitō* 5 (6).
Kano, A. (2011) "Backlash, Fight Back, and Back-Pedaling: Responses to State Feminism in Contemporary Japan," *International Journal of Asian Studies* 8 (1) 41–62.
Kano, A. (2016) *Japanese Feminist Debates: A Century of Contention on Sex, Love, and Labor*, Honolulu: University of Hawai'i Press.
Kano, A. (2018) "Womenomics and Acrobatics: Why Many Japanese Feminists Remain Skeptical About Feminist State Policy," *Feminist Encounters: A Journal of Critical Studies in Culture and Politics*, 2 (1), Article number 06.
Kanō, M. (1985) "Shaen kara no sō tettai o: Gutaiteki kaihō senryaku o teiki suru" (For a Total Withdrawal from Corporate Ties: Proposing a Concrete Liberation Strategy), *Shinchihei*.
Kato, M. (2009) *Women's Rights? The Politics of Eugenic Abortion in Modern Japan*, Amsterdam: Amsterdam University Press.
Lowy, D. (2007) *The Japanese "New Woman": Images of Gender and Modernity*, New Brunswick, NJ: Rutgers University Press.
Mackie, V. (2003) *Feminism in Modern Japan: Citizenship, Embodiment and Sexuality*, Cambridge: Cambridge University Press.
Miura, M. (2016) *Welfare Through Work: Conservative Ideas, Partisan Dynamics, and Social Protection in Japan*, Ithaca: Cornell University Press.
Molony, B. (1993) "Equality Versus Difference: The Japanese Debate over 'Motherhood Protection' 1915–50," in J. Hunter (ed) *Japanese Women Working*, London: Routledge, 122–148.
Morioka, M. (2001) *Seimeigaku ni nani ga dekiru ka: Nōshi, feminizumu, yūsei shisō* (What Life Studies Can Do: Brain Death, Feminism, Eugenic Philosophy), Tokyo: Keisō shobō.
Myōki, S. (2009) *Josei dōshi no arasoi wa naze okorunoka: Shufu ronsō no tanjō to shūen* (What Causes Conflict Between Women: The Birth and Death of Housewife Debates), Tokyo: Seidosha.
Nakao, K. (2009) *"Shinpo teki shufu" o ikiru: Sengo "Fujin kōron" no esunogurafi* (Embodying the "Progressive Housewife": Ethnography of Postwar Fujin kōron), Tokyo: Sakuhinsha.
Nolte, S. H. and Hastings, S. A. (1991) "The Meiji State's Policy Toward Women, 1890–1910," in G. L. Bernstein (ed) *Recreating Japanese Women, 1600–1945*, Berkeley: University of California Press, 151–174.
Norgren, T. (2001) *Abortion Before Birth Control: The Politics of Reproduction in Postwar Japan*, Princeton: Princeton University Press.
Ōsawa, M. (2011) *Social Security in Contemporary Japan*, London: Routledge.
Ōsawa, S. (2015) *Hihyō media ron: Senzen Nihon no rondan to bundan* (On Critical Media: The Japanese Debate Sphere and Literary Sphere in the Prewar Era), Tokyo: Iwanami Shoten.
Otsubo, S. and Bartholomew, J. (1998) "Eugenics in Japan: Some Ironies of Modernity, 1883–1945," *Science in Context* 11 (3–4) 545–565.
Patessio, M. (2011) *Women and Public Life in Early Meiji Japan: The Development of the Feminist Movement*, Ann Arbor: Center for Japanese Studies, University of Michigan.
Rodd, L. R. (1991) "Yosano Akiko and the Taishō Debate over the 'New Woman'," in G. L. Bernstein (ed) *Recreating Japanese Women, 1600–1945*, Berkeley: University of California Press, 175–198.
Sawayama, M. (1998) *Shussan to shintai no kinsei* (Birth and Body in the Early Modern Era), Tokyo: Keisō Shobō.
Shigematsu, S. (2012) *Scream from the Shadows: The Women's Liberation Movement in Japan*, Minneapolis: University of Minnesota Press.
Sievers, S. L. (1983) *Flowers in Salt: The Beginnings of Feminist Consciousness in Modern Japan*, Stanford: Stanford University Press.
Takamure, I. (1926) "Ren'ai sōsei" (Creating Romantic Love), in *Takamure Itsue zenshū*, vol. 7, Tokyo: Rironsha.
Takeda, H. (2005) *The Political Economy of Reproduction in Japan: Between Nation-State and Everyday Life*, London: Routledge.
Ueno, C. (1982) *Shufu ronsō o yomu* (Reading the Housewife Debates), vols. 1–2, Tokyo: Tokyo: Keisō Shobō.
Ueno, C. (1999) "Gendering the Concept of 'Labor'," in H. Wakita, A. Bouchy and C. Ueno (eds) *Gender and Japanese History vol. 2, the Self and Expression/Work and Life*, Osaka: Osaka University Press, 537–538.

Ueno, C. (2009) *The Modern Family in Japan: Its Rise and Fall*, Melbourne: Trans Pacific Press.
Yamaguchi, M. (ed) (1989) *Shiryō: Meiji keimō ki no fujin mondai ronsō no shūhen* (Documents: Women's Issues Debates in the Meiji Enlightenment Era), Tokyo: Domesu Shuppan.
Yamakawa, K. (1918) "Bosei hogo to keizaiteki dokuritsu" (Motherhood Protection and Economic Independence), *Fujin Kōron* 3 (9).
Yosano, A. (1918) "Joshi no tettei shita dokuritsu" (Woman's Complete Independence), *Fujin Kōron* 3 (3).

early 1980s directly corresponded with the perceived lack of specific speech acts and qualities, including argumentation, assertiveness, directiveness, the imperative, and plain forms (with no polite markers or honorifics), as well as the final particles and the first-person pronouns that are associated with "masculinity." Reynolds (1985, 36) thus succinctly sums up the power of language to reproduce gender inequality and captures the existential dilemma that confronts Japanese women:

> A woman's place in Japan is still "in the home." If she steps beyond the domestic boundary, she can find no acceptable place or rank to be identified with. Social rules intended for male members do not tell women how they should behave or speak in order to fit into the establishment. Without identity outside the home, women have no choice but to talk formally and unassertively, as men would when they talk to strangers.
> (Reynolds 1985, 36)

The domination theory of Japanese women's language contrasts with yet another perspective on women's language in conjunction with the pragmatics theory of politeness. This approach problematized the application of a Western universal theory of politeness—in part as a linguistic strategy of face-threat avoidance—to the Japanese linguistic behaviour of politeness (Matsumoto 1988). Ide (1992, 127), for example, argues that women's politer speech does not necessarily index their subordination, but rather "the speaker's prestigious status" (Heinrich 2015; Cook 2011; Fukuda and Asato 2004). This culturalist approach to politeness in particular and women's language in general seems to stand in opposition to the dominance approach mentioned earlier. However, the culturalist argument reveals, perhaps not by design, how women's language is "social capital," or to be more precise, "linguistic capital" unevenly distributed across the society in systematic, durable ways. For those who have access to the linguistic capital of elaborate honorifics through education or "good" upbringing, the public display of the mastery of elaborate honorifics is more indexical of the speaker's class disposition of "elegance and dignity" (Ide 2005), but the *distinction* (Bourdieu 1984) of that class *habitus* presumes the *other* listener's subordinated social status. Linguistic deference can be better understood here as the aestheticization of (and thus the normalization of) class inequality, of social hierarchy and submission, which Ide (2005) calls "*wakimae*," or discernment: knowing one's own social position vis-á-vis the interlocutor.

The domination and cultural approaches actually share the same set of assumptions about the relationship among Japanese language, Japanese society/culture, and Japanese gender. The tenability of both approaches rests on the presumption of "Japan" as homogeneous social space in which Japanese women universally or normatively speak women's language and follow its forms as a matter of course, and that they uniformly have *the same experience and habitus as Japanese women*—be it sexism or *wakimae*. Both approaches assume an unbroken continuity of the subject position of Japanese women from, for example, fourteenth-century court ladies to women in present-day Japan. As will be discussed subsequently, other scholars developed alternative approaches based on recognition of the heterogeneity and diversity of language use and women's subject positions and concrete experience.

The matrix of gender and language since the 1990s

Since the 1990s, Western third-wave feminist scholarship moved away from universal and top-down narratives of domination and oppression and paid more attention to the diversity of, and local specificities of, women's linguistic practices. This materialized in the study of Japanese language and gender by a new generation of scholars as the image of women was significantly reframed from a "passive victim" of oppression or a docile "culture-follower" to an active agent creatively strategizing and even transgressing and resisting. This active subject devises linguistic practices out of the available repertoires and resources in a given social location. In the new framework, even if one seems to be conforming to the given norms, it can be understood as a strategy, a product of negotiation, on the part of the agent, not best conceptualized as habitual conformity. Accordingly, it is argued that language as practiced by the agentful speaker is no longer an inert node in the reproduction of "social structure" but a critical locus in and means by which social structure is collectively laid down as *subjects actively construct their own identities*. Language thus came to be linked up more explicitly with individual identities rather than a mutually interchangeable instance of the given social and cultural identity (as in the strong concept of "subject"). In the Japanese context, the shift to a focus on diversity and action also came from the disavowal of Japan and Japanese people as homogeneous. This, needless to say, became a visceral reality in post-bubble Japan in the 1990s, when the myth of Japan as all middle class and the ever-widening gap between haves and have-nots came to be more visible.

Okamoto and Shibamoto-Smith's (2004) groundbreaking introductory essay in their edited volume, *Japanese Language, Gender and Ideology: Cultural Models and Real People*, ushered in such new approaches, which endow the individual speaker with capacities of resistance and creativity (see the contributions by Hideko Abe; Wim Lunsing and Claire Maree; Laura Miller; Ayumi Miyazaki; Momoko Nakamura, Shigeko Okamoto, Cindi Sturtz-Streetharam). In clear intersections with third-wave feminist sociolinguistics in the West, the volume seeks to complicate the abstract gender binary between women and men, to move beyond the stereotypical linguistic features of "women's language" and thus to recuperate the women's voices that the homogeneous discourse of "Japanese women" or "Japanese women's language" had long erased. Previously the study subjects for language and gender were most often urban, middle-class speakers of standard Japanese—those who would fit the norm of "Japanese women's language" speakers (*other* lives were simply ignored as appropriate sources of "data"). The essays in the volume collectively bring out nuanced and dynamic pictures of heterogeneous linguistic practices and their relationship to gender identities through a wide range of "demographic" particularities, from dialect speakers, those in rural areas, sexual minorities, and urban youth to the speech of mass media and the consumer industries.

The new focus on diversity entails a set of parallel methodological moves, which include the conceptual separation of description from prescription, and practices from norms, or between "cultural models and real people" (Okamoto and Shibamoto-Smith 2004). "Women's language" is recast as "language ideology" that is external to, but inescapably entangled with, local, context-specific linguistic practices. Furthermore, the empirical separation of "language and gender" from "women's language" shifted the focus from how women use women's language to what kind of linguistic practices women *and* men perform in their everyday lives regardless of the presence or the absence of gendered speech. Understanding of the scale of gender also shifted from an institution to individual identities. Finally, this new focus entailed a recognition of the intersectionality of gender as it is refracted by and co-constituted by other axes of difference such as region, age, occupation, and social status. These new insights allowed researchers to recognize that language ideology does not simply dictate local practices in a top-down manner. Language ideology is real but iterative and is inescapably malleable and vulnerable to the active speaker-agent mediating and negotiating its terms in ways that are meaningful for the social location she inhabits. Here, gender is no longer understood as an isolated social category but invariably intersects with other structures of difference, and, accordingly, the strategy of critique has also shifted from destabilizing the unity of Japanese language by introducing the gender difference and inequality internal to it to destabilizing the unity of both language and gender by introducing differences and inequality internal to female gender.

One of the new areas of research that opened up in the new wave of language and gender studies concerns the relationship between language and sexuality. Maree (2008) offers a thoughtful analysis of *onē kotoba*, or what she aptly calls "the language of queens," the hyperfeminine speech forms, performed often by "swishy" gay characters on TV (see also Abe 2010) and shows us how their hyper-women's language use, combined with acts of "malicious wit" (2008, 100), creates an effect of sisterhood with female viewers and readers. More importantly, Maree's work on *onē kotoba* most effectively discloses the epistemic violence inherent in the idea of women's language that hinges upon heteronormativity and the exclusion of those who are other.

Another area of research concerns female dialect speakers to whom "women's language" is not necessarily available and for whom it appears as the speech style of the media and of Tokyo, or somewhere other than where they are. Didi-Ogren (2011) offers a nuanced conversation analysis of a group of female Iwate dialect speakers. Against her initial expectations, "women's language" was not used among them. However, her informants deployed multiple linguistic resources, including the local dialect, to negotiate their social status and roles. SturtzSreetharan's (2004, 2017) study of Kansai dialect male speech, which is often associated with working-class masculinity, brings out an alternative interpretation of masculinity to that which is represented by standard Japanese male speech (see also Itakura 2015). In her thoughtful sociolinguistic analysis of the film *Soshite chichi ni naru* (*Like Father, Like Son*, Koreeda Hirokazu, 2013), Sturtz-Sreetharam (2017) points out how the Osaka dialect spoken by the male protagonist makes him a warm and caring figure, in a subtle but undeniable contrast with the traditional image of a father as being stern and distant expressed in standard Japanese. Here we can appreciate how the Osaka dialect that is often associated with aggressive masculinity, in fact, produces the effect of alternative fatherhood that somehow more realistically captures the figure of the father in the post-recessionary Japanese family.

Scholars have also studied the linguistic practices of women in various nontraditional workplaces, roles, and statuses, especially where women assume the position of authority that would otherwise be associated with the male figure (Dubuc 2012; Takano 2005; Shibamoto Smith 1992; Inoue 2006). How do such women reconcile the perceived role conflict between their gender and their professional responsibilities, and how does it get played out in their linguistic practices? For example, how do they perform male-associated speech acts such as directing and reprimanding? These studies consistently show how women draw on multiple linguistic styles available to them to make their own identity of authority without simply defaulting to male forms.

The new paradigm also foregrounds figures of resistance against "women's language." Miyazaki (2004) carried out a longitudinal ethnographic study among junior high school students, where she worked with girls who use the male first-person pronoun, "boku." It is a defiant refusal to accept linguistic norms. But, as Miyazaki explains, it is not necessarily against authority or the abstract sense of femininity, and also registers a group solidarity, a clear demarcation between "them" and "us" in the social world. Other scholars also explore Japanese subcultures, where language plays significant roles in constructing alternative gender identities. Miller's analysis shows how *kogals*, a name for female, teenage hyper-consumers of fashion, cultivate their aesthetic selfhood through developing and circulating their own slang. Gagné (2008) studies an interesting revival of archaic female speech forms in Japan's Gothic/Lolita subculture, which shows how the Gothic/Lolita persona emerges in the linguistically materialized anachronism, and the reversal of the linear temporality from the past to the present itself co-constitutes its subcultural identity.

The mediatization of "women's language"

In the past, scholars tended to shy away from studying media representations of female and male speech because they were considered secondary and inauthentic as empirical data, as mere representations of real speech. This is not to say that there was no prior study focusing on the social meanings of gendered language in media texts. What is new about more recent studies is their theoretical recognition of the autonomy of media representations of gendered language as constitutive of the reproduction of power relations. In other words, they are no longer treated as "not-so-perfect" representations of "real speech" out there, but as active presentations that perform ideological work (see various contributions in Okamoto and Shibamoto-Smith 2004). Instead of looking for the relationship between the media representation and the supposed empirical reality of actually spoken speech, some scholars now ask what kind of linguistic forms are assigned to what kind of characters and images and what kind of effects are produced.

Kinsui and Yamakido (2015) develop a general framework for such an investigation called *yakuwarigo* or "role language," a robust register that tightly connects a particular speech form and its corresponding character or image (see also Teshigawara and Kinsui 2011). What distinguishes *yakuwarigo* from the regular registers is that it is a media creation with no putative demographic origin. For example, many Japanese speakers would identify the verb-ending form "ja" as that belonging to an elderly speaker, and yet it is highly likely that they have never met any actual elderly person using "ja." Rather than assuming the speech forms used in the media as a direct representation of reality, studies of gendered speech produced in various genres, including romance novels (Shibamoto Smith and Occhi 2009), anime (Hiramoto 2010), manga (Unser-Schutz 2015), self-help literature (Nakamura 2014; Washi 2004; also see the contributions in Bardsley and Miller 2011), girls' magazines, and commodity advertisement (Arima 2003; Miller 2004, 2006; Inoue 2008) and blogs (Nishimura 2016), to name a few, also suggest the importance of zeroing in on how femininity and masculinity are linguistically marked in genre-specific manners.

Recasting women's language not as a statistical summation of empirically existing women repeatedly speaking it, but as an imagined and mediated reality that is not reducible to any empirically existing women, some scholars also turn to how and where such an imaginary is produced and reproduced in the society beyond the obvious sites such as the school and the home. For example, consider the Japanese-as-a-foreign-language classroom, where the fiction of homogeneity of both the Japanese language and Japanese culture is normalized for the sake of pedagogy. Siegal and Okamoto (2003) critically bring to the surface the unreflexive gendered politics of "standard" Japanese-as-a-foreign-language textbooks by examining how "women's language" is taught as the default form for female learners. Kumagai (2014) also observes how Japanese language students learn a reified and hegemonic version of "Japanese culture and language" in their pedagogical interactions with their instructors and brings to our attention the fact that foreign language instruction, far from being apolitical, entails formidable political decisions and responsibilities regarding how Japan is seen and not seen by foreigners (Sato and Doerr 2014).

The fact that a "standard Japanese" exists as a concept, in itself and inevitably, marginalizes its "outside." What is considered worthy to be taught and to be learned by Japanese language learners is the language and culture of an imaginary urban middle-class standard (gendered) Japanese speaker. But what brilliantly transpires in the studies just mentioned is the warped mediation of race through (Japanese) gender and class. What does it mean, for example, for a white American female college student to be taught to learn, if not to speak, "the Japanese female speech?" How is she interpellated by her imagination and use of "women's language," particularly if she visits Japan or converses with native speakers? And what does it mean for a *working-class* or *non-white* Japanese language student in the United States to learn the variation of Japanese language associated with the elite class? How is she interpellated in visiting Japan or speaking with native Japanese speakers? Clearly, these are open-ended questions, the pursuit of which would give us worthwhile insights into "language and gender" (and race and class) in transnational contexts.

Gendered speech also crops up in the space of interlingual translation, and Japanese gender stereotypes get reproduced, ironically enough, through foreign gendered bodies. For example, Inoue examined the Japanese translation of *Gone with the Wind*, in which the protagonist Scarlett O'Hara speaks "women's language," whereas house servants Mammy and Prissy are translated into the Japanese northern dialect with no gendered speech forms (Inoue 2003). In this case, "women's language" as an ideology is reproduced as the index of *whiteness* (see also Nakamura 2014 for the case of *Harry Potter* translation). It is also widely observed that the male speech style as in the first-person pronoun, "ore," is often assigned to the translation of foreign male athletes (see also Ota 2011), rock musicians, and actors.

Conclusion: historicizing women's language

The trope of diversity that underwrites much of the contemporary study of Japanese language and gender has successfully provincialized the notion of "women's language" as an ideological construct (Inoue 2006; Nakamura 2014; Okamoto 2014) that does not represent the sociolinguistic realities of Japanese women. But the point is *not* that we should as sociolinguists focus only on the immediate local context. Given that any linguistic practice generates multiple layers of meanings and interpretations, it is imperative to think about how to theorize the linkage between ideology and practice for the study of gender and language. An ideology, after all, is a social reality. It has "power-effects" and is drawn upon as an instrumentality by real historical actors. Asking where women's language as an ideology originates and how that ideology is iterated, transgressed, resisted, or otherwise drawn upon is a critical step. Historicizing women's language—seeking its "birth" and reproduction through concrete processes of communication, education, and mediation and disclosing its inescapable linkages to power and political projects—makes it possible for us to situate the immediate local contexts as instances in a broader historical and political arc. Thus, we can glimpse an avenue to re-establish the relevance of power and politics to linguistic practice in new ways and thus to conceptualize the empirical speaker-actor both as the subject and the object of women's language as an ideology.

Here is a concrete example of what I mean. Earlier feminist scholars did work on the history of women's language (Endo 2006; Jugaku 1979). Their work presupposes the transhistorical subject of women's language and its unbroken continuity throughout the history of Japanese society. But this is a myth rather than a history, for it does not explain how women's language—or "Japanese women," for that matter—came into being other than presupposing Japanese sexism as a continuous and ubiquitous, but abstract, force. Nakamura's (2014) recent monumental work on the history of the subject of women's language makes a decisive intervention in this regard. While keeping the historical continuity of women's language intact (as an "ideal" of some kind, not an observable statistical pattern), Nakamura cogently shows how at each critical point in history, "women's language" was materially produced out of concrete political projects. In her historical account, sexism is no longer a timeless presence but is a concrete function of historically determinate and material institutional powers. Such a methodological innovation is also shared by Washi's (2004) critical analysis of language policy during WWII and its construction of women's language.

Emphasizing discontinuity over continuity, Inoue focused on the epistemic break in the late nineteenth century when women's language emerged as part of situated projects of national modernization in which language played a central role in producing the modern gendered subject (Inoue 2006). She argues that it was indeed part of the project of national modernity that retroactively strung together disparate instances of gendered speech in the historical past and rendered them into a linearly coherent historical narrative, as the historical continuity and linear temporal progression was the essential qualification of the modern nation-state.

What we are left with is the challenge of how to bring history, politics, and power back into the analysis of the relationship between gender and language. Seeking to understand how "women's language" as a language ideology does political work, or is otherwise entailed in ongoing political projects, is a promising way forward.

Further reading

Endo, O. and Jugaku, A. (eds) (2001) *Onna to kotoba: onna wa kawatta ka, nihongo wa kawatta ka* (Women and Language: Have Women Changed? Has Japanese Language Changed?), Tokyo: Akashi Shoten.

Ide, S. (1979) *Onna no kotoba otoko no kotoba* (Women's Language and Men's Language), Tokyo: Nihon Keizai Tsushinsha.

Ide, S. (ed) (1997) *Joseigo no sekai* (Worlds of Women's Language), Tokyo: Meiji Shoin.

Ide, S. and McGloin, N. H. (1990) *Onnakotoba no sugata* (Aspects of Japanese Women's Language), Tokyo: Kurosio.

Maree, C. (2013) *"Onē kotoba" ron* (On Onē Language), Tokyo: Seidosha.

Nakamura, M. (2012) *Onna kotoba to nihongo* (Women's Language and Japanese Language), Tokyo: Iwanami Shoten.

Nakamura, M. (2013) *Hon'yaku ga tsukuru Nihongo: hiroin wa "onnakotoba" o hanashitsuzukeru* (Japanese Language that Translation Makes: Heroines Continue to Speak Women's Language), Tokyo: Hakutakusha.

Reynolds, K. A. (1993) *Onna to nihongo* (Women and Language), Tokyo: Yushindo.

Sasaki, M. and Nihongo Jendā Gakkai (2006) *Nihongo to jendā* (Japanese Language and Gender), Tokyo: Hitsuji Shobō.

Related chapters

5 Masculinity Studies in Japan
6 Transgender, Non-Binary Genders, and Intersex in Japan
16 Gender and the Workplace
24 Women and Physical Culture in Japanese History
25 Myths of Masculinity in the Martial Arts

References

Abe, H. (2010) *Queer Japanese: Gender and Sexual Identities Through Linguistic Practices*, New York: Palgrave Macmillan.

Arima, A. N. (2003) "Gender Stereotypes in Japanese Television Advertisements," *Sex Roles* 49 (1–2) 81–90.

Bardsley, B. and Miller, L. (eds) (2011) *Manners and Mischief: Gender and Power in Japanese Conduct Literature*, Berkeley: University of California Press.

Bourdieu, P. (1984) *Distinction: A Social Critique of the Judgement of Taste*. Cambridge, MA: Harvard University Press.

Cook, H. M. (2011) "Are Honorifics Polite? Uses of Referent Honorifics in a Japanese Committee Meeting," *Journal of Pragmatics* 43 (15) 3655–3672.

Didi-Ogren, H. K. (2011) "Japanese Women's Language Use and Regional Language Varieties: Evidence from Women's Decision-Making Interactions in Iwate Prefecture," *Gender and Language* 5 (1) 61–87.

Dubuc, C. E. (2012) "When Women Are in Charge: The Language Japanese Women Speak at Work," *Anthropologica* 54 (2) 293–308.

Endo, O. (1995) "Aspects of Sexism in Language," in K. Fujimura-Fanselow and A. Kameda (eds) *Japanese Women: New Feminist Perspectives on the Past, Present, and Future*, New York: The Feminist Press, 29–42.

Endo, O. (2006) *A Cultural History of Japanese Women's Language*, vol. 57, Ann Arbor, MI: University of Michigan, Center for Japanese Studies.

Endo, O. (2008) "The Role of Court Lady's Language in the Historical Norm Construction of Japanese Women's Language," *Gender & Language* 2 (1) 9–24.

Fukuda, A. and Asato, N. (2004) "Universal Politeness Theory: Application to the Use of Japanese Honorifics," *Journal of Pragmatics* 36 1991–2002.

Gagné, I. (2008) "Urban Princesses: Performance and 'Women's Language' in Japan's Gothic/Lolita Subculture," *Journal of Linguistic Anthropology* 18 (1) 130–150.

Heinrich, P. (2015) "The Study of Politeness and Women's Language in Japan," in D. Smakman (ed) *Globalising Sociolinguistics: Challenging and Expanding Theory*, London: Routledge, 178–193.

Hiramoto, M. (2010) "Anime and Intertextualities: Hegemonic Identities in Cowboy Bebop," *Pragmatics and Society* 1 (2) 234–256.

Hiramoto, S. and Wong, A. (2005) "Another Look at 'Japanese Women's Language': A Prosodic Analysis," *Proceedings of the Annual Meeting of the Chicago Linguistics Society* 28 101–112.

Ide, S. (1992) "Gender and Function of Language Use: Quantitative and Qualitative Evidence from Japanese," *Pragmatics and Language Learning* 3 117–129.

Ide, S. (2005) "How and Why Honorifics Can Signify Dignity and Elegance: The Indexicality and Reflexivity of Linguistic Rituals," in S. Ide and T. R. Lakoff (eds) *Broadening the Horizon of Linguistic Politeness*, Amsterdam: John Benjamins Pub, 45–64.

Inoue, M. (2003) "Speech Without a Speaking Body: 'Japanese Women's Language' in Translation," *Language & Communication* 23 (3–4) 315–330.

Inoue, M. (2006) *Vicarious Language: Gender and Linguistic Modernity in Japan*, Berkeley, CA: University of California Press.

Inoue, M. (2008) "Things That Speak: Peirce, Benjamin, and the Kinesthetics of Commodity Advertisement in Japanese Women's Magazines, 1900s-1930s," *Positions: East Asia Cultures Critique* 15 (3) 511–552.

Itakura, H. (2015) "Constructing Japanese Men's Multidimensional Identities," *Pragmatics* 25 (2) 179–203.

Jugaku, A. (1979) *Nihongo to onna* (Japanese Language and Women), Tokyo: Iwanami Shoten.

Jugaku, A. (1999) "Nyôbô kotoba: A Focus Point for Women's Language and Women's History," *Gender and Japanese History* 2 131–161.

Kinsui, S. and Yamakido, H. (2015) "Role Language and Character Language," *Acta Linguistica Asiatica* 5 (2) 29–42.

Kumagai, Y. (2014) "On Learning Japanese Language: Critical Reading of Japanese Language Textbook," in S. Sato and N. Doerr (eds) *Rethinking Language and Culture in Japanese Education: Beyond the Standard*, Tonawanda, NY: Multilingual Matters, 201–217.

Lakoff, R. T. (1975) *Language and Woman's Place*, New York: Harper & Row.

Maree, C. (2008) "Grrrl-Queens: One-Kotoba and the Negotiation of Heterosexist Gender Language Norms and Lesbo (Homo) Phobic Stereotypes in Japan," in F. Martin (ed) *Asiapacific Queer: Rethinking Genders and Sexualities*, Urbana, IL: University of Illinois Press, 67–84.

Matsumoto, Y. (1988) "Reexamination of the Universality of Face: Politeness Phenomena in Japanese," *Journal of Pragmatics* 12 (4) 403–426.

Miller, L. (2004) "Those Naughty Teenage Girls: Japanese Kogals, Slang, and Media Assessments," *Journal of Linguistic Anthropology* 14 (2) 225–247.

Miller, L. (2006) *Beauty up: Exploring Contemporary Japanese Body Aesthetics*, Berkeley: University of California Press.

Miyazaki, A. (2004) "Japanese Junior High School Girls' and Boys' First-Person Pronoun Use and Their Social World," in S. Okamoto and J. Shibamoto Smith (eds) *Japanese Language, Gender and Ideology: Cultural Models and Real People*, Oxford: Oxford University Press, 256–274.

Nakamura, M. (1995) *Kotoba to Feminizumu* (Language and Feminism), Tokyo: Keiso.

Nakamura, M. (2014) *Gender, Language and Ideology: A Genealogy of Japanese Women's Language*, Philadelphia: John Benjamins.

Nishimura, Y. (2016) "Age, Gender and Identities in Japanese Blogs," in S. Leppänen, E. Westinen and S. Kytola (eds) *Social Media Discourse, (Dis)Identifications and Diversities*, Tokyo: Routledge, 263–286.

Ohara, Y. (2004) "Prosody and Gender in Workplace interaction: Exploring Constraints and Resources in the Use of Japanese," in S. Okamoto and J. Shibamoto Smith (eds) *Japanese Language, Gender, and Ideology: Cultural Models and Real People*, Oxford: Oxford University Press, 222–239.

Okamoto, S. (2014) "Rethinking 'Norms' for Japanese Women's Speech," in S. Sato and N. M. Doerr (eds) *Rethinking Language and Culture in Japanese Education: Beyond the Standard*, Tonawanda, NY: Multilingual Matters, 82–105.

Okamoto, S. and Shibamoto-Smith, J. S. (2004) *Japanese Language, Gender and Ideology: Cultural Models and Real People*, Oxford: Oxford University Press.

Ota, M. (2011) "Usain Boruto no 'I' wa, naze 'ore' to yakusareru no ka: supōtsu hōsō no 'yakuwarigo'" (Why Is Usain Bolt's 'I' Translated to 'Ore'? The Role Languages of Sports Broadcasting), in S. Kinsui (ed) *Yakuwarigo kenkyuu no tenkai* (The Development of Role Language Research), Tokyo: Kuroshio Shuppan, 93–125.

Reynolds, A. K. (1985) "Female Speakers of Japanese," *Feminist Issues* 5 (2) 13–46.

Sato, S. and Doerr, N. (eds) (2014) *Rethinking Language and Culture in Japanese Education: Beyond the Standard*, Tonawanda, NY: Multilingual Matters.

Shibamoto Smith, J. S. (1985) *Japanese Women's Language*. Orlando, FL: Academic Press.

Shibamoto Smith, J. S. (1992) "Women in Charge: Politeness and Directives in the Speech of Japanese Women," *Language in Society* 21 (1) 59–82.

Shibamoto Smith, J. S. and Occhi, D. J. (2009) "The Green Leaves of Love: Japanese Romantic Heroines, Authentic Femininity, and Dialect," *Journal of Sociolinguistics* 13 (4) 524–546.

Siegal, M. and Okamoto, S. (2003) "Toward Reconceptualizing the Teaching and Learning of Gendered Speech Styles in Japanese as a Foreign Language," *Japanese Language and Literature* 37 (1) 49–66.

Starr, R. L. (2015) "Sweet Voice: The Role of Voice Quality in a Japanese Feminine Style," *Language in Society* 44 (1) 1–34.

Sturtz-Sreetharan, C. L. (2004) "Japanese Men's Linguistic Stereotypes and Realities: Conversations from the Kansai and Kanto Regions," in S. Okamoto and J. Shibamoto-Smith (eds) *Japanese Language, Gender, and Ideology: Cultural Models and Real People*, Oxford: Oxford University Press, 275–289.

SturtzSreetharan, C. L. (2017) "Resignifying the Japanese Father: Mediatization, Commodification, and Dialect," *Language & Communication* 53 45–58.

Takano, S. (2005) "Re-Examining Linguistic Power: Strategic Uses of Directives by Professional Japanese Women in Positions of Authority and Leadership," *Journal of Pragmatics* 37 (5) 633–666.

Tannen, D. (1996) *Gender and Discourse*, New York: Oxford University Press.

Teshigawara, M. and Kinsui, S. (2011) "Modern Japanese 'Role Language' (*Yakuwarigo*): Fictionalised Orality in Japanese Literature and Popular Culture," *Sociolinguistic Studies* 5 (1) 37–58.

Unser-Schutz, G. (2015) "Influential or Influenced? The Relationship Between Genre, Gender and Language in Manga," *Gender & Language* 9 (2) 223–254.

Washi, R. (2004) "Japanese Female Speech and Language Policy in the World War II Era," in S. Okamoto and J. Shibamoto-Smith (eds) *Japanese Language, Gender, and Ideology: Cultural Models and Real People*, Oxford: Oxford University Press, 76–91.

5
MASCULINITY STUDIES IN JAPAN

Emma E. Cook

Sarariiman (salaryman), *otaku* (geek), *sōshokukei danshi* (herbivorous man), *himote* (undesirable[s]): these are all words that resonate throughout men's studies in Japan today. What is it to be a man in Japan? What constitutes "masculinity," and how does it affect men's lives? How do labour and masculinities continue to intersect? How is masculinity implicated in sex, sexualities, and intimacy? These are some of the driving questions in contemporary Japanese masculinities studies. Masculinity continues to be a topic of significant interest across a variety of disciplines, including sociology, history, and psychology. Indeed, if you Google "masculinities Japan" in Google Scholar in English, you'll get 20,600 results (as of 12 August 2018). In Japanese, 2,640 results come back. If we refine this to the last five years, then the results are 10,700 in English and 756 in Japanese. Given space limitations, this chapter introduces some of the dominant trends in the discipline of masculinities studies (*danseigaku*) in Japan today, primarily covering the 2000s and 2010s, with a particular focus on the trend to explore "alternative" masculinities via labour, caring, intimacy, and sexuality. For readers interested in trends in masculinities studies from the 1980s until the early 2000s, see Taga (2005).

The salaried hegemon: labour, productivity, and masculinities

By far the most dominant discourse with which masculinities studies in Japan continues to grapple, turn to, lean on, or attempt to escape from, is that of the ubiquitous "salaryman." As such, most authors turn to R. W. Connell's (2005) theory of hegemonic masculinity. As Dasgupta (2010, note 4) eloquently put it, hegemonic masculinity is:

> [T]he discourse of masculinity which at a given time in a given society has the greatest ideological power, both in relation to women and femininity/ies, and in relation to other coexisting and intersecting masculinities. Thus, hegemonic masculinity may be regarded as the cultural "ideal" or "blueprint" that has a powerful (and often unarticulated) presence in the lives of men and women. However, at the same time, as Connell stresses, it need not be the most common form, nor the "most comfortable."

In the Japanese context, the white-collar male salaried employee at a large company (the "salaryman") is said to embody this hegemonic type of masculinity. One of the reasons for such continued reference, even for authors writing about alternative masculinities, is that many people in Japan refer to ideals that are embodied in this figure. In particular, there is a continued focus on male productivity, labour, breadwinning, and specific types of familial responsibility. It thus becomes hard to ignore a figure that is ubiquitous even if not, strictly speaking, particularly common. Frühstück and Walthall (2011a) concisely argue that "distinct modes of masculinity become visible only if pitched against an actual or imagined Other" (2011a, 7). The image of the salaried male worker continues, in scholarship on masculinities in Japan, not just as an ideal that is held to be hegemonic, but also as an other against which alternative "types" are measured (Roberson and Suzuki 2003).

"Alternative" masculinities, but still productive...

A significant trend since the early 2000s is a focus on masculinities that are non-hegemonic, "subordinated," or alternative. For example, in their classic edited volume, Roberson and Suzuki (2003) discuss the importance of "dislocating the salaryman doxa." The contributors focus on masculinities and masculine bodies in a variety of topics and contexts, including through beauty work, transgender experiences, fantasy spaces, illness, masculinity within families, and through "what makes life worth living" (*ikigai*), marriage markets, fatherhood, and violence, as well as via explorations of masculinity in relation to class and the nation. Meanwhile, contributors to Frühstück and Walthall's (2011b) edited volume provide an important addition to scholarship on manhood by looking at changing gender ideologies and discourses ranging from early modern Japan of the seventeenth century through to the contemporary period. Topics range from warrior legacies to men at the margins to an exploration of "bodies and boundaries." A focus that runs throughout is on how changes in social roles have prompted various crises of masculinity that are socio-historically, and economically, contingent (see also works by Inoue et al. 1995; Itō 1993, 1996, 2002, 2003; Itō et al. 2011; Taga 2001, 2005, 2006, 2011, 2016; Tanaka 2009, 2015, 2016).

What is clear in much of this work is a strong interlinkage between ideas and ideals of productivity and manhood. Condry (2011), for example, argues that "otaku" (nerds/geeks) are often understood as being an antithesis of the "salaryman," as "failed men" (Galbraith 2015b) (never mind the fact that a man may be simultaneously a salaried full-time employee at a large company and a self-proclaimed otaku). There remains a fundamental assumption in Japan that a man's masculinity is embedded in his productivity (see also Cook 2013, 2016, 2017; Fujimura 2006; Gill 2001, 2003, 2012; Slater and Galbraith 2011).

In recent years, there has also, however, been greater public debate about the costs of working expectations on men's lives and health (Kawanishi 2008; Morioka 2013a; North and Morioka 2016), with some calling for a disentanglement between work and ideals of masculinity. In 2016, a leading masculinities studies scholar in Japan, Tanaka Toshiyuki, published a book aimed at general readership provocatively titled *Otoko ga hatarakanai, ii janai ka!* (A man who doesn't work, it's good, right?!). Tanaka (2016) argues that we need to rethink why and how men work, as well as questioning the idea that "it's natural for men to work." He suggests that men working as full-time salaried employees is seen as common sense in Japan and that this prevents an interrogation of why that is the case, despite significant changes in the economic and employment structure and more diversity in the workforce since the 1990s. Tanaka advocates a slowing down for both men and women through reducing working hours and workdays, as well as providing more flexibility in, and at, work for men and women. Doing so, he argues, would make it easier for both men and women to look after children and to work at the same time. As such, his main argument is that there needs to be greater social recognition and acceptance of diversity in the workforce and in how individuals themselves work. He thus advocates for a lessening in strong social norms that link labour and masculinities.

Changing ideals: caring, "ikumen" and elder care

Hegemonic ideals do, of course, change. In recent years, it is clear that expectations of what men should "do" extend beyond paid work and into domains of intimacy, sex, marriage, and family. For example, expectations of changing male roles in families have been discussed by a number of authors (Ishii-Kuntz 2003, 2013, 2015; Mizukoshi et al. 2016; Nakatani 2006; Tatsumi 2015, 2018), with many focusing in recent years on the figure of the *ikumen*: a neologism that combines the word for childcare (*ikuji*) with the word "men." It is, however, also a play on the word *ikemen*, which refers to a man who is good looking/hot, with the implication that men who are involved in childcare are cool (Mizukoshi et al. 2016).

Whilst Charlebois (2017b) argues that *ikumen*—which he glosses as "stay-at-home dads," though it is more accurately understood as an active and involved father who is typically *not* a stay-at-home dad—can be conceived of as an alternative masculinity, others, such as Ishii-Kuntz (2013, 2015), understand it to be a shifting of hegemonic ideals. Tatsumi (2015, 2018), for example, argues that being an active father continues to presuppose that men will also continue to be first and foremost active and productive workers (see also Vassallo 2017). Moreover, Ishii-Kuntz (2013, 2015) clearly demonstrates the ways in which the *ikumen* discourse, as part of a governmental push spearheaded by the Ministry of Health, Labour and Welfare, is linked to worries about demographic issues (see, for example, https://ikumen-project.mhlw.go.jp/). Indeed, this isn't the first time that the government has advocated men as active fathers: in the 1990s, the "Sam Campaign" suggested, "A man who doesn't raise his children can't be called a father" (2015, 163). It was also linked to the government's "Angel Plan," which sought to increase the birth rate through various projects such as providing more childcare subsidies and places for children in day care (Roberts 2002). Ishii-Kuntz (2015) illustrates how changing ideas indicate a shifting and diversification of hegemonic ideals. It is not necessarily the case that *ikumen* exhibit alternative masculinities, as Charlebois (2017b) claims, but that there are changes to what constitute normative ideals of masculinity which now include involved fathers, even if this can be difficult to enact because of conflicting expectations on men as productive breadwinners who work long hours. As Ishii-Kuntz (2015, 164) notes, "the conduct of fatherhood has not caught up with the culture."

Whilst most research on caring and masculinities focuses on childcare, Umegaki-Costantini (2017) provides an invaluable glimpse of the lives of older men caring for parents-in-law, something traditionally considered a woman's role. In her careful analysis, we can see the various contradictions that the men she worked with expressed about later life caring and the ways they sought to mitigate and come to terms with these contradictions to their sense of masculinity. One such way was the foregrounding of tasks that they felt were linked to masculinities, for example, anything that necessitated physical strength, moving their masculinities away from cerebral work to physical labour and, one could argue, a less elite or more working-class conception of manhood (see, for example, Roberson 2003).

Intimacy, (hetero)sex, and marriage

The discourse of men as failing at intimacy, marriage, or sex is a significant trend in contemporary research. For example, Miles (2017, 2018) explores "economies of intimacy," focusing on men who are considered to be "of no value." She argues that contemporary masculinity in Japan revolves around the idea of "men who can do" (*dekiru otoko*), and she defines masculinity "*as* ability" (2017, 63). This focus on action (see also Cook 2016) sits at the heart of contemporary masculinities, with many of the discourses of manhood revolving around what men are doing or *not* doing. For example, herbivorous men are said not to be "doing" dating or sex right (Charlebois 2017a; Kumagai 2012; Morioka 2008, 2013b; Saladin 2017). Male irregular workers—or at least those from middle-class families—are thought not to be doing work "properly" and by extension often struggle to marry and sustain families (Cook 2013, 2014, 2016, 2017, 2018), and *otaku* are considered to be failing at appropriate expressions of desire and sexuality (Galbraith 2015a, 2015b).

Arguing that male identities in Japan have become "unmoored from traditional lifeways of work and marriage, and have increasingly been focused around the body and modes of public display and self-representation" (Miles 2017, 66), Miles critiques the buzzwords that have come to represent "new" masculinities but in practice obscure the complex lived realities and diverse experiences of manhood in "postmainstream Japan" (2017, 66). Such buzzwords, as Miles rightly points out, are often highly problematic. Moreover, the trends that these buzzwords represent are not so new. For example, in 1996, Itō Kimio argued that there had been a shift in expectations of masculinities, with a move from men who should swagger and exhibit an overt physical masculinity to expressions of "tender-hearted" masculinities. He used *messhii-kun*: men that pay for dinner; *mitsugu-kun*: men that buy gifts for women who may—or may not be—their girlfriends; and *asshii-kun*: men that drive women around, as ostensible chauffeurs, as examples (Itō 1996; non-Japanese readers can read some of Itō's arguments via McLelland and Dasgupta's translated exerpts in Itō 2005). Of course, all three of these still consist of men who are "succeeding" enough with women to take them out for dinner, buy them gifts, or drive them around, but nevertheless these terms indicated a change in what was previously expected. We can also see "softer" masculinities in discussions of popular culture and media icons, as embodied in Johnny's Jimusho (Johnny's Office) idols such as SMAP and Arashi who are supposed to downplay any overt heteronormative masculinity and are not allowed to discuss any romantic relationships in order to appear available to maintain the fiction of these figures as vehicles of female fantasy. They are typically portrayed as approachable, gentle, sensitive, all-round good guys that can slot into what Glasspool (2012, 117) suggests is a "somewhat domestic manhood" (see also Darling-Wolf 2004a).

Buzzwords that index ideas of masculinity continue to be common, and we see this from the increased interest in "*ikumen*" and "herbivorous men" (*sōshokukei danshi*). Although *ikumen*, as already discussed, are more family oriented and caring than the stereotype of the emotionally distant fiscal provider of postwar Japan, most new buzzwords that index masculinities in some way commonly focus on men who are unassertive, uninterested, or uninteresting to women and thus socially problematic (Chen 2012; Miles 2017, 2018; Morioka 2013b; Saladin 2015, 2017; Ushikubo 2008).

Male bodies, masculinities, and sexualities

Men's bodies—and what men do or don't do with them—are also in the spotlight. As Connell argues, "True masculinity is almost always thought to proceed from men's bodies—to be inherent in a male body or to express something about a male body" (2005, 45). There are multiple discourses of male bodies in the scholarship of Japan—of sporting bodies (Barber 2014; Chapman 2004; Light 2003; Manzenreiter 2011, 2013), military bodies (Frühstück 2007; Low 2003; Mason 2011; Satō 2010), commodified bodies (Takeyama 2010; 2016), fantasize-able bodies (Darling-Wolf 2004a, 2004b; Glasspool 2012), and passive/asexual bodies (Charlebois 2017a; Saladin 2015), to name just five.

Lin et al. (2017) argue, however, that in East Asia "the relationship between masculinity and sexuality has been underexplored, with earlier commentators suggesting that masculinity 'leans' on sexuality" (2017, 3). Whilst normative ideals of masculinity in the Japanese context are intimately interlinked with heterosexuality, heteronormative marriage, and procreation, a number of prominent scholars have explored sexuality and masculinities, primarily via analyses of homosexuality, though some work on transgender male experiences also exists (e.g. Lunsing 2003; McLelland et al. 2007).

McLelland (2003, 2005a, 2005b, 2011) reminds readers that during the Tokugawa era, male homosexuality was conceptualized "as a masculine and even masculinizing practice" (McLelland 2000, 24) and that it is only since the Meiji era that male same-sex desire became pathologized or considered unusual or problematic due to post-Meiji social changes and imported discourses of sexual deviance. The implication from this work is that sexual practices were more diverse pre-Meiji and that same-sex practice was, for some men, part of constructing masculinities. During the Meiji period, however, "[T]he issue of sex, both hetero- and homosexual, was seen as a potentially damaging distraction from which a young man needed protection" (McLelland 2000, 24): a radically different discourse than in Japan today where male sexuality is predominantly linked to concerns about population decline. Men who are not heterosexual or not interested in sex or marriage are thus often considered problematic. Dasgupta (2005, 2013, 2017), for example, has argued that some gay men he worked with married but pursued their sexual desires outside the home in order to minimize the impact of discrimination against unmarried adult men in the workplace (see also Lunsing 2001).

Although these discourses go beyond male bodies, it is important to remember that masculinities and sexualities *are* bodily. McLelland (2000, 115), for example, argues that gay magazines in Japan, like straight magazines, "define masculinity through a man's ability to perform sexually." Meanwhile, 15 years on, Castro-Vázquez argues that circumcision, whilst a niche industry, "anchors the gender identity of young men to their genitals" through its commercialization (2015, 29). Men's bodies, sexualities, and sexual practices thus continue to be linked to productivity (in this case bodily productivity) and the expectation that men "do," or can potentially do. If men don't—or don't do the "right" things—then they are "failing" (Castro-Váquez 2015; Galbraith 2015a, 2015b; Gill 2012).

Future directions

Whilst there is a large body of excellent research in masculinity studies in Japan, there are a number of issues and areas that are ripe for further research. Although the co-creation of masculinity and femininity is often acknowledged, and some recent work explores these aspects in more depth (see, for example, Castro-Vázquez 2015; Miles 2017; and contributions in Steger and Koch 2017), most of the recent work in masculinities studies continues to privilege male experiences and discourses of male bodies and actions without also interrogating the complex ways in which women co-construct and reinforce norms and ideals of masculinities. In addition, the intersectionality of masculinities, sexuality, race, ethnicity, and class, as well as transgender experiences, could be further analyzed.

I have argued elsewhere that current masculinities studies scholars also need to perhaps move away from the "salaryman as hegemon" (Cook 2016, 2017). Of course, these ideologies and discourses are important and often emerge in various guises. However, if we rely on this comfortable established argument, we risk obscuring and oversimplifying the complexities of lived experiences and the ways that masculinities are fluid and changeable—not just over the life course—but also in interaction with others in different areas of life at the same time. It is well acknowledged that multiple masculinities exist, but there continues to be a sense that a man has *a* masculinity that he is producing, constructing, and maintaining. Yet individuals themselves may have multiple masculinities or senses of masculinity as they live their lives, making the task of masculinities scholars all the more complex.

Acknowledgements

I would like to dedicate this chapter to the memory of Romit Dasgupta, a leading figure of masculinity studies in Japan until his untimely passing in 2018.

Further reading

Dasgupta, R. (2013) *Re-Reading the Salaryman in Japan: Crafting Masculinities,* London and New York: Routledge.
Frühstück, Sabine and Walthall, Anne (eds) (2011b) *Recreating Japanese Men,* Berkeley and Los Angeles: University of California Press.
McLelland, M., Suganuma, K. and Welker, J. (2007) *Queer Voices from Japan: First Person Narratives from Japan's Sexual Minorities,* Lanham, MD: Lexington Books.
Tanaka, T. (2009) *Danseigaku no Shintenkai (New Developments in Masculinity Studies),* Tokyo: Seikyusha.

Related Chapters

4 Gender and Language
6 Transgender, Non-Binary Genders, and Intersex in Japan
7 Gender and Ethnicity in Urban Japan
11 Intimacy in and Beyond the Family
25 Myths of Masculinity in the Martial Arts
26 The Continuum of Male Beauty in Contemporary Japan
33 Gender, Media, and Misogyny in Japan

References

Barber, C. (2014) "Masculinity in Japanese Sports Films," *Japanese Studies* 34 (2) 135–152.
Castro-Váquez, G. (2015) *Male Circumcision in Japan,* New York: Palgrave Macmillan.
Chapman, K. (2004) "*Ossu!* Sporting Masculinities in a Japanese Karate Dojo," *Japan Forum* 16 315–335.
Charlebois, J. (2017a) "Herbivore Masculinities in Post-Millennial Japan," in Xiaodong Lin, Chris Haywood and Mairtin Mac an Ghaill (eds) *East Asian Men: Masculinity, Sexuality and Desire,* London: Palgrave Macmillan, 165–182.
Charlebois, J. (2017b) "The Shifting Gender Landscape of Japanese Society," in Satoshi Toyosaki and Shinsuke Eguchi (eds) *Intercultural Communication in Japan: Theorizing Homogenizing Discourse,* London and New York: Routledge, 55–70.
Chen, S. (2012) "The Rise of 草食系男子 (Soushokukei Danshi) Masculinity and Consumption in Contemporary Japan," in Cele C. Otnes and Linda Tuncay Zayer (eds) *Gender, Culture, and Consumer Behavior,* London and New York: Routledge, 285–310.
Condry, I. (2011) "Love Revolution: Anime, Masculinity, and the Future," in Sabine Frühstück and Anne Walthall (eds) *Recreating Japanese Men,* Berkeley and Los Angeles: University of California Press, 262–283.
Connell, R. (2005) *Masculinities,* 2nd ed., Berkeley: University of California Press.
Cook, E. E. (2013) "Expectations of Failure: Maturity and Masculinity for Freeters in Contemporary Japan," *Social Science Japan Journal* 16 (1) 29–43.

Cook, E. E. (2014) "Intimate Expectations and Practices: Freeter Relationships and Marriage in Contemporary Japan," *Asian Anthropology* 13 (1) 36–51.
Cook, E. E. (2016) *Reconstructing Adult Masculinities: Part-Time Work in Contemporary Japan*, London and New York: Routledge.
Cook, E. E. (2017) "Aspirational Labour, Performativity and Masculinities in the Making," *Intersections: Gender and Sexuality in Asia and the Pacific* 41. http://intersections.anu.edu.au/issue41/cook.html.
Cook, E. E. (2018) "Irregular Employment, Power, and Intimacy in Japan," in Allison Alexy and Emma E. Cook (eds) *Intimate Japan: Ethnographies of Closeness and Conflict*, Honolulu: University of Hawai'i Press, 129–147.
Darling-Wolf, F. (2004a) "SMAP, Sex, and Masculinity: Constructing the Perfect Female Fantasy in Japanese Popular Music," *Popular Music and Society* 27 (3) 357–370.
Darling-Wolf, F. (2004b) "Women and New Men: Negotiating Masculinity in the Japanese Media," *The Communication Review* 7 285–303.
Dasgupta, R. (2005) "Salarymen Doing Straight: Heterosexual Men and the Dynamics of Gender Conformity," in Mark McLelland and Romit Dasgupta (eds) *Genders, Transgenders and Sexualities in Japan*, London and New York: Routledge, 168–182.
Dasgupta, R. (2010) "Globalisation and the Bodily Performance of 'Cool' and 'Un-Cool' Masculinities in Corporate Japan," *Intersections: Gender and Sexuality in Asia and the Pacific* 23. http://intersections.anu.edu.au/issue23/dasgupta.htm.
Dasgupta, R. (2013) *Re-Reading the Salaryman in Japan: Crafting Masculinities*, London and New York: Routledge.
Dasgupta, R. (2017) "Acting Straight? Non-Heterosexual Salarymen Working with Heteronormativity in the Japanese Workplace," in Xiaodong Lin, Chris Haywood and Mairtin Mac an Ghaill (eds) *East Asian Men: Masculinity, Sexuality and Desire*, London: Palgrave Macmillan, 31–50.
Frühstück, S. (2007) *Uneasy Warriors: Gender, Memory and Popular Culture in the Japanese Army*, Berkeley and Los Angeles: University of California Press.
Frühstück, S. and Walthall, A. (2011a) "Introduction: Interrogating Men and Masculinities," in Sabine Frühstück and Anne Walthall (eds) *Recreating Japanese Men*, Berkeley and Los Angeles: University of California Press, 1–21.
Frühstück, S. and Walthall, A. (eds) (2011b) *Recreating Japanese Men*, Berkeley and Los Angeles: University of California Press.
Fujimura, M. (2006) "Wakamono Sedai no 'Otokorashisa' to sono Mirai" ('Masculine Identity' Among the Generation of Young Men, and Its Future), in Tsunehisa Abe, Sumio Obinata and Masako Amano (eds) *Dansei shi 3: Otokorashisa no gendai shi* (Male History 3: Modern History of Masculinity), Tokyo: Nihon Keizai Hyōronsha, 191–227.
Galbraith, P. W. (2015a.) "Otaku Sexuality," in Mark McLelland and Vera Mackie (eds) *Routledge Handbook of Sexuality Studies in East Asia*, London and New York: Routledge, 205–217.
Galbraith, P. W. (2015b) "'Otaku' Research and Anxiety About Failed Men," in Patrick W. Galbraith, Thiam Huat Kam and Björn-Ole Kamm (eds) *Debating Otaku in Contemporary Japan: Historical Perspectives and New Horizons*, London: Bloomsbury, 21–34.
Gill, T. (2001) *Men of Uncertainty: The Social Organization of Day Laborers in Contemporary Japan*, Albany: State University of New York Press.
Gill, T. (2003) "When Pillars Evaporate: Structuring Masculinity on the Japanese Margins," in J. E. Roberson and N. Suzuki (eds) *Men and Masculinities in Contemporary Japan: Dislocating the Salaryman Doxa*, London and New York: RoutledgeCurzon, 144–161.
Gill, T. (2012) "Failed Manhood on the Streets of Urban Japan: The Meanings of Self-Reliance for Homeless Men," *The Asia-Pacific Journal* 10 1–2.
Glasspool, L. (2012) "From Boys Next Door to Boys' Love: Gender Performance in Japanese Male Idol Media," in Patrick W. Galbraith and Jason G. Karlin (eds) *Idols and Celebrity in Japanese Media Culture*, Basingstoke: Palgrave Macmillan, 113–130.
Inoue, T., Ueno, C. and Ehara, Y. (1995) *Danseigaku* (Studies on Masculinity), Tokyo: Iwanamishoten.
Ishii-Kuntz, M. (2003) "Balancing Fatherhood and Work: Emergence of Diverse Masculinities in Contemporary Japan," in J. E. Roberson and N. Suzuki (eds) *Men and Masculinities in Contemporary Japan: Dislocating the Salaryman Doxa*, London and New York: RoutledgeCurzon, 198–216.
Ishii-Kuntz, M. (2013) *Ikumen Gensho no Shakaigaku: Ikuji Kosodate Sanka heno Kibou o Kanaerutame ni* (Sociology of Child Caring Men: In Search of Realizing Fathers' Involvement in Child-Rearing), Kyoto: Minerva.

Ishii-Kuntz, M. (2015) "Fatherhood in Asian Contexts," in S. R. Quah (ed) *Routledge Handbook of Families in Asia*, London and New York: Routledge, 161–174.

Itō, K. (1993) *Otokorashisa no Yukue* (How Masculinity Is Changing), Tokyo: Shin'yōsha.

Itō, K. (1996) *Dansei-gaku Nyūmon* (Introduction to Men's Studies), Tokyo: Sakuhinsha.

Itō, K. (2002) *[Dekinai Otoko] kara [Dekiru Otoko] Made* (From [Cannot Do Man] to [Can Do Man]), Tokyo: Shogakukan.

Itō, K. (2003) *Otokorashisa toiu Shinwa* (The Myth of Manliness), Tokyo: Nippon Hōsō Kyōkai Shuppankai.

Itō, K. (2005) "An Introduction to Men's Studies," in M. McLelland and R. Dasgupta (eds) *Genders, Transgenders and Sexualities in Japan*, London and New York: Routledge, chapter 10.

Itō, K., Kimura, M. and Kuninobu, J. (2011) *Joseigaku/Danseigaku: Jendāron Nyūmon* (Women's Studies/Men's Studies: An Introduction to Gender Studies), Tokyo: Yūhikaku.

Kawanishi, Y. (2008) "On Karo-Jisatsu (Suicide by Overwork): Why Do Japanese Workers Work Themselves to Death?" *International Journal of Mental Health* 37 (1) 61–74.

Kumagai, K. (2012) "Floating Young Men: Globalization and the Crisis of Masculinity in Japan," *HAGAR Studies in Culture, Policy and Identities* 10 (2) 3–15.

Light, R. (2003) "Sport and the Construction of Masculinity in the Japanese Education System," in Kam Louie and Morris Low (eds) *Asian Masculinities: The Meaning and Practice of Manhood in China and Japan*, London and New York: Routledge, 100–117.

Lin, X., Haywood, C. and Mac an Ghaill, M. (2017) "Introduction," in X. Lin, C. Haywood and M. Mac an Ghaill (eds) *East Asian Men: Masculinity, Sexuality and Desire*, London: Palgrave Macmillan, 1–10.

Low, M. (2003) "The Emperor's Sons Go to War: Competing Masculinities in Modern Japan," in K. Louie and M. Low (eds) *Asian Masculinities: The Meaning and Practice of Manhood in China and Japan*, London and New York: Routledge, 81–99.

Lunsing, W. (2001) *Beyond Common Sense: Sexuality and Gender in Contemporary Japan*, London: Kegan Paul.

Lunsing, W. (2003) "What Masculinity? Transgender Practices Among Japanese 'Men'," in J. E. Roberson and N. Suzuki (eds) *Men and Masculinities in Contemporary Japan: Dislocating the Salaryman Doxa*, London and New York: RoutledgeCurzon, 20–36.

Manzenreiter, W. (2011) "Climbing Walls: Dismantling Hegemonic Masculinity in a Japanese Sport Subculture," in S. Frühstück and A. Walthall (eds) *Recreating Japanese Men*, Berkeley and Los Angeles: University of California Press, 220–240.

Manzenreiter, W. (2013) "No Pain, No Gain: Embodied Masculinities and Lifestyle Sport in Japan," *Contemporary Japan* 25 (2) 215–236.

Mason, M. M. (2011) "Empowering the Would-Be Warrior: Bushidō and the Gendered Bodies of the Japanese Nation," in S. Frühstück and A. Walthall (eds) *Recreating Japanese Men*, Berkeley and Los Angeles: University of California Press, 68–90.

McLelland, M. J. (2000) *Male Homosexuality in Modern Japan: Cultural Myths and Social Realities*, Surrey: Curzon Press.

McLelland, M. J. (2003) "Gay Men, Masculinity and the Media in Japan," in K. Louie and M. Low (eds) *Asian Masculinities: The Meaning and Practice of Manhood in China and Japan*, London and New York: Routledge, 59–78.

McLelland, M. J. (2005a.) *Queer Japan from the Pacific War to the Internet Age*, Oxford: Rowman & Littlefield Publishers, Inc.

McLelland, M. J. (2005b.) "Salarymen Doing Queer: Gay Men and the Heterosexual Public Sphere in Japan," in M. J. McLelland and R. Dasgupta (eds) *Genders, Transgenders and Sexualities in Japan*, London: Routledge, 96–110.

McLelland, M. J. (2011) "Japan's Queer Cultures," in T. C. Bestor and V. L. Bestor (eds) *The Routledge Handbook of Japanese Culture and Society*, London and New York: Routledge, 140–149.

McLelland, M. J., Suganuma, K. and Welker, J. (2007) *Queer Voices from Japan: First Person Narratives from Japan's Sexual Minorities*, Lanham: Lexington Books.

Miles, E. (2017) *Men of No Value: Contemporary Japanese Manhood and the Economies of Intimacy*, Department of Anthropology, PhD Thesis, Yale University.

Miles, E. (2018) "Manhood and the Burdens of Intimacy," in A. Alexy and E. E. Cook (eds) *Intimate Japan: Ethnographies of Closeness and Conflict*, Honolulu: University of Hawai'i Press, 148–163.

Mizukoshi, K., Kohlbacher, F. and Schimkowsky, C. (2016) "Japan's Ikumen Discourse: Macro and Micro Perspectives on Modern Fatherhood," *Japan Forum* 28 (2) 212–232.

Morioka, M. (2008) *Sōshoku Danshi no Ren'Aigaku* (Lessons in Love for Herbivore Men), Tokyo: Media Factory.

Morioka, M. (2013a) *Karōshi wa nani o kokuhatsu shite iru ka. Gendai Nihon no kigyō to rōdō* (Karoshi as an Indictment of Corporations and Work in Japan Today), Tokyo: Iwanami Gendai Bunkō.

Morioka, M. (2013b) "A Phenomenological Study of 'Herbivore Men'," *The Review of Life Studies* 4 1–20. www.lifestudies.org/herbivoremen01.htm

Nakatani, A. (2006) "The Emergence of 'Nurturing Fathers': Discourses and Practices of Fatherhood in Contemporary Japan," in M. Rebick and A. Takenaka (eds) *The Changing Japanese Family*, London and New York: Routledge, 94–108.

North, S. and Morioka, R. (2016) "Hope Found in Lives Lost: Karoshi and the Pursuit of Worker Rights in Japan," *Contemporary Japan* 28 (1) 59–80.

Roberson, J. E. (2003) "Japanese Working-Class Masculinities: Marginalised Complicities," in J. E. Roberson and N. Suzuki (eds) *Men and Masculinities in Contemporary Japan: Dislocating the Salaryman Doxa*, London and New York: RoutledgeCurzon, 126–143.

Roberson, J. E. and Suzuki, N. (eds) (2003) *Men and Masculinities in Contemporary Japan: Dislocating the Salaryman Doxa*, London and New York: RoutledgeCurzon.

Roberts, G. S. (2002) "Pinning Hopes on Angels: Reflections From an Ageing Japan's Urban Landscape," in R. Goodman (ed) *Family and Social Policy in Japan: Anthropological Approaches*, Cambridge: Cambridge University Press, 54–91.

Saladin, R. (2015) "Between *gyaru-o* and *sōshokukei danshi*: Body Discourses in Lifestyle Magazines for Young Japanese Men," *Contemporary Japan* 27 (1) 53–70.

Saladin, R. (2017) "Herbivore Masculinity in Media Discourse: The Japanese TV Drama Ohitorisama," *Intersections: Gender and Sexuality in Asia and the Pacific* 41.

Satō, F. (2010) "Jenda-ka sareru 'posutomodan no guntai'—'atarashisa' wo meguri dōin sareru joseisei/danseisei" (Gendered 'Postmodern Militaries': Utilizing Discourses of Masculinities and Femininities for 'New' Militaries), in K. Kimoto and Y. Kido (eds) *Jenda- to shakai—danseishi/guntai/sekushuariti* (Gender and Society: History of Masculinities, Military and Sexuality), Tokyo: Junposha, 141–169.

Slater, D. H. and Galbraith, P. W. (2011) "Re-Narrating Social Class and Masculinity in Neoliberal Japan: An Examination of the Media Coverage of the 'Akihabara Incident' of 2008," *Electronic Journal of Contemporary Japanese Studies*, 30 September. www.japanesestudies.org.uk/articles/2011/SlaterGalbraith.html.

Steger, B. and Koch, A. (2017) *Cool Japanese Men: Studying New Masculinities at Cambridge*, Zurich: LIT Verlag.

Taga, F. (2001) *Dansei no Jendā Keisei: Otokorashisa no Yuragi no Naka de* (The Gender Formation of Men: Uncertain Masculinity), Tokyo: Tōyōkan Shuppansha.

Taga, F. (2005) "Rethinking Japanese Masculinities: Recent Research Trends," in M. McLelland and R. Dasgupta (eds) *Genders, Transgenders and Sexualities in Japan*, London and New York: Routledge, 153–167.

Taga, F. (2006) *Otokorashisa no Shakaigaku: Yuragu Otoko no Raifukōsu* (Sociology of Masculinity: Life Course of Unstable Men), Kyoto: Sekai Shisōsha.

Taga, F. (2011) *Yuragu Sarañman Seikatsu: Shigoto to Katei no Hazamu de* (Lifestyle of Unstable Salarymen: Between Work and Family), Tokyo: Minerva Shobō.

Taga, F. (2016) *Danshi mondai no jidai? Sakusō suru jendā to kyōiku no poritikusu* (The Age of Men's Problems? The Complicatied Politics of Gender and Education), Tokyo: Gakubunsha.

Takeyama, A. (2010) "Intimacy for Sale: Masculinity, Entrepreneurship, and Commodity Self in Japan's Neoliberal Situation," *Japanese Studies* 30 (2) 231–246.

Takeyama, A. (2016) *Staged Seductions: Selling Dreams in a Tokyo Host Club*, Stanford: Stanford University Press.

Tanaka, T. (2009) *Danseigaku no Shintenkai* (New Developments in Masculinity Studies), Tokyo: Seikyusha.

Tanaka, T. (2015) *Otoko ga Tsurai yo: Zetsubō no Jidai no Kibō no Danseigaku* (It's Hard to Be a Man: Masculinity Studies of Hope in a Generation of Despair), Tokyo: Kadokawa.

Tanaka, T. (2016) *Otoko ga hatarakanai, ii janai ka!* (A Man Who Doesn't Work, It's Good, Right!), Tokyo: Kodansha.

Tatsumi, M. (2015) *"Chichioya no Sodate" saikō: Kea to shite no kosodate to gendai nihon no otokorashisa* (Reconsideration of Fathering: Parenting as Care and Contemporary Japanese Masculinity), Department of Human Sciences, PhD, Osaka Prefecture University.

Tatsumi, M. (2018) "Masculinities of Child-Caring Men 'Ikumen': An Analysis of the Father Figures in Japanese Government Project," *XIX ISA World Congress of Sociology*, Toronto, Canada.

Umegaki-Costantini, H. (2017) "Caring for My Wife's Parents? Reconciling Practices, Masculinity and Family Relations," *Intersections: Gender and Sexuality in Asia and the Pacific* 41. http://intersections.anu.edu.au/issue41/umegaki-hiroko.html.

Ushikubo, M. (2008) *Sōshokukei danshi "ojoman" ga Nihon wo kaeru* (Herbivorous "Ladylike" Men Are Changing Japan), Tokyo: Kodansha.

Vassallo, H. (2017) "Ikumen: Ideologies and Realities of Japan's 'New Papas'," in B. Steger and A. Koch (eds) *Cool Japanese Men: Studying New Masculinities at Cambridge*, Zurich: LIT Verlag, 27–84.

6
TRANSGENDER, NON-BINARY GENDERS, AND INTERSEX IN JAPAN

S. P. F. Dale

"Let this be the final Gender Identity Disorder Conference," the scholar Mitsuhashi Junko proclaimed in her opening remarks at the twentieth Gender Identity Disorder (GID) Conference held in 2018. At a conference founded upon the term "gender identity disorder," Mitsuhashi was making a bold statement by calling for the end of usage of the phrase. As Mitsuhashi stated in her remarks, although she had attended the GID Conference every year since its inception, as a transgender individual, she had never expected to be called upon to address the audience during the opening, had never expected to be given prominence amidst the sea of mostly medical professionals who had all gathered to discuss transgender issues at the (at present) only transgender-related conference in Japan. In her comments, Mitsuhashi was not calling for the end of the conference itself, but rather a shift in naming and framing—a move from "GID" to "transgender," a shift in focus to transgender lives and empowering trans individuals rather than maintaining the current medicalized hierarchy with doctors in charge.

The frameworks through which transgender lives and experiences are understood are in constant negotiation, and Mitsuhashi's statement exemplifies a desire to shift transgender discourse not only semantically, but also institutionally. As Halberstam writes, naming is a powerful act which invokes hierarchy and dominance (2018, 6–7). Naming is an act through which the "other" is created, excluded, and controlled, but also an act through which the individual gains agency and self-determination. Terminology has been at the crux of discussions on trans rights and recognition in recent years, and shifting terminology is seen as key to gaining social acceptance and equality.

Through focusing on terminology, this chapter aims to provide a broad overview of some of the discussions pertaining to trans and non-binary genders in Japan in recent years, as well as to show how some of these discussions intertwine with social and institutional understandings of gender in Japanese society. I explore recent shifts in transgender discourse in Japan and the tenuous relationship that understandings of gender and transgressing gender have with medicalized discourses and gatekeeping. In doing so, I make use of my experiences at the GID Conference discussed previously, as well as my experiences at other events and research on x-gender (*x-jendā*) identity. Following development in local activism as well as global changes in discourse pertaining to trans individuals (in particular changes in the Diagnostic and Statistical Manual of Mental Disorders [DSM] and International Classification of Diseases [ICD] definitions of gender dysphoria), understandings of transgender in Japan are very much in transition. I also briefly explore discussions pertaining to intersex individuals in Japan, but note that rather than being included in a chapter about transgender and non-binary genders, it would be more appropriate to explore intersex in an individual chapter in order to emphasize how discussions pertaining to intersex are quite distinct from those of trans and non-binary issues.

Shifts in transgender frameworks

Mitsuhashi Junko, the scholar cited at the start of this paper, has written that the existence of trans individuals in Japan can be traced back to myths about the creation of Japan (2008). As she explicates, *josō*, or male-bodied individuals "dressing like a woman," is an act that has been prevalent throughout Japanese history. Although *dansō* ("dressing like a man") has also been prevalent throughout Japanese history, there at present does not exist a similar historical study of the practice. The individuals and acts that we may refer to as transgender today have always existed. What has changed, however, are the terms and frameworks through which to understand them.

There have been several key phases in transgender recognition in modern Japan (McLelland 2004, 2005; Mitsuhashi 2003, 2008). Until the mid-1990s, transgender individuals were mostly recognised as entertainers or sex workers, and the terminology that was used reflected this. For example, the term "*dansho*" described male-to-female crossdressing sex workers in the 1940s and 1950s, "blue boy" (*būrū boi*) referred to trans performers in a popular cabaret-style club in the 1960s (Le Carrousel de Paris), and "gay boy" (*gei boi*) was used for male-to-female crossdressing hostesses at drinking establishments (McLelland 2004). There is a notable lack of terminology to refer to transmen, transmasculine, or female-to-male crossdressers, and this also parallels the lack of research carried out about the existence of such individuals. Although most research from a historical perspective has focused on male-to-female crossdressers (or *josōka*), female-to-male crossdressers or transmen have also existed historically (Nagashima 2017; Saeki 2009; Watanabe 2018), but their histories still need to be further unearthed, especially from a sociological and anthropological perspective.

In the 1980s, in tandem with Japan's bubble period, there occurred what Mitsuhashi refers to as the "golden period" of transgender in Japan (2003), when trans individuals started appearing on variety television shows. Although they were featured mainly for entertainment purposes, they reached an audience and level of visibility greater than before. A new vocabulary to refer to trans individuals also developed—Mister Lady (*misutā redi*) and new half (*nyū hāfu*) for male-to-female trans individuals and Miss Dandy (*misu dandei*) for female-to-male trans individuals (Mitsuhashi 2003; Toyama 1999). This was in addition to terms such as *okama* (male-assigned but feminine presenting, often associated with male homosexuality) and *onabe* (female-assigned but masculine presenting), which had been used in the past (and continue to be used today). Although most of the trans individuals who appeared in these shows worked in the trans night-life scene (mostly bars which catered to a heterosexual clientele, which is also indicative of the limited employment opportunities for trans individuals during this period), there were also some individuals employed in "regular" jobs. In my own research, an x-gender informant currently in their 40s told me that they first heard of the term "onabe" from watching one of these variety shows in the 1990s, and the fact that one of the individuals featured was a taxi driver struck them deeply. They describe that show as a turning point in their lives and credit it with showing them that trans people do not have to do night work (*fūzoku*) but can also be employed in other fields.

This understanding of trans individuals as entertainers or objects of entertainment changed abruptly in the 1990s, when the first penis reconstruction surgery was conducted for a transgender man in Japan. From 1965 until 1996, gender reassignment surgery, or any genital modification, was prohibited in Japan. The Eugenic Protection Law, and more specifically the Blue Boy Trial (a trial involving three male-to-female sex workers), strictly forbade the modification of functioning genitals (Ishida 2008; McLelland 2004). In 1995, Japanese surgeons made the news for performing the first successful penis reconstruction surgery on a cisgender man who had been injured in an accident. A transman who read this news wrote to the surgeons and asked if such a surgery could be performed on him (Oe et al. 2011). At this point in time in Japan, there was no legislation regarding surgery or legal gender changes for transgender individuals, and guidelines had to be established in order to allow such surgery to legally take place.

The surgery was eventually conducted in 1998, and in 2003, the Act on Special Cases in Handling Gender Status for Persons with Gender Identity Disorder was passed to allow for legal gender change in Japan. The initial version of this act stated that in order to change one's legal gender, the individual must be above the age of 20, must not be presently married, must not have children, must be sterilized, and must have genitals that resemble that of the other sex (i.e. the sex organs associated with the gender to which they desired to legally transition). In 2007, it was amended to state that one must not have children who are minors. The conditions for changing legal gender were heavily criticized by many trans individuals, in particular those who did not meet them. Many found it unfair and argued that it promoted a very specific image of a trans person that did not match how actual trans people were living. Prominent trans activists Kamikaya Aya and Torae Masai have written about the difficulty they experienced in these negotiations and how they decided to forge ahead with the unfair conditions because they hoped that the initial legislation would help pave the way for future changes (Oe et al. 2011). However, since 2007, no changes have been made, and despite an increasing number of countries allowing trans individuals to change their legal gender without enforcing bodily modification, there do not seem to be any immediate signs of similar legislative changes taking place in Japan.

The guidelines and legislation which were put in force following the 1998 surgery changed not only the medical and legal possibilities of trans individuals, but also provided a new lens through which to view them. The term "*sei dōitsu sei shōgai*" was introduced as the Japanese translation of "gender identity disorder" and became the main term used to describe trans individuals in this new context. A new framework through which to understand trans individuals as individuals born with a specific medical condition emerged, and surgery was described as a "cure." There was a shift from viewing trans individuals as objects of entertainment to objects of pity (Mitsuhashi 2008; Oe et al. 2011). Though the medicalization of trans identities in Japan was relatively recent, media reportage and the fictionalization of trans narratives in popular television dramas led to a widespread recognition of the term. There were reportedly more individuals who went to gender clinics for consultations after hearing about it on television or in the media (Tsuruta 2009; Yonezawa 2003) and who came to understand themselves through this discourse.

The term "*sei dōitsu sei shōgai*" in Japanese also possesses nuances that the English GID does not. Namely, there is a notable difference in nuance between "*shōgai*" and "disorder," as *shōgai* is the term used to translate "disability." The translation of "*shōgai*" for "disorder" is standard in the Japanese translation of DSM (*Nihon seishin shinkei gakkai* 2014). However, the continuity between "disorder" and "disability" allows trans individuals to be imagined on a spectrum of disability, and the kanji for "*sei dōitsu sei shōgai*" also leads to misinterpretation (Sasaki 2017). "*Dōitsu sei*" is the Japanese term for "identity," but as the kanji for "*sei*" is the same as the kanji for "sex/gender," some have misinterpreted "*sei dōitsu sei shōgai*" as meaning that one's gender (sex) does not match. This perhaps has also led to the popular description of transgender as a condition in which one's heart (*kokoro*) does not match one's body (*karada*)—*kokoro no sei to karada no sei ga icchi shinai*.

Despite the undesirable connotations of illness and pathology, disability discourse does help emphasize the services that trans individuals need. The Ministry of Education, for example, released a pamphlet for educators in April 2016 providing information about sexual orientation and gender identity, albeit with a focus mostly on the latter, using the terminology of *sei dōitsu sei shōgai* (Monbukagakushō 2016). What this means is that educators are taught about LGBTQ issues but recognize them as trans issues in a medical framework. Working at a national university in Japan, I have been shocked to hear school counsellors discuss transgender as a disability issue and LGBTQ issues as GID issues. As lesbian activist Oe states, the proliferation of GID discourse also created confusion about other queer identities, and until recently trans individuals have been treated with more social gravitas than LGBQ individuals (Oe et al. 2011).

From April 2018, it became possible for trans individuals to use insurance to cover surgical costs (Fujisawa 2018). Although this move was initially praised by activists, it soon became clear that insurance would only cover sex reassignment surgery (SRS) and not hormone treatment. This limited assistance led to criticism, with many fearing that it would push trans individuals to undergo surgery, although that may not be what they really desire. Many were also puzzled as to the emphasis on surgery over hormone treatment, an emphasis which seemed to push a specific idea of what a trans individual should be. It was also argued that it would be irresponsible to provide only surgery without hormone treatment, as individuals unable to afford hormone treatment on their own may end up suffering further (Kato 2018). In addition, insurance would also cover sterilization procedures—procedures many consider unnecessary (Endo 2017), yet which are mandatory to change one's legal gender in Japan.

Although support services for trans individuals seem to be stealthily increasing, these changes also abide with a specific image of what a trans person—or rather, what a woman or man—should be (Mackie 2001; Norton 2006). It is not possible for trans individuals to change their legal gender in Japan without undergoing sterilization and genital modification. They must conform to a very specific image of what a "biological" woman or man should be and conform to heteronormative social expectations as well. They cannot have a child who is a minor, nor can they be married at the time of changing their legal gender, as after their gender change, their marriage would then legally become a same-sex (in terms of legal gender) marriage, which is not permitted in Japanese law. The ideal trans/woman/man citizen in Japan is as such a heterosexual one, with a very specific body that fits a very specific ideal.

The development of x-gender—non-binary yet binary understandings of gender

Like transgender, non-binary individuals have always existed in Japan, and before it became possible to change one's legal gender, most trans identities were described in non-binary terms. Terms explored in the previous section such as "*nyu hāfu*" and "Miss Dandy" invoke a mixing of genders, and early trans works such as Tsutamori Tsutaru's *Otoko demo onna demo naku* ("Neither a man nor a woman") emphasize an identity that is not distinctly classifiable as woman or man (1993). Non-binary as distinct from or as a subcategory of transgender is a recent development in trans terminology. As McLelland wrote in 2004, "there are many transgender individuals who do not feel 'trapped' in the wrong body, but instead think of themselves as living beyond or between the binary categories of 'male' and 'female'" (McLelland 2004, 2). It was only after GID became the main framework through which to understand transgender that trans identities came to be grasped as more "binary."

Most of Japanese trans history in fact deals with non-binary genders. Keeping this in mind, in this section, I focus on the current (post 2010) discussion of non-binary genders by exploring the term x-gender, which is sometimes used as a stand-in for discussing non-binary genders in general but in some cases also refers to a very specific identity. How the term x-gender has developed and come to be utilized by individuals as well as recognized by the medical institution provides insights into larger social discourses pertaining to gender and sexuality.

I started research on x-gender in 2010, and, as with most identity categories, found that how it is understood and utilized is contingent on the individual. In the years since I started research on x-gender, the term has undergone shifts in general understanding as well as public recognition. In 2010, x-gender was described by an informant as the "minority within minorities," but this is no longer the case. X-gender has gone from an ambiguously defined term with little online presence to a term which is definitively included in discussions of LGBTQ individuals. Educational television programs such as *Hāto TV* (Heart TV) (from 2006 to 2012 known as *Hāto o tsunagō* or "Connecting Hearts") have also featured discussion about x-gender. Articles about x-gender individuals have also popped up in all major newspapers. This increase in media discussion of the term points to more interest in non-binary gender identities. Following GID legislation, most media outlets produced stories of individuals assigned male who always understood themselves to be women, and vice-versa—the focus was on creating a binary tale of clear gender transition. Media producers whom I have spoken with have told me that when they produced a show about LGBTQ issues, they would always receive a lot of feedback from individuals who identified as x-gender, and this made them realize the needs and existence of x-gender individuals.

The term x-gender came into existence as a form of resistance against the binary tales of gender transition which were dominating the news in the 1990s. Tanaka Ray, author of *Transgender Feminism*, says that it also developed as a response to GID discourse. The term likely originated in queer communities in the central-western Kansai region (the prefectures of Osaka, Kyoto, Hyogo, Shiga, Nara, Wakayama, and Mie), and most of the first publications which discussed x-gender (e.g. Poco a poco 2000; ROS 2007; Tanaka 2006; Yoshinaga 2000) were generated in the Kansai area. From the Kansai area, the term then appears to have spread through the Internet. One of the first blogs about x-gender was started by an individual who lives in Kanagawa who read Yoshinaga's book on gender identity disorder which included an interview with an individual who identified as x-gender (the interviewee being Morita, whom I also discuss subsequently), and I met a number of x-gender individuals who first came across the term "x-gender" from reading this blog.

Although definitions of x-gender vary, most hinge upon the categories of "woman" and "man." In one of the first publications which discuss x-gender, *Poco a poco*, a journal published by the LGBTQ organization G-Front Kansai, x-gender is defined as a "term used by individuals who do not fit under the existing categories of male (*dansei*)/female (*josei*), or who are unsure of their sex/gender" (Poco a poco 2000, 128). The key term here is "existing," or already existent, categories of gender—x-gender was meant to express a means of moving away from existent understandings of gender. As Morita Shinichi/Milk, one of the first individuals to publicly use the term x-gender, stated in a documentary interview, a gender-free society which does not discriminate based on sex/gender is the ideal, and, for them, very much connected to x-gender identity (♂ ♀ ⚥ 1999).

Understandings of x-gender have since branched out, and in discussions of x-gender online as well as in publications about LGBTQ issues, x-gender is often discussed as referring to identifying as neither a woman nor a man and as adhering to being *musei* (no sex), *ryōsei* (both sexes), or *chūsei* (literally middle sex, but closer to "androgynous" in meaning). In these definitions, what is noticeable is a reliance on a gender binary in order to define x-gender. In educational material about LGBTQ issues, the use of graphs and charts to describe gender (as well as sexual orientation) has also become more common. In such cases, "woman" and "man" are placed on opposite sides of a spectrum, and x-gender is indicated variously by circling the middle of the spectrum (*chūsei*), both ends of the spectrum (*ryōsei*), or not circling anything (*musei*). Although visualizing a gender spectrum makes the diversity of gendered experiences easier to grasp, it also takes for granted an understanding of gender. What do "woman" and "man" mean, and what is one trying to convey by distinguishing x-gender from these two terms?

In considering the use of the term "x-gender" to articulate identity, I have found that there are three general patterns: x-gender as a form of anti-identity, a means of disrupting the gender binary and questioning the legitimacy of gender-based social norms and institutions; x-gender as a means of articulating an identity that is not categorizable as the individual's understanding of "woman" or "man"; or x-gender as a form of gender identity disorder, a condition one is born with and which requires diagnosis. Although x-gender might have developed as a response to GID, it has since been usurped by GID discourse. The term x-gender developed in a radical queer environment, but its use spread to individuals who did not participate in such communities and whose only contact with queerness was through online discussions and media representations. Many x-gender individuals seek a GID diagnosis, a development which has led the medical profession to pay more heed to non-binary identities, as well as to consider the ramifications of promoting a binary understanding of gender. The theme of the 20th GID conference at which Mitsuhashi spoke was "moving beyond the binary" (*nigenron kara no hishō*), and there was even a special symposium (of which I was a part) about x-gender.

Previous research on GID consultations and diagnoses in Japan describe how doctors sought to confirm stereotypical masculine or feminine traits in diagnosing an individual as male or female (Tsuruta 2009). According to more recent research, however, it seems that these lines of inquiry have changed. Tsuruta notes that doctors now allow patients to craft their own narratives and do not look out for specific tropes about discomfort from a young age or dislike of specifically gendered clothes or colours. Tsuruta quotes one doctor who says, "none of that matters" (2010, 143). Tsuruta also notes that it seems more individuals are unsure of their gender identity and going to gender clinics for the purpose of counselling, whereas in the past most individuals went in with a clear idea of what they desired from diagnosis. In his opening remarks at the GID Conference, the current president of the GID Conference, Harima Katsuki, made light of how many individuals came to him asking him to tell them what gender they were. I have also met x-gender individuals who said they felt a need for diagnosis to be sure of their identity. The reason cited for getting a diagnosis in most cases was "security in one's identity," although some individuals got the diagnosis in order to undergo genital modification surgery. The discourse of GID has become normalized in Japan—it is recognized as a condition that one is born with and that one should receive treatment for. Many individuals come to understand themselves within this GID-framework, and this goes for individuals with non-binary gender identities as well. For them, the discourse of GID provides them with a means of becoming socially recognized.

Some of the individuals who started using the term x-gender in the 1990s are dismayed with its current usage. At the GID conference, as mentioned previously, I participated in a special panel about x-gender. In addition to myself, a representative from Label X (an x-gender organization), an x-gender social worker, a clinic psychologist, and a doctor presented. Given the context, most of the presentations had a medical undertone, and most also discussed x-gender as a "condition" rather than radical identity. During the Q&A session, an individual who had been active in queer activism in the Kansai region in the 1990s spoke of their frustration with the presentations and discussion and how the x-gender that was being discussed did not resonate with the x-gender that they knew and identified with. This sentiment was similar to what I heard when I gave a talk about my research at International Christian University in 2017. Most of the individuals who knew of x-gender in the 1990s were surprised at the understandings of the term that now dominated online and in media discourse and felt a sense of disconnection between the x-gender they knew and the x-gender that now prevailed.

Intersex invisibility

The "I" for "intersex" tends to get tagged on at the end of the LGBTQ acronym, and although there are some intersex individuals who are involved in queer activism, there are others who prefer to keep a distance and who refrain from using intersex terminology and maintain a distinction between intersex and LGBTQ issues and identities. Although there has been some discussion of intersex issues in the media (particularly during the broadcasting of the television drama *IS*, based on a manga series of the same name about an intersex teenager) and academia (mostly in the early 2000s, initiated by intersex activist Hashimoto Hideo), it appears that there is no unified intersex "movement" to speak of. Although there exist some organizations and meet-ups for intersex individuals, these are mostly scattered. Given the lack of discussion on intersex issues in Japan, there is a risk in conflating intersex with discussion of transgender and non-binary issues, as the circumstances which intersex individuals face are different. There is also a risk of oversimplifying the experiences of intersex individuals at a time when their experiences have not really been publicly articulated.

In the early 2000s, intersex activist Hashimoto Hideo started a dialogue about intersex issues by writing about personal experiences as well as introducing the work of Milton Diamond to a Japanese audience (2004). Hashimoto also worked with members of the queer community in Kansai and appeared in a documentary (titled ♂ ♀ ⚥) alongside Morita, mentioned previously. Other than Hashimoto's academic work, first-hand intersex experiences have also been explored in the manga medium by intersex artists such as Arai Shō. Arai's manga discusses not only their own identity and experiences, but also introduces readers to other queer individuals. They emphasize their connections to the queer community, and their blog is even titled "Arai Shō's Queer Everyday" (*Arai Shō no kuia na nichijō*).

Although the authors mentioned previously maintained relationships with and participate in queer communities, there are many intersex individuals who refrain from doing so and who also believe there is a clear distinction between LGBTQ and intersex issues. The organization nexdsd Japan is a clear example of this and has a page on their website discussing the differences between intersex and LGBTQ (Nexdsd Japan 2018). There are also individuals who do not agree with the term "intersex" but prefer instead the medical terminology of "disorder of sex development" (DSD), or *seibun ka shikkan*, to describe their condition (Davis 2015).

On a more personal note, I have also been explicitly told by an intersex individual that she objected to intersex terminology, as well as to how intersex issues had been exploited by LGBTQ activists in order to further their own agenda. It is also because of this experience that I am hesitant to discuss intersex issues in this chapter but feel that it is at least pertinent to discuss how they are often considered in tandem, and how, given the absence of discussion about intersex issues in Japan at present, it would be better to devote more discussion to intersex issues on their own rather than treating them as an addendum to LGBTQ issues.

Frameworks in transition

Changes in LGBTQ legislation are taking place at a quick speed, and since 2015, regions across Japan have started to issue same-sex partnership certificates. Although problems remain, insurance coverage for trans individuals is also a significant step. The past 5 years have seen more social and legal change than the past 50, and many activists are optimistic that more changes will come in the leadup to the 2020 Tokyo Olympics. In fact, many of them view this time frame as their chance to get LGBTQ-related legislation approved. Politicians certainly seem to be interested, and members from all political parties have been present at the Rainbow Parliament (*reinbō kokkai*) lobbying events which have been held for the past two years (2017 and 2018) at the National Diet Building. Politicians from all parties spoke of their devotion to LGBTQ issues, and although one may be tempted to brush this off as lip service, their interest demonstrates that they view these issues as politically lucrative.

Although it is possible to point to historical shifts and developments in trans discourse, it is necessary to note that there has been no universal paradigm shift. GID discourse continues to prevail despite the individuals who oppose it. There are individuals who understand themselves as being x-gender and as having GID and those who use x-gender as a means to proclaim gender as a social construct. There are intersex individuals who oppose the terminology and being tagged on after "LGBTQ," and yet there are also individuals who participate in both communities and thrive in doing so. There are contradictions in terminology and how individuals use terms and mismatches in institutional legislature and how individuals actually live their lives. Transgender discourse is always in transition, but recent developments indicate that transgender legislation may be in transition as well. By the time this chapter is published, one hopes that more meaningful institutional change may have been made.

Related chapters

8   Gender and the *Koseki*
9   Attitudes to Marriage and Childbearing
11 Intimacy in and Beyond the Family
21 Lesbians and Queer Women in Japan

References

♂ ♀ ⚥ (1999) Film. Japan.
Arai, Shō (2018) "Official Blog: Arai Shō No Kuia Na Nichijō." https://ameblo.jp/araishou/.
Davis, G. (2015) *Contesting Intersex: The Dubious Diagnosis*, New York: New York University Press.
Endo, M. (2017) "Seibetsu tekigō shujutsu, Tsui ni hoken teikyō he. Ima kangaeru 'sei no jiko kettei' to wa?" *Wezzy* 30 November. Accessed 20 May 2018. http://wezz-y.com/archives/50933.
Fujisawa, M. (2018) "Seibetsu tekigō shujutsu: horumon chiryō heiyōsha 'hokengai' kōrōsei hōshin," *Mainichi Shimbun* 7 March. Accessed 20 May 2018. https://mainichi.jp/articles/20180306/ddm/008/040/065000c.
Halberstam, J. (2018) *Trans*—A Quick and Quirky Account of Gender Variability*, Oakland: University of California Press.
Hashimoto, H. (2004) *Otoko demo onna demo nai sei*, Tokyo: Seikyusha.
Ishida, H. (2008) "Tsukurareru 'sōten,' kesareru 'sōten'—būrū boi saiban no naisoku ni okeru hō no gaisoku," in H. Ishida (ed) *Sei dōitsu sei shōgai—jendā, iryō, tokureihō*, Tokyo: Ochanomizu shobō, 215–248.
Kato, S. (2018) "Ikizurasa wo kakaete: IDAHO no hi ni kangaeru," *Mainichi Shimbun* 18 May. Accessed 20 May 2018. https://mainichi.jp/articles/20180518/ddl/k08/040/020000c.
Mackie, V. (2001) "The Trans-Sexual Citizen: Queering Sameness and Difference," *Australian Feminist Studies* 16 (35) 185–192.
McLelland, M. J. (2004) "From the Stage to the Clinic: Changing Transgender Identities in Post-War Japan," *Japan Forum* 16 (1) 1–20.
McLelland, M. J. (2005) *Queer Japan from the Pacific War to the Internet Age*, Lanham, MD: Rowman & Littlefield.

Mitsuhashi, J. (2003) "Nihon toransujendā ryakushi (sono 2): sengo no shin tankan," in I. Yonezawa (ed) *Toransujendarizumu sengen*, Tokyo: Shakai hihyō sha, 104–118.
Mitsuhashi, J. (2008) *Josō to nihonjin*, Tokyo: Kodansha.
Monbukagakushō. (2016) "Sei dōitsu sei shōgai ya seiteki shikō/seijinin ni kakawaru, jidō seito ni taisuru kime komaka na taiō tō no jisshi nit suite (kyoshokuin muke)." Accessed 30 May 2018. www.mext.go.jp/b_menu/houdou/28/04/1369211.htm.
Nagashima, J. (2017) *Edo no iseisōshatachi—sekushuaru mainoritei no rikai no tame ni*, Tokyo: Bensei Shuppan.
Nexdsd Japan. (2018) www.nexdsd.com/dsd.
Nihon seishin shinkei gakkai. (2014) "DSM-5 byōmei/yōgō honyaku gaidorain," *Seishin shinkeigaku zasshi* 116 (6) 429–457.
Norton, L. H. (2006) "Neutering the Transgendered: Human Rights and Japan's Law No. 111," *The Georgetown Journal of Gender and the Law* 8 (187) 187–216.
Oe, C., Torai, M., Kamikawa, A. and Fujimura-Fanselow, K. (2011) "Dialogue: Activists and Politicians on Sexuality," in Kumiko Fujimura-Fanselow (ed) *Transforming Japan*, New York: The Feminist Press, 177–196.
Poco a poco. (2000) *Seibetsu to iu mono, koto*, Kyoto: Self Published.
ROS. (2007) *Toransu ga wakarimasen?! Yuragi no sekushuarite kō*. Osaka: At-Works.
Saeki, J. (2009) *"Josō to dansō" no bunkashi*, Tokyo: Kodansha.
Sasaki, S. (2017) *Toransujendā no shinrigaku*, Kyoto: Koyo Shobo.
Tanaka, R. (2006) *Transgender Feminism*, Tokyo: Impact Publishing.
Toyama, H. (1999) *Misu Dandei—otoko to shite ikiru onna tachi*, Tokyo: Shinchosha.
Tsuruta, S. (2009) *Sei dōitsu sei shōgai no esunogurafi—sei gen zō no shakai gaku*, Tokyo: Harvest-Sha.
Tsuruta, S. (2010) "Sei dōitsu sei shōgai no kaunseringu no genjitsu ni tsuite," in Yoshii Hiroaki (ed) *Sekushuariti no tayōsei to haijō*, Tokyo: Akashi Shoten, 125–160.
Tsutamori, T. (1993) *Otoko demo naku onna demo naku*, Tokyo: Keisoshobo.
Watanabe, A. (2018) *Edo no josō to dansō*, Kyoto: Seigensha.
Yonezawa, I. (2003) "Media to toransujendā," in I. Yonezawa (ed) *Toransujendarizumu sengen*, Tokyo: Shakai hihyō sha, 77–83.
Yoshinaga, M. (2000) *Sei dōitsu sei shōgai—seitenkan no ashita*, Tokyo: Shueisha.

7
GENDER AND ETHNICITY IN URBAN JAPAN

Jamie Coates

As John Lie notes, there is a "pervasive conflation of the state, nation, ethnicity, and race in contemporary Japan" (Lie 2001, 144). This chapter traces how issues related to ethnicity in urban Japan are also questions of gender. I interpret these issues from an intersectional perspective (Crenshaw 1991), but due to limited space, mostly focus on providing a critical synopsis of the forms of hegemonic masculinity that have shaped the intersection of race, ethnicity, class, and gender in Japan. For in-depth discussions of sexuality, refer to other chapters in this volume. Dominant narratives of Japanese-ness present a strong association between hegemonic perceptions of gender and national identity, particularly in terms of Japan's image as a homogenous ethnic group. Within this chapter, I present the major historical themes and processes that inform hegemonic perceptions of gender and ethnicity while also trying to account for pivots in Japan's national and ethno-racial identity over the past 200 years.

The emphasis on difference and similarity in the logics of ethnicity shares much in common with how we think about gender. Judith Butler defines gender not so much as a category for analysis as a domain of performances that are then attributed with normative ontological "concreteness" and biological reality (2002 [1990]; also see introduction). Where gender describes the performed and assumed differences between people's bodies, ethnicity describes the performed and assumed differences between socially defined groups. Ethnic identities are fluid, the product of boundary distinctions between in-group and out-group languages, societies, and cultures (Barth 1969), and a primary source of imagined community in the era of the nation-state (Anderson 1991). In a similar way, distinctions between genders are historically, spatially, and culturally contingent.

There is a strong compounding relationship between categories used to discriminate, such as gender, sexuality, ethnicity, class, and race (Crenshaw 1991). From the eighteenth century onwards, for instance, ethnicity was increasingly conflated with biological differences between different social groups around the world (Gossett 1997). This historical process informed how the category of race formed, a category of assumed biological difference that despite holding no scientific credibility remains persistent as a vector of discrimination. East Asia was no exception in the racialization of social difference, with Japanese commentators often leading discussion about the ethno-racial differences between Japan and its neighbours in the nineteenth and twentieth centuries (Dikötter 1997; Takezawa 2011).

Much like the category of race, the gendering of ethnicity and class in popular discourse has served to make differences appear natural or biologically predetermined. Yet we know they are not. Nonetheless, the powerful bodily/biological symbolism of gender and the conflation of race with ethnicity has ensured that these two categories constitute two of the most influential essentialisms endemic to ethno-national identities (Herzfeld 1997). They also consolidate inequalities between genders and/or races because they map the political, social, and economic disparities between ethnic groups and classes onto essentialized bodily categories.

Urban Japan is a useful context to think about the relationship between forms of discrimination because of its central role in the formation of Japanese identity. Japan was home to one of the world's first metropolises, with Edo, now known as Tokyo, reaching a population of over 1 million inhabitants in 1721 (Gordon 2013). This population was largely constituted of Japanese people from central and southern Honshu, who make up the hegemonic image of what Japanese-ness is today. As cities such as Tokyo and Osaka industrialised and expanded from the Meiji period (1868–1912), urban residents and newcomers were increasingly confronted with different forms of Japanese-ness, such as Japanese people from different regions, including Okinawans, historically discriminated groups now referred to as *buraku*, and, within Japan's northern urban areas, the Ainu. Furthermore, a growing number of non-Japanese people became an important part of Japan's urban landscape, such as Chinese-speaking traders and Korean labourers (Sorensen 2005). Consequently, urban Japan has been a key site where Japanese people have encountered, and continue to encounter, difference.

This chapter begins at the historical intersection of gender, race, and ethnicity during Japan's drive to modernize and urbanize. Arguing that hegemonic masculinity largely defined the relationship between ethnicity, race, and gender in modern Japan, I demonstrate how this dynamic continues in contemporary urban contexts. From everyday encounters to media representation, dynamics of in-group and out-group differentiation show how urban masculinities and femininities have played a central role in defining images of Japanese-ness. This dynamic becomes all the more pertinent when considering the position of non-Japanese ethnicities and their efforts to negotiate the highly gendered terrain of ethnicity in urban Japan today.

Masculinity and ethno-national identity in Japan

While Japan's drive to be recognized as a modern nation state from the nineteenth century onwards often made explicit reference to an ethno-racialized concept of ethnicity (*minzoku*), gender was the implicit political and semiotic means through which many visions of ethnicity were consolidated (Germer et al. 2014). As Morris-Suzuki notes (1997), global orientalist visions of Japanese culture as feminine spurred Meiji-era obsessions to present Japan as modern and masculine. Increased regulation of public performances of identity and a widespread retraction of women from public life followed. New sartorial laws banned women from short haircuts and encouraged men to keep their hair short. Industries once dominated by women, such as silk production, were seized by the government and re-industrialized as modern, male, and scientific endeavours (Germer et al. 2014). Patrilineal inheritance laws that once only applied to samurai families were applied to the whole population under the *ie* system (Ueno 1998), and women were barred from political gatherings between 1892 and 1922. They were also not registered as full citizens until after 1945. This legal and political attempt to remove women from public life suggested a desire to present Japan's rise, and Japanese-ness, as a predominantly masculine endeavour in the early twentieth century.

Many of the elements associated with Japanese-ness today can be traced to late eighteenth- and nineteenth-century efforts to distinguish the cultural and geographic boundaries between

Japan and its neighbours (Morris-Suzuki 1997). Epitomised in the *kokugaku* (native/national studies) movement, and the author Motoori Norinaga's work within this field, this earlier period saw the popularization of Japanese-ness as a distinct set of sentiments and aesthetics that differed from other nations (Marra 2007). Motoori's description of Japanese cultural traits depended on "purifying" various popular sentiments and poetics of their non-Japanese associations, particularly Chinese associations. This association between sentiment and ethnicity facilitated images of Japan as a modern nation-state in the coming centuries, and many of the phrases we associate with Japanese ethnic sensibilities today, such as *mono no aware* (the pathos of things) or *shinto* (institutionalized Japanese popular religion), can be traced back to these earlier efforts to distinguish the *magokoro* (pure heart) of an imagined Japanese tradition as an ethnic quality.

To imagine Japanese-ness as distinct from other forms of national identity, particularly through the lens of sentiment and aesthetics, ensured that discussions of Japanese-ness were often gendered. In the second half of the nineteenth century, Japan's relationship with its neighbours and the broader world changed dramatically. Seeing the once hegemonic Chinese empire carved up by Anglo-European colonial powers and subsequently forced into trade relations by the United States, Japan entered a period of reinvention. After the *bakumatsu* civil unrest of 1853–1867, a modern imperial vision of Japanese-ness was popularised. This modernist vision of Japan was coupled with the rearticulation of Japanese masculinity in racialized and ethno-nationalistic ways (Low 2005). The young Meiji emperor's body was refashioned in the clothes and hairstyles of other colonial powers, and young men were inculcated in new "western" forms of deportment (Roden 1980). Official decrees about everyday attire were explicitly connected to reformulating the "national polity" (*kokutai*) as masculine (Dalby 2001). Dalby quotes from the emperor's proclamation about clothing reforms as follows: "We greatly regret that the uniform of our court has been established following the Chinese custom, and it has become exceedingly effeminate in style and character" (2001, 72).

The gendered depiction of Japanese-ness also blended with racialized understandings of Japanese-ness as a matter of blood relation, racially distinct from both "Asia" and "the West" (Young 1997). Yet hierarchies between these distinctions also produced ethno-racial depictions of gender. Japanese soldiers, for example, were presented as white, with European-style hair and clothing that was juxtaposed against non-European and non-Japanese bodies (Low 2005). These depictions were popular in Japanese media representations of the first Sino-Japanese war (1894–195), where Chinese soldiers were presented as physically smaller and cowering in the presence of Japanese soldiers.

Japanese masculinity became a bodily iteration of the phrase *wakon yōsai* (Japanese spirit, Western science), where Japanese-ness was reinscribed as powerful through a combination of future-orientated and "traditional" masculinities. For example, reinvigorated confidence in Japanese-ness and Japanese men's ability to forge a new nation inspired reinterpreting the ethos and role of the samurai class during the late eighteenth and early twentieth century (Benesch 2016). Broadly falling under the term *bushido* (way of the warrior), but also occasionally described as *otoko no michi* (the way of men), the tenets of this masculine ethno-nationalist ethos were largely reinventions of the modern era (see Benesch, this volume). Defined by ideas of loyalty and self-sacrifice, this ethos would be applied to images of the ideal soldier and businessman, which continue as masculine ideals within Japan today (Dasgupta 2013).

Femininity played an important, albeit subordinated, role in how Japanese-ness was imagined too, with forms of hegemonic femininity intersecting with both questions of ethno-racial purity and class. As several Japanese scholars have noted, the early modern period saw the "nationalization of women" (*josei no kokuminka*) (Koyama 1999; Ueno 1998), wherein women's capacity for childbearing was connected to patriotism, epitomized in the phrase "good wife, wise mother" (*ryōsai kenbo*) (Koyama 1999). Over the same period, dominant public portrayals of Japanese women presented them as custodians of an imagined Japanese tradition (Ashikari 2003).

After Japan's defeat in 1945 and subsequent occupation (1945–1952), Allied forces attempted to uncouple the masculine construction of Japanese-ness prevalent before the war. Visions of Japanese "purity" and "vigour" prior to 1945 predominantly focused on the figure of the young man, particularly the soldier (Orbaugh 2007). These figures were seen as promoting Imperialist visions of Japanese-ness, and so propaganda efforts after the war tended to focus on the figures of young women as a means of promoting purportedly liberal democratic ideals (Coates 2016). Yet, despite efforts to decentre masculinity from ideals of Japanese-ness, both by Allied propaganda campaigns and in feminist discourse (see Kano, this volume), urban Japanese men have remained central to depictions of Japan as an active and empowered nation-state.

In the postwar period, the salaryman (*salariiman*) replaced the soldier as the key figure in debates around Japanese-ness and masculinity (Dasgupta 2013). Representing Japan as an economic powerhouse rather than a military power, the salaryman nonetheless came to resemble the soldier. Expected to be loyal, self-sacrificing, a heterosexual patriarch, and productive, the salaryman became a *kigyō senshi* (corporate warrior) (Egami 2011) and continued *bushido* into the corporate world (Roberson 2003). The idealized gendered counterpart of the salaryman in the postwar period became the housewife, who ideologically and economically bridged the relationship between gender, capitalist productivity, and the reproduction of Japanese identity (Borovoy 2005; Bardsley 2014).

It would be an oversimplification to suggest that men simply dominated gender and ethnicity discourse in Japan. Japan's twentieth century saw a robust feminist movement (Mackie 2003), and rapid urbanization afforded a range of opportunities to perform gender in ways that resisted dominant ideologies (Freedman et al. 2013; Sato 2003). The conflation between idealized middle-class gender relations and Japanese-ness also obfuscates regional and class differences among those who identify as Japanese. And the complicated history of marginalized groups indigenous to Japan, such as *buraku* people (Hankins 2014), Okinawans (Christy 1993), and the Ainu (Watson 2014), has shown that there are many ways to discuss Japanese-ness as an ethnic distinction. However, the twentieth century also shows how certain kinds of middle-class masculinity and men became, as Sharalyn Orbaugh notes, "epistemically central" to discussions of Japanese-ness and ethnic identity (2007). In producing ways of thinking about Japanese national identity, men and masculine tropes became the central signifiers around which other ways of being Japanese were related. Discussions of class and ethnicity were often made in reference to masculinity, women's roles in shaping ethnicity were predominantly filtered through relationships they held with men, and divergent gender identities were positioned as non-normative in relation to masculine normativity. The historically central position of masculinity and men in figuring Japan's ethno-racial identity thus helps us understand how various forms of hegemonic masculinity shape the terrain of gender and ethnicity in urban Japan today.

Hegemony and its others in urban Japan today

RW Connell developed the concept of "hegemonic masculinity" to discuss unequal relationships between men, particularly in terms of class and sexuality (2005). The term shares common conceptual goals with "intersectionality" (Crenshaw 1991), because of its interest in the intersection of gender and other forms of inequality, but Connell focuses specifically on how groups of dominant men reproduce their privileged position. Borrowing from Gramsci's notion of hegemony (Gramsci and Hobsbawm 2000), which Gramsci describes as the ability to influence what is seen as intellectually worthy or morally good, hegemonic masculinity describes the taken-for-granted valuations of people in the world, where certain dominant traits are naturalized as the most admirable.

The concept of hegemony intersects with the question of ethnicity in Japan. The popularization of discourse about Japanese-ness (*nihonjinron*) in the postwar period encouraged the perception that Japan was uniquely homogenous, with strongly normative ways of being Japanese. This "hegemony of homogeneity" (Befu 2001) continues to dominate many popular representations of Japan's ethnic makeup today and shapes much of the debate surrounding immigration, gender, and population decline in Japanese media and politics (Burgess 2016; Coates 2016; Suzuki 2017). While three decades' worth of scholarship has worked to challenge the assumed ethnic homogeneity of Japan (Befu 2001; Chapman 2006; Denoon et al. 2001; Douglass and Roberts 2000; Lie 2001; Murphy-Shigematsu and Willis 2008; Morris-Suzuki 2010; Okuda and Tajima 1991; Okuda and Suzuki 2001; Weiner 2009), Japan is still presented as relatively homogenous within international demographic statistics and popular discourse. Indeed, Japan ranks lowest in the OECD for the proportion of immigrants it accepts (Castles et al. 2013), with little over 1.8 percent of the population registered as non-Japanese in 2017 (MOJ, Japan 2017). These figures conceal the fact that many non-Japanese residents have naturalized as Japanese citizens since Meiji records began (Murphy-Shigematsu and Befu 2006) and that Japan is home to a diverse range of identities, from indigenous people such as Okinawans (Christy 1993) and the Ainu (Watson 2014) to regional differences and marginalized communities such as the *buraku* (Hankins 2014). The recent presence of non-Japanese persons in Japan has largely been the result of efforts to temporarily plug gaps in the labour market. Encouraged as labour sources through temporary (or indentured) programmes, the term *immigrant* is very rarely iterated in accounts of non-Japanese residents in Japan (Roberts 2018). Interpreted from a gender perspective, this reticence to encourage non-Japanese settlement in Japan is suggestive of the challenge that immigration poses to the hegemonic position men occupy in economic, ethnic, and gendered terms.

Prior to 1945, those from Taiwan, the Korean peninsula, Manchuria, and various other territories in East Asia fell under the designation of imperial Japanese subjects. This intersection of human mobility and colonial expansion ensured that non-Japanese peoples were posited as "exploitable" under the discourse of Japanese ethno-racial superiority. In particular, the Japanese imperial regime facilitated the indentured sexual exploitation of large numbers of non-Japanese women, now famously referred to as *ianfu*, or "comfort women" (Soh 2008). While the "comfort women" are some of the more extreme cases of exploitation still discussed today, the majority of non-Japanese arrivals in Japan served as a cheap, mobile source of labour, with often-catastrophic effects. For example, it is estimated that some 60,000 Korean laborers died in Japan (Hisako 2014).

The majority of non-Japanese immigrants in Japan up until 1945 came from the Korean peninsula, followed by Chinese-speaking peoples from Taiwan and Northern China. Under the San Francisco Peace treaty of 1951, much of Japan's non-Japanese population were repatriated as part of the Allied forces' efforts to dismantle Japan's Imperial legacy in East Asia. A group of some 200,000 Koreans remained in Japan after 1945, shaping the terrain of minority politics in Japan for decades to come (Morris-Suzuki 2010). Mostly labourers, both indentured and voluntary, these people left a significant footprint on Japan's postwar development. Their impact was partly because of the fraught colonial histories that shaped their lives in Japan; however, it was also due to the way the civil war in the Korean peninsula mapped onto domestic politics (Morris-Suzuki 2007). Forming the bedrock of minority politics in Japan (Chapman 2007), these *Zainichi* Koreans remained the largest group of non-Japanese residents until 2006. *Zainichi* Koreans are the largest multigenerational non-Japanese minority. In 2017, there were roughly 450,000 Koreans registered in Japan, with just under 300,000 registered as "special permanent residents" (*tokubetsu eijūsha*) and a significant number of naturalizations making it difficult to calculate the precise number of people of Korean descent in Japan. *Zainichi* Koreans were significantly discriminated against in the postwar period and continue to be discriminated against by extreme right groups such as the *Zaitokukai* (Organization of Citizens Against the Special Privileges of *Zainichi*). After decades of activism, bolstered by the 1990s popularisation of Korean television and music and the success stories of *Zainichi* Korean entrepreneurs such as Softbank CEO Masayoshi Son, *Zainichi* are slowly coming to be accepted. Today, "little Korea" areas such as Shin Okubo in Tokyo and Tsuruhashi in Osaka, for example, have become popular consumption spaces.

The ethnic Chinese population in Japan can be distinguished by its old established communities and a more recent group of "newcomers" (Liu-Farrer 2011; Tajima 2003). From a 1945 population of roughly 43,000, mostly from Taiwan, Manchuria, and Fujian, the ethnic Chinese population has now become the largest group of non-Japanese residents, with roughly 700,000 mainland Chinese, 50,000 Taiwanese, and more than 100,000 naturalized Japanese citizens of Chinese ethnicity registered in 2017 (MOJ, Japan 2017). From 1985 to 2017, the ethnic Chinese population increased by more than tenfold, inciting mixed feelings in popular Japanese discourse. Early Chinese migrants formed the spaces that are recognized as Chinese in Japan today, such as the Chinatowns in Yokohama, Nagasaki, and Kobe, transitioning from a stigmatized community (Tsu 2011) to a "model minority" celebrated for their social and culinary contributions to Japan (Tsu 1999). However, migrant flows since the 1990s have sparked fears about criminality and Chinese cultural hegemony in new parts of urban Japan, such as Ikebukuro, Tokyo (Coates 2018a).

While *Zainichi* Koreans and Chinese make up the largest non-Japanese ethnic minorities, there are several other large and influential groups whose recent migratory histories reflect continued efforts to plug gaps in Japan's labour market in ways that allow the continuation of the hegemonic masculinities of Japanese men. The migrant population from the Philippines started from a population of roughly 5,000 in the 1960s (Piquero-Ballescas 2013) and has grown to over 250,000 residents in 2017. Predominantly women, and the largest population of those married to Japanese nationals, this group grew in response to a demand for entertainers during Japan's bubble economy and a subsequent demand for elder care professionals in the 1990s. Today, young educated Filipinos in Japan are also sought for their exceptional English-language abilities.

With the decline in the number of manufacturing labourers in Japan in the 1990s, Brazilians and other South Americans with Japanese ancestry (*nikkei*) were enticed to Japan under specialized visas (implemented in 1991) to fill gaps in the labour market (Tsuda 2013) At the time, Japanese policymakers assumed that *nikkei* would settle more easily and cause fewer problems due to their Japanese ancestry. The *nikkei* predominantly settled in the manufacturing areas of Hamamatsu and Toyota, peaking at around 310,000 persons in 2008. After the onset of the Global Financial Crisis that year, fear of Japanese workers being laid off sparked a drastic policy of compensation for *nikkei* returning to South America premised on them not returning to Japan (Tabuchi 2009). The current population is 185,000, suggesting the disposable nature of non-Japanese labourers during times of economic crisis. Bilateral trainee programs have attracted over 230,000 Vietnamese workers in the past ten years (MOJ 2017), who alongside the 70,000 Nepalese migrants (Kharel 2016) make up the fastest growing groups in Japan today.

Despite the divergent histories and proportions of non-Japanese ethnicities in Japan, they share a similar relationship to epistemically central configurations of Japanese-ness, namely hegemonic masculinity and its relation to labour migration. This intersection of gender and ethnicity is particularly evident in popular discourse, as David Pollack outlines in his analysis of the manga *World Apartment Horror* (*Wārudo apātomento horā* , Kon et al. 1991) (Pollack

1993). Non-Japanese men within the text are portrayed as emasculated victims, day labourers, or dangerous, whereas the women are confined to nurturing mother roles and hyper-sexualized victims. While this is a fictional text, it is symptomatic of the ways Japanese popular culture positions the ethnic other in relation to hegemonic Japanese masculine protagonists. Japanese protagonists' ethnic and gendered identities are constructed in relation to exaggerated positive and negative portrayals of non-Japanese characters. Similarly, in film texts prior to the 1990s, *Zainichi* Koreans were often portrayed as emasculated male and sexualized female victims, or as dangerous criminals (Ko 2013), in films such as *Gaki Teikoku* (*Empire of Kids*, Izutsu Kazuyuki 1981) More recently, similar themes have emerged in analyses of the portrayal of Chinese migrants in film and television (Kirsch 2015). These gendered patterns of representation also extend to the ways many non-Japanese people and their cultures are valued as consumable, particularly non-Japanese women's bodies, or the ability for non-Japanese bodies to inspire reinvigorated masculinity through the perception that Asian men represent the vitality of a bygone form of Japanese masculinity (Iwabuchi 2002).

How might these wider discursive regimes relate to the experiences of non-Japanese persons living in Japan today? The central position of Japanese masculine norms ensures that large parts of life are catered towards Japanese male desires and consumption habits. Non-Japanese women have often fit within these gendered structures in ways that resemble their popular cultural portrayal. Nightlife entertainment venues such as girl's bars and *sunakku* (snack bars) hire a significant number of non-Japanese women, with dedicated Korean girls bars popular in southern Osaka (Chung 2012), a growing number of Chinese-run hostess bars in Ikebukuro, and stereotypes of Filipino women predominantly working in hostess bars. These venues serve to "masculinize" their clientele, who are predominantly Japanese businessmen (Allison 1994). Rhacel Salazar Parreñas is careful to point out that most of this work is not transactional sex as its popular representation might suggest, but rather various forms of emotional labour (2011). Nobue Suzuki also argues against seeing Filipino women in Japan as suffering subjects, as a significant number of her research participants attested that their nightlife work was satisfying, with many settling and marrying in Japan (2005). Despite the discursive regimes that influence the gendered lives of non-Japanese women in Japan, being on the edges of hegemonic gender expectations can also be a site of agency, or even an opportunity to challenge extant norms. Researching Chinese women working in Japanese companies, Gracia Liu-Farrer has found that falling outside of normative gender expectations because of being non-Japanese at times allows women to challenge gendered behaviours in the workplace (2009).

For non-Japanese men, their portrayal in the media shapes the way they are treated by formal institutions as well as the opportunities available to them. The image of young Chinese men as either victims or dangerous ensures that they are often the target of police searches and public safety campaigns (Coates 2015). However, these same portrayals have provided career-making cultural scripts for exceptional individuals. In the case of minor celebrity Li Xiaomu, the image of being a dangerous and ambitious Chinese man in the 1990s and early 2000s created a base for his public persona, allowing him to publish a series of memoirs and commentaries on Japanese society (Coates 2018b). Li has positioned himself as an attention-grabbing spokesperson for diversity in Japan and an increasingly legitimated participant in local political debates. The more Li attempts to conform his public persona to a normative Japanese popular cultural milieu, the more he reproduces various hegemonic Japanese masculine tropes, appearing more *salariiman* than Chinese migrant.

From the nineteenth century onwards, the relationship between ethnicity and gender became increasingly imbricated in the Japanese context, resulting in efforts to curb a perceived emasculation of Japanese-ness in the international context. Consequently, Japanese ethnic identities have been specifically focused on maintaining the hegemonic position of Japanese masculinity, both through the discursive position of Japanese femininities and non-normative masculinities and careful boundary maintenance between Japanese and non-Japanese gendered forms. With Japan's rise as an economic power in the second half of the twentieth century, urban intersections of gender and ethnicity continued to support a normative image of Japanese men as economic hegemons and non-Japanese men and women as surplus temporary labour. Within this regime of gender and ethnicity, however, many non-Japanese men and women have shown a capability to navigate these regimes to suit their own needs in urban Japan. The question remains, however, whether their actions will posit a challenge to gender and ethnicity in urban Japan in years to come or whether they will reproduce extant gendered images of what it supposedly means to be Japanese.

Related chapters

5   Masculinity Studies in Japan
11 Intimacy in and Beyond the Family
17 Sex Work
18 Gender, Labour, and Migration in Japan

References

Allison, A. (1994) *Nightwork: Sexuality, Pleasure and Corporate Masculinity in a Tokyo Hostess Club*, Chicago: University of Chicago Press.
Anderson, B. (1991) *Imagined Communities: Reflections on the Origin and Spread of Nationalism*, New York: Verso.
Ashikari, M. (2003) "The Memory of the Women's White Faces: Japaneseness and the Ideal Image of Women," *Japan Forum* 15 (1) 55–79.
Bardsley, J. (2014) *Women and Democracy in Cold War Japan*, London: Bloomsbury.
Barth, F. (1969) *Ethnic Groups and Boundaries: The Social Organization of Culture Difference*, Prospect Heights, IL: Waveland Press.
Befu, H. (2001) *Hegemony of Homogeneity: An Anthropological Analysis of "Nihonjinron"*, Japanese Society Series, Melbourne: Trans Pacific Press.
Benesch, O. (2016) *Inventing the Way of the Samurai: Nationalism, Internationalism, and Bushidō in Modern Japan*, Oxford: Oxford University Press.
Borovoy, A. (2005) *The Too-Good Wife: Alcohol, Codependency, and the Politics of Nurturance in Postwar Japan*, Berkeley, CA: University of California Press.
Burgess, C. (2016) "A Japanese Multicultural Society Still Far Off," *East Asia Forum* (blog). 13 October. www.eastasiaforum.org/2016/10/13/a-japanese-multicultural-society-still-far-off/.
Butler, J. (2002 [1990]) *Gender Trouble*, London: Routledge.
Castles, S., de Haas, H. and Miller, M. J. (2013) *The Age of Migration: International Population Movements in the Modern World*, 5th ed., London: Palgrave Macmillan.
Chapman, D. (2006) "Discourses of Multicultural Coexistence (Tabunka Kyōsei) and the 'Old-Comer' Korean Residents of Japan," *Asian Ethnicity* 7 (1) 89–102.
Chapman, D. (2007) *Zainichi Identity and Ethnicity*, London: Routledge.
Christy, A. S. (1993) "The Making of Imperial Subjects in Okinawa," *Positions: East Asia Cultures Critique* 1 (3).
Chung, H. (2012) "In the Shadows and at the Margins: Working in the Korean Clubs and Bars of Osaka's Minami Area," in D. W. Haines, K. Yamanaka and S. Yamashita (eds) *Wind Over Water: Migration in an East Asian Context*, Oxford: Berghahn Books.
Coates, J. (2015) "'Unseeing' Chinese Students in Japan: Understanding Educationally Channelled Migrant Experiences," *Journal of Current Chinese Affairs* 44 (3) 125–154.

Coates, J. (2016) "Not Multicultural, but a More Diverse Japan?" *East Asia Forum* (blog) 3 December. www.eastasiaforum.org/2016/12/03/not-multicultural-but-a-more-diverse-japan/.

Coates, J. (2016) *Making Icons: Repetition and the Female Image in Japanese Cinema, 1945–1964*, Hong Kong: Hong Kong University Press.

Coates, J. (2018a) "Ikebukuro In-Between: Mobility and the Formation of the Yamanote's Heterotopic Borderland," *Japan Forum* 30 (2) 163–185.

Coates, J. (2018b) "Persona, Politics and Chinese Masculinity in Japan: The Case of Li Xiaomu," in D. Hird and G. Song (eds) *The Cosmopolitan Dream: Transnational Chinese Masculinities in a Global Age*, Hong Kong: Hong Kong University Press, 127–148.

Connell, R. W. (2005) *Masculinities: Second Edition*, Berkeley: University of California Press.

Crenshaw, K. (1991) "Mapping the Margins: Intersectionality, Identity Politics, and Violence Against Women of Color," *Stanford Law Review* 43 (6) 1241–1299.

Dalby, L. (2001) *Kimono: Fashioning Culture*, London: Vintage.

Dasgupta, R. (2013) *Re-Reading the Salaryman in Japan: Crafting Masculinities*, London: Routledge.

Denoon, D., Hudson, M., McCormack, G. and Morris-Suzuki, T. (eds) (2001) *Multicultural Japan: Palaeolithic to Postmodern*, Cambridge and New York: Cambridge University Press.

Dikötter, F. (1997) *The Construction of Racial Identities in China and Japan*, Hong Kong: Hong Kong University Press.

Douglass, M. and Roberts, G. (2000) *Japan and Global Migration*, Honolulu: University of Hawai'i Press.

Egami, G. (2011) *Kigyō Senshi* (Corporate Warriors), Tokyo: Kodansha.

Freedman, A., Miller, L. and Yano, C. (2013) *Modern Girls on the Go: Gender, Mobility, and Labor in Japan*, Redwood City, CA: Stanford University Press.

Germer, A., Mackie, V. and Wöhr, U. (2014) *Gender, Nation and State in Modern Japan*, London: Routledge.

Gordon, A. (2013) *A Modern History of Japan, International Edition: From Tokugawa Times to the Present*, Oxford: Oxford University Press.

Gossett, T. F. (1997) *Race: The History of an Idea in America*, Oxford: Oxford University Press.

Gramsci, A. and Hobsbawm, E. J. (2000) *The Antonio Gramsci Reader: Selected Writings 1916–1935*, ed. David Forgacs, New York: New York University Press.

Hankins, J. (2014) *Working Skin: Making Leather, Making a Multicultural Japan*, Berkeley: University of California Press.

Herzfeld, M. (1997) *Cultural Intimacy: Social Poetics in the Nation State*, New York: Routledge.

Hisako, N. (2014) "Korean Forced Labor in Japan's Wartime Empire," in P. Kratoska (ed) *Asian Labor in the Wartime Japanese Empire: Unknown Histories*, London: Routledge, 112–120.

Iwabuchi, K. (2002) "Nostalgia for a (Different) Asian Modernity: Media Consumption of 'Asia' in Japan," *Positions: East Asia Cultures Critique* 10 (3) 547–573.

Izutsu, K. (1981) *Gaki Teikoku* (Empire of Kids), Tokyo: Art Theatre Guild.

Kharel, D. (2016) "From Lahures to Global Cooks: Network Migration from the Western Hills of Nepal to Japan," *Social Science Japan Journal* 19 (2) 173–192.

Kirsch, G. (2015) *Contemporary Sino-Japanese Relations on Screen: A History, 1989–2005*, London: Bloomsbury Publishing.

Ko, M. (2013) *Japanese Cinema and Otherness: Nationalism, Multiculturalism and the Problem of Japaneseness*, London: Routledge.

Kon, S., Otomo, K. and Nobumoto, K. (1991) *Wārudo apātomento horā* (World Apartment Horror), Tokyo: Kodansha.

Koyama, S. (1999) *Katei no Seisei to Josei no Kokuminka* (The Formation of Home and the Nationalization of Women), Tokyo: Keisō Shobō.

Lie, J. (2001) *Multiethnic Japan*, Cambridge, MA: Harvard University Press.

Liu-Farrer, G. (2009) "'I Am the Only Woman in Suits': Chinese Immigrants and Gendered Careers in Corporate Japan," *Journal of Asia-Pacific Studies* (13) 37–48.

Liu-Farrer, G. (2011) *Labour Migration from China to Japan International Students, Transnational Migrants*, London: Routledge.

Low, M. (2005) "The Emperor's Sons Go to War: Competing Masculinities in Modern Japan," in K. Louie and M. Low (eds) *Asian Masculinities: The Meaning and Practice of Manhood in China and Japan*, London: Routledge, 88–106.

Mackie, V. (2003) *Feminism in Modern Japan: Citizenship, Embodiment and Sexuality*, Cambridge: Cambridge University Press.

Marra, M. F. (2007) *The Poetics of Motoori Norinaga: A Hermeneutical Journey*, Honolulu: University of Hawaii Press.
MOJ, Japan. (2017) "Zairyūgaikokjin tokei tokei hyō" (Resident Foreiegners Statistical Summary). www.moj.go.jp/housei/toukei/toukei_ichiran_touroku.html.
Morris-Suzuki, T. (1997) *Re-Inventing Japan: Nation, Culture, Identity*, Armonk, NY: Routledge.
Morris-Suzuki, T. (2007) *Exodus to North Korea: Shadows from Japan's Cold War*, Lanham, MD: Rowman & Littlefield Publishers.
Morris-Suzuki, T. (2010) *Borderline Japan: Foreigners and Frontier Controls in the Post-War Era*, Cambridge: Cambridge University Press.
Murphy-Shigematsu, S. and Befu, H. (2006) *Japan's Diversity Dilemmas: Ethnicity, Citizenship, and Education*, New York: iUniverse.
Murphy-Shigematsu, S. and Willis, D. B. (2008) "Transcultural Japan: Metamorphosis in the Cultural Borderlands and Beyond," in *Transcultural Japan: At the Borderlands of Race, Gender and Identity*, London: Routledge, 29–70.
Okuda, M. and Tajima, J. (1991) *Ikebukuro no ajiakei gaikokujin- shakaitekijittaihōkoku* (Ikebukuro's Asian Foreigners: A Sociological Report), Tokyo: Mekon Publishing.
Okuda, M. and Suzuki, K. (2001) *Esunoporisu Shinjuku/ikebukuro- rainichi jūnenme no ajiakei gaikokujin chōsakiroku* (Ethnopolis Shinjuku/Ikebukuro: Record of a Ten Year Survey of Asian Residents in Japan), Tokyo: Harvest Publishing.
Orbaugh, S. (2007) *Japanese Fiction of the Allied Occupation: Vision, Embodiment, Identity*, Leiden: Brill.
Piquero-Ballescas, M. (2013) "Philippine Migration to Japan," in *The Encyclopedia of Global Human Migration*, Oxford: Blackwell Publishing Ltd.
Pollack, D. (1993) "The Revenge of the Illegal Asians: Aliens, Gangsters, and Myth in Kon Satoshi's World Apartment Horror," *Positions East Asia Cultures Critique* 1 (3) 677–714.
Roberson, J. E. (2003) *Men and Masculinities in Contemporary Japan: Dislocating the Salaryman Doxa*, New York: Psychology Press.
Roberts, G. (2018) "An Immigration Policy by Any Other Name: Semantics of Immigration to Japan," *Social Science Japan Journal* 21 (1) 89–102.
Roden, D. (1980) "Baseball and the Quest for National Dignity in Meiji Japan," *The American Historical Review* 85 (3) 511–534.
Salazar Parreñas, R. (2011) *Illicit Flirtations Labor, Migration, and Sex Trafficking in Tokyo*, Redwood: Stanford University Press.
Sato, B. (2003) *The New Japanese Woman: Modernity, Media, and Women in Interwar Japan*, Durham: Duke University Press.
Soh, C. S. (2008) *The Comfort Women: Sexual Violence and Postcolonial Memory in Korea and Japan*, Chicago: University of Chicago Press.
Sorensen, A. (2005) *The Making of Urban Japan: Cities and Planning from Edo to the Twenty First Century*, London: Routledge.
Suzuki, E. (2017) "Can Japan Accept Itself as a Nation of Immigrants?" *East Asia Forum* 20 November. www.eastasiaforum.org/2017/11/21/can-japan-accept-itself-as-a-nation-of-immigrants/.
Suzuki, N. (2005) "Filipina Modern: 'Bad' Filipino Women in Japan," in L. Miller and J. Bardsley (eds) *Bad Girls of Japan*, New York: Palgrave Macmillan, 159–173.
Tabuchi, H. (2009) "Japan Pays Foreign Workers to Go Home, Forever," *The New York Times* 22 April. www.nytimes.com/2009/04/23/business/global/23immigrant.html.
Tajima, J. (2003) "Chinese Newcomers in the Global City Tokyo: Social Networks and Settlement Tendencies," *International Journal of Japanese Sociology* 12 (1) 68–78.
Takezawa, Y. I. (2011) *Racial Representations in Asia*, Kyoto: Kyoto University Press.
Tsu, T.Y. (1999) "From Ethnic Ghetto to 'Gourmet Republic': The Changing Image of Kobe's Chinatown in Modern Japan," *Japanese Studies* 19 (1) 17–32.
Tsu, T. (2011) "Black Market, Chinatown, and Kabukichō: Postwar Japanese Constructs of 'Overseas Chinese'," *Positions: East Asia Cultures Critique* 19 (1) 133–157.
Tsuda, T. (2013) *Strangers in the Ethnic Homeland: Japanese Brazilian Return Migration in Transnational Perspective*, New York: Columbia University Press.
Ueno, C. (1998) *Nashonarizumu to jendā* (Nationalism and Gender), Tokyo: Seidosha.

Watson, M. K. (2014) *Japan's Ainu Minority in Tokyo: Diasporic Indigeneity and Urban Politics*, London: Routledge.
Weiner, M. (2009) *Japan's Minorities: The Illusion of Homogeneity*, London: Taylor & Francis.
Young, L. (1997) "The Discourse on Blood and Racial Identity in Contemporary Japan," in F. Dikotter (ed) *The Construction of Racial Identities in China and Japan*, London: Hurst, 199–211.

PART II

Home, family, and the "private sphere"

8
GENDER AND THE *KOSEKI*

David Chapman

Introduction

Legal sex involves the classification of an individual as either male or female for the purposes of the administrative state and in criminal and civil law. Classification by sex as a legal status sits at the intersection of classic jurisprudential questions of personal autonomy, self-ownership, personhood, and the public—private distinction and is relevant to a significant number of legal domains (Hutton 2017).

Legal sex for Japanese nationals is mediated through familial relationships recorded on the Japanese Family Register (*koseki*). In other words, gender/sex (*seibetsu*) is not specifically stated on the *koseki*, but rather an individual is either marked as husband or wife or as son or daughter (Ninomiya 2006; Maree 2014 190). This form of identification institutionalises marriage and the family and positions familial relationships, gender identity, and gender role at the centre of an individual's legal identity. This legislation and its effect are significant because the *koseki* is not only the primary identifier of nationality as Japanese, it is also the basis for identifying individuals and confirming their legal status. As a result, the way in which family is defined and conceptualised within legal and bureaucratic systems in Japan has a profound impact on the everyday lives of Japanese nationals. Moreover, the family registry system (*koseki seido*) facilitates a patriarchal, moralistic, and heteronormative approach in defining what constitutes a legitimate family. Identification through familial relationships and the dogma of an idealised family means that notions of gender/sex are moulded within the *koseki* system and, in turn, these notions form the ideology of family, the problems of which inevitably play out at the interface between individuals and legal-administrative processes.

Endō Masataka is a recent critic of Japan's Family Registry who argues that the problem with the *koseki* is that it is a politically integrated authoritarian process that is in conflict with democratic processes instead of being a means of identification that secures the individual rights, freedom, and protection of its citizens (2013, 304). He adds to a growing body of research activity and increasing social activism concerned with the discriminatory and iniquitous nature of the *koseki* (for example, see Satō and Kaihara 1981; Sakakibara 1992; Fukushima 2001; Ninomiya 2006, 2014; Chapman 2008, 2011; Miyamoto, et. al. 2011; Chapman and Krogness 2014; Mackie 2014; White 2014). Among the revelations emerging from this research is insight into the gendered nature of the *koseki* and how gender is constructed through legislation that works in combination with the *koseki* (for example, see White 2017).

In this chapter, I provide a brief outline of the historical context of the *koseki*, some of the critical issues relating to gender and the *koseki*, and where present research on this topic is situated with some comment on future study within the general context of Japanese society.

A brief history

The roots of the *koseki* system in Japan are ancient, it having been imported from China in the seventh century. Although the structure, incorporation, and social consequences of the *koseki* have changed significantly over time, its role has always been to "identify, categorize and define the population of Japan" (Chapman and Krogness 2014, 3). In feudalistic Japan, the family registration system was differentially administered under distinctive domain structures. There was no centralised system, and different registries, unlike today, included family beyond a two-generational nuclear unit (see Mori 2014). The introduction of a Civil Code in 1898 as part of the modernising process in Japan retained, and indeed, institutionalised a patriarchal approach to family structure through the Household System (*ie seido*). The Household Registry Law (*kosekihō*) enacted in 1871 (effective 1872) became more detailed by 1898 and worked with the Civil Code to ensure a legal framework that enforced the *ie* principles. Although the Civil Code was revised in 1947 (enacted 1948), many believe the tenets of the *ie* system remain (see White 2017; Ueno 2009; Hayakawa 2014; Nishikawa 2000; Nakusō koseki to kongaishi sabetsu 2004), ensuring a patriarchal and moralised approach to defining family within the contemporary Japanese legal system. Patriarchy in Japan, however, does not reduce to "one casual base" (Walby 1989 229) but rather is formed through a complex array of origins and contexts. The tenets of the *ie* system have changed with influences stemming from modernity and capitalism. Since the 1947 revisions, a large part of this change was 1947 revisions to the Civil Code that assumed gender identity and gender roles within "a heteronormative two-generation monogamous nuclear family with children" (Mackie 2014 203–204).

Contemporary Japan and the *koseki*

In contemporary Japan, the *koseki* not only records an individual's details at birth, it is also a mechanism for chronicling marriage, divorce, name changes, gender/sex change, and death. The *koseki* thus follows all Japanese nationals from the very beginning of life through to death, leaving a record of life events. Endō (2013, 37) critically describes this persistent policing of the lives of Japanese through the recording of such events as "coercive power" (*kyōseiryoku*) by which the *koseki* validates an individual's existence. As mentioned previously, central to the power of the *koseki* is the fact that it places the individual within a family unit defined according to state-determined moral codes and dictated by patriarchal approaches. Moreover, in its contemporary form, it is interwoven within the fabric of complex legislation around the Civil Code, Nationality Law, and the Household Registry Law, and it is through the *koseki* that legal sex is proven, confirmed, and determined on multiple occasions during one's lifetime. These factors ensure the authority and control of the *koseki* over the individual and, more broadly, Japanese society. However, in contemporary Japan, conservative definitions of family are at odds with social diversity and do not reflect the lived realities of many Japanese nationals in and outside of Japan. The result is frequent problems for individuals and families that fall outside of the strictly defined legal parameters of family under the *koseki*. The current context and the difficulties encountered are best understood by concrete examples accompanied by informed commentary on the application and interpretation of law. Subsequently, I have included some observations of the more common issues and incongruences related to gender.

Fūfubessei: married couple, separate family names

The fact that familial relationships are used for *koseki* entry means issues relating to legal gender/sex identity in Japan are particularly apparent in relation to marriage. These issues play out in diverse and sometimes quite unexpected ways. One area that has garnered regular attention is that of married couples and family names. Under clause 750 of the 1948 Civil Code, each legally registered household must assume one family name and this must be the name of the designated "head" of the family (*hittōsha*) on the *koseki*. In a legal marriage, this means that either the wife or the husband must give up their family name and adopt their partner's name as the registered household name. In 96 percent of cases, the adopted name is that of the husband (Ministry of Health, Labour and Welfare 2006), who is usually designated as the *hittōsha*. The legislation in this case reflects a general social expectation that family names be passed on through the patrilineal line. Opponents of change in legislation often cite damage to social order (*shakai no chitsujo*) or tradition (*dentō*) as being a reason for dismissing attempts at reform on this issue (Toyoda and Chapman 2017).

Activists in Japan have been fighting this legislation since the 1980s without success. Linda White has conducted extensive ethnographic research on Japanese activists engaged in *fūfubessei* issues. In recent research, she discusses the case of activists Tanaka Sumiko and Fukukita Noboru living in a common law marriage (*jijitsukon*) relationship with real-life experience of the problems encountered with the limited *koseki* definition of family (White 2014). In 1985, the couple had a child that was marked on the *koseki* with the kanji character *ko*, indicating that the birth was out of wedlock. This identification would mean the child would be exposed as illegitimate, a taboo in Japanese society and something that would haunt the child throughout their life. Tanaka and Fukukita have since been involved in a long campaign to address the separate family name issue and fight for the rights of children classified as illegitimate under *koseki* legislation (see White 2014). White underscores the way in which the *koseki* is framed in an ideology of heteronormativity and *ie* normativity which shapes the parameters of the legitimate family in Japan (2014, 252).

Although this is a matter for both members of a relationship, for many women, marriage and the consequent loss of family name mean a loss of identity and connection. For men, adopting their wife's family name can bring their masculinity into question and draw derision from family members for having dishonoured the family name (Toyoda and Chapman 2017; Yamanoue 1994; Miyamoto et al. 2011). Retaining the husband's family name in marriage means the preservation of a patrilineal line of inheritance and identity and, in a conservative social setting, societal enhancement. This, argues White (2017), is a manifestation of marriage inequity entrenched in the Civil Code (*Minpō*) and the Family Registry Law (*koseki hō*). Bringing to light the way in which the *koseki* entrenches the subordination of women in Japanese society is one of the goals of White's research.

Birth registration

In Japan, when a child is born, a medical doctor issues a birth certificate (*shusshō shōmeisho*) where the gender/sex (*seibetsu*) of the child is recorded as either male (*otoko*) or female (*onna*). The parents usually then submit a notification of birth (*shusshō todoke*) to the local ward office within 14 days. This information, which includes the names of the mother, father, and child;

the birth order of the child (first son, first daughter, etc.); and the legitimacy of the child are then entered on the *koseki*. The registration process assumes that the parents of the child are legally married and that the child is the biological offspring of the married parents. The legislation around this process is inflexible and unforgiving and leads to numerous difficulties for those individuals and families that are not included in this strictly prescriptive definition of family. Furthermore, as well as normative notions of family, the legislation favours patriarchy and suffers from systemic inadequacies that disadvantage women in circumstances of divorce, separation, and domestic violence. In these cases, it is not uncommon for children to become temporarily or permanently unregistered (*mukoseki*), and estimates are that 10,000 individuals in Japan are unregistered and therefore without legal identity (Miura n.d.; Akashi City 2015; Ido 2016, 20–21).

The leading cause of children being unregistered in Japan is due to the conditions attached to Article 772. Article 772 can be found under subsection 2 of Judicial Divorce that was established in the Meiji Civil Code of 1896. The conditions are as follows:

(Presumption of Child in Wedlock)
Article 772

(1) A child conceived by a wife during marriage shall be presumed to be a child of her husband.
(2) A child born after 200 days from the formation of marriage or within 300 days of the day of the dissolution or rescission of marriage shall be presumed to have been conceived during marriage.

The problem lies in legislation based on a historical approach to defending patriliny and the presumption of birth during marriage. Alongside the conditions of Article 772 are the requirements of the household registration system, which are complicit in the difficulties that Article 772 creates because birth notification is compulsory for entry into the *koseki*. Parents have three months in which to register their child and, if incomplete, the process of entering the *koseki* (*nyūseki*) at a later date becomes difficult. For women in circumstances of divorce or separation and when escaping domestic violence, difficulties arise because the law presumes that the legal husband is the father of the child. Birth registration would mean the husband would be contacted and informed of the birth, and for this reason, many estranged women in such circumstances choose not to register the birth of their child (Chapman 2019). The result is an unregistered child with no proof of identity or legal status, who is rendered invisible within Japanese administrative and bureaucratic systems. Such circumstances leave the child and mother vulnerable and without access to most basic government services such as health, welfare assistance, and, in many cases, education. If the child remains unregistered into adulthood, they are not able to apply for a passport, driver's licence, or health insurance or to be legally employed. Issues of inheritance and validation of legal status can be extremely difficult for children in this situation: with no proof of identity, the legal frameworks of citizenship, nationality, and familial ties are compromised.

Recent attention has been generated by the general public and through the media in Japan with activists such as Ido Masae (2016) and Sakamoto Yoko (2008) and media outlets such as the Mainichi Shinbun (2015). Like the *fūfubessei* issue explained previously, Article 772 is another example of how the legislation around the *koseki* is particularly impactful on women and interconnected with a patriarchal approach to family dictated by moral frameworks that attempt to ensure birth legitimacy and patrilineality. This has led to some problems being addressed through legislative and procedural change accompanied by efforts of local and federal government agencies providing access to information that assists those in this position (see Chapman 2019).

Same-sex partnerships and the *Koseki*

Same-sex marriage in Japan is not criminalised, nor is there a law that prevents it (Maree 2014, 190). The marriage notification (*konin todoke*) required for legal marriage, like the *koseki*, does not require gender/sex to be entered, but asks for the name of the person who will become the wife (*tsuma ni naru hito*) and the one who will become the husband (*otto ni naru hito*) to be recorded. The Japanese Constitution defines marriage as between "both sexes" (*ryōsei*) and does not strictly specify man and woman, although it is generally agreed to mean this (see Maree 2014, 190–191). As a result, under Japanese law, marriage can only be between two people of different sexes (Taniguchi 2006; Maree 2014, 191). For same-sex partnerships, the *koseki* system provides no room for recognition of legitimacy of a relationship. Same-sex partners are unable to register on the *koseki* as a married couple in the conventional way, leading many in the community to take different approaches in order to have their rights protected within existing conservative legal frameworks. As Maree (2014, 195) explains, adult adoption in Japan, despite the risks listed subsequently, is a popular strategy implemented by same-sex partners. Such a strategy leads to "recognition of familial ties, enjoyment of employment benefits, and establishment of inheritance rights" (Ratliff 2011, 1778; Maree 2014, 194). The risks, however, are that this legal relationship cannot be dissolved, there is no opportunity for compensation, and there is the possibility of prosecution and persecution for incest and contestation by family members with regard to inheritance and choices made on behalf of an incapacitated partner (Maree 2014, 194–195). Other strategies include partnership agreements or notary deeds (*kōseishōshō*), wills and living wills, assigning non-family members as chief mourner (*moshu*), and emergency contact cards, all of which have varying degrees of advantage and disadvantage (see Maree 2014, 196–197).

Although same-sex marriage is not criminalised in Japan, it is not recognised as legitimate or permissible in the eyes of Japanese administrative, legal, and bureaucratic systems. As case in point, in March 2016, Usui Takatoshi from Okuyama applied for marriage registration (*konin todoke*), as many people in Japan do each year. However, unlike the majority of those that apply, his application was rejected. The application was rejected because although Usui identifies as male, he was registered at birth as female, and Japanese legislation does not recognise marriage between two women (Yahoo Japan 1 Aug 2017). Usui appealed this decision by declaring that he was not a woman, even though his familial status on the family registration (*koseki*) defined his gender/sex as female. This rejection stirred feelings of resentment and discomfort for Usui, who believed his individuality was being administered by what he described to be a mechanical process (*watashi toiu jinkaku ga kikaitekini shori sareru koto ni iwakan to ikidori o oboemashita*).

In the article, Usui considers appealing the decision not to allow him to legally marry his female partner even though he identifies as male. However, such an appeal would be unsuccessful because the Act on Special Cases in Handling Gender Status for Persons with Gender Identity Disorder (2003) requires the individual to "have genitals that resemble that of the other sex" for legal sex to be changed, and Usui would not meet this physical legal requirement to be recognised as male by the state. This case brings into the discussion the way gender is determined and highlights the fact that a non-binary option is unavailable in Japan at present. Some research (see Taniguchi 2012, 109) has criticised the lack of a third option in Japan as excluding intersex peoples by only providing for a binary recognition of gender/sex. Although the lack of recognition of non-binary gender identity on birth certificates and related documents is common practice in many countries, options for a non-binary recognition are emerging. For example, Australian Government Guidelines on the Recognition of Sex and Gender (2015, 5) state that, "[s]ex reassignment surgery and/or hormone therapy are not pre-requisites for the recognition of a change of gender in Australian Government records." The same document notes that, "individuals should be given the option to select M (Male), F (Female) or X (Indeterminate/Intersex/Unspecified)" (2015, 4). However, while birth certificates allowing for a third non-binary option are available in South Australia and the Australian Capital Territory, all other states in Australia still adhere to the binary option only. To date, Japanese laws do not recognise or acknowledge a gender spectrum or allow individuals to claim a non-specific gender or intersex category on the *koseki*.

Beyond a binary of gender/sex

Since 16 July 2003, the Act on Special Cases in Handling Gender for People with Gender Identity Disorder (*sei dōitsu sei shōgaisha no seibetsu no toriatsukai no tokurei ni kansuru hōritsu*) (GID) has provided a way for some to have their gender/sex change legally recognised on the *koseki*. Legal provisions dictate that this is allowed providing the individual is 20 years or older, presently single, without children of minor age, has no testicles or has persistent lack of testicular function, and has genitalia similar in appearance to that of the opposite gender/sex (Clause 3). Although outwardly this may seem to be a liberal approach, commentators such Taniguchi (2012) have criticised the Act for its adhesion to societal gender norms. Ninomiya (2014, 169), also critical of the Act, has argued that this approach is problematic for two reasons. First, if successful, the applicant must create a new *koseki*, which means they are automatically deleted from the registry they share with family members. The second problem is related to the status items column (*mibun jikōran*) on the *koseki* where past and present information is contained. Gender/sex change is recorded in this column and is therefore available to third parties in certain circumstances. Another problem encountered by the families in this situation is that the birth order of remaining members in the *koseki* may have to be changed (McLelland 2005, 207–208).

Although same-sex marriage is not legally recognised in Japan, couples that satisfy the requirements of having successfully changed gender/sex (*seitenkan*) are allowed to marry someone who is the same gender/sex as they were previously. In other words, a person who was previously a woman and who is now legally identified as a man is able to marry a woman and vice versa. The marriage is recorded on the *koseki* as legal and legitimate. However, there have been stumbling blocks to such arrangements. For example, in 2009, Maeda Ryō, who had legally changed his gender/sex from female to male on his *koseki*, married in 2008 and, after they discussed the matter, his wife had a child through artificial insemination from a sperm donor. Problems arose when, despite being in a legal marriage, Maeda was not recognised by the local ward office as the father. The reason given was that Maeda's gender/sex change was discovered on his *koseki* and, consequently, officials were alerted that there could be no strict biological father-son relationship. The space where the relationship would have usually been noted (*tsuzukigara*) was left blank. An appeal to the Tokyo Family Court was also rejected on the grounds that Maeda had no reproductive functionality and therefore the child could not be recognised as legitimate (*chakushutsushi*). Eventually, in January 2014, the Supreme Court overturned the ruling and Maeda's name was recorded as the father of his son on the *koseki*. For more on artificial insemination and the *koseki*, refer to Brasor (2006), Ishii (2009) and Mackie (2014, 211–212).

Conclusion

The *koseki* is a mechanism by which the Japanese state attempts to standardise the population. It does this through a complex legal framework that consists of Family Law, the Civil Code, and the Nationality Law within which the Japanese citizen is demarcated and determined. However, the individual citizen is subordinate to the family and codified according to their position or role within an idealised family setting. This ideal family is bounded by normative codes of morality and patriarchy backed up by legislation and regulation. The *koseki* is where this state power and control is concentrated and is inevitably the point of mediation between the agency of the individual and the power of the state.

As this chapter has demonstrated, legal, bureaucratic, and administrative identification of Japanese nationals is processed through the *koseki*. A person's identity is constituted, defined, and confirmed by the *koseki* and/or closely connected documentation. Arbitration of gender identity and the determination of legal sex occur through the Civil Code and Family Law, coded by familial relationships. Even a single-person family, which constitutes the majority of households in Japan at 34.6 percent (Statistics Bureau of Japan 2017), designates the position of the sole family member according to their familial relationship. This is also the case in the creation of new single-person registries (*bunseki*) where the familial relationship is recorded as eldest son/daughter, and so on.

Although recent research in this field has expanded, it is still an emerging area with potential to yield further understanding of the interface between institutional practices and their influence on gender identity. There is much to gain in examining the *koseki* for scholars of gender in Japan, but there are also interesting possibilities for the involvement of scholars of gender studies in general to engage with contexts outside of the Anglosphere. The growing unrest around the disjuncture between conservative legislation relating to gender and the diversifying social reality of what constitutes a family in Japan is also fruitful ground for exploration. Although there is constant legislative change in response to the challenges of this diversity, it occurs at a snail's pace and is often weighed down by conservative policymakers intent on protecting the status quo. The challenges of the *koseki* will be with us for some time to come.

Related chapters

6   Transgender, Non-Binary Genders, and Intersex in Japan
9   Attitudes to Marriage and Childbearing
10   Family, Inequality, and the Work-Family Balance in Contemporary Japan
11   Intimacy in and Beyond the Family
15   Gender and the Law: Progress and Remaining Problems

References

Akashi City. (2015) "Koseki ga nai kata no tame no sapo-to panfuretto" (Support Pamphlet for People Without Household Registration). Accessed 14 January 2018. www.city.akashi.lg.jp/seisaku/soudan_shitsu/mukoseki/documents/20151110mukosekipanhu.pdf.
Australian Government (2015) "Australian Government Guidelines on the Recognition of Sex and Gender." Accessed 16 October 2019. https://www.ag.gov.au/Publications/Pages/AustralianGovernmentGuidelinesontheRecognitionofSexandGender.aspx
Brasor, P. (2006) "Paternity Suits Brought by Moms Symptoms of Family Register Law," *Japan Times* 24 September. Accessed 11 January 2018. www.japantimes.co.jp/news/2006/09/24/national/paternity-suits-brought-by-moms-symptoms-of-family-registry-law/.
Chapman, D. (2008) "Tama-Chan and Sealing Japanese Identity," *Critical Asian Studies* 40 (3) 423–443.
Chapman, D. (2011) "Geographies of Self and Other: Mapping Japan Through the Koseki," *The Asia Pacific Journal* 9 (29) 1–10.
Chapman, D. (2019) "Article 772 and Japan's Unregistered," *Japan Forum* 31 (2) 235–253.
Chapman, D. and Krogness, K. J. (eds) (2014) "The *Koseki*," in D. Chapman and K. J. Krogness (eds) *Japan's Household Registration System and Citizenship: Koseki, Identification and Documentation*, London: Routledge.

9
ATTITUDES TO MARRIAGE AND CHILDBEARING

Ekaterina Hertog

Over the past several decades, Japanese society has experienced significant shifts in family formation trends. Of particular interest for this chapter are marriage and childbearing delays, increased rates of divorce, rising rates of lifelong singlehood, growth in childlessness rates, and fertility rates falling far below two children per woman. These trends have taken place against the background of the high value placed on marriage and families. The large majority of unmarried men and women say that they intend to marry at some point, few people explore alternative partnership forms, few express a desire to remain childless, almost all children are born within marriages, and the large majority of men and women state that they want to have two children (NIPSSR 2015).

The limited attitudinal change against the background of major behavioural shifts presents us with a puzzle. Aiming to make sense of it, this chapter will discuss current research on marriage and childbearing attitudes and relate them to the realities of marriage and childbearing in contemporary Japan. My two primary goals in this chapter are (a) to describe the attitudes to marriage and childbearing in Japan, noting continuities and changes, and (b) to summarize the conflicting material and normative pressures associated with marriage and how these are reflected in men's and women's attitudes to it.

Marriage remains the only socially and normatively sanctioned way of having children in Japan (Hertog 2009), and the link between the two has been strengthening in the past years: more people think of children as the main benefit of marriage, and a growing number of couples marry only after conceiving a child (NIPSSR 2015). Consequently, this chapter will discuss attitudes to marriage and childbearing together, as the two are intimately linked by the widespread assumption that a marriage will be shortly followed by children.

Theoretical framework

Much of the prior research on changes in family formation relies on the second demographic transition (SDT) theory. This theory argues that growing individualization of attitudes to family formation is the core factor behind withdrawal from marriage and diversification of families in developed countries (e.g. Lesthaeghe 1983). The proponents of the SDT framework argue that it is universally applicable (e.g. Lesthaeghe 2014), though the evidence from East Asia, especially Japan, has not been fully consistent with its claims (e.g. Lee et al. 2010). This framework expects continuous liberalization and individualization of attitudes, although it concedes that the pace of change may be different depending on the cultural and structural legacy in a given society.

Indicating a potential shortcoming in the general applicability of the SDT framework, Lee et al. (2010, 186) argue that economic and socio-institutional environment influence not only the pace but also the direction of change when it comes to attitudes to gender equality in Japan. In a marked departure from the SDT predictions, Lee et. al. find that while views about the consequences of women's labour market participation and gender ideology have become more egalitarian between 1994 and 2002 in Japan, beliefs about the importance of women's work have become more conservative. They attribute the traditional attitudes to women's work to the persistent tax disincentives to women's employment, limited career opportunities available to women, lack of affordable childcare, and professionalization of the housewife role. At the same time, Lee et al. (2010) report that both men and women have become more accepting of women's earnings, and the change has been particularly rapid for men, potentially reflecting the economic reality that makes the sole breadwinner role onerous. In a similar challenge to the predictions of the SDT framework, this chapter argues that in Japan, marriage remains a "package" of gender-specific expectations and obligations structured and reinforced by the normative and institutional environment (Bumpass et al. 2009) and is evaluated as such. Therefore, we should not expect a linear change to more liberal and individualistic attitudes predicted by SDT in the absence of change to the dominant social structures.

To explain the links between the labour market and welfare context and the attitudes to marriage and childbearing, this chapter will draw on the work of McDonald (2000; 2013) and Oppenheimer et al. (1997). McDonald's gender equity theory emphasizes the conflict between the growing opportunities open to women outside families and the homemaker role they are expected to play after marriage. This conflict shapes, among other things, their attitudes and transitions to marriage and childbearing. I will use Oppenheimer, Kalmijn, and Lim's work to extend McDonald's approach to men. I will describe the way the conflict between casting men as main breadwinners despite shrinking labour market opportunities makes traditional marriages seem undesirable or out of reach to many Japanese men.

Locating men's and women's marriage and childbearing attitudes within the changing social context, I will demonstrate how the persistently gendered expectations associated with family formation have become unattractive to well-educated young men and women as well as untenable in a growing proportion of partnerships. The declining desirability and feasibility of the Japanese "marriage package" and the dearth of viable alternatives to it explains, in my view, the paradox of withdrawal from family formation against the persistently high desirability of marriage and childbearing in Japan today.

Existing research on marriage attitudes primarily focuses on women, as their expanding access to education and employment is believed to make traditional marriage and family arrangements unattractive to them. The same arrangements are seen as beneficial or even essential to men (e.g. Kaufman and Goldscheider 2007), and therefore men's desire for traditional gendered marriage often remains unquestioned. Research highlighting the difficulties of being the sole breadwinner in a modern economy, however, questions these assumptions (Oppenheimer 2003; Oppenheimer et al. 1997). This overview will, therefore, give equal weight to men's and women's attitudes.

Marriage and childbearing in Japan after 1970

As indicated in the introduction, Japanese marriage and childbearing behaviours shifted dramatically between the 1970s and 2015, with the pace of change accelerating from the mid-1980s to the early 1990s. The average age of first marriage has risen from 27 to 31 for men and from 24 to 29 for women, while the total fertility rate fell from 2.13 to 1.45 between 1970 and 2015. Among 50-year-old men in 2015, 23 percent have never been married, up from 1.7 percent in 1970, when marriage was virtually universal. This change is all the more dramatic in Japan where singlehood almost invariably means childlessness. Unlike singlehood in other post-industrialized countries where young people are increasingly opting for alternative partnership forms, in Japan, singlehood often entails "effective singlehood" that involves celibacy and lack of social interaction with members of the opposite sex in general (Jones 2007).

As a result, later and fewer marriages mean fewer children that tend to be born later. The spacing between children has also lengthened. In the 1970s, almost 90 percent of all children were born within 3 years after marriage. By 2015, this figure had fallen to 73 percent. The link between marriage and childbearing, however, has remained strong throughout these years, with only 2.29 percent of children born outside marriage in 2015, up from 0.93 percent in 1970.

These family formation trends take place against the background of high gender inequality in the public and domestic spheres. While the gender gap in education has almost closed, gender inequality in the labour market is pervasive. Women continue to form the bulk of precarious labour, there is a persistent gender gap in wages, maternal employment rates remain low, and there are few female senior managers and virtually no women on company boards (Estévez-Abe 2013; Nemoto 2016; Yu 2009). In 2018, Japan ranked at 110 out of 149 countries in the Global Gender Gap Report, a testament to its low levels of gender equality (World Economic Forum 2018).

The Japanese government passed the Equal Employment Opportunity Law in 1985 (implemented in 1986) and from the 1990s, the Japanese state has introduced a number of policies aimed to help parents (mostly mothers) to combine work and care responsibilities. Yet the effectiveness of these policies has been limited (Brinton and Mun 2016). Investment in childcare provision in Japan remains considerably below the OECD average (OECD 2017a). In 2003, Japan ranked lowest among 33 countries in terms of public childcare availability (Fuwa and Cohen 2007), and it continues to be characterized by a particularly unequal domestic division of labour even among East Asian countries, in all of which wives do most of the domestic work (Kan and

Table 9.1 Marriage and childbearing trends

Year	TFR [b]	Mean age first marriage [b]		Mean age at first birth [b]	Children born within 3 years of marriage [b] (%)	Never married by 50 [a] (%)		Children born outside marriage [b] (%)
		Men	Women	Women		Men	Women	
1970	2.13	26.9	24.2	25.6	89.1	1.7%	3.33	0.93
1975	1.91	27	24.7	25.7	90.5	2.12	4.32	0.8
1980	1.75	27.8	25.2	26.4	88.7	2.6	4.45	0.8
1985	1.76	28.2	25.5	26.7	88.6	3.89	4.32	0.99
1990	1.54	28.4	25.9	27.0	87.2	5.57	4.33	1.07
1995	1.42	28.5	26.3	27.5	84.5	8.99	5.10	1.24
2000	1.36	28.8	27	28.0	82.2	12.57	5.82	1.63
2005	1.26	29.8	28	29.1	77.6	15.96	7.25	2.03
2010	1.39	30.5	28.8	29.9	76	20.14	10.61	2.15
2015	1.45	31.1	29.4	30.7	73.1	23.37	14.06	2.29

Sources: [a] (Statistics Bureau, various years) [b] (MHLW, various years)

Hertog 2017). In 2015, *The Economist* rated Japan as the third worst economy in which to be a working mother in the OECD (The Economist Data Team 2016). In Japan, it is still common for women to quit full-time jobs upon marriage or childbearing and return to the labour market only several years later, often into dead-end jobs (Nakano 2014, 58–59). Japan's gender wage gap is almost twice the OECD average. Women's limited career opportunities are related to the heavy demands of the "second shift," as wives continue to be responsible for virtually all housework and care work in married couples (Hertog and Kan 2019), and the norms of intensive maternal investment in children remain strong (e.g. Allison 2000). Consequently, married women with children still have to rely on their husbands' earnings, as their own careers remain precarious and marriage and childbearing are typically followed by numerous new responsibilities.

At the same time, the long-term economic stagnation that followed the burst of Japan's economic bubble in the early 1990s has meant that men's ability to be the sole providers in their families has diminished. Over the past two decades, the average income of even full-time employed men, as well as the number of full-time jobs available to recent graduates, fell, while unemployment rates for young men and long-term unemployment among these men have gone up (Brinton 2011; Genda and Hoff 2005; MHLW 2013). Women's improved educational attainment and increasing labour-market participation have also meant that marriages with similar or higher-status men are harder to achieve. The female preference for "marrying up" (Raymo and Iwasawa 2005; Shirahase 2014) means that men with low qualifications are at a particular disadvantage in the marriage market (Raymo and Iwasawa 2005).

These socioeconomic changes make traditional marriages, where a wife becomes a homemaker while the husband is the main or even the only breadwinner, impractical and often impossible. Yet, as women continue to face obstacles to combining careers with families, no clear alternative to the traditional marriage script has emerged, leading to a "drift into singlehood" (Schoppa 2006; Yoshida 2016).

Table 9.2 Trends in social and economic indicators in Japan

Year	Enrolment in 4-year university degrees [b] (%)		Labour force participation rate [a]	Percent working in irregular jobs [b]		Gender wage gap (for regular employees) [b]	Wife's housework share [c] (%)
	Men	Women	Women (15–64)	Women	Men		
1970	27.3	6.5	53.4				
1975	41	12.7	49.7				
1980	39.3	12.3	52.5				
1985	38.6	13.7	54.5				
1990	33.4	15.2	57.1	38.1	8.8	60.2	1991: 93%
1995	40.7	22.9	58.4	39.1	8.9	62.5	1996: 93%
2000	47.5	31.5	59.6	46.4	11.7	65.5	2001: 91%
2005	51.3	36.8	60.8	52.5	17.7	65.9	2006: 90%
2010	56.4	45.2	63.2	53.8	18.9	69.3	2011: 88%
2015	55.4	47.4	66.7	56.3	21.9	72.2	2016: 87%

Sources: [a] (OECD 2017b)

[b] (Gender Equality Bureau 2017)

[c] (Hertog and Kan 2019)

Attitudes to marriage

The second demographic transition theory expects women's greater participation in the public sphere and withdrawal from marriages and childbearing in Japan to be connected via the individualization of attitudes to family formation. For example, Bumpass, Rindfuss, Choe, and Tsuya write, "As the tension continues to build between traditional expectations and changing behaviours, Japanese attitudes are increasingly accepting of behaviours once strongly disapproved, and marriage and childbearing are increasingly being seen as discretionary" (2009, 229; see also Lesthaeghe 2014).

As expected within the SDT framework, marriage in postwar Japan has been redefined as a matter of personal choice. Arranged marriages have become rare, more people agree with the statement that "marriage is not absolutely necessary," and progressively fewer people see social acceptance as one of the benefits of the married state (MHLW 2013, 61, 70, 73; NIPSSR 2015). In spite of this ostensible freedom, changes in other attitudes and plans towards family formation have at most been moderate (see also Kamano 2013). The desire to get married remains high, and most couples state that they would like to have more than two children. A simple tabulation of answers to questions about marriage and family attitudes indicates that a number of attitudes have experienced U-turns. In 2015, roughly as many people as in 1992 agreed that remaining single for life is not a good life choice; that divorce is a step not to be taken for such a simple reason as character incompatibility; and that if a couple lives together, they should get married (see Table 9.3). There is no evidence that cohabitation is becoming a viable alternative to marriage, as a majority of men and women believe children should be born within marriages (NIPSSR 2015). Cohabitation with a loved one, having a family, and having children were the top three reasons for getting married cited by men and women in 2014 (MHLW 2014). Fewer people believe that a married couple *has* to have children, but the proponents of this view still form a large majority of single men and women.

The one sphere where we see a major change is the belief that used to consign women to the home after marriage. This belief has weakened substantially, especially the perception that after marriage the husband should work while the wife should focus on the household. This view was supported by 60 percent of unmarried men and 50 percent of unmarried women in 1992 but is now espoused by only about 30 percent of single men and women.

The traditional division of labour within married families is becoming less desirable and less expected. The majority of singles would like to form families where the wife either quits her job temporarily and then returns to the labour market or where husband and wife both pursue their careers throughout their married lives. In 2015, 73 percent of women said that this would be an ideal life course after marriage, with 64 percent of single women planning to achieve such an arrangement. Seventy-four percent of men would like to have working wives (NIPSSR 2015). Notably, the speed with which these attitudes have been changing has slowed down substantially from late 1990s (see Table 9.4). A recent study by Piotrowski et al. (2019) finds that the liberalization of attitudes towards gender division of labour at home and in the labour market has stalled in Japan in recent decades.

Women's preference for becoming housewives after marriage or childbearing stopped falling in 1997, possibly reflecting the long time they spend on housework and childrearing (see Table 9.2). The proportion of men and women who believe that mothers rather than anyone else should take care of young children fell but is still close to 70 percent for both genders. The economic reality, however, meant that women's expectation to be able to be housewives continued to fall, with only 7.5 percent of women expecting to become housewives in 2015.

Table 9.3 Attitudes to marriage and childbearing

Year	Plan to marry one day [a]		It is not desirable to spend one's life staying single [a]		Once married, one should not divorce just because of character incompatibility [a]	
	Men	Women	Men	Women	Men	Women
1987	91.8	92.9				
1992	90	90.2	65.3	57.6	68	57
1997	85.9	89.1	57.7	49.1	62	47
2002	87	88.3	60.9	53	66	53
2005	87	90	64	56	69.0	58.3
2010	86.3	89.4	64	57	72.3	62.2
2015	85.7	89.3	64.7	58.2	69.2	59.7

	If a couple lives together, they should get married [a]		A married couple should have children [a]		The desired number of children [b]
	Men	Women	Men	Women	
1987					2.23
1992	78.5	72.6	88	85	2.18
1997	69.0	59.3	78	71	2.16
2002	71.6	60.3	76	69	2.13
2005	73.9	62.9	79	69	2.11
2010	73.5	67.4	72.3	62.2	2.07
2015	74.7	70.5	75.4	67.4	2.01

Sources: (NIPSSR 2005, 2010, 2015)

Note

a) Single men and women aged 18–34

b) Married men and women less than 50 years of age

Table 9.4 Expectations of marriage

Year	Even after marriage, one should have their own goals		It is natural to sacrifice half of one's individuality and way of life after marriage		After marriage, the husband should work outside and the wife should take care of the household		When the children are small, the wife should not work	
	Men	Women	Men	Women	Men	Women	Men	Women
1972					83[a]	84[a]		
1992	76.4	78.3	44.7	36.4	61.7	49.7	87.5	87.4
1997	76.5	80.3	45.9	32.6	45.8	31.5		
2002	77.3	81.3	51.8	35.4	40.3	28.9	76.4	77.1
2005	80.2	84.9	56.7	40.1	36.2	28.7	75.9	77.8
2010	81.2	82.4	58.2	45.4	36.0	31.9	73.3	75.4
2015	83.8	88.4	59.3	47.2	30.7	28.6	69.8	73.0

Sources: [a] Retherford et al. (1996)

Everything else (NIPSSR 2005, 2010, 2015)

Men's attitudes to their future wives' labour market participation changed even faster and more dramatically than women's own views between 1987 and 2015. While women were less likely than men to support gender specialization within marriage in the 1980s and 1990s (Raymo and Iwasawa 2008), the situation had reversed by 2015 (see also Lee et al. 2010). In 2015, only around 10 percent of men felt that having a nonworking wife was desirable. In the same year, fewer men than women believed that when children are small their mother should not work, and the difference in the proportion of men and women agreeing with the statement "after marriage, the husband should work outside and the wife should take care of the household" has narrowed to 2 percent, down from 12 percent in 1992. Moreover, while studies published in the 1990s and early 2000s documented a negative association between women's earning potential and their marriage probability, this relationship has reversed and became positive for recent cohorts of women (N. Fukuda 2016, 69–70; S. Fukuda 2013), suggesting that these women are in demand in the marriage market. Piotrowski et al. (2015) also find that women in irregular employment are disadvantaged in the marriage market. In sum, the research cited in this section seems to reflect men's growing unwillingness to be the only earners and women's increased scepticism about their ability to balance work and family responsibilities in the absence of meaningful help from their husbands at home. I will discuss these two mechanisms in the following sections.

The importance of earning power

While single-earner families are a rarity in today's Japan, husbands are still expected to be the main breadwinners, and a life-course where the wife quits her job temporarily to focus on the household while the children are young is still the most expected and the most desired arrangement (see Figures 9.1–9.3). The traditional division of labour is reinforced through extended family, marriage websites (Dalton and Dales 2016), popular culture (Matanle et al. 2014), the press (Bobrowska and Conrad 2017), state policies (OECD 2015), and company practices (Nagase and Brinton 2017).

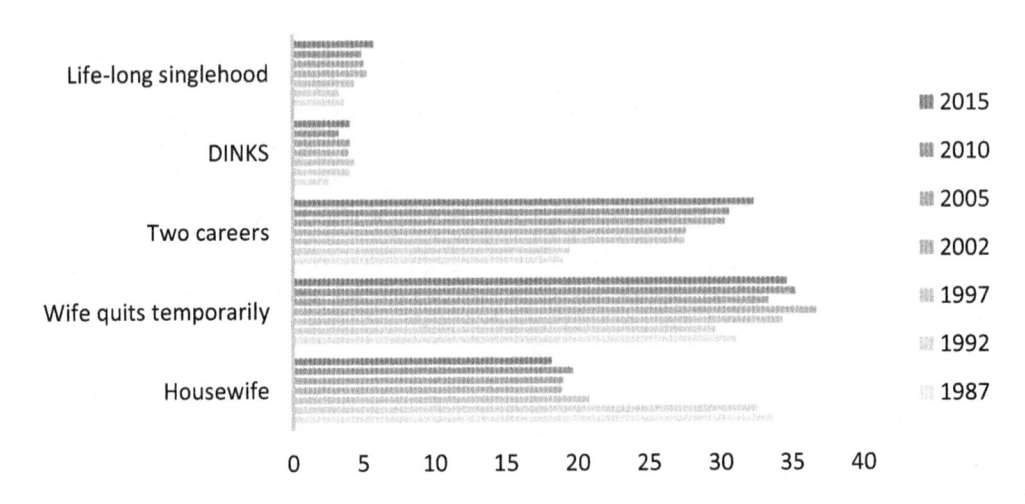

Figure 9.1 Women's perceptions of ideal work-life balance arrangements after marriage

Attitudes to marriage and childbearing

In this environment, young men who have not secured regular full-time employment status are at an extreme disadvantage in the marriage market. Cook (2014) demonstrates that these men wish to get married but feel they cannot do so unless they change their employment status. Following the traditional gender script, these men are adamant "though often conflicted—that on marriage men have to become the main breadwinner" (Cook 2013, 38). Using a survey of 10,000 regular and nonregular unmarried male employees, Uchino et al. (2013) report that men have similar perceptions about marriage and family independently of their employment

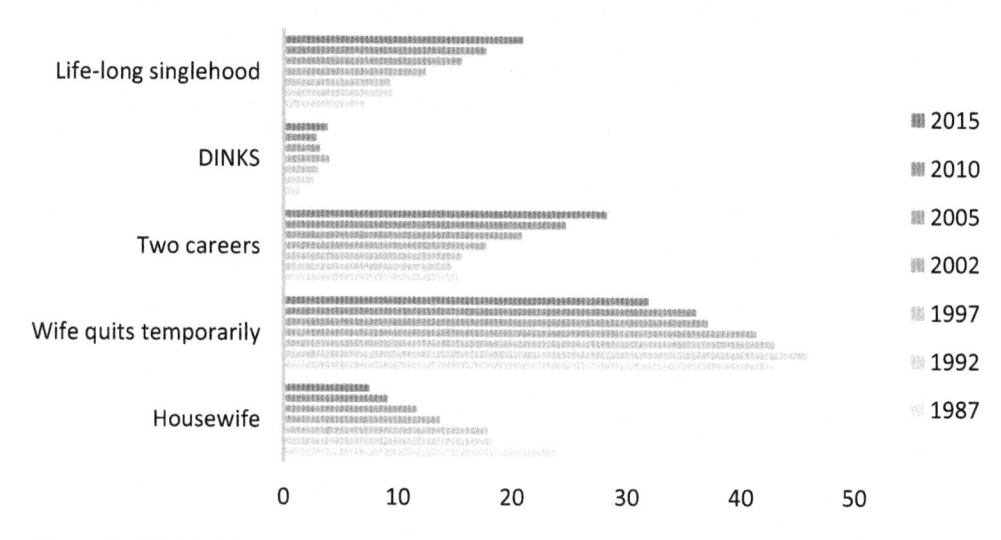

Figure 9.2 Work-life balance actually expected by women after marriage

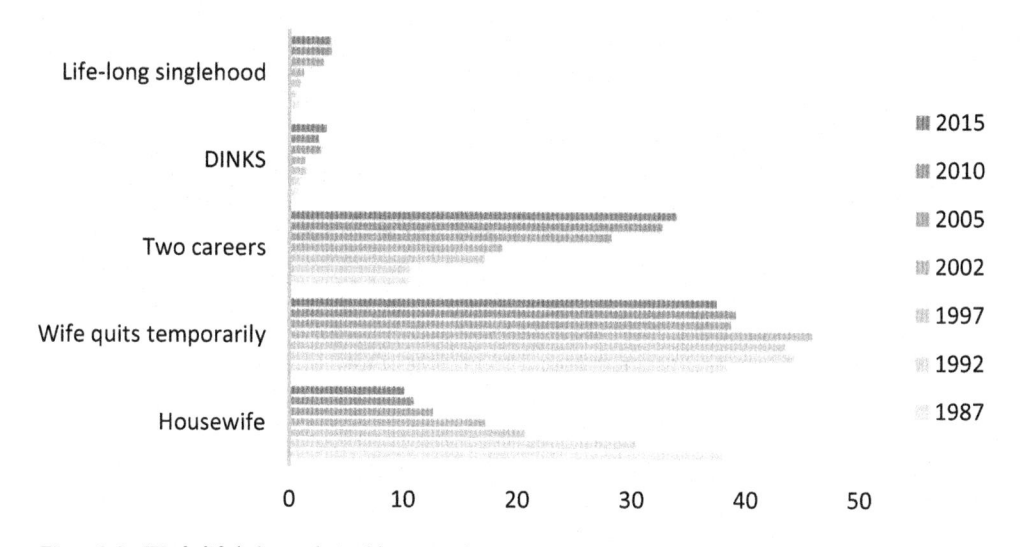

Figure 9.3 Work-life balance desired by men after marriage

type. When it comes to pursuing marriage, however, nonregular employees are passive, and this attitude is associated with their anxiety about employment and income status in the future (see also NIPSSR 2015).

Such attitudes are reinforced by these men's current or prospective female partners (Cook 2013; Honda 2002). In Cook's study, women, irrespective of their own employment status, "made it clear that whilst they might date a man in irregular employment they would not marry or live with him unless he found stable work, regardless of their feelings" (2013, 38). An irregular job was seen as a sign of irresponsibility and incomplete transition to adulthood for men. Moreover, in a reflection of women's own precarious labour market position, a marriage to a man who cannot assume financial responsibility for a family and may lose his job at short notice was perceived as too risky. Finally, many women felt that their parents would never allow such a match. The highly gender-unequal labour market environment remains unfavourable to women (Genda and Hoff 2005). It hence makes securing livelihood via traditional marriage a more straightforward choice for women than trying to maintain a career and be breadwinners in their own right (Mirza 2016). This reality may be behind the reversal in the liberalization trends in many marriage-related attitudes recorded in Table 9.3.

Lower-income and less stably employed men are withdrawing from marriage faster than any other men. As mentioned previously, a smaller negative association is also observed for women in irregular employment compared to women in regular employment (Piotrowski et al. 2015). Women with high earning power are also withdrawing from marriages but at a slower pace compared to women with lower earning potential (Fukuda 2013, 122; Raymo and Iwasawa 2017). We do not have comparable information about high-earning men. Existing research indicates that better-educated and better-earning men and women have growing doubts associated with strongly prescribed gender roles within marriages, namely reduction of personal freedom and autonomy in marriages.

Work-life balance and perceived lack of freedom after marriage

More than 80 percent of single men and women in Japan believe that even after marriage, individuals should be able to pursue their own goals (Table 9.4). In reality, however, men and women expect restrictions of their freedom and individuality after marriage, and the majority of women associate motherhood with self-sacrifice (Nakano 2014, 58). These expectations have strengthened between 1990 and into the decade beginning 2010. Unmarried men in regular employment see marriage as a constraint on their autonomy and free time, which are already limited by their often long working hours and work-centred lives (MHLW 2014; Nemoto et al. 2013). There is somewhat more pressure on men to participate in family life, as around 80 percent of wives said they believe that their husbands should share housework and childcare load with them in 2013, up from 74 percent in 1993. Around 30 percent of wives reported actively expecting men to help and 48 percent expressed their dissatisfaction with the level of men's involvement in domestic work (NIPSSR 2013).

In reality, in 2016, men contributed around 13 percent of total time spent on housework by the couple and around 20 percent of time spent on childcare (Hertog and Kan 2019). The documented gap in housework time between men and women is exceptionally large in Japan for all couples as well as in double-income households (Tsutsui 2015, 173). The rate of increase of husbands' contributions to domestic work has been glacial (Table 9.2). The mismatch between the desire for greater equality at home and the persistently unequal reality is becoming an additional source of stress for regularly employed married men, who feel they should participate more in family life but cannot do so because of their busy schedules (Taga 2017).

As men's working hours remain long, the main responsibility for domestic work falls onto women (e.g. Hidaka 2010; Nemoto 2008). Access to childcare has made balancing work and family easier for women who work only part-time and are able to secure a place in a nursery, but it has not alleviated the total paid and unpaid workload for women in full-time employment (Hertog 2018). Nursery waiting lists also remain long (Japanese Economy Information Division 2005; MHLW 2016). Moreover, there is no formal help available for much more time-intensive housework responsibilities. As a result, for women, marriage and childbearing are associated with loss of financial autonomy and a dramatic increase in domestic workload (MHLW 2014; Mirza 2016; Nemoto 2008). Women's growing ambivalence about their caregiver roles was evident in a *Mainichi Newspaper* report on "The Japanese Population" (2000). According to this report, Japanese women's belief that children taking care of aged parents is a "good custom" or a "natural duty" has been falling since the 1980s (N. Fukuda 2016, 52). Women are also "voting with their feet" by having fewer children with husbands who do not help at home (Nagase and Brinton 2017) and avoiding marriages associated with particularly heavy care burdens (Yu and Hertog 2018). Fuwa (2014) directly links the incompatibility of work and family life in Japan with highly educated women's negative attitudes to marriage.

Given the realities of the Japanese labour market, men and women find it difficult to envisage a nontraditional division of labour in their future families and end up perpetuating the stereotypes of marriageability associated with the opposite sex. Several studies document both genders' dissatisfaction with the dominant cultural roles prescribed for the members of their own sex within marriage—but this dissatisfaction is combined with a persistent aspiration for partners who would conform to these norms (e.g. Nemoto 2008; Nemoto et al. 2013).

The structural constraints that promote marriages as an exchange of gendered obligations, rather than an emotional bond, also diminish its value for personal fulfilment. Emotional closeness is hard to achieve if husbands and wives spend much of the time operating in separate spheres as overtime work and work-related socializing for men, and domestic responsibilities for women, add up to keep them apart.

Reduced marriage pressure

Given the widespread dissatisfaction with and perceived drawbacks of marriage, detailed previously, why would Japanese singles desire marriage at all? Wishing to have a family, wishing to have children, cohabiting with a loved one, and not wishing to be alone in one's old age feature prominently for both men and women (MHLW 2013; NIPSSR 2015). This indicates that marriage remains the only way to secure life-long companionship with a nonrelative. Wanting to reassure one's parents and relatives is also important, suggesting that marriage, to some extent, remains a family enterprise. While somewhat more women than men aged 20 to 39 note these reasons as important for them, the proportions of men and women choosing these answers are broadly similar (MHLW 2013).

Today marriage is hardly seen as "optional" in Japan the way it is in many developed Western countries, but the social pressure to marry by a particular age has declined significantly in recent decades (Nemoto et al. 2013; Yoshida 2016). This opens a loophole that enables Japanese singles to proclaim their desire to eventually form families while postponing the actual family formation to some point in the future (see Ezawa, in this volume).

Given the structural constraints discussed previously, for many singles, marriage and childbearing seem both desirable and at the same time out of reach. In a 2014 survey of singles in seven OECD countries (Japan, South Korea, United States, UK, Germany, France, Sweden), the ratio of young people aged 13 to 29 who have the desire to be married and have children sooner than later was the second highest in Japan (following South Korea). The ratio of those who expected to *actually* be married and raising children by the time they are 40 ranked the lowest (Cabinet Office 2014).

Discussion and conclusion

In recent decades, Japan has undergone a number of changes in its family formation trends, such as later and fewer marriages, growing divorce rates, and fewer children. A cursory look suggests that attitudinal changes have followed suit. Marriages have been redefined as a matter of personal choice rather than a familial institution, and there has been a clear liberalization of attitudes to married women's participation in the labour market. A closer analysis of the available opinion polls reveals, however, that these were the only spheres where we observe individualization and diversification of values related to family formation. We either see very limited change or a U-turn in attitudes related to marriage formation, many of which have been growing more conservative since the early 2000s.

While men and women aspire to a more equal division of labour within marriages, the highly gendered labour market and the insufficient policies to support a work-family balance for husbands and wives continue to make these aspirations impractical. In these circumstances, an extreme division of labour, where the wife shoulders all the domestic work but does not have the stress of maintaining a career, seems to become more attractive to women. The worsening employment conditions for men, however, have led them to embrace the idea of working wives. At the same time, long working hours reduce husbands' ability to support these future wives' careers by helping with domestic work. This mismatch in marriage-related aspirations has meant that single men and women remain open to the idea of marriage and yet ambivalent when it comes to making the actual decision to marry and have a family.

This analysis indicates that structural constraints on the realities of the "marriage package" in contemporary Japan play a major role in influencing individual attitudes to family formation. Marriages based on an equal division of labour at home and in the labour market are favoured by men and women as an ideal family situation. There is, however, a major gap between perceptions of ideal and realistic family arrangements, and this gap can be traced back to the institutionalized labour market constraints. Further analysis using raw data is necessary to explore these findings.

Related chapters

5 Masculinity Studies in Japan
10 Family, Inequality, and the Work-Family Balance in Contemporary Japan
13 Changing Folk Cultures of Pregnancy and Childbirth

References

Allison, A. (2000) *Permitted and Prohibited Desires: Mothers, Comics, and Censorship in Japan*, Berkeley: London: University of California Press.
Bobrowska, S. and Conrad, H. (2017) "Discourses of Female Entrepreneurship in the Japanese Business Press—25 Years and Little Progress," *Japanese Studies* 37 (1) 1–22.
Brinton, M. C. and Mun, E. (2016) "Between State and Family: Managers' Implementation and Evaluation of Parental Leave Policies in Japan," *Socio-Economic Review* 14 (2) 257–281.
Brinton, M.C. (2011) *Lost in Transition: Youth. Work, and Instability in Postindustrial Japan*, Cambridge: Cambridge University Press.

Bumpass, L. L., Rindfuss, R. R., Choe, M. K. and Tsuya, N. O. (2009) "The Institutional Context of Low Fertility," *Asian Population Studies* 5 (3) 215–235.

Cabinet Office. (2014) *Heisei 25 nendo waga kuni to shogaikoku no wakamono no ishiki ni kansuru chōsa* (Survey of Young People's Consciousness in Japan and Other Countries in 2013), Tokyo: Cabinet Office.

Cook, E. E. (2013) "Expectations of Failure: Maturity and Masculinity for Freeters in Contemporary Japan," *Social Science Japan Journal* 16 (1) 29–43.

Cook, E. E. (2014) "Intimate Expectations and Practices: Freeter Relationships and Marriage in Contemporary Japan," *Asian Anthropology* 13 (1) 36–51.

Dalton, E. and Dales, L. (2016) "Online Konkatsu and the Gendered Ideals of Marriage in Contemporary Japan," *Japanese Studies* 36 (1) 1–19.

Estévez-Abe, M. (2013) "An International Comparison of Gender Equality: Why Is the Japanese Gender Gap So Persistent?" *Japan Labor Review* 10 (2) 82–100.

Fukuda, N. (2016) *Marriage and Fertility Behaviour in Japan: Economic Status and Value-Orientation*, Singapore: Springer.

Fukuda, S. (2013) "The Changing Role of Women's Earnings in Marriage Formation in Japan," *Annals of the American Academy of Political and Social Science* 646 107–128.

Fuwa, M. (2014) "Work-Family Conflict and Attitudes Toward Marriage," *Journal of Family Issues* 35 (6) 731–754.

Fuwa, M. and Cohen, P. N. (2007) "Housework and Social Policy," *Social Science Research* 36 (2) 512–530.

Genda, Y. and Hoff, J. (2005) *A Nagging Sense of Job Insecurity: The New Reality Facing Japanese Youth*, Tokyo: International House of Japan.

Gender Equality Bureau. (2017) *White Paper on Gender Equality* (Danjo Kyodou Sankaku Hakusho), Tokyo: Japan.

Hertog, E. (2009) *Tough Choices: Bearing an Illegitimate Child in Japan*, Stanford: Stanford University Press.

Hertog, E. (2018) "Changes in Childcare Availability and Parental Time Use Between 1996 and 2016 in Japan." Paper Presented at the IATUR 2018, Budapest.

Hertog, E. and Kan, M. Y. (2019) "Education and Gendered Division of Domestic Labor over Time in Contemporary Japan." Paper Presented at the Population Association of America, Austin, TX.

Hidaka, T. (2010) *Salaryman Masculinity: The Continuity of and Change in the Hegemonic Masculinity in Japan*, Leiden: Brill.

Honda, Y. (2002) "Jenda to iu Kanten kara Mita 'Freeter'" (Gender Approach to 'Freeter'), in R. Kosugi (ed) *Jiyu no Daisho: Freeter* (The Cost of Freedom: Freeter), Tokyo: Nihon Roudou Kenkyu Kikou (The Japan Institute of Labour), 149–174.

Japanese Economy Information Division. (2005) "Child Day Care Industry in Japan."

Jones, G. W. (2007) "Delayed Marriage and Very Low Fertility in Pacific Asia," *Population and Development Review* 33 (3) 453–478.

Kamano, S. (2013) "Women's Attitudes Toward Marriage, Family and Gender Relationships Since the 1990s in Japan: Analysis of Overtime Changes and Determining Factors," *Journal of Population Problems* 69 (1) 3–41.

Kan, M-Y. and Hertog, E. (2017) "Domestic Division of Labour and Fertility Preference in China, Japan, South Korea, and Taiwan," *Demographic Research* 36 557–587.

Kaufman, G. and Goldscheider, F. (2007) "Do Men 'Need' a Spouse More than Women? Perceptions of the Importance of Marriage for Men and Women," *Sociological Quarterly* 48 (1) 29–46.

Lee, K. S., Tufis, P. A. and Alwin, D. F. (2010) "Separate Spheres or Increasing Equality? Changing Gender Beliefs in Postwar Japan," *Journal of Marriage and Family* 72 (1) 184–201.

Lesthaeghe, R. (1983) "A Century of Demographic and Cultural Change in Western Europe: An Exploration of Underlying Dimensions," *Population and Development Review* 9 (3) 411–435.

Lesthaeghe, R. (2014) "The Second Demographic Transition: A Concise Overview of Its Development," *Proceedings of the National Academy of Sciences of the United States of America* 111 (51) 18112–18115.

Matanle, P., Ishiguro, K. and McCann, L. (2014) "Popular Culture and Workplace Gendering Among Varieties of Capitalism: Working Women and their Representation in Japanese Manga," *Gender, Work and Organization* 21 (5) 472–489.

McDonald, P. (2000) "Gender Equity in Theories of Fertility Transition," *Population and Development Review* 26 (3) 427–439.

McDonald, P. (2013) "Societal Foundations for Explaining Low Fertility: Gender Equity," *Demographic Research* 28 981–994.

Ministry of Health, Labour and Welfare. (2013) *Heisei 25-nenban kōsei rōdō hakusho: wakamono no ishiki o saguru* (White Paper on Labour and Welfare: Understanding Young People), Tokyo: Ministry of Health, Labour and Welfare.

Ministry of Health, Labour and Welfare. (2014) *Heisei 26-nendo kekkon kazoku keisei ni kansuru ishiki chōsa hōkoku-sho* (Report of the 2014 Survey on Marriage Family Formation Attitudes), Tokyo: Ministry of Health, Labour and Welfare.

Ministry of Health, Labour and Welfare. (2016) *Hoikujo-tō kanren jōkyō torimatome wo kōhyō shimasu* (A Summary of the Situation of Nurseries and Related Issues) [Press release], Tokyo: Ministry of Health, Labour and Welfare.

Ministry of Health, Labour and Welfare (various years) *Jinkō dōtai tōkei* (Demographic Statistics), Tokyo: Ministry of Health, Labour and Welfare.

Mirza, V. (2016) "Young Women and Social Change in Japan: Family and Marriage in a Time of Upheaval," *Japanese Studies* 36 (1) 21–37.

Nagase, N. and Brinton, M. C. (2017) "The Gender Division of Labor and Second Births: Labor Market Institutions and Fertility in Japan," *Demographic Research* 36 339–370.

Nakano, M. (2014) *"Ikukyū sedai" no jirenma: josei katsuyō wa naze shippai suru no ka*, Tōkyō: Kabushiki Kaisha Kōbunsha.

National Institute of Population and Social Security Research (2005) *13th Basic Survey of Childbearing Trends* (Dai jugokai shussei dōkō kihon chōsa), Tokyo: National Institute of Population and Social Security Research.

National Institute of Population and Social Security Research (2010) *14th Basic Survey of Childbearing Trends* (Dai jugokai shussei dōkō kihon chōsa), Tokyo: National Institute of Population and Social Security Research.

National Institute of Population and Social Security Research (2013) *5th National Survey of Family Trends* (Daigokai zenkoku katei dōkō chōsa), Tokyo: National Institute of Population and Social Security Research.

National Institute of Population and Social Security Research (2015) *15th Basic Survey of Childbearing Trends* (Dai jugokai shussei dōkō kihon chōsa), Tokyo: National Institute of Population and Social Security Research.

Nemoto, K. (2008) "Postponed Marriage: Exploring Women's Views of Matrimony and Work in Japan," *Gender and Society* 22 (2) 219–237.

Nemoto, K. (2016) *Too Few Women at the Top: The Persistence of Inequality in Japan*, Ithaca: ILR Press.

Nemoto, K., Fuwa, M. and Ishiguro, K. (2013) "Never-Married Employed Men's Gender Beliefs and Ambivalence Toward Matrimony in Japan," *Journal of Family Issues* 34 (12) 1673–1695.

OECD (2015) "Japan Policy Brief" [Press release].

OECD (2017a) "OECD Family Database."

OECD (2017b) "Labour Force Statistics: Indicators by Sex and Age."

Oppenheimer, V. K. (2003) "Cohabiting and Marriage During Young Men's Career-Development Process," *Demography* 40 (1) 127–149.

Oppenheimer, V. K., Kalmijn, M. and Lim, N. (1997) "Men's Career Development and Marriage Timing During a Period of Rising Inequality," *Demography* 34 (3) 311–330.

Piotrowski, M., Kalleberg, A. and Rindfuss, R. R. (2015) "Contingent Work Rising: Implications for the Timing of Marriage in Japan," *Journal of Marriage and Family* 77 (5) 1039–1056.

Piotrowski, M., Yoshida, A., Johnson, L. and Wolford, R. (2019) "Gender Role Attitudes: An Examination of Cohort Effects in Japan," *Journal of Marriage and Family* 81 (4) 863–884.

Raymo, J. M. and Iwasawa, M. (2005) "Marriage Market Mismatches in Japan: An Alternative View of the Relationship Between Women's Education and Marriage," *American Sociological Review* 70 (5) 801–822.

Raymo, J. M. and Iwasawa, M. (2008) "Changing Family Life Cycle and Partnership Transition—Gender Roles and Marriage Patterns," in F. Coulmas (ed) *The Demographic Challenge: A Handbook About Japan*, Leiden: Brill.

Raymo, J. M. and Iwasawa, M. (2017) *Diverging Destinies: The Japanese Case*, Singapore: Springer.

Retherford, R. D., Ogawa, N. and Sakamoto, S. (1996) "Values and Fertility Change in Japan," *Population Studies* 50 (1) 5–25.

Schoppa, L. J. (2006) *Race for the Exits: The Unraveling of Japan's System of Social Protection*, Ithaca, NY and London: Cornell University Press.

Shirahase, S. (2014) *Social Inequality in Japan*, Abingdon: Routledge.

Statistics Bureau. (various years) "Census."
Taga, F. (2017) "Dilemma of Fatherhood: The Meaning of Work, Family, Happiness for Salaried Male Japanese Workers," in B. G. Holthus and W. Manzenreiter (eds) *Life Course, Happiness and Well-being in Japan*, London: Routledge.
The Economist Data Team (2016) "The Best—and Worst—Places to Be a Working Woman: The Glass-Ceiling Index," *The Economist* 3 March.
Tsutsui, J. (2015) *Shigoto to kazoku: Nihon wa naze hatarakizuraku uminikui no ka*, Tōkyō: Chūō Kōron Shinsha.
Uchino, J., Iijima, A. and Takahashi, T. (2013) *An Analysis of Unmarried Men's Attitudes to Marriage and Family Focusing on Non-Regular Employees: Empirical Evidence from Survey Data*, ESRI Discussion Paper Series. Tokyo: Cabinet Office.
World Economic Forum. (2018) "The Global Gender Gap Report 2018." www.weforum.org/reports/the-global-gender-gap-report-2018. Yoshida, A. (2016) "Unmarried Women in Japan: The Drift into Singlehood," in *Routledge Research on Gender in Asia Series*, London: Routledge.
Yu, W. H. (2009) *Gendered Trajectories: Women, Work, and Social Change in Japan and Taiwan*, Stanford: Stanford University Press.
Yu, W. H. and Hertog, E. (2018) "Family Characteristics and Mate Selection: Evidence from Computer-Assisted Dating in Japan," *Journal of Marriage and Family* 80 (3) 589–606.

10

FAMILY, INEQUALITY, AND THE WORK-FAMILY BALANCE IN CONTEMPORARY JAPAN

Aya Ezawa

The work-family balance is a topic that attracts considerable attention in Japan today, as a growing number of women not only work when single but also wish to continue working and pursuing a career while working as a mother. Also, for heterosexual men, their partners' ability to work is of increasing importance, as employment stability and lifetime employment can no longer be taken for granted, and the costs of child rearing and education are central concerns among many families with children in contemporary Japan. There are significant challenges in combining work and family in Japan today.

What makes the topic of the working lives of families interesting is that child bearing and working parenthood are both private and personal, yet at the same time public issues, nestled at the intersection of the state, the market, and family life. Whether one chooses to have a child, stay home, or work as a parent may appear in the first instance as a personal decision. Yet social policies and government support in the form of family allowances, subsidized childcare, or regulations which support working parents can also generate incentives and disincentives for combining work with having a family. Likewise, the structure of the economy, labour laws, and company practices affect the working conditions of parents. Family strategies also play an important role in the setting of priorities between, for instance, staying home to be able to spend more time with a pre-school-aged child or ensuring a second income in order to be able to finance the rising costs of children's education. Social policy regimes and work environments, as well as families' engagement with them, are thus important factors that shape family lifestyles and the work-family balance.

In this chapter, I examine the relationship between the state, market, and family life in Japan from several angles, beginning with an overview of the role of domesticity and child rearing in the building of the modern Japanese nation-state, followed by an examination of the consolidation of a gendered division of labour in the family and the postwar Japanese economy, and leading up to a discussion of the empirical realities of working parents and family life in contemporary Japan.

Family, domesticity, and modernity

One of the characteristic aspects of the period of modernization during the Meiji era (1868–1912) was that government policies at the time not only invested in the building of a modern nation-state with a Constitution and National Diet, and modern infrastructure and industry, but also took an active interest in the family and women's role in the shaping of a modern Japanese nation and its future citizens (Nolte and Hastings 1991; Uno 2005; Koyama 2014; see also Germer et al. 2014). Central to government campaigns at the time was the ideal of the "good wife, and wise mother" (*ryōsai kenbo*), which underscored women's contribution to the nation in the form of dedication to the well-being of the family, efficient household management, and the education of children (Uno 1993a). Contrasting women's marginal role in the education of their children until then, educational thinkers during the Meiji period stressed women's duty and responsibility in child rearing and the importance of making women into "educated mothers" who would contribute to the development of the nation by raising "superior" children (Koyama 1991).

The "good wife, wise mother" ideal was promoted through primary school education, which became mandatory for children of both sexes from 1873. Children not only learned basic skills in reading, writing, and mathematics, but were also taught specific values, attitudes, and skills, in line with the gender roles expected of them as adults (Nolte and Hastings 1991). The ideal of the housewife and mother was also promoted by Daily Life Improvement Campaigns (*seikatsu kaizen undō*) initiated by the Ministry of Education, which took the form of exhibitions, public lectures, and social education showcasing how to approach the role of the wife and mother in an efficient and effective manner. In promoting the role of the "good wives, and wise mothers," the government made mothers and their role in the family an integral element of Japan's path toward modernization (Koyama 1999; Garon 1997).

To be sure, the ideal of the "good wife, wise mother," in targeting primarily middle-class mothers, could hardly describe the actual lifestyles of the majority of mothers at the time, for whom work was a self-evident element of their everyday life. While single women worked in factories, married women often did piece work at home, such as assembling match boxes, shaving toothpicks, sewing sandal straps, or polishing metal wares, to contribute to the family income (Uno 1993b). Concerned with working mothers' inability to look after their children, the government invested in the building of public day care centres in the early twentieth century, which provided care for the children of working families while also educating children about the value of hard work and parents about health and savings (Uno 1999).

That policy makers promoted the ideal of the "good wife, wise mother" in parallel with the establishment of public day care centres is not necessarily a contradiction in terms. Rather, the contrasting treatment of middle-class women and working-class mothers indicates that the promotion of the "good wife, and wise mother" ideal was not simply about the domestication of women and childcare; working mothers were, in fact, not chastized for their employment but rather encouraged to devote themselves to productive work, as frugal and diligent workers, while leaving their children in care (Uno 1999). What seemed to matter most was not that children were raised by their mothers per se, but that children received an appropriate upbringing regardless of their mothers' work status. In promoting the "good wife, wise mother" ideal, and building day care facilities for working mothers, policy makers recognized the instrumental role of mothers in raising healthy and productive citizens and strengthening the nation, making child rearing not just a private but a public issue.

Family life and the gender division of labour in postwar Japan

Family life in the postwar period underwent a number of significant changes. The postwar constitution assured equal rights to men and women and granted women suffrage as well as the right to divorce. Whereas large and extended families with four or more children were common in wartime Japan, the average number of children per family dropped dramatically as women gained more control over reproduction with the legalization of abortion (Norgren 2001). By the 1960s, a nuclear family consisting of a married couple and two children had become the norm (Ochiai 1996).

Yet, there were also important continuities. While the ideal of the "good wife, wise mother" lost its appeal (Uno 1993a), it came to be replaced by a new family ideal consisting of a hard working "salaried" husband and a full-time "professional" housewife devoted to the well-being of her spouse and children (Vogel 1963). The "salaryman," a white-collar employee working in a large corporation or a government office, became a central symbol of the rising middle class, with a lifestyle characterized by secure employment and the promise of affluence. Housewives married to salarymen were not just considered housewives but were expected to play a central role in ensuring children's success in school; their commitment to housework and child rearing has also been likened to a profession that requires knowledge, skills, and dedication, just like that of their salaried husbands (Vogel 1978; Imamura 1987; Hendry 1993). Due to its association with affluence and modernity, the role and lifestyle of the housewife continues to have a strong appeal, despite expanding educational and employment opportunities for women (Goldstein-Gideoni 2012) and the fact that employment has remained a normal part of life for most working-class women (Kondo 1990; Roberts 1994; see also White 2002).

The role of the housewife and gendered division of labour were fostered by social policies, which relied on and reinforced a male breadwinner ideal at a time when educational and employment opportunities for women were expanding (Yokoyama 2002; Shimoebisu 1994). Tax and pension schemes created financial incentives for married mothers to limit employment to part-time work and offered advantages, particularly to the families of men with management positions in large corporations who could support their family on a single salary (Osawa 2002). Low-income families, by contrast, received little government support. A child allowance (*jidō teate*) for low-income families was introduced at a very late stage of the development of Japanese social policies (in 1972; Oshio 1996), and offered only a limited amount of support.

Company policies and practices, likewise, have reinforced a gendered division of labour in the workplace and in the home. Before the introduction of the Equal Employment Opportunities Law (EEOL) in 1986, women were offered few career opportunities in large corporations, under the assumption that they would quit with marriage and childbirth (Ogasawara 1998). Women's educational attainment increased considerably in postwar Japan, yet employment and career opportunities did not expand at the same pace (Brinton 1993; see also Kurotani 2014). Large companies are also known to have encouraged the wives of employees to support their spouses by taking care of the household in order to make sure employees would arrive at work physically and psychologically well rested (Gordon 1997; Meguro and Shibata 1999). That is to say, companies not only demanded loyalty and long work hours from their employees but also counted on their spouses to commit themselves to household and children to allow employees to dedicate themselves fully to their job.

As a consequence, an M-shaped curve in women's employment has remained remarkably persistent throughout most of the postwar period (Iwai and Manabe 2000). The tendency for women to enter employment after the completion of their education, withdraw from work during their child-bearing years, and return as part-time employees when children reach elementary school age has only recently begun to recede, contributing to a gradual "flattening" of the M-shaped employment curve (MHLW 2015). Nevertheless, even though continued employment among mothers is growing, those who do pursue employment (approximately one third of married mothers) remain a minority among mothers to date (IPSS 2010).

Prime Minister Abe's Womenomics policies have, among others, stressed the importance of advancing women's position in the workplace by investing in childcare and supporting women's employment and advancement toward senior positions in government and the economy in recent years. Yet the ability to benefit from these policies tends to be limited to a minority of highly educated elite women who already have considerable resources at their disposal (Dalton 2017). Waiting lists for a place in a day care centre also continue to hamper many women's ability to remain employed (Shibata 2016). Above all, mothers who wish to embrace equal opportunities and pursue a career not only need to work "like a man" but also need to manage child rearing and housework, as men's participation in housework and childcare often remains limited even when their partners are employed (MHLW 2015).

Beyond policies and regulations, the demands placed on employees, particularly in large corporations, have been viewed as a key issue hampering married mothers' ability to balance work and family (Brinton 2001). That is, in a setting where long work hours are considered key indicators of an employee's loyalty and performance, prioritizing work over family becomes a necessity for those eager to pursue a career. But while it allows male employees to assert their identity and status by working overtime, it can also become a source of discouragement for women with children (Nemoto 2013). While women may not lack in ambition to pursue a career, a culture of long work hours, combined with a persistent gendered division of labour in the home, and high expectations toward motherhood mean that work and family remain very difficult to combine for women in contemporary Japan. This conflict not only limits women's employment opportunities but also affects their views of having children (Rosenbluth 2007; Nemoto 2008).

The difficulties of balancing work and family in the current corporate environment also have implications for men. The lifestyle of the salaryman, with his extremely long work hours and life-long commitment to the company, has been subject to question, particularly among a younger generation of men who see little appeal in becoming a workaholic and absent father and husband (Roberson and Suzuki 2003). Corporate cultural practices have also been argued to have an impact on employees' health with, at times, fatal consequences (North 2011). Yet there are few alternatives. Due to the recession, there has been a significant increase of *freeters*—young people employed in casual and part-time work—in part due to a lack of opportunities for permanent employment (Brinton 2011; Kosugi 2003), which has also posed challenges to their masculinity and status as adult men (Cook 2016). Other studies have likewise underscored the importance of the role of the breadwinner for salarymen's masculinity (Hidaka 2010). Even if men wish to be more involved in child rearing, the bottom line often remains that men feel responsible as breadwinners; the loss of employment is equated with "social death" (Dasgupta 2013, 83).

Men's focus on work and company life and absence from family life has been so obvious that the postwar Japanese family has been considered a quasi-single mother family. As Kasuga's ethnographic study of single fathers (1989) has shown, the main challenge single fathers in the 1980s faced was that they were not expected to be capable of parenting their own children. Although some groups of fathers have come to embrace the role of the father (Ishii-Kuntz 2003), the take-up rate of paternity leave among fathers to date remains extremely low. Men in Japan are highly socially isolated because of the centrality of work in their lives, and men of working age have a high suicide rate (Minashita 2015). The incompatibility of work and family thus not only disadvantages women but has also marginalized men from family life.

The persistence of a rigid gendered division of labour in postwar Japanese society has had wide-ranging repercussions not only for women's employment opportunities but also men and women's experiences of work and family life. The reinforcement of this gendered division of labour through government policies and company practices has privileged a male breadwinner model and families able to afford to live comfortably on a single income but has also made it difficult to pursue lifestyles outside of this model.

Family and social inequality in contemporary Japan

The challenges faced by families in contemporary Japan are, however, not limited to the work-family balance and its gender implications. Contrasting the public discourse on Japan as a middle-class society and a preoccupation with the middle-class salaryman family during the bubble economy, with the onset of the Heisei recession in the early 1990s, income inequality and class stratification began to attract growing attention (Tachibanaki 2005; Sato 2000; Seiyama 2008; Hashimoto 2010; Ishida and Slater 2010). Class and stratification have become increasingly visible in the form of disparities in the living conditions of families (e.g. Yamada 2004) and child poverty. Japan's "familialist" welfare regime, viewed from this perspective, not only promoted a gender division of labour but also stratification among families in Japan (Shirahase 2017). Whereas the early postwar family was construed as a unit of security, in post-bubble Japan, family has become a major risk in everyday life (Takeda 2014, 106).

The OECD Economic Survey of Japan (2006) presented a child poverty rate of 14 percent for the year 2000, which significantly exceeded the OECD average, drawing attention to the existence of child poverty in Japan. The report not only revealed a high level of child poverty in Japan but also highlighted the relationship between the difficult working conditions of mothers and the well-being of children. According to the report, Japan's child poverty rate was boosted by the high poverty rate among single-mother households, who were found to be more likely to live in poverty if they work, as compared to if they do not (OECD 2006).

The high poverty rate of single mothers in Japan underscores the implications of the reinforcement of a male breadwinner model and the incompatibility of work and family for the well-being of women and children. More than 80 percent of single mothers are working, regardless of their children's age (84.5 percent in 2010; MHLW 2011), yet single mothers' average household income in 2010 amounted to only 44.2 percent of the income of other households with children (MHLW 2011). Despite a high work participation rate, 58.7 percent of single mothers in Japan in 2009 were estimated to live in poverty (Abe 2014, 10).

To be sure, there are a range of policies in place which support single mothers and their children, from the dependent children's allowance (*jidō fuyō teate*), which offers cash assistance to single mothers with a low or no income, special loans for educational and other purposes, and waivers for utility fees, as well as programs and subsidies to acquire qualifications in order to facilitate employment and a better income (cf. Ezawa and Fujiwara 2005). As low-income families, single mothers are also eligible for child allowance and subsidized public day care services. While single mothers have received more government support than other low-income families, their high work participation rate and high poverty rate underscore the limits of current policies supporting single mothers in Japan today (Akaishi 2014).

Educational attainment is also an important factor to consider (cf. Ezawa 2010), as single mothers with a low educational attainment are more highly represented among divorcees and single-mother households (Fujiwara 2008). Single mothers with a low educational attainment often have fewer resources at their disposal: they are less likely to have made agreements about child support payments (MHLW 2011) and receive less support from their families (Iwata 2001). While single mothers who are university graduates earn on average an income of ¥2.97 million per year, senior high school graduates earn considerably less (¥1.69 million per year) and are also more likely to work in part-time and irregular work than university-educated single mothers (MHLW 2011). In addition, only highly educated single mothers or those who have become a single mother at a relatively young age are likely to experience a substantial salary increase after becoming a single mother; on average, single mothers' living conditions tend to become increasingly difficult over time (Abe 2008, 135–137).

The repercussions of motherhood on women's incomes are also noticeable among two-parent families. As a panel study conducted by the Institute for Research on Household Economics during the Heisei recession has shown, for many families, the birth of children not only comes with additional costs but, as mothers find it difficult to combine work with family, also results initially in a lower household income when mothers quit working after giving birth. The interruption of employment due to childbirth has also been found to have long-term consequences for mothers' income and increases the likelihood of a family experiencing poverty (Higuchi 2004, 219).

Limited resources and constrained household finances can furthermore affect children's educational performance. Studies of families who live in public housing units and who rely on public assistance have shown that children's educational opportunities were not only limited by household finances but also due to parents' lack of time, cultural capital, and knowledge on how to support their children's education (Kudomi 1993; Hasegawa 2014). Even if mothers do their best in caring for their children in addition to holding up a full-time job, deprivation experienced in childhood has been found to have consequences for children's life course, achievements, and health in the long term (Abe 2008).

The institutionalization of the salaryman family, composed of a full-time housewife and a salaryman employed in a large corporation and their children, therefore, not only maintains a gendered division of labour but also reinforces social and economic disparities in Japanese family life. Families with a full-time housewife have always constituted a minority among families (Osawa 2002). While their lifestyle has not been exclusive to the middle class, it is mostly among families with breadwinners who work in large corporations that remaining a full-time housewife and relying on a single breadwinner is associated with material comfort (Nihei 2010). Single-mother households and low-income families, by contrast, continue to struggle with the fact that combining work and family remains difficult and that the presence of children and interruption of work with childbirth have long-term consequences for mothers' earnings and the household income.

Conclusion

Contrasting the carefree image of the middle-class housewife and the salaryman of the early postwar period, contemporary newspaper headlines are more likely to discuss soup kitchens for children and the realities facing families living in poverty. The "discovery" of family poverty encourages us to critically review scholarship on the postwar Japanese family, which has predominantly focused on middle-class families and highly educated women during the Bubble Economy, and directs our attention to the diversity of families and family lifestyles in contemporary Japan. While scholarship on minorities, gender, and sexual orientation has grown considerably in the past decades, there is still room for greater attention to the economic and social disparities in Japanese family life which have been documented and discussed widely in Japanese scholarship (e.g. Aoki 2003; Abe 2008; Kodomo no hinkon hakusho henshū īnkai 2009; Nakusō! Kodomo no hinkon zenkoku network 2012; Abe 2014; Matsumoto et al. 2016). Above all, the emergence of child poverty as a public issue in Japan allows us to critically assess the social consequences of Japan's welfare regime and company system, not only for men and women's ability to combine work and family life, but also for the living conditions of families and children in contemporary Japan.

Related chapters

5 Masculinity Studies in Japan
9 Attitudes to Marriage and Childbearing
16 Gender and the Workplace
39 Beyond the "Parasite Single"

References

Abe, A. (2008) *Kodomo no hinkon* (Children and Poverty), Tokyo: Iwanami Shinsho.
Abe, A. (2014) *Kodomo no hinkon II* (Children and Poverty II), Tokyo: Iwanami Shinsho.
Akaishi, C. (2014) *Hitorioya katei* (Single Parent Households), Tokyo: Iwanami Shinsho.
Aoki, O. (ed) (2003) *Gendai nihon no 'mienai' hinkon* (The Invisibility of Poverty in Contemporary Japan), Tokyo: Akashi Shoten.
Brinton, M. C. (1993) *Women and the Economic Miracle*, Berkeley, CA: University of California Press.
Brinton, M. C. (2001) "Married Women's Labor in East Asian Economies," in M. C. Brinton (ed) *Women's Working Lives in East Asia*, Stanford, CA: Stanford University Press, 1–37.
Brinton, M. C. (2011) *Lost in Transition*, Cambridge: Cambridge University Press.
Cook, E. (2016) *Reconstructing Adult Masculinities: Part-Time Work in Contemporary Japan*, London and New York: Routledge.
Dalton, E. (2017) "Womenomics, 'Equality' and Abe's Neo-Liberal Strategy to Make Japanese Women Shine," *Social Science Japan Journal* 20 (1) 95–105.
Dasgupta, R. (2013) *Re-Reading the Salaryman in Japan: Crafting Masculinities*, London and New York: Routledge.
Ezawa, A. (2010) "Motherhood and Class: Reproductive Strategies Among Japanese Single Mothers," in H. Ishida and D. Slater (eds) *Social Class in Contemporary Japan: Structures, Sorting and Strategies*, London and New York: Routledge, 197–221.
Ezawa, A. and Fujiwara, C. (2005) "Lone Mothers and Welfare-to-Work Policies in Japan and the United States: Toward an Alternative Perspective," *Journal of Sociology and Social Welfare* 32 (4) 41–63.
Fujiwara, C. (2008) "Single Mothers and Welfare Restructuring in Japan: Gender and Class Dimensions of Income and Employment," *The Asia Pacific Journal: Japan Focus* 6 (1).
Garon, S. (1997) *Molding Japanese Minds: The State in Everyday Life*, Princeton: Princeton University Press.
Germer, A., Mackie, V. and Wöhr, U. (eds) (2014) *Gender, Nation, and State in Modern Japan*, Oxford and New York: Routledge.
Goldstein-Gideoni, O. (2012) *Housewives of Japan*, New York: Palgrave Macmillan.
Gordon, A. (1997) "Managing the Japanese Household: The New Life Movement in Postwar Japan," *Social Politics* 4 (2) 245–283.
Hasegawa, Y. (2014) *Kakusa shakai ni okeru kazoku no seikatsu/kosodate/kyōiku to arata na kon'nan* (New Issues in Family Life, Child Rearing, Education in an Unequal Society), Tokyo: Junposha.
Hashimoto, K. (2010) *Kazoku to kakusa no sengoshi* (A Postwar History of Family and Economic Disparity), Tokyo: Seikyusha.
Hendry, J. (1993) "The Role of the Professional Housewife," in J. Hunter (ed) *Japanese Women Working*, London: Routledge, 224–241.
Hidaka, T. (2010) *Salaryman Masculinity: Continuity and Change in Hegemonic Masculinity in Japan*, Leiden: Brill.
Higuchi, Y., Ota, K. and The Institute for Household Economics (2004) *Joseitachi no heisei fukyō* (Women and the Heisei Recession), Tokyo: Nihon Keizai Shimbunsha.
Imamura, A. (1987) *Urban Japanese Housewives*, Honolulu: University of Hawaii Press.
IPSS, National Institute of Population and Social Security Research (2010) *Report on the Fourteenth Japanese National Fertility Survey, vol. 1: Marriage Process and Fertility of Japanese Married Couples*, Tokyo: National Institute of Population and Social Security Research.
Ishida, H. and Slater, D. (2010) "Social Class in Japan," in H. Ishida and D. Slater (eds) *Social Class in Japan: Structures, Sorting, and Strategies*, London: Routledge, 1–29.
Ishii-Kuntz, M. (2003) "Balancing Fatherhood and Work: Emergence of Diverse Masculinities in Contemporary Japan," in J. E. Roberson and N. Suzuki (eds) *Men and Masculinities in Contemporary Japan*, London and New York: RoutledgeCurzon, 198–216.

Iwai, H. and Manabe, R. (2000) "M-jigata shūgyō pataan no teichaku to sono imi" (The Hardening of the M-Shaped Work Pattern and Its Meaning), in K. Seiyama (ed) *Nihon no kaisō system 4: jendâ/shijô/kazoku*, Tokyo: Tokyo Daigaku Shuppankai, 67–91.

Iwata, M. (2001) "Ribetsu boshikazoku to shinzoku no shien: hahaoya no gakureki kara mita kaisōsei" (Family Support Among Divorced Single Mother Families: Considering Social Class from the Perspective of Mothers' Educational Attainment), *Kyōiku fukushi kenkyū* (7) 57–72.

Kasuga, K. (1989) *Fushikatei o ikiru* (Life as a Single Father), Tokyo: Keiso Shobo.

Kodomo no hinkon hakusho henshû înkai (ed) (2009) *Kodomo no hinkon hakusho* (White Paper on Child Poverty), Tokyo: Akashi Shoten.

Kondo, D. K. (1990) *Crafting Selves*, Chicago: University of Chicago Press.

Kosugi, R. (2003) *Escape from Work*, Melbourne: Trans Pacific Press.

Koyama, S. (1991) *Ryōsai kenbo no kihan* (The Norm of the Good Wife and Wise Mother), Tokyo: Keiso Shobo.

Koyama, S. (1999) *Katei no seisei to josei no kokuminka* (The Rise of the Family and Women's Citizenship), Tokyo: Keiso Shobo.

Koyama, S. (2014) "Domestic Roles and the Incorporation of Women into the Nation-State: The Emergence and Development of the 'Good Wife, Wise Mother' Ideology," in A. Germer, V. Mackie and U. Wöhr (eds) *Gender, Nation and State in Modern Japan*, Oxford and New York: Routledge, 85–100.

Kudomi, Y. (1993) *Yutakasa no teihen ni ikiru* (Living on the Lower Ranges of Affluence), Tokyo: Aoki Shoten.

Kurotani, S. (2014) "Working Women of the Bubble Generation," in S. Kawano, G. S. Roberts and G. S. Long (eds) *Capturing Contemporary Japan*, Honolulu: University of Hawaii Press, 83–104.

Matsumoto, I., Yuzawa, N., Hirayu, M., Yamano, R. and Nakajima, T. (2016) *Kodomo no hinkon handbook* (Handbook of Child Poverty), Tokyo: Kamogawa Shuppan.

Meguro, Y. and Shibata, H. (1999) "Kigyōshugi to kazoku" (Corporatism and the Family), in Y. Meguro and H. Watanabe (eds) *Koza Shakaigaku: 2 Kazoku*, Tokyo: Tokyo Daigaku Shuppankai, 59–88.

MHLW, Ministry of Health, Labor and Welfare (2011) *Zenkoku boshi setai to chôsa kekka hôkoku* (Nationwide Survey on Fatherless Families), Tokyo: Ministry of Health, Labor and Welfare.

MHLW, Ministry of Health, Labor and Welfare (2015) *Heisei 24 nen ban hataraku josei no jitsujō* (The Circumstances of Working Women in 2015), Tokyo: Ministry of Health, Labor and Welfare.

Minashita, K. (2015) *'Ibasho' no nai otoko, 'jikan' no nai onna* (Males without "a place of their own" and women without "time"). Tokyo: Nihon Keizai Shinbun Shuppansha.

'Nakusō! Kodomo no hinkon' zenkoku network (ed) (2012) *Daishinsai to kodomo no hinkon hakusho* (Child Poverty and the Great East Japan Earthquake), Tokyo: Kamogawa Shuppan.

Nemoto, K. (2008) "Postponed Marriage: Exploring Women's Views of Matrimony and Work in Japan," *Gender and Society* 22 (2) 219–237.

Nemoto, K. (2013) "Long Working Hours and the Corporate Gender Divide in Japan," *Gender, Work and Organization* 20 (5) 512–527.

Nihei, N. (2010) "Sanchōme no gyakko/yonchōme no yuyami (The Backlight of 3 Chome/the Twighlight of 4 Chome)," in K. Hashimoto (ed) *Kazoku to kakusa no sengoshi*, Tokyo: Seikyusha, 79–110.

Nolte, S. H. and Hastings, S. A. (1991) "The Meiji State's Policy Toward Women, 1890–1910," in G. L. Bernstein (ed) *Recreating Japanese Women, 1600–1945*, Berkeley: University of California Press, 151–174.

Norgren, T. (2001) *Abortion Before Birth Control: The Politics of Reproduction in Postwar Japan*, Princeton, NJ: Princeton University Press.

North, S. (2011) "Deadly Virtues: Inner-Worldly Asceticism and Karoshi in Japan," *Current Sociology* 59 (2) 146–159.

Ochiai, E. (1996) *The Japanese Family System in Transition*, Tokyo: LTCB International Library Foundation.

OECD, Organization for Economic Co-operation and Development (2006) *Economic Survey of Japan 2006: Income Inequality, Poverty, and Social Spending*, Paris: OECD.

Ogasawara, Y. (1998) *Office Ladies and Salaried Men: Power, Gender, and Work in Japanese Companies*, Berkeley, CA: University of California Press.

Osawa, M. (2002) "Twelve Million Full-Time Housewives: The Gender Consequences of Japan's Postwar Social Contract," in O. Zunz, L. Schoppa and N. Hiwatari (eds) *Social Contracts Under Stress*, New York: Russell Sage Foundation, 255–277.

Oshio, M. (1996) *Kazokuteate no kenkyū* (Research on the Family Allowance), Tokyo: Horitsubunkasha.

Roberson, J. E. and Suzuki, N. (2003) "Introduction," in J. E. Roberson and N. Suzuki (eds) *Men and Masculinities in Contemporary Japan*, London and New York: RoutledgeCurzon, 1–19.

Roberts, G. S. (1994) *Staying on the Line: Blue Collar Women in Contemporary Japan*, Honolulu: University of Hawaii Press.

Rosenbluth, F. M. (2007) *The Political Economy of Japan's Low Fertility*, Stanford: Stanford University Press.

Sato, T. (2000) *Fubyōdoō shakai nihon* (Japan as an Unequal Society), Tokyo: Chuko Shinsho.

Seiyama, K. (ed) (2008) *Readings: sengo nihon no kakusa to fubyōdoō: hendo suru kaisō kōzo* (Readings: Economic Disparities and Inequality in Postwar Japan: The Changing Class Structure), vol. 1, Tokyo: Nihon Tosho Center.

Shibata, H. (2016) *Kosodate shien ga nihon o suku* (Child Care Support Will Save Japan), Tokyo: Keiso Shobo.

Shimoebisu, M. (1994) "Kazoku seisaku no rekishiteki tenkai. Ikuji ni taisuru seisaku taiō no hensen" (The Historical Development of Family Policies: Changes in Child Care Policies), in Shakai hosho kenkyujo (ed) *Gendai kazoku to shakai hoshō*, Tokyo: University of Tokyo Press, 251–272.

Shirahase, S. (2017) "Economic Inequality Among Families with Small Children in Japan: Who Provides Welfare to Children?" in D. Chiavacci and C. Hommerich (eds) *Social Inequality in Post-Growth Japan*, London and New York: Routledge, 107–120.

Tachibanaki, T. (2005) *Confronting Income Inequality in Japan*, Cambridge, MA: MIT Press.

Takeda, H. (2014) *The Political Economy of Reproduction in Japan*, London and New York: Routledge.

Uno, K. S. (1993a) "The Death of the 'Good Wife, Wise Mother'?" in A. Gordon (ed) *Postwar Japan as History*, Berkeley, CA: University of California Press, 293–322.

Uno, K. S. (1993b) "One Day at a Time: Work and Domestic Activities of Urban Lower-class Women in Early Twentieth Century Japan," in J. Hunter (ed) *Japanese Women Working*, London: Routledge, 37–68.

Uno, K. S. (1999) *Passages to Modernity: Motherhood, Childhood, and Social Reform in Early Twentieth Century Japan*, Honolulu: University of Hawaii Press.

Uno, K. S. (2005) "Womanhood, War and Empire: Transmutations of 'Good Wife, Wise Mother' Before 1931," in B. Molony and K. S. Uno (eds) *Gendering Modern Japanese History*, Cambridge, MA: Harvard University Press, 493–519.

Vogel, E. F. (1963) *Japan's New Middle Class*, Berkeley, CA: University of California Press.

Vogel, S. H. (1978) "Professional Housewife: The Career of Urban Middle Class Japanese Women," *Japan Interpreter* 12 16–43.

White, M.I. (2002) *Perfectly Japanese: Making families in an era of upheaval*, Berkeley: University of California Press.

Yamada, M. (2004) *Kibō kakusa shakai* (A Society of Unequal Hope), Tokyo: Chikuma Shobo.

Yokoyama, F. (2002) *Sengo nihon no josei seisaku* (Women's Policies in Postwar Japan), Tokyo: Keiso Shobo.

11
INTIMACY IN AND BEYOND THE FAMILY

Allison Alexy

When, in the spring of 2007, the Japanese Minister of Health, Labor, and Welfare referred to women as "baby-making machines" (*umukikai*)—and errant ones, at that—the outcry was immediate. Japanese newspapers reported the phrase as further evidence of Prime Minister Abe's inexperienced and gaffe-prone cabinet (Caryl and Kashiwagi 2007). Commentators described it as an explanation as to why governmental family policy was not solving any problems: precisely because the government seemed to view women as machines, it was unprepared to address the myriad social, occupational, and familial concerns that shape a woman's decision to have a baby. Feminists decried it as further unnecessary evidence of rampant sexism in Japanese society. For the international media, the story lay at a happy intersection of sexism portrayed as extreme and uniquely Japanese and a particular brand of Japanese kookiness that has become a saleable commodity (Walsh 2007). The quote got a lot of attention, but Minister Yanagisawa ultimately was able to keep his job.

Despite such clueless phrasing, such attention to intimate decisions, ideals, and action taking place within and beyond marital relationships is not unusual, in Japan or elsewhere. In Japan, intimacy, and issues broadly related to it, are at the heart of contemporary questions about what it means to be a good or successful person, how to balance personal desires with responsibilities, and the future of the nation. Not only is the aging population of baby-boomers stretching social services like the pension and healthcare systems, but younger people are waiting longer to have children, having fewer children overall, and are increasingly likely to forgo having children at all. On a national scale, these private decisions manifest in a failing social safety net because the Japanese government has long relied on families to provide support that is, in other countries, conveyed through governmental welfare systems (Goodman 2002). Same-sex intimacies and gender non-conforming individuals are prompting further questions about previously unmarked, heteronormative families (Dale 2019).

Attention to intimacy within and beyond family relationships reflects the centrality of "family" as a key symbol in modern Japan. Since the 1868 Meiji reorganization of the nation-state, "family" has been used as a central idiom through which to unify the Japanese population. In the contemporary moment, intimate practices and patterns are likewise held up as both the causes and effects of catalytic social change. As people debate the future of the nation and reflect on the types of intimate relationships they want and the relationships that are possible to create, intimacy is the hinge between the personal and political, as well as private and national concerns.

Defining "intimacy" in a Japanese context

An intimate relationship, Zelizer argues, is not merely close but also clearly marked as such; it is close in demonstrable, recognizable ways with "particularized knowledge received and attention provided" (2010, 268). Moreover Berlant (2000) convincingly argues that intimacy is never only as private as it might feel. Political and governmental attention, not to mention moral panics, regularly focus on intimate lives and practices, from same-sex marriage to abortion rights or citizenship acquired through family membership. Despite its feeling, intimacy is never *only* private; it exists at the centre of public consciousness (Faier 2009, 14; Ryang 2006).

Emphasizing the actions involved in intimacy, Plummer (2003, 13) says "[i]ntimacy exists in the doing of sex and love, obviously, but also in the doing of families, marriages, and friendship, in child bearing and child rearing, and in caring for others." Building from these careful phrasings, in this chapter, I define intimate relationships as those 1) marked by particular emotional, physical, or informational closeness, or aspirations for such; 2) taking place within realms commonly understood to be "private," itself a constructed category; 3) often, though not always, framed through bonds of love and/or sexual desire and contact.

The most direct translations of terms about intimacy from English are not necessarily at the centre of contemporary Japanese discussions. For instance *bekkon*, *shin'ai*, and *shitashimi* all gloss the idea of intimacy. They describe relationships that are particularly close or familiar and can be used to describe a range of intimate relationships from friendships to parent-child bonds to sexual partnerships. In the contemporary moment, there is a similar range of vocabulary used to talk about romantic love, including *ren'ai*, *ai*, *daisuki*, and *rabu*, the latter of which is a loan word from English. There is regular debate about which terms are best used to describe different forms and styles of love, and people regularly switch between these terms when they're discussing intimacy. In many confessions or expressions of love, for instance, people are more likely to use "I really like you" (*daisuki*), such that *ren'ai* or *ai* can, at times, sound a bit more formal or conservative.

Families in a "family nation"

From the beginning of Japan's modernity, the creation of particular family forms has been a national project. Japan's modern period began in 1868, with the Meiji Restoration, a time of political turbulence and national reinvention, when families, both literal and symbolic, were moved to the centre of the new nation. In their attempts to build a new nation that could repel powerful threats to its sovereignty, statesmen built national cohesion and patriotic loyalty to the emperor by describing the national population as one large family (*kazoku kokka*, literally "family nation") (Gluck 1985). At the same time, the Meiji Constitution also legally restructured individual families to conform to invented but supposedly traditional forms (Ikegami 1995). These laws, which defined patrilineal primogeniture as required, were made manifest in the newly universal "stem family" system (*ie seido*) and the concurrent "household registration" (*koseki*) system that tracked all citizens through their family membership (see Chapman in this volume). Although the legal restrictions of the *ie* system were abolished after World War II, scholars have argued that it continues to play a tremendously powerful role in shaping people's expectations of how families should be organized (Ueno 2009). For instance, familial roles such as "oldest son" (*chōnan*) or "daughter-in-law" (*yome*) continue to have substantial social resonance (Harris and Long 1993). Such common social tropes of family roles continue to impact Japanese people today, even as families are reshaped in light of changing patterns of intimacy (White 2002).

Family intimacies in the postwar period

Japan's postwar economic recovery—described as miraculous until the 1990s Heisei recessions burst that bubble—was structured through intimate relationships. Although academic and public attention was frequently directed at the white-collar male *salaryman* and other male labourers as agents of the economic miracle, in practice these workers were facilitated through structures of heteronormative intimacy (McLelland 2012; Plath 1980). Because salarymen and other male workers were required to work very long hours, stay out late to build working relationships, and generally be available to their employers, their lives and work habits were only made possible through domestic labour and assistance (Kurotani 2005). Within middle and upper class families, men could not work without wives taking care of basic needs like preparing food, cleaning clothes, and paying bills. At the same time, precisely because companies were offering so-called "lifetime employment" to a minority of male workers, other categories of workers were needed to be easily laid off. Especially between the 1960s and early 1990s, female workers often filled this role, acting as part-time or dispensable labourers that enabled employers to spend financial resources on other workers (Brinton 1993). Such patterns of gendered employment are visible in the M-curve graph, named because it shows how female labour force participation changes over the course of a woman's life: typically women worked before marriage or children, at which point many dropped out of paid work, before returning after children get older (Brinton 1993; Ezawa in this volume). These labour structures were often combined with patterns of same-sex socializing that meant husbands and wives rarely spent leisure time together (Imamura 1987; Ishii-Kuntz and Maryanski 2003). During Japan's economic miracle, social intimacies built in workplaces, such as work teams and junior/senior (*kōhai/sempai*) relationships, were used to make workers feel like part of the corporate "family" (Kelly 1991; Kondo 1993).

Despite such practices separating spouses in the contexts of labour and socializing, in other important ways, these spheres were fundamentally connected, often through structures of dependencies. Because labour norms often discriminated against married women or mothers to push women out of full-time labour, the average woman was unable to find a career that enabled her to support herself. Men, on the other hand, were not often taught basic domestic necessities like how to do laundry or cook nutritious meals. Even if a particular man had domestic skills or knowledge, the demands of his work schedule would likely make it impossible for him to feed and clothe himself. Thus, Edwards (1989) argues, Japanese spouses in the 1970s and 1980s were linked together partially through their "complementary incompetence"—her need for a financially viable salary and his for the domestic assistance required to earn such a salary.

These older forms of marital intimacy embody what I label *disconnected dependence*. In this term, I am trying to capture both the centrifugal and centripetal forces that were commonly exerted on Japanese marital relationships. Gendered labour policies, heteronormativity, the demands placed on male employees, and family norms pushed men and women to be structurally dependent on each other. And yet these strong social centripetal forces were met, in practice, with equally common disconnections between the spouses. While they might need each other, many spouses didn't want to spend too much time together. Indeed, the ethnographic record contains many examples of Japanese wives suggesting that a good husband is "healthy and absent" or that husbands at home are bothersome and under foot (Smith and Wiswell 1982, 179; Vogel with Vogel 2013). In these ways, discursively and in practice, typical marital relationships for most of the postwar era have been framed through *disconnected dependence:* spouses absolutely needed each other and fully recognized that dependence but often led social and emotional lives that were largely disconnected from each other.

Contested intimacies in millennial Japan

Intimacy stands at the centre of personal, public, and political debates about how best to conceptualize and construct relationships in Japan. Even more than the risks from earthquakes or tsunami, in recent decades, severe threats have come from the simultaneous problems of a rapidly falling fertility rate and aging population (see Vainio in this volume). As people have fewer children at older ages, politicians, academics, and policy-makers have been attempting to figure out why people are less inclined or able to have children and what incentives might be used to change their minds (Coleman 2008; Schoppa 2006; Takeda 2004). With fewer children, Japan's demographic pyramid is quickly becoming top-heavy, and the aging workforce's pension benefits and health care costs will soon be too much for younger workers and taxpayers to sustain (Traphagan and Knight 2003). Why, exactly, Japanese people are having fewer children remains an open question, but these intimate choices are both reflecting and contributing to major social shifts.

Beyond the falling birth rate, profound and ongoing social shifts occurring in recent decades have prompted both personal and public questioning about what used to be basic social norms. Throughout much of the postwar period, there was a strong sense of mainstream, unmarked social norms that located people in particular forms of families, school, and work: a heterosexual, middle-class couple, including a breadwinner husband and stay-at-home wife, children deeply involved in the educational system, within an extended family network shaped by gendered roles defined through the stem family system (*ie seido*). For instance, for much of the postwar period, a responsible and loving father might demonstrate his feelings by working so hard as to remove himself from a family's daily life (Allison 1994; Hidaka 2010). Love, care, and intimacy were demonstrated through behaviours that might, at first, seem to include none of those feelings.

In recent decades, starting in the early 1990s, these very norms have been called into question, challenged, or rendered impossible. The falling birth rate is matched by a rising age at marriage and shifting divorce ideologies (Alexy 2011; Rosenberger 2013). Many men and women are not content with marital lives like their parents' and are trying to negotiate new standards for intimacy within and beyond marriage (Aoyama et al. 2014). Gay, lesbian, and queer people still face substantial discrimination but have been working to increase their visibility, decrease stigma, and legally formalize their relationships (Maree 2014; McLelland 2000; see also Dale, Wallace, and Baudinette in this volume). The "lifetime" careers previously imagined as ideal are perceived to be evaporating, and potential employees are more likely to be offered contract or part-time positions, reflecting both labour market restructuring and governmental policies (Brinton 2010; Cook 2016). People are increasingly likely to live alone, especially in old age, and older people are negotiating their changing sexual relationships (Hirayama and Ronald 2006; Moore 2010). These new patterns are taking place within popular rhetoric that describes Japan as a society newly lacking "connections" (*muen shakai*; literally, bond-less or disconnected society), where people who were once tied to extended families, paternalistic employers, or a supportive education system might now float in relative isolation (Allison 2013; Miyamoto 2012; Toivonen 2013). A more positive interpretation of these trends can be found in the popular buzzwords "independence" (*jiritsu*), "self-responsibility" (*jiko sekinin*), and "being true to oneself" (*jibunrashisa*), which are commonly suggested as attributes necessary for success and happiness in the contemporary moment (Fukushima 2001; Hook and Takeda 2007). Indeed, to be freed from restrictions or requirements can be both positive and negative, releasing people from rigid social norms but increasing potential precarity, allowing new possibilities but disrupting the social safety net.

How to save heterosexual marriages

Among the heterosexually married couples with whom I conducted research, these intimate shifts manifest in new suggestions about how to strengthen relationships. In mid-2000s Japan, one prominent tip proffered to improve marriages or reduce the risk of divorce suggested that people actively work against the idea that love and affection should be un- or understated. On television programs, in advice books, and in private counselling sessions or semi-public support groups, many counsellors advised spouses to verbalize their love for each other—out loud and on a regular basis (Ikeuchi 2002; TBS Broadcast Staff 2006). This tip is frequently summarized as a deceptively simple command: "Say 'I love you' to your spouse." Counsellors are not the only people engaging the possibility that new styles of communication might improve marriages, and many people who did not feel comfortable enacting the suggestion nevertheless were aware of it as an increasingly common piece of advice.

The perceived need to communicate love and affection in such explicit—and verbal—ways reflects new models for relationality between spouses. While the earlier norms suggested the best style of intimacy was for spouses to be fused into one body (*ittai*), thereby obviating the need for any verbal communication, these newer models suggest that even if spouses feel like they shouldn't have to verbally communicate with each other, such communication is vitally necessary for a healthy relationship. Spouses who say "I love you" to each other are not just verbalizing their love but are also simultaneously demonstrating their need to talk, thus attesting to the lack of any fusion between selves. Needing to speak suggests that spouses are fundamentally separate beings who, nevertheless, work to care for each other. In contrast to the older patterns of relationality and intimacy, this pattern of *connected independence* emphasizes the complicated web of connections and disconnections through which spouses build a relationship with each other. In this model for intimacy, spouses are ideally linked through emotional and affective ties rather than highly gendered structures of labour. Saying "I love you"—both having loving feelings and being able to share them out loud—marks relationships as aspiring to this newer kind of ideal type (Alexy 2019).

Queer, lesbian, gay, trans, and bi intimacies

Scholarship across disciplines documents same-sex, queer, lesbian, and gay intimacies in Japan throughout history and in the current moment. Much of this work complicates the terms used to label these relationships, suggesting not just troubles caused by translation to and from English but also the deeply embedded cultural nuances that shift over time and context (McLelland 2005). When scholars describe the range of experiences, connections, and desires within queer intimacies, many highlight the complicated conflicts between discourse and practices, between popular perceptions and extant discrimination toward queer people. For instance, Maree (2014, 187) identifies both academic and mainstream misperceptions that Japan is unusually tolerant of same-sex issues because "Japan has no laws criminalizing homosexuality or sexual acts between persons of the same sex . . . Japan is often positioned as being queerer earlier than so-called western nations." However, as Maree goes on to explain, the family registration system (*koseki*) designs all families to be fundamentally heteronormative, which presents many problems for same-sex partners who want to start legal families together or receive any of the myriad benefits that come through family membership (Maree 2014; Ninomiya 2006). In other contexts as well, Japan's long history of same-sex loving relationships represented in art or literature, which continues through the present day, does not bring substantial relief to overt and implicit discrimination faced by queer people on a daily basis (Chalmers 2002; McLelland et al. 2007). For instance, the strong social norms surrounding heterosexual marriage can put substantial pressure on people to enter into "paper" marriages that make their home life appear to conform to social expectations (Lunsing 1995). Gay salarymen report that not having a wife presents a serious threat to career advancement—even more, potentially, than not being straight (Dasgupta 2005).

Parents and children

Within the broader scholarship about family lives in contemporary Japan, scholars have focused specifically on relationships between parents and children. Continuing social norms that delineate a male breadwinner and female caregiver mean that many children are more likely to have a primary, daily relationship with their mothers, particularly in early childhood. Ivry (2009), for example, narrates how common beliefs suggest that a child not raised by their mother in the first three years of life will go on to have problems, which makes women less likely to continue work after having a baby. In this belief system, being a good mother is about being present to assist and aid one's children on a daily basis (Ivry 2009; Seaman 2011). But women continue to prefer having children as part of a married couple, partially because many believe that having a husband enables a wife to be as indulgent as she wants, and perhaps needs, to be with her children (Hertog 2009).

Within common Japanese idealizations of family lives, *skinship* plays an important role linking parents, children, and siblings. A neologism Tahhan (2014, 11) translates as "intimacy through touch," skinship describes love and affection expressed through breast-feeding, co-sleeping, bathing together, or play (Caudill and Plath 1966). Although scholars have found that Japanese children tend to be in more frequent direct contact with their mothers, parenting norms and expectations of fathers are shifting, potentially changing gendered household dynamics and intimate practices within the family.

In the early 2000s, reconfigured models for fatherhood coalesced around the neologism *ikumen*, a complimentary term for "a man who raises [children]" or an "involved father" (Ishii-Kuntz 2015, 164). This new ideal is an explicit repudiation of previous models for fatherhood and parenting, suggesting that good fathers connect with their children as measured through time and emotional bonds. Although statistical measures make clear that *ikumen* ideals have not translated into radically revised gendered responsibilities in families, in contrast to the norms common a generation before, younger fathers emphasize their involvement in their children's lives.

Paid intimacies and sex work

Sexual contact in exchange for money in Japan is often categorized within the broad category of *mizu shōbai*. A euphemism literally meaning "water business," this term encompasses businesses offering a wide range of intimate contact, including bars, strip clubs, host and hostess clubs, and people performing sexual acts. Because only coitus is rendered illegal by anti-prostitution laws, sex workers and the establishments where they work can freely advertise other acts (Allison 1994; Takeyama 2016). During the height of Japan's economic bubble, such spaces of groping and sexualized jokes were, at least for some large companies, vital to business both because of the male relationships fortified via hostesses and the company's co-optation of male employees' leisure time (Allison 1994). Doing research with female sex workers in the early 2010s, Koch (2016) found rhetoric of female care and healing of male workers to be especially prevalent. Although Allison's ethnographic portrait of the elite club where she worked remains a touchstone, newer research makes clear how unusually elite that space was. In general, women working as hostesses in Japan are likely to be foreign, making citizenship and legal status vitally important issues (Faier 2009). Particularly because Japan is such a wealthy country, migration—often formally illegal—to work in the sex industry is a prominent phenomenon, with risks of discrimination and violence for immigrant workers (Matsui 1995; Perreñas 2011).

Paid intimacies are not just, however, the provision of women serving men. In recent decades, host clubs have been growing in popularity in Japan. These involve male hosts catering to female clients in patterns that are parallel to, but not simply inverted forms of, hostess clubs. Takeyama (2016) argues that male hosts are likely to understand themselves as self-responsible entrepreneurs and as the embodiment of the contemporary model for "ideal subjecthood" enacting "postindustrial consumer logic and neoliberal values" (Takeyama 2010, 232). Research about LGTBQ sex workers and their clients is a topic worthy of future consideration.

Conclusions

For most of the postwar period, heterosexual marriage has been a powerfully normative social force marking people as responsible social adults (*shakaijin;* literally, "social person"). The vast majority of people got married, and ethnographers have demonstrated that heterosexual marriage was used as evidence of a person's "normalcy." In the current moment, however, both the centrality of heterosexual marriages and the particular forms those relationships should take are being implicitly and explicitly called into question. Japan's rising average age at first marriage and the increasing number of "never-married" people surely include both those who explicitly reject marriage and those who might very much want to get married but have not found the right person or an acceptable situation. Extant scholarship on Japan makes clear the ways in which seemingly personal and private decisions about intimate needs and wants link with larger political, social, and economic issues.

Related chapters

5   Masculinity Studies in Japan
6   Transgender, Non-Binary Genders, and Intersex in Japan
7   Gender and Ethnicity in Urban Japan
8   Gender and the *Koseki*
9   Attitudes to Marriage and Childbearing
12 Rural Gender Construction and Decline: Negotiating Risks Through Nostalgia
13 Changing Folk Cultures of Pregnancy and Childbirth

References

Alexy, A. (2011) "Intimate Dependence and Its Risks in Neoliberal Japan," *Anthropological Quarterly* 84 (4) 895–917.
Alexy, A. (2019) "What Can Be Said? Communicating Intimacy in Millennial Japan," in A. Alexy and E. E. Cook (eds) *Intimate Japan: Ethnographies of Closeness and Conflict*, Honolulu: University of Hawai'i Press, 91–111.
Allison, A. (1994) *Nightwork: Sexuality, Pleasure, and Corporate Masculinity in a Tokyo Hostess Club*, Chicago: University of Chicago Press.
Allison, A. (2013) *Precarious Japan*, Durham: Duke University Press.
Aoyama, T., Dales, L. and Dasgupta, R. (eds) (2014) *Configurations of Family in Contemporary Japan*, London and New York: Routledge.
Berlant, L. (ed) (2000) *Intimacy*, Chicago: University of Chicago Press.

Brinton, M. C. (1993) *Women and the Economic Miracle: Gender and Work in Postwar Japan*, Berkeley and Los Angeles: University of California Press.

Brinton, M. C. (2010) *Lost in Transition: Youth, Work, and Instability in Postindustrial Japan*, Cambridge: Cambridge University Press.

Caryl, C. and Kashiwagi, A. (2007) "The Good Son Falters: Japan's Abe Regime in Decline," *The Asia-Pacific Journal: Japan Focus* 5 (2) 1–5.

Caudill, W. and Plath, D. (1966) "Who Sleeps by Whom? Parent-Child Involvement in Urban Japanese Families," *Psychiatry* 29 (4) 344–366.

Chalmers, S. (2002) *Emerging Lesbian Voices from Japan*, London and New York: Routledge.

Coleman, L. (2008) "Family Policy: Framework and Challenges," in F. Coulmas, H. Conrad, A. Schad-Seifert and G. Vogt (eds) *The Demographic Challenge: A Handbook About Japan*, Leiden: Brill, 749–764.

Cook, E. E. (2016) *Reconstructing Adult Masculinities: Part-Time Work in Contemporary Japan*, London and New York: Routledge.

Dale, S. P. F. (2019) "Gender Identity, Desire, and Intimacy: Sexual Scripts and X-Gender," in A. Alexy and E. E. Cook (eds) *Intimate Japan: Ethnographies of Closeness and Conflict*, Honolulu: University of Hawai'i Press, 164–180.

Dasgupta, R. (2005) "Salarymen Doing Straight: Heterosexual Men and the Dynamics of Gender Conformity," in M. McLelland and R. Dasgupta (eds) *Genders, Transgenders and Sexualities in Japan*, London: Routledge, 168–182.

Edwards, W. (1989) *Modern Japan Through Its Weddings: Gender, Person, and Society in Ritual Portrayal*, Stanford: Stanford University Press.

Faier, L. (2009) *Intimate Encounters: Filipina Women and the Remaking of Rural Japan*, Berkeley and Los Angeles: University of California Press.

Fukushima, M. (ed) (2001) *Aremo kazoku koremo kazoku: ko o daiji ni suru shakai* (This Is a Family, That Is a Family: Toward a Society That Values Individuals), Tokyo: Iwanami Shoten.

Gluck, C. (1985) *Japan's Modern Myths: Ideology in the Late Meiji Period*, Princeton: Princeton University Press.

Goodman, R. (ed) (2002) *Family and Social Policy in Japan: Anthropological Approaches*, Cambridge: Cambridge University Press.

Harris, P. B. and Long, S. O. (1993) "Daughter-in-Law's Burden: Family Caregiving and Social Change in Japan," *Journal of Cross-Cultural Gerontology* 8 (2) 97–118.

Hertog, E. (2009) *Tough Choices: Bearing an Illegitimate Child in Japan*, Stanford: Stanford University Press.

Hidaka, T. (2010) *Salaryman Masculinity: The Continuity of and Change in the Hegemonic Masculinity in Japan*, Leiden and Boston: Brill.

Hirayama, Y. and Ronald, R. (eds) (2006) *Housing and Social Transition in Japan*, London and New York: Routledge.

Hook, G. D. and Takeda, H. (2007) "'Self-Responsibility' and the Nature of the Postwar Japanese State: Risk Through the Looking Glass," *The Journal of Japanese Studies* 33 (1) 93–123.

Ikegami, E. (1995) *The Taming of the Samurai: Honorific Individualism and the Making of Modern Japan*, Cambridge: Harvard University Press.

Ikeuchi, H. (2002) *Koware kake fūfu no toraburu, kaiketsu shimasu* (Couple's Troubles and Their Resolutions), Tokyo: Magajin Housu.

Imamura, A. E. (1987) *Urban Japanese Housewives: At Home and in the Community*, Honolulu: University of Hawai'i Press.

Ishii-Kuntz, M. (2015) "Fatherhood in Asian Contexts," in S. R. Quah (ed) *Routledge Handbook of Families in Asia*, London: Routledge.

Ishii-Kuntz, M. and Maryanski, A. R. (2003) "Conjugal Roles and Social Networks in Japanese Families," *Journal of Family Issues* 24 (3) 352–380.

Ivry, T. (2009) *Embodying Culture: Pregnancy in Japan and Israel*, New Brunswick: Rutgers University Press.

Kelly, W. W. (1991) "Directions in the Anthropology of Contemporary Japan," *Annual Review of Anthropology* 20 395–431.

Koch, G. (2016) "Producing *iyashi*: Healing and Labor in Tokyo's Sex Industry," *American Ethnologist* 43 (4) 704–716.

Kondo, D. (1993) "Uchi no kaisha: Company as Family?" in J. Bachnik and C. Quinn (eds) *Situated Meaning: Inside and Outside in Japanese Self, Society, and Language*, Ithaca: Cornell University Press, 169–191.
Kurotani, S. (2005) *Home Away from Home: Japanese Corporate Wives in the United States*, Durham: Duke University Press.
Lunsing, W. (1995) "Japanese Gay Magazines and Marriage Advertisements," *Journal of Gay and Lesbian Social Services* 3 (3) 71–88.
Maree, C. (2014) "Sexual Citizenship at the Intersections of Patriarchy and Heteronormativity: Same-Sex Partnerships and the Koseki," in D. Chapman and K. J. Krogness (eds) *Japan's Household Registration System and Citizenship: Koseki, Identification and Documentation*, London and New York: Routledge, 187–202.
Matsui, Y. (1995) "The Plight of Asian Migrant Women Working in Japan's Sex Industry," in K. Fujimura-Fanselow and A. Kameda (eds) *Japanese Women: New Feminist Perspectives on the Past, Present, and Future*, New York: The Feminist Press, 309–319.
McLelland, M. J. (2000) *Male Homosexuality in Modern Japan: Cultural Myths and Social Realities*, London and New York: Routledge.
McLelland, M. (2005) *Queer Japan from the Pacific War to the Internet Age*, Lanham: Rowman & Littlefield.
McLelland, M. (2012) *Love, Sex, and Democracy in Japan during the American Occupation*, New York: Palgrave Macmillan.
McLelland, M., Suganuma, K. and Welker, J. (2007) *Queer Voices from Japan: First Person Narratives from Japan's Sexual Minorities*, Lanham: Lexington Books.
Miyamoto, M. (2012) *Wakamono ga muenkasuru: shigoto fukushi komyuniti de tsunagu* (Young People Without Ties: Connecting Work, Welfare, and Community), Tokyo: Chikumashobō.
Moore, K. L. (2010) "Sexuality and Sense of Self in Later Life: Japanese Men's and Women's Reflections on Sex and Aging," *Journal of Cross-Cultural Gerontology* 25 (2) 149–163.
Ninomiya, S. (2006) *Koseki to jinken* (Family Register and Human Rights), Osaka: Buraku Kaihōjinken Kenkyūjo.
Perreñas, R. S. (2011) *Illicit Flirtations: Labor, Migration, and Sex Trafficking in Tokyo*, Stanford: Stanford University Press.
Plath, D. W. (1980) *Long Engagements: Maturity in Modern Japan*, Stanford: Stanford University Press.
Plummer, K. (2003) *Intimate Citizenship: Private Decisions and Public Dialogues*, Seattle: University of Washington Press.
Rosenberger, N. (2013) *Dilemmas of Adulthood: Japanese Women and the Nuances of Long-Term Resistance*, Honolulu: University of Hawai'i Press.
Ryang, S. (2006) *Love in Modern Japan: Its Estrangement from Self, Sex and Society*, London and New York: Routledge.
Schoppa, L. J. (2006) *Race for the Exits: The Unraveling of Japan's System of Social Protection*, Ithaca: Cornell University Press.
Seaman, A. C. (2011) "Making and Marketing Mothers: Guides to Pregnancy in Modern Japan," in J. Bardsley and L. Miller (eds) *Manners and Mischief: Gender, Power, and Etiquette in Japan*, Berkeley and Los Angeles: University of California Press, 156–177.
Smith, R. and Wiswell, E. L. (1982) *The Women of Suye Mura*, Chicago: University of Chicago Press.
Tahhan, D. A. (2014) *The Japanese Family: Touch, Intimacy and Feeling*, London: Routledge.
Takeda, H. (2004) *The Political Economy of Reproduction in Japan*, London and New York: Routledge.
Takeyama, A. (2010) "Intimacy for Sale: Masculinity, Entrepreneurship, and Commodity Self in Japan's Neoliberal Situation," *Japanese Studies* 30 (2) 231–246.
Takeyama, A. (2016) *Staged Seductions: Selling Dreams in a Tokyo Host Club*, Stanford: Stanford University Press.
TBS Broadcast Staff. (2006) *Jukunen rikon 100 no riyū* (100 Reasons for Later-Life Divorce), Tokyo: Shōnensha.
Toivonen, T. (2013) *Japan's Emerging Youth Policy: Getting Young Adults Back to Work*, London and New York: Routledge.
Traphagan, J. W. and Knight, J. (eds) (2003) *Demographic Change and the Family in Japan's Aging Society*, Albany: State University of New York Press.
Ueno, C. (2009) *The Modern Family in Japan: Its Rise and Fall*, Melbourne: TransPacific Press.

Vogel, S. H. and Vogel, S. K. (2013) *The Japanese Family in Transition: From the Professional Housewife Ideal to the Dilemmas of Choice*, Lanham: Rowman & Littlefield.
Walsh, B. (2007) "In Japan, a Revolution over Childbearing," *Time* 5 February.
White, M. I. (2002) *Perfectly Japanese: Making Families in an Era of Upheaval*, Berkeley and Los Angeles: University of California Press.
Zelizer, V. (2010) "Caring Everywhere," in E. Boris and R. S. Perreñas (eds) *Intimate Labors: Cultures, Technologies, and the Politics of Care*, Stanford: Stanford University Press, 267–279.

12
RURAL GENDER CONSTRUCTION AND DECLINE
Negotiating risks through nostalgia

Anna Vainio

Gender relations have stood at the centre of investigation into contemporary Japan for some decades; however, along with Japan's postwar development, intellectual interest has shifted from rural areas to the rapidly expanding cities. Despite rapid urbanisation, ideas of gender in Japan continue to echo rural traditionalism and ideas of harmony rather than equality and have remained remarkably static across society. Social and economic structures remain stratified along gendered lines. I argue in this chapter that a core basis of this continued gendered regime can be located in the rural household structure as a "natural" representation of gender in Japan. Rather than seeing the rural setting as representing outdated modes of social relations and values contained in the periphery of Japan's modernity, I outline the continuing vital role the countryside plays in forming Japanese national identity and the persistent impact it has on the construction and performance of gender today. Though they often stem from rural traditionalism, gender identities and hierarchies are not contained in rural societies alone.

Nevertheless, no discussion on the Japanese countryside today would be complete without addressing the issue of acute and crippling socioeconomic decline. The emptying countryside, rural decline, and economic and social precarity are intensifying a sense of risk and loss, and holding onto the nostalgic past brings psychic comfort and a sense of stability into the contemporary situation of instability. Naturalised and traditionalist ideas of the countryside therefore affect the ways in which gender is negotiated today in rural families, and this is reflected in national discourses on gender and in policies on rural revitalisation.

Instability is experienced in Japan as a whole; however, the urgency of decline and the importance rural society plays in the Japanese psyche and identity (Robertson 1988) place rural inhabitants, faced with the crippling decline first hand, in a position of double pressure. They are not only responsible for the continuation of their own lineage but are the protectors of Japanese culture itself through their own succession. Therefore, seeking stability in an increasingly precarious society (Allison 2013) is integrally linked to ideas of gender both on national and household levels. Revival of traditional ideas of gender as an essential and natural part of the nostalgic past is directing people to seek answers to contemporary instability by gazing into the perceived stability of the past.

Rural orientation and politics of gender

The countryside has played a significant role in Japan's modernisation, not only economically, but as the imagined repository of Japanese history, culture, and national identity. Many Japanese people can still pinpoint the exact location of their family's rural origin, even if little direct contact with the village remains (Imamura 2010), an indication of a strong sense of rural orientation toward the "native home," or *furusato* (Traphagan 2000). The *furusato* as an imaginary representation of the ideal past has been framed as a place for nurturing and healing in the midst of rapid modernisation for generations (Schnell 2005; Robertson 1988; Ivy 1995). As a result, it has come to stand in stark contrast with modern urbanisation, carrying a sense of dissatisfaction with the present.

Furusato is not a physical place, nor is it a specific point in time. Rather it is a representation of an imagined authentic Japaneseness (Robertson 1991), simultaneously existing in the past as nostalgia and as a utopian goal on the fringes of capitalist prosperity (Ivy 1995, 12). As a representation of a natural and harmonious state of affairs, the *furusato* becomes an ideal model for personhood, social relations, and traditions located in the Japanese countryside, thus creating an emotional connection between the rural space and the entire nation.

As a result, *furusato* has become one of the most powerful and persistent symbols of Japaneseness, where the countryside is marked in contrast to urban and increasingly Westernised life. These rural-urban juxtapositions are abundantly utilised and perpetuated in marketing, media, and tourism across the nation (Creighton 1997; Knight 1995), designed to evoke a sense of nostalgia and yearning. Even the recent contents tourism boom, travel behaviour motivated by popular culture and "Cool Japan" (Seaton et al. 2017), fluidly incorporates the traditionalist *furusato* tropes and imagery into their marketing, despite being chiefly inspired and constructed by contemporary film, manga, and television dramas. Proving itself an effective tool in rural revitalisation initiatives (Gasparri and Martini 2018; Greene 2016), contents tourism continues to replicate and reinforce the ideas of sociality, naturalness, and harmony and the perceived superiority of rural lifestyles.

The notion of *furusato* has also been utilised by nativist and conservative projects, critiquing rampant modernisation and Western influence (Robertson 1988; Schnell 2005). The perceived authenticity of the rural lifestyle and society is intimately linked with the nature and climate of the Japanese isles (connecting symbolic and actual naturalism), whose unique composition is argued to have formed the very character and way of life of its people (Martinez 2010). Gender relations are central to these ideas of rural naturalism.

Gendered social relations are codified in rural settings as representations of harmonious society (Robertson 1988). The love and yearning for the rural home contained in the very idea of *furusato*, with its perceived idyllic lifestyles and communal affairs, provides a sensation similar to motherly love and feeling of belonging (Creighton 2007; Robertson 1988; Knight 1998). In contrast, social hierarchy and power revolve around male symbolism. *Daikoku bashira*, the central pillar upholding the roof in a traditional Japanese farmhouse, symbolises male strength and reliability and is a word commonly used to describe the role Japanese men should assume in their families and in society at large (Gill 2003). This symbolism of the rural home and society suggests a cultural and social state where the feminine and masculine complete each other in a natural and harmonious way. The nurturing feminine sphere of the home is protected and upheld through the masculine strength and social reliability.

The family stands at the centre of this naturalistic ideology, with traditional gender relations stemming from the rural household organisation representing an imagined authentic Japaneseness. In this context, the family becomes a cultural asset occupying political importance and urgency for its protection (Schnell 2005; Robertson 1988). It is therefore crucial for any discussion on rural gender construction in the Japanese context to pay attention to the connection between the rural setting and family relations as a politically induced process enforcing gender inequality.

The rural *ie* as the vessel of gender organisation

Gender and family as analytical concepts are not unequivocally connected. But due to the legal and ideological position the family institution occupies in any society, gender is negotiated in strong association with the family (Coltrane et al. 2008; Carter 2014). While in contemporary Japan, the urban nuclear family occupies a dominant position, and as a result is the subject of the majority of academic research on Japanese families today, the traditional stem family, or the *ie*, nevertheless remains worthy of investigation (Imamura 2010). Ochiai (2009 288) even goes as far as to state that the *ie* in fact continues to be "regarded as the symbol of Japanese cultural identity."

Even though the *ie* has become closely associated with the countryside and is often seen as providing the foundation for Japan's persistent gender stratification (Imamura 2010), the origins of the *ie* system nevertheless lie elsewhere. Emerging from feudal Japan, the *ie* has its origins in the household model of the samurai class, emphasising filial piety and patriarchy. Until the Meiji Restoration, gender relations in rural society among peasants had remained more fluid, based on ability rather than status. Both men and women held a variety of roles within the household hierarchy as both labour and managers (Smith 1983). The new Meiji state adopted the *ie* of the samurai classes as the legal foundation for organising a modern family for the new modern nation, thus introducing the rural population and other classes to values and practices largely alien to them up until then (Imamura 2010; Ochiai 2009; Smith 1983). Rural society was therefore brought into the sphere of gender stratification as part of the state's modernisation project.

The *ie* of the Meiji era was part of a modernisation process aiming to standardise the family institution. As such, it is an invented institution designed to support the new modern state and its political and economic goals (Schnell 2005). The *ie* was, however, never geographically uniform, and multiple forms of household organisation, marriage, succession, and inheritance patterns have existed throughout history, accommodating a variety of gender roles and befitting the diversity of economies and lifestyles across the Japanese islands (Ochiai 2009). However, the model for the Meiji *ie* came most closely to resemble a narrow section of rural society, the traditional rice-cultivating households of the northeastern parts of the country, resting on the absolute succession of the eldest child and the patriarchal power of the household head (Ochiai 2009; Schnell 2005; Knight 1995).

The Meiji goal was to integrate the family into the state, both ideologically and economically. Women's roles in families and society at large were reduced, and for the first time, their lower status was enshrined into law. Similarly, Confucian values emphasising filial piety, previously not a strong part of rural societies, entered into the core curriculum of compulsory education and were thus disseminated throughout the population (Smith 1983; Schnell 2005). Women's roles became defined by household management and motherhood, while men were recruited to public service and labour for the state (Imamura 2010). The rigid gender harmony within the *ie* was therefore integrated into the structures of the state (Molony and Uno 2005; Smith 1983) and was replicated in the postwar period, demonstrating its effectiveness by producing miraculous economic growth (Sekiguchi 2010; Mathews 2003). Gender harmony—based on rigid distinctions in gender roles—therefore became an inseparable part of Japan's postwar capitalism.

The Meiji leaders incorporated the rural household and its idealised gender harmony into the state as an essential part of Japan's modernisation. But the countryside was not immune to the rapid socioeconomic changes taking place in society. Postwar high fertility combined with expanding industrialisation and widening professional opportunities led to rapid urbanisation, rendering Japan's primarily rural society into an urban one in less than a century (Knight 1994; Matanle and Rausch 2011). Continuation of primogeniture in the rural homes offered few opportunities for additional children of the *ie* to establish themselves (Imamura 2010), eventually leading to an acute rural decline, destabilising the family institution at the heart of Japanese social and economic continuity.

Is the *ie* dead?

Today, livelihoods are dependent on education and professional opportunities rather than inherited family trades where land, property, equipment, and business rights are passed on as a single unit to the eldest child (Orpett-Long 2014). As a result, a majority of young people born in rural areas spend extended periods of time in the cities engaging in education and professional development that is often necessitated by the institutional organisation and narrow scope of opportunities in rural regions (Matanle 2008; Matanle and Rausch 2011). Exercising one's duties toward the household has therefore become increasingly difficult, rendering succession into a privilege rather than the norm, one that only a few can manage to uphold today.

Succession has been further complicated not only by diversification of life courses, but by the lowering national fertility rate that has placed the majority of children in the position of a first born (North 2009). Since the Japanese household system is patriarchal but not patrilinear (Imamura 2010) and an increasing number of marriages are formed between two eldest children, the changing demographic conditions are placing more succession pressure on both eldest sons and eldest daughters. This can lead to conflicting interests when trying to uphold filial duties toward the families of both partners. Additionally, while historically most marriages were formed by finding a suitable partner within close proximity to one's own household (Smith 1983; Knight 1994), most marriages today are formed in urban areas where partners from different regions meet (Kumagai 2008). This growing geographical distance between the families of each partner is likely to also exacerbate the other complications presented to succession.

Statistically, co-resident multigeneration households are now a minority across Japan (MIC 2017). The decline in the traditional markers of the *ie* has led some researchers to argue that the stem family has lost much of its former glory and meaning (Maeda 2004; Izuhara 2000), but writing the *ie* off as an archaic cultural institution might be foolish (Schnell 2005; Ochiai 2009). It could be argued that due to the modernisation of the family unit and rise of the nuclear family, the countryside and the traditional household as representations of the natural and harmonious order of social relations have even strengthened. The distance they have acquired from most peoples' everyday reality may in fact be elevating their position as the nostalgic ideal past that people long for in an era of uncertainty.

Upholding a vanishing ideal

Compared to other industrialised nations, equalisation of gender relations appears not to have taken place in Japan to the degree expected, and preservation of historical gender relations within Japanese families has remained persistent (North 2009). Research indicates that gender ideology and relations codified in the rural *ie* have changed remarkably little during this time and continue to be the foundation for a gender consciousness that preferences patriarchal prestige and gendered division of labour (North 2009; Boling 1998; Lock 1993; Traphagan 2006; Tanaka 2007; Tanaka and Iwasawa 2010). Even though nuclearisation of the family today has decreased the influence of patriarchy at home and women's position in society and the labour market is widely accepted, men and women are still exposed to these values in employment and family life (White 2002; Schoppa 2006; Mathews 2003). The interplay between traditionalism and gender therefore remains relevant in contemporary Japan.

While nuclear families today occupy a dominant position even in rural regions, North (2009, 40) finds that family-level strategies nevertheless remain geared toward upholding the perceived natural division of labour and gender hierarchy that are fostered through the idea of a homogenised *ie*. This is illustrated by the persistence of gendered division of labour in Japanese families characteristic of the traditional stem family ideal (North 2009; White 2002). Researchers further argue that this gaze into the past may imply a strategy of risk avoidance, where the increasing uncertainty experienced in Japanese society today may induce people to seek a semblance of stability from the cultural codes and practices of the past. The acute decline of the rural regions (Allison 2013; Matanle and Rausch 2011), the hub of Japan's cultural authenticity, places these practices in danger of extinction, needing protection.

Caution should therefore be exercised when discussing Japanese families and gender merely in the context of the nuclear family, without reference to the traditional stem family. The family represents an important approach to understanding the way in which gender is constructed and performed in contemporary rural Japan today and why, despite the statistical disappearance of the rural ideal, it still retains strong significance in society at large. Gender remains central to family continuation, heavily influencing the expected behaviour and life courses of men and women (Traphagan 2000, 2006). Today gender is increasingly negotiated in the ever-widening gap between ideology and reality, increasing the tension between generations at the intersection of pressure for succession and the realities of decline. But in an era of increased risk and uncertainty, are Japanese families holding onto tradition, or embracing change to save themselves, their ancestors, and ideas of "Japaneseness"?

Negotiating succession

Succession has particularly heavy importance for those left to guard the family homes in the countryside. Family continuation is still viewed by many as a form of duty that ensures a permanent home for the ancestors (Traphagan 2006). Failure to do so leaves them disconnected and discontent (Tanaka 2007). The current generation is also often a part of a lineage that traces back centuries in the same location, having sustained natural disasters, famines, and wars, symbolising resilience and permanence. Therefore, the mundaneness of gradual economic decline and the slow vanishing of communities and families can be hard to comprehend and emotionally testing. As a result, obligations toward the family are typically triggered by the older generation who can at times vigorously exert their power in demanding that filial duties be upheld (Traphagan 2008). After all, no one wants to be the last generation that failed the family or to be abandoned in the afterlife by their children.

Aside from emotional concerns over tradition and permanence, family continuation is a practical consideration as well. The influence of the urban nuclear family today has transformed the primary direction of family obligations toward the younger generation (Traphagan 2006), with many increasingly relying on institutional care for the older members of the family. But due to the rising elderly population in the countryside, the demand for old-age care is on the rise and not equally available or accessible across the country (Tanaka and Iwasawa 2010). While others today welcome old-age independence, free from the expected burden of taking care of grandchildren in exchange for their own care in the future (Izuhara 2000; Traphagan 2006), others, particularly elderly male caregivers, can be disproportionately affected by lack of familial care (Tanaka and Iwasawa 2010). The breakdown of the filial cycle and family continuation can give rise to assumed social stigma and shame that affect rural men more than women, as care has not been seen as part of their gendered responsibilities (North 2009; Tanaka and Iwasawa 2010).

The younger generation can as a result be fiercely steered toward remaining or returning to the rural country home when it is deemed possible from the older generation's perspective. This pressure is not gender specific, but related to assumed ideas of adulthood and duty, with eldest sons and unmarried daughters being particularly susceptible to parental influence and power (Traphagan 2000). If prolonged stay in the urban setting cannot be justified within the framework of traditional thinking (marriage, employment), the influence exerted by the older generation can override the personal desires of the younger generation in favour of conformity and parental control (Traphagan 2000). The result is a tense intrafamily relationship where values and gender norms emerging from different socioeconomic realities between the generations are reflected in conflicting ideologies on the meaning of family, adulthood, and responsibility.

Equal to filiality, which is internally imposed and acted on, rural society is also governed by the outward appearance of appropriateness, the social gaze, or *sekentei* in Japanese. Both filiality and *sekentei* strengthen established ideas of gender. Gendered expectations on the first son to succeed his father and the daughter-in-law to take care of her husband's parents remain stable and are seen as not only instrumental for continuation and care, but as helping the family to maintain respectability in the eyes of others (North 2009; Tanaka and Iwasawa 2010). While less visible in the cities, *sekentei* remains influential in the countryside due to the proximity and intimacy of social relations in the rural context (Tanaka and Iwasawa 2010). Both men and women alike are found to be strongly compliant in this narrative, even if it goes against their own interests (North 2009).

While succession is strongly associated with male responsibility, it is the female sphere that can offer a fruitful avenue for understanding its complexities. While women's position in Japanese families was legally and ideologically placed below men in the prewar period, in terms of property rights and legal authority, for instance, it has also been the site where the majority of gender negotiations and progress have occurred across the postwar era. The countryside has not been immune to these trends. The traditional power relationship between the female members of the household is illustrative of this shift. Many women today see co-residence as undesirable, but find themselves pressured to uphold traditional duties as *yome* (daughter-in-law) (Traphagan 2000), a role that has a long-documented history of tension in Japanese families (Imamura 2010). Many instead prefer to negotiate a middle-ground solution where the generations live apart yet retain a mutual agreement on care and family obligations that do not contradict the outward appearance of filiality.

Women themselves are active in simultaneously challenging and reinforcing established gender roles. Rural women in particular have for a long time presented contradictory marriage preferences for their offspring, wanting their daughters to escape the rural social gaze while supporting their sons' enforcement of it. Itamoto (1988, in Knight 1995) explains that while most rural mothers want their son and daughter-in-law to co-reside with them, for their daughters, they wish for a different life and try to ensure a more satisfying match than they themselves had. Rural gender order can therefore be an inhibiting factor for women to remain, as they are being both pulled and pushed toward a life different to their mothers'.

Contemporary anxiety over the continuation of the household has in some cases begun to turn *sekentei* into an impetus for change. Some mothers, for instance, are explicitly raising their sons to engage in housework and caring duties to reflect changing attitudes and realities, which is also a way to improve their marriage potential among the depleting stock of young people in rural areas (North 2009). In a competitive rural marriage market where men increasingly outnumber women (Knight 1995: Traphagan 2000), successfully securing a marriage for one's offspring that includes continuation of the family and old-age security for oneself can therefore be seen as a matter of personal and social prestige.

Rural regions are having to adjust to changing conditions, and it is clear that a modern nuclear family is increasingly preferred in the countryside, together with a desire for greater opportunities amidst rural decline. Long-term strategies for ensuring succession and care are implemented on the family level in various ways. Crucially, however, any functional changes to the family unit are still ideologically justified through the lens of tradition. Traphagan (2000) argues that as a result, today the younger generation exists in a liminal state between nuclear and traditional family values and try to negotiate their way through these two states in order to maintain (even limited) levels of satisfaction for themselves and the older generation. The importance of appropriate social appearance and protection of family lineage are still ideologically intact, which has ensured that identity and the performance of gendered duties have remained relatively static and unchanging despite diminishing returns in vanishing rural societies.

Rural revitalisation and the role of the countryside in the future

The conflicting sense of urgency and status quo is reflected in rural revitalisation, a catch-phrase mobilising local communities and igniting their sense of hope for a better future across rural Japan. The widening gap between ideology and socioeconomic realities in the rural country home represents a perceived risk not only to the continuation of individual families but to the continuation of Japanese culture itself. The traditional family stands as the guardian of tradition through its own succession, and revitalisation initiatives have skilfully utilised the strong emotive connection Japanese people retain toward rural areas and the traditional family institution. Gender harmony remains at the centre of this imagery.

While rural connection is still deemed important, the reality of the countryside has for some time been distant from the everyday lifeworlds of most Japanese people (Knight 1998). But far from the countryside losing its relevance, this gap is being filled with the nostalgic and pseudo-rural imaginary, with a somewhat baffling lack of urgency toward the very real demise that is taking place. Martinez (2010), upon discussing environmental protection in the Japanese context, offers an analysis of "nature as an aesthetic concept" that provides a fitting analogy for rural society. She argues that because nature in Japan is primarily an aesthetic concept, its destruction can be justified "as long as one beautiful pine or rock formation is wrapped as if sacred" (Martinez 2010, 196). Similarly, the strength of rural nostalgia justifies the half-hearted political commitment to tackling rural decline and securing the diversity of lifestyles and regional cultures (Love 2013). As long as nostalgic rural society is upheld as a representation of the ideal, urgency toward saving the breadth and diversity of rural society becomes muffled.

Neoliberal revitalisation has targeted economic progress while simultaneously promoting social and cultural stability and the human and social relationships perceived as natural. Focus has shifted onto communities themselves by framing rural inhabitants as producers, actors, and protectors of the diversity and authenticity of their living culture, proving a useful justification for the Japanese government's hands-off approach and emphasis on personal responsibility and nostalgic longing for the past (Love 2013; Knight 1994). Responsibility for survival has been individualised, placing traditional families and rural communities centre stage as actors of revitalisation and diverting attention away from structural inequalities and economic peripheralisation.

The idea of gender harmony has been invigorated in revitalisation. Gendered symbolism and language are often strongly present in these initiatives, with a particular focus on women. Activities perceived as feminine and maternal, such as traditional food and folk crafts, are associated with recovery and actively incorporated into the grand narrative of rural vitality, enforcing nostalgic and romantic notions of the countryside (Knight 1998; Creighton 1997). Women, particularly mothers, are seen as the nurturing life force of rural society and central to revitalisation success. Gender division and traditional femininity therefore become virtues to be upheld rather than renegotiated with gender equality as a goal. Lack of any serious negotiations of gender equality in the rural setting can be justified as disturbing the home-grown character of revitalisation efforts and local cultural heritage.

Risk and crisis have remained continuous themes in Japanese society throughout its contemporary history, where the preference for status quo and a distinct conservatisation of the sociopolitical climate can be witnessed. The "lost decade" of the 1990s, continued economic distress, social precarity, and the 2011 triple disaster have strengthened political appetite for nativism, and a shift in public discourse toward conservatism and self-reliance has become increasingly noticeable (Koikari 2017). This shift has reinvigorated intellectual and political revitalisation of filial piety and conservative narratives of gender (Yoda 2000), individualising decline and risk and placing more attention on self-responsibility as a response to Japan's economic, social, and cultural stagnation.

Conclusions

This chapter has argued that the decline of the countryside bolsters rather than relaxes established gender norms and identities; the very precariousness of Japanese society is further pushing populations to gravitate towards traditional values. The strength of the rural imaginary places families in a double bind, protecting not only their own lineages but culture itself, making them complicit in upholding gender hierarchy as a part of the process. As rural decline and demographic change intensify, they push families toward a nuclear structure and performance, but the ideology codified in and symbolised by the stem family has nevertheless remained remarkably stable. The statistical disappearance of the stem family therefore appears to be less of an indicator of the construction and performance of gender than the ideological foundation of gender harmony and filial power upon which it is built.

Given the place that rural societies occupy in the national psyche, rural ideals remain the ideological pillars that appear the most stable. Temporally, the rural ideal is framed simultaneously as nostalgia and utopia, where anything in between represents uncertainty and dissatisfaction. Gender, too, is negotiated in the present that is framed as forever temporary and unstable, leaving people in a space of suspension and instability between two poles resting on principles of traditionalism. From this perspective, holding onto the traditional forms of life and social conventions may represent a seemingly rational response of risk avoidance and management for rural inhabitants that is also incorporated into national narratives of revitalisation and growth.

But the notion of stability and naturalism in the rural ideal is deeply damaging for various reasons. Gender construction is guided by both geographic and social dimensions in Japan, placing particularly heavy pressure on rural families and communities as protectors and guardians of national culture and tradition. Validation of gender hierarchy as a natural and ideal character of Japanese life and society overall provides a convenient distraction from exploring the depths of rural decline and gendered inequality in society at large.

Related chapters

9 Attitudes to Marriage and Childbearing
11 Intimacy in and Beyond the Family
13 Changing Folk Cultures of Pregnancy and Childbirth
18 Gender, Labour, and Migration in Japan

References

Allison, A. (2013) *Precarious Japan*, Durham, London: Duke University Press.
Boling, P. (1998) "Family Policy in Japan," *Journal of Social Policy* 27 (2) 173–190.
Carter, M. J. (2014) "Gender Socialization and Identity Theory," *Social Sciences* 3 (2) 242–263.
Coltrane, S. and Adams, M. (2008) *Gender and Families*, Plymouth: Rowman & Littlefield Publishers Inc.
Creighton, M. (1997) "Consuming Rural Japan: The Marketing of Tradition and Nostalgia in the Japanese Travel Industry," *Ethnology* 36 (3) 239–254.
Creighton, M. (2007) "Changing Heart (Beats): From Japanese Identity and Nostalgia to Taiko for Citizens of the Earth," in C. Kwok-bun, J. W. Walls and D. Hayward (eds) *East-West Identities: Globalization, Localization, and Hybridization*, Boston and Leiden: Brill.
Gasparri, D. and Martini, A. (2018) "Amachan: The Creation of Heritage Tourism Landscapes in Japan After the 2011 Triple Disaster," in C. Palmer and J. Tivers (eds) *Creating Heritage for Tourism*, London: Routledge.
Gill, T. (2003) "When Pillars Evaporate: Structuring Masculinity on the Japanese Margins," in J. E. Roberson and N. Suzuki (eds) *Men and Masculinities in Contemporary Japan: Dislocating the Salaryman Doxa*, London and New York: RoutledgeCurzon.
Greene, B. (2016) "Furusato and Emotional Pilgrimage: Ge ge ge no kintarō and sakaiminato," *Japanese Journal of Religious Studies* 43 (2) 333–356.
Imamura, A. (2010) "Family Culture," in Y. Sugimoto (ed) *The Cambridge Companion to Modern Japanese Culture*, Cambridge: Cambridge University Press.
Ivy, M. (1995) *Discourses of the Vanishing: Modernity, Phantasm, Japan*, Chicago, London: University of Chicago Press.
Izuhara, M. (2000) "Changing Family Tradition: Housing Choices and Constraints for Older People in Japan," *Housing Studies* 15 (1) 89–110.
Knight, J. (1994) "The Spirit of the Village and the Taste of the Country: Rural Revitalization in Japan," *Asian Survey* 34 (7) 634–646.
Knight, J. (1995) "Municipal Matchmaking in Rural Japan," *Anthropology Today* 11 (2) 9–17.
Knight, J. (1998) "Selling Mother's Love: Mail Order Village Food in Japan," *Journal of Material Culture* 3 (2) 153–173.
Koikari, M. (2017) "Re-Masculinizing the Nation: Gender, Disaster, and the Politics of National Resilience in Post-3/11 Japan," *Japan Forum* 31 (2) 143–164.
Kumagai, F. (2008) *Families in Japan: Changes, Continuities and Regional Variations*, Lanham: University Press of America.
Lock, M. (1993) "Ideology, Female Midlife, and the Graying of Japan," *Journal of Japanese Studies* 19 (1) 43–78.
Love, B. (2013) "Treasure Hunts in Rural Japan: Place Making at the Limits of Sustainability," *American Anthropologist* 15 (1) 112–124.
Maeda, D. (2004) "Social Filial Pity Has Made Traditional Filial Piety Much Less Important in Japan," *Geriatrics and Gerontology International* 4 74–76.
Martinez, D. P. (2010) "On the 'Nature' of Japanese Culture, or, Is There Japanese Sense of Nature?" in J. Robertson (ed) *A Companion to the Anthropology of Japan*, Oxford: Blackwell Publishing Ltd.
Matanle, P. (2008) "Shrinking Sado: Education, Employment and the Decline of Japan's Rural Regions," in P. Oswalt (ed) *Shrinking Cities: Complete Works 3: Japan*, Berlin: Project Office.
Matanle, P. and Rausch, A. (2011) *Japan's Shrinking Regions in the 21st Century: Contemporary Responses to Depopulation and Socioeconomic Decline*, Amherst, MA: Cambria Press.
Mathews, G. (2003) "Can a 'Real Man' Live for His Family? *Ikigai* and Masculinity in Today's Japan," in J. E. Roberson and N. Suzuki (eds) *Men and Masculinities in Contemporary Japan: Dislocating the Salaryman Doxa*, London and New York: Routledge Curzon.

Ministry of Internal Affairs and Communications (MIC) (2017) "Japan Statistical Yearbook 2017." www.stat.go.jp/english/data/nenkan/66nenkan/index.htm.

Molony, B. and Uno, K. (eds) (2005) *Gendering Modern Japanese History*, Cambridge, MA: Harvard University Press.

North, S. (2009) "Negotiating What's 'Natural': Persistent Domestic Gender Role Inequality in Japan," *Social Science Japan Journal* 12 (1) 23–44.

Ochiai, E. (2009) "Two types of Stem Household System in Japan: The *Ie* in Global Perspective," in A. Fauve-Chamoux and E. Ochiai (eds) *The Stem Family in Eurasian Perspective: Revisiting House Societies, 17th to 20th Centuries*, Bern: Peter Lang.

Orpett-Long, S. (2014) "Aging of the Japanese Family: Meaning of Grandchildren in Old Age," in S. Kawano, G. S. Roberts and S. Orpett-Long (eds) *Capturing Contemporary Japan: Differentiation and Uncertainty*, Honolulu: University of Hawai'i Press.

Robertson, J. (1988) "Furusato Japan: The Culture and Politics of Nostalgia," *International Journal of Politics, Culture, and Society* 1 (4) 494–518.

Robertson, J. (1991) *Native and Newcomer: Remaking a Japanese City*, Berkeley, Los Angeles and Oxford: University of California Press.

Schnell, S. (2005) "Rural Imaginary: Landscape, Village, Tradition," in J. Robertson (ed) *Companion to the Anthropology of Japan*, Oxford: Blackwell Publishing Ltd.

Schoppa, L. (2006) *Race for the Exits: The Unraveling of Japan's System of Social Protection*, Ithaca: Cornell University Press.

Seaton, P., Yamamura, T., Sugawa-Shimada, A. and Jang, K. (2017) *Contents Tourism in Japan: Pilgrimages to "Sacred Sites" of Popular Culture*, Amherst, MA: Cambria Press.

Sekiguchi, S. (2010) "Confucian Morals and the Making of a 'Good Wife and Wise Mother': From 'Between Husband and Wife There Is a Distinction' to 'As Husbands and Wives Be Harmonious'," *Social Science Japan Journal* 13 (1) 95–113.

Smith, R. J. (1983) "Making Village Women into 'Good Wives and Wise Mothers' in Prewar Japan," *Journal of Family History* 8 (1) 70–84.

Tanaka, K. (2007) "Graves and Families in Japan: Continuity and Change," *The History of the Family* 12 (3) 178–188.

Tanaka, K. and Iwasama, M. (2010) "Aging in Rural Japan—Limitations in the Current Social Care Policy," *Journal of Aging and Social Policy* 22 (4) 394–406.

Traphagan, J. W. (2000) "The Liminal Family: Return Migration and Intergenerational Conflict in Japan," *Journal of Anthropological Research* 56 (3) 365–385.

Traphagan, J. W. (2006) "Power, Family, and Filial Responsibility Related to Elder Care in Rural Japan," *Care Management Journals* 7 (4) 205–212.

Traphagan, J. W. (2008) "Constraint, Power, and Intergenerational Discontinuity in Japan," *Journal of Intergenerational Relationships* 6 (2) 211–229.

White, I. M. (2002) *Perfectly Japanese: Making Families in an Era of Upheaval*, Berkeley, Los Angeles and London: University of California Press.

Yoda, T. (2000) "Rise and Fall of Maternal Society: Gender, Labour, and Capital in Contemporary Japan," *The South Atlantic Quarterly* 99 (4) 865–902.

13
CHANGING FOLK CULTURES OF PREGNANCY AND CHILDBIRTH

Manami Yasui

TRANSLATED BY LUCY FRASER AND MADELEIN SHIMIZU

The third revolution in childbirth and the present day

This chapter will discuss themes related to pregnancy and childbirth in modern and contemporary Japan, exploring how pregnancy and childbirth-related folk cultures have changed along with the evolution of obstetric medicine, as well as how new folk cultures are being created. Particular attention will be given to death in childbirth—namely newborn, foetal, and maternal death. The declining birth rate in recent years has led to changes in experiences of miscarriage and stillbirth. Whereas in the past, these experiences were deemed best forgotten as soon as possible, an increasing number of parents now wish to have some form of ritual service to come to terms with the death of a beloved child. Historically, women needed to prepare themselves for the possibility of death in childbirth, leading to early-modern folktales warning that maternal death would result in the appearance of a type of *yōkai* (supernatural apparition) known as an *ubume*, which is the ghost of a woman who died in pregnancy or childbirth. However, maternal mortality in modern Japan has declined dramatically since then, and maternal mortality is now seen as an adverse event that should never occur. This paper will focus on these changes, elucidating the changing awareness of pregnancy and childbirth, as well as changing attitudes regarding foetuses and childbirth. Recent research in the field of *yōkai* and the supernatural will be integrated into the discussion, allowing analysis of historical understanding of foetal death and maternal death from a gender studies perspective.

Childbirth in Japan underwent two revolutionary periods of change from the Meiji period (1868–1912) (Fujita 1979). The First Revolution in Childbirth refers to changes that occurred around 1900 when the emergence of midwives led to a decline in infant and maternal mortality. Midwives in this period were required to pass a midwifery examination, held in accordance with nationwide midwifery regulations issued in 1899. Nishikawa Mugiko calls these "modern midwives" (Nishikawa 1997). The Second Revolution in Childbirth indicates the period that began in the 1960s when the percentage of total births occurring in the presence of an attending physician reached 41.9 percent (Fujita 1979, 142). In this era, the location of childbirth gradually shifted from the mother's home to hospitals, clinics, and other medical facilities. This change in the location of childbirth occurred over a period of almost 20 years from the 1950s into the 1960s. Obstetricians at hospitals adopted various medical practices, such as the use of medications to induce labour, episiotomy, scheduled delivery, caesarean delivery, and painless delivery, further increasing reliance upon medical care during childbirth. In 1980, 95.7 percent of all births occurred at medical facilities, with this figure rising to 98.8 percent in 1990. This increase shows that the establishment of medical facilities as the place for childbirth was almost complete by this time (Yasui et al. 2009, 58).

I have previously referred to this continuing situation as the Third Revolution in Childbirth (Yasui 2013). The current accepted belief is that a hospital is the place to give birth, but this thinking has created a range of contradictions and issues, such as women in some areas not being able to give birth at their hospital of choice. One reason for this phenomenon originated in the late 1990s, when the number of facilities providing medical care for childbirth declined. Obstetrician numbers began to decline due to factors including resignations resulting from the large number of malpractice suits and demanding work conditions in the field, and fewer medical students were showing interest in specializing in obstetrics.

Technological advances in reproductive medicine have also created major changes to the circumstances surrounding childbirth itself. This has also brought changes to interpersonal relationships between the mother experiencing childbirth and her family, and medical professionals and other related personnel. In the past, childbirth occurred with the support of the family and community. Now, it has become more individualized, developing into something that is the responsibility of a couple and becoming further individualized to the point where the mother herself must bear the burden alone. This development creates situations where mothers become isolated and solely responsible for childrearing, leading to conditions such as postnatal depression in some cases. It is clear that these factors are making the current circumstances surrounding childbirth even more difficult.

A number of steps need to be taken in response to this situation. I argue that the Third Revolution in Childbirth indicates possible solutions to these issues by maximizing the role of the midwife in contemporary obstetric care (Yasui 2013). In the past, midwives used to visit the homes of women to assist with childbirth. The same midwife would provide support during pregnancy, childbirth, and the postpartum period. This allowed new and expectant mothers to discuss any concerns they had directly with the midwife. In the present day, however, the number of birthing centres operated by midwives is extremely small. The percentage of births occurring at birthing centres is less than 1 percent of all births. Midwife education in Japan is an optional extra year of study available to nurses, in addition to the required three-year nursing curriculum, making it difficult to train midwives who are capable of acting independently.

Since 2008, the Ministry of Health, Labour and Welfare has encouraged hospitals to establish midwife-led birthing centres within their facilities, with attendance by obstetricians in the hospital only in emergency situations. However, the number of such facilities does not seem to be on the rise. The establishment of this kind of birthing centre requires a significant change in thinking—obstetricians must allow midwives to act independently, and midwives must reduce their reliance on obstetricians and accept responsibility for patient care. The full utilization of midwives could potentially reduce the burden on obstetricians, improve levels of satisfaction among new and expectant mothers, and improve contemporary obstetric care. However, in reality, the field has not yet progressed to this stage.

Utilizing the wisdom of folk cultures in the present day

Given this background, here I seek to identify knowledge contained within childbirth-related folk cultures, focusing on the past roles of midwives, and to analyze the possibility of utilizing this knowledge in the present day. First of all, I will consider how mothers in the past spent the post-partum period, an aspect of care that has been the focus of particular attention in contemporary obstetrics. The following example concerns an interview-based survey I carried out in Nara Prefecture (Yasui 2013). The survey found that women who became midwives during the post-WWII baby boom did more than just assist with childbirth at the mother's home. They made daily visits to the new mother's home for a period between seven and ten days in order to bathe the newborn. These midwives reportedly visited a number of homes per day, travelling by bicycle (Yasui 2013, 122). Although bathing a newborn is something that could easily be done by a family member instead of a midwife, responses to the survey indicated that the new mother's family looked forward to these daily visits. The new mother was able to ask the midwife questions about childrearing and post-partum health directly, and casual conversation between the two contributed to lifting the mood of the new mother. In effect, this was a post-partum home visiting service carried out by midwives and could be used as reference for contemporary post-partum care.

Another custom worth considering is that of housing new mothers in a special hut during childbirth and the post-partum period. These huts, known as *ubuya*, were established within the grounds of private homes or in small communities. *Ubuya* existed to isolate the new mother from her family and other community members, as the blood from childbirth was considered *kegare*. The notion of *kegare*, meaning impure, unclean, or polluted, was an important element of Japanese folk beliefs until at least the 1980s and could provoke a strong emotional or even physical response (Namihira 2009, 4–5). Ordinary people were well aware of the *kegare* associated with death, and they could also be strongly conscious of *kegare* as arising from childbirth and menstruation, which took a variety of forms from region to region (Namihira 2009, 21). Most of the *ubuya* huts fell out of use from the Meiji period onward, with a few remaining into the post-war period. By the 1960s, none of the remaining *ubuya* were used for this purpose (Itabashi 2014, 29). Itabashi Haruo wrote that the custom of giving birth and spending the post-partum period in the *ubuya* facilitated *bekka* or *betsubi*, the custom of using a separate flame to cook food for the new mother due to the perceived uncleanliness of childbirth. Women in the community would speak with the new mother when delivering food to her in the *ubuya*; these conversations were used to provide words of support and to pass on childrearing knowledge and other information. Itabashi noted that this consistent communication with the new mother was valued by the local women as a form of mutual aid and cooperation. Itabashi thereby reinterpreted the custom of new mothers being housed in *ubuya* from the perspective of facilitating post-partum recovery and enabling mutual aid (Itabashi 2014, 48).

I also interviewed subjects in the Shiraki area in Tsuruga City, Fukui Prefecture, finding that new mothers previously did not return home immediately after being discharged from hospital; they stayed in an *ubuya* (Yasui 2014, 183–184). This custom reportedly continued into the mid-1970s, long after hospital births became the norm. In recent times, it has become increasingly common for new mothers to give birth in a hospital and then be required to take sole responsibility for caring for their newborn and housework immediately after being discharged from hospital. Given this situation, the recuperative care and mutual aid inherent in the *ubuya* custom provides an important perspective when considering how to provide post-partum care in the present day.

Medical anthropologist Namihira Emiko has identified *kegare* (uncleanliness) as a significant indicator of the level of support provided for childbirth in the past (1984). Namihira says that the concept of childbirth as unclean has faded almost completely in recent times, and she identifies the search for an alternative indicator as a major challenge for contemporary researchers (2009). I would argue that "safety" has replaced "uncleanliness" as an indicator. In clinical practice, safety has become the ultimate priority. This also applies to new and expectant mothers and their families. In the past, expectant mothers visited local shrines and so on to pray for a safe delivery. Now, the prevailing belief is that medical care itself provides safety. As a result, new and expectant mothers rely more heavily on obstetricians, based on the belief that their safety is assured if they place their care into the hands of a physician. The women's liberation movement in the 1970s brought the concept of active birth to Japan: the idea that women can utilize their bodies to participate fully in the birthing process (Yasui 2013, 188). This concept has now faded from public awareness, although it remains in some circles. In this era of the Third Revolution in Childbirth, awareness regarding childbirth has changed in a variety of ways, and suitable responses are required to deal with these changes.

Foetal death and *mizuko kuyō*

Here I focus on death in childbirth: infant death, foetal death including miscarriage and stillbirth, and maternal death. *Nihon San'iku Shuzoku Shiryō Shūsei* (Imperial Gift Foundation Boshi-Aiiku-Kai 1975) is an important compilation of information about childbirth-related customs in each prefecture from the early Meiji period to the early Showa period (late nineteenth century to the 1930s). According to this publication, in cases of miscarriage and stillbirth, the foetus was buried or otherwise disposed of together with the afterbirth (*ena*, the placenta). This indicates that the foetus was considered to be the same as the afterbirth, or, alternatively, that the afterbirth was seen to be part of the foetus.

With the arrival of modern ideas about hygiene, the afterbirth was required to be disposed of in a hygienic manner. Laws and other regulations stipulating methods for afterbirth disposal were established nationwide in the 1920s. Analysing examples from Nara Prefecture, I found that, previous to these changes, the afterbirth was often buried under the floor of the mother's home or in other locations (Yasui 2014, 82–88). After notions of hygiene became widely accepted, the afterbirth was incinerated or buried in a cemetery (Yasui 2014, 88–106). The survey revealed that locations subsequently selected for the disposal of the afterbirth were places thought to be gateways to the spiritual realm such as burial mounds and cemeteries.

Suzuki Yuriko writes that, in the past, there was a widespread tendency to see the foetus and the afterbirth as one. From the mid-1970s onward, the foetus inside the mother's body began to be visualized, creating an awareness of the foetus as a "child" (Suzuki 2018). This change is partly due to the adoption of ultrasound devices in prenatal check-ups from the 1980s into the 1990s. The use of this technology gradually became widespread, allowing clear images of the foetus to be viewed by parents. As a result, dead foetuses that had previously been disposed of together with the afterbirth now began to be dealt with on an individual basis. One of these methods was *mizuko kuyō*.

Mizuko kuyō refers to a new folk culture that emerged in the early 1970s, the practice of holding memorial rites for foetuses lost through miscarriage, stillbirth, and abortion. The origins of *mizuko kuyō* can be traced back to increased access to abortion in Japan. In 1948, the Eugenic Protection Law was enacted (replacing The National Eugenic Law of 1940); revisions just one year later (1949) made abortion accessible for economic reasons, and revisions in 1952 in effect shifted decisions regarding abortion away from government agencies and towards the discretion of doctors and medical associations (Ogino 2008, 170). These revisions resulted in a dramatic rise in the number of abortions from the 1950s onward (Ogino 2008, 175). It is important to note that women who had undergone abortions were not the ones who originally asked temples to perform memorial rites for aborted foetuses. The requests were made by doctors and other medical professionals who were involved in carrying out abortions, as well as afterbirth service providers responsible for the treatment and disposal of foetal remains (Suzuki 2014). These professionals worked in the medical field, with some involved in the latest reproductive medicine, yet they seemingly wished to somehow ease their consciences. These feelings drove them to create *mizuko kuyō* as a religious rite. Temples were quick to respond to demand for such services, with *mizuko kuyō* spreading throughout Japan in the mid-1980s. *Mizuko kuyō* coincided with growing interest in occult matters. Daytime variety programs on television presented *mizuko kuyō* as a supernatural phenomenon, focusing on the possibility of being cursed by the spirit of the foetus, and criticizing temples carrying out such services for commercial purposes.

A large body of research into *mizuko kuyō* has already been carried out, beginning soon after the phenomenon emerged (Morikuri 1995; Takahashi 1999). The subject attracted the interest of researchers in the United States and Europe, with William R. LaFleur placing a particular focus on the use of water in the *mizuko kuyō* ritual (1992); *mizuko* literally means "water-child." Those carrying out *mizuko kuyō* rites might scoop up water from a basin using a ladle, pouring the water over a *jizō* statue. LaFleur, focussing on the symbolic meaning of this water, writes that "the child who has become a mizuko has gone quickly from the warm waters of the womb to another state of liquidity" and that "the water-child has reverted to a former state but only as preparation for later rebirth in this world" (1992, 24).

Although the number of abortions has declined in recent years, *mizuko kuyō* has not disappeared altogether in Japan. According to Suzuki Yuriko, of the 83 Buddhist head temples in Japan (excluding new religions), 33 clearly indicate that they provide *mizuko kuyō* rituals (2014). Some temples even have a website where women who have experienced abortion can post comments. Commenters on these sites do not use the word *mizuko*, instead describing the aborted foetus as "returning to the sky." The symbolism of water is completely absent from this expression. Some women who have undergone abortions give names to their aborted foetuses, or sign their posts with "------'s Mama." These expressions show a clear change toward awareness of an aborted foetus as a "child" (Yasui 2016).

It is uncertain whether *mizuko kuyō* will continue for both aborted foetuses and those that died due to miscarriage or stillbirth, or whether a new alternative will emerge. However, it is clear that these changes are related to the changing image of the foetus among the public. More recently, ultrasound devices widely used in prenatal check-ups can provide realistic 3D photographs of the foetus and "4D" video images. The foetus inside the uterus is now seen by the parents as a "child" with a name.

Perinatal bereavement care and the creation of new rituals

In recent years, there has been an increasing need for bereavement care in the obstetric field for mothers and their families after miscarriage, stillbirth, and infant death. From an academic standpoint, bereavement care begins with Freud's concept of the "work of mourning" as an important process in bereavement (Okonogi 1979, 155; Shimazono 2018, 38). Bereavement care refers to the process by which those who are experiencing profound grief after the death of a close friend or loved one can be somewhat soothed through others spending time with them, listening to them, and being there for them in their grief.

Theological scholar Shimazono Susumu notes that bereavement care in Japan first gained attention after the 2005 JR Fukuchiyama Line train crash in Amagasaki City, in the Kansai region (2018, 47). Hundreds of people, including many young people, were injured when the train derailed. Another possible starting point for the acceptance of bereavement care in Japan was the Great Hanshin Earthquake that occurred in Kobe—also in the Kansai region—in 1995. Since the Great East Japan Earthquake occurred on 11 March 2011, bereavement care has begun to be carried out in a wide variety of venues and situations. In some instances, bereavement care is carried out by members of religious groups or clinical psychologists. In others, care is provided by regular members of the public.

As mentioned previously, bereavement care in the field of obstetrics is now regarded as necessary due to significant changes in thinking regarding foetal death due to miscarriage, stillbirth, or other causes. Older mothers or those whose pregnancies are the result of fertility treatments feel a pregnancy itself is precious. Therefore, miscarriage and stillbirth have become causes of new levels of grief and shock for women. Many are convinced that hospital births are safe and, given the rapid advancement of reproductive technologies, there is a tendency to believe that mothers can be saved from any potential adverse event. Reportedly, these beliefs have exacerbated the tendency for women to blame themselves for miscarriages or stillbirths—they feel guilty and are convinced that they are somehow to blame. Miscarriages and stillbirths are now seen as unthinkable by new and expectant mothers in an era where the "safe" and "celebratory" environment of childbirth is backed up by advanced medical technologies (Yasui 2018, 7–10; Suzuki 2018, 116)

Currently, many medical facilities provide bereavement care in the case of neonatal death, miscarriage, or stillbirth (Endō 2018, 136–146). However, the nature of that bereavement care can vary widely between facilities. At some facilities, mothers can hold their stillborn foetus, dress the foetus in baby clothes, or take photographs. Some facilities create bereavement care working groups including clinical psychologists as part of their programs, while others provide care according to a manual. In the past, most hospitals did not allow mothers to see their stillborn foetuses due to concern that the shock would be too much for them. Given this history, it is clear that a significant change in awareness has occurred among medical professionals toward more patient-focused care (Yasui 2018, 9–12; Satō 2018, 126–129).

Another noteworthy development is volunteer activities by women who have experienced miscarriage or stillbirth. These women sew baby clothes for stillborn foetuses and send them to medical facilities to ease the suffering of women who are facing the same grief. There are also self-help groups that are actively providing support. One example is Satō Yuka in Sendai City, Miyagi Prefecture. After suffering the trauma of a stillbirth, she created With You (With Yū), a group for families who have lost children due to miscarriage, stillbirth, neonatal death, or other causes in 2002. Satō continues to be active in this community, focusing mainly on the Sendai area. A survey carried out by the group collected detailed responses from members about what was the most traumatic aspect of being at the hospital after a miscarriage or stillbirth and what brought them comfort (Satō 2018). The survey revealed that some women who experienced stillbirth or miscarriage had been deeply hurt by offhand comments from medical professionals, including obstetricians, nurses, and midwives. In contrast, others reported feeling comforted by the words of medical professionals.

Satō also outlines in detail specific methods by which mothers can express their grief after experiencing the death of a child due to miscarriage or stillbirth. These include rituals marking the birth of the child, collecting family photographs, and creating handmade photo albums, as well as spending quality time with family members. Specifying these actions, effectively providing a model by which family members who experience the same trauma can carry out rituals or discuss the death of a child, is intended to allow mothers and family members to feel less alone and assist them in accepting the death of the child. In the same way, new rituals are being created within the field of contemporary obstetrics to assist mothers and family members in accepting neonatal death and foetal death due to miscarriage or stillbirth, allowing them to bid farewell to the child. Evidence shows that many medical facilities carry out these rituals in a neutral manner wherever possible, without relying on elements from Buddhism, Christianity or other religions, focusing instead on methods that allow the family to grieve in their own way.

One might assume that bereavement care did not exist in Japan until recently, but this is not the case. One early example is offered by Suzuki Yuriko. Up to the 1960s, when most women gave birth at home, family members and relatives who had a miscarriage or stillbirth in the past would comfort women who had recently gone through the same, encouraging them to forget the experience as soon as possible, and assuring them that they would be able to conceive again after miscarriage (Suzuki 2018). As such, good support structures were in place for women who experienced miscarriage and stillbirth. From the 1970s onward, some women carried out *mizuko kuyō* after being advised to do so by their families. Although miscarriage or stillbirth was not spoken about outside the family, such methods ensured that women who had these experiences were not alone in their grief.

Cultural anthropologist Matsuoka Etsuko has written about experts in bereavement care, saying that modernization has led to the loss of the "collective experience" provided by folk society in the form of traditional Japanese concepts of the supernatural, rituals, and so on. She adds that bereavement care has shifted from folk society into a specialized field, making it something that will be learned as a specialized skill (Matsuoka 2018). In this way, it is only natural that the "collective experience" provided by folk society that has been lost to time can be recreated in the obstetric field, not with traditional concepts of the supernatural or rituals and such, but with new rituals that continue to emerge.

Maternal death in childbirth

I have previously carried out analysis of rituals and customs related to pregnancy, childbirth, and the post-natal period passed down through folklore in modern Nara Prefecture (Yasui 2011). This analysis shows that the number of rituals related to the post-natal period far exceeds those related to pregnancy. This phenomenon could result from a view of pregnancy and childbirth that assumed that the birthing process would be smooth if the mother went about her daily life in a normal manner. In contrast, post-birth rituals and customs are specified in detail, in particular the custom of new mothers having their activities restricted for a period of 21 days after birth to allow them to rest and recuperate. The "unclean" nature of childbirth was used as the reason for this practice. This reflects a view that the way a woman spent the post-natal period was an important factor in ensuring her physical health. This view could be attributed to the fact that death due to childbed fever (postpartum infections) was common, even after the emergence of modern midwives mentioned previously, and the maternal mortality rate remained high. People understood from experience that women needed to recuperate properly after childbirth to ensure they recovered the physical condition necessary to carry out their everyday housework and work in the fields and so on. Here I examine how maternal death has been treated. The section titled "maternal death" in the *Nihon San'iku Shuzoku Shiryō Shūsei* (Imperial Gift Foundation Boshi-Aiiku-Kai 1975, 330) includes examples of beliefs such as "if a woman who dies in pregnancy is buried, she will become an *ubume* and will not be able to move on into the afterlife" or "if a pregnant woman dies, the foetus must be removed from her body and the mother and child must be buried separately."

Maternal death was seen as being doubly unclean—combining the uncleanliness of childbirth and the uncleanliness of death. As a result, people feared that women who died in pregnancy or childbirth would be transformed into a type of *yōkai* called *ubume*, which would bring misfortune upon members of the family. This was a popular subject in *ukiyo-e* woodblock prints. Many *ukiyo-e* artists in the Edo Period became popular because of their depictions of *ubume* and numerous other *yōkai*, which are supernatural creatures, apparitions, or objects. The typical representation of an *ubume* was a woman holding a child and wearing a straw skirt stained red with blood. Pictures included elements of folk culture such as *nagare kanjō*—a piece of cloth suspended between four poles intended to assist the spirit of the dead woman to attain Buddhahood. Folk culture related to maternal death is captured in these early-modern images of *yōkai* (Yasui 2015, 2017a; 2017b).

As a result, folk culture traditions in a number of regions included the custom of burying the foetus separately from the mother: the mother's stomach would be cut open and the foetus removed and buried separately to ensure she would not transform into an *ubume* (Yasui 2003, 2014). The fact that this seemingly bizarre custom spread throughout many regions shows that its purpose was to prevent misfortune befalling the family as a result of the dead mother transforming into an *ubume*. However, as the maternal death rate declined, this custom rapidly lost its appeal. Thanks to comprehensive contemporary obstetric care, the maternal mortality rate in 2015 was low, at just 3.8 deaths per 100,000 births. Expectant mothers and their families now have a tendency to see death in pregnancy or childbirth as something that will not happen to them. However, the fact remains that 39 women died in pregnancy or childbirth in Japan in 2015. When maternal death does occur, it is seen as an "incident," bringing profound shock and grief to both those involved and society as a whole. Investigations are carried out into the causes of such deaths, often resulting in malpractice suits. For instance, an incident of a woman dying during childbirth in Nara Prefecture in 2006 was covered prominently in the media (kicked off by a *Mainichi Shinbun* newspaper article headlined "Byōin ukeire kyohi" [Refused admittance] 2006). This, combined with media reports around stillbirth in 2007, stirred citizen debate and action and changes in procedures around high-risk pregnancies implemented by the Nara Prefectural Government (Nara Prefectural Government 2018, 163).

Gender and the world of *yōkai* and the supernatural

In recent years, the study of *yōkai* has gained wide attention in the field of folk culture studies, both in Japan and overseas. In particular, Komatsu Kazuhiko has built a theoretical framework to position *yōkai* and the supernatural world as a field of academic study. Komatsu plays a central role in the development of this field: he has published numerous research papers investigating *yōkai* in ancient to modern sources, as well as in popular culture including games and anime. Komatsu published *An Introduction to Yōkai Culture: Monsters, Ghosts, and Outsiders in Japanese History* in Japanese in 1994 (translated into English in 2017), which became an essential reference for understanding *yōkai* culture.

Yōkai have been visually depicted since ancient times, but they became popular after representations of numerous *yōkai* with names began to emerge, beginning with picture scrolls in the middle ages, and particularly in the Edo Period, in the latter half of the eighteenth century, with the development of woodblock printing techniques. At the time, the Western concept of natural history studies had been brought to Japan. As a result, *yōkai* were classified and ordered (Kagawa 2002), and encyclopaedia-like catalogues of *yōkai* began to be published by Toriyama Sekien and others.

Analysis of this *yōkai* culture from a gender perspective allows us to explore Japanese culture at a deeper level. For example, among the many scrolls and pictures featuring *yōkai*, ghosts—another form of *yōkai*—are most often portrayed as female. Japanese literature scholar Tanaka Takako has raised the question of why ghosts are portrayed as women in Japan (1997), but the answer has not been fully explored. The origin of this typical visual portrayal of ghosts as female can be directly linked back to the previously mentioned *ubume yōkai*. I have investigated the historical and social factors behind the emergence of the *ubume yōkai*, focusing on legends related to *ubume* and the burial customs that were carried out due to fear of *ubume* (Yasui 2004). My studies also suggest the possibility of a transcultural comparison of the representation of ghosts of women who died in childbirth in both Japanese culture and East Asian cultures (Yasui 2017a, 2017b). I am also using concrete examples to investigate how body parts are visually represented in the process of praying for a safe birth or recovery from illness (Yasui 2017a, 2017b).

Michael Dylan Foster pioneered the study of *yōkai* from a gender perspective (2003, 2007). Through his analysis of *kuchi-sake-onna*—a vengeful feminine-presenting *yōkai* that was sighted all over Japan from December 1978 to the summer of the following year—Foster adds his own perspectives to previous studies exploring connections between *Izanami* (goddess of creation and death), *yamamba* (mountain witches), *yuki-onna* (a ghostly snow-woman), *ubume*, *Oiwa-san* (the ghost of a mistreated woman named Oiwa), *kuwazu nyōbō* (a woman with a second mouth concealed behind her hair), and others. Foster states that these *yōkai* have an important common trait of being *ayashii onna*, sinister or suspect women (*ayashii* uses the first character of the word *yōkai*) (2003, 639) and that "such interpretations promote a sense that woman is always already monster" (2007, 702). In short, in a male-dominated society, women are always viewed negatively as the "other." Foster concludes that the minority status of women means they are were not recognised as human and that this was a factor in women being portrayed as *yōkai*.

From an iconographic perspective, *yōkai* are symbolic of the minority status of women, but I see such representations as also positioning women as objects of the gaze, noting that elements of sexuality have been emphasized for the enjoyment of those viewing illustrations and images of *yōkai*. This can be seen in the representations of female ghosts: while the late eighteenth century works of Maruyama Ōkyo (1733–1795) feature terrifying female ghosts, sensual, provocative female ghosts have also been popular subjects among artists such as Utagawa Kuniyosi (1798–1861), Tsukioka Yoshitoshi (1839–1892), Kawanabe Kyōsai (1831–1889), and so on. This re-evaluation of *yōkai* from a gender perspective reveals a number of interesting elements that are relevant to the study of Japanese culture and the *yōkai* that emerged from it.

This chapter has discussed folk cultures related to pregnancy and childbirth, with a particular focus on death in pregnancy or childbirth as the result of miscarriage, stillbirth, abortion, and maternal death. This discussion has examined past folk customs and practices, as well as individual awareness, revealing new information about changes occurring in the modern era and the present day. It has identified elements of past folk customs related to pregnancy and birth that could be utilized in contemporary obstetric care. It has also focused on the creation of new customs related to miscarriage and stillbirth. While this also includes new folk cultures that emerged in the 1970s such as *mizuko kuyō* as a memorial ritual after foetal death, including abortion, I hope to have shown that other folk cultures are now replacing them, such as the bereavement care currently being carried out at hospitals and other facilities. A research focus on death in childbirth can assist in clarifying perspectives on childbirth and perspectives on death. Linking this topic to recent research in the field of *yōkai* makes it possible to perceive more clearly changes to the view of death in childbirth through the modern period to the present day.

Related chapters

9   Attitudes to Marriage and Childbearing
32 Gender and Visual Culture

References

Endō, M. (2018) "Sanka iryō no genba kara" (Obstetric Care—Report from the Field), in M. Yasui (ed) *Kodomo o ushinatta kanashimi o idaite—gurīfu kea o mijika ni* (Intimate Grief Care—Embracing Sorrow at the Loss of a Child), Tokyo: Bensei Shuppan, 136–146.

Foster, M. D. (2003) "Watashi, kirei? Josei shūkanshi ni mirareru 'Kuchi-sake-onna'" (Am I Pretty? The 'Kuchi-sake-onna' Legend as Seen in Women's Weekly Magazines), in K. Komatsu (ed) *Nihon yōkaigaku taizen*, Tokyo: Shōgakkan, 635–667.

Foster, M. D. (2007) "The Question of the Slit-Mouthed Woman: Contemporary Legend, the Beauty Industry, and Women's Weekly Magazines in Japan," *Signs* 32 (3) (Spring) 699–726.

Fujita, S. (1979) *Osan kakumei* (Revolutions in Childbirth), Tokyo: Asahi Shimbun-sha.

Imperial Gift Foundation Boshi-Aiiku-Kai (1975) *Nihon san'iku shūzoku shiryō shūsei* (Collection of Documents Related to Birth and Childrearing in Japan), Tokyo: Dai'ichi Hōki.

Itabashi, H. (2014) "Ubuya shūzoku ni miru kegare, kyōjo, kyūyō" (Uncleanness, Mutual Aid and Recuperation in the Birthing Hut Tradition), in M. Yasui (ed) *Shussan no minzokugaku, bunka jinruigaku* (Folklore Studies and Cultural Anthropology of Childbirth), Tokyo: Bensei Shuppan, 29–53.

Kagawa, M. (2002) *Edo no yōkai kakumei* (The Yōkai Revolution in Edo), Tokyo: Kawade Shobō Shinsha.

Komatsu, K. (2017) *An Introduction to Yōkai Culture: Monsters, Ghosts, and Outsiders in Japanese History*, trans. H. Yoda and M. Alt, Tokyo: Japan Publishing Industry Foundation for Culture.

LaFleur, W. (1992) *Liquid Life: Abortion and Buddhism in Japan*, Princeton: Princeton University Press.

Matsuoka, E. (2018) "Gurīfu kea to shite no tsūka girei" (Bereavement Care as a Rite of Passage), in M. Yasui (ed) *Kodomo o ushinatta kanashimi o idaite—gurīfu kea o mijika ni* (Intimate Grief Care—Embracing Sorrow at the Loss of a Child), Tokyo: Bensei Shuppan, 79–81.

Morikuri, S. (1995) *Fushigidani no kodomotachi* (Children of the Mysterious Valley), Tokyo: Shinjinbutsu Ōraisha.

Namihira, E. (1984) *Kegare no kōzō* (The Structure of Uncleanliness), Tokyo: Seidosha.

Namihira, E. (2009) *Kegare* (Uncleanliness), Tokyo: Kodansha Gakujutsu Bunko.

Nara Prefectural Government. (2018) "Nara hoken iryō keikaku: shūsanki iryō" (Nara Prefecture Public Medical Care Plans: Perinatal Care), *Nara ken* (Nara Prefecture). www.pref.nara.jp/secure/194743/05-09iryokeikaku.pdf.

Nishikawa, M. (1997) *Aru kindai sanba no monogatari—Noto, Takeshima Mii no katari yori* (Tale of a Modern Midwife, as Told by Takeshima Mii in Noto), Toyama: Katsura Shobō.

Ogino, M. (2008) *Kazoku keikaku e no michi—kindai nihon no seishoku o meguru seiji* (The Road to Family Planning—Politics and Reproduction in Modern Japan), Tokyo: Iwanami Shoten.

Okonogi, K. (1979) *Taishō sōshitsu* (Object Loss), Tokyo: Chūō Kōronsha.

Satō, Y. (2018) "Ryūzan, shizan ni mukiau" (Facing Miscarriage and Stillbirth), in M. Yasui (ed) *Kodomo o ushinatta kanashimi o idaite—gurīfu kea o mijika ni* (Intimate Grief Care—Embracing Sorrow at the Loss of a Child), Tokyo: Bensei Shuppan, 120–132.

Shimazono, S. (2018) "Gurīfu kea no rekishi to Nihon de no tenkai" (The History of Bereavement Care and Its Application in Japan), in M. Yasui (ed) *Kodomo o ushinatta kanashimi o idaite—gurīfu kea o mijika ni* (Intimate Grief Care—Embracing Sorrow at the Loss of a Child), Tokyo: Bensei Shuppan, 37–55.

Suzuki, Y. (2014) "Mizuko kuyō—taiji seimei he no shiza" (Mizuko Kuyō—A Perspective on Foetal Life), in M. Yasui (ed) *Shussan no minzoku-gaku, bunka jinrui-gaku* (Folklore Studies and Cultural Anthropology of Childbirth), Tokyo: Bensei Shuppan, 141–186.

Suzuki, Y. (2018) "Kanashimi ni yorisou—minzokugaku no tachiba kara" (Being There During Grief—A Folklore Studies Perspective)" in M. Yasui (ed) *Kodomo o ushinatta kanashimi o idaite—gurīfu kea o mijika ni* (Intimate Grief Care—Embracing Sorrow at the Loss of a Child), Tokyo: Bensei Shuppan, 106–119.

Takahashi, S. (ed) (1999) *Mizuko kuyō—gendai shakai no fuan to iyashi* (Mizuko Kuyō—Anxiety and Comfort in Today's Society), Otsu: Kōrosha.

Tanaka, T. (1997) "Josei no yūrei ga ooi no wa naze ka (Why Are Most Ghosts Female?)" in *Bessatsu Taiyō 98: Yūrei no shōtai* (Bessatsu Taiyō No. 98: The True Nature of Ghosts), Tokyo; Heibonsha, 44–47.

Yasui, M. (2003) "Research Notes: On Burial Customs, Maternal Spirits, and the Fetus in Japan," *U.S.-Japan Women's Journal* 24 102–114.

Yasui, M. (ed) (2009) *Umu, sodateru, tsutaeru—mukashi no o-san, ibunka no o-san ni manabu* (Birth, Raise, and Transfer Knowledge—Learning from Childbirth in the Past and in Other Cultures), Tokyo: Fūkyōsha.

Yasui, M. (ed) (2011) *Shussan, ikuji no kindai—Nara-ken fūzoku-shi o yomu* (Childbirth and Childrearing in the Modern Era—Reading Nara Prefecture's 'Folk Custom History'), Kyoto: Hōzōkan.

Yasui, M. (2013) *Shussan kankyō no minzokugaku—dai-san-ji o-san kakumei ni mukete* (Folklore Studies of the Childbirth Environment—Toward a Third Revolution in Childbirth), Kyoto: Shōwadō.

Yasui, M. (2014) *Kai'i to shintai no minzokugaku—ikai kara shussan to ko-sodate o toinaosu* (Folklore Studies of the Supernatural and the Body—Re-Evaluating Childbirth and Childrearing from the Supernatural Realm), Tokyo: Serica Shobō.

Yasui, M. (2015) "Kai'i no imēji o otte—ubume to tengu o chūshin ni" (In Pursuit of the Image of the Supernatural—Focusing on Ubume and Tengu), in Tenri Daigaku Kōkogaku and Minzokugaku Kenkyū Shitsu (eds) *Mono to zuzō kara saguru kai'i, yōkai no sekai* (Investigating the Supernatural and the World of Yōkai Through Items and Depictions), Tokyo: Bensei Shuppan, 18–40.

Yasui, M. (2016) "Tataru mizuko kara mama no shugorei e—21-seiki no mizuko kuyō" (Transformation of Mizuko from a Curse into a Guardian Spirit—Mizuko Kuyō in the Twenty-First Century), *Ishibashi Hyōron Cultures/Critiques* supplement, 349–355.

Yasui, M. (2017a) "Minkan shinkō ni miru shintai no zuzōka, zōkeika—yōkai-ga no haikei o motomete" (Depictions and Modelings of the Body Seen in Japanese Folk Religion: Connections to Yōkai Images) in Tenri University Archaeology and Folklore Research Lab (ed) *Mono to zuzō kara saguru kai'i, yōkai no tōzai* (Investigating the Supernatural and the East-West of Yōkai Through Items and Depictions), Tokyo: Bensei Shuppan, 111–138.

Yasui, M. (2017b) "Depictions and Modelings of the Body Seen in Japanese Folk Religion: Connections to Yokai Images," *Advances in Anthropology*, Special Issue on Folk Life and Folk Culture (July) 79–93.

Yasui, M. (2018) "Kodomo no shi, taiji no shi e no gurīfu kea o kangaeru" (Thoughts on Grief Care for the Loss of a Child or Unborn Child," in M. Yasui (ed) *Gurīfu kea o mijika ni—Kodomo o ushinatta kanashimi o idaite* (Intimate Grief Care—Embracing Sorrow at the Loss of a Child), Tokyo: Bensei Shuppan, 1–12.

14
RELIGION AND GENDER IN JAPAN

Yumi Murayama and Erica Baffelli

Is the issue of religion and gender still important in today's secular society? In the Japanese context, the answer is definitely yes. As surveys show (Inoue 2003; Ishii 2007), the number of people in Japan declaring an affiliation to a specific religious organization is declining, yet the religious influence on society and on individual lives should not be underestimated. Buddhist and Shinto ideologies in particular, as well as folk religious practices, still assert certain gender stereotypes and presuppositions today. Conversely, scholars have also argued that religion could provide a way for some women to achieve agency.

Prominent Japanese feminist scholars of religion Kawahashi Noriko and Kuroki Masako (2004) describe this ambivalence of religion vis-à-vis liberation of women as a "mixed blessing": religion could and often does manifest itself as a male-dominant system or oppressive dogma, yet women or other minorities who are at the bottom of the religious hierarchy also discover ways to affirm and assert their existence, by reinterpreting and recreating their religious traditions. This chapter focuses on a few themes emerging from the intersections of women's lives and religion in contemporary Japan, with a particular emphasis on current debates, especially those amongst scholars in Japan. We also advocate the importance of an ethnographic approach in order to emphasize women's agency.

"Women, come out of the ring!"

As we will discuss later in this chapter, two central issues in the discussion of religion and gender in Japan concern practices of exclusion based on ideas of pollution. A recent news story provides a striking example of these practices. In early April 2018, during the Spring Sumo tournament, the mayor of Maizuru collapsed due to a brain haemorrhage while delivering a speech in the sumo ring. Several members of the public rushed into the ring to attempt to save his life, including a few women, and at least one of them was a nurse (Nihon Keizai Shinbun 2018). As she was giving him CPR, a man's voice came over the loudspeaker repeatedly yelling "Women, come out of the ring" (New York Times 2018); sumo rings are considered sacred spaces and are formally barred to women. The event fuelled a public debate regarding whether saving a life should have priority over what was defined as anachronistic and unjustified discrimination against women.

This was not the first time that the public was reminded of the controversial tradition of barring women from the sumo ring. In 1990, for example, then chief cabinet secretary Moriyama Mayumi was not allowed by the Sumo Association to grant a prize to the winner on behalf of the prime minister because of her gender. Again, in 2000, the female governor of Osaka, Ota Fusae, was not allowed to present a trophy at the end of a tournament in the city as is customary in the case of male mayors. And on the very next day of the tournament at Maizuru described previously, the (female) mayor of Takarazuka city in Hyogo offered to give a speech from the ring as (male) mayors do in their cities, but her request was denied.

A few weeks after the mayor's collapse in Maizuru, the chairperson of the Sumo Association, Hakkaku Nobuyoshi, officially apologized for "the confusion caused by the incident" and stated that it was inappropriate for the referee to make such announcement when a life was at risk, and that an exception should have been made for women entering the ring in this case (Japan Sumo Association 2018). He also explained that the main reason for the banning of women is that the ring is a "sacred place of wrestling and discipline for men." The chairman denied that the exclusion of women from the sumo ring was connected to views related to female pollution. Although the historical origin of this exclusion is unclear, the idea of banning women from a sacred place is a familiar trope in the religious Japanese context where exclusion is based on a code of purity.

Mountain asceticism and the exclusion of women

One of the most debated issues in the study of Japanese religions from a gender perspective is the exclusion of women from sacred spaces (*nyonin kekkai*). Beyond the sumo ring, women have also been excluded from sacred mountains or main halls of temples and shrines. Some local festivals also excluded women from playing certain roles in performances, justifying this on doctrinal ground that some deities would not appreciate women performing men's roles. Mountains have been considered a particular sacred space for the religious training of men in some religious systems. In *shugendō*, which incorporates mountain ascetic practices, and esoteric Buddhism, for example, the practitioner interacts with deities on sacred mountains to acquire powers from nature (Suzuki 2002, 2). However, this training has long been available only to men, with women prohibited from crossing certain defined boundaries in the mountains. In the second half of the nineteenth century, the Meiji government issued a series of edicts to rearrange Japanese religious institutions and formally abolished *shugendō* practices including the exclusion of women, yet both survived with the support of local believers. The situation has been changing in the last few decades, however, and local festivals are becoming more inclusive, while sacred spaces in temples, shrines, or mountains have begun to open to women. These changes are reflected in recent ethnographic studies focusing on the life of mountain practitioners, such as female ascetics (*shugenja*) and female practitioners performing oracles and rituals (*miko*) (Kanda 2001; Kobayashi 2011, 2017).

Justifications for the exclusion of women from sacred mountains can be summarized in three main points. First, women are seen as polluted due to their association with blood during menstruation and childbirth. Second, mountain asceticism is described as sacred training for men, and the presence of women could be a distraction. Finally, and often less discussed, is that the deity of the mountain is considered to be female and abhors the presence of women; trespassing may cause divine vengeance. Some of these justifications appear in other cultural forms, such as the previously discussed chairperson of the Sumo Association, who denied pollution as a reason for excluding women from the ring while arguing for the second (distraction caused by the presence of women). This latter explanation is often supported and justified by comparing this practice with monastic traditions in other religious contexts (Suzuki 2002, 48).

Exclusion is justified in different ways, but the criticism of these exclusions as discriminatory is often rejected by practitioners, who claim that these are practices connected to "tradition" and therefore should be respected as such. For example, Sanjōgatake of Mt. Ōmine is the only mountain in Japan where the entire area is prohibited for women. Human rights activists have attempted to challenge this exclusion, which is also extended to female hikers, yet the local residents and *shugendō* confraternities strongly resist and actively oppose changes. Historians, anthropologists, and religious studies scholars have addressed gender issues related to ascetic practices from the point of view of exclusion of women from sacred areas and the perceived ritual impurity of women's bodies (Miyata 1998; Nishigai 2012; Suzuki 2002); however, women's voices on these issues have been largely overlooked.

Kobayashi Naoko, in her ethnographic work, has argued for the importance of including women's voices in the discussion of ascetic practitioners to avoid stereotypical assumptions about female practitioners and to elucidate the complexity of the process of exclusion. In her analysis on contemporary Shugen confraternities (lay religious associations), she shows how female practitioners, although not allowed to go into Sanjōgatake itself, trained in other areas of the mountain side by side with male practitioners, kindling close ties with those who oppose the opening of the mountain path to women. Kobayashi's work describes how these women encounter the female activists pushing to open up the mountain, when they themselves did not hold strong positions on this demand. While the practitioners were excluded from decision-making processes within their confraternities, their interpretations of exclusion were ultimately based on their faith in gods and buddhas, who, in their view, have the ultimate say about whether women should be guided into restricted areas.

Women: unclean or sacred?

One of the reasons for female exclusion from sacred places is the essentialist view of women as impure due to their reproductive functions. The idea of impurity or pollution has been studied and extensively debated in folklore studies, yet the exact meaning of the word *kegare*—which is often translated as dirt, pollution, or impurity—is still contested amongst scholars. Sakurai Tokutarō defined *kegare* as dwindling of life power (*ke*: life, *gare*: to wither; 1982). Namihara Emiko explained *kegare* using the concept of liminality, building on van Gennep's theory of rites of passage as developed by Victor Turner (1969). According to Namihira, *kegare* emerges from a liminal stage of ambivalence and invokes a feeling of disgust. For example, bodily fluids, such as blood and excrement, or material cut off from the body, such as nails, hair, and dead skin, are *kegare*, because life used to circulate in them while attached to the body, but they have now separated from it (Namihira 1984). Regarding the *kegare* of menstrual and childbirth blood, Miyata Noboru suggests that it originated from the fear of blood, which renders it a reminder of death (2010, 133). Originally, the *kegare* from blood was not considered permanent.

The notion of female pollution began to limit women's role in Buddhist and Shinto rituals and their status in religious institutions from around the ninth century. Previously, both male and female Buddhist monasteries had developed, following the same monastic rules (Ushiyama 1996). As male monks began to dominate the administration of the temples, the nuns and nunneries gradually lost their status within institutionalized Buddhism. This political shift coincided with the spread of the idea that women were inherently more sinful and it was more difficult for them to reach enlightenment. This idea of karmic inferiority of women to men regarding enlightenment combined with the notion of *kegare* exacerbated the exclusion of women from playing important ritualistic roles (Ushiyama 1990). In Shinto shrines, also, priestesses gradually disappeared in the development of institutional orders (Takatori 1979).

While the idea of female pollution and sinfulness took root in the Japanese religious landscape, in folklore studies, women are often romanticized as bearing "special spiritual powers," attributed to their reproductive capacity and emotional nature. This essentialist view of women and biologically determined female mystical power (such as, for example, the ability to discern the will of a spirit or to enter altered state of consciousness) was presented in the influential work of the so-called founding father of ethnography in Japan, Yanagita Kunio, but his approach has been widely criticized and deconstructed in later studies (Yoshie 1988; Kawahashi 2005; Kobayashi 2017). In her study of female *shugenja*, Kobayashi warns against this romanticized image which tends to present women who practice asceticism as heroic figures while ignoring individual stories (2017). In her analysis, Kobayashi discusses how female practitioners performing ascetic practice are often presented in the media as seeking "to reset their lives" after traumatic experiences (2017, 104) and how some senior female practitioners are lauded for being "pious women" (2017, 105) able to master such physically demanding training. However, she argues, these representations tend to obscure discriminatory practices that still perpetuate in the mountain ascetic tradition (2017, 105).

A different perspective is offered by studies on the religious culture of Okinawa, where, unlike the case of *shugendō*, the concern over pollution from menstrual period and childbirth is not evident. Anthropologists working on Okinawa have claimed that the importance of gender has been disregarded by previous studies. Before annexation by Japan in 1879, Okinawa was an independent kingdom called Ryūkyū, where the religious sphere of the female and the political sphere of the male were interdependent and of equal value. Female ritual specialists, divine priestesses (*kaminchu*), played a central role in state rituals. The divine priestess performed rituals for the community, and both men and women were under her authority. The degree of the significance of their sacred status and role is the subject of scholarly debate (Kawahashi 2017), with Kawahashi pointing out the danger of downplaying women's roles based on a secularist prejudice (2017, 91). Another example of women's leadership in the Okinawan context is provided by the figure of *yuta*, divination and healing specialists, who are mainly, but not exclusively, female and play an important role as healers and mediators between clients and deities or ancestors (Wacker 2003).

Women in contemporary Buddhist institutions

Although several studies have focused on the lives and experiences of nuns in Japanese Buddhism, the ethnographical study of nuns, female priests, or *bōmori* (the spouses of priests of the Jodo Shin School, whose status has been recognized ever since the founding of the sect in the twelfth century) from a gender perspective has gained momentum in the last decade (Heidegger 2010; Kuroki 2011; Starling 2013; Rowe 2017). This attention to gender issues has also developed inside the Buddhist tradition itself. About 20 years ago, women in modern Japanese Buddhist organizations created an interdenominational network to reimagine and reform Buddhism from the perspective of gender. A book published in 1999 by the Tōkai-Kanto Network for Women and Buddhism, *Bukkyō to jendā: onnatachi no nyōzegamon* (*Buddhism and Gender: Thus Have I Heard*), and its sequels represent important publications for this network (Josei to Bukkyō Tōkai Kantō Nettowāku, 1999, 2004, 2011). The authors include nuns, scholars, and wives of Buddhist priests reconsidering and reconstructing the teaching of Buddha and the history and tradition of Buddhism in light of their own experience.

One interesting debate that has emerged concerns the role of *jizoku* (women living in temples because they married Buddhist priests) (Kawahashi 1995, 2003, 2017). Japanese Buddhist schools had long been complacent about the existence of these "wives." An edict issued in 1872 by the government allowed priests to be married, but although this is legal, it does not resolve the incongruity with doctrines requiring celibacy. To date, several Buddhist denominations have never officially recognized the existences of priests' spouses, despite this being public knowledge and fully accepted by parishioners.

The priests are living between the ideal of world-renunciation and the reality of marriage, with the result being the marginalization of women both doctrinally, by claiming that they are an obstacle to the path to enlightenment, and institutionally, by being denied recognition. In her study of *jizoku* in Sōtō Buddhism—a Zen school and one of the largest traditional Buddhist orders in Japan with "approximately 14,500 temples and over 16,000 priests" (Kawahashi 2017, 56)—Kawahashi criticized this situation as a "fictitious celibacy" (1995). It was only in 1995 that the existence of *jizoku* was acknowledged in an amendment to the Sōtō Constitution. Even then, *jizoku* are defined as "persons other than priests who follow the religious tenets of this school and who reside in a temple" (Kawahashi 2017, 59). It is not clear whether the spouses are part of the clergy or lay parishioners. Despite this lack of clarity, these women are expected to take care of the temple administration and to support the work of the husband/priest. Priests' wives in Sōtō Buddhism voiced their disappointment regarding their neglected status in a series of public debates held in several occasions between 2006 and 2011. Kawahashi's ethnographic accounts of these debates challenges the idea of priests' wives as passive victims of oppressive religious organizations, illustrating instead how they came together to reclaim their role within the tradition.

New religions and mobilization of women

In comparison to established religions, such as Christianity or Buddhism, some scholars have claimed that so-called "new religions" (*shinshūkyō*)—an umbrella term including a variety of different groups established since the nineteenth century—present nontraditional views of women. Several groups emerging in the late nineteenth and early twentieth centuries were founded or co-founded by a female leader, such as Nakayama Miki (1798–1887) of Tenrikyō, Deguchi Nao (1837–1918) of Ōmoto, Kitamura Sayo (1900–1967) of Tenshō Kōtai Jingukyō, and Kotani Kimi (1901–1971) of Reiyūkai. Some of these figures gained popularity by challenging commonly held views regarding the role of women and their bodies. For example, Nakayama Miki rejected the connection of pollution to menstruation and childbirth (Tenrikyō Church Headquarters 1977 127–128). Nakayama also criticized and rejected dietary restrictions and other practices regarding pregnant women's bodies, such as the belief that wearing a belt around the stomach will guarantee the delivery of a healthy baby. Instead of observing these customs, Nakayama herself became a living-god to protect pregnant women through childbirth. Nakayama's teachings are seen by some scholars as egalitarian, although heterosexual conjugal relationships were prioritized (Horiuchi 2012).

Many scholars, however, have questioned whether these founders' teachings sufficiently challenge the patriarchal structure of Japanese society (Nakamura 1981; Hardacre 1994a; Yamashita 2002; Ambros 2015). Moreover, after the death of the founder, the leadership in these denominations usually became dominated by men, and the more revolutionary and provocative messages promoted by female founders were toned down and replaced with more conventional doctrine and rituals. This was also due to the fact that in the early twentieth century, newly established organizations struggled to receive recognition and acceptance by the government and tended to adapt to normative gender roles. Today, many new religious organizations encourage heteronormative practices and often promote the role of women as subservient to the husband. As expressed in several new religious movements' teaching, wives will achieve self-realization through faith and submission (Inose 2017; Watanabe 2002), as well as devotion to the organization. Gender roles are now given a religious significance, which might give some women a sense of worth that they could not find in society (Hardacre 1984). In particular, their gender role is expressed in their contribution to the running of the organization and its activities, and they are considered the most active members in these groups (Igeta 1992).

Such mobilization of women is visible, for example, in the proselytism strategies, political mobilization, or volunteer activities of some of the largest new religious organizations, activities which are often organized and powered by female members. In the case of Sōka Gakkai, for example, the Married Women's Division has been defined by Levi McLaughlin as "the engine powering the organization" (2009, 217), and it plays a crucial role in the organization's day-to-day operation, including electioneering for its affiliated political party Kōmeitō. Paola Cavaliere observes that many women who are involved in volunteer work hosted by religious organizations eventually find self-realization and a venue to exercise their political agency in society (2015). However, the fact that the mobilization of women is based on free labour by volunteers suggests that religious organizations are not separate from the wider Japanese social structure that expects men to be the primary (or sole) breadwinner.

After the Great East Japan Earthquake in 2011, religious figures from various denominations, both traditional and "new," appeared in the media and started to promote the social-capital of religion for secular Japanese society. At the same time, media attention to volunteer activities helped some religious organizations to promote their image. Feminist scholars of religion in Japan, however, have expressed their concern that the discourse about religion and social contribution (*shakai kōken*) may obscure issues regarding gender discrimination that should be addressed by religious organizations. These organizations have the organizational structure and members to mobilize volunteer work, and there is a need for them to make a contribution, especially after a natural disaster strikes. However, scholars have pointed out that emphasizing their positive contribution to society may cover up the inequality within their organizations and teachings, which may now affect the larger society as they advance into the public sphere. (Komatsu 2014; Kawahashi and Kobayashi 2017; Inose 2018).

Recent developments inside and outside established religions

The study of Christianity from a gender perspective has also seen some significant contributions by Japanese scholars. In Protestant Christianity, methodologies of feminist theology and biblical interpretation have been imported and developed in the Japanese context (Kinukawa 1994; Yamaguchi 2006). Regarding the issue of the ordination of women, Miki Mei (2017), who is an Anglican priest herself, outlines the history and issues surrounding the ordination of female priests in the Anglican Church in Japan. In particular, she shows how discussions and consultations inside the Anglican-Episcopal Church of Japan (Nippon Sei Ko Kai) led to a modification of the church Canons in 1998 in order to allow the ordination of women. Miki argued that this opened a new path as "women clearly became aware of, and raised their voices against, marginalization due to sexual discrimination" (2017, 52). With the translation of Patrick S. Cheng's *Radical Love: An Introduction to Queer Theology* by Kudo Marie into Japanese in 2014, and the rise of social awareness of LGBT+ issues, discussions on queering theology and Christian experiences are also beginning to spread in Japan. For example, Horie Yuri is a scholar and an activist and a leading figure in the movement for improving LGBTQ rights in Japanese Christianity (Horie 2006, 2015).

While women practitioners have created supportive networks in order to make their voices heard by institutions, others find more liberating practices outside established religious institutions. Komatsu Kayoko's ethnography of women engaging in spirituality-related practices, such as Reiki, hypnotherapy, energy work, and past life therapy, shows how those women, experiencing the social pressures of being both professionals and mothers, found "spirituality" useful for both self-affirmation and finding a place where they can relate to each other and experience mutual recognition (2017). Some of them describe in negative terms their experiences in established religions, mentioning particular problems with not being able to find positive role models, priests lacking in understanding and empathy, a sense of being forced into conformity, a sense of rejection, and male dominance in hierarchies (Komatsu 2017, 131–133). These reasons suggest that for at least some Japanese women, mainstream religious organizations in contemporary Japan reflect normative views of gender roles that are seen as old fashioned and not adequate to their spiritual needs.

The scope of the study of Japanese religion from a gender perspective should also be extended beyond the geographical boundary of the nation. Kuroki Masako's work on the religious experiences of Japanese women in immigrant communities in the United States is one early attempt in this area. Kuroki analyzes the situation of women who can be described as multiple minorities and how their social position affected their experience of Christianity (Kawahashi and Kuroki 2004).

Finally, Japanese scholars have also pointed out that the gender power imbalance that is visible in most religious organizations is also reflected in the field of religious studies (Kawahashi et al. 2013; Inose 2018). Female scholars of religion are still a minority. This is also due to the gender gap in the leadership and ministry within many religious denominations, as a number of scholars of religion are in fact clergymen. It makes even more urgent and pressing the importance of encouraging debate and new research in these areas.

Further reading

Inoue, N. (2017) *Japanese New Religions in the Age of Mass Media*, trans. N. Havens and C. Freire C. www.kokugakuin.ac.jp/assets/uploads/2017/06/JapaneseNewReligions.pdf

Jaffe, R. (2001) *Neither Monk nor Layman: Clerical Marriage in Modern Japanese Buddhism*, Princeton: Princeton University Press.

Kawahashi, N. (2006) "Gender Issues in Japanese Religions," in C. Chilson and S. L. Swanson (eds) *Nanzan Guide to Japanese Religions*, Honolulu: University of Hawaii Press, 323–335.

Kawahashi, N. and Kuroki, M. (eds) (2003) *Japanese Journal of Religious Studies 30* Special Issue: "Feminism and Religion in Contemporary Japan."

Lebra, W. P. (1966) *Okinawan Religion: Belief, Ritual and Social Structure*, Honolulu: University of Hawaii Press.

Reader, I. (2011) "Buddhism in Crisis? Institutional Decline in Modern Japan," *Buddhist Studies Review* 28 233–263.

Related chapters

5 Masculinity Studies in Japan
6 Transgender, Non-Binary Genders, and Intersex in Japan
10 Family, Inequality, and the Work-Family Balance in Contemporary Japan
13 Changing Folk Cultures of Pregnancy and Childbirth

References

Ambros, B. (2015) *Women in Japanese Religions*, New York and London: New York University Press.
Cavaliere, P. (2015) *Promising Practices: Women Volunteers in Contemporary Japanese Religious Civil Society*, Leiden: Brill.
Cheng, P. S. (2014) *Radical Love*, trans. M. Kudo, Tokyo: Shinkyō Shuppan.
Hakkaku, N. (2018) "Rijichō danwa" (President's Address), *Japan Sumo Association* 28 April. www.sumo.or.jp/IrohaKyokaiInformation/detail?id=268.
Hardacre, H. (1984) *Lay Buddhism in Contemporary Japan: Reiyūkai Kyōdan*, Princeton: Princeton University Press.
Hardacre, H. (1994) "Shinshūkyō no josei kyōso to jendā" (Female Founders of New Religions and Gender), in H. Wakita and S. B. Hanley (eds) *Jendā no nihonshi* (Gender and Japanese History), Tokyo: University of Tokyo Press, 119–152.
Heidegger, S. (2010) "Shin Buddhism and Gender: The Discourse on Gender Discrimination and Related Reforms," in U. Dessì (ed) *Social Dimensions of Shin Buddhism*, Leiden: Brill, 165–208.
Horie, Y. (2006) *"Lesbian" to iu ikikata: Kirisutokyo no iseiaishugi o tou* (Live as a Lesbian: Questioning Christianity and Its Heterosexism), Tokyo: Shinkyo Shuppansha.
Horie, Y. (2015) *Lesbian Identities*, Kyoto: Rakuhoku Shuppan.
Horiuchi, M. (2012) "Jendā no shiten kara mita kyōso den" (Lives of Founders of Religious Organizations from a Gender Perspective), in K. Hatakama (ed) *Katarareta Kyōso: kinsei kingendai no shinkōshi* (Narrating Religious Founders: Early Modern and Modern Religious History), Kyoto: Hozokan.
Igeta, M. (1992) "'Shufu' no matsuru senzo: Jūzokusuru shutai" (Ancestors Celebrated by Housekeepers: Subordinated Agency), in T. Wakimoto and K. Yanagawa (eds) *Gendai Shūkyōgaku 4 Ken'i no Kōchiku to Hakai* (Contemporary Religious Studies 4: Constructing and Deconstructing Power), Tokyo: Tokyo University Press.
Inose, Y. (2017) "Gender and New Religions in Modern Japan," *Japanese Journal of Religious Studies* 44 (1) 15–35.
Inose, Y. (2018) "Jendā to Shūkyō: Sono kakawari wo tou toi ni chūmoku shite" (Gender and Religion: Considering the Question of How It Influences), *Gendai Shūkyō*, 201–223.
Inoue, N. (2003) *Japanese College Students' Attitudes Towards Religion*, Tokyo: Kokugakuin University Press.
Ishii, K. (2007) *Dētabukku: Gendai nihon no shūkyō* (Databook: Religion in Contemporary Japan), Tokyo: Shinyōsha.
Josei to Bukkyō Tōkai Kantō Nettowāku (Women and Buddhism Tōkai Kantō Network) (1999) *Bukkyō to jendā: Onna tachi no nyoze gamon* (Buddhism and Gender: Women's "Thus I Hear"), Osaka: Toki Shobō.
Josei to Bukkyō Tōkai Kantō Nettowāku (Women and Buddhism Tōkai Kantō Network) (2004) *Jendā ikōru na Bukkyō o mezashite: Zoku onna tachi no nyoze gamon* (Aiming Toward Gender-Equal Buddhism: Women's "Thus I Hear" cont.), Osaka: Toki Shobō.
Josei to Bukkyō Tōkai Kantō Nettowāku (Women and Buddhism Tōkai Kantō Network) (2011) *Shin Bukkyō to jendā: Josei tachi no chosen*, Tokyo: Nashinokisha.
Kanda, Y. (2001) *Miko to shugen no shūkyōminzokugakuteki kenkyū* (A Religious and Folklore Study of Female Shamans and Mountain Ascetics), Tokyo: Iwatashoin.
Kawahashi, N. (1995) "Jizoku (Priests' Wives) in Sōtō Zen Buddhism: An Ambiguous Category," *Japanese Journal of Religious Studies* 22 161–183.
Kawahashi, N. (2003) "'Feminist Buddhism' as Praxis: Women in Traditional Buddhism," *Japanese Journal of Religious Studies* 30 291–313.
Kawahashi, N. (2005) "Folk Religion and Its Contemporary Issues," in J. Robertson (ed) *A Companion to the Anthropology of Japan*, Oxford: Blackwell Publishing, 453–466.
Kawahashi, N. (2017) "Embodied Divinity and the Gift: The Case of Okinawan *Kaminchu*," in M. Joy (ed) *Women, Religion, and the Gift*, Switzerland, Cham: Springer, 87–102.
Kawahashi, N. and Kobayashi, N. (2017) "Editors' Introduction: Gendering Religious Practices in Japan: Multiple Voices, Multiple Strategies," *Japanese Journal of Religious Studies* 44 (1) 1–13.
Kawahashi, N., Komatsu, K. and Kuroki, M. (eds) (2013) "Gendering Religious Studies: Reconstructing Religion and Gender Studies in Japan," in Z. Gross, L. Davies and A. Diab (eds) *Gender, Religion and Education in a Chaotic Postmodern World*, New York: Springer, 111–123.
Kawahashi, N. and Kuroki, M. (2004) *Konzai suru Megumi* (Mixed Blessing), Tokyo: Jinbun Shoin.
Kinukawa, H. (1994) *Women and Jesus in Mark: a Japanese Feminist Perspective*, New York: Orbis Books.

Kobayashi, N. (2011) "Gendering the Study of Shugendo: Reconsidering Female Shugenja and the Exclusion of Women from Sacred Mountains," *Japanese Review of Cultural Anthropology* 12 51–66.

Kobayashi, N. (2017) "Sacred Mountains and Women in Japan: Fighting a Romanticized Image of Female Ascetic Practitioners," *Japanese Journal of Religious Studies* 44 (1) 103–122.

Komatsu, K. (2014) "Shūkyō ha hitobito no kizuna wo tsukuriagerunoka: Social Capital ron to jendā no shitenkara" (Can Religion Create a Bond Between People: Critiquing Social Capital Theories from a Perspectives of Gender Studies), *Kiyō* 6 61–74.

Komatsu, K. (2017) "Spirituality and Women in Japan," *Japanese Journal of Religious Studies* 44 (1) 123–138.

Kuroki, M. (2011) "A Hybrid Form of Spirituality and the Challenge of a Dualistic Ender Role: The Spiritual Quest of a Woman Priest in Tendai Buddhism," Japanese Journal of Religious Studies 38 (2) 369–385.

McLaughlin, L. (2009) *Sōka Gakkai in Japan*, PhD diss., Princeton University.

Miki, M. (2017) "A Church with Newly-Opened Doors: The Ordination of Women Priests in the Anglican-Episcopal Church of Japan," *Japanese Journal of Religious Studies* 44 (1) 37–54.

Miyata, N. (1998) *Hime no Minzokugaku* (Ethnology of *Hime*). Tokyo, Seidosha.

Miyata, N. (2010) *Kegare no Minzokushi* (Ethnography of Pollution), Kyoto: Chikuma Gakujyutu Bunko.

Nakamura, K. (1981) "Revelatory Experience in the Female Life Cycle: A Biographical Study of Women Religionists in Modern Japan," *Japanese Journal of Religious Studies* 8 (3–4) 187–205.

Namihira, E. (1984) *Kegare no Kōzō* (Structure of Pollution), Tokyo: Seidosha.

Nishigai, K. (2012) *Edo no nyoninkō to fukushi katsudō* (Women's Confraternity and Social Welfare in Edo). Kyoto: Rinsen Shobō.

Rich, M. (2018) "Women Barred from Sumo Ring Even to Save Man's Life," *New York Times* 5 April. www.nytimes.com/2018/04/05/world/asia/women-sumo-ring-japan.html.

Rowe, M. (2017) " Charting Known Territory – Female Buddhist Priests." *Japanese Journal of Religious Studies* 44 (1) 75–101.

Sakurai, T. (1982) *Nihon Minzoku Shūkyōron* (Theory of Japanese Folk Religion), Tokyo: Shunjūsha.

Starling, J. (2013) "Neither Nun nor Laywoman: The Good Wives and Wise Mothers of Jōdo Shinshū Temples," *Japanese Journal of Religious Studies* 40 (2) 277–301.

Suzuki, M. (2002) *Nyonin kinsei* (Exclusion of Women), Tokyo: Yoshikawa Kobunkan.

Takatori, M. (1979) *Shintō no Seiritsu* (Foundation of Shinto), Tokyo: Heibonsha.

Turner, W. Victor. (1969) *The Ritual Process: Structure and Anti-Structure*. Chicago: Chicago, Aldine Pub. Co.

Ushiyama, Y. (1990) *Kodai Chūsei Jiin Sosiki no Kenkyū* (A Study of Ancient and Medieval Temple Organization), Tokyo: Yoshikawa Kōbunkan.

Ushiyama, Y. (1996) "'Nyonin Kinsei' Saikou (Re-Thinking Women's Exclusion)," *Sangaku Shugen* 17 1–11.

Wacker, M. (2003) "*Onarigami*: Holy Women in Twentieth Century," *Japanese Journal of Religious Studies* 30 (3–4) 339–359.

Watanabe, M. (2002) "Shinshūkyō to josei" (New Religion and Women), in T. Inoue, C. Ueno and Y. Ehara (eds) *Iwanami joseigaku jiten* (Iwanami Dictionary of Women's Studies), Tokyo: Iwanami Shoten, 259–260.

Yamaguchi, S. (2006) *Mary and Martha: Women in the World of Jesus*, Oregon: Wipf and Stock.

Yamashita, A. (2002) "Tenrin-o and Henjo-nanshi: Two Women Founders of New Religions," *Japanese Religions* 25 (1) 89–103.

Yoshie, A. (1988) "Tamayorihime saikō "Imo no Chikara" hihan (Reconsidering Tamayorihime: Critiquing "Female Spirituality")" in K. Ōkuma and J. Nishiguchi (eds) *Miko to Megami: Siñzu josei to Bukkyō* (Shamans and Goddesses: Women and Buddhism Series), Tokyo: Heibonsha, 51–90.

PART III

Work, politics, and the "public sphere"

PART III

Works, politics and the bioaesthetic

15
GENDER AND THE LAW
Progress and remaining problems

Stephanie Assmann

Since the onset of the Abe administration in 2012, Prime Minister Shinzō Abe has pledged to prioritize the professional and societal development of women. This approach is entailed in the Abe policy entitled *womenomics*, the third component of a three-dimensional economic growth strategy, which seeks to implement structural reforms, a liberalization of the labour market, and an increasing participation of women and migrants in the labour force. The term *womenomics* preceded the efforts of the Abe administration to promote the employment of women. It was coined in 1999 by Kathy Matsui, an analyst at Goldman Sachs, with the objective to integrate women more effectively into the labour force and to remove structural obstacles that prevent the implementation of gender equality (2014).

Abe has pledged to create "a society in which women can shine" and has advocated ambitious goals for 2020, including a rise in the labour participation rate of women between the ages of 25 to 44 from 68 percent (2012) to 73 percent in 2020 and a target of 30 percent representation of women in economic and political leadership positions (Matsui 2014, 7). In 2012, merely 6.9 percent of all leadership positions were occupied by women (Holdgrün 2017, 144). In Abe's vision, women should also be encouraged to return to their workplaces earlier after childbirth, moving from the 38 percent of women who returned to work after the birth of their first child in 2010 to 55 percent by 2020. Childcare is a particular focus of *womenomics*. Parents face difficulties in finding childcare facilities. In April 2013, 22,741 children were waiting to be enrolled at a day care facility; this figure rose to 23,167 children in April 2016 (MHLW 2017a). Abe has pledged to create more day care spots and also aims at more active involvement of fathers. In 2011, only 2.6 percent of fathers took parental leave; this figure should rise to 13 percent by 2020 (Matsui 2014, 7).

Gender inequality persists

Despite these ambitious targets, sceptical voices question whether *womenomics* is an adequate strategy to improve gender equality. Since the enactment of the Equal Employment Opportunity Law (*danjo koyō kikai kintō-hō*) (hereafter: EEOL) in 1986 and the advancement of the Basic Act for A Gender-Equal Society (*danjo kyōdō sankaku shakai kihon-hō*) in 1999, significant progress has been made towards gender equality. However, the advancement of gender equality remains unsatisfactory with regard to women's participation in the labour market and their representation in political decision-making processes. The Gender Inequality Index (GII) of 2015, published by the United Nations Development Programme (UNDP), provides data on the three areas of reproductive health, empowerment, and economic activity. Japan overall ranks very high, in seventeenth place (out of 188 countries). With respect to reproductive health and secondary education, Japan ranks high. It ranks low, however, in terms of representation of women in the National Parliament. It only achieves a mid-range standing with regard to the labour force participation rate (UNDP 2015). In a similar vein, the 2016 World Economic Forum's Global Gender Gap Report, which examines the gap between men and women in four key categories of health, education, economy, and politics, ranks Japan at the 114th position (out of 144 countries). Japan scored almost complete equality in health and education, a middling ranking in terms of labour force participation and an extremely low score for political empowerment (World Economic Forum 2017).

Part 1: gender-related legislative frameworks

This chapter has two objectives. First, I will give an overview of legal frameworks with regard to recruitment, promotion, childcare, and part-time work. Second, I will investigate intersections between legislation, corporate governance, and human resource practices. Factors such as the deregulation of the labour market impede gender equality, whereas human resource practices such as diversity management may provide an opportunity to reconsider gender-related policies.

The Labor Standards Law

The equal treatment of workers and employees with respect to wages and working hours and the payment of equal wages to both genders is stipulated in Japan's basic employment law, the Labor Standards Law (*rōdō kihon-hō*), enacted in 1947. However, in the postwar period, gender equality in the workplace was not a priority. During the high economic growth period (1955–1973), a male-centred employment system, which combined lifetime employment with seniority-based promotion and payment schemes, was perceived to be more beneficial for economic progress than the advancement of gender equality. A division of gender roles allowed men to pursue demanding corporate careers and assigned women to the domestic sphere as homemakers and mothers (Osawa 2011). Lifetime employment schemes remain common in contemporary Japan but increasingly coexist with fragmented employment such as part-time work, contract-based employment, and temporary jobs.

The Equal Employment Opportunity Law

In 1986, the EEOL was enacted. This was initially a result of *gaiatsu* to comply with international demands to acknowledge the necessity of gender equality. *Gaiatsu* can be translated as external pressure, more specifically as "an explicit or tacit attempt by foreign countries to make Japan do what it would not otherwise do" (Miyashita 1999, 697). The term *gaiatsu* has often been used to describe external pressure from the United States on Japan in the fields of foreign policy or trade. With regard to the implementation of gender equality, the International Women's Year in 1975 and the United Nations Decade for Women (1976–1985) sparked debates about gender equality in women's groups and among journalists that led the Japanese government to comply with international norms (Bishop 2005, 112). In 1980, Japan ratified the Committee on the Elimination of All Forms of Discrimination against Women (CEADW), which led to the enactment of the EEOL. This legal framework applies exclusively to the private sector. The National

Public Service Act (*kokka kōmuin-hō*), enacted in 1947, applies to public servants and addresses employment, promotion, payment, retirement, and other working conditions. Like the Labor Standards Law, the National Public Service Act includes a "principle of equal treatment" with respect to race, religious faith, sex, social status, family origin, and political opinion in Article 27 (Assmann 2010, 139).

In 2016, the EEOL celebrated its 30th anniversary, which provides an opportunity to reflect upon the progress of gender equality and remaining tasks. Despite flaws such as a lack of compliance, the EEOL remains Japan's main legal framework for the private sector aimed at equal treatment in recruitment, promotion, and pay and protection for both genders from harassment and discrimination.

The first revision of the EEOL in 1997 abolished discrimination against women in all stages of professional development from job interviews and recruitment procedures to promotion. The second revision of the law in 2007 was more comprehensive. It included measures against practices of indirect discrimination such as hiring upon height, weight, or physical strength. Furthermore, mobility clauses that had made the willingness to accept nationwide transfers a condition for recruitment or promotion were abolished. Moreover, terminating women's employment during pregnancy or within one year after childbirth is now illegal. If a woman's employment is discontinued during pregnancy or after childbirth, it is the responsibility of the company to prove that pregnancy or childbirth was not the reason for terminating employment (Imano 2006, 46).

In 1989, the first case of sexual harassment was settled at the Fukuoka District Court and ended with a landmark victory of the victim, Haruno Mayumi (Okunuki 2017). Eighteen years later, the 2007 revision of the EEOL introduced the prevention of sexual harassment of both genders. The inclusion of men was a step forward from the EEOL as a tool to protect women from work-related discrimination towards the implementation of equality between genders. However, the revision of 2007 also pursued *positive action*—the Japanese equivalent of *affirmative action*—which included the pursuit of numerical targets of women's occupation. The integration of positive action programs reflects the ongoing debate between equality and difference in gender studies. Whereas difference theorists argue that women's specific roles and responsibilities in the private sphere need to be taken into consideration when drafting equality policies, equality theorists argue that the goal of equality policies needs to be complete gender neutrality, whereby "women are enabled to participate with men as equal citizens in the public sphere" (Pilcher and Welehan 2017, 43). In contrast, a third—and increasingly accepted—approach moves beyond this strictly oppositional model and recognizes that equality can entail the affirmation of difference expressed in policies such as affirmative action programs that guarantee the representation of minorities or oppressed groups (Pilcher and Welehan 2017, 43). This affirmation of difference is also reflected in the recent revision of the EEOL in 2017, which prevents discrimination related to pregnancy, childbirth, and/or parental leave. This is a response to cases of maternal harassment (*mata hara*) that women have experienced at their workplaces prior to, during, or after pregnancy and childbirth (MHLW 2017b; Ueno 2017, 24). Measures against maternal harassment demonstrate that 30 years after the enactment of the EEOL, discrimination against women remains a prevalent issue.

The Act of Promotion of Women's Participation and Advancement in the Workplace

The Act of Promotion of Women's Participation and Advancement in the Workplace (*Josei no shokugyō ni okeru josei katsuyaku no suishin ni kansuru hōritsu*, abbreviated to *josei katsuyaku suishin-hō*) is one of the most far-reaching instruments for the promotion of gender equality in the workplace to date. Enacted in 2016, this policy symbolizes a renewed shift from an emphasis on the integration of both genders toward a stronger encouragement of women's employment. The act requires companies with more than 301 employees and prefectural and municipal governments to set numerical targets for the employment and promotion of women. In this context, companies need to disclose the number of women employees, the duration of employment for both genders, the number of working hours of all employees, and finally the number of women in responsible positions (*kanrishoku*) (Ueno 2017, 24; Holdgrün 2017, 147). Furthermore, companies are required to develop a long-term strategy to improve the situation of women with regard to these four points and provide potential measures to improve the situation of women. Although the *josei katsuyaku suishin-hō* requires larger companies to provide transparency regarding their efforts to promote gender equality, the act does not require middle-sized and small enterprises with less than 300 employees to do so. Smaller companies are merely asked to co-operate with the objectives of this act (*doryoku gimu*), but they are not subject to sanctions if they fail to do so (Holdgrün 2017, 148).

The Basic Act for a Gender-Equal Society

Whereas the EEOL specifically targets the implementation of gender equality on the labour market and The Act of Promotion of Women's Participation and Advancement in the Workplace demands numerical targets, the Basic Act for a Gender-Equal Society, enacted in 1999, pursues a broader approach. The act encourages the equal participation of both genders in all areas of life, including family and professional life. A gender-equal society is very broadly defined as a society in which both men and women, as equal members of society, are given opportunities to freely participate in activities in any fields of society and thereby equally enjoy political, economic, social, and cultural benefits as well as sharing responsibilities (MOJ 2016).

The Basic Act for a Gender-Equal Society can be seen as the first stage of implementing work-life balance measures. The EEOL and the Basic Act for a Gender-Equal Society together form a comprehensive legal framework for implementing gender equality in all areas of private and public life.

The Child Care and Family Care Leave Laws

As stated earlier, childcare is a particular concern in *womenomics*. However, legislation for childcare dates back to 1991, when the Child Care Leave Law (*ikuji kaigo kyūgyō-hō*, hereafter: Child Care Law) was enacted. This law came into effect in 1992 and enables parents and care-givers to take childcare leave until the child is one year old. Furthermore, the law puts limitations on overtime work and late-night work and enables employees to take up to five days of leave to care for sick or injured children. The Child Care Law has been revised four times. In 1995, the law included other family members who are in need of care. In 1999, the law was renamed the Act on the Welfare of Workers Who Take Care of Children and Other Family Members Including Child Care. Childcare measures were no longer simply a recommendation but an obligation for companies.

Since then, the Child Care Law has yielded success: in 2008, 99.8 percent of all companies with 500 or more employees and 97.2 percent of companies with 100 to 499 employees implemented child and family care measures. However, the implementation of childcare proved more difficult for smaller companies. Whereas companies with fewer than 100 employees had a childcare implementation rate of 82.6 percent, only 56.5 percent of companies with fewer than 30 employees had introduced childcare measures (MHLW 2008).

After the 2008 revision, which went into effect in 2010, employers were required to establish a short working hour system and exemptions from overwork for employees raising children below the age of three years. Furthermore, the revised Child Care Law enabled both parents to take childcare leave until the child is one year and two months of age. Childcare leave to care for sick or injured children was expanded to five days per year and per child. The 2008 revision seeks a more active involvement of fathers. Fathers are encouraged to take two full months of childcare leave after the birth of a child. The latest revision of the Child Care Law, which went into effect in January 2017, enables parents to take days of childcare leave in half days (as opposed to full days). Another significant change of the 2017 revision is the inclusion of foster parents who plan to adopt or are in the process of adopting a child (Japan Times 2016; Baker and Kenzie 2016).

Part 2: intersections between legislation and corporate governance

The legal frameworks outlined previously intersect with laws that impede the implementation of gender equality, such as the spousal tax system. The frameworks also coincide with developments such as the gradual deregulation of the labour market, which results in more part-time work settings that include dispatch work, contracted work, and other forms of temporary employment. Diversity management practices that aim to integrate employees of different ethnicities, ages, and cultural backgrounds have gained greater significance and may result in a shift from the focus on gender equality towards the integration of older employees and non-Japanese employees.

The spousal tax law

One reason for the slow advancement of gender equality is the spousal tax system (*haigūsha kōjo*), which provides income tax deductions to main income earners for their spousal dependents. In order to benefit from the spousal tax system, the dependents—in most cases wives—need to keep their income below 1.03 million yen per year (MacNaughtan 2015; Matsui 2014, 15). Incomes below 1.03 million yen remain tax free, but higher incomes of dependent spouses lead to the regular taxation of the incomes of both partners and to the loss of benefits such as health insurance that cover the household head and all dependents.

This system was created in 1961 at the height of the economic high growth period, when men tended to be the main income providers, whereas women were confined to the domestic sphere or engaged in part-time jobs. A spousal tax system is common in a number of variations in other countries, among them Germany, France, and the United States. In Germany, under the policy of the *Ehegattensplitting*, enacted in 1958, married couples are treated as one economic unit regardless of the spouses' individual incomes (DIW 2017, *Ehegattensplitting*). Similar tax deduction systems for married couples are in place in the United States of America, Poland, and Luxemburg. In France—under the system of *Quotient familial*—families with dependent children are treated as one economic unit (DIW 2017, *Familiensplitting*). In 1986, a special spousal tax system (*haigūsha tokubetsu kōjo*) was implemented in Japan, which provided progressive tax deductions for working dependents with an income between 1.03 million yen and 1.41 million yen per year. Dependent spouses with a yearly income of more than 1.41 million yen receive no tax deductions and are subject to regular taxation. This anachronistic spousal tax system leads

Pie chart data

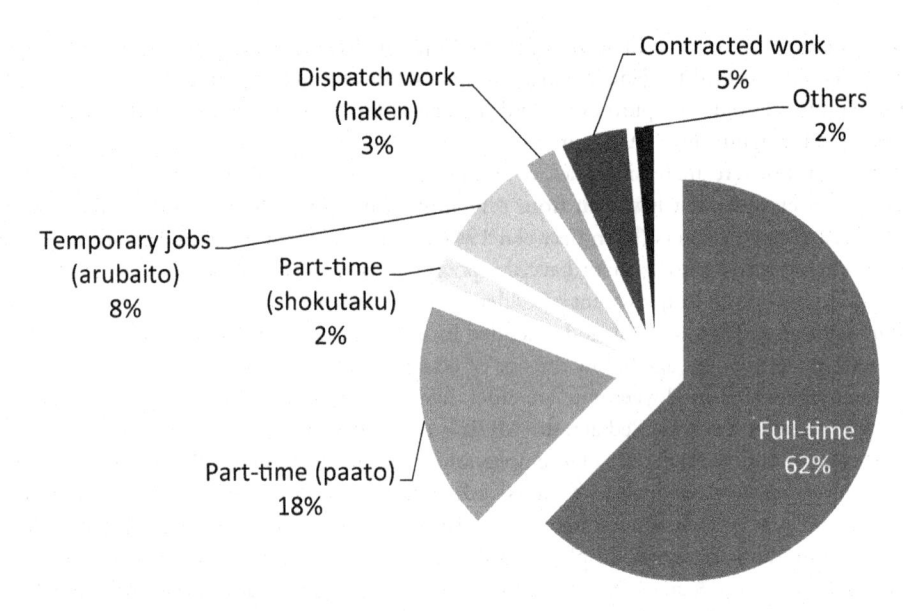

- Full-time: 62%
- Part-time (paato): 18%
- Temporary jobs (arubaito): 8%
- Contracted work: 5%
- Dispatch work (haken): 3%
- Part-time (shokutaku): 2%
- Others: 2%

Figure 15.1 Shares of full-time and part-time employees

Source: This graph is based on data compiled by the Ministry of Health, Labor and Welfare (MHLW 2016a), Hi-seiki koyō no genjō to kadai (Non-Regular Employment. Current Situation and Tasks), www.mhlw.go.jp/file/06-Sei sakujouhou-11650000-Shokugyouanteikyokuhakenyukiroudoutaisakubu/0000120286.pdf. (accessed on October 24, 2018)

and again in 2015. The act seeks to prevent discrimination against part-time employees and enables employees to make a transition from part-time employment to full-time employment. Besides this, the act seeks to prevent hourly income differences between part-timers and full-timers.

In 2015, 16,340,000 persons were part-time workers, which amounts to approximately one-third of the entire working population in Japan (MHLW 2016b). Approximately 70 percent of all part-timers are women. However, part-time employment is also on the rise among men, particularly among younger and older men (MHLW 2016b). The 2015 revision requires employers to prevent discrimination against part-time employees. However, the benefits of the act remain questionable because transitions from part-time employment to full-time employment remain rare (Weathers 2005, 83). Instead, the perpetuation of limited contracts is common. A personal interview with a 36-year-old part-time woman employee in Sapporo illustrates this:

> After graduating from a two-year college, Ms. K. worked as a full-time ground staff member for an airline in Chitose, Hokkaido. When she got married and had a child, she quit her job and moved to Sapporo with her husband. After a divorce, Ms. K. worked in a series of part-time employment positions. Her previous employer, a home for senior citizens, promised to give Ms. K. a full-time and permanent contract after a trial period of three months. Despite the successful completion of the trial period, this transition never materialized, which prompted Ms. K. to quit. Currently, Ms. K. works six hours per day as an administrative assistant at a university in Sapporo. Her hourly salary is 1,250 yen. She receives a new one-year contract every year for a period of five

years. After five years, Ms. K. has to leave the university. She can re-apply, but employment would be subject to the same conditions. After a maximum period of (a further) five years, the employment will be terminated.

(Personal communication on 10 August 2015)

The previous quotation illustrates the struggles of part-time employees in their hope and search for permanent employment.

The Labor Dispatch Law

Men are also increasingly affected by non-regular employment settings. Between 1990 and 1999, the share of men in non-regular work settings rose from 8.7 percent to 11 percent. The precariousness of male employment became visible for the first time in 2008 after the financial crisis, when 500 temporary male workers assembled for shelter and food in Hibiya Park in Tokyo after they had been laid off (Assmann and Maslow 2010). The Labor Dispatch Law (*rōdōsha haken-hō*), enacted in 1986, has contributed significantly to the deregulation of the labour market. The law was gradually expanded with regard to applicable occupations and the duration of employment. However, the most recent reform of the law, enacted in September 2015, abolished all 26 applicable specified job categories. The revised law requires employers to seek renewal of the employment contract, secure employment opportunities when the end of a contract is reached, or pay a financial compensation to the temporary staff if the temporary employment is terminated prior to the expected date. However, the revised dispatch law also enables the dispatch of regular employees with no specified contractual time limit. What appears to be a protection of dispatch workers could become a trap for workers that keeps them in dispatch work permanently (Okunuki 2015).

Womenomics: new affirmation of difference

Gender equality legislation has moved beyond the stage of responding to external pressure from the international community. Since the enactment of the EEOL, the implementation of gender equality has made significant progress. However, *womenomics* does not (yet) represent a genuine commitment to gender equality. Rather it needs to be seen as a strategy toward the stronger integration of women in the workforce with the objective to remain economically competitive in times of globalization and demographic challenges. The recent enactment of prevention clauses against maternal harassment as part of the EEOL and efforts to promote women's employment such as the Act of Promotion of Women's Participation and Advancement in the Workplace move away from an emphasis on the equality of both genders which was evident in the Basic Act for a Gender-Equal Society and show a new affirmation of difference which illustrates that there is still a long way to go until gender equality is firmly integrated into corporate governance. *Womenomics* intersects with the increase of neoliberal employment practices that put the employment conditions and prospects of both genders at a disadvantage. Furthermore, *womenomics* does not address the need to move beyond an exclusive focus on gender and include the integration of employees who are diverse with respect to age, gender, and nationality. In order for a strategy like *womenomics* to be successful, it is necessary to embrace the increasing diversity of the workforce and to remove obstacles that neoliberal employment practices pose to the stability of all employees regardless of gender.

Related chapters

5 Masculinity Studies in Japan
7 Gender and Ethnicity in Urban Japan
10 Family, Inequality, and the Work-Family Balance in Contemporary Japan
16 Gender and the Workplace
18 Gender, Labour, and Migration in Japan

References

Anderson, Mōri and Tomotsune Law Firm (2012) "The Latest Labor and Employment Law Bulletin (Partial Amendment to Act on Stabilization of Employment of Elderly Persons/Partial Amendment to Act on Promotion of Employment of Persons with Disabilities (No. 32)." www.amt-law.com/asset/en/pdf/bulletins7_pdf/LELB32.pdf
Assmann, S. (2010) "The Long Path Towards Gender Equality in Japan: The Revision of the Equal Employment Opportunity Law and Its Implementation," in P. Haghirian (ed) *Innovation and Development in Japanese Management and Technology*, Basingstoke: Palgrave Macmillan, 139–156.
Assmann, S. (2016) "Diversity in the Japanese Firm," in P. Haghirian (ed) *Routledge Handbook of Japanese Business and Management*, London and New York: Routledge, 224–235.
Assmann, S. (2014) "Gender Equality in Japan: The Equal Employment Opportunity Law Revisited," *The Asia-Pacific Journal* 12 (45) 2. http://apjjf.org/2014/12/45/Stephanie-Assmann/4211.html.
Assmann, S. and Maslow, S. (2010) "Dispatched and Displaced: Rethinking Employment and Welfare Protection in Japan," *The Asia-Pacific Journal* 15 (3–10). http://apjjf.org/-Stephanie-Assmann/3342/article.html.
Baker and McKenzie. (2016) "Amendments to the Child and Family Care Leave Act and the Equal Opportunity Act." www.bakermckenzie.co.jp/en/newsletter/cat/employment.
Bishop, B. (2005) *Globalisation and Women in the Japanese Workforce*, Abingdon and New York: Routledge Curzon.
Deutsches Institut für Wirtschaftsforschung (DIW) (2017) "Familiensplitting." https://www.diw.de/de/diw_01.c.411706.de/presse/glossar/ehegattensplitting.html.
Holdgrün, P. S. (2017) "'Womenomics' und Abes Vision einer Gesellschaft brillierender Frauen: Politikwandel oder Papiertiger?" (Womenomics and Abe's Vision of a Society in Which Women Can Shine: Political Change or Paper Tiger?), in G. Vogt and S. Heinrich (eds) *Japan in der Ära Abe. Eine politikwissenschaftliche Analyse* (Japan in the Era Abe. An Analysis in Political Science), Munich: Iudicium, 139–159.
Imano, H. (2006) "Hataraku josei" (Working Women), in Nihon Fujin Dantai Rengo-kai (ed) *Josei hakusho 2006. Kakusa shakai to josei* (Women's White Book 2006. The Divided Society and Women), Tokyo: Horupu Shuppan, 34–47.
Ito, P. (2016) "Japan and Its Immigration Policies Are Growing Old," *East Asia Forum* 7 June. www.eastasiaforum.org/2016/06/07/japan-and-its-immigration-policies-are-growing-old/.
Japan Times. (2016) "Foster Parents Allowed Child Care Leave Under New Law," *Japan Times* 31 March. www.japantimes.co.jp/news/2016/03/31/national/social-issues/japan-enacts-new-law-allowing-foster-parents-take-child-care-leave-starting-2017/#.WcoX9VeFX8s.
MacNaughtan, H. (2015) "Womenomics for Japan: Is the Abe Policy for Gendered Employment Viable in an Era of Precarity?" *The Asia-Pacific Journal* 13 (12) 1. http://apjjf.org/2015/13/12/Helen-MacNaughtan/4302.html.
Matsui, K., Suzuki, H., Tatebe, K. and Tsumugi, A. (2014) "Japan: Portfolio Strategy. Womenomics 4.0: Time to Walk the Talk." 30 May. www.goldmansachs.com/insights/pages/macroeconomic-insights-folder/womenomics4-folder/womenomics4-time-to-walk-the-talk.pdf.
Ministry of Education, Culture, Sports and Technology (MEXT) (*Monbukagakushō*) (2018) "Heisei 30 nendo gakkō kihon chōsa sokuhō" (2018 Basic School Statistics. An Overview). www.mext.go.jp/component/b_menu/other/__icsFiles/afieldfile/2018/08/02/1407449_1.pdf.
Ministry of Health, Labor and Welfare (MHLW) (*Kōsei Rōdōshō*). (2008) "Introduction to the revised Child Care and Family Care Leave Law". www.mhlw.go.jp/english/policy/affairs/dl/05.pdf.
Ministry of Health, Labor and Welfare (MHLW) (*Kōsei Rōdōshō*). (2009) "Tomobataraki setai no zōka" (Increase of Dual Income Households). www.mhlw.go.jp/shingi/2009/02/dl/s0224-8h_0005.pdf.

Ministry of Health, Labor and Welfare (MHLW) (*Kōsei Rōdōshō*). (2014) "Danjo-kan no chingin kakusa no kaishō no tame no gaidorain. Sono chingin, koyō kanri, minaoshite mimasenka?" (Guidelines for Dissolving Gender-Specific Wage Differences. Aren't Wages and the Administration of Employment Worth Improving?" www.mhlw.go.jp/bunya/koyoukintou/seisaku09/pdf/02.pdf.

Ministry of Health, Labor and Welfare (MHLW) (*Kōsei Rōdōshō*). (2016a) "Hi-seiki koyō no genjō to kadai" (Non-Regular Employment: Current Situation and Tasks). www.mhlw.go.jp/file/06-Seisakujouhou-11650000-Shokugyouanteikyokuhakenyukiroudoutaisakubu/0000120286.pdf.

Ministry of Health, Labor and Welfare (MHLW) (*Kōsei Rōdōshō*). (2016b) "Pāto-taimu rōdō-hō no aramashi" (Outline of the Part-Time Employment Act). www.mhlw.go.jp/stf/seisakunitsuite/bunya/0000061842.html#ri-fu.

Ministry of Health, Labor and Welfare (MHLW) (*Kōsei Rōdōshō*). (2017a) "Taiki jidō kaishō ni muketa torikumi" (Measures Toward Fewer Children on Waiting Lists for Daycare Places). https://www8.cao.go.jp/shoushi/shoushika/whitepaper/measures/w-2016/28pdfgaiyoh/pdf/column02.pdf.

Ministry of Health, Labor and Welfare (MHLW) (*Kōsei Rōdōshō*). (2017b) "Ninshin, shussan nado ni kansuru harasumento no bōshi setchi no naiyō ni tsuite" (Concerning the Content of Measures to Prevent Harassment with Regard to Pregnancy and Childbirth). https://www.mhlw.go.jp/file/05-Shingikai-12602000-Seisakutoukatsukan-Sanjikanshitsu_Roudouseisakutantou/0000124003.pdf.

Ministry of Justice (*Hōmushō*) (MOJ). (2016) "Convention on the Elimination of All Forms of Discrimination Against Women Statement by the Head of the Delegation of Japan for the Seventh and Eighth Periodic Reports." 16 February. http://www.gender.go.jp/international/int_kaigi/int_teppai/pdf/statement7-8_e.pdf.

Miyashita, A. (1999) "Gaiatsu and Japan's Foreign Aid: Rethinking the Reactive-Proactive Debate," *International Studies Quarterly* 43 695–732.

Nakatani, I. (2013) "Drastic Change in Immigration Policy Off the Japanese Election Agenda," *East Asia Forum* 21 July. www.eastasiaforum.org/2013/07/21/drastic-change-in-immigration-policy-off-the-japanese-election-agenda/.

North, S. (2014) "Limited Regular Employment and the Reform of Japan's Division of Labor," *The Asia-Pacific Journal* 12 (15) 1. www.japanfocus.org/-Scott-North/4106.

Okunuki, H. (2015) "Legal Change Will Make Temp Purgatory Permanent for Many Japanese Workers," *Japan Times* 27 September. www.japantimes.co.jp/community/2015/09/27/issues/legal-change-will-make-temp-purgatory-permanent-many-japanese-workers/#.WdCVL1eFX8s.

Okunuki, H. (2017) "NS Solutions Case Is Latest Battle in Long War Against Sexual Harassment," *Japan Times* 1 October. www.japantimes.co.jp/community/2017/10/01/issues/case-latest-battle-long-war-sexual-harassment/#.WdHSXFeFX8s.

Osawa, M. (2011) *Gender-Equality and the Revitalization of Japan's Society and Economy Under Globalization*, World Development Report 2012, Gender Equality and Development.

Pilcher, J. and Welehan, I. (2017) *Key Concepts in Gender Studies*, Los Angeles, London and New Delhi: Sage.

Ueno, C. (2017) "Neoriberarizumu to jendā" (Neoliberalism and Gender), *Jendā Kenkyū* (Research on Gender) 20 21–33.

United Nations Development Programme (UNDP). (2015) "Gender Inequality Index (GII)." http://hdr.undp.org/en/content/gender-inequality-index-gii.

Weathers, C. (2005) "In Search of Strategic Partners: Japan's Campaign for Equal Opportunity," *Social Science Japan Journal* 8 (1) 69–89.

World Economic Forum. (2017) "The Global Gender Gap Report 2017. Japan." https://www.weforum.org/reports/the-global-gender-gap-report-2017.

16
GENDER AND THE WORKPLACE

Helen Macnaughtan

This chapter argues that the Japanese workplace is deeply gendered despite the incremental development of employment legislation and calls for gender equality. The Japanese government and corporate institutions have institutionalised a gendered system of employment that shows little sign of dissipating. The system is based on drawing social and economic advantages from a gendered division of labour, with women and men occupying complementary (re)productive roles at work and at home. This results in an employment model that continues to reproduce inherent gender bias in workplace attitudes, behaviours, and practices. Throughout the postwar decades, this has created a systematically segregated core male and peripheral female workforce. While there are signs of gradual progress for women, there is at the same time a resistance to any deeper momentum that could effectively weaken gender segregation. This chapter questions the degree to which recent focus on expanding female employment in Japan is enough to dismantle gender segregation or challenge mainstream male employment. It first offers an ideological framework for understanding how workplace gendering continues to be reproduced in Japan, then outlines how the gendered employment model developed during the postwar decades, and ends with an analysis of how this continues to play out for women and men in the Japanese workplace.

(i) Gender ideology and work

The postwar decades of economic growth up until the 1990s were crucial in establishing the current employment system. During that period, two distinctly different but complementary systems emerged: a mainstream system for men founded on notions of lifetime employment and a peripheral system for women that institutionalised non-regular categories of work and designated them as a buffer labour force (Macnaughtan 2005). In this process, the segregation of women and men was neatly achieved; moves by the Japanese government to save costs on social welfare placed the burden of care on women and enabled Japanese organisations to secure stable and well-paid employment for men (Nemoto 2016). Despite incremental progress in employment legislation seeking to promote gender equality, the gendered segregation of work in Japan is still persistent and evident (Assmann 2014; Macnaughtan 2015; Aronsson 2015; Dalton 2017).

The model that underpins this deep-seated division of labour is the ideology of the male breadwinner, with men assigned primary responsibility for productive roles in the economy and women for reproductive roles within the family unit and more broadly in society (Macnaughtan 2015). There is general agreement in the literature that the male breadwinner model has substantially eroded in most advanced countries since the 1970s (Lewis 2001), but Japan remains a notable exception, where the ideology remains distinctly embedded in society, reinforcing everyday workplace practices and continuing to undermine seemingly gender-equal employment reforms. The argument that economic development accompanied by female empowerment and higher rates of female employment narrows the gender gap holds in most OECD nations (OECD 2014). Although the total female labour force participation rate in Japan now rivals that of other OECD nations, this has not produced significant change to the gendered status of employment nor to the assessment of gender equality outcomes. Japan continues to rank low (114 out of 144 nations) in the annual World Economic Forum global gender gap index (WEF 2017). This is because Japan has retained the nuclear male breadwinner model longer than other advanced economies, with mechanisms supporting the model continuing to underpin discourse and practices located within corporations. The model remains strong within the Japanese economy, where there is insufficient investment in market resources to replace female domestic labour in areas such as childcare and healthcare, and where the income packages of regular male employees combined with the spousal tax system encourage women to predominantly focus on household activities (Saito 2014; Macnaughtan 2015). In societies where the male breadwinner model is strong, it is common for women to contribute high levels of unpaid domestic labour, have broken career paths, and work part-time (Pascall 2010). This is evident in Japan and works to undermine the effectiveness of gender equality legislation and so-called female-focused or family-friendly policies.

Japanese companies and government policy makers seek to gain economic advantage from the incorporation of more women in work under the broad guise of "womenomics" (Macnaughtan 2015). However, they are not providing access to the types of work that could enhance economic outcome as well as challenging gendered norms. Women are encouraged to work more, but core workplace practices remain focused around the ideal of the male breadwinner employee. This perpetuates a cycle of gendering in employment practices and behaviours, ultimately resulting in a majority of women choosing to opt out of the system of regular employment, meaning that mainstream practices within organisations remain dominated by men and by ideological expectations of how men should work. The outcome is that neither sex is provided with concrete opportunities to challenge the way they are expected to work. Men are also neglected in the broader analysis of gender and employment in Japan by both policy makers and employers (Roberson and Suzuki 2003; Frühstück and Walthall 2011). This reinforces gender segregation in employment and results in a tension that arguably restricts the choices of, and discriminates against, both sexes.

The significance of male breadwinner ideology is evident when assessing the impact of legislation. The implementation of the Equal Employment Opportunity Law (EEOL) in 1986 ironically enabled companies to segregate male and female regular employees into general (*sōgoshoku*) and clerical career tracks (*ippanshoku*) on the normative notion that women's domestic labour required protection from the demands of regular employment. This offering of a protective status of employment to women was viewed as "preferential treatment" for women and therefore not a violation of the EEOL (Yamada 2013). As a result, discrimination against women was legitimised, as companies effectively restricted the long-term career access of female regular workers by placing them in *ippanshoku* tracks, with jobs predominantly confined to clerical and support roles. In turn, this reinforced the stability of employment for men, with the *sōgoshoku* track overwhelmingly composed of male employees and offering business-focused roles and advancement to managerial positions. Although the EEOL has undergone several revisions since 1986, it still does not adequately recognise marital status as grounds for discrimination. Although dismissal due to marriage is now prohibited, companies can continue the practice of offering regular positions of employment to unmarried women and non-regular positions to married women within the parameters of the EEOL (Yamada 2013). In this way, the EEOL, which ostensibly seeks to remove gender discrimination in the workplace, continues to enable the institutionalisation of segregated, gendered employment tracks in Japanese organisations. Government policy focuses on how to enable women to work within normative expectations of their caring roles, at the same time offering little alleviation to the rigours of regular employment for men, effectively curtailing their contribution to domestic labour. There is therefore inertia within the postwar system that is constraining any real progress in workplace practices while supporting broader ideological gender norms in society.

(ii) Gendered employment system

The Japanese style of employment that emerged in the postwar decades had gender segregation at its core. High economic growth in the 1960s led to a labour shortage and subsequent demand for women to alleviate this and enter the workforce. The prior establishment of lifetime employment in the 1950s had offered stability of employment for male workers, protecting them as core labour, while women were encouraged into paid work within the context of their role as household dependents (Macnaughtan 2005). It was noted early on in the literature that lifetime employment was usually associated with men and non-regular employment with women (Vogel 1963). This division of labour was described as a freedom or liberation for women vis-à-vis their male counterparts (Rohlen 1974), which spared them from being relocated for work (Clark 1979), while legislation was observed to be formulated based on a core ideology that female workers needed to be treated distinctly differently to male workers (Kamiya 1995). The evolution of this system harnessed women as a crucial force for economic growth, as both a supply of inexpensive labour to industry and nurturers of the human capital of their husbands and sons (Brinton 1993). However, this protection of women came at a cost, as their primary status as carers in the family unit and their constrained contribution as non-regular workers ultimately made them an unreliable long-term investment in the eyes of employers (Sako and Sato 1997; Macnaughtan 2005). These normative assumptions and workplace practices combined to keep postwar employment deeply segregated along gender lines (Brinton 2015; Osawa 2000, 2002; Macnaughtan 2006); the practices that underpin this show little erosion over time.

Research on the employment of Japanese women has documented their increased presence in the workplace but noted a persistence of the M-curve (see Figure 16.1) and their visible role as part-time workers (Broadbent 2003; Macnaughtan 2006). There are two distinctly separate but intertwined forces that have intensified government focus on women and employment: economic necessity and demographic transition. With the labour shortages and rapid economic take-off of the 1960s, and faced with the prospect of potentially having to import labour to cope with demand, Japan's political and business leaders turned to women. Their assimilation into employment was set up to reap economic advantage rather than challenge gender roles (Macnaughtan 2005, 2015). In the last two decades, women have again been encouraged to expand their employment participation within efforts to revitalise the economy, address the declining supply of labour under depopulation, and alleviate the economic burden of an aging population. Women are persistently under-utilised in the economy and remain a pool of labour that can repeatedly be called upon by policymakers to "save" Japan when deemed necessary, particularly when the less palatable alternative might be immigrant labour (Shinkawa 2012). Policy remains

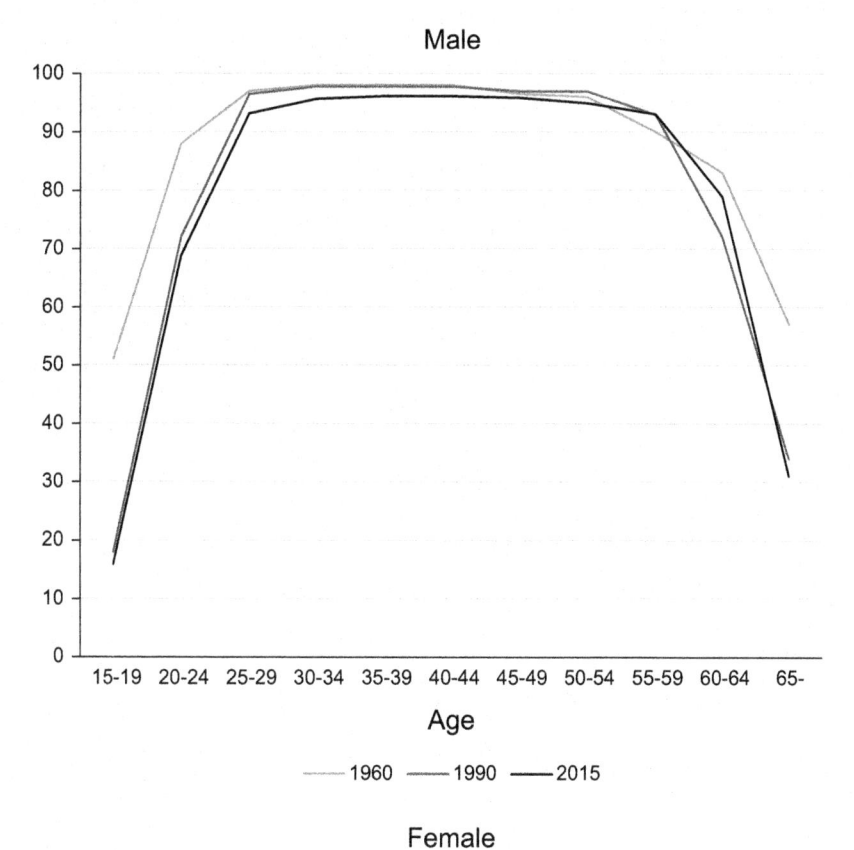

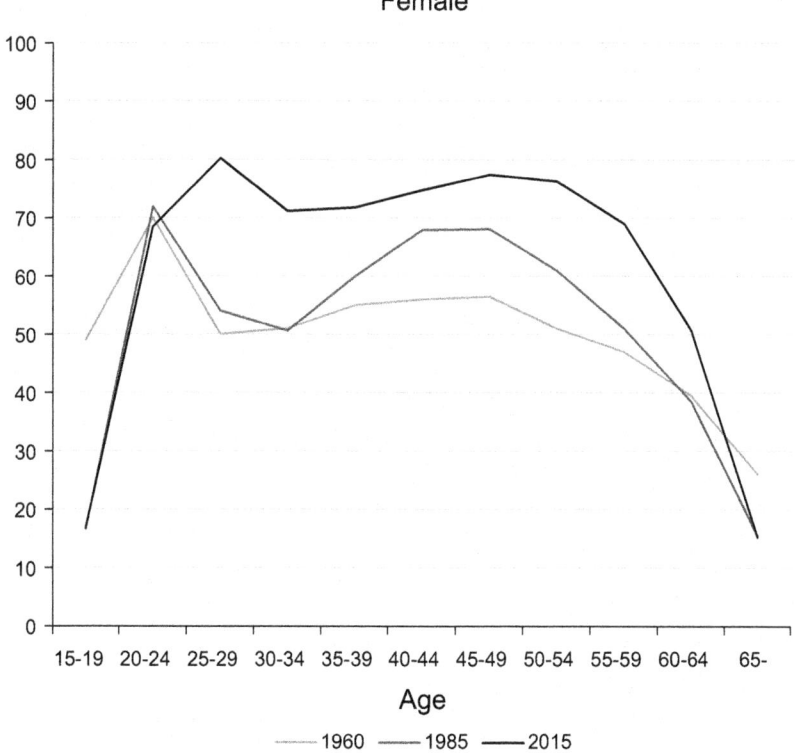

Figure 16.1 Male and female labour participation rate: 1960, 1985, 2015

focused on increasing female contribution to the economy without substantially dismantling the segregation of the breadwinner model.

This segregation manifests in the M-curve pattern of female employment vis-à-vis the inverted-U pattern for males (Figure 16.1). Choice and opportunity differ for women and men during their life-course, with a significant portion of women continuing to opt out of employment in the prime child-rearing years of life. This dip in the M and the high proportion of non-regular employment for older cohorts (Figure 16.2) indicates that motherhood and opting in and out of the market pose barriers to continuous regular employment. These barriers persist even within a momentum for change. As can be seen in Figure 16.1, the M-curve began to take shape in the 1960s and was well established by 1985 (the year the EEOL was passed). By 2015, a higher proportion of women were working due to growing demand for their labour, increased social acceptance of working women, better availability of parental leave, and lower fertility leading to a shortening of the average number of years required for early childcare. Under these trends, the M-curve has flattened. While these changes point to progress for women, depth of progress cannot be assumed. The rising proportion of older women working and the decline in the proportion opting out in the peak reproductive years does not necessarily correlate to

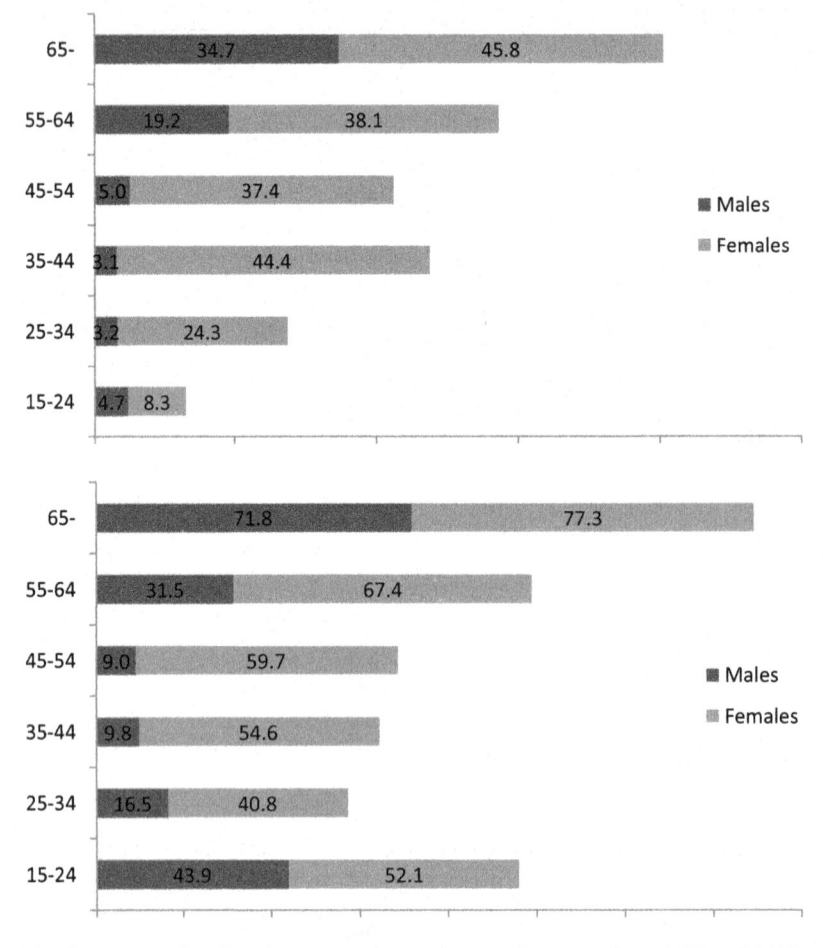

Figure 16.2 Percentage of workers in non-regular employment by age and sex: 1985 and 2015

enhanced career opportunities. A significant proportion of well-educated women (25–30 percent) in the peak reproductive age cohorts are not participating in the labour market at all. The flattening of the dip in the M-curve is partly attributable to fewer women opting for parenthood, while the proportion of women resigning from their jobs upon childbirth remains high at 48 percent (Macnaughtan 2015).

The number of women working has been increasing for some decades, and the proportion of total employees who are women reached 43.9 percent in 2015 (JILPT 2016). However, there is significant gendering at play in employment status. Women constitute more than two-thirds (68.1 percent) of all non-regular employees and less than one-third (31.5 percent) of all regular employees (Annual Labor Force Survey 2016). This predominance of women in non-regular employment cannot be overstated. In recent years, some authors have argued that the growth in non-regular employment signifies that the model of postwar lifetime employment is increasingly obsolete or in decline (e.g. Holzhausen 2000; Watanabe 2003; Hamaaki et al. 2012; Kawaguchi and Ueno 2013). An analysis by gender suggests otherwise. It is true that non-regular employment has increased and now represents 37 percent of total employment (JILPT 2016), and 20 percent of all men are now in non-regular employment. However, for women, the proportion is significantly higher at more than 55 percent (JILPT 2016) and there is considerable gender and age disparity. Figure 16.2 shows that for both sexes, there is an increased likelihood of non-regular employment in the younger and older age cohorts compared to 1985. However, it is important to note the low levels of non-regular employment for men in the prime productive years (25–55 years of age) against a deteriorating situation for women. Younger cohorts of women also predominate in temporary agency employment and in administrative work (Gottfried 2014). The data indicate that employment remains highly gendered and that regular employment continues to be the domain of men.

Despite the strengthening of the EEOL over the past 30 years, there has been little increase in the rate of regular employment of women for all age cohorts and no significant increase in the participation of married women with young children (Abe 2013), while the proportion of older women in non-regular categories of work has increased. This indicates that the ideological and structural framework within which female employment operates has not significantly changed since the 1960s, and the opportunity to combine family and career remains limited. In direct relation, Japanese men therefore have little choice but to opt to be the main breadwinner and pursue continuous employment, particularly in the years when family formation takes place. Crucial to this perpetuation of a gendered rigidity of lifecycle employment and opportunity for men and women is the role played by workplace practices.

(iii) Gendering in the workplace

As detailed in Assmann's chapter in this volume, there are persistent barriers impeding the progress of gender equality: spousal taxation, access to childcare, and the limitations of legislation. Alongside these, the impediments to deconstructing gender segregation in employment are to a large extent due to corporate practices. The Japanese-style career path model developed in large organisations throughout the postwar period relies on an internal labour market with key criteria including graduate recruitment, long-term in-house training, continuous years of service, job rotation and relocation, and a commitment to long working hours. Allocation of projects and promotion decisions are based on these criteria and in most cases restricted to regular employees. With traditional gender norms dictating that women are still expected to take on the greater share of household responsibilities, this makes it difficult for women to compete with men and meet the criteria required for a career path. And because a significant proportion resign upon childbirth, the linear career model that starts at graduate recruitment even limits career opportunities for experienced women who return to work, particularly if they change their company of employment. The internationally low proportion of female managers in Japanese companies reflects the barriers to gender equality intrinsic within the Japanese-style career model, with women facing institutionalized prejudice in the workplace (Aronsson 2015). As women opt out, their prospects are hampered, and their employers' view of their long-term "unreliability" is confirmed and the cycle of segregation reinforced (Nemoto 2016). This also places added pressure on men to pursue permanent jobs and work long hours, thereby reinforcing core criteria and behaviour at the heart of workplace culture. Here I discuss several such corporate practices and cultures: segregated career tracks, performance and promotion, motivation, long working hours, and the correlation of work with masculinity.

Under the pressures of a declining population and emerging labour shortage, Japanese companies now actively compete to recruit from a highly educated female labour pool. Increasing numbers of women are recruited at entry level and in theory are able to compete with male counterparts for career opportunities. However, the gendered characteristics of corporate practice that were embedded during the 1960s continue to shape employment for both sexes. Women accounted for only 11.6 percent of recruits into the main career track in medium and large organisations in 2012, while 65.1 percent of women employed ten years previously had already quit, and in 48.9 percent of companies, all of the female main career track employees hired ten years previously had quit (GEB 2013). Tracking creates indirect discrimination, and the current legislation is not strong enough to prevent its use. Even in companies that do not have formal career tracks, there are far higher levels of men compared to women in their permanent headcount, and they simultaneously hire a large pool of educated women as temporary workers (Nemoto 2016). Such practices have a negative impact on the efficient allocation of human capital in the Japanese economy. Nakano (2014) notes that highly educated women are channelled within a "gender order in the workplace" (*shokuba no jendā chitsujo*) that fails to motivate them, leading to high levels of dissatisfaction, with only a minority who can accept the gender order remaining in continuous employment.

Performance and promotion criteria also create and reproduce gender distinctions through everyday practices (Shire 2000). Spatial positioning of men and women's workspaces reflect male status, distinctly gendered criteria are used for performance evaluations, highly skilled assignments are allocated to men before women, and normative messages are signalled to women that they are expected to resign upon marriage. Men are evaluated on criteria including decision-making and analytical skills, while women are evaluated on temperament, grooming, and manners (Shire 2000). Women have to work arguably harder than men to prove their worth and are judged on a longer time frame within an unconscious bias of a "wait and see" employer mindset (Yamaguchi 2016; Komagawa 2016). The outcome is women resigning, opting for non-career jobs to accommodate caring responsibilities, or even side-lining themselves from promotion opportunities. The result is a lack of visible female role models who have continuously made their way up to senior positions, ensuring the career pipeline appears unattainable in the eyes of younger female cohorts. This absence of female business leaders further reinforces top-down gender biases and decision-making by male leaders (Nemoto 2016).

The Japanese workplace can be a demotivating environment in which to juggle full-time work and parenthood. The focus on continuous service as a determinant of career opportunity makes it difficult for either sex to fit back into a demanding working culture after taking parental leave. The continued employment rate of women upon or before their first childbirth remains persistently low at 38 percent, while only 2.6 percent of men in private companies take their childcare leave entitlement (GEB 2016). Expectations of long working hours, loyalty, and commitment in Japanese companies are well known. Everyday requests are made to work overtime at short notice, as well as intermittent rotations of roles, transfers, and relocations (Sato and Imai 2011). This uncertainty in terms of time and location makes it difficult for men to contribute to domestic labour, meaning women have to take on the majority of the burden, thereby limiting their ability to compete with men in the workplace. Government policy is not yet alleviating long work hours, and there is insufficient capacity of early childcare places (Abe 2011; Lee and Lee 2014; Kawabata 2014). There is also a shortage of childcare workers, with the government only nominally raising wage levels in the sector and reluctant to meet the shortfall of care workers via immigration (Song 2015). This points to a clear lack of policy seeking to marketise the unpaid care labour done by Japanese women.

The expectation of long work hours for regular male workers overrides the implementation of gender equality policy and tends to ignore the issue of the gendering of unpaid domestic labour. To achieve gender equality, men need to be the target of equality opportunities, too, and so far there have been limited attempts to rebalance male employment. One example is the government's promotion of the *ikumen* (men who do childcare) project since 2010, which has had mixed reception (Mizukoshi et al. 2016). Japanese fathers continue to rank lowest amongst OECD nations in time spent on unpaid childcare and housework (JILPT 2016). However, to simply criticise Japanese men for not doing more neglects an analysis of the relationship between employment and domestic labour. Time-use data of women and men in the 30s and 40s age cohorts (the key reproductive years when family formation and childcare take place) provide an explanation as to why policy is not contributing to gender equality outcomes. In 2015, average hours of work per day for job-holders was 9.3 hours for men in their 30s and 9.22 hours for men in their 40s. For women, it was 6.14 hours for those in their 30s and 6.33 hours for those in their 40s. In addition, 33 percent of all male job-holders worked 10+ hours per day, and 19 percent of men in their 30s and 40s worked 60+ hours per week (NHK 2015; GEB 2015). If we compare this with data on domestic labour, men spend on average 54 minutes per weekday on domestic labour compared to women, who spend 4.18 hours per day (NHK 2015). This points to a clear gender divide. The culture of long working hours for men is not changing, and the average working hours for men in their 30s and 40s have actually increased since 1995, when it stood at 9.0 and 8.36 hours, respectively (NHK 2015). The average working hours for women have slightly increased since 1995 as well, but the gender gap remains. Although the labour force participation rate of women has risen, there is no significant change in the sharing of domestic work by married couples (Tsutsui 2016). The tension is clear. Asking men to do more at home if they are employed in the long-hours culture of regular employment is impossible. Asking women to work more in that workplace culture if they shoulder the burden of care is equally impossible. Even as the proportion of families with dual income couples increases in Japan, both workplace and household behaviours continue to be oriented toward preserving traditional notions of gender roles and perpetuating significant inequalities in domestic labour.

The persistence of a gendered ideology framing employment structures, and the continued reinforcement of workplace practices, criteria, and behaviours described in this chapter, contribute to the coupling of Japanese masculinity with work. Much of the literature on gender and employment has focused on slow progress and conditions for women (Kimoto 2005; Nemoto 2016; Aronsson 2015; Dalton 2017). Far less attention has been paid to men, masculinity, and employment, and the image, ideal, and challenges of the stereotype of the postwar salaryman model of masculinity remain pervasive (Roberson and Suzuki 2003; Hidaka 2010; Dasgupta 2013). The image of the salaryman is one of an over-worked corporate employee, taxpayer for the nation, and absent father. Even in the more recent literature on male precarity and in cases where men opt out of regular employment, Cook (2016) notes that men continue to refer to the salaryman as a dominant symbol of what it is to be a normative adult man in society. Despite economic stagnation since the 1990s and generational shifts in attitudes toward work, gaining regular employment is still a status that a majority of men try to achieve once they graduate (Dasgupta 2013), and the category of regular employee in Japanese corporations is still strongly connected to social status, income levels, and career opportunity (Chiang and Ohtake 2014). These pressures on masculinity reinforce the segregation of men into regular employment. The gendering of the workplace for both women and men therefore takes place both consciously (recruitment, tracking, career development, reward, promotion) as well as unconsciously (task allocation, motivation, communication, commitment, loyalty) and aggregates to create a situation where both sexes are constrained by norms governing work and family life.

Conclusion

The current Japanese workplace environment seems to be making progress toward equality but still makes it difficult for women to engage in and men to opt out of continuous employment within a persistently male-focused model. Such difficulties lead to women themselves reinforcing the expectation of the male breadwinner. With little change to internal corporate career structures, gender equality targets merely encourage women to slot into a male-focused employment model. Women are finding this demotivating and opting out or, at best, refusing to work in the way that men are expected to do. At the same time, the system offers little choice for Japanese men, and there has been little significant change in the expectations placed on men to gain regular employment and commit to certain workplace practices. Japan's gender dividend of segregation is therefore still in operation, and corporate Japan is a key player in perpetuating that gendered status quo. Nevertheless, the norms of gender inequality for women offset opportunity compared to men. Although men may not have freedom to opt in and out of the workplace as women can, this means they still find better jobs than women, who are an increasingly high proportion of low-paid non-regular workers. Demographic trends will continue to pressure the system for change. However, the postwar model of segregation will remain resilient in Japan so long as gendered norms and ideologies governing workplace practice and behaviour remain.

Related Chapters

5 Masculinity Studies in Japan
10 Family, Inequality, and the Work-Family Balance in Contemporary Japan
15 Gender and the Law: Progress and Remaining Problems

References

Abe, Y. (2011) "Family Labor Supply, Commuting Time, and Residential Decisions: The Case of the Tokyo Metropolitan Area," *Journal of Housing Economics* 20 (1) 49–63.
Abe, Y. (2013) "Long-Term Impacts of the Equal Employment Opportunity Act in Japan," *Japan Labor Review* 10 (2) 20–34.
Annual Report on the Labor Force Survey (2016) www.stat.go.jp/english/data/roudou/report/2016/index.html.
Aronsson, A. (2015) *Career Women in Contemporary Japan: Pursuing Identities, Fashioning Lives*, New York: Routledge.
Assmann, S. (2014) "Gender Equality in Japan: The Equal Employment Opportunity Law Revisited," *The Asia-Pacific Journal* 12 (45) 2.
Brinton, M. C. (1993) *Women and the Economic Miracle: Gender and Work in Postwar Japan*, Berkeley, CA: University of California Press.

Brinton, M. C. (2015) " Japanese Low Fertility and the Low Labor Force Participation of Married Women: The Role of Rigid Labor Markets and Workplace Norms." *Research Institute of Economy, Trade, and Industry (Japan)* October.

Broadbent, K. (2003) *Women's Employment in Japan: The Experience of Part-Time Workers*, London: RoutledgeCurzon.

Chiang, H. and Ohtake, F. (2014) "Performance-Pay and the Gender Wage Gap in Japan," *Journal of the Japanese and International Economies* 34 71–88.

Clark, R. (1979) *The Japanese Company*, New Haven, CT: Yale University Press.

Cook, E. (2016) *Reconstructing Adult Masculinity: Part-Time Work in Contemporary Japan*, Abingdon, Oxon and New York: Routledge.

Dalton, E. (2017) "Womenomics, 'Equality' and Abe's Neo-Liberal Strategy to Make Japanese Women Shine," *Social Science Japan Journal* 20 (1) 95–105.

Dasgupta, R. (2013) *Re-Reading the Salaryman in Japan*, Abingdon, Oxon: Routledge.

Frühstück, S. and Walthall, A. (2011) *Recreating Japanese Men*, Berkeley: University of California Press.

Gender Equality Bureau (2011; 2013; 2015; 2016) "Women and Men in Japan", http://www.gender.go.jp/english_contents/pr_act/pub/pamphlet/women-and-men.html.

Gottfried, H. (2014) "Precarious Work in Japan: Old Forms, New Risks?" *Journal of Contemporary Asia* 44 (3) 464–478.

Hamaaki, J., Hori, M., Maeda, S. and Murata, K. (2012) "Changes in the Japanese Employment System in the Two Lost Decades," *ILR Review* 65 (4) 810–846.

Hidaka, T. (2010) *Salaryman Masculinity: The Continuity of and Change in the Hegemonic Masculinity in Japan*, Leiden and Boston: Brill.

Holzhausen, A. (2000) "Japanese Employment Practices in Transition: Promotion Policy and Compensation Systems in the 1990s," *Social Science Japan Journal* 3 (2) 221–235.

JILPT (2016) *Labor Situation in Japan and Its Analysis*, Tokyo: The Japan Institute for Labour Policy and Training.

Kamiya, M. (1995) "A Decade of the Equal Employment Opportunity Act in Japan: Has It Changed Society?" *Law in Japan: An Annual* 25 40–83.

Kawabata, M. (2014) "Childcare Access and Employment: The Case of Women with Preschool-Aged Children in Tokyo," *Review of Urban and Regional Development Studies* 26 (1) 40–56.

Kawaguchi, D. and Ueno, Y. (2013) "Declining Long-Term Employment in Japan," *Journal of the Japanese and International Economies* 28 19–36.

Kimoto, K. (2005) *Gender and Japanese Management*, Melbourne: Trans Pacific Press.

Komagawa, T. (2016) "Gender-Based Job Segregation and the Gender Gap in Career Formation: Focusing on Bank Clerical Staff since the Postwar Years," *Japan Labor Review* 13 (3) 58–79.

Lee, G. H. Y. and Lee, S. P. (2014) "Childcare Availability, Fertility and Female Labor Force Participation in Japan," *Journal of the Japanese and International Economies* 32 71–85.

Lewis, J. (2001) "The Decline of the Male Breadwinner Model: The Implications for Work and Care," *Social Politics* 8 (2) 152–170.

Macnaughtan, H. (2005) *Women, Work and the Japanese Economic Miracle: The Case of the Cotton Textile Industry, 1945–1975*, London: Routledge Curzon.

Macnaughtan, H. (2006) "From 'Postwar' to 'Post-Bubble': Contemporary Issues for Japanese Working Women," in P. Matanle and W. Lunsing (eds) *Perspectives on Work, Employment and Society in Japan*, Basingstoke: Palgrave Macmillan, 31–57.

Macnaughtan, H. (2015) "Womenomics for Japan: Is the Abe Policy for Gendered Employment Viable in an Era of Precarity?" *The Asia-Pacific Journal: Japan Focus* 13 (12).

Mizukoshi, K., Kohlbacher, F. and Schimkowsky, C. (2016) "Japan's Ikumen Discourse: Macro and Micro Perspectives on Modern Fatherhood," *Japan Forum* 28 (2) 212–232.

Nakano, M. (2014) *'Ikukyū Sedai' no Jirenma Josei Katsuyō wa Naze Shippai Suru no Ka?* (Why Is the Utilisation of Women Dilemma Failing in the 'Childcare Generation'?) Tokyo: Kobunsha Shinsho.

Nemoto, K. (2016) *Too Few Women at the Top: The Persistence of Inequality in Japan*, Ithaca, NY: Cornell University Press.

NHK (2015) "Hōsō Kenkyū to Chōsa" (Broadcasting Research and Survey).

OECD (2014) "Enhancing Women's Economic Empowerment Through Entrepreneurship and Business Leadership in OECD Countries." www.oecd.org/gender/Enhancing%20Women%20Economic%20Empowerment_Fin_1_Oct_2014.pdf.

Osawa, M. (2000) "Government Approaches to Gender Equality in the Mid-1990s," *Social Science Japan Journal* 3 (1) 3–19.

Osawa, M. (2002) "Twelve Million Full-Time Housewives: The Gender Consequences of Japan's Postwar Social Contract," in O. Zunz, L. Schoppa and N. Hiwatari (eds) *Social Contract Under Stress: the Middles Classes of America, Europe and Japan at the Turn of the Century*, New York: Russell Sage Foundation, 255–278.

Pascall, G. (2010) "Male Breadwinner Model," in *International Encyclopedia of Social Policy*, London and New York: Routledge.

Roberson, J. E. and Suzuki, N. (2003) *Men and Masculinities in Contemporary Japan: Dislocating the Salaryman Doxa*, London: RoutledgeCurzon.

Rohlen, T. P. (1974) *For Harmony and Strength: Japanese White-Collar Organization in Anthropological Perspective*, Berkeley, CA: University of California Press.

Saito, O. (2014) "Historical Origins of the Male Breadwinner Households Model: Britain, Sweden and Japan," *Japan Labor Review* 11 (4) 5–20.

Sako, M. and Sato, H. (1997) *Japanese Labour and Management in Transition*, London and New York: Routledge: LSE.

Sato, Y. and Imai, J. (2011) *Japan's New Inequality: Intersection of Employment Reforms and Welfare Arrangements*, Tohoku: Tohoku University: Center for the Study of Social Stratification and Inequality.

Shinkawa, T. (2012) "Substitutes for Immigrants? Social Policy Responses to Population Decreases in Japan," *American Behavioural Scientist* 56 (8) 1123–1138.

Shire, K. (2000) "Gendered Organization and Workplace Culture in Japanese Customer Services," *Social Science Japan Journal* 3 (1) 37–58.

Song, J. (2015) "Labour Markets, Care Regimes and Foreign Care Worker Policies in East Asia," *Social Policy and Administration* 49 (3) 376–393.

Tsutsui, J. (2016) "Female Labor Participation and the Sexual Division of Labor: A Consideration on the Persistent Male-Breadwinner Model," *Japan Labor Review* 13 (3) 80–100.

Vogel, E. (1963) *Japan's New Middle Class: The Salary Man and His Family in a Tokyo Suburb*, Berkeley: University of California Press.

Watanabe, T. (2003) "Recent Trends in Japanese Human Resource Management: The Introduction of a System of Individual and Independent Career Choice," *Asian Business and Management* 2 111–141.

World Economic Forum (WEF) (2017) "The Global Gender Gap Report 2018." www.weforum.org/reports/the-global-gender-gap-report-2017.

Yamada, S. (2013) "Equal Employment Opportunity Act, Having Passed the Quarter-Century Milestone," *Japan Labor Review* 10 (2) 6–19.

Yamaguchi, K. (2016) "Determinants of the Gender Gap in the Proportion of Managers Among White-Collar Regular Workers in Japan," *Japan Labor Review* 13 (3) 7–31.

17
SEX WORK

Toru Takeoka

In the context of Japan, sex work can be defined as a continuum of work satisfying sexual orientation or curiosity, around which it is hard to set a clear boundary. While we can acknowledge that work such as prostitution is sex work, Japan contains a much wider array of sex-related work that does not always fall under the same legal and social regulations and approbation as sex work. Such boundary cases include *kyabakura* (cabaret clubs), which do not include direct sexual services but involve conversation and drinking with staff members, and *seku-kyaba* (sexy *kyabakura*), in which customers can touch the worker's body, though there is no sexual service provision, based on the *kyabakura* style of interaction. While both *kyabakura* and *seku-kyaba* are objects of laws regulating the sex industry, nonregulated forms of business are continuously emerging. This is also the case with pornographic materials. This chapter provides a short history of attitudes to sex work in Japan before turning to a mapping of the contemporary sex work landscape and issues facing sex workers and communities associated with sex work.

Historical perspectives: from Edo to contemporary Japan

Japan accommodated formal and informal institutions of the sex industry in the Edo period (1603–1868), which were accepted by both Japan's feudal government and the people. In Edo (present-day Tokyo), these were spatially organised around the legal Yoshiwara district and illegal red-light districts known as *okabasho*; similar systems of legal and illegal but tolerated sex work existed in other cities. Yoshiwara district entertainers known as geisha were regarded as engaging in ambiguous work, which included both the performing of dance and music and prostitution (Ishii 1967). This ambiguity dates back to the medieval role of the *yūjo* (prostitute, lit. "play woman"). The term *yūjo* was used throughout the Edo period, but it is not known whether these workers were accepted or stigmatised during that era, partly because of the scarcity of historical sources (for a recent contribution, see Tsuji 2017).

Scholarship on the Yoshiwara and *yūjo* has tended to romanticise cultural aspects of the industry, such as the subtle communication techniques of workers, the "courtesy" of the customers, and the sophisticated protocol between them (such as "geisha did not eat or drink at all with customers she did not know") (Nishiyama 1985; Ishii 1967). From the 1990s, however, research on urban history began to flourish in Japan, and the spatial and social structures of sex work became an object of study from the perspective of researchers of urban Edo.

Just after the Edo feudal government was formed (1603), the Yoshiwara red-light district was established with the official blessing of the Tokugawa Shogunate. Permission for the business of the Yoshiwara was exclusive, and other businesses without permission were unofficial—that is, illegal. The governance system of the Yoshiwara was fully incorporated into the urban administrative organisation of Edo, including the management of *yūjo*. Unregistered sex workers were restricted to the *okabasho*.

During the Edo period, there was a hierarchy among sex workers from street prostitutes to courtesans (*tayū*), a term derived from *noh* theatrical performance. Those working at the upper levels of the hierarchy of sex workers also played music, sang, and danced, and they are said to have had a certain degree of autonomy from the obligation to provide sexual services (Ishii 1967). Yet these aspects should not be overly romanticised. The cultural sides of sex work in Tokugawa Japan were limited to a higher social stratum and earlier era. Upper-class workers had the option not to provide sexual services even if customers paid for these services, while lower-class workers had no such option. It is also noteworthy that regardless of the worker's class, the sex industry was the central objective of human trafficking, although this often took the form of a sales contract wherein a daughter worked for ten years in return for her poor parents receiving considerable amounts of money (Nishiyama 1963; Ishii 1967). Male prostitutes called *kagema*, whose major customers were men, were also well known at that time (Leupp 1997; Pflugfelder 2007).

The official blessing given by the Shogunate was also part of a policing and security enforcement plan, as criminals often fled to the Yoshiwara (Yoshida 2006). The monopoly of sex work by Yoshiwara brothel owners also served the Tokugawa's interest in terms of generating stable tax revenues and assisting in the control of public morality. Actual law enforcement against unregistered prostitutes outside the Yoshiwara was undertaken by private citizens, and arrested sex workers were turned in to the Yoshiwara for three years of indentured servitude (Tsukada 1992). The Yoshiwara and the *okabasho* sex workers were therefore not unconnected. There were networks among *okabasho* and between the *okabasho* and the Yoshiwara. Some unregistered prostitutes moved up the career ladder to become registered *yūjo* in the Yoshiwara, at the very centre of the Shogunate's organised order of sex work.

With the dawn of the Meiji Period (1868), sex work in Japan entered a new stage of prohibition. At first in 1872, forced prostitution was prohibited. The sex industry throughout the Edo period had been based on human trafficking, and through some revisions to the law, the Meiji government began to see sex work as based on voluntary will, though in practice this did not get rid of the practice of indenture. Thereto this concept was ambivalent. Although it freed trafficked women from forced sex work, at the same time it generated accusations of loose morals against workers because they were seen as voluntarily engaging in sex work (Fujime 2011).

The Meiji period also saw significant changes to familial relationships, which impacted understandings of sex work. Upper-class men's marriages especially were arranged through and based on the *ie* institution, in which three generations lived together in a rigid family hierarchy with strict inheritance policies. "Modern" Japanese men saw arranged marriage as an old-fashioned conservative ritual and looked for "true love" in affairs with geisha (Izumi 1895; Koyano 2007), as in the Edo period *geisha* were the object of romantic love. Geisha, at that time at least, were not directly associated with sexual services, even if customers may have expected such. In contrast with the coercive nature of arranged marriage, romantic love affairs with geisha by "mutual agreement" were sought by "modern" men, including famous novelists. They believed that "true love" could not be found in marriage but should be pursued in love affairs outside the marriage. So the Japanese sex industry accommodated a complex gradation of performances of romantic love and sexual services. In this era, a Westernised style of clubs called "cafés" also emerged throughout Japan, providing sexual services, even though they were seen as different from places explicitly devoted to sexual service (Fujino 2001; Koyano 2007).

During the period between the outbreak of the Sino-Japanese war (1931) and the end of World War II (1945), it is well known that there were "military comfort women" (*jūgun ianfu*) in the territories under Japan's control. Comfort women—or victims of Japan's system of enforced sexual slavery—consisted of captive Japanese women and colonised peoples. Prior to the war, a number of Japanese women called *karayuki-san* had travelled abroad to engage in sex work and sometimes found themselves cheated by their employers or forced unexpectedly into certain kinds of work. Japan, as a developing country with a poor population, was at that time a source of women for trafficking, not the destination country it became after the war. Destinations for these Japanese women ranged from Shanghai and Singapore to the United States, Canada, Australia, and even Africa (Koyano 2007). Japan's expansive prewar history of exploitation of women for sex was not unrelated to the emergence of the "comfort system."

The assumption of male entitlement to sex also continued after the end of the Second World War. With the collapse of the imperial system and the influx of Allied Occupation forces, the Japanese government gave instructions to establish comfort women facilities called the Recreation and Amusement Association (RAA). The RAA was declared off limits to the Allied occupation within a year, partly because of epidemics of sexually transmitted diseases (Fujino 2001). However, after this officially sanctioned prostitution system closed, a number of sex workers previously employed at the RAA continued to engage in sex work both for non-Japanese and Japanese customers, even though the Supreme Commander for the Allied Powers (SCAP) set new orders abolishing forced prostitution in 1946 (Kramm 2017). Millions of soldiers had died, and widows and their children were suffering from poverty under foreign occupation after unconditional surrender in the devastated land after air raids. That is why a variety of women became sex workers at that time (Kovner 2012). Sex industry around US bases is omnipresent around the world and Okinawa has been no exception. Since the occupation by the US in 1945 until today, Okinawa has suffered a disproportionate volume of US forces settlement and therefore militarised sex work and violence (Mackie and Tanji 2015).

Even after SCAP's order, prostitution continued not to be criminalised until 1958, insofar as it was regarded as voluntary. The Prostitution Prevention Act was passed in 1956, partly enacted in 1957, and fully enacted in 1958, in response to a perceived "boom" in prostitution in the early 1950s (Fujime 2011). Japan had, for the first time in its history, fully prohibited prostitution. The contemporary history of sex work in Japan started in 1958, as legal restrictions drove changes in the organisation of the industry and led to the variety of different forms it takes today.

The framework of The Prostitution Prevention Act is still valid. Concerning the characteristics of the Act, the following points are noteworthy. First, sex workers and customers themselves are exempt from criminal punishment. The major objects of punishment are organisers of prostitution, or "pimps." Second, only organised prostitution, which takes unspecified customers for profit, is prohibited (Article 2 and 12). Therefore, a contract with a specified person identified as a "lover," even if a sexual affair is included, is not illegal from the viewpoint of the Act.

Third, and this is the most important point from the perspective of analysing the contemporary sex-work scene in Japan, the definition of an act of prostitution is limited to penetrative genital sexual intercourse, that is, penis-in-vagina sex. Other sexual acts, such as masturbation, oral sex, or anal sex, are clearly not criminalised under certain conditions, even if those acts are provided for profit. This distinctive character of prohibition has resulted in the development of varied forms of clubs and establishments within the sex industry in Japan.

According to published statistics by the National Police Agency, there were 64,600 entertaining clubs and 31,900 sexual-service clubs in 2016 in Japan, if only licensed or registered clubs are counted (Keishichō Seikatsu Anzen kyoku Hoan ka 2017). The number of sex workers, however, is inconsistent in official statistics and can be estimated at hundreds of thousands throughout Japan. Statistics about sex work are undeveloped in general (Takeoka 2017).

It is worth noting as the most recent trend that new technologies and social media have transformed the sex industry. The transformation can be summarised as the move from service provision at premises to call-girl style backed up by the Internet and mobile devices. The call-girl-style industry puts women in vulnerable workplaces such as a hotel room or client's home (Aoyama 2015). According to the public statistics given previously, the majority of the sex industry in Japan is call-girl style nowadays instead of premises-style as in the past.

Features of sex work in Japan

Sex work in contemporary Japan can be discussed in the context of three different features: indoor/outdoor, individual/collective, and sexual service/entertainment service. As Ronald Weitzer points out in his review of sex work, sex-work studies in general have a strong tendency towards focusing on outdoor (i.e. street) prostitution undertaken by individuals (2009). With the exception of a few decades after the end of WWII and the particular prominence of the "pan-pan" girl (a stigmatising term which indicates a street prostitute whose major customers were officers and soldiers of SCAP. See also Kovner (2012) in Occupation-era Japan), outdoor sex work is less common in Japan. There have been various kinds of sex work, but almost all of them have been undertaken inside buildings.

Of course, not all aspects of this work are indoors. For example, soliciting is typically conducted outdoors through touts who call in passers-by. Touts in Japan work on a kind of economic contract that is not necessarily in written form. Most commonly, touts do not recruit women for sex work, and there is a division of labour between touts and recruiters (Takeoka 2017). Touts work outdoors not for individual sex workers but for clubs.

Clubs have considerable importance in sex work in Japan. Almost all sex workers work in some sort of club, ranging from hostess clubs (see subsequently) to *de facto* brothels. The individual relationships between sex workers and pimps common in many countries are replaced by the collective relationships between clubs and touts or recruiters. Both touts and recruiters are paid by the clubs; however, touts do not have contact with individual sex workers. Recruiters (almost all men) will enlist a woman on the street for sex work (usually offering work in a hostess club initially) and introduce her to a club; the club then pays the recruiter as well as the new worker. The recruiter keeps in touch with the worker even after the introduction is complete and keeps trying to introduce her to clubs that are more profitable for him—that is, clubs with sexual services. Because of the severe social stigma attached, women are reluctant to engage in sexual services, and that sort of club continuously complains about worker shortages despite relatively high pay compared with the general labour market (Takeoka 2017). This is where the need for recruiters arises.

At clubs providing entertainment services, the actual working space is also collective. Of course, this is not the case with clubs providing sexual services. Sexual services are provided in individual rooms, but entertainment services typically take place in a large undivided room with tables and chairs. What is noteworthy here is that the collectiveness of the actual working scene can often be the basis for cohesion amongst workers. In the 2000s, for example, hostesses organised a union called *kyabakura-union* (Asahi Shinbun 2009, 37). Sexual-service workers, however, not infrequently prefer an individual working style to a collective one, which helps avoid peer pressure, group politics, or restrictions on freedom (Takeoka 2017). In contrast with the individualism of sexual-service workers, workers in entertainment services have created an information exchange about actual working conditions and the atmosphere of clubs they have worked in. Occasionally, they even move from one club to another on a colleague's recommendation or invitation.

For the services provided in sex work, a central distinction can be drawn between sexual services and entertainment services. Sexual services can be defined as a service in which sexual pleasure is provided through physical contact and usually ends in ejaculation on the male customer's part. Entertainment services are far more difficult to define than sexual services. According to the Act Regulating the Gambling and Sex Industry, which was reformed in 1984, any communication between staff and a customer beyond casual greetings can be regarded as entertainment. Clubs providing entertainment services must acquire business permission; in one case, a relatively moderate club with a license only for serving alcohol, in which a hostess had talked with customers, was accused of being an unlicensed business for providing entertainment (Matsuzawa 2012).

The most typical entertainment services are *kyabakura* clubs, though the demarcation is ambiguous. In *kyabakura*, mainly male customers pay considerable fees to drink with hostesses. There is little physical contact between client and worker. A hostess is chosen by the customer, and then has to take a seat beside them at least for a while. Popular hostesses can be requested by many customers at the same time; in this case, their entertainment time—that is, time spent talking with a customer at a neighbouring seat—becomes shorter.

The male counterpart of the *kyabakura* is the host club, in which male hosts provide entertainment services mainly for female customers (Takeyama 2016). Host clubs acquired a high profile in the 1990s through popular culture. In contrast to the relatively settled mood of *kyabakura*, the host club can be characterised by its conviviality, represented by the ritual of taking a long drink from a champagne bottle, or a "champagne tower," a tower built up of cocktail glasses filled with champagne. If a customer orders a champagne bottle, various hosts approach her table and drink the bottle quickly. This costs hundreds of thousands of yen, while the "champagne tower" costs millions of yen. Both *kyabakura* and host clubs sell pseudo-romantic love in a somewhat convivial and gregarious atmosphere. Therefore, this type of entertainment club is not unrelated to sexual affairs. For example, the colloquial term *makura-eigyo* (pillow sales) is widely known as a tactic whereby female and male workers are engaged by customers in exchange for sexual intimacy, usually at arm's length from the club.

For clubs engaging in sexual services, the relationship between services and law becomes a conundrum. By and large, the Japanese sex industry is quite law abiding. Workers avoid penetrative genital intercourse and provide other kinds of services leading to ejaculation. However, it is an open secret that in a certain type of club known as a "soap land," workers engage in penetrative genital intercourse as a standard service.

While soap land clubs are broadly recognised as violating the Prostitution Prevention Act, other and varied forms of sexual-service clubs avoid penetrative genital intercourse and customers accept alternative services. For example, an *ime-kura* (short for "image club," meaning fantasy club) recreates various kinds of mock situations such as a train, classroom, or hospital as the locale of the services; this can stimulate a customer's sexual fantasy. *Onakura* ("onanism" masturbation club) provides a separate room where by looking through a mirror on both sides the worker and customer can masturbate together, while *deriheru* (delivery health) arranges for workers to visit a customer's residence or hotel room. These various forms of sexual services have existed since just after the enactment of the Prostitution Prevention Act (see Sinclair [2006] for an excellent but rare visual source on the variety of sexual-service clubs). Yet this diversity in the Japanese sex industry is not always easily understood, and has yet to have a comprehensive scholarly explanation.

Critical issues and topics

As Rosen and Venkatesh (2008) point out, there has been a tendency within sex-work studies in general to focus on discussion of whether sex work is an individual right or whether the practice exploits (mainly) women. This is also the case in Japan, especially during and after the boom in discussion of *enjo-kōsai* (compensated dating) (Kinsella 2014). *Enjo-kōsai* became a social problem in the mid-1990s as high school girls engaged in dating adult men for profit, using new technologies such as pocket pagers or cell phones. A number of such encounters may have been simple "dating" (*kōsai*), but the term *enjo-kōsai* was more usually used to suggest sexual affairs. Although similar phenomena have emerged throughout the second half of the twentieth century in Japan, public discourse on *enjo-kōsai* was conducted in tones of amazement, anger, and great curiosity—at times bordering on a moral panic.

Enjo-kōsai can be evaluated from today's perspective as the ultimate in "free will sex work." The connection between sex work and poverty had loosened throughout the second half of the century until the dawn of *enjo-kōsai*. Girls involved in *enjo-kōsai* pursued the practice not because of absolute monetary necessity but for fun, to experience relationships with others, because of peer pressure, and as part of a consumption culture that involved luxurious designer goods, which some have argued is based on anomie (Miyadai 2006).

The case of minors engaging in sex work has been a crucial problem in debates over sex work. Even after popular concern about the *enjo-kōsai* phenomenon burned out, a series of services collectively called "JK business" emerged around 2010. "JK" is an abbreviation of *joshi-kōsei* (high-school girl). JK business includes "JK massage," "JK photo sessions," "JK walking" (taking a walk with a high-school girl), and so on. Each service is characterised by a setting that allows customers to be alone with a high school girl, which of course may lead to sexual affairs. It has been hard to regulate these businesses or their participants using existing law, even though some local governments enacted a variety of restrictive codes from 2015.

Japan is also thought to have a huge market in pornography (Yano Keizai Kenkyujo 2016); however, reliable estimations of its size are not available, partly because of the vague definitions of pornographic imagery. On the train, one can see advertisements for magazines with photos of swim-suited young women every day. Models employed by this kind of magazine often include young teens. It is not illegal in Japan to employ minors as swimsuit models unless the images are excessively revealing.

It is hard to define "pornography," however, especially in the context of Japan in which non-government-based bodies and review panels "self-regulate" their media content by themselves. Here, however, it would suffice to explain it as materials to stimulate sexual desire, often with representation of sexual acts, used in masturbation (for more detailed argument, see Hambleton in this volume and McLelland [2015]).

Hardcore pornography (known as "adult video" or *AV* in Japanese when it takes the form of moving images) includes sexual intercourse or similar acts. AV is far more rigorous in terms of refusing to employ minors than soft pornography. However, while recruitment to soft pornography usually has ties to entertainment agencies involved with TV or some formal sector of the entertainment industry, recruitment to hardcore pornography is undertaken by recruiters associated with the sex industry clubs (Fujii 2008).

The protection of human rights is fairly underdeveloped in the pornography industry and in the sex industry as a whole in Japan. In 2016, the problem of women being coerced into pornography was presented as a human rights issue and broadly recognised as a social problem (Asahi Shinbun 2016, 37). Globally, Japan has also been one of the most notorious destinations of human trafficking related to sex work and is well known as a source and transit country. As noted previously, street prostitution is fairly rare in Japan, but the exceptions include workers from overseas who may have been trafficked. Their workplaces range from entertainment clubs and massage parlours to the street itself. The whole process of sex trafficking is said to have some association with organised crime, *bōryokudan* (crime syndicates) or *yakuza* (gangsters) (Oshima and Francis 1988). Initially, trafficked women were predominantly from Thailand and the Philippines but are starting to have more diverse origins. Some come to Japan often not knowing they are going to engage in sex work, under contracts of servitude that incur debts of millions of yen; however, others strategically come to Japan with a certain degree of agency (Parreñas 2011; Aoyama 2009; Pendleton 2015), all of which make understanding of and advocacy for migrant sex work more nuanced and complicated.

Current contributions and research

Academic research on sex work remains underdeveloped in Japan. One exception is scholarship on "clubs"—sophisticated and highly priced clubs without sexual services—usually located in luxury areas of Tokyo such as Ginza, Akasaka, and Roppongi. Matsuda Saori is a leading researcher on this kind of club, in addition to scholars writing in English, such as Allison and Gagné (Matsuda 2006, 2008; Allison 1994; Gagné 2010, 2016); much of their work focuses on subtle gendered relationships in the service area. Journalistic publications such as that of Fujii (2008) document the economic aspect of sex workers in entertainment services for a more general readership.

On a similar category of club, but in which migrant hostesses work, Parreñas and Aoyama accomplished important ethnography (Parreñas 2011; Aoyama 2009). After the Trafficking in Persons (TIP) Report by the US Department of State first listed Japan as a Tier 2 country in 2001, Parreñas and Aoyama grasped the subtle but critical change in the situation of migrant sex work in Japan. Tier 1 countries are explained in the TIP Report as the countries "whose governments fully meet the Trafficking Victims Protection Act's (TVPA) minimum standards" and Tier 2 countries are those "whose governments do not fully meet the TVPA's minimum standards, but are making significant efforts to bring themselves into compliance with those standards." As the latest update of TIP report 2018 first listed Japan as a Tier 1 country, the Japanese government has achieved some improved regulation on trafficking, which decreased the number of migrant hostesses and changed circumstances surrounding migrant sex work.

The context and customs of the sex-work club can reflect gendered behaviours and gender-related issues in Japanese society at large, as well as having their own logics. Recently published work by Takeyama, based on fieldwork in a host club, is noteworthy as a fairly rare academic source (2016). Takeyama's ethnographic study reveals key aspects of male sex workers' lives, female customers' emotions and purchasing power based on women's recent social advancement, and the social situations that try to draw money from people by stimulating their aspirations, in a continuing economic downturn.

When compared to research on entertainment services, research on sexual services has considerably more space to investigate. In a valuable quantitative study (quite rare in Japan), Kaname and Mizushima (2005) interviewed 126 workers engaged in sexual services. I have dealt recently with the urban structure of Kabuki-chō, the most infamous red-light district in Japan, focusing on both entertainment services and sexual services, as well as the social structure that circumscribes both services and sex-work-related occupations (Takeoka 2017). Another valuable recent study is an ethnography of a call-girl style sado-masochism club by Kumada (2017). Since 2015, journalistic work on low-wage sex workers, who usually are not affiliated with clubs, has been published frequently, although most of it is sensational and the surveys reported are neither systematic nor theoretical (Ogiue 2012; Suzuki 2014). The documentary film *Boys for Sale (2017)* by Ian Thomas Ash is rare and precious material focusing on male prostitution in gay bars, which interviews several workers and questions their approaches to their career in, understanding of, and social relations in the work.

Historical research may recently be the most flourishing domain on sex work. Especially on the après-guerre situation around the 1940s and 1950s, Kovner (2012), Kramm (2017), Fujino (2001), Fujime (2011), and Norma (2008) provide significant perspectives and insights.

Future research directions

Here I would like to present three directions for fruitful research in the future. Each direction is related to narrow definitions of sex work and gender studies. Keeping the intersectionality of gender, sex work, and society in mind means research on sex work will be a promising and productive field that can clarify the structure of Japanese society and envisage better relationships between the individual and society.

First, regarding both entertainment services and sexual services, we are severely lacking in quantitative knowledge. This is a problem of not only accessibility but also theoretical underdevelopment in the field. As long as we are poor at generating contextualised concepts and theoretical frameworks, it is not clear what we should investigate or what we should organise under which categories.

Second, comprehensive understanding including both Japanese workers and foreign workers is scarce. They have tended to be treated separately. Recently, however, the number of foreign visitors to Japan who become involved in the sex industry as customers has been increasing. In the lead-up to the 2020 Tokyo Olympic and Paralympic Games, this trend may change the ethnoscape of sex work in Japan, as well as clubs' acceptance of foreigners.

Third, studies of policing practices in general are underdeveloped in Japan, and in the specific case of sex work this area of research is still awaiting further exploration. To investigate the legal environment of Japanese sex work, it is essential to take into account the fact that clubs are more common than independent individual workers. As described previously, sex work in clubs accounts for a substantial portion of the Japanese sex industry. The fact that clubs provide the majority of venues determines the frameworks for regulating sex work, and vice versa.

Sex work has been one of the most common aspects of popular culture in Japan, featuring in Edo-period cultural materials such as *ukiyo-e* woodblock prints, Kabuki theatre, and *rakugo* performance. Culture, obviously, is gendered, and its constellation involving marriage, family, sexuality, and work also includes sex work. Each of these elements cannot be separately understood. The meaning of marriage at a certain time in history must be grasped by evaluating its positional value in relation to family, sexuality, work, and sex work, for instance. Studies of sex work thereby serve as both a reference point and a starting point for comprehending gender and Japanese culture.

Further Reading

Inoue, S. (1999) *Ai no Kukan* (The Space of Love), Tokyo: Kadokawa Shoten. An inspiring collection of historical investigation into the spatial structure of sexuality.

Kageyama, S. (2008) *Chukai Fueihou* (Commentary on ARAEB), Tokyo: Tokyo Horei Shuppan. The only exhaustive commentary on the Act regulating the sex industry.

Nagai, Y. (2015) *Teihon Fūzoku-Eigyo Torishimari* (Standard Book on the Regulation of the Sex Industry), Tokyo: Kawade Shobo Shinsha. A comprehensive historical work on the regulating framework of the sex industry, covering the whole twentieth and early twenty-first century.

Taniguchi, K. (1997) *Sei o Kau Otoko* (Men Buying Sex), Tokyo: Pandora. A rare document interviewing Japanese clients of prostitutes in various Southeast Asian countries.

Related Chapters

8 Gender and the *Koseki*
16 Gender and the Workplace
35 Gendered Desires: Pornography and Consumption

References

Allison, A. (1994) *Nightwork: Sexuality, Pleasure, and Corporate Masculinity in a Tokyo Hostess Club*, Chicago: The University of Chicago Press.
Aoyama, K. (2009) *Thai Migrant Sex Workers from Modernisation to Globalisation*, London: Palgrave Macmillan.
Aoyama, K. (2015) "The Sex Industry in Japan: The Danger of Invisibility," in M. McLelland and V. Mackie (eds) *Routledge Handbook of Sexuality Studies in East Asia*, London and New York: Routledge, 281–293.
Asahi Shinbunsha. (2009) "Kyabakura-yunion kessei" (Kyabakura-Union Organized), *Asahi-Shinbun* 12 December, 37.
Asahi Shinbunsha. (2016) "AV Shutsuen- Kyōyō, Higai-Sōdan 22ken" (Coerced Acting on Porno Movie, 22 Counseling by Victim), *Asahi Shinbun* 16 November, 37.
Ash, I. T. (director) (2017) *Boys for Sale* (Online streaming).
Fujii, Y. (2008) *Kyaba-jo Kyūyo-Meisai no Himitsu* (Secrets of the Pay Statements of Sex Worker Entertainers), Tokyo: Kodansha.
Fujime, Y. (2011) *Sei no Rekishi-gaku* (Historiography of Sex), Tokyo: Fuji Shuppan.
Fujino, Y. (2001) *Sei no Kokka-kanri* (State Management of Sex), Tokyo: Fuji Shuppan.
Gagné, N. O. (2010) "The Business of Leisure, the Leisure of Business: Rethinking Hegemonic Masculinity Through Gendered Service in Tokyo Hostess Clubs," *Asian Anthropology* 9 (1) 29–55.
Gagné, N. O. (2016) "Feeling like a 'Man:' Managing Gender, Sexuality, and Corporate Life in After-Hours Tokyo," in T. Zheng (ed) *Cultural Politics of Gender and Sexuality in Contemporary Asia*, Hawai'i: University of Hawai'i Press.
Ishii, R. (1967) *Yoshiwara*, Tokyo: Chuo Koronsha.
Izumi, K. (1895) "Ai to Kon'in" (Love and Marriage), in *Gendai Nihon Bungaku Taikei 5* (System of Modern Japanese Literature), Tokyo: Chikuma Shobō.
Kaname, Y. and Mizushima, N. (2005) *Fūzoku-jō Ishiki-Chōsa* (Survey of Sex Workers' Attitudes), Tokyo: Potto Shuppan.
Keishichō Seikatsu-Anzen-kyoku Hoan-ka (National Police Agency Community Safety Bureau Safety Division) (2017) "Heisei 28 nen ni okeru Fūzoku-Kankyo no Genjo to Fūzoku Kankei Jihan no Tor-ishimari Jokyo tou nit suite" (On the Regulating Situation of Public Morals and Crimes Related to Public Morals in 2016). www.npa.go.jp/safetylife/hoan/h28_fuzoku_jihan.pdf.
Kinsella, S. (2014) *Schoolgirls, Money and Rebellion in Japan*, Oxon: Routledge.
Kovner, S. (2012) *Occupying Power: Sex Workers and Servicemen in Postwar Japan*, Stanford: Stanford University Press.
Koyano, A. (2007) *Nihon Baishun-shi* (History of Prostitution in Japan), Tokyo: Shincho-sha.
Kramm, R. (2017) *Sanitized Sex: Regulating Prostitution, Venereal Disease, and Intimacy in Occupied Japan, 1945–1952*, Oakland: University of California Press.
Kumada, Y. (2017) *Sei-Fūzoku Sekai o ikiru "Onnanoko" no esunogurafi* (An Ethnography of "Girls" Living in the World of Sex Work), Tokyo: Akashi Shoten.
Leupp, G. P. (1997) *Male Colors: The Construction of Homosexuality in Tokugawa Japan*, Berkley and Los Angeles: University of California Press.
Mackie, V. and Tanji, Y. (2015) "Militarised Sexualities in East Asia," in M. McLelland and V. Mackie (eds) *Routledge Handbook of Sexuality Studies in East Asia*, London and New York: Routledge, 60–73.
Matsuda, S. (2006) "Hosutesu no Idō o Kangaeru" (Considering the Mobility of Hostesses), Gendei Fūzoku Kenkyukai (ed) *Gendai Fūzoku Kenkyukai Nenpo* (Annual Review of Contemporary Manners), Tokyo: Shinjuku Shobo.

Matsuda, S. (2008) "Hosutesu-tachi wa nani o uru?" (What Are Hostesses Selling?), in S. Inoue (ed) *Seiyoku no Bunkashi 2* (Cultural History of Sexual Desire 2), Tokyo: Kodansha.

Matsuzawa, K. (2012) "Gurē Zon ga Nakunaru Shakai" (Society Losing Grey Areas), in R. Isobe (ed) *Odotte-wa Ikenai Kuni Nihon* (Japan, the Country You Cannot Dance in), Tokyo: Kawade Shobo Shinsha.

McLelland, M. (2015) "Sex, Censorship and Media Regulation in Japan: A Historical Overview," in M. McLelland and V. Mackie (eds) *Routledge Handbook of Sexuality Studies in East Asia*, London and New York: Routledge, 402–413.

Miyadai, S. (2006) *Seifuku-Shojo-tachi no Sentaku* (Choices Girls in Uniform Made), Tokyo: Asahi Shinbunsha.

Nishiyama, M. (1963) *Kuruwa* (Red Light District), Tokyo: Shibundo.

Nishiyama, M. (1985) *Kinsei Fūzoku to Shakai* (Early Modern Manners and Society), Tokyo: Yoshikawa Kobunkan.

Norma, C. (2008) "A Past Re-Imagined for the Geisha: Saviour of the 1950s Japanese Sex Industry," *Traffic* 10 37–56.

Ogiue, C. (2012) *Kanojo tachi no warikiri* (Prostitution of Them), Tokyo: Fusosha.

Oshima, S. and Francis, C. (1988) *HELP kara mita Nihon* (Japan Viewed from HELP), Tokyo: Asahi Shinbunsha.

Parreñas, R. C. (2011) *Illicit Flirtations: Labor, Migration, and Sex Trafficking in Tokyo*, Stanford: Stanford University Press.

Pendleton, M. (2015) "Transnational Sexual Politics in East Asia," in M. McLelland and V. Mackie (eds) *Routledge Handbook of Sexuality Studies in East Asia*, Oxon: Routledge, 21–34.

Pflugfelder, G. M. (2007) *Cartographies of Desire: Male-Male Sexuality in Japanese Discourse*, Berkeley and Los Angeles: University of California Press.

Rosen, E. and Venkatesh, S. A. (2008) "A 'Perversion' of Choice: Sex Work Offers Just Enough in Chicago's Urban Ghetto," *Journal of Contemporary Ethnography* 37 (4) 417–441.

Sinclair, J. (2006) *Pink Box: Inside Japan's Sex Clubs*, New York: Abrams.

Suzuki, D. (2014) *Saihinkon Joshi* (The Poorest Girls), Tokyo: Gentosha.

Takeoka, T. (2017) *Ikinobiru Toshi* (Surviving City), Tokyo: Shinyosha.

Takeyama, A. (2016) *Staged Seduction: Selling Dreams in a Tokyo Host Club*, Stanford: Stanford University Press.

Tsuji, H. (2017) *Chusei no Yūjo* (Medieval Yūjo), Kyoto: Kyoto Daigaku Syuppan-kai.

Tsukada, T. (1992) *Mibunsei-shakai to Shimin-shakai: Kinsei Nihon no Shakai to Hou* (Status Society and Civil Society: Society and Law of the Early Modern Japan), Tokyo: Kashiwa Shobo.

Weitzer, R. (2009) "Sociology of Sex Work," *Annual Review of Sociology* 35 213–234.

Yano, Keizai Kenkyujo (2016) "Adaruto-muke Shijo ni Kansuru Chosa-Kekka 2016" (Report on Adult Market 2016). www.yano.co.jp/press/download.php/001498.

Yoshida, N. (2006) "Yukaku Shakai" (Society of Yukaku Red Light District), in T. Tsukada (ed) *Toshi no Shuen ni Ikiru* (Living in Urban Margins), Tokyo: Yoshikawa Kobunkan.

18
GENDER, LABOUR, AND MIGRATION IN JAPAN

Helena Hof and Gracia Liu-Farrer

For over three decades, Japan has been struggling with the issues of both immigration and the status of women in the workforce. Low fertility rate and population ageing have turned labour shortage into an economic threat, making importing foreign labour and maximizing women's economic participation necessary to sustain Japan's economic growth. Meanwhile, changing economic, political, and ideological landscapes brought about by globalisation force both the government and wider society to ameliorate institutional frameworks for immigration as well as to improve women's chances on the labour market. However, on both issues, the political will is feeble and actual improvements are inadequate. On the one hand, a sense of reluctance surrounds the question of immigration. Though the country recognises the necessity to bring in foreign workers, it is unwilling to imagine changes to the cherished Japanese ways of life. Immigration is still seen as a threat to national identity. On the other hand, despite what the Abe government propagates, gendered workplace practices and institutional constraints prevent women from making significant advancement both economically and politically. This ambivalence toward immigration and the inertia in women's labour market progress manifest themselves in the conditions experienced by immigrant women—those foreign women who have entered Japan as both productive and reproductive labour. By reviewing scholarship on female migration into Japan in the past three decades, this chapter highlights the challenges Japan faces in relation to the conditions of both women and migrants.

After a brief introduction of controversial practices surrounding immigration, this chapter presents two major categories of female labour migration phenomena in Japan discussed in scholarly research. We label the first category "gendered labour migrants." The foreign women in this category are brought in to fulfil the productive and reproductive labour that Japanese women have vacated or are unable to supply. Their presence and plight epitomise the country's ambivalent stance towards immigration and the consequences of an inflexible migration regime. This category has attracted the most scholarly attention. The second category of women migrants in Japan includes those so-called "skilled professional workers" who enter Japanese companies as white-collar workers. It is important to note, though, that many women who enter through the first category have tertiary education and are skilled professionals, too. This second group, the female white-collar employees, are confronted with the gender hierarchy typical for Japanese workplaces but at the same time are contesting these boundaries, with uneven outcomes. In the final section, we reflect on these two inflows of female labour to Japan and conclude that while foreign women are confronted with gender barriers in Japanese society and to some extent face multiple constraints by being both foreign and female, their increased presence in various institutions in Japan, from the most intimate to the most public, might accelerate Japanese society's transformation from within.

Labour migration to Japan

Japan had been considered a negative case of migration among postwar industrial countries (Bartram 2000). During the economic boom in the 1960s and 1970s, it had mostly relied on the reserve of rural labour to supply the rapidly expanding urban industry. In the 1980s bubble economy, labour shortages threatened economic development. Nonetheless, the Japanese government has been reluctant to institute immigration policies (Komai 2001; Iguchi 2001). In spite of the demand for labour by Japanese businesses, Japan's migration regime is characterised by the persistent "side doors" (Kajita 1995) for labour import and selective migration policies.

As a first "side door," the return of ethnic Japanese from South America, or *nikkeijin*, allowed the Japanese government to incorporate them as "Japanese" rather than foreign workers into the labour force during the economic boom (e.g. Tsuda 2003, 2009; Takenoshita 2015). Second, "trainee" and "technical intern" programmes have disguised labour migration as training for foreign nationals of developing countries. Under these schemes, 228,588 technical interns—mainly from China—were registered in Japan in 2016 (Ministry of Justice 2017a; Kamibayashi 2010). Most work in low-wage agricultural jobs or the food industry, and their mobility in Japan is strictly controlled (Akaishi 2010). Finally, international education has become an effective channel for labour import (Liu-Farrer 2009a, 2011a). Foreign students, mostly from Asian countries, constitute a significant share of Japan's part time work force. Approximately one-third of foreign students (12,325 out of 42,643) who graduated from Japanese educational institutions in the 2015 academic year (from 1 April 2015 to 31 March 2016) found employment in Japan (JASSO 2017).

The other characteristic of Japan's labour migration policies is selectivity. While the front door remains closed to foreign labour, it is open wide for highly skilled foreigners (Oishi 2012). In 2012, a new point-based visa category was introduced to attract "highly skilled foreign professionals" and provides a direct path to permanent residency. However, given the high criteria for academic credentials and professional accomplishments, only 1,810 people had this status in 2016. The majority of skilled foreigners (161,154) held the "Engineer/Specialist in Humanities/International Services" visa in 2016 (Ministry of Justice 2017a). As the name indicates, it is a broad category. While the majority of the engineers are recruited directly from overseas, the people in "Humanities and International Services" are more likely international students who graduated from Japanese universities (Liu-Farrer 2013; Debnár 2016). Aside from supplementing the labour force for small and medium-sized firms, these immigrants often find themselves in an "occupational niche" (Liu-Farrer 2011b). Chinese workers, for example, are most likely in positions dealing with transnational businesses with Chinese speaking regions (Liu-Farrer 2011b), while Europeans and North Americans, regardless of their linguistic background, often find themselves pigeon-holed as English teachers or hired because their non-East Asian appearances add a global flavour to the organisation (Debnár 2016; Hof 2018).

Despite the lack of frameworks for immigration, in 2016, over 2.3 million foreign nationals lived in Japan. The foreign population has become a substantial part of Japan's workforce. From restaurants and supermarkets to farms, fishing boats, and assembly lines, foreign workers have been contributing invaluable labour to the Japanese economy. With rapid population ageing, sectors such as nursing and elderly care are in desperate need of migrant labour. We now turn to the gendered structure of such necessary foreign labour.

Gendered labour migration

From plantation workers to tradesmen, labour migrants in Asia were historically male (Amrith 2018; Komai 2001). Changing labour market structures brought by globalisation since the 1980s have feminised migration (Castles and Miller 1993). Women move, typically from developing countries, to supplement productive and reproductive labour traditionally occupied by women in more developed countries (Oishi 2005). In 2016, more than half of the total foreign resident population (2,382,822) in Japan were women (1,247,741), and women also accounted for the majority of Asian migrants (Ministry of Justice 2017b).

Three patterns of labour flows have shaped not only the demographic profiles of Japan's immigrants but also the debate on female migration in the past few decades. The first pattern is the immigration of so-called "entertainers" since the late 1970s. Supposedly dancers or singers, in reality most of these migrants became hostesses in bars and clubs, with some becoming sex workers. Most entertainers have been women from Southeast Asian countries, especially the Philippines, but some also came from Eastern Europe and Latin America. The second pattern is international marriage migration. Since the 1980s, many Asian women have been brought in to marry Japanese men, especially those in depopulated rural areas in Japan. China was a major sending country of international brides (Chung et al. 2016; Le Bail 2017). Finally, we are witnessing the development of a new trend of female labour migration in Japan—the recruitment of nurses and caregivers to staff Japan's hospitals and nursing homes. This highly scrutinised migration flow takes place through bilateral agreements, which have brought in limited numbers of Indonesian, Filipino, and Vietnamese women.

Women who arrive in Japan through these channels represent the typical feminised migrant labour. In the past three decades, researchers have drawn attention to these migrant women's vulnerability. More recently, however, many studies have tried to illustrate the complexity of these forms of labour migration and the agencies women migrants demonstrate in the migration process.

Entertainers: the stigmatised labour

"Entertainer" visa-holding migrants were not only the first gendered immigration stream to postwar Japan but also represent the first "side door" of labour migration (Kajita 1995). These visas provided the most accessible means for Filipino women, including some transgender women, to enter Japan from 1980 to 2005 (Ballescas 1992; Komai 2001; Douglass and Roberts 2003; Takeda 2005; Okada 2014). They were usually recruited by agents and worked in Japan's entertainment industry as dancers, singers, and hostesses. Some were engaged in sex work, an industry in which other migrant women can be found, including Thai women who mostly entered Japan as tourists and worked illegally, which made them more vulnerable to exploitation (Piper 2002). In total, 1,917,063 people entered Japan on entertainer visas between 1979 and 2005, and the majority were Filipinas. Amidst concerns of visa abuses, with the intervention of the US State Department, this visa category became more strictly regulated and increasingly unavailable to Filipinas after 2005. The human rights abuse of entertainers was globally publicised through the United States' 2004 *Trafficking in Persons Report*. Amidst global criticism, the Japanese government drafted *Japan's Action Plan of Measures to Combat Trafficking in Persons* (Ministry of Foreign Affairs of Japan 2004), and stringent controls over the issuing of entertainment visas became effective from 2006, resulting in a drastic decline of entertainers newly arriving from the Philippines. The number of Filipinas who entered as entertainers decreased drastically, especially after 2011.

Early studies on this migration trend focused on its exploitative nature and incidents of abuses and argued that it merely reversed the earlier trend of sex tourism by Japanese (men) to the Philippines (Ballescas 1992; Douglass and Roberts 2003; Tyner 2009). Filipina entertainers filled the entertainment jobs vacated by Japanese women who were able to leave such stigmatised industries thanks to the economic boom (Piper 2002). More recent research, for example by Faier (2009) and Parreñas (2011), serve as correctives to dominant sex worker and victim narratives. These studies demonstrate that entertainer work can be experienced as empowering because these women are chosen for their singing and dancing skills and consider themselves professionals. Moreover, their jobs allow them to financially support their families at home. Regardless of the context of research—Faier (2009) observing Filipina entertainers as brides of rural families, Parreñas (2011) focusing on those working as urban hostesses—these studies stress women's agency. They emphasise that these women are making choices. They *choose* to migrate and *can decide* whether they want to meet clients privately. While migrants' intimate encounters with male Japanese clients who sometimes become their boyfriends are unequal from the outset, Faier (2009) demonstrates the opportunities for romance and love that open up through entertainment work. Some of the Filipina brides become accepted as "ideal *oyome-san*" (Faier 2009, 242)—that is, ideal wives and daughters-in-law—for their working-class husbands and these husbands' natal families in Japan's rural prefectures. Nevertheless, women's initial stigmatisation as immoral workers and their frustrations with (their lack of) the Japanese language remind us of the downside of their economical migration and the impenetrability of Japanese society and the domestic labour market. Moreover, migrants' roles as homemakers and mothers in traditional Japanese households underline the continuation of patriarchal gender norms.

Mail-order brides: the invisible labour

The other gendered migration flow to Japan that started in the 1980s was spurred by (mainly rural) Japanese men's struggles to find marriage partners. There is a gender imbalance in international marriages in Japan, with the vast majority consisting of foreign brides (especially Chinese women and Filipinas) and Japanese grooms. Numbers peaked in the early 2000s, when more than 30,000 marriages between foreign women and Japanese men were registered, in contrast to less than 10,000 marriages between foreign men and Japanese women (Le Bail 2017).

A whole industry flourished around finding foreign women who were willing to marry Japanese men and stay in rural areas. Women from developing countries in Asia have often turned to marriage migration when other access channels to developed countries were not available. Nakamatsu investigated such match-making agencies (2003) and pointed out that many of them were staffed by former marriage migrants. After coming to Japan, these foreign women not only provide reproductive labour, they also form a significant part of the labour force in depopulated rural areas which are in desperate need of productive labour (Le Bail 2017).

Against earlier portrayals of these women as the voiceless victims of Asian neighbouring countries' backward economic status, Suzuki (2003, 413) argues that by having love affairs or becoming entrepreneurs, some of these women are able to "dislocate[e] the borders surrounding mail order brides as merely 'sexually constrained victims.'" Nakamatsu (2003) illustrates that the majority of the Asian women she studied engage in paid work such as textile production and are sometimes able to gain control over household decisions and the family budget. The gendered Japanese labour market, however, means that these women—some being professionals in their home countries—are usually denied a professional career. They often face discrimination and are assigned menial tasks. Nevertheless, earning their own income enhances their self-esteem and increases their power at home vis-à-vis their Japanese spouse and in-laws. These women have settled in Japan and have become a visible part of the blue-collar labour force.

Nurses and caregivers: the demanded labour

The most recent and so far the most "controlled" influx of feminised labour migration is that of female nurses and caregivers. Japan faces an ever-growing need for caregivers for its senior population. Reluctantly, the government adopted bi-national Equal Partnership Agreements (EPAs) with Indonesia in 2008, the Philippines in 2009, and Vietnam in 2014 in order to meet the rising demand for caregivers. Next to population ageing, Japanese women's growing participation in paid work created a need for caregivers who could replace the unpaid care work formerly provided by Japanese housewives.

Vogt (2018, 37), however, argues that the government policies are "designed to fail." The migrant workers are confined to work in the institutionalised health-care sector. Yet, a substantial part of health care in Japan is organised at the community level. Furthermore, the top-down approach implemented by the government fails to build trust between the actors involved, leading to resentment by the families in need, misunderstanding if not discrimination on the side of the Japanese staff and health care institutions, and frustration and eventually departure of the foreign care workers. The low numbers of foreign nurses—791 Indonesian health-caregivers between 2008 and 2011, 532 Filipino health-caregivers from 2009 to 2011—underscore the structural problems of the EPA scheme (Vogt 2018, 37). Foreign care workers only receive a conditional status as assistants until they pass the Japanese-language national exam for nurses. Uncertain if they can pass the test (the condition for bringing in their family members), provided a poor salary as assistants despite their qualifications in their home countries, and with limited free time used for studying the language, they often find that other destination countries are more attractive (Ogawa 2012). Employers are likewise reluctant to hire these foreign nurses due to concerns over language proficiency and professional skills and some Japanese families' xenophobic attitudes towards foreign nurses (Vogt 2018).

In summary, these three patterns of migration—entertainers, international marriages, and care work—represent the dominant trends of feminised migration into Japan. All three involve women from developing countries in Asia who migrate to Japan to fulfil the historically prescribed gender roles for Japanese women. These women's plights reflect the embedded vulnerability in feminised migration in Japan as well as Japan's inadequate frameworks to address its labour shortage and to protect migrants. However, while often targets of exploitation and discrimination, these women are not mere victims. Rather, they strategize to combat precarious conditions, to destigmatise themselves, to strive for economic independence and upward mobility. By infiltrating the most intimate spheres, they might even serve as transformative forces in Japanese society (Burgess 2004; Suzuki 2003; Faier 2009). After reviewing the first group of female labour migrants to Japan, we now turn to migrant women in Japan's white-collar labour force.

Foreign women in Japanese "white-collar" workplaces

Acker (1990, 152) claimed that organisational structures in the white-collar workplace are inherently gendered: "While women's bodies are ruled out of order, or sexualised and objectified, in work organisations, men's bodies are not." According to scholars of gender studies and the sociology of work, the ideal worker, thus, is a man. Whereas in Western countries, this man is supposedly white (Delgado and Stefancic 2001), in Japan, he is Japanese (Dasgupta 2003). A foreign woman at a Japanese workplace, being not only non-Japanese but also female, is the opposite of the ideal Japanese worker. Moreover, Japanese gender norms expect women—foreign ones included (Debnár 2016)—to manage the household and support their working husbands, even if they are employed full-time themselves. As such, on the one hand, working foreign women face the same challenge of combining household duties with a demanding work schedule as working Japanese women do. On the other hand, being foreign adds another layer of complication to their career mobilities in Japanese workplaces.

Research about foreign women in Japanese white-collar workplaces is emerging. A few early studies focus mostly on company-assigned expatriates who enjoyed a somewhat privileged status cushioned by home-country contracts (Napier and Taylor 2002). In recent years, with more and more foreign women university graduates being recruited to work in Japanese companies, how they experience Japanese workplaces has become increasingly important. Existing studies present several main findings. First, being foreign might free these women from the gendered expectations of Japanese society and allow them to pursue careers. Many immigrant women in Japan, especially the highly educated, come from countries with different gender role expectations and have a stronger sense of gender equality (Liu-Farrer 2009b). As a result, a rising number of educated foreign women, especially those who speak Japanese, have chosen to enter Japanese firms as permanent employees and pursue a career-track destined for managerial positions—a labour market choice less common for Japanese women (Liu-Farrer 2009b, 2011a; Achenbach 2017; Hof 2018).

Second, their unique cultural capital gives foreign women some leverage in their corporate career. Aside from their university degrees and Japanese language proficiency, these foreign women are fluent in at least one more foreign language and functional in both sending and receiving countries' social and cultural contexts. This renders them favourable international sales staff or employees in the transnational sector (Liu-Farrer 2009b; Hof 2018). Chinese women are often sent on business travel (usually to China), a practice less common for Japanese female employees. Furthermore, proficiency in foreign languages and a foreign look appeal to Japanese firms which hope to boost their global image by hiring foreign graduates (Conrad and Meyer-Ohle 2018).

Third, while foreign women are able to secure jobs in Japan, their obvious difference from the majority of Japanese staff members creates dilemmas. Language is an important factor. Some foreign workers, especially those from non-*kanji* countries, can speak Japanese but lack sophisticated use or adequate knowledge of these Chinese characters (Hof 2018; Suzuki 2017). If they also look "foreign," they stand out among East Asian employees. Such a combination of racial and cultural "foreignness" makes them visible, sometimes singles them out, and threatens to marginalise them. The authors have observed several such instances (Liu-Farrer and Hof 2018). For example, one blonde woman informant was invited to a client meeting by the manager of a team she did not belong to because this particular client was a fan of a blonde Japanese comedian and the team manager thought that the woman's attendance would please the client. While this woman acknowledged that it was an unusual privilege for a junior employee to meet such an important client and that her attendance was valued by the manager, she was uncomfortable with the fact that it was her physical attributes that invited such attention. Moreover, as Hof's research shows, these women's visibility also invites exclusion, envy, and sometimes harassment. A few women assumed that colleagues' distancing behaviour was related to the attention they received from team managers. In a few cases, visibly different women were verbally harassed on grounds of their appearance (Hof 2018).

Finally, despite this exceptionalism, foreign women still confront the gender stratification of corporate Japan. Chinese (and Southeast Asian) women's careers are largely confined to small or medium-sized companies. These come with a lower salary and package and less promotional opportunities than in the big firms (Liu-Farrer 2011b; Achenbach 2017). A much smaller number of white women, equipped with the educational credentials they obtained from mostly elite Japanese universities, sometimes enter prestigious companies. However, when they encounter the rigid gendered structures of these companies, most women transfer to smaller (and thus less financially attractive) firms within the first two years. Foreign women therefore often find themselves constrained by the same sexual segregation as Japanese women. They also suffer from the male-dominant environment and the lack of female—and foreign—role models. Ultimately, these struggles manifest in a pattern of job transfers from Japanese to foreign-owned firms or less hierarchical start-ups and sometimes women's migration to another country which they perceive less gender discriminative (Hof 2018).

Conclusion and recommendations for future directions

Japan is confronted with an immigration dilemma, wrestling with anachronistic gender norms, and troubled by persistent sexual segregation in its workplaces. Immigrant women's experiences in Japan reflect these struggles. Here we introduced two broad categories of women immigrants: those who come to fulfil particular gendered labour as entertainers, marriage migrants, and care workers, and foreign women who enter corporate Japan. Regardless of their migration channels, educational backgrounds, and countries of origin, immigrant women inevitably bump against the gender and ethnic barriers of Japanese society. However, because they are a much-needed labour force, foreign women can challenge the rigid structures by asserting their subjectivity in the intimate realm and making their voices heard in the corporate field. Their struggles call attention to the lack of equity of the migration regime, as well as the inertia of Japanese gendered workplaces.

Though there have been many studies of women's labour migration and immigrant women in Japan, one group of women are ostensibly missing from extant literature. Those are the so-called "dependents"—people who enter Japan as spouses or children of student and work visa holders. In 2016, there were close to 150,000 "dependents" in Japan, and women spouses make up the majority. These women not only make sacrifices for the sake of their husbands' jobs and education, but also serve as an important casual labour force. Future studies need to account for these women's migration and labour experiences in Japan. Moreover, immigration to Japan is evolving. Migrants are coming from a wider range of ethnic backgrounds and countries of origin; international students and skilled workers from Vietnam and Nepal, for instance, have increased rapidly. The migration experiences and mobility outcomes of these new stocks of immigrants, particular those of women, can shed light on the future of Japan as an immigrant country and the possibility of social transformation. Finally, the Japanese government has introduced new policies to allow the recruitment of foreigners for housekeeping services in so-called national strategic zones. Studies are needed to understand how effective these policies are and how migrant women entering Japan via this scheme are experiencing their new lives in Japan. As we suggest, migrant women's presence signals possible ways for change. Through their defiant voices, progress for working women and foreign workers might be accelerated. In one migrant woman's words, "I believe in Japan they don't expect direct answers from a woman. So if [such an answer] comes they are like, 'Wow, okay we are on the same eye level.' [This is] maybe because they wouldn't expect this if you are foreigner and woman."

Related chapters

5   Masculinity Studies in Japan
7   Gender and Ethnicity in Urban Japan
10 Family, Inequality, and the Work-Family Balance in Contemporary Japan
12 Rural Gender Construction and Decline: Negotiating Risks Through Nostalgia
16 Gender and the Workplace
17 Sex Work

References

Achenbach, R. (2017) *Return Migration Decisions: A Study on Highly Skilled Chinese in Japan*, Wiesbaden: Springer.
Acker, J. (1990) "Hierarchies, Jobs, Bodies: A Theory of Gendered Organizations," *Gender and Society* 4 (2) 139–158.
Akaishi, J. (2010) *Nyūkoku kanri seisaku (1990 nen taisei) no seiritsu to tenkai* (Implementation and Development of the Immigration Policies of the 1990 Constitution), Kyoto: Nakanishiya Shuppan.
Amrith, S. S. (2018) "Colonial and Postcolonial Migrations," in G. Liu-Farrer and B. S. A. Yeoh (eds) *Routledge Handbook of Asian Migrations*, Oxon and New York: Routledge, 21–32.
Ballescas, R. P. (1992) *Filipino Entertainers in Japan: An Introduction*, Tsukuba: The Foundation for Nationalist Studies.
Bartram, D. (2000) "Japan and Labor Migration: Theoretical and Methodological Implications of Negative Cases," *International Migration Review* 34 (1) 5–32.
Burgess, C. (2004) "(Re) Constructing Identities: International Marriage Migrants as Potential Agents of Social Change in a Globalising Japan," *Asian Studies Review* 28 (3) 223–242.
Castles, S. and Miller, M. J. (1993) *The Age of Migration: International Population Movements in the Modern World*, London: Palgrave Macmillan.
Chung, C., Kim, K. and Piper, N. (2016) "Marriage Migration in Southeast and East Asia Revisited Through a Migration-Development Nexus Lens," *Critical Asian Studies* 48 (4) 463–472.
Conrad, H. and Meyer-Ohle, H. (2018) "Brokers and the Organization of Recruitment of 'Global Talent' by Japanese Firms—A Migration Perspective," *Social Science Japan Journal* 21 (1) 67–88.
Dasgupta, R. (2003) "Creating Corporate Warriors: The 'Salaryman' and Masculinity in Japan," in K. Louie and M. Low (eds) *Asian Masculinities: The Meaning and Practice of Manhood in China and Japan*, London and New York: Routledge Curzon, 118–134.
Debnár, M. (2016) *Migration, Whiteness, and Cosmopolitanism. Europeans in Japan*, New York: Palgrave Macmillan.
Delgado, R. and Stefancic, J. (2001) *Critical Race Theory: An Introduction*, New York: New York University Press.
Douglass, M. and Roberts, G. S. (2003) "Japan in a Global Age of Migration," in M. Douglass and G. S. Roberts (eds) *Japan and Global Migration: Foreign Workers and the Advent of a Multicultural Society*, Honolulu: University of Hawaii Press, 3–37.
Faier, L. (2009) *Intimate Encounters: Filipina Women and the Remaking of Rural Japan*, Berkeley, CA: University of California Press.
Hof, H. (2018) "'Worklife Pathways' to Singapore and Japan: Gender and Racial Dynamics in Europeans' Mobility to Asia," *Social Science Japan Journal* 21 (1) 45–65.
Iguchi, Y. (2001) *Gaikokujin rōdōsha shinjidai* (A New Epoch of Foreign Labour), Tokyo: Chikuma Shobō.
Japan Student Services Organization (2017) "Heisei 27 nendo gaikokujin ryūgakusei shino jōkyō gakui juyo chōsa kekka" (Survey Results on Foreign Students' Career Course and Academic Degrees in 2015). www.jasso.go.jp/about/statistics/intl_student_d/__icsFiles/afieldfile/2017/04/17/degrees15_1.pdf.

Kajita, T. (1995) "Characteristics of the Foreign Worker Problem in Japan: To an Analytical Viewpoint," *Hitotsubashi Journal of Social Studies* 27 1–26.

Kamibayashi, C. (2010) "The Temporary Foreign Worker Programme in Japanese Style: the 20 years' history of the Technical Internship Programme (TIP)," *Hosei University Institute of Comparative Economic Studies Working Paper Series*, 155 1–19.

Komai, H. (2001) *Foreign Migrants in Contemporary Japan*, trans. J. Wilkinson, Melbourne: Trans Pacific Press.

Le Bail, H. (2017) "Cross-Border Marriages as a Side Door for Paid and Unpaid Migrant Workers: The Case of Marriage Migration Between China and Japan," *Critical Asian Studies* 49 (2) 226–243.

Liu-Farrer, G. (2009a) "Educationally Channelled International Labor Migration: Post-1978 Student Mobility from China to Japan," *International Migration Review* 43 (1) 178–204.

Liu-Farrer, G. (2009b) "'I Am the Only Woman in Suits': Chinese Immigrants and Gendered Careers in Corporate Japan," *Journal of Asia-Pacific Studies* (Waseda University) 13 37–48.

Liu-Farrer, G. (2011a) *Labor Migration from China to Japan: International Students, Transnational Migrants*, London: Routledge.

Liu-Farrer, G. (2011b) "Making Careers in the Occupational Niche: Chinese Students in Corporate Japan's Transnational Business," *Journal of Ethnic and Migration Studies* 37 (5) 785–803.

Liu-Farrer, G. (2013) "Chinese Newcomers in Japan: Migration Trends, Profiles and the Impact of the 2011 Earthquake," *Asian and Pacific Migration Journal (APMJ)* 22 (2) 231–257.

Liu-Farrer, G. and Hof, H. (2018) "Ōtebyō: the Problems of Japanese Firms and the Problematic Elite Aspirations," *Journal of Asia-Pacific Studies* (Waseda University) 34 65–84.

Ministry of Foreign Affairs of Japan (2004) "Japan's Action Plan of Measures to Combat Trafficking in Persons." www.mofa.go.jp/policy/i_crime/people/action.html.

Ministry of Justice (2017a) "16-12-01-1 Kokuseki chīki betsu zairyū shikaku (zairyū mokuteki) betsu sōzairyū gaikokujin" (Total Number of Foreigners in Japan by Nationality and Residence Status). www.e-stat.go.jp/stat-search/files?page=1&layout=datalist&lid=000001177523.

Ministry of Justice (2017b) "16-12-02-1 Kokuseki chīki betsu nenrei danjo zairyū gaikokujin" (Foreigners in Japan. By Nationality, Age, and Gender). www.e-stat.go.jp/stat-search/files?page=1&layout=datalist&lid=000001177523.

Nakamatsu, T. (2003) "International Marriage through Introduction Agencies: Social and Legal Realities of 'Asian' Wives of Japanese Men," in N. Piper and M. Roces (eds) *Wife or Worker? Asian Women and Migration*, Lanham: Rowman & Littlefield Publishers, Inc., 181–201.

Napier, N. and Taylor, S. (2002) "Experiences of women professionals abroad: comparisons across Japan, China and Turkey," *The International Journal of Human Resource Management*, 13 (5) 837–851.

Ogawa, R. (2012) "Conceptualizing Transnational Migration of Care Workers: Between 'Skilled' and 'Unskilled'," *ASIEN, The German Journal on Contemporary Asia* 124 95–114.

Okada, T. (2014) "Nihon ni okeru toransu jendā no firipinjin entāteinā" (Filipino Transgender Entertainers in Japan), *Waseda daigaku jendā kenkyū* 21 (3) 51–63.

Oishi, N. (2005) *Women in Motion: Globalization, State Policies, and Labor Migration in Asia*, Stanford, CA: Stanford University Press.

Oishi, N. (2012) "The Limits of Immigration Policies: The Challenges of Highly Skilled Migration in Japan," *American Behavioral Scientist* 56 (8) 1080–1100.

Parreñas, R. S. (2011) *Illicit Flirtations: Labor, Migration, and Sex Trafficking in Tokyo*, Stanford, CA: Stanford University Press.

Piper, N. (2002) "Global Labour Markets and National Responses: Legal Regimes Governing Female Migrant Workers in Japan," in D. S. Gills and N. Piper (eds) *Women and Work in Globalising Asia*, New York: Routledge, 188–208.

Roberts, G. S. (2018) "An Immigration Policy by Any Other Name: Semantics of Immigration to Japan," *Social Science Japan Journal* 21 (1) 89–102.

Suzuki, N. (2003) "Transgressing 'Victims' Reading Narratives of 'Filipina Brides' in Japan," *Critical Asian Studies* 35 (3) 399–420.

Suzuki, N. (2017) "Nihon kigyō de hataraku josei gaikokujin shain no jendā to kyaria keishiki. Moto ryūgakusei de bunkei sōgōshoku shain no bāi" (Career Development Processes and the Gender Role of Foreign Female Employees Working for Japanese Companies: Interviews with Those Who Have Graduated from University in Japan), *Journal of Gender Studies Ochanomizu University* 20 55–72.

Takeda, J. (2005) *Filipin josei entāteinā no laifu sutōrī* (Female Filipino Entertainers' Life Stories), Nishinomiya: Kansei Gakuin Daigaku Shuppankai.

Takenoshita, H. (2015) "Labor Market Structure, Welfare Policy, and Integration: Brazilian Immigrants during the Economic Downturn," in Y. Ishikawa (ed) *International Migrants in Japan: Contributions in an Era of Population Decline*, Melbourne: Trans Pacific Press, 234–255.

Tsuda, T. (2003) "Domesticating the Immigrant Other: Japanese Media Images of Nikkeijin Return Migrants," *Ethnology* 42 (4) 289–305.

Tsuda, T. (2009) *Diasporic Homecomings: Ethnic Return Migration in Comparative Perspective*, Stanford: Stanford University Press.

Tyner, J. A. (2009) *The Philippines: Mobilities, Identities, Globalization*, New York and London: Routledge.

Vogt, G. (2018) *Population Aging and International Health-Caregiver Migration to Japan*, Switzerland, Cham: Springer.

19
WOMEN IN ELECTORAL POLITICS

Emma Dalton

In 2017, Japan dropped three places in the World Economic Forum's Global Gender Gap Report to 114 out of 144 countries, mainly because of its low representation of women in politics. The Inter-Parliamentary Union places Japan last amongst OECD countries and at number 157 out of 187 countries in its ranking of female representation in national legislative assemblies (based on single and lower house figures). Female representation in other levels of government varies widely, from a high of 36 out of 128 on the Tokyo metropolitan to some 20 percent of town and village assemblies with zero representation of women. Yet overall female representation in governments is low: 9.6 percent in prefectural and municipal councils, 14.2 percent in city and ward councils, and 9.2 percent in town and village assemblies (Miura 2016a, 3).

Why is it that a country advanced in technology, human rights, and many other developmental indices has such a dismal record in empowering women, especially politically? While we may assume more "developed" countries like Japan have better track records in promoting equality and women's advancement, in fact, high representation of women in politics is no longer concomitant with "development." There are 49 countries in the world with female political representation of 30 percent or more, and of these, 33 are "developing" or "least developed" as characterized by the World Bank (Rosen 2017, 83). This chapter examines the situation in Japan by first providing a brief outline of the history of women's participation in politics. An exploration of reasons for Japan's enduring gender inequality in the realm of political representation follows. The chapter then turns to the interesting and sometimes contested arguments for increasing women's political representation—arguments about the nature of democracy and the impact women can have on policy-making processes—and concludes with a summary of the direction in which women in Japanese politics are heading.

Context and history

Discourses about Japanese femininity and women's roles in the public sphere that emerged during the Meiji Era in the late 1800s were set against a backdrop of the beginnings of modernisation and industrialisation. Gendered roles were intrinsically linked to the (changing) interests of the nation-state. From 1890, women's political participation was formally prohibited. Women were prohibited from joining political organisations or attending political lectures. This was not because of a belief that women were weak or inferior to men but because of the state's desire to limit women's activities to those within the home and family. Women engaged in reproductive and productive activities that served the state's interests by (re)producing forces for labour and the military and engaging in economic labour. For example, women were encouraged to cultivate thrifty consumer habits to drive the economy (Garon 1993, 30–32) as well as to foster morals within the population. In the early twentieth century, the authorities began to realise that these activities could benefit society more if women were able to extend these activities from the private sphere to the public sphere as well.

While the industrialising and increasingly militaristic state attempted to appropriate women's roles for state interests, women themselves organised and fought for the right to participate in civic life, such as the suffragists, led by Ichikawa Fusae. In addition, some (socialist) women protested the prohibition on women's political activity by joining such organisations as the *Heiminsha* (Commoners' Society), writing articles in socialist publications, and contributing to the developing labour movement. Although socialist women criticised the feminist movement, including the suffrage movement, for being bourgeois, they eventually joined feminists to campaign for political rights (Mackie 1997, 141). At this time, nevertheless, many women's groups that campaigned for political rights, with the exception of some socialist women, based their arguments primarily on those that supported state interests. For the Women's Christian Temperance Union and for many of the suffragists, women's votes would "clean up" electoral corruption and make a better Japan (Mackie 2003, 63). Theirs was an argument based on what they could do for Japan rather than one based on a sex-equality philosophy. In this way, many women's groups fed from and supported state-sanctioned images of Japanese womanhood. Women were connected to notions of charity, integrity, and the home. With the outbreak of war, all women's groups were mobilised into patriotic organisations and the fight for political rights was subsumed under obligations to serve one's country (Mackie 2003, 109).

Japanese women gained civil rights during the US-led Occupation between 1946 and 1952, including the right to vote and run for political office. This put them in a better position from which to pursue political goals. Women were still, however, constructed as the political "Other," in the sense that their appropriate role was in the domestic rather than the public, political sphere. For example, the Civil Information and Education Unit (CIE) of the Supreme Commander for the Allied Powers (SCAP) was in charge of educating women about how "democratic" families functioned. The family that was presented as the democratic norm was the American middle-class family (Koikari 2002, 36). Women's organisations that had been mobilised during the war for nationalist indoctrination were "democratised" by a group of women in the CIE who travelled the country visiting local areas and educating the women. In this way, SCAP encouraged women's public activity, but only on the assumption that it was carried out within the framework of the idealised roles of mother and wife, thus giving no legitimacy to radical and/or working-class women from the discourse of emancipation. The occupying forces held conservative beliefs about gender roles that kept "women in their place" within the patriarchal order by discouraging women's collective action against male domination and explicitly and implicitly encouraging women's political activities as an extension of their roles as wives and mothers (Pharr 1987, 236).

Women voted and ran for office for the first time in the 1946 general election. Thirty-nine women were elected, constituting 8.4 percent of successful candidates. The following year, the electoral system was altered to medium-sized electoral districts where voters cast a single vote for a single candidate, a system that favoured candidates who had the backing of a large party (Mackie 2003, 126). The Lower House election held in 1947 following the revisions saw the number of women plummet to 3.2 percent—a figure that barely changed for over half a decade. The 1946 figure of 8.4 percent was only surpassed nearly 60 years later in 2005, when it rose to 9 percent. Furthermore, there was no increase in the number of women in the Lower House

Women in electoral politics

until after the 1993 electoral reform when it rose from 2.7 percent to 4.6 percent in 1996. The electoral system has thus been identified as being a major contributor to the success or failure of women candidates. In 1993, the Lower House electoral system changed from medium-sized electoral districts to a hybrid system of single-seat constituencies and proportional representation. Single-seat member seats have been identified as being difficult for women and other minority candidates to win. In a single-member district, political parties have to choose one candidate to win, and this requires nominating a candidate they believe will have the broadest appeal and therefore be most likely to win (Matland 1998, 76). Typically, a candidate reflecting the characteristics and qualifications of the previous successful representative, who in most places is usually a man, will be selected to run (Norris 2006, 206).

Proportional representation seats, however, are well-recognised around the world as being easier for women to win (Norris 2006, 201). Results from elections since the Japanese electoral reforms in 1993 support this claim. When approximately the same number of women run in both types of seats, they are more likely to win the PR seats. However, the same data indicate a smaller percentage of women winning elections than running in them, something political scientist Miura Mari (2016b, 28) claims is a result of the single-member districts being particularly difficult for most women to succeed in.

In Graphs 1 and 2, we can see the trajectory of women's representation in the Lower and Upper Houses. The sharp rises in 2005 and 2009 were the result of measures taken by then Liberal Democratic Party (LDP) leader and Prime Minister Koizumi Jun'ichirō (2005) and then opposition Democratic Party of Japan (DPJ) leader Ozawa Ichirō (2009). Due to a lack of ongoing support for many of the women elected at that time, few remained in office very long. Measures like those implemented by Koizumi and Ozawa need to be permanent and they need to be followed up if we are to see sustainable change. Permanent measures that acknowledge the invisible barriers in politics that women face are mostly lacking in Japan, with the exception of the recently adopted Gender Parity Law (see Conclusion for a discussion of this). The next section discusses these barriers.

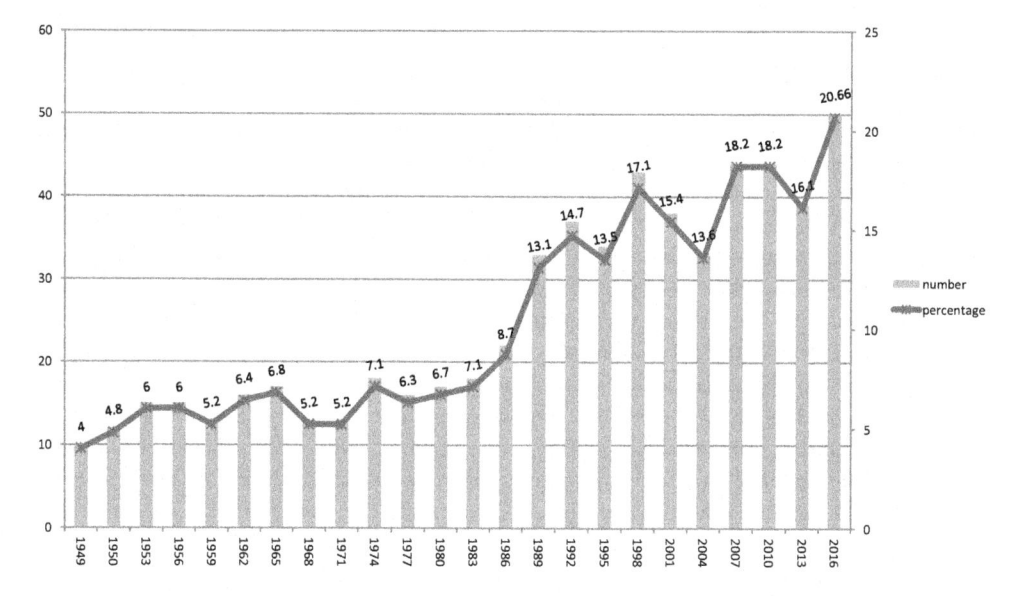

Figure 19.1 Women in upper house

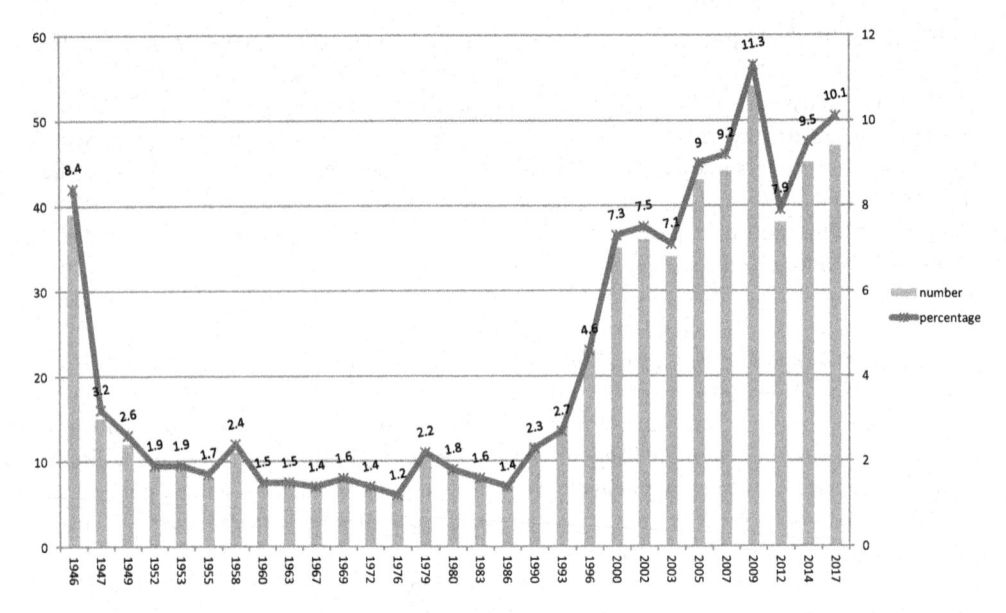

Figure 19.2 Women in lower house

Stubborn obstacles: why so few women?

Obstacles preventing women from participating fully in politics can be divided into those that are *institutional* and those that are *cultural*. In the previous section, we saw an example of an institutional barrier: the electoral system. There are other obstacles too, all of which intersect to make it difficult for women to make a stronger impact on politics and thus ensure the world of politics remains male dominated.

Institutional obstacles

As outlined previously, Japan's electoral system is a significant institutional barrier to increased female political representation. The electoral system is often criticised for being organised in a way that favours incumbents and others who have ties to the political machine (Kubo and Gelb 1994, 133; Tsujimura 2007, 28–29; Iwanaga 2008, 116–117). These people are usually men. A more open electoral system that does not compel candidates to rely so heavily on money and male-dominated networks would provide women and other minorities further opportunities to make inroads into the political world. Other, related institutional obstacles include political parties (Norris 1993, 320–330) and, in particular, party rules and culture (Caul 1999, 94). The LDP has been in power in Japan almost continuously since its inception in 1955, apart from an eight-month interlude in 1993–1994 and for three years after the DPJ took control in 2009. Its conservative stance towards women's social roles along with party rules that favour incumbents have made for a political culture that is quite hostile to women (Dalton 2015). Between 1980 and 1993, the LDP had no women in its Lower House seats. Traditionally, LDP rules have made it difficult for women to run in elections by preferring to give priority to incumbents and by requesting long lists of names of faction members and new recruits into the party (Kubo and Gelb 1994, 126). This is difficult for women candidates, who typically did not have the political networks considered desirable because of their tendency to occupy social roles such as unpaid mothers and wives (Yamaguchi 2002, 12) and their concentration in low-paid and often part-time work. More recently, however, the LDP has seen a number of women rise to powerful positions within the party, indicating that the party is not averse to seeing women succeed once they are in office.

Nevertheless, political parties are understood as being the gatekeepers to participation in political office (Paxton et al. 2007, 270), and a major reason for women's continued under-representation is that women are not fielded often as candidates. Part of the problem here is that political parties, including the LDP, do not make special efforts to find suitable women candidates. Another part of the problem is that women do not volunteer to run for candidacies often enough. This is where institutional and cultural barriers collide, as we will see subsequently.

Cultural obstacles

Cultural obstacles include things like social norms and values that shape ideas about appropriate career choices for women or the notion that politics is a world for men. Cultural obstacles prevent women from not only running for office but also from advancing in their careers and climbing the political ladder.

According to some politicians, one of the first obstacles women must overcome to pursue a career in politics is opposition from family (Hayashi 2016, 82–83; Shiomura 2016, 92–94). A career in politics is time consuming and takes people away from their families. If a woman is married with children, she will almost certainly meet with opposition from her husband and perhaps her parents and/or parents-in-law. In a culture where a woman's identity is firmly bound up with family and motherhood, choosing a labour- and time-intensive career is frowned upon. Reconciling family responsibilities with effectively representing their constituents is also difficult. This is not unique to Japan. A survey conducted between 2006 and 2008 by the Inter-Parliamentary Union of 272 parliamentarians from 110 countries revealed that while only 6 percent of male politicians around the world do not have children, a much larger 28 percent of women politicians are childless (Inter-Parliamentary Union 2008, 9). According to the same survey, women are more than twice as likely to be single than men. In Japan, 13 percent of men and 29 percent of women politicians are childless (Miura 2016b, 34). Yet childless women politicians are often pressured by both their constituents and their colleagues to have children, so they can "represent women" better (Kobayashi 2015, 67). Single men are also pressured to marry, but not necessarily to have children, thus indicating gendered expectations on women politicians and the strength of the maternal discourse in Japan. Women are therefore in a double bind, where they are pressured to have a family to appear approachable and knowledgeable in everyday matters, but their career makes it very difficult to have a family. Some women politicians, such as leading suffragist Ichikawa Fusae, first female political party head Doi Takako, and Tokyo governor Koike Yuriko, have enjoyed huge support and popularity without having a husband or children, suggesting that voter concerns about the marital status of female representatives may not be as significant as is often presumed.

The introduction of a childcare centre in the Diet in 2010 (Japan Times 2010) points to a culture that until then had, for the most part, ignored working mothers' needs but is now slowly changing. While these changes are positive, other events and incidents suggest that there is a long way to go until the culture is truly welcoming of women as equals and not "space invaders" (Puwar 2004). This boys' club culture, as it is often called, is fertile ground for sexual harassment, a problem emerging in Japan and around the world as a serious impediment to women's ability to exercise full citizenship.

In recent years, a few incidents closely covered by the media have shone a light on to a boys' club culture that permeates Japanese politics. First was the sexual harassment of Tokyo metropolitan assemblywoman Shiomura Ayaka. This incident received a great deal of both domestic and international press due to its public nature. Shiomura was heckled by male members of the Tokyo assembly as she gave a speech about her party's policies regarding making Tokyo an easier place to live for women. The sexist heckling enjoined Shiomura to "hurry up and have a baby," among other things. The media coverage began by spotlighting the case and seeking out the perpetrator. Shiomura (2016, 89–91) believes that after Suzuki Akihiro from the LDP admitted to the heckling, the media covered his apology comprehensively and then turned on her. They hounded her, some journalists going so far as to knock on the front door to her home and force themselves inside.

The media's commitment to harassing women who have already been violated was again spotlighted in 2017 with the story of journalist Itō Shiori's alleged rape by another journalist, Yamaguchi Noriyuki. Itō took the unusual and brave step of speaking out in public about her accusation of Yamaguchi raping her two years previously. She went further and claimed her reports to the police had been covered up and the case dropped because of Yamaguchi's close relationship to Prime Minster Shinzō Abe. While Itō is not a politician, her world is one that operates in close contact with politics and her alleged attacker, Yamaguchi, is in fact the author of a pro-Abe book called *Sōri* (Prime Minister), published in 2016. The boys' club mentality that underpins the Japanese political world (and its collusive relationship with certain sections of the media) is part of what led Itō to speak out. It is this boys' club mentality that ensures the sexual harassment of women in politics and those who work in close contact with politicians has, for a long time, remained hidden.

Women's organisations in Japan have begun working to unveil the problem. In the wake of the 2014 Tokyo metropolitan assembly incident, the Alliance of Feminist Representatives (*Femigiren*) conducted a survey on municipal council members to uncover the extent of sexual harassment in local politics, results that were replicated in a similar survey conducted by the New Japan Women's Association (*Shin Nihon Fujin Kai*) in the same year (New Japan Women's Association 2015). The results show that sexual harassment of women politicians in local politics is widespread and serious. *Femigiren* found that 52 percent of respondents had experienced sexual harassment in their workplace (Femigiren 2015). Sexual harassment of women politicians has been identified as a form of violence against women and a hindrance to women's advancement and to their political ambitions (Krook 2017; National Democratic Institute 2017). It has thus been conceptualized by activists, scholars, and practitioners as an impediment to democracy in that it disables the full participation of women in policy-making processes. Sexual harassment of women has the effect of sending the message to women that they do not belong, and it can discourage women from running from office (Krook 2016, 16). The lack of women in politics is a reflection of a dysfunctional democracy, if we understand representativeness as a central element of democracy. The lack of women in political decision-making roles also leads to a bias in the kinds of policies that are prioritised. The question of what changes when more women participate is addressed next.

Women's impact: what changes when women are at the table?

Numerous studies around the world have demonstrated that when women are at the political bargaining table, they act in the interests of women more often than men. What this means is that policies relating to women because of their social positions *as women* (this includes, among others, mothers, carers to the young and elderly, poorly paid casual workers, and victims of sexual and/or domestic violence) are raised. The issue of what constitutes "women's issues" remains a contested one (Celis and Childs 2012), but many studies continue to prove that women representatives behave differently to male representatives and often in ways that prioritise issues that are more likely to affect woman than men. For example, in the Swedish national parliament, an increase in the number of women led to an increased emphasis on social welfare issues (Wangnerud 2000, 85). In the United Kingdom, studies have shown that women representatives act differently to men and their presence results in more policy debate on issues that women have typically seen as more important, such as women's health (Catalano 2009, 66). Similar results were found in Japan: in Tokyo metropolitan councils, women representatives are found to actively advocate for women by making statements that include mention of women as the group being represented (Yoon and Osawa 2017, 56).

Recent research in Japan has shown that women representatives are more likely than men to focus on issues that are directly relevant to women and also that they have different preferences on major issues, such as nuclear power and constitutional reform (Yoon and Osawa 2017, 46; Oyama 2016, 230–234). Data from the UTokyo-Asahi Survey (UTAS) conducted by Taniguchi Masaki of the Graduate Schools for Law and Politics, the University of Tokyo, and the Asahi Shimbun, which surveys attitudes and values of successful candidates in general elections on certain policy issues, shows a gender difference in policy priorities. In 2009, the issues prioritised by men and women were similar, but there was a gendered difference in the level of support for each topic. The top policy priorities for both men and women candidates in the 2009 Lower House election were "economic recession counter-measures," "health," "old age pensions," and "employment," but while "economic recession counter measures" and "old-age pensions" were the most important for men, "employment" and "health" were the top two priorities for women (cited in Oyama 2016, 220–222). The 2012 survey—conducted after the triple disaster of 3.11's earthquake, tsunami, and nuclear incident—showed a slight shift towards a gendered difference in policy priorities—women prioritised disaster relief/prevention, childcare/education issues, and work/employment, while men were more likely to prioritise diplomacy/security, pension/health, and finance (cited in Oyama 2016, 222).

On a national level, women representatives' approaches to women's issues have led to, for example, the introduction of the anti-domestic violence law in Japan in 2001. In addition, the content of the Basic Law for a Gender-Equal Society, implemented in 1999, would arguably not have been as progressive were it not for the work of Dōmoto Akiko and Doi Takako, women who were leaders of the coalition government parties New Party Sakigake and Japan Socialist Party, respectively, at the time the law was planned (Osawa 2000, 5).

If elected women are more likely to represent issues that affect women, then there is a democratic imperative for women to be a part of the political decision-making processes in government. Some countries have acknowledged this and implemented affirmative action measures to ensure women are present. These measures also recognise that women as a group have suffered and continue to suffer discrimination (often invisible) and attempt to counter the results of this discrimination. These measures include electoral gender quotas, as seen in Scandinavian countries, many South and Central American countries, and South Korea; reserved seats, as seen in India; and the most common type, political party quotas, as seen in Australia, the United Kingdom, Brazil, and many more. The effects of gender quotas are mixed, but the remarkable increase in the proportion of women in elected to lower house seats of government across the globe in the last 20 years from just 12 percent in January 1997 to an average of 23.5 percent as of December 2017 (Inter-Parliamentary Union 2017) has occurred concurrently with the spread of gender quotas to more than 100 countries (Rosen 2017, 83). In recent years, the campaign to have electoral quotas implemented in Japan is gaining momentum. Challenges remain, however.

Conclusion: where to from here?

The movement in Japan to introduce electoral quotas began in 1994. Many are tired of waiting for change and believe that if gender quotas are not introduced in Japan, the country will get further and further "left behind" by the rest of the world (Miura 2016c, 349). In January 2015, a group of cross-partisan Diet members was formed with the objective of legalising an electoral quota system for the purpose of increasing the number of women elected to the Diet. The alliance created a bill, which the four opposition parties submitted to the Diet on 30 May 2016. The bill was aimed at ensuring political parties field equal numbers of male and female candidates. The governing LDP and *Komeitō*, along with *Ishin no Kai*, opposed the words "equal numbers" (*dōsū*) in the bill and created their own, with the less binding phrase "as equal as possible" (*dekiru kagiri kintō*). After revisions, the bill received cross-partisan support in 2017 and was passed in May 2018. The successful bill, known as the Gender Parity Law, mandates that political parties must "endeavour" (*tsutomeru*) to make sure numbers of men and women candidates are "as equal as possible." It has no binding power and thus results will depend on the action of political parties.

Based on cross-national research of quotas, the effectiveness of a gender quota depends very much on its suitability for that country and its correct implementation. For a quota to be effective in its purpose of increasing the number of women elected to office, it typically needs a specific target (like 30 percent or more) and sanctions for non-compliance (Rosen 2017, 97). Japan's cross-partisan bill contains neither. For a bill like this to be effective, political party leaders need to be concerned about the issue, supportive of affirmative action as a concept, and willing to act. In light of the dominance of the LDP, which shows consistent indifference towards the idea of a gender quota, the potential effectiveness of this bill is questionable. In fact, in the 2019 Upper House elections - the first election to be held since the implementation of this law - a mere 15 percent of the LDP candidates were women. This is in contrast to 71 percent for the SDP and 55 percent for the JCP. The success of the cross-partisan alliance containing some well-connected and influential politicians, like political veteran and senior member of the LDP Noda Seiko, who are committed to affirmative action for the purpose of increasing women in office is nevertheless a hopeful sign. Noda (2018, cited in Nannichi 2018, 4) states, "I want the bill to effect an 'awakening' about increasing the number of women." In this sense, perhaps the bill should be regarded as one of the first steps in the consciousness-raising that is required to drive substantive change. It is a welcome step towards addressing the enduring problem of gender inequality in Japanese politics.

Appendix
POLITICAL PARTY GLOSSARY

Liberal Democratic Party (LDP): *Jijūminshutō*
Democratic Party (DP): *Minshutō* (formerly known as Democratic Party of Japan)
Social Democratic Party (SDP): *Shakai Minshutō* (formerly known as the Japan Socialist Party)
Japan Restoration Party: *Nippon Ishin no Kai* (often referred to simply as *Ishin no Kai*)

Related chapters

10 Family, Inequality, and the Work-Family Balance in Contemporary Japan
15 Gender and the Law: Progress and Remaining Problems
20 Demanding Publics: Women and Activism

References

Catalano, A. (2009) "Women Acting for Women? An Analysis of Gender and Debate Participation in the British House of Commons 2005–2007," *Politics and Gender* 5 (1) 45–68.
Caul, M. (1999) "Women's Representation in Politics: The Role of Political Parties," *Party Politics* 5 (1) 75–98.
Celis, K. and Childs, S. (2012) "The Substantive Representation of Women: What to Do with Conservative Claims?" *Political Studies* 60 (1) 213–225.
Dalton, E. (2015) *Women and Politics in Contemporary Japan*, Oxon and New York: Routledge.
Femigiren. (2015) *Jijitai Gikai ni Okeru Seisabetsu Taiken Ankēto, Hōkokushū* (Report on the Questionnaire about Sexual Discrimination Experience in Municipal Legislative Councils), Tokyo: Femigiren.
Garon, S. (1993) "Women's Groups and the Japanese State: Contending Approaches to Political Integration, 1890–1945," *Journal of Japanese Studies* 19 (1) 5–41.
Hayashi, K. (2016) "Josei ga kaeru, Nihon no shakai" (Women Will Change Japanese Society), in R. Akamatsu (ed) *Josei Giin ga Fuereba Shakai ga Kawaru* (Society Will Change with More Women Representatives), Tokyo: Pad Women's Office, 78–105.
Inter-Parliamentary Union. (2008) "Equality in Politics: A Survey of Men and Women in Parliaments." http://archive.ipu.org/PDF/publications/equality08-e.pdf.
Inter-Parliamentary Union. (2017) "Women in National Parliaments." www.ipu.org/wmn-e/classif.htm.
Iwanaga, K. (2008) "Women's Political Representation in Japan," in K. Iwanaga (ed) *Women's Political Participation and Representation in Asia*, Copenhagen: NIAS Press, 101–129.

Japan Times. (2010) "Lower House Facility to Open Its First Child Care Center Next Month," *Japan Times* 6 August. http://search.japantimes.co.jp/mail/nn20100806a6.html.
Kobayashi, A. (2015) "Sukāto o fumaretsuzukeru" (Skirts Still Being Stepped on), *AERA* 1542 (56).
Koikari, M. (2002) "Exporting Democracy: American Women, 'Feminist Reforms' and the Politics of Imperialism in the U.S. Occupation of Japan, 1945–1952," *Frontiers* 23 (1) 23–45.
Krook, M. L. (2016) "Violence Against Women in Politics." Paper Presented at the International Political Science Association World Congress, Poznan, Poland.
Krook, M. L. (2017) "Violence Against Women in Politics," *Journal of Democracy* 28 (1) 74–88.
Kubo, K. and Gelb, J. (1994) "Obstacles and Opportunities: Women and Political Participation in Japan," in J. Gelb and M. L. Palley (eds) *Women of Japan and Korea*, Philadelphia: Temple University Press, 120–149.
Mackie, V. (1997) *Creating Socialist Women in Japan. Gender, Labour and Activism, 1900–1937*, Cambridge: Cambridge University Press.
Mackie, V. (2003) *Feminism in Modern Japan. Citizenship, Embodiment and Sexuality*, Cambridge: Cambridge University Press.
Matland, R. E. (1998) "Enhancing Women's Political Participation: Legislative Recruitment and Electoral Systems," in A. Karam (ed) *Women in Parliament: Beyond Numbers*, Stockholm: International Institute for Democracy and Electoral Assistance, 65–88.
Miura, M. (2014) "Nihon ni okeru kuōtasei seiritsu no seijiteki jōken" (Political Conditions for Implementing a Quota in Japan), in M. Miura and M. Eto (eds) *Gender Quotas in Comparative Perspectives: Understanding the Increase in Women Representatives*, Tokyo: Akashi, 235–260.
Miura, M. (2016a) "Introduction," in M. Miura (ed) *Nihon no Josei Giin Dō Sureba Fueru no ka* (How to Increase Women Representatives), Tokyo: Asahi Shinbun, 3–12.
Miura, M. (2016b) "Josei ga giin ni naru toiu koto" (When Women Become Representatives), in M. Miura (ed) *Nihon no Josei Giin Dō Sureba Fueru no ka* (How to Increase Women Representatives), Tokyo: Asahi Shinbun, 13–62.
Miura, M. (2016c) "Conclusion," in M. Miura (ed) *Nihon no Josei Giin Dō Sureba Fueru no ka* (How to Increase Women Representatives), Tokyo: Asahi Shinbun, 347–354.
Nannichi, K. (2018) "Danjokōhosha 'kintō' e hōan futatabi" (Reattempt with the Bill Concerning 'Equal' Male and Female Candidates), *Asahi Shinbun* 2 February, 4.
National Democratic Institute (2017) "#NotTheCost: Stopping Violence Against Women in Politics Program Guidance."
New Japan Women's Association (2015) "Watashi ga Kanjita Sabetsu"—Zen Josei Chihō Giin Ankēto no Kekka ni tsuite (Results of Questionnaire to All Women Local Council Members). www.shinfujin.gr.jp/survey/2015date/2015_councilwoman_questionnaire.pdf.
Norris, P. (1993) "Conclusions: Comparing Legislative Recruitment," in. J. Lovenduski and P. Norris (eds) *Gender and Party Politics*, London: Sage, 309–330.
Norris, P. (2006) "The Impact of Electoral Reform on Women's Representation," *Acta Politica* 41 197–213.
Ōsawa, M. (2000) "Government Approaches to Gender Equality in the Mid-1990s," *Social Science Japan Journal* 3 (1) 3–19.
Oyama, N. (2016) "Josei giin to dansei giin wa nani ga chigau no ka" (What Is the Difference Between Female and Male Representatives?) in M. Miura (ed) *Nihon no Josei Giin Dō Sureba Fueru no ka* (How to Increase Women Representatives), Tokyo: Asahi Shinbun, 217–270.
Paxton, P., Kunovich, S. and Hughes, M. M. (2007) "Gender in Politics," *Annual Review of Sociology* 33 263–284.
Pharr, S. J. (1987) "The Politics of Women's Rights," in R. Ward and Y. Sakamoto (eds) *Democratizing Japan: The Allied Occupation*, Honolulu: University of Hawaii Press, 221–252.
Puwar, N. (2004) *Space Invaders: Race, Gender and Bodies Out of Place*, Oxford: Berg.
Rosen, J. (2017) "Gender Quotas for Women in National Politics: A Comparative Analysis Across Development Thresholds," *Social Science Research* 66 82–101.
Shiomura, A. (2016) *Josei Seijika no Riaru* (The Reality of a Women Politician), Tokyo: East Press.
Tsujimura, M. (2007) "Seiji sankaku to jendā kuōta: Kuōta sei no gōhōsei o chushin ni" (Political Participation and Gender Quotas: A Focus on the Constitutionality of Gender Quotas), in S. Kawato and H. Yamamoto (eds) *Seiji Sankaku to Jendā* (Political Participation and Gender), Sendai, Japan: Tohoku University, 5–42.
Wangnerud, L. (2000) "Testing the Politics of Presence: Women's Representation in the Swedish Riksdag," *Scandinavian Political Studies* 23 (1) 67–91.

Yamaguchi, M. (2002) "Josei tachi no senkyo to seiji sanka: Jissenteki michishirube" (Women's Participation in Elections and Politics: Practical Signposts), in F. Ichikawa Memorial Association (ed) *Ichikawa Fusae Seijisanka Sentā de Manabu: 47nin no chosen* (Learning at the Ichikawa Fusae Political Participation Centre: The Challenge of 47 Women), Tokyo: Ichikawa Fusae Kinenkai, 10–16.

Yoon, J. and Osawa, K. (2017) "Advocating Policy Interests in Local Politics: Women's Subtantive Representation in Japan and South Korea," *Asian Women* 33 (2) 43–67.

20
DEMANDING PUBLICS
Women and activism

Chelsea Szendi Schieder

The main focus of this chapter is what has often been called "women's activism" in Japan, with the caveat that both the terms "women" and "activism" are not fixed categories and require attention to historical context. "Gender" is a useful but relatively new scholarly analytical category and one with its own roots in feminist activist scholarship (Scott 1999). A great deal of the earlier literature that worked through what now might be considered the gendered meaning of activism tended to focus on "women's movements" (Inoue 1963; Tatewaki 1957), and foundational literature on gender and activism in Japan in English introduces audiences to such issues through the figures of prominent female activists (Hane 2003; Sievers 1983; Hane 1988). Although social expectations of gendered behaviour define not only cis-gender female activists, key debates in what was long studied as women's activism created the conditions that made broader critiques of gendered expectations in political participation possible.

Within this chapter, "activism" refers to engagement by non-institutional actors to bring about political or social change. This understanding of activism relies upon a modern mode of politics in which the public is understood to be part of the national political project. This has not always meant that marginalized groups had access to the vote or even to political debate. A persistent theme in women's activism has been the enduring limits to full political participation by women based on gendered understandings of citizenship in particular. However, modern political institutions that appealed to enlightenment ideas of natural rights offered an understanding of political participation that made it possible for many women to make demands as the "public."

This chapter gives an overview of the history of women and activism through a roughly chronological account of major social movements in modern Japanese history organized by the following themes: gendered understandings of political and activist subjects, tensions between radical leftist and liberal women activists, the gendered implication of mothers' activism, gendered marginalization and exclusion among activists, and the transnational influences of gendered activism.

Gendered understandings of political subjects and activist subjects

Gendered exclusion was at the core of the modern Japanese state. The legal systems put into place by elites from 1868 to 1898 established the parameters of political participation for the populace at large. The political context of the early Meiji Period was in many ways a time in which an expanding number of people, usually but not exclusively men, negotiated the boundaries of who could or could not access rights.

While most people living under the Meiji state did not enjoy democratic rights, ideas from the West about natural rights, equality, and individualism influenced political discussions. In 1873, a group of elite men established the Meiji Six Society (*Meirokusha*), and their commitment to explore "modern" ideas created a public sphere in which the merits of democracy and natural rights could be debated. This was an elite male public sphere, however, and while the Meiji liberals of the *Meirokusha* at times proposed a new mode for gender relations, they tended to think of granting women "equal rights" within marriage, rather than in politics (Mackie 2003a, 24).

While "modern" ideas about new institutions and natural rights influenced the tenor of political conversations, Confucianism also retained a strong intellectual influence. Confucianism tended to define women as inherently passive subjects and demanded obedience of them. However, Confucian ideas about a "mandate from heaven" that only legitimized benevolent rule galvanized activism in the Meiji Period as well. When wealthy farmers mobilized by demanding benevolent rule and also natural rights, they formed the Freedom and People's Rights Movement (*Jiyū minken undō*) in the 1870s to challenge the continued rule of elites (Irokawa 1967, 181). While most members of the Movement were male, the movement also shaped the early experience of women like Fukuda Hideko, who would go on to participate in more radical activist movements (Hane 1988, 29–50).

Two key laws implemented in the late Meiji Period defined the gendered limits for political subjects in modern Japan: the 1890 Law on Political Associations and Assembly (*Shūkai oyobi seisha hō*) and the 1898 Meiji Civil Code (*Meiji minpō*). The 1890 Law on Political Associations and Assembly prohibited women from "engaging in any political activity, whether it be attending a political meeting, holding one, or joining a political party" (Mackie 2003a, 35). Article Five of the 1900 Public Peace Police Law (*Chian keisatsu hō*) also prohibited women from participating in political activity. As such, repealing Article Five became a focus for women's activism in the Meiji Period.

Whereas marriage and inheritance practices in pre-Meiji Japan had differed across regions and classes, the 1898 Meiji Civil Code instituted a patriarchal family form. Under this law, women were incompetents and the male head of the household wielded tremendous power over all members of the family. This family structure became a common target for activist women, and criticism of the family system alone could constitute an act of protest.

The Meiji legal code not only restricted women's participation in politics, it also prohibited minors, police, and military men from engaging in political activities and forbade the organizing of labour strikes. The state did not recognize basic democratic freedoms, and only men who paid a certain amount of taxes were permitted to participate in politics. The Commoner's Society (*Heiminsha*) formed in 1903 precisely to challenge that class-based exclusion, and more radical strains of socialist and anarchist thought also shaped activism in the late Meiji Period.

The time saw a proliferation of women's socialist journals such as *Nijūseiki no Fujin* (*Twentieth Century Woman*, founded in 1904) and *Sekai Fujin* (*Women of the World*, founded in 1907 and closed due to government pressure in 1909). However, many socialist activists did not challenge the "implicit notions of gender identity" as they were constructed in the Meiji Period; even within radical movements, women often acted as "wives" and "helpmates" (Mackie 2003a, 6). Government suppression proved to be a bigger threat to the movement in any case, as a series of mass arrests decimated the Left in Japan by 1930 (Hane 1988, 27).

While limits to women's participation in politics and activism certainly defined the gendered context for activism in the Meiji Period, Marnie Anderson has critiqued the historiography of women's activism in the late nineteenth century in Japan. Historians often rely upon women who wrote—who demonstrated "literary agency"—and tend to underestimate those women's links with male activists while also dismissing women who did not write as "passive appendages of men" (Anderson 2011). This has made for an incomplete history of how women and men actually participated in activism together.

Historians' focus on "literary agency" has meant that early feminist journals such as *Seitō* (Bluestockings), founded in 1911 by an elite group of women, has figured prominently in studies about the political and social role of women in Meiji-era Japan (Bardsley 2007; Lowy 2007; Sievers 1983). The journal offered women a space to debate issues important to women and to advocate for women as intellectuals as well as citizens. The journal featured heated debates about female sexuality, suffrage, and the issue of state assistance for mothers. Contributors advocated a diverse set of ideological positions *vis-à-vis* proper gender relations and political solutions (Mackie 2003b, 45–72). The vigorous debate in the pages of *Seitō*, then, points to another longstanding tension in women's activism in modern Japan based on various ideas about the ultimate goals of women's political participation, a tension perhaps best explored through thinking what marked the difference between "radical leftist" and "liberal" women activists.

Tensions between "radical leftist" and "liberal" women activists

While gendered understanding about who belonged in politics and even in activism continually excluded women from understandings about the "public," tensions also developed among women with different ideological goals. In 1922, modifications to Article Five of the Public Peace Police Law made it possible for women to organize to demand women's suffrage. The 1920s in Japan saw an explosion of various "women's" organizations, which varied widely in terms of aims and strategies. For some women who demanded suffrage, access to the existing state was the end of activism in itself, while female socialists and anarchists often saw women's political participation as just one aspect of a much larger struggle against state authority and economic exploitation.

The modification of Article Five of the Public Peace Police Law was itself the result of activism spearheaded by the New Women's Association (*Shin fujin kyōkai*), founded in 1920 by Hiratsuka Raichō, Ichikawa Fusae, and Oku Mumeo. Radical women from outside the group criticized its lack of a socialist perspective (Mackie 2003a, 104). Internal differences of opinion soon split the group as well (Ichikawa 1972, 68). Ichikawa went on to found the League of the Attainment of Women's Political Rights (Suffrage League/*Fujin sanseiken kakutoku kisei dōmeikai*) in 1924. Women's Leagues affiliated with the proletarian parties that proliferated after the 1925 Enactment of Universal Manhood Suffrage also multiplied. New women's groups included socialist women's groups like the *Sekirankai* (Red Wave Society, founded in 1921) and the *Yōkakai* (Eighth Day Society, founded in 1922).

To examine the points of difference that defined a more radical leftist "socialist" female activist position from the "liberal" position of the women's suffrage activists, it is worth looking closely at a set of demands outlined by socialist Yamakawa Kikue and the Women's Division of the Political Studies Association, which was affiliated with prominent communists and the Labour Union Council. The 1925 demands overlapped with the demands of women in the Ichikawa Fusae-led Suffrage League but also demonstrated some distinct differences. Like many advocates for full female political participation, Yamakawa decried the contemporary head-of-household system and women's lack of rights in the family and marriage, demanded workplace accommodations for women and mothers, and called for the abolition of licensed prostitution.

In contrast to the female activists of the Suffrage League, Yamakawa called for equal education and employment opportunities and standard living wages for women *and* the people of the colonies (Faison 2017, 22–23). Yamakawa and her comrades insisted on a socialist program, and their leftist beliefs entailed not only changes to the institutions that marginalized women in public economic institutions but also changes that would extend the rights enjoyed by ethnically Japanese men to colonized men and women.

In 1931, a year after the First National Women's Suffrage Conference of April 1930, a limited Bill for Women's Suffrage passed the lower house. While groups that had supported the Conference included rather radical groups, such as the Proletarian Women's League, support for the Bill on the part of lawmakers probably rested on their gendered assumption that women might prove a conservative force and mitigate the power of more radical male voters (Mackie 2003a, 131).

As the nation geared up for war following the September 1931 Manchurian Crisis, it became increasingly difficult to voice dissent in Japan. Female activists engaged in the suffrage movement had different reactions to the rise of an increasingly authoritarian militarist state. In 1940, leading suffrage activist Ichikawa dissolved the Suffrage League and joined the state-sponsored All Japan Women's League (*Dainihon fujinkai*). After the war, Ichikawa "claimed that it was in order to cause women's abilities to be recognized with the aim of acquiring the right to political participation within the framework of national policy" that she participated in the enforcement of the wartime state's policies (Loftus 2013, 44). Ichikawa prioritized women's access to political institutions over a more radical critique of the applications of political power.

In spite of the various political positions women took in the prewar period, as radicals, liberals, and as patriotic militarists, after Japan's 1945 defeat, the Allied Occupation of Japan (1945–1952) inaugurated a gendered political culture that construed female participation in an essentializing way, specifically understanding women as nonviolent. The US occupying authorities, primarily Douglas MacArthur, demanded women's suffrage as a pillar of postwar democracy and based his opinion on ideas popular in the United States about women as a moderating political force. On the Japanese side, Prime Minister Shidehara Kijūrō agreed, and argued to sceptical Japanese lawmakers that women were non-ideological, politically moderate, and had a simplicity that could benefit that nation (Koikari 2008, 49–50). Japan's wartime experience and the particular ways in which women were imagined to figure in its resolution offered women a privileged place from which to speak as new citizens when the Japanese parliament amended the electoral law in December 1945 to give women the vote.

The gendered implications of postwar mothers' activism

Because of the gendered exclusions of the prewar and wartime state, any political participation by women in those periods may constitute "activism." In the postwar period, women gained the legal right to vote, run for office, and participate in politics. Barriers to women's full participation remained, although many of them were based on informal and cultural ideas about the proper place for women in public and in politics. In part because of gendered expectations of women's social role and in part as a strategy to amplify women's voices, a dominant mode for postwar women's activism has been what might be called "matricentric activism," or activism as mothers (Maxson 2017).

Women, in their roles as defenders of domestic space and survival, spearheaded key postwar activist movements associated with consumer rights and the peace movement. Soon after the war, demonstrations organized to demand more equitable systems of food distribution and democratic representation often featured female speakers with infants strapped to their backs

(Loftus 2013, 53). On 8 March 1947, International Women's Day, the newly formed Women's Democratic Club (*Minshu fujin kurabu*) mobilized women to counter government corruption in the face of black markets and rampant inflation. In September 1948, women organized as the Federation of Housewives (*Shufuren*) in the wake of nationwide confrontations between women and authorities over the availability of staple foods. The official organ of *Shufuren*, *Shufuren-dayori*, published a 5 December 1948 article that declared, "The greatest success of the Federated Housewives' movement to date has been the establishment of a pipeline into government officialdom so that the voice of female consumers can be heard in quarters that have heretofore been reserved for business elites only" (Loftus 2013, 52). This gendered framing, in which women defended daily household needs against "male" government officials and other expert elites, influenced many of the key activism movements in the postwar period.

Women became some of the most visible supporters of anti-war, anti-nuclear, and environmental movements. These included the anti-US military base struggles from the 1950s onward, the mass demonstrations against the revision and adoption of the US-Japan Security Treaty in 1960, and the protests against wrongdoing by powerful corporations at Miike in the 1960s and Minamata in the 1970s (Onnatachi no ima o 'tō' kai 1987, 1990; Miike 'tankō' shufukai 1973).

When nuclear testing became a galvanizing issue worldwide in the 1950s, Japanese women played a key role in the transnational mobilization of "mothers" against war and specifically nuclear weapons. Hiratsuka Raichō organized the Mother's Congress (*Hahaoya taikai*) in Japan in 1955 in the wake of the "Lucky Dragon incident," in which a tuna fishing boat was contaminated from the fallout of a US nuclear test at Bikini Atoll in 1954. Raichō, as a leader in Japan and as vice-president of Women's International Democratic Federation (WIDF), advocated for a World Congress of Mothers and made the appeals of Japanese women central to the creation of that event. Japanese women's voices were amplified because of their global image as victims of atomic warfare (Mackie 2016).

It has been argued that female activists in postwar Japan fought to reclaim motherhood, which had been co-opted by the wartime state (Maxson 2017). Acting as mothers remains a powerful strategy available to women in postwar Japan, and gendered ideas about motherhood can also mobilize otherwise apolitical women. In the wake of the March 2011 meltdown at the Fukushima Daichi Nuclear Power Plant, scholars were quick to note the various gendered frames women, particularly mothers, stepped into as new activists and how their activism built upon a longer tradition of female environmental activism in postwar Japan (Freiner 2013; Holdgrün and Holthus 2014). But women's perceived lack of expertise also made activist women vulnerable to claims that mothers were engaging in anti-nuclear activism based on hysterical misperceptions (Kimura 2016). There are other drawbacks to organizing women as wives and mothers: mobilizing gendered expectations about women as wives and mothers to criticize state and corporate authority can reinforce gendered stereotypes about women's concerns and labour belonging to the domestic sphere. It can also collapse different categories of female experiences into one essentialized ideal of "women," with "housewife" in particular a privileged socioeconomic position in the postwar period. Robin LeBlanc has also noted, based on her work on "housewife" (*shufu*) activism in the 1990s, how the *shufu* identity was often considered outside public life and politics, not only by politicians and housewives themselves, but also by sociologists and political scientists who researched political and social movements (1999).

In the 1970s, women's liberation (*ūman ribu*) activists, who identified themselves as leftist radicals, launched a critique of social definitions of femininity, which included an inherent link with maternalism and motherhood. This movement insisted upon the political importance of issues that had previously been considered outside of the realm of politics and activism, particularly the nature of femininity, and the liberation of female sexuality (Shigematsu

2012; Mackie 2003b). Whereas many women's movements in the prewar and postwar period had employed the term *fujin* to indicate "women," women's lib activists rejected that term's middle-to-upper-class connotations. They instead embraced the more raw and provocative term *onna* to describe themselves (Shigematsu 2012, 16). They also rejected the common female activist strategy that framed women as victims, noting that it obscured the capacity women had to commit violence and also how women had been complicit in violent institutions in the past (Shigematsu 2012).

Gendered marginalization and exclusion among activists

Scholars of activism in Japan have recently attempted to understand women's activism through critical approaches to the gendered assumptions that have historically marginalized female activism. Vera Mackie has traced how prewar labour unions tended to employ masculine definitions of workers and labour activists, and Christopher Gerteis argues that postwar union activism also privileged a masculinist agenda (Gerteis 2010; Mackie 2003a). These exclusions among leftist labour activists tended to turn on gendered assumptions about women as wives and mothers, and therefore supporters of male labour and activism, rather than participants on their own terms.

The youth-based New Left that emerged in the late 1950s and expanded rapidly across campuses in the 1960s in Japan offered a challenge to the established Left's hegemony over radical activism. The movement embraced a more expansive definition of human liberation, employed a more radically democratic organizational style, and attracted many female students as well as male students in its disruptive protests to state and university authorities. But it also replicated gendered expectations. While men could perform the roles of the heroic street activists, women often found themselves in charge of support duties, preparing food, jail support, and mimeographing fliers (Schieder 2017).

Partly in response to this continued gendered marginalization within activist movements, the women's liberation (*ūman ribu*) movement emerged in the early 1970s and asserted the centrality of feminist critique of imperialism and capitalism. This movement insisted upon the political importance of issues that had previously been considered outside of the realm of politics and activism, particularly the nature of female sexuality and selfhood (Shigematsu 2012; Mackie 2003b; Onnatachi no ima o tō kai 1996). Radical feminism in Japan has perpetuated some of the exclusions that undergird the contemporary gender order in Japan, most notably of lesbians and of ethnic minorities (Welker 2017; Seo 2017). At the same time, radical feminism in the 1970s in many ways created the discursive environment and the networks that would later make other activist movements based on more expansive notions of gender and intersectionality possible. James Welker has noted that *ribu*'s creation of women-only spaces and discursive attention to both female subjectivity and to women's erotic subjectivity made lesbian feminism (*rezubian feminizumu*) possible (Welker 2017, 51).

In contemporary Japan, many people who do not feel that they fit into the existing hegemonic gendered binary are struggling to define themselves. That struggle often includes "resisting the old paternalism (of experts, professionals, the press or even self-proclaimed leaders of minority rights' groups)" as individuals "are stressing their rights to self-determination and expression." At the same time, this emphasis on individual difference often eschews group identities and collective forms of organizing (McLelland and Dasgupta 2005, 8). "Transgender" (*toransujendā*) entered the Japanese language along with information about queer activism and queer studies in 1996. S. P. F. Dale's work on "x-gender" (*x-jendā*) explores how people in local queer organizations in Japan have negotiated their personal identities while demanding the elimination of gender discrimination in society at large. The internet has played a big role in spreading the idea of *x-jendā*, often through blogs that share personal stories. It will be interesting to see how this develops into a social movement demanding change or whether it shifts understandings of what constitutes activism (Dale 2012; see also Dale, this volume).

Both domestic and external pressures through shifting global norms have legitimized efforts to create policy changes to promote "gender equality" in Japan since the 1990s. However, such changes also prompted a backlash among conservative and right-wing groups that opposed the mainstreaming of gender equality policies, particularly from 2002 to 2006 (Yamaguchi 2017). While women seem disproportionately active and visible in contemporary anti-globalization, anti-war, and anti-discriminatory movements in Japan (Chan 2008), conservative women are also activists, although they demonstrate a different approach toward negotiating gender norms (Osawa 2015).

Transnational issues and women's activism

As mentioned previously, there has been a historical tension between women activists who demanded more influence and access to state-level decision-making and women activists who criticized the state as it existed from a more radical positions, ranging from communist and socialist to anarchist and nihilist. In working through historical instances in which the state committed violence, particularly gendered violence, there have also been various positions taken among women activists that have demonstrated the complex position of Japanese women activists *vis-à-vis* women and women activists in nations subjected to Japanese imperial state violence.

The issue of the Japanese imperial military's system of sexual slavery has become a flashpoint for various views concerning the historical position of Japanese women as victims of state discrimination and simultaneously as those who discriminated against and victimized other ethnicities. This was a core idea for the women who founded the Asian Women's Conference Fighting Against Invasion=Discrimination (*Shinryaku=Sabetsu to tatakau Ajia fujin kaigi* in 1970 (Iijima and Germer 2014). The female victims of Japan's militarist violence, particularly women often forced into sexual slavery to service the Imperial military (the so-called "comfort women") were often colonized ethnic minorities, and the activist movement demanding redress for their suffering has been shaped by Japanese academics and activists—many of them women—concerned about Japanese exploitation of other Asian people, resident Korean (*zainichi*) women in Japan, and South Korean academics and activists. Many feminist activist groups in Japan protested what they saw as the exploitation of women in other Asian countries through war and also sex tours of Japanese men from the 1970s onward, and in 1977, a group of women in Tokyo founded the Asian Women's Association (*Ajia no Onnatachi no kai*) (Mackie 2003b, 202–204). At the same time, the women of *zainichi* communities had often felt alienated from the women's liberation movement in Japan and had focused on activism on behalf of their ethnic communities, often as "mothers" (Seo 2017, 234). Yoon Jung-ok, a South Korean scholar and activist, researched the "comfort women" issue and introduced *zainichi* female activists to the idea that "comfort women" had been victims not only of colonial aggression but also of patriarchy (Seo 2017, 236). The broader movement demanding redress for female victims of wartime sexual violence involved a transnational network of feminist activists and scholars, which organized a Women's International War Crimes Tribunal on Japan's Military Sexual Slavery in 2000 that brought together prosecution teams from nine countries to examine evidence and testimonies. While the Tribunal did not have legal authority, it did influence the global community's discussions of how armed conflict includes specifically gendered sexual violence (United Nations 1998). The movement for redress has not been free from controversies over legacies of colonial exploitation or how to understand ethnic or feminist belonging (Wöhr 2017).

Related chapters

3   Debates in Japanese Feminism
6   Transgender, Non-Binary Genders, and Intersex in Japan
19 Women in Electoral Politics

References

Anderson, M. (2011) "Women's Agency and the Historical Record: Reflections on Female Activists in the Nineteenth-Century Japan," *Journal of Women's History* 23 38–55.
Bardsley, J. (2007) *The Bluestockings of Japan: New Woman Essays and Fiction from Seitô, 1911–1916*, Minneapolis: University of Michigan Center for Japanese Studies.
Chan-Tiberghien, J. (2004) *Gender and Human Rights Politics in Japan: Global Norms and Domestic Networks*, Stanford: Stanford University Press.
Dale, S. P. F. (2012) "An Introduction to X-Jendâ: Examining a New Gender Identity in Japan," *Intersections: Gender and Sexuality in Asia and the Pacific* 31 1–17.
Faison, E. (2017) "Women's Rights as Proletarian Rights: Yamakawa Kikue, Suffrage, and the 'Dawn of Liberation'," in J. C. Bullock, A. Kano and J. Welker (eds) *Rethinking Japanese Feminisms*, Honolulu: University of Hawai'i Press, 15–33.
Freiner, N. (2013) "Mobilizing Mothers: The Fukushima Daiichi Nuclear Catastrophe and Environmental Activism in Japan," *ASIANetwork Exchange* 21 1–15.
Gerteis, C. (2010) *Gender Struggles: Wage-Earning Women and Male-Dominated Unions in Postwar Japan*, Cambridge, MA: Harvard University Asia Center.
Hane, M. (1988) *Reflections on the Way to the Gallows: Rebel Women in Prewar Japan*, Berkeley: University of California Press.
Hane, M. (2003) *Peasants, Rebels, Women, and Outcastes: The Underside of Modern Japan*, Lanham, MD: Rowman & Littlefield.
Holdgrün, P. and Holthus, B. (2014) "Gender and Political Participation in Post-3/11 Japan," *DIJ Working Papers* 14, German Institute for Japan Studies.
Ichikawa, F. (1972) *Watashi no fujin undô* (My Women's Movement), Tokyo: Akimoto Shobo.
Iijima, A. and Germer, A. (trans.) (2014) "From Personal Experience to Political Activism in the 1970s: My View of Feminism," in A. Germer, V. Mackie and U. Wöhr (eds) *Gender, Nation and State in Modern Japan*, New York: Routledge.
Inoue, R. (ed) (1963) *Gendai fujin undô shi nenpyô* (Timeline of Modern Women's Movements), Tokyo: San'ichi Shobo.
Irokawa, D. (1967) "Freedom and the Concept of People's Rights," *Japan Quarterly* 14 175–183.
Kimura, A. H. (2016) *Radiation Brain Moms and Citizen Scientists: The Gender Politics of Food Contamination after Fukushima*, Durham: Duke University Press.
Koikari, M. (2008) *Pedagogy of Democracy: Feminism and the Cold War in the U.S. Occupation of Japan*, Philadelphia: Temple University Press.
LeBlanc, R. M. (1999) *Bicycle Citizens*, Berkeley: University of California Press.
Loftus, R. P. (2013) "Resenting Injustice: Yoshitake Teruko—From Ampo to Women's Lib," in *Changing Lives: The "Postwar" in Japanese Women's Autobiographies and Memoirs, Asia Past & Present: New Research from AAS*, Ann Arbor: Association for Asian Studies, Inc, 85–106.
Lowy, D. (2007) *The Japanese "New Woman": Images of Gender and Modernity*, New Brunswick, NJ: Rutgers University Press.
Mackie, V. (2003a) *Creating Socialist Women in Japan: Gender, Labour and Activism, 1900–1937*, Cambridge: Cambridge University Press.
Mackie, V. (2003b) *Feminism in Modern Japan: Citizenship, Embodiment, and Sexuality*, Cambridge: Cambridge University Press.
Mackie, V. (2016) "From Hiroshima to Lausanne: The World Congress of Mothers and the *Hahaoya Taikai* in the 1950s," *Women's History Review* 25 (4) 671–695.

Maxson, H. (2017) "From 'Motherhood in the Interest of the State' to Motherhood in the Interest of Mothers: Rethinking the First Mothers' Congress," in J. C. Bullock, A. Kano and J. Welker (eds) *Rethinking Japanese Feminisms*, Honolulu: University of Hawai'i Press, 34–49.

McLelland, M. and Dasgupta, R. (2005) *Genders, Transgenders and Sexualities in Japan*, London: Routledge.

Miike tankō shufukai (ed) (1973) *Miike shufukai nijūnen* (Twenty Years of the Miike Housewives' Association), Tokyo: Rōdō Daigaku.

Onnatachi no ima o tou kai (ed) (1987) *55-nen taisei seiritsu to onnatachi* (The Establishment of the 1955 System and Women), Jūgoshi nōto sengohen, Kawasaki: Inpakuto Shuppankai.

Onnatachi no ima o tou kai (ed) (1990) *Onnatachi no 60-nen Anpo* (Women's 1960 US-Japan Security Treaty), Jūgoshi nōto sengohen, Kawasaki: Inpakuto Shuppankai.

Onnatachi no ima o tou kai (ed) (1996) *Zenkyōtō kara ribu e* (From Zenkyōtō to Lib), Jūgoshi nōto sengohen, Kawasaki: Inpakuto Shuppankai.

Osawa, K. (2015) "Traditional Gender Norms and Women's Political Participation: How Conservative Women Engage in Political Activism in Japan," *Social Science Japan Journal* 18 45–61.

Schieder, C. S. (2017) "Left Out: Writing Women Back into Japan's 1968," in J. E. Pieper-Mooney and T. Chaplin (eds) *The Global 1960s: Convention, Contest and Counterculture, Decades in Global History*, New York: Routledge, 140–158.

Scott, J. W. (1999) *Gender and the Politics of History*, New York: Columbia University Press.

Seo, A. (2017) "Toward Postcolonial Feminist Subjectivity: Korean Women's Redress Movement for 'Comfort Women'," in J. C. Bullock, A. Kano and J. Welker (eds) *Rethinking Japanese Feminisms*, Honolulu: University of Hawai'i Press, 230–250.

Shigematsu, S. (2012) *Scream from the Shadows: The Women's Liberation Movement in Japan*, Minneapolis: University of Minnesota Press.

Sievers, S. (1983) *Flowers in Salt: The Beginnings of Feminist Consciousness in Modern Japan*, Stanford: Stanford University Press.

Tatewaki, S. (1957) *Nihon no fujin: Fujin undô no hatten wo megutte* (Japanese Women: Concerning the Development of a Women's Movement), Tokyo: Iwanami shinsho.

United Nations Division for the Advancement of Women Department of Economic and Social Affairs. (1998) "Sexual Violence and Armed Conflict: United Nations Response," *Women 2000*, New York.

Welker, J. (2017) "From Women's Liberation to Lesbian Feminism in Japan: Rezubian Feminizumu Within and Beyond the Ūman Ribu Movement in the 1970s and 1980s," in J. C. Bullock, A. Kano and J. Welker (eds) *Rethinking Japanese Feminisms*, Honolulu: University of Hawai'i Press, 50–67.

Wöhr, U. (2017) "A Touchstone for Transnational Feminism: Discourses on the Comfort Women in Japan," *Japanstudien* 16 (1) 59–90.

Yamaguchi, T. (2017) "The Mainstreaming of Feminism and the Politics of Backlash in Twenty-First-Century Japan," in J. C. Bullock, A. Kano and J. Welker (eds) *Rethinking Japanese Feminisms*, Honolulu: University of Hawai'i Press, 68–85.

21
LESBIANS AND QUEER WOMEN IN JAPAN

Jane Wallace

When I began my PhD research on lesbian, gay, bisexual, and transgender (LGBT) communities in Japan, I was discouraged by a relative lack of scholarship on lesbians and queer women within the scholarship of gender and sexuality in Japan. Reading through what seemed to be scant literature on the topic appeared to confirm these accounts. As Maree (2007, 291) points out, "it would be safe to say that Lesbian Studies has never seriously been placed on the Japanese academic agenda." Over the last decade, Izumo Marou and Claire Maree (2003), Claire Maree (2007, 2015), and James Welker (2010, 2017) have made key contributions to addressing this imbalance. There are, however, a number of reasons for the relative absence of scholarship on queer women, including the fact that lesbian and queer women's communities have historically carved out spaces outside the academy in which to produce their own work (Maree 2007; Welker 2010). It is important, however, not to fall into despair about the potential of the field. Whilst relatively few in number, the existing literature is as diverse and as complex as the lived experiences of the people it seeks to understand.

After a brief discussion of the politics of naming, this chapter is divided thematically, presenting the reader with snapshots of scholarship across three subfields. The first section will discuss historical studies of lesbians and queer women. The second section will give an overview of first-person narratives, with particular focus on the issue of *tōjisha-sei* (being directly concerned with an issue). The final section will focus upon sociological studies of lesbians and queer women in Japan. The chapter will conclude with a discussion of the significance of existing scholarship and other writing and some suggestions for future directions.

Naming queer women's identities and communities

Although transliterations of loan words such as *rezubian* (lesbian) seem on a surface level to be identical in meaning to their English counterparts, they do not always carry the same connotations. Indeed, the politics of naming queer women's identities has a long history to which this chapter must attend.

During the rise of the Women's Liberation Movement in the 1970s, and again during the so-called "gay boom" of the 1990s, lesbian feminists engaged directly with the meaning of the word "lesbian" (Maree 2015). However, Sugiura (2007, 127) has argued that it was not until the 1990s that the word *rezubian* took on the meaning of women-loving-women, as distinct from the earlier designation of *onabe* (pot), which usually referred to "masculinized women." The word "lesbian" continues to evolve, with many individuals preferring to identify as *bian*, which avoids the negative connotations "*rezu*" (lez, which is similar in tone to "dyke"). "Lesbian" is also often associated with pornography made for heterosexual men, which means that some individuals shy away from its use (Horie 2008; Kakefuda 1992; Tamagawa 2017). Hence, "lesbian" is used in this chapter as a close approximation of the Japanese *rezubian* and refers to individuals who self-identify as *rezubian*/lesbian in its many meanings.

The word *kuia* (queer), has not yet entered mainstream use in Japan, and tends to be used mainly within scholarship and activist groups. It is not entirely unproblematic to apply this word to the Japanese context. However, it does open up linguistic space in which to include non-heterosexual women who do not find room for themselves under the label "lesbian." "Queer" includes, but is not limited to, bisexual+, pansexual, sexually fluid, and non-monosexual identifying individuals. In this chapter, "women" and "woman" include all who identify as such, regardless of their gender assigned at birth, day-to-day strategies of identification, or current legal registration status.

It would be difficult to argue that there is a single monolithic lesbian community in Japan. The development of organised community groups for lesbians and queer women has a long history in Japan, with the establishment of *Wakakusa no kai* (Young Grass Club) in 1971 as a significant moment. There continue to be a number of online and face-to-face lesbian community groups active in Japan, including *Regumi Sutajio*, which was established in 1987 (Regumi Sutajio 2013). There are also active women-only bar scenes, particularly in larger cities such as Tokyo, Osaka, and Nagoya. However, with lesbians and queer women spread across the country, communities are often created online or through a sense of shared experiences and values. The communities discussed here are loose groupings of individuals who find collective belonging through the shared experiences of identifying as a lesbian or queer woman in Japan.

Lesbian and queer women's histories

Historical writing is one of the most well-developed areas of scholarship, documenting the long history of lesbian and queer women's organising and community building in Japan. However, much lesbian and queer women's history writing has occurred on the fringes of academia. As Maree (2007, 293) has argued, "lesbian studies" as it is in Japan, "lives in shared histories of community events, in activism and in writings by woman-loving women." Many of these histories can be found in special collected editions brought together by community groups such as Regumi Sutajio and the writers of *Subarashii onna tachi* (*Wonderful Women*, a newsletter written by a group of women who broke away from Young Grass Club). A seminal early example of such a publication is *Onna o ai suru onnatachi no monogatari* (Stories of Women Who Love Women) (Bessatsu 1987), which was brought to fruition by Sawabe Hitomi. The volume established the shape of community-based writing that continued well into the 2000s with a focus on personal experiences and the inclusion of artwork, interviews, and surveys. This special issue is perhaps most significant in the role it played as access point for many lesbian and queer women into the community at the time (Welker 2010; Yajima 1999). Welker (2010) notes that many women cite reading this volume as being the first realisation of the extent of the lesbian community in Japan. As many respondents in my own study stated, in a time before the rapid sharing of information online, much knowledge was shared through printed materials of this kind. The magazine also set the tone for future publications of this ilk, as can be seen in a 2001 edition of the now discontinued lesbian magazine *Anīsu* (Anise) (*Anīsu* 2001). Although written over a decade later, the *Anīsu* special edition brought together the history of the lesbian community using similar techniques of experience-based interviews and documentary materials.

Despite the contribution of magazines such as *Onna o ai suru onnatachi no monogatari* and *Anīsu* to our understanding of lesbian histories in Japan, piecing together these accounts into a coherent whole can be tricky. As Welker (2010) noted, it is often necessary to look to alternative modes of history-telling, such as the tradition of *zadankai* in intellectual and literary publishing in Japan. These are essentially transcriptions of round-table discussions, published alongside essays and other formats more familiar to non-Japanese readers (see also Kano in this volume). An example of one such *zadankai* was published in the May 1997 issue of *Gendai shisō* (Contemporary Thought), which featured Izumi Marō, Hara Minako, Tsuzura Yoshiko, and Ochiya Kumiko. Discussion covered the development of lesbian feminism in Japan, including tensions over the balance between political activism and the creation of networking and socialisation spaces. This debate emerged from the fact that Young Grass Club was originally set up as a social space, but lesbian feminists within the club wanted to undertake more focused activism (Izumo et al. 1997).

What will strike the reader when looking at these sources are the number of debates which continue to circulate within contemporary lesbian and queer spaces. For example, Izumo (Izumo et al. 1997, 60) talked personally about tensions within *Subarashii onna tachi* related to the telling of "dark" (*kurai*) experiences of being a lesbian in Japan. Izumo discusses the telling of these negative experiences as a "political strategy" and as a way of unpicking the complexity of the problems facing same-sex-attracted women in Japan. Debate was central to lesbian feminism, as it was to the wider feminist movements in Japan (see Kano in this volume). How to deal with personal trauma, and its role within activism, is a question that continues to resonate now. For example, during my own fieldwork, one activist respondent who actively engaged with the mainstream media described how they would intentionally withhold negative experiences during interviews because they felt that these stories didn't seek visibility in constructive ways.

For some lesbian feminists such as Sugiura Ikuko, however, how the public would understand lesbianism was not the major concern. Sugiura was instead interested in the ways in which community discourses of lesbianism have changed over time and the emergence of lesbianism as a political choice in the 1970s. Based on documentary evidence and oral histories, Sugiura's "Lesbian Feminist Activism in Japan" (2008) succeeds in shifting the focus towards the notion of identifying as a lesbian as a political choice and the impact of this upon lesbian communities. At the time of this shift in the 1970s, these discursive changes created tension within lesbian and feminist community groups between those who identified as "innate" (*nekkara*) lesbians and those who made the choice to identify as lesbian only as part of their political feminist strategies (Maree 2015).

Sugiura (2015) has also sought to trace a detailed history of discourses of female same-sex sexual desire from the Taishō period (1912–1926) to the 1990s and examine discourse within Japanese lesbian *mini-komi*, self-published magazines like *Subarashii onna tachi* which became popular in Japanese lesbian communities in the 1970s (Sugiura 2017). Of particular significance here is a section in the latter article discussing the politics of naming. As part of Young Grass Club's newsletters, featured individuals were categorised into "types," such as "looks female—bottom" and "looks boyish—top" (Sugiura 2017, 167). These designations were criticised by lesbian feminists such as Izumo Marō (Izumo et al. 1997) for their re-inscription of the male/female binary, with individuals taking on set gender-roles, and for the way in which they conflated same-sex attraction with sexual intercourse. In conflating same-sex attraction with sexual intercourse, these discourses fed in to the gratuitous sexualisation of same-sex-attracted women which has its roots in the so-called perverse press of the 1950s (McLelland 2005). Tensions surrounding designations such as *tachi* (literally "standing," with the connotation "butch", *tachi* may also derive from *tachiyaku* in Kabuki) and *neko* ("cat," equivalent to "femme") included disagreements over the gender presentations considered acceptable and whether designations of *tachi* and *neko* re-inscribed the male/female binary. These discussions were also underway in Anglophone contexts, and it is possible that Sugiura and others were influenced by the translation of works such as Lillian Federman's *Odd Girls and Twilight Lovers*, which was translated by Tamioka Akemi and Hara Minako in 1996. Federman's (1991) work chronicles many of the debates related to naming and categorising as they developed in the United States, and Hara Minako was one of the scholars who appeared in the 1997 edition of *Gendai shisō* which criticized these paradigms (Izumo et al. 1997).

When studying community histories through the works of groups like *Subarashii onna tachi*, we must be cautious about how these histories are used within the communities they discuss. Taking a step back from the simple plotting of events allows us to see that these groups were highly complex, with a range of political and other agendas. Welker (2017, 148) has noted that these community-based histories often refer anachronistically to pre-modern sexual practices and use "utopian" claims about the near future as a strategy for community building. Historians have described these strategies as "recuperative histories," and their use in Japan's lesbian and queer women communities is by no means unique. In Welker's discussion of their self-motivated historical projects (2010, 2017), we begin to see a portrait of Japanese lesbian communities as deeply complex, internationally connected, yet locally situated and constructed. Lesbian and queer communities of women in Japan were more than simple adopters of so-called Western paradigms of gender and sexuality.

Tōjisha-sei and the politics of naming

Any researcher working on LGBT experiences in Japan will soon discover the ubiquitous nature of first-person narratives and debates around naming. The adoption of first-person narratives functioned as a tool in creating solidarity while nevertheless creating and sustaining a complex politics of naming.

During the 1970s, the concept of *tōjisha* was taken up within civil society groups, particularly by disability rights groups, and was later adopted within lesbian and gay liberation movements (McLelland 2009; Nakanishi and Ueno 2003). The term originated in the legal sphere, and can be translated as the "person directly concerned" with a legal case; however, it soon came to take on a wider social meaning. Talking from the position of lived experience, authors and activists developed *tōjisha* narratives as a means to centre the needs of those affected by issues; they quickly became an important tool in solidarity building within minority communities. As a result of the mobilisation of person-centred discourses within lesbian and other movements, the question of who can speak for whom has been a key concern.

The seminal lesbian text in this subfield is Kakefuda Hiroko's *Rezubian' de aru to iu koto* (On Being a "Lesbian," 1992). In this text, Kakefuda both explores the wider political and social context of lesbian cultures and examines how this is experienced on the terrain of the *tōjisha*. For Kakefuda, the label of lesbian can never be anything other than a reluctant and temporary strategy of visibility; she notes how the word has often been associated with the heterosexual male gaze in contexts including pornography. She argues that heterosexist Japanese society systematically erases the lived experiences of lesbians and queer women, with women in Japan held essentially in "moratorium" until they become fully fledged adults through marriage with a man (Kakefuda 1992, 102). In a section subtitled "Towards Words That Allow Me to Speak as a Lesbian," Kakefuda (1992, 50) recounts an interaction with a friend who became frustrated at being asked to speak on behalf of gay people. Kakefuda notes the tension between wanting to give a balanced account, whilst at the same time feeling personally discriminated against on a day-to-day basis. This echoes the debates that emerged amongst the writers of *Subarashii onna tachi* over the extent to which they should share "dark" stories in a *mini-komi* that had the word "wonderful" in its title (Izumo et al. 1997). Kakefuda asks similar questions about the responsibilities that lesbians and queer women have to reveal their personal stories and about how to prevent these stories becoming hollow "papier-mâché" versions of the truth (Kakefuda 1992, 52). In adopting her own *tōjisha* platform to work through these issues, Kakefuda set out many of the key debates which have continued into the contemporary period.

Deployment of personal narrative to consider the meanings of the category of "lesbian" can also be found in Horie Yuri's *Rezubian aidentifīzu* (Lesbian Identities 2015). Horie engages directly with Kakefuda by echoing her questioning and unpacking the meaning of the word "lesbian" in 1992 and by exploring Kakefuda's subsequent flight from public life in 1997. Kakefuda said that she was "escaping" from a situation in which the diversity of lesbian existence was homogenised and erased within heterosexist Japanese society. Whilst Horie (2015, 31–33) has sympathy for Kakefuda's position, agreeing that "[A]ll too soon, words spoken from the standpoint of one 'lesbian' spin out and make a representative of abstracted versions of 'lesbians'," she also argues that it is important to move forward from this impasse and explore "the possibilities that are connected to our anger." Horie encourages us to understand the historical contexts that have led to debates over *tōjisha* and the politics of naming and to use these debates to move forwards, both in scholarship and in communities.

The politics of naming are not confined to scholarly writing, with more mainstream work also taking up these issues. One figure who does this is Makimura Asako, an ex-model turned writer who came out as a lesbian in 2012. Makimura has published four books, including 2016's *Gei kappuru ni moetara meiwaku desuka?* (Is It OK Ask a Gay Couple?). This book is written for a general audience, and includes illustrations and definitions of key terms such as "sexual preference." Makimura uses personal anecdotes to answer questions about lesbian lives in an irreverent, accessible manner. In contrast, Makimura (2015) wrote a recent article for *Gendai shisō* in which she rejects the position of LGBT *tōjisha*, in the form of a break-up letter addressed "Dear 'LGBT'." While acknowledging the benefits of organising under the community grouping of LGBT, Makimura decries the way in which LGBT has become a product used to sell diversity and inclusion. In simultaneously rejecting the label of LGBT *tōjisha*, but continuing to write from a queer women's *tōjisha* perspective in her later book, Makimura highlights the ambivalence and tensions that often surround the notion of *tōjisha*. Indeed, it is perhaps more productive to think of *tōjisha* as a flexible category of belonging, through which individuals are able to move as the necessity arises. This flexibility should not detract from the authenticity of self-presented voices but rather reminds us of the complexity of experience grouped under more generic terms like "lesbian" and "queer women."

This complexity was often echoed by many of the queer women in my own research who regularly emphasised the flexibility of sexuality and sexual identities. Many of the queer women I interviewed had identified in manifold ways during their lives and were open to the notion that they may identify differently in the future. For example, one respondent had identified first as "probably not straight," then "bisexual," and had recently settled on "lesbian." Some respondents talked about how designations such as *tachi* and *neko* put them off attending women-only events and groups. Others talked about how their bisexual or pansexual identifications and/or relationships with transgender and/or non-binary individuals had resulted in direct exclusion from community events. Awareness of this nuance and complexity highlights the breadth of lived experience and the contested nature of belonging within lesbian and queer women's communities in Japan.

Sociological studies of lesbians and queer women

Despite the gay boom of the 1990s, in which media coverage of gay and lesbian lives surged, it was not really until the early 2000s that sociological studies of lesbians and queer women emerged. One of the earliest monographs in English to take lesbian subjectivities in Japan as its topic was Chalmers's (2002) *Emerging Lesbian Voices from Japan*, which draws heavily on the work of Kakefuda. Chalmers's book was based on six years of research on what she calls "same-sex attracted women" and the ways in which they dealt with heterosexist systems in their day-to-day lives. Approaching the research from a feminist perspective, Chalmers (2002, 7) argued that media representations of lesbianism in Japan at the time was, "... firmly in the category of anti-family, anti-reproduction, anti-social, transgressing normal (*futsū*) female bodily behaviour ... and more commonly, it [lesbianism] has simply been ignored." For Chalmers, the social issues faced by lesbian women in Japan are not only bound up in heteronormative social systems but also in a patriarchal legal system that controls women's basic rights and systematically erases their existence. Lesbians and queer women in Japan, then, are faced with issues because of their gender as well as their sexuality.

In 2006, Diana Khor and Kamano Saori edited a special issue of the *Journal of Lesbian Studies*, which collected diverse scholarship on East Asian lesbians and queer women and which sought to intervene in and challenge several key blind spots of lesbian studies and lesbian communities in Japan. Iino Yuriko (2006), for example, used documentary evidence from the 1992 meeting of the Asian Lesbian Network to illustrate the historical and continued erasure of *Zainichi* Japanese (Japanese people of Korean descent living in Japan—a community that numbers in the hundreds of thousands) within lesbian communities. Horie Yuri (2006) focused on a case study of homophobic discourses in the United Church of Christ in Japan to offer an essential corrective to the notion that religious discrimination against lesbians and queer women in Japan does not exist. Lesbians and queer women in Japan face a myriad of social issues, which are now beginning to be explored in scholarship.

Kamano and Khor's significant contributions to the sociological study of lesbians and queer women in Japan should not be overlooked. In addition to the special issue of *Journal of Lesbian Studies*, they have also explored how lesbian couples meet and form relationships while living with the fear of being "found out" (Kamano and Khor 2008) and the ways in which "passing" as female friends allowed lesbians to access important social capital, including housing, while erasing important aspects of their identities (Kamano and Khor 2011). These offer important details about the ongoing structural obstacles that lead to invisibility and erasure of lesbians and queer women in Japan.

Other work based on qualitative interviews and ethnographic work with lesbian communities has been published over the last decade or so. In 2008, for example, Sugiura Ikuko, Kamano Saori, and Yanagihara Yoshie interviewed a number of female same-sex couples with the aim of establishing their legal needs. The authors explore the kinship networks of female same-sex couples and the impacts that these have upon their decision for or against seeking legal protections through marriage, which is not currently legal in Japan, or through adult adoption. The household registration system in Japan allows for an adult to adopt a non-blood relative through a simple legal process carried out at the local government office. This adult adoption system is sometimes used by same-sex couples in Japan to set up new legal families—for example, one of the respondents in my study had legally adopted their partner, creating a new legal household in a shared name. Sugiura et al. (2008) identified a number of reasons why couples may not wish to seek legal recognition in this way. These include fear of causing trouble for their parents, trust that their blood kin will protect their legal rights should the need arise, and lack of support from one or the other of the couple's parents. These are important issues to consider as relationship recognition becomes an increasing concern, with growing numbers of Japanese local governments establishing local same-sex relationship schemes, and a nascent debate about same-sex marriage.

Despite the potential of the works discussed previously to add empirical knowledge about the lives and beliefs of lesbian and queer women in Japan, sociological and anthropological studies remain comparatively scant. There are many reasons this might be the case. It is possible, for example, that the lack of legal protection for lesbians and queer women in Japan (such as overt national legislation outlawing discrimination based on sexual orientation) makes participation in research projects difficult. In my own research, I found that many of my respondents were not able to be fully open about their sexuality in their daily lives, and participation in research was undertaken with caution and only after reassurance from networks of trusted friends and community members. The relative dearth of research should not act as a deterrent to future researchers but rather encourage us to develop mutually productive research designs with lesbian and queer women.

Significance and future directions

Japanese society is currently experiencing significant social change. Super-ageing, the increase in irregular and part-time work, and hollowing-out in rural areas all present social issues related to gender and sexuality (for an overview of these general social issues, see Allison (2013); Vainio in this volume). These contexts raise significant issues for lesbian and queer women in Japan. With ageing LGBTQ communities, how should elder-care be organised? How can queer mothers provide social support networks for each other as local communities become fractured? How can lesbians and queer women find financial security in increasingly precarious employment? What effects will localised same-sex partnership agreements have on women who live outside of these jurisdictions or who cannot afford certification fees? Moreover, regardless of ongoing debates surrounding activist strategy within sexual minority communities, the persistent lack of legal protections for sexual minorities in Japan remains an area of deep concern. Lesbians and queer women continue to find themselves at a financial disadvantage in comparison to their male counterparts (Nijiiro Diversity and CGS at ICU 2016). This general lack of legal protection alongside the effects of gendered financial disparities are key impacts on lesbian and queer women's lives and suggest that the issues facing these communities are not unique but related to wider social developments in Japan. At the same time, they can perpetuate their invisibility and erasure. It is for this reason that lesbian studies, alongside wider studies of queer women, should remain an essential focus for sexuality and gender studies in Japan.

What I hope has become apparent in reading this chapter is that lesbians and queer women have a long history of organising and creating collective spaces of belonging in Japan. These communities are by no means a new phenomenon, regardless of the extent to which these communities are (mis)represented and (not) discussed in the mainstream media and academia. Recent shifts in the Japanese mainstream media towards discussing sexually diverse lives under the homogenising umbrella term LGBT should not distract us from this long history, nor from lively and productive debates that continue to circulate amongst queer communities of women. This is not to suggest that lesbians and queer women should not be considered as part of wider sexual minority collectivities in Japan. Rather, we should not allow the specific issues facing lesbians and queer women to be subsumed under hegemonic discourses that seek to erase these long histories and homogenise queer experiences.

In order to continue producing scholarship which pushes forward the boundaries of existing work, we may need to adopt flexible and creative approaches. Participatory, action-based research, conducted across a broad cross-section of lesbian and queer-identifying women can go some way towards contributing to this empirically vital and theoretically productive field of research. This approach should be about centring the lived experiences and self-told histories of those who have lived through the developments outlined previously, in a way which is sensitive to both the complex histories and continuing needs of lesbian and queer women in Japan. The study of lesbians and queer women in Japan is one of rich potential and broad possibilities, if only we have to courage to stand on the shoulders of those who have gone before us.

Further reading

For a detailed exposition of the development and current status of queer women's cultures see Maree's (2015) "Queer Women's Culture and History in Japan". Although it courted some controversy from within the lesbian community in Japan, Iino Yuriko's (2008) *Rezubian de aru "watashitachi" no sutōrī* ("'Our' Lesbian Story") gives a lucid, well-researched history of lesbians and queer women in Japan. Izumo Marō and Claire Maree's (2003) *Love Upon the Chopping Board* is a memoir of the authors' lives together, indicative of *tōjisha-sei* writing, and has been translated into English. Yajima's (1999) *Life Stories of Women Who Love Women* is a veritable trove of qualitative data from lesbians and queer women in Japan.

Related chapters

3   Debates in Japanese Feminism
6   Transgender, Non-Binary Genders, and Intersex in Japan
11 Intimacy in and Beyond the Family
12 Rural Gender Construction and Decline: Negotiating Risks Through Nostalgia

References

Allison, A. (2013) *Precarious Japan*, Durham: Duke University Press.
Anīsu 2001 natsugō tokushū: 1971–2001 komyuniti no rekishi (Anise 2001 Summer Special: Community History 1971–2001) (2001) Tokyo: Tera Shuppan.
Bessatsu, T. (1987) *Onna o ai suru onnatachi no monogatari* (Stories of Women Who Love Women), Tokyo: JICC Shuppankyoku.
Chalmers, S. (2002) *Emerging Lesbian Voices from Japan*, London: RoutledgeCurzon.
Federman, L. (1991) *Odd Girls and Twilight Lovers: A History of Lesbian Life in Twentieth-Century America*, New York: Columbia University Press.
Horie, Y. (2006) "Possibilities and Limitations of 'Lesbian Continuum,'" *Journal of Lesbian Studies* 10 (3–4) 145–159.
Horie, Y. (2008) "Kurōzetto kara deru koto no fu/kanōsei – rezubian no aida ni sotei sareru bunkiten o megutte (Im/Possibilities of Coming Out of the Closet: Regarding the Divergent Points Assumed Amongst Lesbians)," *Kaihō shakaigaku kenkyū* (The Liberation of Humankind: A Sociological Review) 22 102–118.
Horie, Y. (2015) *Rezubian aidentitīzu* (Lesbian Identities), Kyoto: Rakuhoku Shuppan.
Iino, Y. (2006) "The Politics of 'Disregarding'," *Journal of Lesbian Studies* 10 (3–4) 69–85.
Iino, Y. (2008) *Rezubian de aru 'watashitachi' no sutōrī* ('Our' Lesbian Story), Tokyo: Seikatsushoin.
Izumo, M., Hara, M., Tsuzura, Y. and Ochitani, K. (1997) "Nihon no rezubian mūvumento" (Japan's Lesbian Movement) *Gendai Shisō* 25 (6) 58–83.
Izumo, M. and Maree, C. (2003) *Love Upon the Chopping Board*, Melbourne: Spinifex.

Kakefuda, H. (1992) '*Rezubian' de aru to iu koto* (On Being a 'Lesbian'), Tokyo: Kawade Shobo Shinsha.
Kamano, S. and Khor, D. (2008) "'How Did You Two Meet?' Lesbian Partnerships in Present-Day Japan," in S. Jackson, L. Jieyu and W. Juhyun (eds) *East Asia Sexualities: Modernity, Gender & New Sexual Cultures*, London: Zed Books, 161–177.
Kamano, S. and Khor, D. (2011) "Defining Lesbian Partnerships," in K. Fujimura-Fanselow (ed) *Transforming Japan: How Feminism and Diversity are Making a Difference*, New York: Feminist Press, 147–163.
Makimura, A. (2015) "Haikei LGBT to iu gainen san e" (Dear 'LGBT'), *Gendai Shisō* 43 (16) 72–74.
Makimura, A. (2016) *Gei kappuru ni moetara meiwaku desuka? kikitai! kedokikenai! LGBTs no koto* (Can I Ask a Gay Couple? I Want to Ask About LGBT, but I Can't!), Tokyo: East Press.
Maree, C. (2007) "The Un/State of Lesbian Studies: An Introduction to Lesbian Communities and Contemporary Legislation in Japan," *Journal of Lesbian Studies* 11 (3–4) 291–301.
Maree, C. (2015) "Queer Women's Culture and History in Japan," in M. McLelland and V. Mackie (eds) *Routledge Handbook of Sexuality Studies in East Asia*, Abingdon: Routledge, 230–243.
McLelland, M. (2005) *Queer Japan from the Pacific War to the Internet Age*, Oxford: Rowman & Littlefield.
McLelland, M. (2009) "The Role of the '*Tōjisha*' in Current Debates About Sexual Minority Rights in Japan," *Japanese Studies* 19 193–207.
Nakanishi, S. and Ueno, C. (2003) *Tōjishashuken* (The Reign of *tōjisha*), Tokyo: Iwanami Shoten.
Nijiiro Diversity and Center for Gender Studies at International Christian University. (2016) *LGBT ni kansuru shokuba kankyō ankēto 2016* (2016 Survey of the Conditions of LGBT People in the Workplace). www.nijiirodiversity.jp/wp3/wp-content/uploads/2016/08/932f2cc746298a4e76f02e3ed84 9dd88.pdf.
Regumi Sutajio. (2013) *Kai no shōkai* (About Us). http://regumi.sakura.ne.jp/retsushin/about/.
Sugiura, I. (2007) "Lesbian Discourses in Mainstream Magazines of Post-War Japan: Is *Onabe* Distinct from *Rezubian*?" *Journal of Lesbian Studies* 10 (3–4) 127–144.
Sugiura, I. (2008) "Nihon ni okeru rezubian feminizumu no katsudō: 1970 nedai kōhan no meireki ni okeru" (Lesbian Feminist Activism in Japan: At the Dawn of the Late 1970s), *Jendā kenkyū* 11 143–170.
Sugiura, I. (2015) "Josei dōsei ai' gensetsu o meguru rekishiteki kenkyū no tenkai to kadai" (Discourses of "Female Same-Sex Love"—Developments and Issues in Historical Studies), *Wako University Bulletin of the Faculty of Human Studies* 8 7–26.
Sugiura, I. (2017) "Nihon ni okeru rezubian minikomishi no gensetsu bunseki: 1790 nendai kara 1980 nendai zenhan made" (A Discourse Analysis of Lesbian Mini-komi in Japan: From the 1970s to the Mid 1980s), *Wako University Bulletin of the Faculty of Human Studies* 10 159–178.
Sugiura, I., Kamano, S. and Yanagihara, Y. (2008) "Josei kappuru no seikatsu jittai ni kansuru chōsa bunseki—hōteki hoshō nīzu o saguru tameni" (An Analysis of the Everyday Reality of Female Same-Sex Couples—Exploring the Need for Legal Protections), *Japanese Sexual Research Congress Report* 20 (1) 30–54.
Tamagawa, M. (2017) "Coming Out of the Closet in Japan: An Exploratory Sociological Study," *Journal of GLBT Family Studies* (Online first) 1–31.
Welker, J. (2010) "Telling Her Story: Narrating a Japanese Lesbian Community," *Journal of Lesbian Studies* 14 (4) 359–380.
Welker, J. (2017) "Toward a History of 'Lesbian History' in Japan," *Culture, Theory, and Critique* 58 (2) 147–165.
Yajima, M. (1999) *Joseidōseiaisha no raifusutorī* (Life Stories of Women Who Love Women), Tokyo: Gakubunsha.

PART IV

Cultures of play
Leisure, music, and performance

22
GENDER AND MUSICAL SUBCULTURES IN JAPAN

Rosemary Overell

As in most late-capitalist nations, music scenes have formed a key site for the cultivation of emerging and often resistant cultural formations in Japan. In this chapter, I use the term *subcultures* to unpack some key ideas in recent Japanese anthropological, sociological, and cultural studies engagements with such formations. A key thread which runs through this scholarship is how subcultural participation works as a challenge to perceived Western—particularly North American—cultural hegemony in Japan. While the subcultures discussed here (hip-hop, mod [fans of British music, such as the Rolling Stones and the Small Faces, from the 1960s and known for their "dapper" attire], reggae/dancehall, metal and punk) all claim to carve out a space away from Japanese pop (J-pop) music's culture industry, many of the scenes re-inscribe normative patriarchal structures within the bars, "livehouses" (*raību hausu*, the Japanese word for music venues), and clubs where their music is performed, distributed, and consumed. Nonetheless, as the studies outlined subsequently demonstrate, women subculturalists actively push against gendered norms in often novel and radical ways.

The following chapter will give some initial insight into gendered dynamics in Japan's music subcultures. I have picked only a few subcultural formations here, based on central texts in the field. There is, of course, much more written, and there are other musical scenes. For further information, I recommend the reader refer to the reference list.

Researching Japanese subcultures, scenes, and communities

Before launching into an outline of subcultural studies of music in Japan, it is worth noting the context in which subcultural studies of Japan arise and asking whether this largely Anglophone framework is useful for the study of Japanese music. Subcultural studies have had significant clout in English-language academic studies of cultural production. Ostensibly beginning with the Chicago School's work on "corner boys" (Park et al. 1925), the "subcultural turn" is exemplified by the work of Hall and Jefferson (1975), Hebdige (1979), and others from the Birmingham School (Gelder 2007). For theorists like Hall, Hebdige, Cohen (1972), and Willis (1978), subcultural formations presented a resistance to dominant culture. For these thinkers, *style*—the clothes worn by subculturalists, the music they produced, and the way they moved through city-spaces—was the key mode in which struggle was borne out and made visible. Here, subcultural identity was necessarily working class. Further, the subcultural subject was always already male.

This Birmingham approach has been widely contested: for its obvious sexism due to a lack of engagement with women subculturalists, but also for its lack of nuance around the mechanics of subcultural class-identity (Bennett and Kahn-Harris 2004; McRobbie and Garber 1975; Muggleton and Weinzierl 2003). This has also been addressed in Japanese studies critiques of subcultures, particularly in Laura Miller's work (2004). As styles came and went, and "gushed up" from the underground to mainstream culture, the power of subcultural resistance was also challenged. Nonetheless, the notion of a "sub-" or underground cultural formation, presenting a trenchant (if not romanticised) critique of capitalism and the status quo, remains within cultural studies of music.

Thornton's (1995) take on the club scene in London remains an important discussion on gender and subcultures. Here, she uses Bourdieu's notion of "cultural capital" to suggest that post-1980s subcultures are a mirror economy of bourgeois norms and practices. Her case study demonstrates that—while often feigning working-class authenticity—clubbers were largely middle class and articulated and gate-kept a complex field of signifiers (slang, dress style, dance moves) indicative of one's "subcultural capital," or status. Key to this, as in Bourdieu's original model, is the enactment of distinction, particularly from popular music fans as a type of *habitus*.

There have also been numerous post-subcultural studies hinging on terms such as "scene" and "community" (Bennett and Kahn Harris; Muggleton and Weinzierl), but these are often analyses of unconventional cultures or styles. Notably, this is no longer bound to an identifiable working-class identity. Rather, discussions of musical formations which do not apparently conform to popular styles focus on other outsider markers of identity, linked to race, gender, sexuality, or ability. Work since the 1980s has revolved around questions of how music might (or might not) be a site for the production of some sort of struggle around cultural norms such as middle-classness, whiteness, patriarchy, and heteronormativity.

These movements in cultural studies of music in Anglophone work have influenced how many scholars approach Japanese music cultures (Mōri 2007; Tōya 2003). While there has been no extensive English-language study of what might map onto Birmingham's working-class subcultures in Japan (though the motorcycle groups [*bōsōzoku*] discussed by Kersten [1993] could be one example), there have been numerous engagements with music cultures that produce divergent styles and provide a sense of belonging for non-conforming Japanese people. Broadly speaking, such work has focused on musicians and spaces that are outside of the realm of major record labels, sometimes called "indies" (*indīzu*) in Japan. Academic work in this area looks at a broad range of genres from reggae, to hip-hop, to metal. While such studies, such as those discussed subsequently, follow the Birmingham School's formula situating aesthetic, or style, as a key signifier of divergence from the mainstream, they also incorporate more recent understandings of nondominant identities and how these might flourish (or not) in a specifically Japanese context.

A key site for discussion has been how gendered identity circulates in Japanese music cultures. That is, discussions of how non-cis heterosexual male subjects' participation in music cultures have focused on whether spaces of musical play, consumption, and production offer a different sort of—and potentially more liberating—site for the production of gendered identity. The following forms a survey of key academic work in this area.

Japanese pop music (J-pop) is, much like Western pop, dominated by idols (*aidoru*), many of who are women. Stevens (2008) notes the rise of women pop-stars (outside of the *enka* genre of sentimental ballad music) from the 1980s. Boy- and girl-bands also form a significant portion of the pop market. Fans of *aidoru*—whether solo or in boy or girl bands—are also generally women (Stevens 2008). Female *aidoru* and pop-stars are heavily feminised and regularly present as *kawaii* (cute) young girls wearing "girly" clothes and makeup (Aoyagi 2005; Yano 2013). This

J-pop context is important to bear in mind when considering how women in the subcultures discussed in this chapter subvert or conform to these norms.

Genba girls

Ian Condry (2006) tackles Japan's hip-hop culture; while avoiding the label "subculture," his notion of *genba* (scene) works in a similar way. Referring to nightclub sites and informal hip-hop event spaces, *genba* encompasses the people and practices around Japanese hip-hop (Condry 2006, 87–110). Condry acknowledges the dynamic between underground emcees from the "bowels of Tokyo" (2006, 1) and major-label artists. Nonetheless, within the Oricon (Japan's billboard charts) J-pop-scape, hip-hop remains marginal or relegated to rap breaks in boy-band songs. Though Japanese hip-hop draws on American style, Condry suggests that the *genba* of the Japanese scene—with "samurai" rappers and "yellow B-Boys"—potentially resists the cultural hegemony of J-pop through its references to the Western subcultural style of hip-hop complemented with local, Japanese lyrics and cultural references (2006, 11). He dubs this a form of "glocalisation" (drawing on Robertson 1995)—where a globally circulating cultural object is localised outside of its original context. As Condry and others (Dexter 2016; Morris 2013) point out, however, such resistance hinges on a problematic appropriation of an often-stereotyped "black" hip-hop culture. In some cases, too, Japanese hip-hop uses African-American style to promote nationalist themes and ideas. I will discuss this in more detail subsequently in reference to Sterling's (2010) work on Japanese reggae.

The male Japanese rappers and scenesters Condry interviews rehearse a familiar discourse that "real" hip-hop or subcultural cache lies in male-led production, distribution, and consumption (Rose 1994). Women are dismissed as *ningyō* (dolls or puppets) who slavishly follow J-pop trends (Condry 2006, 167), similar to the "Sharons and Tracys" Thornton describes as déclassé in her work. Hip-hop is regularly deemed *otokorashii* (manly) and bound to the tough "hardcore" style of male emcees (Condry 2006, 164–165). Girls in the *genba* can get by through what Condry coins *cutismo* (2006, 165): a kind of cute toughness where women may be the main attraction of an R&B cross-over act (singing the hook, etc.). Nonetheless, their power still depends on adherence to feminine stereotypes.

Condry does find a handful of women emcees who reject cuteness in favour of American-style female rap aesthetics. Rather than performing vulnerable *kawaii* female identity, Ai and Riko (Condry's interviewees) foreground an active female sexuality. Most notable is Ai's reclamation of the slang term for sexually active women as "yellow cabs" (they will pick up anyone) (2006, 176). In Ai's hip-hop, yellow cab becomes a signifier for female agency and "women in the driver's seat" (2006, 176). This challenges dominant Japanese gender hierarchies as well as the strictures of *genba* gender. However, Riko and Ai also offer an arguably conservative understanding of their resistance as a form of nonconformist, but no less neoliberal, individualism. Riko narrates her success as a standard neoliberal fable of hard ork and gumption paying off. Her position as a marked and excluded "daughter of a communist" is overcome through her devotion to hip-hop music and her eventual job as an MTV-Japan VJ. She tells Condry that her emceeing's message is "girl, do what you want to do.... You can be a mechanic or a truck driver. My attitude is, together as women let's challenge ourselves to do what we want" (2006, 177). Riko also frames her corporate success on MTV as resistant. She talks about her role as a VJ as giving her space to "express an opinion," unlike her former job on public television provider NHK—the women on which she likens to "passive muppets" (2006, 175). Condry's case study demonstrates the complex politics of gendered subcultures and the taken-for-granted authenticity of individualized narratives in late-capitalist societies such as Japan.

Modettes

Christine Feldman (2009) finds a similar male dominance at work on the Japanese mod rock scene. She notes the limitations of subcultural frameworks as indicative of outsider status through her account of the thorough commodification of mod culture exemplified by Twiggy credit cards and a transplanted local version of the Cavern Club in Shibuya. Nonetheless, like Condry's hip-hop fans, the mods with whom Feldman talks feel their engagement with "British" rock music of the 1960s is a mode for resisting dominant "American" popular culture in Japan (2009, 173). Feldman's study found that Japanese mods take the masculine gendering of the mod subculture as given. One popular niche media magazine argued that "Mod culture is boys' culture" and that women (Modettes) were at best "accessories" (Feldman 2009, 166). Interviewees showed the same rhetoric echoed by Modettes themselves—even those in bands and DJs at themed mod club nights—effacing their modness (2009, 177).

Feldman also posits that, despite their interaction with a subcultural scene, mod girls follow the hegemonic *kawaii* aesthetic (2009, 182). Despite this, Feldman follows Aoyagi's (2005) argument that cuteness can potentially be empowering for young women as a form of resistance to the "mature" (masculine) culture of the salaryman—a kind of softer "cutismo." The childlike performance of modettes presents a subcultural refusal of the nine-to-five world characterised by women working as OLs (office ladies) in corporate offices (2005, 180; see also Hendry 2009, 169, 179; Gregory 2012).

Dancehall divas

Marvin D. Sterling (2010) also finds resistance to hegemonic modes of Japanese femininity in his analysis of dancehall and reggae subcultures. Like the mods, some "Japarege" (*Japarege*) fans imagine their subcultural participation as a challenge to American cultural imperialism via a *jibun sagashi* (search for the self) through an engagement with Rastafarian culture. Like Japanese hip-hop, this rehearses a mythology of neoliberal individualism. More problematically, though, Japarege culture often hinges on an appropriation of black cultural forms (including mimicry of Jamaican *patois*), which Sterling notes is a "structurally facilitated indifference" (2010, 28) to the Afro-Jamaican people from whom they borrow. Nonetheless, Sterling understands Japanese dancehall as a "performative field" (drawing on Victor Turner 1987)—as a nuanced site which can produce subcultural challenges to Japanese mainstream culture, whilst also, at times, reproducing racist stereotypes (2010, 29).

Like the modettes, the subcultural capital afforded "donettes" (female dancehall fans and particularly dancers) allows women a space to accrue status outside their, in this case working-class, professions. Unlike the modettes in Feldman's study, the donettes were not usually OLs. Rather, they were unskilled shop assistants or beauticians (Sterling 2010, 116). Sterling notes that dancehall can potentially become an "autonomous space" where women might "express their womanhood in positive ways" (2010, 103), especially through dancing. In dancehall more broadly, dancing and the structured event of Dancehall Queen contests are a highly feminised space. In Japan, too, it is important for women Japarege fans to participate in these events to gain scenic ("subcultural," in Thornton's terms) capital.

While Sterling interviews a small number of women who DJ or run sound systems, the key mode for women's participation in Japanese dancehall is through dancing. However, as Sterling points out, the site of the Dancehall Queen contest works differently than in, say, Jamaica or the United States. This is because of how race intersects with gender in the hybrid space of Japanese reggae. Participation in Japanese dancehall—through its association with black culture—can generate negative perceptions of Japanese dancehall "divas." This is because of what Sterling discusses as broader racism towards black people in Japanese culture but also due to associations which he posits as existing in Japanese media culture between dancehall and pornography (a key source for Sterling's discussion of women in Japarege is a film called *X Rated Dance Hall Girls*). Despite their relatively low economic position, most Japanese dancehall queens approach the subculture as a *shumi* (hobby), demonstrating a playful reflexivity around signifiers of Japanese womanhood. Notably, the Japanese dancehall queens expressed understandings of their participation in the scene as "empowering" partly due to an understanding of Jamaican dancehall queens as "ethnically" stronger than Japanese women (2010, 117; 124). While this is of course a problematic echoing of racist stereotypes around black women, it presents a counterpoint to accepted notions of Japanese womanhood. Sterling discusses this in terms of a resignification around ideals of feminine beauty—where a fuller-figure might be valued more than in dominant Japanese culture (2010, 123)—but also as an alternative economy where women might, in a handful of cases, eke out a profession as a dancehall queen (Junko Kudo, who won the National Dancehall Queen competition in Jamaica in 2002, being a key example). This functions, according to Sterling, as a performative field where subcultural participation for Japanese women works as a challenge to both Western, and Japanese, ideals of modern womanhood through the embrace of what is broadly considered a "licentious" mode of leisure activity—"wining" (Jamaican slang for provocative dancing) at dancehall events (2010, 142).

Punks

Jennifer Milioto Matsue discusses another male-dominated scene, the *angura* (underground) hardcore punk subculture in Tokyo (2009). Here, she reflects on the gendered politics of the subculture from her position as both an academic and a punk band-member. Her autoethnography is highly self-reflexive, and she describes her own sense of empowerment through participation in making live music (2009, 21–23). As with other subcultures, elements of hegemonic patriarchy exist in hardcore—even within what she dubs a "playground" outside normative nine-to-five culture. Nonetheless, the women she interviews—both musicians and fans—regard the punk *angura* as a "safe space" (2009, 84) to push against normative Japanese female identity (95). She describes participants who are able to take on "masculinized roles, powerfully striding across the stage and screaming" (2009, 84). She chronicles gigs called (in English) "No dicks: punk is no dicks!!" Matsue and her key female informant, the drummer for a band called Jug, read such moments and events as liberating. Nonetheless, as Matsue points out, the enactment of forthright "striding and screaming" also adheres to the subculture's generic requirements of hardcore aggression, loudness, and (albeit usually feigned) violence. The "no dicks" event, for example, was not a women-only live show. Rather, the appropriation of a crass English word (like Japarege's echoing of Buju Banton's homophobia, discussed in the next section) signified subcultural adeptness at hardcore argot and aesthetics. Perhaps more so than *genba* girls, modettes and dancehall divas are the hardcore women divergent from hegemonic Japanese femininity, at least in Matsue's estimation. Matsue chronicles *onna no ko bando* (girls' bands) representation in subcultural micro-media as "loud" and "noisy" (2009, 97), moving away from the demure expectations to which mainstream Japanese women are still pressured to adhere (Allison 2013; Gregory 2012). The women Matsue encounters are a far cry from the pop *aidoru* described by Stevens. As Matsue points out, hardcore women "typically sported everyday clothes on stage—jeans and a t-shirt, simple shoulder-length hair and no makeup" (Matsue 2009, 97). Matsue goes on to say that this style demonstrated a deliberate nonconformity to "ideal" femininity embodied in female J-pop singer style (2009, 97). While the *genba* girls, modettes, and certainly the donettes reproduced particular modes of heteronormatively desirable femininity, particularly in their dancing, the *onna no ko bando* members foregrounded their subcultural capital in adherence to masculine punk aesthetics and performance.

Metal machismo

So far, I have summarized how subcultural studies of Japanese music account for women's participation. However, any discussion of Japanese patriarchal formations must also consider how male subjectivity is produced. As hooks (2000) and others (Connell 2000, 2005; Cremin 2017) note, patriarchy has a detrimental effect on men as well as women. In Japan, the pressure for men to conform to the *salaryman* track has been thoroughly documented (Roberson and Suzuki 2003). Even if following their *ikigai* (dream, or reason for living [see Mathews 1996 for a detailed discussion of *ikigai*]) or *jibun sagashi* in Sterling's terms, Japanese men generally conform to heteronormative standards and align themselves with imagined ideals of "Japaneseness" (Allison 2013; Louie and Low 2003). Of course, there are significant exceptions to this—as discussed by McLelland (2005) and Sugunuma (2012) particularly. Nonetheless, though the latter discusses nightclubbing culture, these works (and others on non-heteronormative cultures) do not directly address music. Sterling does discuss heterosexism briefly, noting that the broader homophobia of reggae lyrics is regularly echoed in Japarege (2010, 108). Nonetheless, he suggests that it is difficult to discern whether references to "Boom Bye Bye" (a notorious anti-gay tune by Jamaican Buju Banton) are homophobic "machismo" (2010, 109) or a concern with "getting dancehall right" (2010, 109) through the rehearsal of what are seen as authentic subcultural signifiers.

My own work on extreme metal music in Osaka (2014) focuses on how male musicians and fans negotiate their *ikigai* of playing and enjoying metal music in terms of Japanese patriarchy. Metal, like hip-hop and dancehall, is globally dominated by men. So too is noise music—a subculture closely related to metal in Japan. Novak (2013) has written an excellent account of noise in his book *Japanoise: Music at the Edge of Circulation*. While his ethnography and subcultural history are lively and present a convincing case for noise as a subcultural affront to neo-liberal capitalism in Japan, it is puzzling how little he accounts for the gendered dynamics of the scene. *Japanoise* describes noise as a scene presided over by "godfathers" (2013, 125, 251)—noisicians, such as Merzbow and Masonna, whose apparent lack of dexterity with technology now circulates as a signifier of noise subcultural capital. The discourse around technical expertise (though inverted) is never unpacked in terms of gender, despite the persistent popular mythology that men are technically capable and women are not. The musicians discussed are almost all men. While this does reflect the Japanese noise scene, this is unreflexively presented without an unpacking of why this might be the case. Merzbow, understandably, provides a focus for much of *Japanoise* but despite his long collaboration with female noisician Reiko A, she is mentioned only once (2013, 134). In fact, Merzbow's status as the "father" of noise is sometimes uncritically rehearsed by Novak. This not only undercuts Novak's (and many noisicians') argument that noise challenges the Western paradigm of individual genius but also seriously marginalises the presence of women in the scene.

Japan's metal scene has more men than women participants. Nonetheless, I suggest that in the moment of performance, in small livehouses (venues) across Shinsaibashi and Namba, metallers experience a "brutal belonging" which might exceed the bounded masculine signifiers so important to metal. Like metal elsewhere, Osaka's scene depended on images of women being abused in lyrics, fliers, and album covers, alongside representations of "strong men"— often associated with right-wing Japanese politics in the form of Japanese Imperial Army logos and imagery. Interviewees, too, also regularly expressed racist, nationalist politics. More emphatically perhaps than the hip-hoppers and Japarege fans above, Osaka-based metalheads rejected American culture as a signifier of mainstream culture, insisting that their subcultural participation worked as a challenge to Western cultural imperialism (Overell 2014, 139–140). Sometimes, Osaka-based metallers even dubbed their subcultural practices *yamato damashii*, a nationalist concept of "Japanese spirit" or soul. In this case, masculine identity was entangled with, and articulated through, appeals to nationalism. Despite their rejection of the *salaryman* citizenship of most men their age, these men adhered to Japanese patriotism through their dedication to metal as an expression of their *yamato damashii*.

Nonetheless, my ethnography regularly revealed an ambivalence around these representations (language, images, and other signifiers) of Japanese masculinity. In the circle pit, in the movement between audience and performer in the space of the live show more-than-representational affects potentially challenge the idea of a solid, bounded male identity (Overell 2014, 73–76). I accounted for this through moments of interviewees' inability to express their experiences in the pit and performing. These were some of the few moments in interviews where masculinity—entwined with nationalist discourse—was not expressed. Despite such more-than-representational, or affective, moments, the men interviewed were quick to return to gendered representations and articulations of live performances as demonstrations of male sexual prowess. One interviewee was keen to point out that, for him, drumming was "like an orgasm . . . real samurai power" (2014, 52). Engaging with this tension between strong articulations of masculinity and the more ambivalent, affective site of the live performance is an important intervention in Japanese subcultural studies of gender, because it accounts for the hegemonic power of patriarchy in Japan in terms of men's positions but also Japanese patriarchy's entanglement with imagined, nationalist ideals of an imagined idealized Japaneseness.

Conclusion

The handful of Japan-focused studies discussed previously demonstrate one of the key tensions of subcultural studies more broadly: that it is impossible to consider cultural formations around music without attention to the global rhythms of patriarchal late capitalism. I wish to conclude by reflecting on the gendered dynamics through which Japanese subcultural style has been taken up in non-Japanese spaces, focusing on one example: Yung Lean, a Swedish rapper who has some global success. Lean coined the term "sad boys rap" in 2012 as a way of describing his Stockholm-based crew's "emotional" rap style. Lean's songs are deliberately slowed down, mumbled verses over minimal beats. The themes focus on heartbreak, the use of depressant drugs (codeine, morphine, and ketamine), and mental illness. Lean's emphasis on a vulnerable male rap identity is arguably divergent from mainstream hip-hop style embodied by A$AP Rocky and Tay K (though, post-Lean, this is changing with rappers such as Lil Xan and Le1f coming to the fore). Most interesting for this chapter, however, is the Sad Boy crew use of Japanese subcultural signifiers. Like pop stars such as Avril Lavigne and Gwen Stefani, and hip-hop group Wu Tang Clan, they draw on Japanese street style fashions and *otaku* (nerd) culture and include *kanji* on their merchandise in an arguably Orientalist manner. But Lean and the Sad Boys have also collaborated with Japanese hip-hop crews MonyHorse, Junkman, and PETZ on the track "Tokyo Drift" (2015), where all the rappers identify as "sad boys." We could read this as a straightforward case of Orientalist appropriation—the exotic Otherness of the Japanese crew adding authenticity to Lean's subcultural status. There is no doubt that Lean and the Sad Boys operate in terms of Orientalism, not least in how they homogenise "Asian-ness" into a generalized mesh of signifiers ranging from ginseng to koto music and Tibetan chant samples. Still more problematic is the

Sad Boys' apparent rehearsal of the sexist and racist stereotype of the less-than-manly Asian male (unpacked and critiqued in detail in Louie and Low 2003). Though the Sad Boys, and particularly Lean, gesture to Japanese male subcultural identity, they seem to draw an affinity between their own vulnerable masculinity and the figure of the Asian male. I suggest this is perhaps too neat an equation. MonyHorse et al., rhyming in Japanese in "Tokyo Drift," display braggadocio and the hardness Condry's hip-hop scene-members emphasised (2006). Despite their references to benzos (benzadrine-based narcotics) and repping (representing) "sad boy" identity, their out-of-jointness with Lean and his Swedish crew is perhaps indicative of a continuum of masculinity (see Cook's and Monden's chapters in this volume) in the Japanese context. Further, for the Sad Boys and Lean, vulnerability is an asset and key signifier of authentic sad boy masculinity. Key to this is an affiliation with Japanese subcultural representations. While this might appear an idiosyncratic example, I argue it also demonstrates the ability for subcultural style—mediated via gender and race—to flow from Japan to Europe and America in a potentially disruptive manner akin to what Lionnet and Shih dub "minor transnationalism" (2005).

Related chapters

23 Gender in Digital Technologies and Cultures
27 Performing Gender: Cosplay and Otaku Cultures and Spaces
33 Gender, Media, and Misogyny in Japan

References

Allison, A. (2013) *Precarious Japan*, Durham: Duke University Press.
Aoyagi, H. (2005) *Islands of Eight Million Smiles: Idol Performance and Symbolic Production in Contemporary Japan*, Cambridge: Harvard University Asia Centre.
Bennett, A. and Kahn-Harris, K. (eds) (2004) *After Subculture: Critical Studies in Contemporary Youth Culture*, Houndmills: Palgrave Macmillan.
Cohen, S. (1972) *Folk Devils and Moral Panics: The Creation of the Mods and Rockers*, London: MacGibbon & Kee.
Condry, I. (2006) *Hip-Hop Japan: Rap and the Paths of Cultural Globalisation*, Durham: Duke University Press.
Connell, R. W. (2000) *The Men and the Boys*, Berkeley: University of California Press.
Connell, R. W. (2005) *Masculinities*, Berkeley: University of California Press.
Cremin, C. (2017) *Man-Made Woman: The Dialectics of Cross-Dressing*, London: Pluto Press.
Dexter, T. L. (2016) "Niggers and Japs: The Formula Behind Japanese Hip-Hop's Racism," *Social Identities* 22 (2) 210–225.
Feldman, C. (2009) *"We Are the Mods": A Transnational History of a Youth Subculture*, New York: Peter Lang.
Gelder, K. (2007) *Subcultures: Cultural Histories and Social Practice*, London: Routledge.
Gregory, L. (2012) "Women in a Bubble: Three Theoretical Perspectives on Japanese OLs' Experience at Work," *Studies on Asia* IV 2 (2) 184–199.
Hall, S. and Jefferson, T. (eds) (1975) *Resistance Through Rituals: Youth Subcultures in Postwar Britain*, London: Hutchinson.
Hebdige, D. (1979 [1987]). *Subculture: The Meaning of Style*, London: Routledge.
Hendry, J. (2009) *Understanding Japanese Society*, London: Routledge.
hooks, b. (2000) *Feminism Is for Everybody: Passionate Politics*, London: Pluto Press.
Kersten, J. (1993) "Street Youths, Bôsôzoku and Yakuza: Subculture Formation and Societal Reactions in Japan," *Crime and Delinquency* 39 (3) 277–295.
Lionnet, F. and Shih, S. (eds) (2005) *Minor Transnationalism*, Durham: Duke University Press.
Louie, K. and Low, M. (2003) *Asian Masculinities: The Meaning and Practice of Manhood in China and Japan*, London: Routledge.
Mathews, G. (1996) *What Makes Life Worth Living? How Japanese and Americans Make Sense of Their Worlds*, Berkeley: University of California Press.

Matsue, J. M. (2009) *Making Music in Japan's Underground: The Tokyo Hardcore Scene*, New York and London: Routledge.
McLelland, M. J. (2005) *Queer Japan from the Pacific War to the Internet Age*, Lanham: Rowman and Littlefield.
McRobbie, A. and Garber, J. (1975) "Girls and Subcultures," in S. Hall and T. Jefferson (eds) *Resistance Through Rituals: Youth Subcultures in Postwar Britain*, London: Hutchinson, 209–222.
Miller, L. (2004) "Those Naughty Teenage Girls: Japanese Kogals, Slang, and Media Assessments," *Journal of Linguistic Anthropology* 14 (2) 225–247.
Mōri, Y. (2007) *Popyura ongaku to shihonshugi* (Popular Music and Capitalism), Tokyo: Serica-shoba.
Morris, D. Z. (2013) "The Sakura of Madness: Japan's Nationalist Hip-Hop and the Parallax of Globalised Identity Politics," *Communication, Culture and Critique* 6 (3) 459–480.
Muggleton, D. and Weinzierl, R. (eds) (2003) *The Post-Subcultures Reader*, Oxford: Berg.
Novak, D. (2013) *Japanoise: Music at the Edge of Circulation*, Durham: Duke University Press.
Overell, R. (2014) *Affective Intensities in Extreme Music Scenes: Cases from Australia and Japan*, London: Palgrave Macmillan.
Park, R. E., Burgess, E. W. and McKenzie, R. D. (eds) (1925) *The City*, Chicago: University of Chicago Press.
Roberson, J. E. and Suzuki, N. (2003) *Men and Masculinities in Contemporary Japan: Dislocating the Salaryman Doxa*, London: Routledge.
Robertson, R. (1995) "Glocalisation: Time-Space and Homogeneity-Heterogeneity," in M. Featherstone, S. Lash and R. Robertson (eds) *Global Modernities*, London: Sage, 25–44.
Rose, T. (1994) *Black Noise: Rap Music and Black Culture in Contemporary America*, Middletown: Wesleyan University Press.
Sterling, M. D. (2010) *Babylon East: Performing Dancehall, Roots Reggae, and Rastafari in Japan*, Durham: Duke University Press.
Stevens, C. S. (2008) *Japanese Popular Music: Culture, Authenticity and Power*, New York: Routledge.
Sugunuma, K. (2012) *Contact Moments: The Politics of Intercultural Desire in Japanese Male-Queer Cultures*, Hong Kong: Hong Kong University Press.
Thornton, S. (1995) *Club Cultures: Music, Media and Subcultural Capital*, Middletown: Wesleyan University Press.
Tôya, M. (ed) (2003) *Popyura ongaku e no manazashi* (A Look At Popular Music), Tokyo: Keisô shobo.
Turner, V. (1987) *The Anthropology of Performance*, New York: PAJ Publications.
Willis, P. (1978) *Profane Culture*, London: Routledge and Kegan Paul.
Yano, C. (2013) *Pink Globalisation: Hello Kitty's Trek Across the Pacific*, Durham: Duke University Press.

23
GENDER IN DIGITAL TECHNOLOGIES AND CULTURES

Jennifer Coates and Laura Haapio-Kirk

Digital technology affords new modes of engaging with gender, often in ways that challenge extant inequalities through simulation and transformation. Yet digital iterations of gender do not make a radical break with pre-existing lived experiences and practices and can even support the development of conservative or exclusionary gender ideologies rather than proliferation of difference. Furthermore, the major research activity around Japanese digital cultures to date has tended to cleave to disciplinary boundaries without a great degree of cross-reference, and so key approaches and definitions central to the study of digital technologies and cultures vary across different fields. This problem is exacerbated by the ubiquity of digital technologies in various aspects of Japanese life.

For the purposes of this chapter, we will define the digital as "all that which can be ultimately reduced to binary code but which produces a further proliferation of particularity and difference" (Horst and Miller 2013, 3). To date, scholarship on Japanese digital technologies and cultures has clustered around the fields of art history, anthropology, media studies, film studies, communications, and cultural studies. Digital popular culture products, including online games, computer games, streamed television and film content, and other entertainments, have been the focus of much scholarship, though the dominant approach tends towards textual analysis, positioning these studies closer to classic media studies than research on digital technologies in Japan. As a number of chapters in this volume assess media texts with a significant digital component, we will focus more closely on the gendered impacts and implications of digital technologies in contemporary Japan.

Anthropologists and digital film researchers specializing in documentary genres have recently stressed the relevance of digital media for health and medical issues. In relation to Japan, digital media texts and scholarship on digital media and digital devices have tended to focus on the health challenges of a super-aging society and health issues related to the aftermath of the triple disaster in Fukushima in March 2011. The case study presented in the second part of this chapter demonstrates this interdisciplinary approach to studying digital technologies and cultures in Japan. First, however, we will introduce some of the key areas, disciplines, and topics around which scholarship on Japanese digital technologies and cultures has been developing. It is our hope that the overviews to follow, as well as the pioneering case study, will inspire researchers to develop interdisciplinary approaches for further study of Japanese digital cultures, particularly in relation to gender.

Gender in the digital arts

Counter to the trends in anthropology and documentary film studies noted previously, other fields have seen less overlap and cooperation. For example, the digitization of existing art works and artefacts has become a major focal point in the field of art history, but is rarely brought into conversation with other areas of digital scholarship. The digitization boom changing the face of art history in the twenty-first century has been driven by Japanese institutions such as the Art Research Center at Ritsumeikan University in Kyoto and the Research Institute for Cultural Properties at Tokyo University. Outside Japan, significant digitization activities are being pursued by institutions with Japanese art collections such as the British Museum, the Fitzwilliam Museum at Cambridge University, and the Metropolitan Museum in New York. The digitization of historic art and cultural materials relates to gender in a number of significant ways, yet there has been little overlap between digital art historical scholarship and the media and cultural studies work that takes gender as a central issue for the study of digital media, gaming, and the design of digital-born art and cultural materials, including technological aides such as robots.

In the most basic terms, digitization of historical materials is changing the gender make-up of the field, incorporating a significant number of digital native researchers from younger generations and, in the process, a larger number of female researchers than the field has previously seen. But it is not only the back rooms of galleries and research facilities that are changing. Digitization of aged materials allows for greater variety in what can be studied and shown to the public by changing how those materials can be displayed. Scholars and the general public alike can now view a large number of pre-modern and early modern Japanese art works through catalogues and databases featuring high-resolution images of recently cleaned and restored works, as well as images of works considered too fragile to be publicly displayed. With the development of three-dimensional (hereafter 3D) scanning technologies, a number of collections provide even greater access, in terms of detail viewable, to online visitors than to visitors within the physical gallery space, allowing online audiences a researcher's view of certain objects.

The increasing number of Japanese art works available for public view has a significant gendered aspect. Ever since Chino Kaori's seminal paper "Gender in Japanese Art" (1996), Japanese art history has included consideration of key art works and their production histories in the context of gender. At the Eastern Regional Conference of the Art History Association of Japan (*Bijutsushi gakkai*) in 1993, Chino argued that an idea of "the feminine" had been appropriated by male elites and used to mask the power held by men in patriarchal feudal periods of Japanese history. Her argument constituted such a significant intervention in the field that she was required to explain "the very concept of 'gender'" to her audience at that time (Mostow 2003, 8). Chino argued that certain eras of Japanese art production, such as the Heian era, have been perceived as "feminine," drawing a distinction between sex and gender to demonstrate how men in positions of power have historically deployed a self-definition as feminine to obscure the precise origins and location of the power that they held. Chino's argument shows the deeply gendered aspects of the ancient art works now on display to a global audience thanks to digitization. Digital databases and catalogues now allow scholars all over the world to continue Chino's pioneering work placing Japanese history of art within the context of gender.

While Chino's argument was largely illustrated by examples from the Heian, pre-modern, and early modern eras of Japanese art production, contemporary Japanese art history continues to explore gender issues. In the field of digital-born art, that is, artworks that rely on binary code for their material existence and development, gender features frequently in relation to three key concepts: space, law, and the nature of human imagination. A number of digital-born art works consider the human body in public space from the perspective of how people use buildings and their technologies, as well as who can occupy what kinds of space and how. These questions are of course deeply gendered. For example, Igarashi Megumi, the artist better known as Rokudenashiko (literally, "good-for-nothing girl") has clashed repeatedly with Japanese obscenity law over her silicone moulds, casts, and 3D printed replica of her own genitals (McLelland 2018). From tiny key chain ornaments to a full-size canoe, Rokudenashiko has produced numerous molds and sculptures shaped like her vulva, challenging viewers and lawmakers alike to define where and how the female body can be depicted in public spaces such as trains, schools, rivers, and other locations outside the art gallery.

On 8 May 2016, the Tokyo District Court handed down a mixed verdict on Rokudenashiko's artistic activism, following her arrest in July 2014, and trial for obscenity. A 400,000-yen fine was imposed for distributing 3D printer data over the Internet, but Rokudenashiko was acquitted on charges of "displaying obscene materials publicly" (McKnight 2017, 251). Rokudenashiko's 3D printed replica of her vulva ironically uses digital technologies to critique popular media and pornographic representations of the female body marred by another kind of digital interference, in the form of the pixilation (*bokashi*) that covers the genital areas of both men and women in erotic and pornographic photographic images produced and sold in Japan (Hambleton 2016, 5). In this way, her irreverent digital-born art uses the master's tools to attempt the dismantling of the master's house, if those tools are understood as digital technologies of representation and the house is understood as a sphere of gendered representational practices perpetuating a sense of shame around sex organs and the normalization of restrictive and often heteronormative depictions of human bodies. Digital-born art has been at the forefront of much recent art activism that protests the treatment and control of human bodies in designed living spaces such as cities, workplaces, and legal frameworks.

Gendered by design: digital devices, aides, and robots

Rokudenashiko's work shares concerns with another area of digital-born art that reflects how we imagine the ideal body and its functions. In *Robo Sapiens Japanicus: Robots, Gender, Family, and the Japanese Nation*, anthropologist Jennifer Robertson considers the design principles of digital aids such as robots from a gender perspective, coining the term "robo-sexism" (Robertson 2017, 89–97). Robertson argues that digital initiatives in household and workplace aides, in the form of humanoid or human-like robots, entrench earlier discriminatory ideas about gendered labour. Robots are developed to "perform a repertoire of roles that maintain the status quo" (Robertson 2017, 89–90), and, as such, often take over roles pejoratively stereotyped as women's work. Consequently, such robots and digital aides have been imagined almost exclusively as taking the form of a stereotypical, idealized, biologically female body.

In extreme cases, Robertson writes, this has even restricted the development of technology itself. Roboticist Takahashi Tomotaka, who introduced the "Female Type" robot in 2006, claims that previous generations of robots had taken the form of machines, men, or boys, because "female-like robots posed greater technical difficulties" (quoted in Robertson 2017, 102). Takahashi cites the perceived requirement for female-gendered robot casings to be slim and curvy as the major complication in the development of female-type robots, suggesting that the normalization of aestheticized ideal images of women to which Rokudenashiko attributes her motivation for her art activism also operates in the world of robotics design. Robertson argues that the "gendered upbringing and everyday behaviour" of roboticists themselves is reproduced in the gendered names and forms that they give to robots designed for certain types of work (2017, 90). As such, *Robo Sapiens Japanicus* is a good example of the interdisciplinary scholarship developing between anthropology, design, and architecture that interrogates the role of gender in the digital technologies and cultures of Japan today.

Gender and digital spaces

A related strand of anthropological scholarship on gender and the digital draws from communication studies work to consider the impact of digital devices such as mobile phones, portable screens, and other daily use objects that connect the user to a digital sphere, world, or space. A diverse range of studies have considered gender as a factor in how mobile phones are used (Ono and Zavodny 2005) and the "digital divide" in gendered access to mobile technologies and the Internet. In 2001, for example, a Japanese government survey found higher rates of Internet use among men with higher incomes, as opposed to women with lower, or no, income (Freeman 2003, 244). By 2007, however, scholarship had begun to place greater consideration on the content of digital and online media, as well as the form in which such media is presented. Ethnographers, communications studies researchers, and media studies scholars of computer games and online gaming cultures began to argue for new potentials stemming from the use of digital devices and consumption of digital media. For example, Larissa Hjorth suggests that the use of *kawaii* cute culture to "humanize dehumanized technologies" occurs alongside the shifting of gender inequalities "through changing technological platforms and industries" (2007, 378). While some of these shifts may be positive developments in the direction of lessening gender inequalities, we must also remain aware of the areas of the digital sphere that are increasingly experienced as less safe for users who do not occupy the hegemonic position of cis-gendered male users of digital technologies and digital spaces.

Scholarship on these areas of the digital sphere, including digital media and video games featuring ultra-violence and sexual assault, has sometimes struggled to deal with the age-old question of to what extent what we see affects how we think and behave. In his examination of the computer game *RapeLay* (2006), which allows the game player to rape female characters, Patrick Galbraith questions whether "fantasy itself" is "a problem" (2017, 105). Galbraith makes a distinction between the production and reception of sexually violent material involving human actors and the production of virtual violence such as that of the computer game. Asking, "Is it all right to fantasize about sexual violence or, as some critics argue, does such fantasy normalize sexual violence against women?" (2017, 105). Galbraith uses digital media content to consider cultural approaches to sexual fantasy, play, and harm in Japan. In suggesting that sexual fantasy be afforded more space in the everyday public sphere, however, little consideration is given to the other gendered bodies inhabiting that sphere and how the dissemination of digital content influences the non-digital environment in which it is disseminated, as well as the digital and online spaces inhabited by a variety of users of digital technologies. Without conflating the consumption of violent imagery with increased levels of actual violence perpetrated in the material world by game players, we can still insist that violence perpetrated in the digital sphere is likely to make that sphere less comfortable, welcoming, or attractive to game players of the gender, race, or positionality against which the violence is disproportionately levelled. By extension, we must question whether spaces that drive out difference can be conducive to the development of a fair and equal society.

A number of recent studies do give consideration to the everyday material world in which computer gamers live, work, and relate, as well as the connections and overlapping aspects of this world with the everyday physical world pre-existing the digital age, in which many of our extant norms and expectations were formed. For example, Ben Whaley's research on the "social narrative" of action puzzle game *Catherine* reveals the use of computer games to reflect and explore "the changing nature of romantic relationships and gender roles in Japanese society" (2018, 99). While director Hashino Katsura explores the "universal themes" of love and marriage in the story, Whaley argues that the protagonist is designed to challenge standard ideas, and ideals, of masculinity, moving across a spectrum of possible image, identity, and behaviours that encompasses the salaryman and the opposing "herbivore man" (2018, 102). While it may be rare, as Whaley argues, to see such consideration of the changing nature of gender and the family in a "mass-market commercial video game" (2018, 103), scholarly consideration of such narratives is enlightening and even refreshing in a field that can tend towards a focus on the darker side of digital media content. Like similar innovations in digital film, these examples reveal the value of digital technologies and worlds for solving the very concrete and material problems that we face offline as well as on.

Gender and digital culture in film and media

Like gaming culture, the digital age has changed cinema cultures, exhibition, and content in Japan. Mitsuyo Wada-Marciano argues that digital technologies have "transformed cinema's production, distribution, and consumption patterns," bringing Japanese cinema to ever more global markets (2012). Increasing the visibility of Japanese cinema, particularly those genres less likely to have a cinema theatre release, by bringing films to international film festivals and streaming sites has also increased the visibility of female filmmakers. Director Kawase Naomi, founder of the Nara Film Festival, credits the streaming website Netflix with the potential to revitalize the Japanese film industry by backing little-known and experimental filmmakers (South China Morning Post 2017). It is striking to note that many of these filmmakers are female, particularly in the context of the few women directors working on feature film over the long history of the Japanese studio system. For example, in *Ten Years Japan* (Jū nen 2018), which expands on the Netflix-hosted *Ten Years* anthology film franchise begun in Hong Kong, three of the five young directors introduced by Koreeda Hirokazu are female. New digital platforms such as Netflix are diversifying the Japanese cinema landscape by supporting work by new female artists, as well as more experimental work by senior female directors like Kawase.

In terms of film content, digital cinema has democratized documentary filmmaking, making it possible for grassroots concerns to be brought to a wider public (Kamanaka et al. 2018). In recent years, the single biggest issue in amateur, semi-professional, and professional documentary filmmaking has been the aftermath of the triple disaster that struck Fukushima in March 2011 in the form of an earthquake, tsunami, and the failure of the Fukushima Daiichi nuclear power plant. While a number of documentary films have focused on the impact on farmers, the largest number deal with the health implications of nuclear fallout. Unsurprisingly, this has become something of a gender issue, with digital documentary films communicating the concerns of activist groups formed by mothers of young children living in the area suffering from thyroid gland cancers. In documentary films such as *A2-B-C* (dir. Ian Thomas Ash 2013) and *Coda: Ryuichi Sakamoto* (dir. Steven Nomura Schible 2017), digital cameras are used to record the use of devices such as Geiger counters, now a part of everyday life in certain areas of Fukushima prefecture. The voices of mothers of affected children are commonly amplified in these narratives, gendering the testimonies of sufferers just as the classical narrative films of the 1950s gendered nuclear issues feminine by focusing on female characters (Coates 2018). Today digital technologies are used to make invisible threats and issues such as radiation and inequality more visible. As filmmaker Kamanaka Hitomi observes, the day-to-day experience of dealing with such invisible threats often becomes women's work (2018, 22).

Digital filmmaking allows filmmakers to bring these stories more directly to a wide audience, often circumventing classic studio system era production and distribution models. While this trend is supported by newly emerging digital devices that significantly reduce the costs and physical difficulties of filmmaking, it has not been the only catalyst for greater representation of women filmmakers. Rather, the independent documentary sector has been noted for its higher number of women from the 1930s. As Hikari Hori has shown, militarism and the development of the "culture film" (*bunka eiga*) in 1930s and 1940s Japan created a rare opportunity for women directors and editors to find work in the Japanese film industry. After the war, however, women were discouraged from taking up these roles in the postwar studio system (Hori 2018, 138). The development of digital filmmaking devices and digital streaming sites is increasing the representation of women on both sides of the camera, but digital technologies rarely drive social change entirely in and of themselves. Public attitudes and governmental initiatives play a large part in increasing the effectiveness of digital technologies, as the case study presented in the second part of this chapter demonstrates.

Digital devices, gender, and aging in contemporary Japan

The second part of this chapter presents a contemporary case study in order to show how digital technologies are being used to research gender-related social issues. The comparative multi-sited Anthropology of Smartphones and Smart Ageing project at University College London (UCL) conducted research on smartphone use and ageing in the city of Kyoto and rural Kochi prefecture from 2017 to 2019, investigating how the smartphone is used by middle-aged people (45–70 years old) in an era of changing aspirations and expectations around mid-life. Compared to other sites included in the study, what became apparent in the Japanese case was the inherently gendered nature of mobile phone usage. In both the rural and urban sites it was more commonly women who stayed abreast of the latest developments in mobile phone technology. They were more likely than men to have replaced their flip-style feature phones (*garakei*) with smartphones, primarily because female study participants were more invested than men in the affective labour of digital communication with friends and relatives. The gendered practice of care-at-a-distance and co-presence through the smartphone among primarily mothers and daughters in Japan was documented by Ohashi et al. (2017). Through an exploration of family communication via the messaging application LINE, their study demonstrated how the visually affective nature of LINE stickers fostered intimate forms of digital kinship. However, this affordance of expressions of intimacy is not new but has long been documented in association with older mobile communication technology in Japan. Ito et al. (2005) argued that from its inception, Japan's *keitei* culture made previously tacit emotions more explicit.

LINE is the most popular mobile messaging application in use today in Japan, with 78 million monthly active users in its home country as of October 2018 (Statista 2018). A distinctive feature of messaging on LINE, compared with other messaging applications such as WhatsApp, is the use of stickers or graphics which are sent as an individual message rather than embedded in text, as is common with emojis (see Figure 23.1). Sun Sun Lim argues that visual communication through LINE stickers allows users to "attain communicative fluidity" (Lim 2015) and express feelings which might otherwise be difficult to put into words. The affective quality of this visual form of communication not only has the potential to "humanize cold technology" (Hjorth 2007, 378), as in *kawaii* culture discussed previously, but for the women in the UCL study, the technology itself provided the potential to foster warmer and more personal relationships through *kawaii* LINE stickers. This was especially important when communicating across age categories, which would typically require a degree of formality. With middle-aged women

Figure 23.1 Stickers used in messaging app LINE
Source: Image by Laura Haapio-Kirk.

often returning to the workforce after raising children, many of the study's participants found that the majority of their colleagues were significantly younger than themselves, and they would use respectful distancing language at work, which reminded them of the age gap. However, on work LINE groups, these boundaries were overcome through the use of LINE stickers, which expressed meaning without the user having to type words. For example, one research participant described their use of the app in this way.

> I think that LINE stickers are quite useful when speaking to various generations. Because stickers make communication more approachable, warmer. You can use it across all ages. It's not that LINE makes us feel younger but more that it makes us not even think about our age.

By not having to conform to traditional modes of formal language, the selection of a particular LINE sticker to express a phrase or a sentiment became a kind of leveller, bypassing otherwise required modes of conduct and "warming up" otherwise cool relationships. While these women consider the affective nature of LINE stickers to be important for their relationships, to the extent that they are willing to pay for particular sets of stickers, Stark and Crawford (2015) critique this commodification of affective labour and also note the valuable data which companies can gather from the use of such affective markers.

Women in the UCL study purchased LINE stickers of their favourite cartoon characters and sometimes found sets with their own names embedded within them. The women instantly knew which friend had sent a message because of the style of the sticker: some people chose cute ones, whereas others opted for more comedic styles, depending on which they felt aligned most with their personality and tastes. In this way, LINE stickers appeared to be a way to express personality and extend more of oneself into the digital sphere. This personalization of LINE mirrored the way that the exterior of the phone was often decorated, especially by women. Phone charms, cases, and real stickers were applied according to the owner's tastes. This habit of aesthetic personalization of the smartphone was a continuation of how people treated their *garakei*, yet participants in the UCL study noted increased closeness and attachment to their smartphones since they felt that they had greater control over how they could craft the phone's interior to match their personality. One woman explained:

> I feel more towards the smartphone. I want to have it near me always. I feel shy about showing people my apps. It's kind of like a bookshelf, it shows my personality. You would only put the covers of the books you want to show in the front too. The smartphone is who I am.

Mid-life can by a trying time for Japanese women, when they increasingly take on the responsibility of care for elderly parents, often at the same time as returning to work and experiencing shifting relationships with spouses and children (see Takeda 2004; Oshio 2014; Lock 1993). One participant shared her feelings about this change: "It's really hard and sad to see your own mother and father deteriorate, especially if they get dementia. It's like a tunnel without an ending." As one ages, the ability to draw on the comfort of friends through trying times, such as experiencing sickness or caring for elderly parents, becomes increasingly important. In particular, messaging allowed many research participants to feel supported.

> If I have a particularly hard day with my mother, smartphones can give me a quick window to reach out to my friends and get sympathy. That aspect of being able to

reach out to someone right at that second when you need them is a great thing about smartphones, and receiving stickers that tell me "It's okay!!" is great.

The smartphone is integral to lightening the load of being a middle-aged woman in Japan and the responsibilities this represents. Female-to-female peer support fulfilled a need for empathy, which was sometimes perceived as lacking from male partners. One study participant noted that:

> I think the way women and men think are different. The support my husband gives me is different from my girlfriends because women to women, they know what to say and the things you want to hear. I feel more understood when speaking with my friends. Men are more logical. I am not seeking for, you know, an answer. I just want someone to listen to me.

The term *kodokushi* (solitary death) has become a recognised social issue in rapidly ageing Japan (Nozawa 2015), where elderly people are increasingly living alone with infrequent social contact. In this context, middle-aged participants in the UCL study, especially women, expressed the feeling that the smartphone was integral to reducing loneliness when looking towards the future when they themselves will be elderly and may have limited social support and restricted mobility. Conversely, the study found indications of a rejection of the smartphone among older men, often for reasons of cost and practicality. Many middle-aged and older male participants said that their *garakei* served them well enough, often explaining that they had all their work contacts on their *garakei* and therefore switching would be troublesome. For men approaching or just post-retirement, maintaining this connection to their working lives through the *garakei* was especially important. In rural Kochi, men would typically see friends and acquaintances at a local bar (*izakaya*), and they would use their mobile phone minimally to arrange such meetings. In the cases where male participants did own smartphones, they would often protest that they did not know how to use them or that they only used their smartphone for playing games, keeping their *garakei* for making calls because it was cheaper. While smartphones continue to reduce in price, monthly data bills are still costly in Japan, so for men who often do not feel as strong a need to be socially connected through the smartphone, the *garakei* remains a popular choice.

Finally, the UCL study reveals how the digital world influences recent flows of migration from urban to rural Japan, which also appears to be a gendered process. Over the past eight years, since the March 2011 earthquake, the Internet has been a major source of news at a time when mistrust of government information was widespread. Ohashi et al. (2017) note how Twitter became a vital source of up-to-date and trusted information in the post-3.11 context. One woman who made the move to rural Kochi from Tokyo explained: "I would follow news about the disaster coming from foreign sources, such as from France, because they would tell us more about what is actually happening than our own news channels." Another mother who moved to rural Kochi with her two young children explained that she had been inspired by the blog of a woman who had recently made the move:

> When the earthquake happened I picked up both of my children, one under each arm. I was so scared, and I felt so helpless. I knew then that I did not want to stay in the city where I was dependent on others for everything, and where my food could come from contaminated land. I was inspired by reading blogs by other women who had moved with their families to the countryside and could grow their own food and be more self-sufficient.

Blogs and social media provided a glimpse into another possible life for these women and their families, and as such they held great potential to contribute towards processes of rural repopulation and regeneration.

Conclusion

While digital technologies and cultures continue their fast-paced development, an overview of the field remains challenging and a conclusion even more so. This chapter has attempted to bring together diverse areas of scholarship on digital technologies and cultures in Japan, identifying areas of commonality across disciplinary boundaries. We have focused more on digital technologies than the content of digital media texts, in part due to the comprehensive scholarship in media studies, communications studies, film studies, and anthropology that provides in-depth contents analysis of games, television, film, and animated entertainments. Instead we aimed to demonstrate the interconnected nature of the digital and physical aspects of life in Japan today, insisting on remaining aware of historical contexts in order to understand the promising yet relatively limited degree to which technological innovation has so far been converted into concrete social change in gender roles, norms, and expectations.

While digital technologies and cultures will be central to future developments in gender in Japanese culture, we must remain aware of the elements of digital cultures that reflect, or even actively entrench, gender inequalities and gendered labour. While female digital technology users are relied on by others to maintain family and social bonds through smartphones, for example, or while women use apps to seek emotional support from other women while shouldering the burden of caring duties, we must ask whether digital technologies are really changing gender roles to any great degree. What would it mean to hand such women's work over to a female-shaped robot or hologram? As we argued in the early stages of this chapter, digital iterations of gender do not make a radical break with pre-existing lived experiences and practices. The challenge for scholars is to remain aware of these constraints and push for greater understanding of the many roles and potentials of digital technologies and cultures, currently studied behind disciplinary boundaries. An interdisciplinary approach in a global context like that of the UCL study will allow for a nuanced understanding of the possibilities and constraints presented by digital technologies and cultures in Japan today.

Related chapters

9   Attitudes to Marriage and Childbearing
11 Intimacy in and Beyond the Family
18 Gender, Labour, and Migration in Japan
27 Performing Gender: Cosplay and Otaku Cultures and Spaces
32 Gender and Visual Culture
33 Gender, Media, and Misogyny in Japan
34 Representing Girls in Cinema
35 Gendered Desires: Pornography and Consumption

References

Chino, K. (1996) "Gender in Japanese Art," *Aesthetics* 7 49–68.
Coates, J. (2018) "Mediating Memory: Shōjo and War Memory in Classical Japanese Cinema," *Cultural Studies* 32 (1) 105–125.

Freeman, L. (2003) "Mobilizing and Demobilizing the Japanese Public Sphere: Mass Media and the Internet in Japan," in F. J. Schwartz and S. J. Pharr (eds) *The State of Civil Society in Japan*, Cambridge: Cambridge University Press, 381–411.

Galbraith, P. W. (2017) "*RapeLay* and the Return of the Sex Wars in Japan," *Porn Studies* 4 (1) 105–126.

Hambleton, A. (2016) "When Women Watch: The Subversive Potential of Female-Friendly Pornography in Japan," *Porn Studies* 3 (4) 427–442.

Hjorth, L. (2007) "The Game of Being Mobile: One Media History of Gaming and Mobile Technologies in Asia-Pacific," *Convergence* 13 (4) 369–381.

Hori, H. (2018) *Promiscuous Media: Film and Visual Culture in Imperial Japan, 1926–1945*, New York: Cornell University Press.

Horst, H. A. and Miller, D. (2013) "The Digital and the Human: A Prospectus for Digital Anthropology," in H. A. Horst and D. Miller (eds) *Digital Anthropology*, London and New York: Berg.

Ito, M., Okabe, D. and Matsuda, M. (eds) (2005) *Personal, Portable, Pedestrian*, Cambridge, MA: The MIT Press.

Kamanaka, H., Katsuya, H., Long, M. R. and Anson, A. (2018) "Fukushima, Media, Democracy: The Promise of Documentary Film," *Japan Focus: The Asia Pacific Journal* 15 (16) 3. https://apjjf.org/2018/16/Kamanaka.html

Lim, S. S. (2015) "On Stickers and Communicative Fluidity in Social Media," *Social Media + Society* 1 (1). https://doi.org/10.1177/2056305115578137

Lock, M. (1993) "Ideology, Female Midlife, and the Greying of Japan," *Journal of Japanese Studies* 19 (1) 43–78.

McKnight, A. (2017) "At the Source (Code): Obscenity and Modularity in Rokudenashiko's Media Activism," in M. Steinberg and A. Zahlten (eds) *Media Theory in Japan*, Durham: Duke University Press.

McLelland, M. (2018) "The Case of a Good-for-Nothing Kid and Her Pussy," in G. Meikle (ed) *The Routledge Companion to Media and Activism*, London: Routledge.

Mostow, J. (2003) "Introduction," in J. Mostow, N. Bryson and M. Graybill (eds) *Gender and Power in the Japanese Visual Field*, Honolulu: University of Hawaii Press.

Nozawa, S. (2015) "Phatic Traces: Sociality in Contemporary Japan," *Anthropological Quarterly* 88 (2) 373–400.

Ohashi, K., Kato, F. and Hjorth, L. (2017) "Digital Genealogies: Understanding Social Mobile Media LINE in the Role of Japanese Families," *Social Media + Society*. https://doi.org/10.1177/2056305117703815

Ono, H. and Zavodny, M. (2005) "Gender Differences in Information Technology Usage: A US-Japan Comparison," *Sociological Perspectives* 48 (1) 105–133.

Oshio, T. (2014) "The Association Between Involvement in Family Caregiving and Mental Health Among Middle-Aged Adults in Japan," *Social Science and Medicine* 115 121–129.

Robertson, J. (2017) *Robo Sapiens Japanicus: Robots, Gender, Family, and the Japanese Nation*, Oakland, CA: University of California Press.

South China Morning Post. (2017) "Netflix Could Fix Japan Film Financing, Director Naomi Kawase Says," *South China Morning Post*. www.scmp.com/culture/film-tv/article/2097494/netflix-could-fix-japanese-film-financing-director-naomi-kawase-says

Stark, L. and Crawford, K. (2015) "The Conservatism of Emoji: Work, Affect, and Communication," *Social Media + Society*. https://doi.org/10.1177/2056305115604853

Statista. (2018) "Number of Monthly Active LINE Users in Japan as of 3rd Quarter 2018 (in millions)," *The Statistics Portal* (online). www.statista.com/statistics/560545/number-of-monthly-active-line-app-users-japan/

Takeda, Y., Kawachi, I., Yamagata, Z., Hashimoto, S., Matsumura, Y., Oguri, S. and Okayama, A. (2004) "Multigenerational Family Structure in Japanese Society: Impacts on Stress and Health Behaviors Among Women and Men," *Social Science and Medicine* 59 (1) 69–81.

Wada-Marciano, M. (2012) *Japanese Cinema in the Digital Age*, Honolulu: University of Hawai'i Press.

Whaley, B. (2018) "Who Will Play Terebi Gēmu When No Japanese Children Remain? Distanced Engagement in Atlus' Catherine," *Games and Culture* 13 (1) 92–114.

24
WOMEN AND PHYSICAL CULTURE IN JAPANESE HISTORY

Keiko Ikeda

On 19 July 2011, *The Japan Times* published an article entitled, "Japan celebrates Women's World Cup win: '*Nadeshiko*' lift nation with surprise victory over Americans." *Nadeshiko* is the nickname of the Japan women's national football (soccer) team and is an abbreviation of *Yamato-nadeshiko*, a compound noun combining the term *Yamato*, signifying "ancient Japan," and *nadeshiko*, a pink frilled carnation symbolizing grace and beauty. It is perhaps unsurprising that the name of the women's team evokes nationalism, given that the term "Blue Samurai" is used for the men's team (*The Japan Times* 2011). *The Guardian* newspaper also commented on this victory with a nod to history. "In wartime, the term '*Yamato Nadeshiko*' was used to describe women who displayed the traditional virtue of silent sacrifice in the nation's cause, an etymology that seems a little at odds with the fearless exploits of their modern-day footballing counterparts" (McCurry 2011).

The contradictory nickname represents the complex history of physical culture and gender in Japan. Traditional notions of women's virtue may have been challenged, but ideas of gender have regularly shifted between complicated ideals of tradition and modernization. These contradictions can be traced back to the late nineteenth century when modern physical education was established in Japan. Before this period, women's physical activities were mostly restricted to the traditional arts, such as dancing at folk festivals, sacred religious rituals, and *bushi* (warrior) class women's swordplay called *naginata* (long halberd), which was practiced in the Edo period as self-defence and in preparation for emergencies. Evidence for women's involvement in other physical activities is scarce; at most, they were expected to be spectators, not practitioners (Guttmann and Thompson 2001, 29–30).

This began to change after the Meiji Restoration, when secondary education for girls was formally institutionalized with the Imperial Rescript on Education of 1890. Educational aims were based on images of ideal womanhood, such as *ryōsai kenbo* (good wife, wise mother). This ideal was linked to the ideology of imperial nation-building, a belief that healthy and wise mothers were needed for the emerging Japanese empire. This was an "invented tradition" (Hobsbawm 1983, 1), a new social code attempting to ground an emerging imperialist ideology in the past in order to legitimate that ideology. As a complement to men's "simple manliness" (*shitsujitsu gōken*), domestic affairs were imagined as women's "territory" and women were generally excluded from other social activities (Koyama 1999, 20–27; Muta 2000, 36–40; Ikeda 2014, 97).

A girls' secondary education system was firmly established and linked with the context of a nationalistic policy by the time of the First Sino-Japanese War (1894–5). The ideal of *ryōsai kenbo* led to the introduction of girl students' active participation in physical activities, eventually including track and field athletics, gymnastics, dance, indoor baseball, croquet, lawn tennis, table tennis, marching games, volleyball, basketball, and swimming. Organized competitive sports for women flourished in the Taisho era (1912–1926). The games and exercise taught at schools came to involve more masculine physical exertion (Ikeda 2010, 539–541; Ikeda 2014, 97), partly as a result of Western influence.

The *ryōsai kenbo* ideal emerged from a blend of Eastern Confucian ideas about traditionally restrained women and the idea of the Victorian woman imported from the United Kingdom, the "angel in the house" (Fukaya 1990, 11; Koyama 1991, 1–9; Inose 1992, 95–105). Meiji Japan was strongly influenced by British culture, especially following the 1902 Japanese-Anglo Alliance against Russia. When Elizabeth Phillips Hughes, the first Principal of the Cambridge Training College for Women (C.T.C., now Hughes Hall in Cambridge University), visited Japan to undertake educational research from 1901 to 1902, she praised the Japanese modernization ideology that mixed the best of Western values with traditional Japanese culture (Hughes 1902a, 1–10; Hughes 1902b; Bottrall 1985, 33–34). Her influence on Japanese education was obvious. Hughes spoke to Japanese audiences about the significance of women's roles for a new age through outdoor activities like climbing and rowing, organized games such as tennis and hockey, and gymnastics, which (in Hughes' view) encouraged proper character, self-restraint, cooperation, and healthy bodies for women. She also mentioned a woman's role at home as a wise mother responsible for the discipline of young children, suggesting the need for domestic science: "It is more important for women to administrate politics at home than for the country" (Hughes 1902a, 24–29).

Many visiting educational specialists to Japan contributed to the development of modern physical education for girls. Higher Women's Normal Schools (Colleges of Education) in Tokyo and Nara were the top educational establishments for daughters of the elite members of Japanese society before World War II and played major roles in developing women's physical education and disseminating Western-style girls' physical education. Graduates of the colleges themselves then began teaching at schools, furthering this influence. For example, Miss Akuri Inokuchi (1870–1931, also known as Aguri Inokuchi) was sent by the Japanese Ministry of Education to study at Smith College, a prominent women's liberal arts college in Massachusetts, under the guidance of Miss Senda Berenson, and returned to Japan to become a professor at Tokyo Women's Higher Normal School (later Ochanomizu Women's University). Here she introduced the Swedish system of exercise that had been adopted as women's gymnastics at Smith College. This system involved light exercises, such as calisthenics, with no apparatus. Her reports were collected in an influential book entitled *Theory and Practice of Physical Education*, published by the Japanese Investigation Committee for Gymnastics and Games in 1905 (Inokuchi 1906, 103–126; Koshimizu 1981, 103–126; Shindō 1986, 115–123; Ikeda 2010, 541). The course that Inokuchi proposed included Swedish gymnastics and Western-style sports and activities like tennis, dance, baseball, the discus, and the javelin (Nikaidō et al. 1957, 65; Nishimura 1981, 165–168; Ikeda 2010, 541).

At institutions like Tokyo Women's Higher Normal School, girls wore bloomers, a uniform for gymnastics that became widespread due to the influence of the activities of Mrs Amelia Bloomer (1818–1894), an American women's rights activist in the second half of the nineteenth century (Noun 1985, 595–600). Inokuchi was responsible for the introduction of bloomers to Japan. Tunics, another form of popular athletic wear for women, were brought to Japan by

Tokuyo Nikaidō, who had studied at Martina Bergman-Österberg's Physical Training College in London in 1913.

While influences from North America and England resulted in Japanese girls and women learning modern sports, a traditional education in classic Japanese poetry, the Japanese harp, sewing, handicraft, housework, and cooking was still considered important. Some graduates commented that their experience of school sports was like a dream, a time and space separated from their real lives at home (Yoshida 2000, 129–136; Ikeda 2010, 543–544). Hargreaves (1994, 77–78) points out that conventional sex divisions in Japanese colleges were similar to those in operation at overseas institutions, such as Österberg's college. The Victorian idealization of the role of a woman in the family—training for a future life as a wife and mother—was a central feature of the version of feminism associated with the profession of women's physical education in both England and in Japan (Ikeda 2014, 98–99).

The varied influence of Euro-American sporting cultures in Japan can be seen across five categories of women's physical activity. First, recreational games taking place in gardens and backyards and using various implements, for example, croquet or badminton, became a status symbol for upper-middle-class elite women in England. These had negligible influence on Japanese women's sporting activities due to the significantly different organization of private space in Japan. Very few Japanese people, even the upper classes, had access to lawns and other open spaces. One exception was croquet, which was slightly better known at girls' secondary schools and Western missionary schools (Hargreaves 1994, 64; Ikeda 2016, 60).

However, organized sports played during school lunchtimes or at social clubs, such as hockey and tennis, proliferated. These derived from social activities in the suburbs, and later influenced extracurricular activities at schools for middle-class girls in England, before being transferred to Japan by leading Japanese educational specialists who had studied abroad. The emergence of these activities may best be understood with reference to the work of leading Japanese sociologist Ueno Chizuko, who proposed two models of women's advancement. In Ueno's reading, the social position of women could be advanced in societies that remained dominated by men through the strategic deployment of certain aspects of femininity such as motherhood and maternity. Women could use their subordinate position for strategic advantage. In these approaches, women's rights were acceptable, so long as women did not venture beyond their designated feminine sphere or directly challenge masculine dominance. This contributed to the development of secondary education for women, as secondary schools for girls were initially opened as part of a process of separating the sexes for educational activities (Ueno 1998, 92–93), as well as the emergence of separate sporting activities coded as feminine. In contrast, Ueno points out that in a time and space where the public sphere and social power remained controlled by men, women who actively pursued an agenda of equality with men continued to encounter difficulties (Ueno 1998, 92–93).

This second model of women's advancement is represented in the third of our gendered physical culture typologies. Games played at working-class factory-clubs such as football were pursued within a "unisex model" with equality marked through dress; women more often played these games in "menswear" rather than bloomers or tunics. Historically, women's participation in such activities was only possible when men were not present. Football clubs increased in British military factories for working-class women during and after World War I. However, the English Football Association abolished women's football in 1921 after men returned from the war, and women's football was officially banned for the next 50 years (William 2003, 6; Ikeda 2016, 61–62). Football clearly belonged within the male sphere, and women's participation in it was forced underground. While these more direct models challenging male dominance had little historical influence in Japan, this model reasserted itself later in the twentieth century, as women's demands for equal access became increasingly prominent.

Middle- and upper-class sports like women's cricket constitute our fourth grouping. These were first witnessed in the United Kingdom in the eighteenth century but declined in the nineteenth century except at girls' public boarding schools in which the curriculum was almost identical to that of boys at similar public schools (Hargreaves 1994, 64). Most British sport of the period was expected to be amateur, excluding workers from participation in an elite pastime for middle-class men. This extended to some elite girls' sports. In Japan, one example of this is the emergence of indoor baseball for women in a few higher educational schools for elite women (Yoshida 2000, 132; Ikeda 2016, 62–63).

The last grouping is perhaps most significant in considering Western influences on women's physical activity in Japan. The emergence of school physical education saw callisthenics, Swedish exercises, and musical gymnastics introduced, with physical progress checked through regular physical examinations by a qualified doctor who prescribed treatment by exercise to cure postural defects (Hargreaves 1994, 64–65). British girls' PE classes were a means of producing modern healthy female bodies that fit the imperialist and social Darwinist ideals of the time. A healthy woman was most important as a mother able to birth a healthy (male) soldier and future administrator for the Empire. Modern concepts of health and social Darwinism as the survival of the fittest spread overseas in tandem with the British Empire. Similarly, Japanese educational specialists and administrators who studied abroad also strongly encouraged physical activities through girls' PE (Nikaidō et al. 1957, 65; Nishimura 1981, 161–168; Ikeda 2010, 541) for the purpose of producing healthy soldiers and administrators to strengthen the militarily and economically strong future Japanese Empire (Ikeda 2016, 63–64).

The second and fifth of the previous typologies had the most influence upon late nineteenth- and early twentieth-century attitudes to Japanese women's physical activity. The aforementioned concept of *ryōsai kenbo* mapped perfectly onto these models of physical education borrowed and adapted from Victorian Britain. The alliance of these external models with that domestic ideal helps to explain why such frameworks of physical education have been sustained in Japanese society for over a century.

"Liberal education" and the internationalization of organized women's sports during the Taisho Era

Ryōsai kenbo education helped to produce exceptional women. In 1911, Hiratsuka Raichō set up the famous journal of Japanese feminism, *Seitō* (Blue Stocking), referring to the Blue-Stocking Society for Literature established in mid-eighteenth-century London. This brought the image of "new women" to greater public prominence and exerted a significant influence on both women's and men's thoughts on marriage (Ikeda 2010, 540–541, 2014, 99). Hiratsuka had graduated from Nihon Joshi Daigakkō (now Japan Women's University), the founder of which, Naruse Jinzō (1858–1919), had encouraged the Delsarte system (an expressionistic form of gymnastics invented by Francois Delsarte of France, 1811–1871) and other physical activities for women (Naruse 1896, 213; Ikeda 2010, 540, 2014, 99). Students also enjoyed playing lawn tennis and basketball (Baba 2011, 79). While Hiratsuka's feminism did not directly influence further developments in women's physical education, it stimulated the atmosphere of liberal education for women in society in general and encouraged greater freedom for women in different areas of life—a new "spirit of the age" (Ikeda 2014, 99).

After the Taisho period, fascist and totalitarian ideology came to dominate Japanese education (Irie 1993, 131; Ikeda 2010, 545). In parallel, national women's sporting events were developed, with the first Women's Federal Athletic Meeting being held in Tokyo in 1922. Two years later, the first meeting of the Women's Olympic Games of Japan in Osaka and the Meiji-Jingu Athletic Meeting in Tokyo were held. Track and field, basketball, volleyball, and tennis featured in the latter meeting, which continued until 1943 with formal participation confined to students of upper secondary schools (Ikeda 2001, 606).

The Japan Association of Physical Education for Women was formed in 1926, followed by the Japan Women's Sport Federation (JWSF). By 1930, this Federation was affiliated as a sub-organization of the Federation Sportive Feminine Internationale (FSFI) (Raita 1999, 123). Also in 1926, Hitomi Kinue (1907–1931) participated in the second Women's World Games organized in Gothenburg, Sweden, by FSFI. Hitomi was the only Japanese woman to compete and the first to succeed in an international sports competition, winning gold medals in the long jump and the standing long jump, as well as silver medals in the discus and the 100-yard dash and subsequently writing two books, *The Traces of Spikes (1929)* and *Reach the Goal (1931)* (Hitomi 1929, 1931; Ikeda 2014, 100).

Fascism, maternal feminism, and the restoration of *budō*

The period leading to World War II, when the West was increasingly perceived as an enemy, saw the re-emergence and popularization of some traditional aspects of Japanese physical culture. Traditional Japanese martial arts, *budō*, were introduced into primary and secondary schools: *judō* and *kendō* (Japanese fencing) for boys, and *naginata* (Japanese long sword) and *kyudō* (traditional archery) for girls. Although *budō* had already been taught in most schools prior to this revival, it became formally regulated with the purpose of consolidating martial spirit. *Budō* was adopted for women's physical education in the 1930s and continued during the war, with the aim of providing disciplined training of both the mind and the body in the absence of conscription for women (Irie 1986, 146–147; Ikeda 2010, 545). The Ladies' Society for the National Defence of the Japanese Empire (*Dai-Nihon Kokubō fujinkai*), for example, was formed for this purpose in 1932, following the Manchurian Incident (Ikeda 2010, 545). In the 1930s, even feminism fell under the influence of fascism, becoming known as maternal feminism (Ueno 1998, 31–34, 38–49).

A key figure in this imperial direction was Fujimura Toyo, a female physical educationalist who had studied in Germany. She argued that, "in order to foster the nation with a vigorous and plucky character, firstly, we have to educate women since they have to become mothers and teachers in the near future." In her *Women's Physical Education*, words and phrases such as "the consciousness of the home front" and "to welcome *Hitlerjugend* (Hitler Youth)" added to the wider fascist discourse in which totalitarianism advanced. However, Fujimura also wrote about practical things, such as women's need to physically prepare for childbirth, practising certain postures through lumbar-region abdominal training. This conflation of maternalism and feminism with nationalist ideologies was a common feature of fascist Japan (Kaminuma 1967, 81–82; Ikeda 2006, 95), as was the popularization of women sportspeople. By the early 1930s, the swimmer Maehata Hideko had succeeded Hitomi as Japan's leading female sportswoman, winning silver medals in the 200-m breaststroke in the Olympics in Los Angeles in 1932 and Berlin in 1936. Newspaper, radio, and TV reported her win so fanatically that she temporarily became a media star. Following Maehata's brilliance, sports were quickly taken over by the world of national defence (Ikeda 2001, 606, 2014, 100–101).

The influence of fascism on sport continued to grow in the 1940s through print media. A book published by the Society of Physical Education for the Japanese Empire in 1940, for example, argued for a nationalistic justification for girls' physical education. An advertisement in the same book for *budō* for elementary school education highlighted the book's "explication of the true ethos of *budō*, the pivot of the national spirit" (Dainihon taiiku gakkai 1940). Magazine articles on physical education also clearly suggested the purpose of *budō* as "the best teaching material for contributing to moulding people for the Japanese Empire," idealizing nationhood, the fascist woman, and "maternal feminism" (Sato 1940, 3–6).

In the period leading up to war, and particularly after the war in the Pacific broke out on 8 December 1941, localized organizations were established to maintain a spirit of solidarity and to unite the country. Both martial arts and Western sports activities were organized within a simulated army or sport-corps called *hōkokutai* or *hōkoku-dan*. It was the duty of all staff and students to demonstrate their allegiance to the Japanese Empire through these activities (Ikeda 2010, 547). Physical education for women during World War II continued to emphasize maternal feminism and the importance of women having a strong spirit for the sake of the nation.

Following a 1940 instruction from the Ministry of Education, *hōkoku-dan* and *hōkoku-tai* were formed in almost every school, and the policy was fully implemented in August 1941. Although girls were not conscripted, girl students were imbued with the spirit of the home front and games were taken over by a militaristic sports organization. The *hōkoku-dan* at Japan Women's University comprised six sections: general affairs, culture, life, training, labour service, and the national defence drill, which had divisions for air drill, first aid, nursing, and the distribution of food (Japan Women's University 1981, 106). At Tokyo Women's Higher Normal School, the *hōkoku-tai* included *kyūdo*, *naginata*, swimming, skiing, athletics, tennis, table tennis, basketball, volleyball, touring, and *tairen* (a mass game of militaristic physical training and gymnastics). In war, the physical activities in *hōkoku-dan* became more predominant than other sporting activities (Ochanomizu Women's University 1984, 201–202). Similar organizations existed at several other women's schools and colleges, and Western-style physical education, dancing, and competitive sports for women all lost popularity. Then, after the war, the rejection of the wartime system of education became the starting point of a new era (Ikeda 2014, 101).

The postwar revival of women's sporting cultures

After World War II, Japanese civil law was revised according to the new Constitution of Japan (1947), with Japan's new democracy underpinned by equal status for women and men. World War II had damaged the Japanese people both economically and psychologically, but the end of the war opened up new opportunities and consciousness of women's sports rose to a new level. Great athletes, such as Hitomi, had already shown that individual women could be successful sports people, a trend that continued. Physical educators such as Miura Hiro (1898–1992) also became more prominent, building on their earlier efforts to improve the standards of women's physical educators and instructors. Starting in the Taisho period, Miura had sought to improve women's health and strength through modern dance and new aesthetic gymnastics influenced by figures as diverse as Isadora Duncan (1878–1927), Rudolph Laban (1879–1958), Emile Jaques-Dalcroze (1865–1950), Rudolf Bode (1881–1970), Elizabeth Marguerite de Varel Mensendieck (1864–1957), and Mary Wigman (1886–1973). Miura's ideas and practice continued through the war but became more influential after 1945 through teacher education (Kunieda 1981, 203–221; Yamamoto 2001; Ikeda 2014, 101).

The proportion of women in the Japanese workforce slowly increased from 36.9 percent to 39.4 percent from 1950 to 1990. Alongside this, female athletes, sports instructors, and sports educators also became more prominent. After the 1964 Tokyo Olympic Games in particular, many competitive sports became popular for both men and women. Moreover, they diversified and flourished: female rugby players, bodybuilders, yachtswomen, boxers, karate practitioners, and ice hockey players have all become common since 1970. The first Tokyo International Women's Marathon was held in 1979, leading to a boom in popularity, with runners like Masuda Akemi and Arimori Yuko becoming national celebrities. A Japanese women's mountaineering team climbed Mount Everest for the first time in 1975. In 1977, another famous sportswoman, the professional golfer Higuchi Hisako, won the US Open, becoming the first Japanese woman to do so (Ikeda 2014, 102).

The Olympic Games saw growing numbers of Japanese women participating and winning medals. The all-Japan team of women volleyball players won a gold medal in 1964 (Tokyo) (Macnaughtan 2014, 134–156). In 1992 at Barcelona, Iwasaki Kyoko won a gold medal in the 200-meter breaststroke at the age of 14, the youngest gold medallist ever. In winter sports, Hashimoto Seiko was chosen as the representative of all Japanese Olympic competitors in 1994, the first time a woman had been so honoured. The 1998 Nagano Winter Olympic Games also produced many young women medal winners, including Satoya Tae, who won gold in the freestyle mogul (Ikeda 2001, 607, 2014, 102). In the twenty-first century, women's participation and wins in international athletic events are no longer considered unusual.

Changes in perspectives on gender and developments towards equality with men have also been achieved through the inauguration and work of organizations at national and international levels, for example, the Japan Association of Physical Education for Women (JAPEW), the Japanese Association for Women in Sport (JWS), and the International Working Group on Women and Sport (IWG) (Hargreaves 2000). Academic research has also reinforced work towards women's equality in sports through specialized academic congresses. In 2001, the First Asian Conference on Women and Sports was held in Osaka, involving scholars from the Philippines, Nepal, Sri Lanka, Hong Kong, Mongolia, Cambodia, South Korea, Singapore, Malaysia, Thailand, Syria, and Indonesia. The same year, the "Osaka Five-Year Plan: Asian Action Plan for Gender Equity in Sport" was unanimously adopted (Itani et al. 2001, 284–311; Raita 2001, 2–58; Ikeda 2014, 102), reaffirming key developments in the global promotion of gender equality and women's participation in sport, such as the principles of the Brighton Declaration (at the first World Conference on Women and Sport in 1994) and the Windhoek Call for Action (at the second World Conference on Women and Sport in 1998). Then, in 2002, a preparatory committee for the Japan Society for Sport and Gender Studies (JSSGS) was set up, followed by the first congress of the study of Sport and Gender Studies held at the Dawn Centre, an institution dedicated to the promotion of independence and equal opportunity for men and women. Academics from physical education and sports studies initiated the event, and all together, 61 academics from a wide variety of fields such as history, sociology, pedagogy, psychology, anthropology, and literature attended. Three years later, the JSSGS was officially inaugurated (Yamaguchi 2012, 23; Ikeda 2014, 102). JSSGS publishes an annual journal, the *Journal of Sport and Gender Studies*. The tenth issue, published in May 2012, celebrates the achievements of the society over the previous decade (Mizuno 2012, 2–3; Yamaguchi 2012, 23–28; Ikeda 2014, 102).

In contemporary Japan, most sports are played recreationally by both men and women, and great progress has been made towards increased participation of women. However, the media continue the legacy of "Samurai Japan" for men's sports and *Yamato Nadeshiko* for women's sports, as noted previously, an interesting manifestation of the longevity of gender-biased idioms and images. However, traditional gender divisions are being constantly undermined and reinvented. The old and the new still coexist in many ways, despite the World Cup triumph having opened up a new world of women's professional football, symbolizing new possibilities for women and new relations of gender in all areas of sport and life.

Japan placed 110th in the World Economic Forum's global gender equality rankings for 2018, a small rise from 114th in 2017, due to continued poor scores for political empowerment, such as the proportion of women among lawmakers and Cabinet ministers, low annual income equality, and the proportion of women in managerial positions (*The Japan Times* 2018). This is the lowest rank on gender issues among developed countries. However, Japanese women's athletic achievements do not accord with this ranking. The 2016 Rio de Janeiro Summer Olympic Games produced many women gold medallists such as Kanato Rie (swimming), Tosaka Eri, Ichō Kaori, Kawai Risako and Doshō Sara (wrestling), Tachimoto Haruka (judo), and Takahashi Ayaka and Matsutomo Misaki (badminton). The great woman wrestler Yoshida Saori, who won 13 consecutive championships across Olympic Games and other world championships, was awarded the People's Honour Award by the Cabinet in November 2012, followed by another great woman wrestler, Ichō Kaori, who was awarded the same honour in October 2016. The 2018 winter Olympic games produced many women medallists such as Arakawa Shizuka (figure-skating), also a gold medallist in the 2006 Torino Winter Olympic Games; Asada Mao (figure-skating); Kodaira Nao, Tabata Maki, and Hozumi Masako (speed-skating), also silver medallists in the 2010 Vancouver Winter Olympic Games; and Takeuchi Tomoka (snowboard), also a silver medallist in the 2014 Sochi Winter Olympic Games.

Leading women athletes are symbolically fighting domestic conventions and institutions that remain rooted in the traditional hierarchies of athletic organizations constructed by Japan's male-dominated society. The continuation of this male dominance is particularly visible when cases of harassment are revealed. In 2014, in response to a series of such reports, the Japan Sport Council (JSC) "launched an email-based consultation service for Olympic, Paralympic and other promising amateur athletes in 2014, giving victims a place to report violent incidents and power and sexual harassment" (Kobayashi 2018). While issues remain, women's outstanding feats in physical culture remind us that issues of gender equality in Japanese society are wider than what happens in workplaces or in relation to economic and political empowerment.

References

Baba, T. (2011) "Nihon Joshi Daigakkō de mananda 'Atarasii onna' tachi to taiiku supōtsu" ('New Women' Educated at Nihon Joshi Daigakkō and PE & Sports), in The Society of "New Women" (ed) *"Seitō" to sekai no "Atarashii onna" tachi* ("Blue Stocking" and "New Women" in the World), Tokyo: Kanrin Shobō.
Bottrall, M. (1985) *Hugh's Hall 1885–1985*, Cambridge: Rutherford Publications.
Dainihon Taiiku Gakkai (ed) (1940) *Taiiku-to-kyōgi* (Physical Education and Athletic Sports), 19–9 [advertisements].
Guttman, A. and Thompson, L. (2001) *Japanese Sports: A History*, Honolulu: University of Hawai'i Press.
Fukaya, M. (1990) *Ryōsai-kembo-shugi-no-kyō-iku* (Education Based on the Principle of Ryōsai-Kenbo), Nagoya: Reimei Shobo.
Hargreaves, J. (1994) *Sporting Females: Critical Issues in the History and Sociology of Women's Sports*, London: Routledge.
Hargreaves, J. (2000) *Heroines of Sport: The Politics of Difference and Identity*, London: Routledge.
Hitomi, K. (1997 [1929]) "Supaiku no ato" (The Trace of Spikes), in *Hitomi Kinue: Honoo no Supurintā* (Hitomi Kinue: Sprinter on Fire), Tokyo: Nihon Tosho Center.
Hitomi, K. (1997 [1931]) "Gōru ni hairu" (Reach the Goal) in *Honoo no Supurintā* (Hitomi Kinue: Sprinter on Fire), Tokyo: Nihon Tosho Center.
Hobsbawm, E. (1983) "Introduction: Inventing Traditions," in Eric Hobsbawm and Terence Ranger (eds) *The Invention of Tradition*, Cambridge: Cambridge University Press.
Hughes, E. P. (1902a) "Modern British Ladies II," *Onna* [*Women*] 2 (3) 24–29.
Hughes, E. P. (1902b) "Taisōhō ni tsuite" (On the Methods of Gymnastics), trans. X, *Taiiku* (*Physical Education*) 103 1–10.
Ikeda, K. (2001) "Japan," in K. Christensen, A., Guttmann and G. Pfister (eds) *International Encyclopedia of Women & Sports*, New York: Berkshire Reference Works and Macmillan Reference, 604–607.

Ikeda, K. (2006) "The Body and Grass-Roots Fascism During World War II: 'The Topos' of the Emperor in a Personal-Body-Mechanism in Japan," *International Journal of Eastern Sports & Physical Education* 4 (1) 91–103.

Ikeda, K. (2010) "'*Ryōsai-kembo*', 'Liberal Education' and Maternal Feminism Under Fascism: Women and Sports in Modern Japan," *The International Journal of the History of Sport* 27 (3) 537–552.

Ikeda, K. (2014) "From *Ryosaikenbo* to *Nadeshiko*: Women and Sports in Japan," in Jennifer Hargreaves and Eric Anderson (eds) *Routledge Handbook of Sport, Gender and Sexuality*, London and New York: Routledge, 97–105.

Ikeda, K. (2016) "An Analysis of Gender-Biased Spaces in Terms of the Studies of British Sport History," *Journal of Sport and Gender Studies* 14 (March) 58–69.

Inokuchi, A. (1906) *Taiiku no riron oyobi jissai* (Theory and Practice of Physical Education), Tokyo: Kokkō.

Inose, K. (1992) *Kodomotachi no Daieiteikoku* (The Children and the British Empire: The British Interpretation of "Hooligan" at Turn of the Century), Tokyo: Chuokoron shinsha.

Irie, K. (1986) *Nihon fashizumu ka no taiiku shisō* (The Philosophy of Physical Education Under Japanese Fascism), Tokyo: Fumaido Publishing.

Irie, K. (1993) *Taishō jiyū taiiku no kenkyū* (The Study of Liberal Physical Education in Taisho Period), Tokyo: Fumaido Publishing.

Itani, K., Tahara, J. and Raita, K. (eds) (2001) *Josei-supōtsu-hakusho* (A White Paper on Women's Sports), Tokyo: Taishukan Publishing.

The Japan Times (2011) "Japan Celebrates Women's World Cup Win: "*Nadeshiko*' Lift Nation with Surprise Victory Over Americans," *The Japan Times*, 19 July.

The Japan Times (2018) "Japan Rises Four Places to Lowly 110th in WEF's Global Gender Equality Rankings," *The Japan Times* 18 December. Accessed 14 January 2019. www.japantimes.co.jp/news/2018/12/18/national/japan-rises-four-places-110th-wefs-global-gender-equality-rankings/#.XDwVUbxoRhF

Japan Women's University (ed) (1981) *Zusetsu Nihon Joshi Daigaku no ayumi* (An Illustrated History of Japan Women's University), Tokyo: Japan Women's University.

Kaminuma, H. (1967) *Kindai Nihon joshi taiikushi josetsu* (The Exordial Book of the History of Modern Japanese Girls' Physical Education), Tokyo: Fumaido Publishing.

Kobayashi, Y. (2018) "Sports Council to Launch LINE App-Based Harassment Consultation Service for Athletes," *The Mainichi* 28 December. Accessed 14 January 2019. https://mainichi.jp/english/articles/20181228/p2a/00m/0sp/013000c

Koshimizu, H. (1981) "Inokuchi Akuri [Akuri Inokuchi]," in Josei Taiikushi Kenkyūkai (ed) *Kindai Nihon joshi taiikushi* (Modern Japanese History of Girls' Physical Education) Tokyo: Nihon Taiikusha, 103–126.

Koyama, S. (1991) *Ryōsai kenbo to iu kihan* (The Standard of Ryōsai kenbo) Tokyo: Keisō shobō.

Koyama, S. (1999) *Katei no seisei to josei no kokuminka* (Generation of the Concept of Home and Nationalization of Women), Tokyo: Keisō shobō.

Kunieda, T. (1981) "Dansu ni yoru jidōchūshinshugi no jissen" (Children-Centrism through Dance Education), in Josei Taiikushi Kenkyūkai (ed) *Kindai Nihon joshi taiikushi* (Modern Japanese History of Girls' Physical Education), Tokyo: Sports and Physical Education Publishing Co., 197–221.

Macnaughtan, H. (2014) "The Oriental Witches: Women, Volleyball and the 1964 Tokyo Olympics," *Sport in History* 34 (1) 34–156.

McCurry, J. (2011) "Women's World Cup Victory Brings Joy to Japan," *The Guardian*, 18 July. www.theguardian.com/world/2011/jul/18/japan-womens-world-cup-reaction-joy

Mizuno, E. (2012) "2011 o furikaette" (Looking Back to the Year 2011), *Journal of Sport and Gender Studies* 10 2–3.

Muta, K. (2000) "Ryōsai kembo shisō no omoteura" (Two Sides of the Ideology of *Ryōsai Kenbo*), in T. Aoki, S. Kawamoto, K. Tsutsui, T. Mikuriya and T. Yamaori (eds) *Onna no bunka* (*Women's Culture*), Tokyo: Iwanami Shoten Publishers, 23–46.

Naruse, J. (1983 [1896]) *Joshi taiiku* (Girls' Education), Tokyo: Nihontosho Center.

Nikaidō, S., Tokura, H. and Nikaidō, S. (1963 [1957]) *Nikaidō Tokuyo den* (A Biography of Tokuyo Nikaidō), Tokyo: Fumaido Publishing.

Nishimura, A. (1981) "Nikaidō Tokuyo" [Tokuyo Nikaidō], in Josei Taiikushi Kenkyūkai (ed) *Kindai Nihon joshi taiikushi* (Modern Japanese History of Girls' Physical Education), Tokyo: Nihon Taiikusha, 151–176.

Noun, L. (1985) "Amelia Bloomer, a Biography," *The Annals of Iowa* 47 (7) 575–617.

Ochanomizu Women's University (ed) (1984) *Ochanomizu Joshi-Daigaku hyaku-nenshi* (A Hundred-Year History of Ochanomizu Women's University), Tokyo: Publishing Committee for a Hundred-Year History of Ochanomizu Women's University.

Raita, K. (1999) "The Movement for the Promotion of Competitive Women's Sport in Japan 1924–35," *The International Journal of the History of Sport* 16 (3) 120–134.

Raita, K. (2001) (ed) *Abstracts of the First Asian Conference on Women and Sports*, issued by The First Asian Conference on Women and Sports.

Sato, U. (1940) "Kokumingakkō taiikuka budō (zoku)" (The *Budō* in the Curricula for Physical Education for National Elementary Schools: Sequel), *Taiiku to kyōgi* (Physical Education and Athletic Sports) 19 (9) 3–6.

Shindō, K. (1986) *Inokuchi Akuri joshi-den* (A Women's History Biography of Akuri Inokuchi), Akita: Onkokan.

Ueno, C. (1998) *Nashonarizumu to jendā* (Nationalism and Gender) Tokyo: Seidosha.

Williams, J. (2003) *The Games for Rough Girls?: A History of Women's Football in England*, London: Routledge.

Yamaguchi, R. (2012) "Nihon supōtsu to jendā gakkai: Jūnen no sōkatsu to kadai" (The Japan Society of Sport and Gender Studies: The Summary of the Last Decade and the Agenda for the Future), *Journal of Sport and Gender Studies* 10 23–28.

Yamamoto, T. (2001) "Miura Hiro no senkanki taiiku e no omoide [Hiro Miura's Memory of Physical Education During the War]," paper presented to Spring Seminar for the Historical Research Section of Japan Society of Physical Education, Health and Sport Sciences, Hitotsubashi University, 12 May 2001.

Yoshida, A. (2000) "Kōtō jogakkō to joshi gakusei" (Girls' Upper Secondary School and Girl Students: Westernized Modernity and Modern Japan), in T. Aoki, S. Kawamoto, K. Tsutsui, T. Mikuriya and T. Yamaori (eds) *Onna no bunka* (Women's Culture), Tokyo: Iwanami Shoten.

25
MYTHS OF MASCULINITY IN THE MARTIAL ARTS

Oleg Benesch

The relationship between masculinity and the martial arts is close and complex in all societies. In the context of Japan, the investigation of this relationship takes place at the intersections of gender, nationalism, sport, philosophy, and even religion. At the same time, the investigation of Japanese martial arts benefits from a historical approach, as the relationship between masculinity and martial arts has changed significantly over time. Furthermore, for many martial artists, claims to historical lineages are an essential element of appeals to legitimacy, even if these are often idealized and even mythical. This chapter looks at three key periods to provide an overview of the role that masculinity has played in the Japanese martial arts: the Edo period (1603–1868), the Imperial period (1868–1945), and the postwar era since 1945.

One of the most fundamental and controversial issues throughout the periods treated here concerns the role of the martial arts in Japanese society. While associated debates have changed considerably over time, they remain highly relevant and are important for the relationship of the martial arts to evolving conceptions of masculinity. In broad terms, the role of the martial arts as an embodiment and performance of the masculine ideal met with distinct challenges in each of the three periods considered here. In the Edo period, the greatest challenge to the martial arts was the peaceful nature of Tokugawa society. This placed a heavy burden for self-justification on the ruling warriors—popularly known as samurai today—who still defined themselves as a military class. In formulating theories to legitimize their exalted status, many samurai drew heavily on nostalgia for the warfare of earlier ages, stressing the importance of military preparedness even after decades or centuries of peace. The rhetorical emphasis on the unique martial nature of the samurai remained constant, even as commoners became increasingly influential and also participated in martial arts on their own terms.

In the decades of modernization and empire-building that followed the Meiji Restoration of 1868, the discrediting and abolition of the warrior class were compounded by new challenges from Western sports and increasing engagement with foreigners in physical contests. As part of this process, the martial arts were reinvented, codified, and organized in ways that were highly modern yet stressed their older roots. The martial arts became a storehouse of an idealized masculine national tradition that was closely tied to the modern military and Japanese cultural and imperial expansion. Following Japan's defeat in the Pacific War and the subsequent Allied Occupation led by the United States, the martial arts suffered due to their connections with militarism and the former Imperial state. The challenges they faced in the postwar period included not just greater competition from "foreign" sports but the necessity of adapting to unprecedented levels of participation from foreigners, women, and other traditionally marginalized groups. This invariably caused tensions with existing interests, as these developments drastically revised and undermined earlier notions of masculinity. Different martial arts have dealt with these challenges with varying degrees of success, with some continuing to resist major changes well into the twenty-first century.

Recent decades have seen increasing recognition of the martial arts as a legitimate subject of academic study from a wide range of disciplines. The founding of the interdisciplinary journal *Martial Arts Studies* in 2015 has been a significant step in this development. On Japanese martial arts specifically, broader recent studies in English include Denis Gainty's *Martial Arts and the Body Politic in Meiji Japan* and Cameron Hurst's *Armed Martial Arts of Japan*. Dedicated studies of swordsmanship and gunnery provide deeper analysis of these fields (Bennett 2015; Friday and Humitake 1997; Walthall 2011; Wert 2016). Other scholarship has begun to revise commonly held assumptions regarding the spiritual underpinnings of the martial arts, especially Zen Buddhism (Benesch 2011, 2014, 2016; Yamada 2001).

Early modern martial arts

The role of the martial arts in the early modern period was closely related to the characteristics of Japanese society and government at the time. On the one hand, martial virtues were at the core of the warrior rule established under the Tokugawa shogunate (1603–1868). The official Tokugawa code for the warrior houses stressed the importance of maintaining a balance between civil and martial virtues (*bun-bu*), building on far older Chinese concepts of statecraft (De Bary et al. 2006, 12–14). For the Tokugawa, this balance was initially intended to serve the transition from the warfare of the previous centuries to a new age of stability. As the Edo period progressed, it became known as the "Great Peace," and Japan experienced almost no warfare between the mid-seventeenth and mid-nineteenth centuries. In spite of the lack of practical applications for the martial arts, samurai still saw themselves as warriors and sought to legitimate their rule on this basis (De Bary et al. 2006, 159–176). The dominant samurai images that emerged and were theorized in the Edo period were on a spectrum that included both the rough warriors of the sixteenth century and idealized Confucian gentlemen of ancient times (Benesch 2014). In this sense, the samurai ideal was almost always nostalgic, even as its specific manifestations were highly diverse.

This diversity could be seen in the great proliferation of terms for warrior behaviour and ethics, which were retrospectively gathered together under the umbrella term bushido (*bushidō*; the way of the warrior) around the turn of the twentieth century. During the early modern period, bushido was just one of dozens of overlapping or even synonymous terms and is itself found in only a handful of texts. The almost universal—if anachronistic—usage of bushido to describe early modern warrior behaviour has led to a popular impression of homogeneity among samurai that obscures their great diversity. This diversity also applied to the practice of the martial arts as part of the balance of civil and martial virtues. During the Edo period, many warriors were under- or unemployed, and those that were fortunate enough to have stable positions fulfilled largely bureaucratic tasks. As a result, maintaining the desired balance between scholarship and martial arts required dedication and was often difficult to incorporate into the routine of daily life. Those warriors with bureaucratic positions were often accused of neglecting their martial training, while others focused their energies on the martial arts and dismissed reading and intellectual pursuits as effete and not becoming of warriors (Benesch 2011). By the end of the Edo period, the seemingly irreconcilable division between these groups was a common lament among those concerned with the state of society and the nation in the face of domestic and foreign threats.

Even at the end of the Edo period, however, solutions to the problems of warrior society appealed to the balance of civil and martial virtues, and there was little doubt that Japan's fate rested on the abilities of the (reformed) male warriors who led society. Amidst the diversity of the warrior class over the course of the period, their superiority and masculine nature were widely accepted. One of the many early modern concepts later subsumed into the bushido "tradition" included the "way of men" (*otoko no michi*), while the popular saying "flowers are cherry blossoms and men are warriors" (*hana wa sakuragi, hito wa bushi*) epitomized the martial nature of the Japanese masculine ideal. The masculine warrior ideal also fed into an emerging proto-nationalism which cast Japan as a martial country, as opposed to "civil" China (Benesch 2011). This view drew upon Japan's successful repulsion of the Mongol Invasions in the thirteenth century, the devastating invasions of Korea in the 1590s, and also the reality that Japan was ruled by a warrior government. The masculine martial identity was replicated at various regional levels, as warriors often sought to portray themselves as more masculine than their counterparts in other domains. The early seventeenth-century text *Hagakure*, for example, includes harsh criticism of the effete warriors of Kyoto and Osaka, while itself drawing on an idealized martial history of the Nabeshima family in rural Kyushu (De Bary et al. 2006, 387–393). In contrast, the eighteenth-century resident of Edo known by the pen name Buyō Inshi focused his ire on warriors from wealthy domains, whom he accused of acting like courtiers and even having "become like women" (Buyō 2014, 43).

Many early modern warriors saw martial masculinity as separate from the practice of martial arts. Instead, they interpreted the role of the warrior as maintaining proper comportment and ethics and thereby serving as a model for society. For others, however, the martial arts were of primary importance and scholarly pursuits dismissed as "bookish weakness" (*bunjaku*). In this environment, just as print culture flourished and appealed to members of all classes, the Edo period saw a great proliferation of martial arts schools among both warriors and commoners. A growing body of scholarship has begun to consider martial arts in early modern Japan in similar ways to the development of sport in contemporary Europe—as a pursuit that provided an outlet for competitive urges but which also provided no small amount of cultural capital and was increasingly commercialized (Thompson 1998; Walthall 2011; Wert 2016). Michael Wert examines these developments, and further argues that early modern martial arts were treated as sports from their inception and were never intended to transmit practical combat skills (Wert 2016). Indeed, the most popular forms of martial arts in the Edo period focused on swordsmanship and other traditional weapons that firearms had rendered effectively obsolete as instruments of warfare. During the Tokugawa peace, swords became established as symbols of the warrior class, and warriors carried them as such, but firearms were strictly controlled. Even among the schools of gunnery that developed in the Edo period, the focus was often on forms that showcased skill and claimed exclusive knowledge but would have had limited application on the battlefield (Walthall 2011).

Through their association with the warrior class, the martial arts provided access to both cultural capital and elite masculinity, contributing to their popularity among commoners. By the early nineteenth century, the proliferation of martial arts schools for non-warrior audiences prompted the shogunate to pass several edicts in an ultimately unsuccessful attempt to suppress this activity (Wert 2016). These legislative moves may instead have had the opposite of the desired effect, as they enhanced the exclusivity of the martial arts by expressly restricting them to warriors, thereby increasing their cultural capital and cementing their status as symbols of an elite masculinity. That said, exclusivity was not merely imposed from above, and masculinity can be notoriously fragile. One of the most interesting and contentious issues in the martial arts, from the early modern period to the present day, is that of competition between schools and styles. While challenging other schools can enhance one's own reputation in case of victory, the risks that defeat posed to reputation were too great for most schools to countenance. As a result, even though there was considerable exchange between martial artists, even from different regions, formal competitions tended to be restricted to closely regulated bouts within schools and status groups in ways that would minimize the potential loss of face (Wert 2016).

In the last decades of the Edo period, foreign threats and domestic instability led to an increased focus on national defence, including a "remilitarization" of the martial arts. Officials such as the prominent reformer Yokoi Shōnan (1809–1969) lamented the general weakness of the samurai, as well as the irreconcilable gap between those who practiced martial arts and those who focused on intellectual pursuits (Yokoi and Miyauchi 1968). Increasingly frequent and deadly skirmishes between rival groups in the 1850s and 1860s lent the martial arts an edge that they had not had in at least two centuries. This was accompanied by a revival of "authentic" *seppuku* as a method of suicide, as opposed to the formalized method of execution by decapitation that it had largely become in the Edo period (Rankin 2011). Although certainly very real, the widespread violence against rivals and foreigners at the end of the Tokugawa period also had distinctly performative aspects tied to an idealized martial masculinity based on a nostalgic view of the Japanese past.

Imperial developments

The collapse of the Tokugawa order in the Meiji Restoration of 1868 can be seen as one point in a longer period of transition that occurred at different rates in different spheres of Japanese life, society, and politics. In the case of the warriors, their military abilities were subject to increasingly harsh criticism, and their reputational decline continued after 1868 (Sonoda 1990). Warrior privileges and stipends were gradually abolished in a series of reforms which met with growing resistance from those individuals who were unwilling or unable to adapt to the new order. This culminated in the Satsuma Rebellion of 1877, in which thousands of disgruntled former warriors gathered around the Restoration hero Saigō Takamori (1828–1877) and rose against the government. The new imperial army was able to crush the uprising only with considerable loss of life, and it was telling that both sides relied on modern weaponry, rather than swords and the traditional martial arts. Even the practice of gunnery underwent great changes in the years around the Restoration, as the existing schools were largely supplanted by European drill (Jaundrill 2016).

The violence of the Satsuma Rebellion contributed to the widespread dislike of the former warrior class in Meiji society. This also affected the martial arts, even if many schools continued to practice as before. The crisis and abolition of the samurai removed them as the embodiment of the martial masculine ideal, especially after the Satsuma Rebellion. In addition, while the demise of the former class structure meant that commoners were now free to practice the martial arts, the reduced exclusivity of the latter also diminished their attractiveness. Westerners represented a further challenge to the former martial masculine ideal, even if their absolute number was relatively low and they were largely restricted to the treaty ports. The journalist and politician Ozaki Yukio (1858–1954) was one thinker who was especially concerned with Japanese developments relative to Britain, writing that "The English nature is also seen in the way in which the women view the opposite sex. They seem to find robust, well-built men the most handsome—in sharp contrast to Japanese women, who see handsomeness in pale and sickly actor types" (Ozaki 2001, 108).

Ozaki was particularly concerned by what he perceived to be a vacuum in the masculine ideal that had appeared in Japan with the decline of the warrior class. At the same time, Ozaki shared the widespread belief that a noble martial spirit had existed in Japan long before, even if it had been almost completely lost in the present. In the late 1880s, Ozaki was at the forefront of an influential movement to recover this ancient warrior ideal. Here, Ozaki was convinced that the English gentleman was the ideal model for the Japanese male at the time. Echoing the Victorian ideology that the modern gentleman was the direct heir of medieval chivalry, Ozaki proposed that Japan channel its own "feudal knighthood"—the warriors of old—to create a native equivalent of English "gentlemanship". As it was ostensibly based on samurai ideals, Ozaki accordingly called this new ethic "bushido," appropriating an obscure early modern term. By the 1890s, the passage of time had dulled much of the virulent anti-warrior sentiment, making it possible to symbolically appropriate them in positive ways. In addition, Japan's success in the Sino-Japanese War of 1894–95 was accompanied by an unprecedented wave of nationalism. In this environment, the martial ethic of bushido reached unprecedented popularity. While Ozaki had initially proposed bushido as a response to the English gentlemanly ideal, by 1901, the great promoter of bushido and professor of philosophy at Tokyo Imperial University, Inoue Tetsujirō (1856–1944), dismissed European chivalry as mere "woman-worship" and as vastly inferior to Japan's "ancient" bushido (Benesch 2014).

Martial artists were among the greatest promoters of bushido during its period of rapid growth after the Sino-Japanese War. One reason for this was tactical, as a wide range of interests sought to capitalize on the tremendous popularity of bushido at the time. These included writers, playwrights, and musicians, as well as promoters of Buddhism, Christianity, and Shinto (Benesch 2014, 124–137). Bushido was incorporated into the military and civilian education systems in the first decade of the twentieth century, further raising its profile. Promoters of a wide range of martial arts theorized about their schools' relationship to bushido, while supporters of baseball also expounded about the role of their sport in the cultivation and realization of the Japanese samurai spirit (Blackwood 2008). Although the notion of "samurai baseball" continues to be influential in the present day, the rehabilitation of the samurai image and the rise of bushido presented a unique opportunity for the martial arts due to their long-standing links with the former warrior class (Benesch 2014).

Just as the association of the martial arts with the dominant masculinity in the form of the samurai had resulted in a crisis in the early Meiji period, the symbolic rehabilitation of the samurai from the 1890s onward also provided a major boost for the martial arts. Just as the samurai had to be reinvented in order to be rehabilitated for the nation, so did the martial arts. In the case of the samurai, this involved recasting their ideals not as the domain of an exclusive class, but as the spiritual heritage of all Japanese—especially men. This was further tied to the new masculine image of the victorious soldier of the Imperial Japanese Army. While the modern soldier was being cast and trained as the spiritual heir of the idealized samurai, the army also used its organization and propaganda to promote an image of the hardy rural youth who was physically stronger and less susceptible to dangerous liberal thought than were urban recruits (Yoshida 2002). Although these views were contradictory and often did not reflect reality, they helped contribute to a new "national" masculine ideal of the Japanese soldier who also embodied ancient martial virtues, a portrayal that became accepted on a global level through Japan's surprising victory in the Russo-Japanese War of 1904–1905 (MacKenzie 1999).

The transformation of the martial arts was similar in scope to the reinvention of the samurai, and the two had a reciprocal influence. The growth of bushido in the 1890s was closely tied to a simultaneous flourishing of martial arts organizations, although most of these were ultimately incorporated into the Greater Japan Martial Virtue Association (*Dai-Nippon Butokukai*) by the start of the twentieth century (Gainty 2013). While some martial arts had existed in forms that were close to modern sports for decades and even centuries, the late nineteenth century saw many of them become more formally organized and standardized across the country. Judo (*judō*) was the most prominent example of this shift and was developed in its modern form from a variety of earlier schools of unarmed combat (*jūjutsu*) by the educator Kanō Jigorō (1860–1938). In addition to the standardization of rules and equipment, judo and other martial arts underwent a change from being mere "techniques" (*jutsu*) to "ways" (*dō*) that emphasized more spiritual elements. This could also be seen in the development of kendo from earlier fencing schools (*kenjutsu*) and in the widespread acceptance of the term "*budō*" to exclusively refer to the martial arts from the 1890s onward. Kanō himself explained this shift in emphasis by stating that while earlier martial artists had focused on practical fighting, his new judo stressed the importance of "mental and moral training" (Lindsay and Kano 1889, 204).

The new emphasis on intangible elements in the martial arts meshed well with the national agenda that focused on the uniqueness and superiority of the "Japanese spirit," often referred to as "*Yamato damashii*." This not only gave the martial arts additional patriotic legitimacy, but it allowed them to recover a certain exclusivity that had been lost with the collapse of the Tokugawa order. Now, exclusivity was tied more closely to "Japaneseness" than class, but the symbolic rehabilitation of the samurai represented the resurrection of a similar martial masculine ideal of earlier times. This ideal was perhaps no more nor less removed from the reality of the samurai than popular views had been in Tokugawa times, but it was now supported by the apparatus of the modern state for ideological dissemination and was in some ways more attainable than it had been under the ostensibly rigid class system of the early modern period.

The codification and standardization of larger martial arts schools provided greater scope for competition than in earlier times, but this was still tightly regulated, and bouts between different styles continued to pose threats to reputation and masculinity and were therefore largely proscribed. This dynamic was further complicated by a new international angle, as both Japanese and foreign fighters sought to compete with and learn from one another. Western wrestlers who travelled to Japan to fight featured in national newspapers, and bouts could attract thousands of spectators. In the other direction, Japanese instructors taught judo techniques throughout the Americas and Europe, and also engaged in some competitions. In spite of their popularity, the reputational stakes meant that these fights were not usually sanctioned by official martial arts schools, and fighters who participated could be (at least temporarily) suspended for engaging in them. Furthermore, as these were fora for bringing together the sensitive dynamics of masculinity, race, and nationalism, accounts of these matches vary widely between different observers (Stevens 2013). In this regard, another subject that would benefit from a treatment that fully considers these points of intersection is the high-profile adoption of "jiu-jitsu" by suffragettes in Britain at the start of the twentieth century.

Masculinity and martial arts after 1945

The connections between the martial arts and the imperial state continued to grow throughout the first half of the twentieth century and were encapsulated in the militaristic bushido that was a key pillar of the Imperial ideology until 1945. After Japan's surrender, the US-led Occupation authorities banned all suspected symbols of militarism, including the martial arts. Plays and films with samurai themes were also banned, discrediting the former warrior class for the second time in less than a century. The Greater Japan Martial Virtue Association was disbanded, and the martial arts were removed from schools to be replaced by baseball and other "democratic" sports.

The criticism and prohibition of martial arts contributed to the crisis of Japanese masculinity that accompanied defeat and occupation (Benesch 2014).

Even before the end of the Occupation, however, movements were underway to rehabilitate both the samurai and martial arts as emblems of Japan's pre-Imperial past. The role these symbols played in the service of the Imperial state was dismissed as a corrupt aberration, and efforts were made to find the "true" character of the samurai and martial arts in the pre-modern period (Benesch 2014). At the same time, the postwar era also saw an increased search for a universal value of the Japanese martial arts, and many of them reached international prominence. This also meant increased participation in the martial arts by foreigners and women, further challenging the existing connections between the martial arts and a Japanese masculinity. The opening up of the martial arts reduced their exclusivity and created potential for competitions that could threaten reputations as well as the previous dominance of the adult Japanese male.

The various martial arts experienced and reacted to these shifts in very different ways. In the case of judo, its Olympic debut in Tokyo in 1964 reflected its successful spread and acceptance as a global sport, and while Japan took three gold medals, the Dutch competitor Anton Geesink's victory in the Open Division was a national disappointment (Skya 2014). Although Japan continues to be the most successful country in judo at the Olympics, its dominance has gradually declined. The debut of women's judo as an official Olympic sport in Atlanta in 1996 was another pivotal moment in the sport, and further showed how far judo had developed over the preceding 50 years. There is a still a pronounced masculine culture within judo, which has contributed to concerns over its reintroduction into public junior high schools in Japan in 2012, but the connections between this masculinity and national identity, or even gender, are not as rigid as they once were.

Conclusions

As with cultural activities in many societies, the martial arts in Japan have also been traditionally defined by their exclusivity, which was closely tied to the dominant masculinity. During the early modern period, by definition this ideal was only attainable by the very small percentage of the population who were adult male samurai, but commoners also sought to benefit from this cultural capital by engaging in martial arts training. Even within warrior groups, exclusivity was furthered by the proliferation of martial arts schools that competed over lineages, styles, and hidden teachings.

In the Imperial period, when the abolition of the class structure ostensibly opened the martial arts to all Japanese, exclusivity was maintained through rigorous examinations, as well as through the increased emphasis on the "spiritual" elements of the martial arts. This was most clearly embodied in the discourse surrounding bushido from the 1890s onward. This was also the period when the first major connections were drawn between Zen Buddhism and the samurai, as a spiritual basis for the martial arts was retroactively projected upon earlier practices (Benesch 2016). The emphasis on spiritual aspects also served to distinguish the martial arts from foreign sports, even if promoters of baseball formulated bushido-infused versions of their sport. In this sense, the exclusivity of the martial arts, and the associated masculine status bestowed by their practice, were largely national and gendered, being restricted to Japanese males.

These exclusivities began to break down further after 1945 with the internationalization of Japanese martial arts, both at home and abroad, sometimes in dramatic circumstances. This shift was also associated with the increased "sportification" of many martial arts as competitions and training methods diversified, with judo perhaps the best example of this process. One of the major fissures running through scholarship on the martial arts in Japan, especially, relates to their status as either competitive sports or methods of self-cultivation, although these two viewpoints are not necessarily incompatible. As Kris Chapman has argued in the context of karate, by focusing on self-cultivation and spiritual elements of martial arts practice, especially the "way," the door can be opened to women and other practitioners who were traditionally excluded by a masculinity based purely on physical attributes such as strength. Chapman explores how an emphasis on self-cultivation in the martial arts provides scope for practitioners to subvert the established masculinity (Chapman 2004). At the same time, this shift in emphasis from strength, victory, and pure physical achievement can also serve to protect certain spheres of the martial arts from women, foreigners, and other groups who may challenge existing power structures. By tying the ability to comprehend the "way" of a martial art to characteristics of gender and nationality, the continued dominance of those who exhibit a traditional masculinity can be maintained.

The ongoing popular interest in the martial arts, epitomized by the global success of mixed martial arts, reflects the important role that the martial arts continue to play. The media dominance of these new forms also contributes to ongoing debates concerning their relationship to the "traditional" martial arts, as well as the role of the martial arts in broader society. In this context, further examination of the martial arts can provide an important window on historical and contemporary conceptions of gender and masculinity in Japan on a national and transnational level.

Related chapters

5   Masculinity Studies in Japan
16 Gender and the Workplace
24 Women and Physical Culture in Japanese History

References

Benesch, O. (2011) "National Consciousness and the Evolution of the Civil/Martial Binary in East Asia," *Taiwan Journal of East Asian Studies* 8 (1–15) 129–171.
Benesch, O. (2014) *Inventing the Way of the Samurai: Nationalism, Internationalism, and Bushido in Modern Japan*, Oxford: Oxford University Press.
Benesch, O. (2016) "Reconsidering Zen, Samurai, and the Martial Arts," *The Asia-Pacific Journal* 14 (17–7) 1–22.
Bennett, A. (2015) *Kendo: Culture of the Sword*, Berkeley: University of California Press.
Blackwood, T. (2008) "Bushidō Baseball? Three 'Fathers' and the Invention of a Tradition," *Social Science Japan Journal* 11 (2) 223–240.
Buyō, I. (2014) *Lust, Commerce, and Corruption: An Account of What I Have Seen and Heard, by an Edo Samurai*, trans. M. Teeuwen, K. Wildman Nakai, F. Miyazaki, A. Walthall and J. Breen, New York: Columbia University Press.
Chapman, K. (2004) "Ossu! Sporting Masculinities in a Japanese Karate Dōjō," *Japan Forum* 16 (2) 315–335.
De Bary, W. T., Gluck, C. and Tiedemann, A. E. (eds) (2006) *Sources of Japanese Tradition: 1600 to 2000 Volume Two, Part One*, New York: Columbia University Press.
Friday, K. F. and Humitake, S. (1997) *Legacies of the Sword: The Kashima-Shinryu and Samurai Martial Culture*, Honolulu: University of Hawaii Press.
Gainty, D. (2013) *Martial Arts and the Body Politic in Meiji Japan*, New York: Routledge.
Hurst, G. C. III (1998) *Armed Martial Arts of Japan: Swordsmanship and Archery*, New Haven: Yale University Press.
Jaundrill, C. (2016) *Samurai to Soldier: Remaking Military Service in Nineteenth-Century Japan*, Ithaca: Cornell University Press.
Lindsay, T. and Kano, J. (1889) "Jiujutsu," *The Asiatic Society of Japan* 16 192–207.

MacKenzie, S. P. (1999) "Willpower or Firepower? The Unlearned Lessons of the Russo-Japanese War," in D. Wells and S. Wilson (eds) *The Russo-Japanese War in Cultural Perspective, 1904–05*, London: MacMillan Press.

Ozaki, Y. (2001) *The Autobiography of Ozaki Yukio: The Struggle for Constitutional Government in Japan*, trans. F. Hara, Princeton: Princeton University Press.

Rankin, A. (2011) *Seppuku: A History of Samurai Suicide*, Tokyo: Kodansha International.

Skya, W. (2014) "Review, Denis Gainty, *Martial Arts and the Body Politic in Meiji Japan*," *Journal of Japanese Studies* 40 (2) 396–400.

Sonoda, H. (1990) "The Decline of the Japanese Warrior Class, 1840–1880," *Japan Review* 1 73–111.

Stevens, J. (2013) *The Way of Judo: A Portrait of Jigoro Kano and His Students*, Boulder: Shambhala.

Thompson, L. A. (1998) "The Invention of the *Yokozuna*," in S. Vlastos (ed) *Mirror of Modernity: Invented Traditions of Modern Japan*, Berkeley: University of California Press.

Walthall, A. (2011) "Do Guns Have Gender? Technology and Status in Early Modern Japan," in S. Frühstück and A. Walthall (eds) *Recreating Japanese Men*, Berkeley: University of California Press.

Wert, M. (2016) "Swordsmanship and Society in Early Modern Japan," in R. von Mallinckrodt and A. Schattner (eds) *Sports and Physical Exercise in Early Modern Culture*, London: Routledge.

Yamada, S. (2001) "The Myth of Zen in the Art of Archery," *Japanese Journal of Religious Studies* 28 (1-2) 1–30.

Yokoi, S. and Miyauchi, D. Y. (trans) (1968) "Kokuze Sanron. The Three Major Problems of State Policy," *Monumenta Nipponica* 23 (1–2) 156–186.

Yoshida, Y. (2002) *Nihon no guntai: heishi tachi no kindai shi*, Tokyo: Iwanami Shinsho.

26
THE CONTINUUM OF MALE BEAUTY IN CONTEMPORARY JAPAN

Masafumi Monden

Recalling his first encounter with Japanese actor Okada Masaki at the shooting of their TV drama based on a popular *shōjo manga* (girls' comics, 2007), actor Ikuta Toma described 17-year-old Okada as "a boy with beautiful (*kirei na*) face" who looked *kawaii* (cute) (Kurozu 2016). While the alternative term *kakkoii*, describing a cool handsomeness, is frequently used to describe male appearance, *kirei* or *utsukushii*, which translate as "beautiful" in English are also commonly used for attractive men as well as women. This may be surprising for those who are unfamiliar with Japanese culture, for beauty is often regarded in English-speaking cultures as a female-gendered term. This chapter examines male beauty in contemporary Japan, specifically related to the fully clothed body. I argue that male beauty is often understood, especially outside Japan, in a binary of muscular maturity and slender youthfulness. However, in reality, male beauty is a continuum, as recent TV commercials created for the Shiseido men's grooming product line Uno indicate. These advertisements offer a male image that is situated somewhere in the middle of the continuum between a rugged, mature, and brawny image thought to be preferred by men, to the slender, delicate, and youthful images designed to appeal to women. These different modes of male beauty in Japanese popular culture also signal a degree of flexibility in appreciating male beauty in Japan, though of course also this appreciation depends on the sexual orientation and class of those evaluating beauty.

Male beauty in Japan

Male physical beauty is often discussed in binary. Kenneth R. Dutton (1995, 343), in relation to the Western ideal of the male body, argues that:

> there are, broadly, two prototypes for the traditional depiction of the male body-as-object—one of them stressing its heroic, super-masculine traits, the other presenting features associated with the passive object of desire. Heavy muscularity in the "heroic" mode is conceptually quite distinct from the muscularity associated with youthful potency and the lithe and slender physique of the "aesthetic" mode.

The "heroic" super-mesomorph body is primarily a form of dominance-display aimed at other men rather than a form of aesthetic pleasure (Dutton 1995, 345; Ueno 2015a, 131). A slender, adolescent-like male body can be interpreted as signalling a childlike non-threatening quality and thus denying messages of aggression (Dutton 1995, 306; Ueno 2015b, 118), but risks being labelled, often in a derogatory way, as "feminine" or "effeminate." The Japanese concept of ideal masculinity, partly influenced by Chinese traditional *wen-wu* masculinity, which involves "both excelling in literature (*wen*) and military skills (*wu*)"—a combination of both *yin*/feminine and *yan*/masculine attributes in an ideal male (Chen 2011, 53)—offers a more nuanced approach.

Dutton's idea of the "aesthetic" male body comes with a caveat in that it is, contrary to the assumption of being lithe and slender, still characterized by muscularity. While some argue that the youthful male body is increasingly apparent in Anglophone advertisements and media (Dutton 1995, 343; Bordo 1999, 185), from a Japanese perspective, even if these men have cute, boyish faces, their bodies are emphatically muscular (Seki 1996, 50; Monden 2015, 53). We can therefore infer that a muscled physique is still part of preferred male aesthetics, especially in mainstream Euro-American cultures. This male body is, moreover, displayed frequently without clothes, adding further significance to its physical muscularity. Indeed, when discussing male beauty, a male nude body (or at least partially clothed body) is often at the centre of discussion (e.g. Dutton 1995; Krauss 2014).

European civilizations have long treated the naked body as an object of aesthetic importance, and modish fashion of each era has left traces on how nudity was (artistically) conceived (Hollander 1978). In other words, the favoured visualization of the human nude has always been influenced by contemporary fashion. Here, we might ask a question: how is beauty defined in contemporary Japanese culture where the idea of nudity has been differently treated (Morris 1994 [1964]) and images of "beautiful" men with fashionable looks are prevalent in everyday culture (Monden 2015)?

In Japanese culture, too, male beauty is often discussed in terms of contrast and binary. In his collection of essays *Binan e no ressun* (*Lessons for Beautiful Men* 1994), Hashimoto Osamu argued that the standard of male beauty differs according to many factors including milieu, but also the beauty preferred by men themselves and that preferred by (presumably heterosexual) women. For Hashimoto (1994, 26), the kind of beauty preferred by (a group of) men tends to be a brawny, mature, and often rugged physique, while that preferred by (a group of) women would be characterized by an almost adolescent, "feminine," genteel face and a lithe body. The latter is a more genuine beauty, as the former is largely reflective of the ego of (often unbeautiful) men themselves (Hashimoto 1994, 44). In this sense, a "genuine" male beauty that is based purely on aesthetic appreciation has similar qualities to conventional "feminine" beauty (Hashimoto 1994; Inagaki 1986 [1973]) and differs from "male specific" beauty which is marked by muscularity (Katsura 1963, 145).

Male beauty similar to that of "feminine" beauty, evoking an aesthetic of androgyny, has long been appreciated in Japan, especially the beauty of a *shōnen* (adolescent boy). Writer Inagaki Taruho (1973 [1986], 39), famous for his *Shōnen'ai no bigaku* (*Aesthetics of a Love of Adolescent Boys*, 1968), argues that fundamental human beauty lies in the *shōnen*, which due to its ephemerality will soon be consumed by beautiful women. While this kind of ephemeral beauty is a feature of both the *shōnen* and *shōjo* (adolescent girl), that associated with the *shōnen* is seen as rarer, because physically boys undergo more dramatic and apparent changes in secondary sexual characteristics when maturing than girls, like having their voice break and growing facial hair (Sunaga 2002, 9). Writer and TV critic Mori Mari (1994 [1979], 37), whose series of novellas about homoerotic relationships between beautiful males has gained her a cult status in Japanese literary circles, also articulates her ideal *bishōnen* (beautiful boy) as one who can also be considered as a *bishōjo* (beautiful girl) when he wears a girl's dress, and vice versa for her ideal beautiful girl. Beauty may be subjective, and this is only Mori's idiosyncratic definition of human beauty, but nevertheless her influence on the 1970s *shōjo manga* is well documented (Aoyama 1988). *Shōjo manga* has a strong role in articulating a preferred male beauty in Japan (for example, a beautiful young man is often described as "as if (he) popped out from pages in *shōjo manga*") and this idea of an idealized beauty with an androgynous quality is important.

In Japanese culture, the (nude) human body was not widely regarded as an object of aesthetic appreciation (Morris 1994 [1964]), 202), and a beautiful boy was first and foremost perceived as an object for sexual commodification (Saeki 2016). This changed after the Meiji restoration (1868), when European art introduced to Japan the concept of appreciating the human body in art (Saeki 2016). Since then, male beauty, especially the boyish kind, has been appreciated by men and women alike (Miller 2011; Aoyama 2005; Hartley 2015). For instance, naïve, melancholic male beauty was appreciated in the pre-Pacific War era, as the examples of Origuchi Nobuo's semi-biographical novel *Kuchibue* (*Whistle* 1914) and Takabatake Kashō's *jojōga* (lyrical illustrations) indicate. After the war, a cuter and more perky portrayal of boys with large eyes and slender bodies was introduced with Naitō Runé's illustrations in fashion magazine for teens, *Junia soreiyu* (Junior Soleil, Naitō 2005, 75–79), subsequently influencing the style of beautiful boy characters in *shōjo manga*. In mainstream contemporary Japanese culture such as advertising and *manga*, the acknowledgement of the female gaze in appreciating the male body (McLelland 2000; Miller 2006) and the frequent fear of female scrutiny in fashion media for men (Bardsley 2011; Monden 2015) have been reported. While there is more than one type of male body that exists in the cultural imagination in Japan, a slender and smooth male body has dominated as an aesthetically pleasing example (Miller 2006, 151). These slender male bodies, with their display of boyish charm, allow Japanese men to deny mature masculinity while remaining "masculine" (Seki 1996, 92–93).

Kazumi Nagaike (2012) argues that male celebrities with boyish features, such as members of Japanese boy *aidoru* (idol) group Arashi, embody a female idealization of non-threatening male figures. This is because men like the members of Arashi are biologically male, but their youthful appearance implies that they are yet to fully bloom into sexually mature manhood (Nagaike 2012, 104; Seki 1996). In this reading, an apparent lack of mature, sexual masculinity in Arashi has been seen by their fans, the majority of them women, as desirable precisely because they are unthreatening, creating the impression that they will not seek to dominate women in the traditional mode of a patriarchal society.

Laura Miller (2006, 151) instead has argued that this "aesthetic" male type can also appear desirable to many Japanese women as realistically and erotically attractive. Thereby, this apparent "lack" of sexuality among young men might still appear erotically charged to a certain group of individuals. In either case, importance is attached to the fact that the aesthetic appreciation of young men like the members of Arashi in Japan is not necessarily centred on their nude bodies, despite the occasional display in women's magazines like *an an*. As I touched on previously, the naked body was not always an object of fascination and eroticism in Japanese culture, and generally nudity and body shape have not been important in Japanese aesthetics. In contemporary Japanese culture, nudity, particularly female nudes but also male nudes, as indicated by the example of aforementioned Arashi members, are undeniably sexually charged (e.g. Miller 2006, 76). But (heterosexual) women's aesthetical judgement of male beauty tends to prefer a clothed body (Monden 2015, 55–56). This raises a question surrounding the relationship triangle of human beauty, eroticism, and sexual desire.

Beauty, eroticism, and sexual desire

In reconciling these positions, it is important to recognize the different contexts of individual consumers and what they might find stimulating and also to define eroticism versus sexuality.

Many authors link physical beauty to sexuality, sexual attractiveness, and sexual desirability. As Arthur Marwick (2004, 11) argues, beauty in human beings is what arouses sexual desire by looking, though everything that is sexually arousing does not have to be beautiful. Likewise, male beauty with emphatically masculine attributes such as a muscled body is frequently seen as synonymous with male sexual appeal (Katsura 1963, 145). While this chapter does not deny such a relationship, it demonstrates that it is simplistic and limited. As Immanuel Kant defines, beauty can also be something we contemplate from a distance, without desire for ownership (Tōhata 2012, 96).

Here it is useful to distinguish eroticism from sexual desire. The meaning of eroticism varies across culture and time period; however, we might broadly define it as relating to desire and the aesthetics of desire, a delayed or postponed promise of gratification, as opposed to the immediacy of sexualization. Eroticism is within the realm of aesthetics. It is about gazing and contemplating from distance, relying on suggestion and allusion, but never being explicit (Scruton 2009, 159). In contrast, sexualization jumps from visual apprehension to the use of a particular instance of male beauty for carnal gratification (whether direct or otherwise). Sexualization explicitly reduces people to bodies, taking away their individuality and making them into objects of sexual fantasy (Scruton 2009, 165). It is also important that obscuring the body using clothes and fashion, as George Simmel (1997 [1905]) has argued, gives a body individuality. Of course, there is no single way that male beauty is appreciated in Japan; however, I argue that Japanese culture offers one way of appreciating (male) physical beauty that is focused on a fully clothed body which is not immediately linked to sexual desire, such as the near absence of nudes in Edo-period woodblock prints (which are therefore not seen as erotic; see Screech 2009 [1999]).

The popularity of youthful male beauty has been read by some as a refusal by young men to embrace the traditional masculine values of the salaryman (Miller 2006; Bardsley 2011, 11–16; Ueno 2015b, 118). Despite some stylish, nice-looking salarymen existing in reality, in the collective consciousness the middle-aged, mid-level corporate salaryman has been associated with a somewhat dowdy hegemonic masculinity in post-Pacific War Japan (Dasgupta 2013, 9). The salaryman aesthetically symbolized a rather unattractive, undesirable, authoritarian mode of mature masculinity (Bardsley 2011). The adoption of a youthful-looking, stylish, non-threatening masculinity by young men (and, significantly, its appreciation by a large number of females) is seen by some as a "delicate revolt" against what has become a social stereotype. Ueno Chizuko (2015b, 118) also sees the increase of male consciousness of physical beauty as related to men's refusal to embrace mature masculinity, which has, as we have seen, been strongly tied to the image of salarymen in modern Japan.

In more recent times, the idea of repudiating the salaryman as a motivation of fashionability among young men seems to have declined. Partly this might be due to the changes among young men and their attitudes towards their work and professional careers, with single-company careers now much rarer. However, the power dynamic between youth and maturity seems to be changing in Japan. Since around 2006, the media has reported the increasing lack of assertiveness, competitiveness, and even ambition among young male workers (Ushikubo 2008; Nihei 2013; Dasgupta 2013, 158). This change is often associated with the bursting of the economic bubble in the early 1990s and subsequent collapse of the promise of lifetime employment (Taga 2003, 139; Dasgupta 2013, 39). Rather than sacrificing themselves to a company which no longer assures stability in their lives, men in younger generations are believed to have shifted their attention to life outside the work environment, including increasing interests in their appearance and hobbies, which in turn have affected their choice of employment and working styles (see, for example, Cook 2013; Dasgupta 2013, 40). While the salaryman himself has not been eradicated, his image as a middle-class, white-collar, work-oriented and bread-winning male (e.g. Roberson 2005; Taga 2003) seems to have altered. However, caution is necessary here, as such "new" portrayals of young Japanese men could, to a certain degree, be a media creation. Irrespective of the validity of this claim, however, ideas of beauty in relation to male maturity and youthfulness seem to be undergoing reconsideration in recent times. This shift is also reflected in Japanese popular culture. A prime example is Shiseido's series of TV commercials for the men's cosmetic products brand, Uno.

Takenouchi Yutaka: mature male beauty with boyish innocence in Uno

The cosmetics industry is one of the industries that spend the most on advertising in Japan, relying on celebrities and stars like *aidoru* and actors to promote their products (Karlin 2012, 76). In Japanese television advertising, celebrities are used as "image characters," and this image "becomes a source of pleasure achieved through identification" (Karlin 2012, 79). Since in contemporary society, men use cultural ideals of the male body as a point of reference in their perceptions of their own bodies and hence their self-identities (Gill et al. 2005, 39; Wienke 1998), it is informative to observe images of the male body and beauty in Japanese television commercials.

Shiseido is one of the biggest cosmetic companies in Japan; its production of men's cosmetics and toiletries dates as far back as to the early 1900s (Fukuhara 1969, 101). In March 2016, Shiseido created a new series of ads for Uno, their men's cosmetic and haircare products range, with popular and high-profile actors 45-year-old Takenouchi Yutaka (1971–), 28-year-old Kubota Masataka (1988–), and 23-year-old Nomura Shūhei (1993–) as the main leads.

In the second series of the commercials, the "*otona jizai*" (adult freely) version (first aired April 2017), Kubota and Nomura are young employees, working under Takenouchi in what appears as a stylish, sunny, foreign-owned architecture office. In the commercials, the two young men scrutinize Takenouchi on different occasions, and they describe Takenouchi by referring to binaries: "picking the best of mature sexiness" (a profile in serious mien, working) and "boyish innocence" (facing the young men, and hence the camera, with a cheeky smile, eating a cherry out of chocolate parfait, itself connoting childlike femininity in Japan), or professional strictness and male tenderness, for example. Takenouchi is portrayed as a male figure that amalgamates all these opposing qualities, and, obviously, the commercial's message is that this is an attractive male figure that young men (the young actors and the commercials' target audiences alike) can aspire to emulate. Strikingly, Shiseido Uno's commercials present both, rather than either/or, mature and young male types of beauty.

The commercial reveals Takenouchi's slightly wrinkled face and stubble, as well as his low, deep voice, all of which connote mature masculinity. Takenouchi is the only one of the three who wears a three-piece suit, another emblem of sophisticated maturity associated with classic masculinity. Takenouchi is a highly attractive male actor and former fashion model, and the qualities he embodies, coupled with his lean, slender body, prevent the image from becoming too masculine or virile. His slender build also suggests that unlike the Anglo-European cultural norm, attractive modes of male maturity do not require muscularity. Even in advertisements for men's grooming and cosmetics products, the male body is often presented as rugged, hard, and well-muscled in Anglophone culture (Negrin 2008, 158; Bordo 1999). Moreover, men have frequently been portrayed as machine-like: virile, hard-bodied, yet apathetic in the Anglophone media (Attwood 2005, 84). The connotation of such an instrumentalization of the male body is in line with "an insistence on sexual difference and a refusal of male eroticization evident throughout the modern period" (Attwood 2005, 85). This "hypermasculine" visual discourse presumably reassures its male viewers, its target audience, of their "masculinity" while aligning with or endorsing the conventional assumption that taking an interest in one's appearance and cosmetics are "feminine" concerns. The commercial's focus on Takenouchi's relationship with the two young men, instead of instrumentalization of his body, delineates his personal, intimate aspects and hence presents this mature masculinity as both desirable and approachable. While there are parallels here with the "metrosexual" construct of younger men in Anglophone cultures, there are also subtle differences.

Mature male beauty as embodied by Takenouchi is obviously the look that young men like Kubota and Nomura are expected to admire, aspire to, and emulate. In one scene, Kubota and Nomura's narration notes that Takenouchi is so attractive and accomplished that "even we as blokes would fall in love with him," referring to the concept of a younger man admiring a mature male figure rather than a woman, and in a mainstream and therefore presumably platonic or heterosexual fashion. This is a male image situated somewhere in the middle of the male beauty continuum as defined by Hashimoto (rugged, mature, and brawny versus slender, delicate, and youthful). However, this series of Shiseido Uno commercials not only focuses on mature male beauty as desirable and objectified, but as being of equal regard as young male beauty and appearance.

Boyish male beauty

The younger men, Kubota and Nomura, embody emphatically youthful masculinity. They are clean-shaven, smooth-skinned with clear complexions, and their eyes are much bigger and rounder than Takenouchi's. Both of the young men have frequently played the role of college and even high school students in their acting careers. Kubota and Nomura represent "ectomorphic" adolescent beauty even though they are in their mid- to late 20s. This creates a sense that Kubota and Nomura are boyish even though they wear business suits—a symbol of "a confident adult masculinity" (Hollander 2016 [1994], 83) that accentuates "a man's sensual anatomy" (Breward 1999, 47). Even though they are cast as salarymen in the second series of commercials, their visuality still exudes schoolboy qualities, signalling childlike freedom from responsibility and incompleteness.

While the narrative of the commercials in the "adult freely" version objectifies Takenouchi as a highly attractive and inspiring mature male, it often cuts back to the shots where both Kubota and Nomura's faces are captured in medium to close-up shots. In theories of visual analysis, the direct gaze of the participant is often read as demanding something from the viewer, while the indirect gaze can indicate that the participant is the object of the viewer's gaze (Kress and van Leeuwen 1996, 118–119). The direct gaze of a male model in a commercial, for instance, can be read as persuading the viewer of "identification with the look of the male model" (Nixon 1996, 178). In these commercials, the younger men's youth is contrasted with Takenouchi's mature beauty and his renowned low, deep voice. The frequent cut backs to close-ups of these two young men also suggest that not only Takenouchi, but Kubota and Nomura, are the intended objects of the (viewer's) gaze, so that, given the boyish qualities of these two latter actors, they are presented as attractive and admiring.

The significance of the Shiseido Uno commercials is that they present two different types of male beauty—one mature and the other boyish, not so much contesting but in harmony with one another. Given that Kubota and Nomura, with their ectomorphic bodies and images associated with their acting roles, and with their attitudes (e.g. surveying their boss with admiration in a comical way) signal their almost schoolboy youthfulness. Moreover, Takenouchi had occupied a similar position as Kubota and Nomura fifteen to twenty years prior, giving him the quality of a romantic lead and meaning that he himself is not, in a conventional sense, too "masculine," thereby bridging the gap between the conceptions of mature and youthful male beauties as defined by Hashimoto. Instead of depicting him as a virile, "hypermasculine" salarymen as Japanese popular culture targeted at mature men would have conventionally done (Dasgupta 2000, 198), the Shiseido commercials present the mature male beauty of Takenouchi as closer to the young men rather than the other way around: as one of Takenouchi's charms is that he still retains a "boyish innocence." While this series of TV commercial highlights the binary of youthful and mature male beauties, it also signals the continuity of this boyish, youthful, and cute male beauty even once its exemplars reach adulthood.

The commercial's last shot shows the three men lined up at the mirror, doing their hair in what appears to be the rest room of their office. The two young men's hair in particular is styled in a more businesslike fashion, with their bangs slicked back. These complementary modes of male beauty in Japanese popular culture, one mature and the other youthful, signal a degree of flexibility in appreciating male beauty. It is interesting to note the context of the shot compared to the majority of Anglophone cosmetic and fragrance ads, which often tend to portray the subject in a state of near or total undress while using the product, featuring the muscularity of the body.

Conclusion

Male beauty is often understood in terms of a binary organization of muscular maturity and slender youthfulness. In Japanese culture, a similar binary is also seen, but the female gaze and by implication female aesthetic preference has played a strong role in defining male beauty. Such a female gaze tends to prioritize a slender and ectomorphic, beautiful body that is fully clothed, and hence this is different to the display of the mature muscled or unclothed body that is often a feature of Western concepts of ideal masculinity. The appreciation of the beauty of the fashioned male body and apparently innocent look in contemporary Japan question the widely assumed equation of human beauty and sexual desire. Rather than seeing beauty only through its link with sexuality and desire of ownership, this idea allows a calibration of beauty that is focused purely on aesthetic appreciation, thereby offering a more nuanced and complex mechanism of appreciating (male) beauty.

Recent commercials for Shiseido's Uno offer two kinds of male beauty, finessing the established binary of the mature and youthful. As we have seen, rather than presenting these as in negation of or contrast to one another, the Shiseido commercials present them as congruous. This corresponds with well-reported changes in young men's attitudes towards work and life in contemporary Japan and consequently reconsidering the perception of older men who are different from the stereotyped, and perhaps increasingly anachronistic, image of the aesthetically undesirable salarymen. Shiseido Uno's conceptualization and subsequent visualization of the male image via the bodies of highly attractive male actors offers an image that is situated somewhere in the middle of the male beauty continuum. This resolution of traditionally binary modes of male beauty in Japanese popular culture also signals the opportunity for flexibility in appreciating male beauty in contemporary Japan.

Related chapters

5   Masculinity Studies in Japan
16 Gender and the Workplace
25 Myths of Masculinity in the Martial Arts

27 Performing Gender: Cosplay and Otaku Cultures and Spaces
31 Cuteness Studies and Japan
33 Gender, Media, and Misogyny in Japan

References

Aoyama, T. (1988) "Male Homosexuality as Treated by Japanese Women Writers," in G. McCormack and Y. Sugimoto (eds) *The Japanese Trajectory: Modernization and Beyond*, Cambridge and New York: Cambridge University Press, 186–204.
Aoyama, T. (2005) "Transgendering *Shōjo* Shōsetsu: Girls' Inter-text/sex-uality," in M. McLelland and R. Dasgupta (eds) *Gender, Transgenders and Sexualities in Japan*, London and New York: Routledge, 49–64.
Attwood, F. (2005) "'Tits and Ass and Porn and Fighting': Male Heterosexuality in Magazines for Men," *International Journal of Cultural Studies* 8 (1) 83–100.
Bardsley, J. (2011) "The Oyaji Gets a Makeover," in J. Bardsley and L. Miller (eds) *Manners and Mischief Gender, Power, and Etiquette in Japan*, Berkeley, Los Angeles and London: University of California Press, 114–135.
Bordo, S. (1999) *The Male Body: A New Look at Men in Public and in Private*, New York: Farrar, Straus and Giroux.
Breward, C. (1999) *The Hidden Consumer: Masculinities, Fashion and City Life 1860–1914*. Manchester: Manchester University Press.
Chen, Y. (2011) *Warriors as the Feminised Other: The Study of Male Heroes in Chinese Action Cinema from 2000 to 2009*, PhD Thesis, University of Canterbury.
Cook, E. (2013) "Expectations of Failure: Maturity and Masculinity for Freeters in Contemporary Japan," *Social Science Japan* 16 (1) 29–43.
Dasgupta, R. (2000) "Performing Masculinities? The 'Salaryman' at Work and Play," *Japanese Studies* 20 (2) 189–200.
Dasgupta, R. (2013) *Re-Reading the Salaryman in Japan: Crafting Masculinities*, New York: Routledge.
Dutton, K. R. (1995) *The Perfectible Body: The Western Ideal of Male Physical Development*, New York: Continuum.
Fukuhara, Y. (1969) "Masu shōhin to shite no tenkai" (Men's Cosmetics as Product for Mass Consumers), *Chemical Review* 2 (5) 101–103.
Gill, R., Henwood, K. and McLean, C. (2005) "Body Projects and the Regulation of Normative Masculinity," *Body & Society* 11 (1) 37–62.
Hartley, B. (2015) "A Genealogy of Boys Love: Girls Viewers of the *Bishōnen* Body in the Pre-War Images of Takabatake Kashō," in M. McLelland, K. Nagaike, K. Suganuma and J. Welker (eds) *Boys Love Manga and Beyond: History, Culture, and Community in Japan*, Jackson: University Press of Mississippi, 21–41.
Hashimoto, O. (1994) *Binan e no ressun* (Lessons for Beautiful Men), Tokyo: Chūō kōron-sha.
Hollander, A. (1993 [1978]) *Seeing Through Clothes*, New York: Viking Press.
Hollander, A. (2016 [1994]) *Sex and the Suits*, New York and London: Bloomsbury.
Inagaki, T. (1986 [1973]) "Nisemono to shite no bijo" (A Beautiful Woman as an Imitation), in T. Inagaki (ed) *Bishōjo ron* (Studies of the Beautiful Girl), Tokyo: Ushio shuppan, 28–49.
Karlin, J. G. (2012) "Through a Looking Glass Darkly: Television Advertising, Idols, and the Making of Fan Audiences," in P. W. Galbraith and J. G. Karlin (eds) *Idols and Celebrity in Japanese Media Culture*, London: Palgrave Macmillan, 72–93.
Katsura, Y. (1963) "Dansei no bi" (Male Beauty), in K. Kamei and I. Yoshikawa (eds) *Bi no yūwaku* (Seduction of Beauty), Tokyo: Kawade shobō, 143–148.
Krauss, K. (2014) *Male Beauty: Postwar Masculinity in Theatre, Film, and Physique Magazine*, New York: State University of New York Press.
Kress, G. and van Leewen, T. (1996) *Reading Images: The Grammar of Visual Design*, London and New York: Routledge.
Kurozu, N. (2016) "Intabyū: Ikuta Tōma x Okada Masaki" (Interview: Tōma Ikuta with Masaki Okada), Cinemacafé.net 3 August. www.cinemacafe.net/article/2016/08/03/42430.html.
McLelland, M. (2000) "No Climax, No Point, No Meaning? Japanese Women's Boy-Love Sites on the Internet," *Journal of Communication Inquiry* 24 (3) 274–291.
Marwick, A. (2004) *A History of Human Beauty*, London & New York: Hambledon Continuum.

Miller, L. (2006) *Beauty Up: Exploring Contemporary Japanese Body Aesthetics*, Berkeley: University of California Press.

Miller, L. (2011) "Cute Masquerade and the Pimping of Japan," *International Journal of Japanese Sociology* 20 (1) 18–29.

Monden, M. (2015) *Japanese Fashion Cultures: Dress and Gender in Contemporary Japan*, New York and London: Bloomsbury Academic.

Mori, M. (1994 [1979]) *Besuto obu Dokkiri Channeru* (The Best of Dokkiri Channel), Tokyo: Chikuma shobō.

Morris, I. (1994 [1964]) *The World of the Shining Prince: Court Life in Ancient Japan*, New York, Tokyo and London: Kodansha International.

Nagaike, K. (2012) "Johnny's Idols as Icons: Female Desires to Fantasize and Consume Male Idol Images," in P. W. Galbraith and J. G. Karlin (eds) *Idols and Celebrity in Japanese Media Culture*, London: Palgrave Macmillan, 97–112.

Naitō, R. (2005) *Subete o nakushite—tenraku no ato ni* (I Have Lost Everything—After the Fall), Tokyo: Shōgakkan.

Negrin, L. (2008) *Appearance and Identity*, New York: Palgrave Macmillan.

Nihei, C. (2013) "Resistance and Negotiation: "Herbivorous Men" and Murakami Haruki's Gender and Political Ambiguity," *Asian Studies Review* 37 (1) 62–79.

Nixon, S. (1996) *Hard Looks: Masculinities, the Visual and Practices of Consumption*, New York: St. Martin's Press.

Roberson, J. (2005) "Fight!! Ippatsu!! 'Genki' Energy Drinks and the Marketing of Masculine Ideology in Japan," *Men and Masculinities* 7 (4) 365–384.

Saeki, J. (2016) "Kagirinaku josei ni chikai shōnen tachi" (Boys Who Are Almost the Same as Women), *Bijutsu techō* 68 (1035) 50–51.

Screech, T. (2009 [1999]) *Sex and the Floating World: Erotic Images in Japan, 1700–1820*, London: Reaktion.

Scruton, R. (2009) *Beauty*, Oxford: Oxford University Press.

Seki, O. (1996) *Binan-ron, josetsu* (The Theory of Beautiful Male, An Introduction), Tokyo: Natsume shobō.

Simmel, G. (1997 [1905]) "The Philosophy of Fashion," trans. K. H. Wolff, in D. Frisby and M. Featherstone (eds) *Simmel on Culture*, London: Sage Publications.

Sunaga, A. (2002) *Bishōnen nihon shi* (Japan's History of Beautiful Boys), Tokyo: Kokusho kankokai.

Taga, F. (2003) "Rethinking Male Socialisation: Life Histories of Japanese Male Youth," in K. Louie and M. Low (eds) *Asian Masculinities*, Abingdon: Routledge Curzon.

Tōhata, K. (2012) *Bi to shinsou shinrigaku* (Aesthetics and Depth Psychology), Kyoto: Kyoto University Press.

Ueno, C. (2015a [1989]) "Shisen no seijigaku" (Political Studies of the Gaze), in C. Ueno (ed) *Hatsujō sōchi* (The Erotic Apparatus, new edition), Tokyo: Iwanami shoten, 123–136.

Ueno, C. (2015b [1998]) "Ratai no kigō-gaku" (Semiotics of Nudity) in C. Ueno (ed) *Hatsujō Sōchi* (The Erotic Apparatus, new edition), Tokyo: Iwanami shoten, 92–122.

Ushikubo, M. (2008) *Sōshoku-kei danshi [ojō -man] ga Nihon o kaeru* (Herbivorous Men [Ladylike Men] Change Japan), Tokyo: Kōdansha +a shinsho.

Wienke, C. (1998) "Negotiating the Male Body: Men, Masculinity, and Cultural Ideals," *The Journal of Men's Studies* 6 (3) 255–282.

27
PERFORMING GENDER
Cosplay and otaku cultures and spaces

Emerald King

At the end of 2016, the newly established Tokyo Comic Con caused a stir when they posted a set of conduct rules that included a prohibition on male-to-female crossdressing at the event. Online communities were quick to register their outrage on forums such as Reddit at what seemed to them to be blatant discrimination. The situation was further exacerbated when it became apparent that there was no mandate against female-to-male crossdressing. The rule was quickly lifted (Reddit's r/anime 2016), but not before a string of commentary appeared online across a number of popular culture and niche sites such as *Anime News Network* and *Kotaku*, as well as more mainstream news media outlets in languages other than Japanese or English, including *Weekendavisen* (a Danish broadsheet which regards itself as the world's oldest newspaper, Weekendavisen n.d.).

This chapter will give a brief overview of gender and gender performance in cosplay and otaku culture and spaces (otaku is used here both in the Japanese language meaning—a fan with an extreme knowledge of an often small or obscure branch of, for example, popular culture, and the English language meaning—a self-designated fan of Japan-specific-brand geek- and nerd-related popular culture). In keeping with the themes this collection, this chapter focuses on cosplay and cosplay-related events in Japan. However, in order to give some context and contrast, reference will also be made to events across Australasia, Europe, North America, and East Asia. Many cosplay events outside of Japan began as homages to Japanese traditional and popular culture, and although many have shifted focus as they have grown, there remains some inherent kernel of "Japaneseness" at the heart of many popular cultural cosplay conventions and events.

As a starting point, let us look at the reportage surrounding the Tokyo Comic Con's initial cosplay rules. In order to understand why Tokyo Comic Con would even contemplate rules that would be viewed as discriminatory, it is necessary to give a brief overview of cosplay and crossplay (crossdressing whilst in cosplay) as it has risen to the predominant form of fannish dressing up around the world over the past 30 or so years.

Cosplay spaces and zones

Cosplay differs from country to country and from state to state. Convention rules, accepted social conduct, social media usage, trends in popular series and characters, and the emphasis on costume construction, role play, and performance vary between sites of cosplay—something that many cosplay scholars and reporters are only just starting to address. Despite cosplay, superhero films, and shōjo-style fashions becoming more widely accepted and somewhat mainstream in many places around the world, there are still glaring misconceptions that are held as true by the general non-geek, nerd, or otaku public. Peter Harmsen's "Duften af samurai" (The Scent of Samurai), which was published in *Weekendavisen* a month after Tokyo Comic Con's initial cosplay rules banning men crossdressing were listed, concentrates on idealized *bishōnen* and historical practices of Socratic love between samurai (Harmsen 2016). A report in *The Daily Mail* on Melbourne Oz Comic Con in 2015 claimed that cosplay had finally arrived in Australia—hot off the plane from America (Lewis 2014)—some 13 years after the first cosplay, anime, and Japanese popular culture convention in Australia was held in the same city in 2001.

In 2013, Katrien Jacobs proposed that cosplay and related activities take place within a set "zone:"

> As a theory of liminality suggests, the Cosplay zone is a space of fan-driven entertainment and identity transgression that involves strict boundary-policing by authorities and by peer groups themselves.[...] At the same time, the Cosplay zone offers access to fringe venues, as well as support and tolerance between these "misfits" and queer activism, which is where the potential for social change is located.
>
> *(Jacobs 2013, 22–24)*

In my own work, I have written on the links between shōjo (girlhood) space, as theorized by Honda Masuko, and cosplay (King 2016, 2019). Honda speaks of girlhood as taking place in a liminal "bower" where delicate hothouse flowers are able to bloom freely amongst "ribbons, frills or even, lyrical word chains [which] flutter in the breeze as symbols of girlhood" (Honda 2010, 20). Within this space, girlhood is allowed to bloom and develop unrestrained by societal restrictions or demands until the girl is ready to emerge into adulthood. The shōjo space can be revisited or remembered, even after leaving.

In both Jacobs's "zone" and the shōjo space, cosplay only occurs safely and successfully in a set, negotiated, and clearly defined location: the frame of a camera lens, the set of a photography shoot, the booth of a cosplay *purikura* machine (Miller 2017, 104–113), the masquerade floor of a popular culture convention, the cosplay competition stage, and select social media platforms such as Cure World Cosplay, Cosplayers Global (heavily linked to the World Cosplay Summit [WCS] see subsequently), Instagram, Tumblr, Facebook, and DeviantART. As Jacobs notes, these spaces are heavily regulated—not only by conventions and organizations, per the cosplay rules at various conventions discussed previously, but also by other cosplayers, event attendees, and the broader social media audience. Jacobs's work with cosplayers active in Hong Kong, Taiwan, and mainland China highlights how there can be an even higher level of policing involving government supervision in cosplay and popular cultural events.

In order to consider the stage as one of these settings, let us first look briefly at the competitions that take place centre stage. Many cosplay competitions in North America, Australia, New Zealand, and parts of Europe require either a two- to three-minute skit performance or a stage display or "walk on." Skit competitions include WCS in its heats across 36 counties and its finals in Japan, Madman National Cosplay Championship (MNCC) in Australia and New Zealand, and the Clara Cow Cosplay Cup (4C) across Europe and North America. Costume-based competitions seem to be more prevalent in American-based competitions, as seen at regional Comic-Cons throughout America, Oz Comic-Con in Australia, and the Chicago Comic and Entertainment Expo (C2E2) Crown Championships of Cosplay. Cosplay skits can and have incorporated fight scenes, dance numbers, and singing, as well as magic tricks, quick costume changes, and flying through the air, all set to an audio track which may include voice acting, sound effects, and an accompanying backing video. Jacobs reports that in China, skits usually take the form of "a 20-minute drama that is written by the Cosplay team" (Jacobs 2013, 27).

As with other competitions globally, these skits are submitted to the event prior to the performance to be vetted for standard, appropriateness, and adherence to the competition's rules. Skits are rarely performed with live audio. Instead, audio and video content is submitted to events well ahead of time. This move to pre-recorded audio and lip-synced performances allows the cosplayers to perform with sound effects and full musical score, as well as avoiding the logistical nightmare of providing microphones for 100 or more cosplay competitors. Pre-recording vocals also allows cosplayers to use other vocals to "maintain the dignity of character" (Silvio 2006, 111) by coercing friends or acquaintances with either better vocal acting skills or who are the same gender as the characters being portrayed to record a character's lines. Early submission also allows events to check that audio files work. In mainland China, this convention is what allows the Communist government to regulate the content of cosplay dramas for sexual, political, or other undesirable content (Jacobs 2013, 27).

It is within these spaces that Jacobs observed a small group of cosplayers negotiating queer gender and sexual identities. Taking the liminal nature of cosplay to the extreme, members of this group were able to circumvent strict parental and government control on the mainland by renting a "tiny sub-divided apartment in the outer reaches of Hong Kong (the 'New Territories') where [they were] able to store [their] costumes" and get dressed before events (Jacobs 2013, 40–41). Jacobs's interviews reveal that for these cosplayers active in mainland China and Hong Kong, "acts of cross-dressing are more common for the gays and lesbians" in a cosplay group (Jacobs 2013, 36). While these cosplayers might not be open about their gender or sexuality, even amongst their peers, there is a tacit understanding and acceptance.

In New Zealand, the cosplay space or zone provides a safe space for transgender and/or non-heterosexual individuals to engage and play with their gender identity when they may not be able to do so in their everyday life due to personal choice, familial pressures, and/or other mitigating circumstances (from discussions on Facebook cosplay group "Older Cosplayers New Zealand" in 2015). Harleynyx is a New Zealand cosplayer and photographer who identifies as part of the LGTBQ+ community. In a piece commissioned for another New Zealand cosplayer's honours thesis in design, they raise many of the same concerns as Jacobs' cosplayers.

> Being LGBTQ+ can make daily life stressful—often we find ourselves watching our words, watching for signs that individuals may be safe to be out around, and careful of who we expose certain aspects of our self to. For some, we are concerned for our safety if we "pass" convincingly or not. To those who disregard the concepts of passing and being closeted, still we watch for people who would harm us for our inherent being. [. . .] Often, costume gives us a literal mask, and a security barrier, to cover ourselves with as we explore where our comfort and identity may truly lie.
>
> *(Harleynyx 2018)*

In cosplay spaces around the world, character and gender are tried on, discarded, recreated, and revisited with such regularity that it can be easy for LGTBQ+ cosplayers to experiment with their own gender identity, regardless of whether they are out to their parents and friends.

Cosplay rules and guidelines

The webpage for Tokyo Comic Con proclaims, in a large comic book font, that in 2016 "the world's largest pop culture event finally arrived in Japan" (What's Comic Con? *Komikkukon to wa* 2017; it should be noted that Tokyo Comic Con is not affiliated with any of the American Comic Cons). Given that the main Comic-Con held annually in San Diego attracts over 130,000 visitors, how did the Japanese organizers, if they are affiliated with the various Comic-Con franchises, get their cosplay regulations so wrong? (Although, as we will see, popular culture conventions in Europe and Anglophone settings such as Australia and the United States are not without controversy.) Conjecture on *Reddit*, *Ni Chanel*, and the *Anime News Network* (ANN) as to the context of the ban fell into two camps. One Redditor summed up the whole situation by citing the *ANN* article: "Tokyo Comic-Con bans male crossplay. Staff concerned of 'attracting a large number of stereotypically unattractive men dressed as women' and costumes that are 'not passing'" (Reddit's r/anime 2016). However, based on Tokyo Comic Con's statement published when the ban was lifted, it seems that the official reason was a worry that men would use the wrong changing room. It is likely that both are true, and both are grounded in sentiment that could be read as homophobic or transphobic, but which most likely fall under the banner of *meiwaku*—annoyance or disruption—and a preference for avoiding it.

Cosplay and otaku spaces in Japan are heavily regulated both by event organizers and by participants themselves. The original Tokyo Comic Con rules were, as noted previously, directed towards male crossdressers (*josō* lit. in women's clothing) rather than women doing *dansō* (lit. in men's clothing). Comic Market (also known as Comiket), Japan's biggest and longest-running manga event, has always dictated where cosplay costumes can and cannot be worn, where photographers can take their photos, and the sorts of photos can be taken (for example, no low-angle or "up skirt" shots) (Comic Market 2017a, 2017b). There are no rules relating to crossdressing, although regulations do state that underwear must be worn and that genetically female chests must be at least one-third covered, including the nipples. Excessive gore and/or nudity are banned, as is the wearing of real military or emergency services uniforms. These rulings are reportedly for the cosplayers' safety. By allowing photographs only to be taken in set locations, congestion in hallways and egresses is avoided in the midst of crowds of 590,000 and above. Having all cosplay photography in one spot allows photographers to be monitored and ensures that cosplayers themselves do not become overly fatigued (Zenko 2013).

Tokyo Comic Con's current cosplay and photography rules (see Tokyo Comic Con 2017a, 2017b) share significant guidelines with Comiket and the WCS rules for public attendees. Unlike Comiket and Tokyo Comic Con, which are events based around trading halls and showrooms—both amateur and corporate—WCS is a ten-day summit with public and private cosplay events, the culmination of which is a cosplay skit competition between teams from nearly 40 countries around the world. Of these three popular culture events, arguably the largest in Japan, only WCS now has rulings on crossdressing. These rules, aimed at the attendees and not the summit representatives, do not prohibit men or women from crossdressing, but ask that if they do, they "stay true to the spirit of the original character"; that legs, armpits, and faces be clean-shaven and that appropriate wigs and makeup be worn (World Cosplay Summit 2017). It should be noted that while *dansō* is commonplace amongst WCS representatives, *josō* is relatively rare. In 2017, Team Spain's Tobi Cosplay wore a qipao-style dress for the Ohs Street parade (an optional event for WCS delegates) to portray Xelloss from *Slayers* (1995), a crossdressing trickster priest. The most sensational example of *josō* in WCS to date is 2018's winning Chun Li worn by Luis of the Banana Boys cosplay duo who represented team Mexico. Before a panel of judges made up of each country's organizers, Luis explained how he had learned to pad, tuck, and paint his body to achieve Chun Li's iconic curves and neck-crushing-thighs (personal observation, Nagoya 2018). However, in both 2017 and 2018, we are looking at one individual out of a field of 64 cosplayers and a possible 192 costumes worn over the ten-day event.

Japanese popular culture events take place in a liminal conceptual space carved out of the everyday norms and expectations of Japan's rigid vertical social hierarchy. As Edmund Hoff noted in 2012, "much is made of the strict regulations at events in Japan [which may] be attributed to an orderliness in a society where one is constantly reminded that . . . one must refrain from *meiwaku*" (162). At the top of the WCS English language cosplay rules, there is a message in red-coloured font to cosplayers from outside Japan stating that the rules at WCS may be different from their home country (World Cosplay Summit 2017). In many countries, such as Australia, New Zealand, and the United States, a convention day starts with travelling to the venue in costume. In Japan, cosplayers must never attempt to arrive at or leave events in costume (see, for example, Baird 2016)—large signs at events like Comiket remind cosplayers to change before leaving (*Sora News* 2014). Hoff notes that this has not always been the case. At early cosplay events held 30 years ago, cosplayers were able to "cosplay everywhere" (Hoff 2012, 149) (somewhat ironically, this is now the official slogan of WCS). Currently Tokyo Comic Con, Comiket, and WCS events all provide ticketed change and cloakrooms for attendees, and their use is enforced.

It should be noted that Tokyo Comic Con and WCS are not the only conventions to police gender-related aspects of cosplay. *ANN* points out that the 2003 cosplay rules at Supanova, an Australian convention that has hosted both the Madman National Cosplay Championship (MNCC) and the Australian preliminaries for the World Cosplay Summit (WCS), once requested that cosplayers planning to crossdress email in advance so as to avoid "extreme cases of cross players" (*Supanova* 2004). In the early 2000s, cosplay was still a fledgling hobby in Australia—Manifest (Melbourne Anime Convention), said to be Australia's first dedicated cosplay and popular culture convention, was first held in 2001. The idea of dressing up as an anime or comic book character in public was only just becoming acceptable; crossdressing in white patriarchal middle Australia, particularly male-to-female crossdressing, was much more risqué. Indeed, up until 2001, it had been illegal for men to wear women's clothing after dark in some Australian states (see, for example, Angle 2011).

Extreme cases of crossplayers

On the surface, crossplay is the simple act of dressing as a character featured in an anime, manga, games, fiction, or film text, who is of a different gender to the cosplayer. Often the goal is to "pass" as the character through wigs, makeup, posture, body hair cultivation or removal, binding or tucking of genitals or visible secondary sex characteristics, and, of course, clothing and footwear. A 2009 survey of Australian cosplayers posted on DeviantART (an online art community) revealed that for most women in the cosplay community, crossplay was simply another skillset to learn and perfect, involving skills such as armour construction, wig styling, or pattern drafting. Reasons that women respondents gave for crossplaying also highlighted an ongoing gender imbalance in the representation of women and non-male characters in popular culture. Many respondents explained that they would rather cosplay male characters, as the designs and storylines were better than those for their women or young girl counterparts. For these women cosplayers, character and costume design were more important than any concerns relating to gender. During the first decade of the 2000s, there was also something of a belief that the best portrayals of beautiful *bishōnen* characters were by women (Okabe 2012, 238).

Norris and Bainbridge discuss cosplay in terms of drag (2009). Indeed, crossplayers do sometimes take on the role of drag queens or drag kings to subvert, critique, or parody the original character. Like drag performers, cosplayers who dress outside of their gender (and, indeed, cosplayers dressing in their own gender) take on characteristics that are hyperfeminine or hypermasculine, "revealing the socially constructed nature of gender roles yet concomitantly reinforcing them" (Leng 2013, 90).

However, passing is not always the aim for men who crossplay. Takeuchi Naoko's *Bishōjo senshi Serā Mūn* (*Pretty Soldier Sailor Moon*, 1991–1997; 2015–2018) is perhaps the most cosplayed series. The character designs provide cosplayers with the opportunity to portray a well-known character as an individual or as a duo, trio, or group of 5, 6, 10, 11, or more. Takeuchi's obsession with 1990s designers means that each character has a large wardrobe of street clothes, school uniforms, Sailor Scout uniforms, and eveningwear, giving cosplayers a wide range of choice. The huge cast of heroes, allies, villains, and bystanders also allows for a range of face types, personalities, genders, and, to a certain extent, body shapes. The original Japanese language anime and manga series boasts a number of characters who are gender ambiguous, crossdressers, gay, or lesbian. The iconic nature of the Sailor Scout sailor suit— short, coloured skirt and matching sailor bib with white gloves, leotard, and brightly coloured high-heeled shoes or boots—has also meant that the designs are easily parodied across a wide range of media and fan works. Canonical works of note include Neo Sweden's Nobel Gundam mecha in *Kidō Butōden Ji Gandamu* (*Mobile Fighter G Gundam*, 1994); a team of giant robots in the shape of Takeuchi's magical girl protagonists complete with high heels and long sculpted foam antennae.

Arguably the most (in)famous Sailor Moon cosplayer is the hirsute, paddle-wielding figure of Sailor Bubba. The man known as Sailor Bubba made his first appearance at the 1999 Anime Central convention in Chicago, Illinois (Tomberry, "Sailor Bubba"). His notoriety rose to the point that in 2004 Anime Central made bobble-head doll versions of his cosplay and sold them at the convention. In 2010 an actor dressed as Sailor Bubba appeared in the drama series *Leverage* (season 3, episode 3, first aired 27 June 2010). At the same time that Sailor Bubba was active, Man-Faye appeared on the scene: another hirsute male crossdresser in a skimpy outfit—this time Faye Valentine's yellow hot pants and bra, worn under a loosely tied red shirt from 1998 anime *Kaubōi Bibappu* (*Cowboy Bebop*). Man-Faye first emerged in 2001 and was a regular figure at American anime and popular culture conventions. Man-Faye's propensity for performing his "ass wave" superpower lead to his appearance on *The Tonight Show* in 2006; it also resulted in his being banned from Anime Expo in 2004 for two years when he accidentally flashed a member of the public (Tomberry, "Man Faye").

Sailor Bubba and Man-Faye were both loved and hated. A 2003 forum on *Cosplay.com* criticised Man-Faye for poorly representing cosplayers (Cosplay.com 2003). It was these "extreme" cosplayers that Supanova was cautious about allowing into their event, resulting in their request that crossplayers email event organizers in advance. While Sailor Bubba and Man-Faye were somewhat reviled, beardy men in girls' clothing have become a mainstay of the cosplay scene globally. In 2014, *The Daily Mail* covered Melbourne Oz Comic Con, focussing their report on crossplayers and genderbent costumes with a focus on three muscular men in the garb of petite, female characters: Zeke, a body builder who dressed in pigtails and cut-off jean shorts as Misty from *Pokemon*; Sunday Cosplay, who wore a large pink gown with a Batman cowl as Princess Batman; and Miley Gyrus, wearing nothing but three pairs of white underwear to recreate Miley Cyrus's *Wrecking Ball* music video (Lewis 2014). Following in the footsteps of performers such as Ladybeard (Richard Margary), an Australian entertainer and pro-wrestler based in Japan, and Sailor Suit Ojiisan (Kobayashi Hideaki), who has been wearing a sailor suit uniform since 2010 (see, for example, Coello 2014), these beardy crossdressers are held up as icons within the cosplay and even wider community.

Beautiful cross-dressers

Both Leng (working in the United States) and Okabe (Japan) note that, per the 2009 DeviantART Survey (Australia) introduced previously, crossplay is held to an even higher standard, with "good" or successful crossplay being highly admired and "bad" crossplay (some would argue that Man-Faye is a "bad" crossplayer) being harshly criticized, usually in online forums. Okabe's work with Japanese cosplayers reveals a hierarchy within the Japanese cosplay community that is only hinted at in Leng and Jacob's respective fieldwork. Interviews conducted in Japanese reveal a lower or higher status through a shift in polite language usage by informant cosplayers. When talking about beautiful crossplayers, Okabe notes that one of his informants, already using polite language, shifted to an even higher register of respect, humbling themselves in relation to the crossplayer they were discussing (Okabe 2012, 238). In this way, we can see that this kind of gender performance, even though many of the requisite steps to crossplay are the same as cosplay, is assigned a higher value by some cosplayers than just dressing as a character of the same gender. Some cases, particularly in media and other outside coverage, prioritize male-to-female crossdressing over female-to-male crossdressing (as in *The Daily Mail* story) (Leng 2013, 104).

Harleynyx points out those born female are more able to "experiment publicly" with gender, character, and costume than those who are genetically male:

> In fashion, male-influenced androgyny has had far less stigma than a more feminine neutrality. We don't perceive femininity to be neutral, the default setting, and as such by crossplaying individuals place themselves (in society's eye) into "the other".
>
> *(Harleynyx 2018)*

Those cosplayers who create *josō* crossplay and who do not engage in the beardy Pantomime Dame style of crossplay mentioned previously (King 2013) are often held to a much higher standard than those performing *dansō*. In both cases, the cosplayer in question will alter their physical appearance. They will use: a wig to emulate their chosen character's hair style; contacts to change their colour and give the illusion of smaller or larger eyes; makeup and contouring to change their face shape (softening or strengthening their jaw line and altering the shape and size of their nose); corsets to control their waist or body shape (either to give themselves a classic hourglass or to help form a squarer torso); padding to give the illusion of curves or muscles and bulges; and tucking, binding, or taping to hide away breasts or penises—and this is before a costume garment and shoes are even considered. For women crossplayers who do *dansō*, much of this work is accepted, if not expected, daily behaviour. But, as Harleynyx points out, for men to go through these processes is perceived as somehow strange or demeaning in mainstream society. I noted previously that Norris and Bainbridge look at cosplay through the lens of drag. However, as Rachel Leng points out, "drag is marginalized by mainstream society, whereas crossplay practices, particularly M2F [male to female] crossplay, appears to be endorsed by the community from which it emerges" (Leng 2013, 92). While I agree with what Leng says, I would like to emphasize that this is not necessarily the case across all cosplay communities worldwide and that on the whole, as Harleynyx notes, *dansō* is more universally accepted.

Measuring cosplay

I have used the term "successfully" previously in this chapter, but what is a successful cosplay and how is it measured? In the terms of a cosplay made for a competition, success is measured by whether the cosplayer wins an award. Competitions are judged by a group of experts, usually forming a panel made up of experienced cosplayers or cosplay idols and popular culture- or game-related industry representatives. Cosplayers are judged according to a set of rules that award points for, for example, accuracy in recreating a costume, the construction of the garment, and the cosplayer's onstage presence. How then, are non-competition costumes or costumes that have been purchased rather than constructed judged? Leng proposes that for crossplayers in the United States, success is measured "by compliments from other cosplayers as well as the number of photography requests" (Leng 2013, 104). In his work with a group of Japanese cosplayers, Daisuke Okabe notes that a "cosplayer's assessment of her own costume is meaningless on its own."

The standards that define the quality of cosplay are not based on individual assessment, nor are they based on assessments accessible to the general public. It is considered more meaningful to create an outfit that garners acclaim from a few community members than from the general public. Whether a cosplay outfit is "good" or "bad" is meaningless if taken out of the context of a peer review by members of the subcultural community (Okabe 2012, 238). Within the Japanese cosplay community, beautiful crossdressing and costumes that recreate a "character's appearance down to even subtle details" are "particularly appreciated" (Okabe 2012, 238).

Conclusion

In the 2009 DeviantART survey introduced previously, only three male cosplayers gave a reason behind their choice to cosplay (or not cosplay) women characters: one respondent said that they were too hairy for crossplay, one said they only cosplayed characters who they were attracted to and so would never crossplay, and the third proclaimed that they would only crossplay to be a "trap" (with the specific aim of deceiving heterosexual men in order to surprise or disgust their victim by revealing the cosplayer's true gender) or for the "LOLs" (King 2013). It seems that in the decade that has passed, attitudes towards gender performance and crossdressing have shifted as cosplay has entered new locales and laws have changed to better reflect current social mores.

Cosplayers in various communities around the world and online create and negotiate spaces where they are able to cosplay the characters that they love, regardless of age, skin colour, and, perhaps most importantly, gender. It should be noted that issues of race, skin colour, and black/yellow/white face in cosplay are too complex to be discussed here but require further study. This notwithstanding, for the majority of cosplayers, dressing as the favourite character is more important than questions of gender. As Jacobs notes, "the liminal zone of Cosplayers is indeed also a by-product of capitalism which offers a type of gender play that can be easily cast aside and forgotten" (Jacobs 2013, 31). If crossplay is examined as a separate act to cosplay, it becomes clearly apparent that "gender is constructed and never static," meaning that crossplay can provide a platform for temporary liberation from pre-established orders (Locke 2016, 13). Cosplay spaces then become a site of play and experimentation where gender identities can be tried on and experienced, or perfected and later utilized in everyday life.

Related chapters

6   Transgender, Non-Binary Genders, and Intersex in Japan
26 The Continuum of Male Beauty in Contemporary Japan
30 Gender, Manga, and Anime
31 Cuteness Studies and Japan

References

Angle, M. (2011) "Tasmania's Parliament Legalises Cross-Dressing," *The World Today* 16 March. www.abc.net.au/worldtoday/stories/s261378.htm

Baird, D. (2016) "What It Takes to Be a Cosplayer at Comiket," *Tokyo Cheapo* 16 August. https://tokyocheapo.com/lifestyle/how-to-comiket-cosplayer/

Coello, J. (2014) "When Ladybeard Meets 'Sailor Suit Old Man', It's an Explosion of Manly Cuteness," *Sora News 24* 25 February. https://en.rocketnews24.com/2014/02/25/when-ladybeard-meets-sailor-suit-old-man-its-an-explosion-of-manly-cuteness%e3%80%90photos%e3%80%91/

Comic Market (2017a) "C93 *kosupure oyobi satsuei no chūi jikō*" (Note Regarding Cosplay and Photography at Comiket #93), *Comiket* 18 December. www.comiket.co.jp/info-p/C93/C93cosplay.html

Comic Market (2017b) "Information for Overseas Attendees in Comic Market 93 Catalog" *Comiket* 8 December. www.comiket.co.jp/info-a/TAFO/C93TAFO/cmkfor.html

Cosplay.com (2003) "What's the Big Deal on Man-Faye," *Cosplay.com* 23 September. www.cosplay.com/showthread.php?t=21476

Harleynyx (2018) "Safety Dance—The LGBTQ+ Community Within Cosplay," (no page numbers) in M. McLisky (ed) *Convention: Identity and Embodiment*, Unpublished Honours Thesis.

Harmsen, P. (2016) "Duften af samurai" (The Scent of Samurai), *Weekendavisen* 4 November.

Hoff, E. (2012) "Cosplay as Subculture: In Japan and Beyond/*Cosupure subukarucha Nihon to kaigai*," *Tōkai Gakuen Daigaku Kenkyū kiyō* (Tokai Gakuen University Research Bulletin) 17 (31 March) 149–166.

Honda, M. (2010) "The Genealogy of *Hirahira*: Liminality and the Girl," in T. Aoyama and B. Hartley (eds) *Girl Reading Girl in Japan*, London and New York: Routledge, 19–37.

Jacobs, K. (2013) "Impersonating and Performing Queer Sexuality in the Cosplay Zone," *Participations: Journal of Audience and Reception Studies* 10 (2) 22–45.

King, E. L. (2013) "Girls Who Are Boys Who Like Girls to Be Boys. . . : BL and the Australian Cosplay Community," *Intersections: Gender and Sexuality in Asia and the Pacific* 32. http://intersections.anu.edu.au/issue32/king.htm.

King, E. L. (2019) "*Sakura ga meijiru*: Unlocking the Shōjo Wardrobe—Cosplay; Manga; 2.5D Space," in J. Berndt, K. Nagaike and F. Ogi (eds) *Shōjo Across Media: Multidisciplinary Approaches*, Lexington, KY: The University Press of Kentucky.

King, E. L. (2016) "Tailored Translations—Translating and Transporting Cosplay Costumes Across Texts, Cultures, and Dimensions," *Signata: Annales des sémiotiques/Annals of Semiotics* 7 361–376.

Leng, R. (2013) "Gender, Sexuality, and Cosplay: A Case Study of Male-to-Female Crossplay," *The Phoenix Papers: First Edition* (April) 89–110. http://fansconf.a-kon.com/dRuZ33A/wpcontent/uploads/2013/04/Gender-Sexuality-and-Cosplay-byRachel-Leng1.pdf

Lewis, M. (2014) "Three Pairs of Underpants, a Crop Top and a Sledgehammer: Gender-Bending Cosplayer Who's Turned Himself into Miley Gyrus (And He's Not the Only Man Dressing Like a Lady)," *The Daily Mail* 11 July. www.dailymail.co.uk/femail/article-2687013/Dude-looks-like-lady-From-Miley-Cyrus-Pokemon-meet-gender-bending-men-cosplay-arent-ones.html#ixzz38vcK3S00

Locke, E. (2016) "To Be or Not to Be the Queerest of Them All: Investigating the Freedom of Gender Performativity Within the Queer Space of Cosplay/Cross Play," *3rd Kanita Postgraduate International Conference on Gender Studies 2016*, unpublished conference paper, 11–22.

Miller, L. (2017) "*Purikura*: Expressive Energy in Female Self Photography," in A. Freedman and T. Slade (eds) *Introducing Japanese Popular Culture*, New York: Routledge, 104–113.

Norris, C. and Bainbridge, J. (2009) "Selling *Otaku*? Mapping the Relationship Between Industry and Fandom in the Australian Cosplay Scene," *Intersections: Gender and Sexuality in Asia and the Pacific* 20 (April). http://intersections.anu.edu.au/issue20/norris_bainbridge.htm

Okabe, D. (2012) "Cosplay, Learning, and Cultural Practice," in M. Ito et al. (eds) *Fandom Unbound: Otaku Culture in a Connected World*, New Haven: Yale University Press, 225–248.

Reddit's r/animeboard (2016) "Male Crossplaying Banning Rule Is Cancel[l]ed at Tokyo Comic Con," 26 October. www.reddit.com/r/anime/comments/59hl3m/male_crossplaying_banning_rule_is_canceled_at/

Silvio, T. (2006) "Informationalized Affect: The Body in Taiwanese Digital Video Puppetry and Cosplay," in F. Martin and L. Heinrich (eds) *Embodied Modernities: Corporeality, Representation, and Chinese Cultures*, Honolulu, HI: University of Hawaii Press, 195–217.

Tokyo Comic Con (2017a) "What's Comic Con?/*Komikkukon to wa*" http://tokyocomiccon.jp/english/whatscc.html

28
GENDER IN JAPANESE LITERATURE AND LITERARY STUDIES

Laura Clark and Lucy Fraser

An excellent range of monographs, book chapters, journal articles, encyclopaedia entries, and more are available in English to introduce researchers to gender studies perspectives on modern Japanese literature. These serve as entry points into the vast body of work in Japanese, and Japanese literary and academic works are increasingly being made available in translation. This chapter offers a glimpse into the field of gender and Japanese literature, with a focus on postwar and contemporary texts and criticism. The first two sections reflect on how gender in literature is constructed as a matter for women, whereas up until relatively recently, gender for male authors and their creations has been left unmarked. This existing focus on "women" as "gender studies" in literature is vital, as it addresses ongoing gaps in the recognition of women's writing and mounts important critiques of stereotyping and the effacement of women both as authors and as characters. However, this focus risks perpetuating the structure of men as an unquestioned "norm" versus women as the "deviation" in need of investigation. As such, we aim to provide a broader approach to the topic of gender and literature by also introducing studies and works that raise issues of men and masculinity. The second half of the chapter targets some examples of "genre" and forms of "popular fiction" and reveals the complex gendered engagements present in the literary creations themselves, as well as how scholars have found this to be a useful lens.

This chapter focuses on the work on Japanese literature and literary criticism available for readers of English. However, it should be noted that the literary and critical work that is available in English translation is not simply a straightforward reflection of the shape of Japanese literature and literary criticism scenes. The selection, publication, and promotion of translated literature depends on factors beyond the critical acclaim or popularity enjoyed by a text in Japan: it is affected, for example, by availability of copyright, opportunities and support provided by government and other funding bodies, perceived marketability (especially in relation to the work's imagery of Japan), the personal or research interests of translators (many of whom are academics, some with highly specialized and sometimes esoteric fields of study), and much more (see Fowler 1992). Therefore, the kinds of works available in English and the kinds of critical engagements that those works receive have complex contexts and value judgements at all levels.

Laura Clark and Lucy Fraser

"Women's literature"

The bounds of the once-powerful notion of *jun bungaku*—"pure" or "high" literature—were traditionally determined by the *bundan* or literary establishment via literary prizes and literary criticism and commentary in periodicals and other print media. Modern women authors were excluded from this category, with the few exceptions of novelists such as Higuchi Ichiyō (1872–1896), Enchi Fumiko (1905–1986), and the poet Yosano Akiko (1878–1942) (see Campana in this volume). Yet the most celebrated piece of classic Japanese literature is *The Tale of Genji*, which was written by the court lady Murasaki Shikibu in the Heian period (794–1185). Many other significant classical works of prose and poetry had female authors. This history has provided women writers with a kind of literary lineage to reach back to, or conversely, to be compared unfavourably with (Mostow 2001). These issues and more are insightfully addressed by the significant and varied contributions included in *The Woman's Hand: Gender and Theory in Japanese Women's Writing* (eds. Schalow and Walker 1996).

Regardless of the feted classical women authors, subsequent eras saw less work from women. The flourishing world of literary, poetic, and theatrical production in the Edo period (1601–1868) was dominated by male authors. The Meiji restoration of 1868 and the Meiji period (1868–1912) of "modernisation" saw the sudden influx of new writing pieces and styles, instigating a literary revolution led by (male) figures such as Mori Ōgai (1862–1922), and Natsume Sōseki (1867–1916). However, changing views on women's roles and educational reform increased female literacy and participation in the realm of letters (Copeland and Ortabasi 2006), as particularly illustrated in the feminist female-authored *Seitō* (Bluestocking), a "New Women's" journal of the 1910s (Bardsley 2007). Work by modern women authors was labelled in various ways, but from the beginning of the twentieth century, it came to be segregated as *joryū bungaku* (women's style of literature). This term, which implies a particular "feminine" literary style, had by the middle of the century become the standard means for assessing women's literary production (Ericson 1997, 76). As Hartley (2016) notes, this terminology was not only essentialist, but also served to delegitimise writing by women.

Many debates around this approach are featured in *Woman Critiqued: Translated Essays on Women's Writing* (ed. Copeland 2006), an invaluable volume of translated essays from the 1890s through to the 1990s. It captures both affirmations of and challenges to the idea of a particular female style, including, for example, a 1966 essay by the renowned modern author Mishima Yukio (1925–1970) that makes the claim that "the mind of the woman [. . .] is inhibited by the gravitational pull of the womb" (2006, 83). *Woman Critiqued* also includes a translated extract from *Danryū bungakuron* (On Men's Literature), one of the most famous and fierce critiques of the notion and treatment of *joryū bungaku*. This was the collected series of roundtable discussions conducted by three feminists in 1989: sociologist Ueno Chizuko (1948–); psychology, gender, and sexuality researcher Ogura Chikako (1952–); and poet, novelist, and critic Tomioka Taeko (1935–). The discussants make free and easy with the revered names of the modern Japanese canon, from decadent anti-naturalist Tanizaki Jun'ichirō (1886–1965) to Japan's first winner of the Nobel Prize for literature in 1968, Kawabata Yasunari (1899–1972). The confident, playful approach and the ironic title exposed and ridiculed the way that women authors have been treated by a male-dominated literary establishment, as well as articulating problems with men's fictional representations of women.

In line with international feminist movements in academic research emerging from the 1980s, edited collections in English often analyse female authors within the context of gender issues. Key authors include Enchi Fumiko, who became known for her feminist writing and exploration of supernatural or shamanistic themes in her works (e.g. Bargen 1996); Hayashi

Fumiko (1903–1951) with her depiction of the urban working-class (e.g. Brown 2001); the acclaimed Ōba Minako (1930–2007) (e.g. Wilson 2013); the "anti-novel" author Kurahashi Yumiko (1935–2005) (e.g. Aoyama 1994; Sakaki 2001); the provocative and experimental writer Kanai Mieko (1947–) (e.g. Aoyama 2006; Orbaugh 1999); and the somewhat controversial Yamada Eimi (1959–) (e.g. Cornyetz 1996). Other critics, such as Vernon (1987), examine the works of women, as well as making comparisons with how women are depicted in literature written by men. The idea of "transgressive" women has also been useful, with a number of edited collections seeking to highlight challenging women and the challenges that women face, from literary and multidisciplinary perspectives (Bullock 2010; Cornyetz 1999; Marran 2007; Miller and Bardsley 2005; Miller and Copeland 2018). Efforts from scholars and translators have also led to an increase in translated short story collections that celebrate Japanese women's writing (selected examples include Birnbaum 1982; Tanaka and Hanson 1982; Layne 2006; Lippit and Selden 2015). Male authors have typically dominated in short story collections that do not have a stated focus on women, though there is an increasing but not yet equal inclusion of female authors.

An examination of the intricacies of issues surrounding women writers and their literary (and sometimes actual) lineage and the "pure" literature canon is undertaken in *The Father-Daughter Plot* (eds. Copeland and Ramirez-Christensen 2001). This is an apt approach for the Japanese literary scene, which has long featured complex networks of literary families such as father Dazai Osamu (1909–48) and daughter Tsushima Yūko (1947–2016), and father Mori Ōgai (1862–1922) and daughter Mori Mari (1903–87). Another significant pairing is the "high culture" critic Yoshimoto Taka'aki (1924–2012) and his daughter, the bestselling author Yoshimoto Banana (1964–). Yoshimoto Banana, along with Murakami Haruki (1949–), is known for challenging the (already dubious) borders of "pure" versus "popular" fiction, which have been disintegrating for decades. The generational shift that these authors were seen to embody, away from socially and politically engaged literature, was lamented by prominent figures such as author Ōe Kenzaburō (1935–) (Japan's second Nobel Prize for Literature winner) and critics such as Masao Miyoshi (1991). Yoshimoto's hugely popular work was accused of sentimentalism and empty consumerist imagery. These critiques are highly gendered, tied to cultural anxieties surrounding the figure of the *shōjo* (girl) she invoked through young female protagonists and stylistic associations with girls' novels and manga (Aoyama 2010; Kawasaki 2010; Saitō 2006; Sherif 1999; Treat 1993; see also Ting, and Taylor-Jones and Thomas-Parr in this volume). It is striking that although similar critiques have been levelled at Murakami Haruki, whose work has now exceeded Yoshimoto's in popularity both domestically and internationally, they have evinced far less anxiety regarding his challenges to masculine norms and ideals (see the "Men's literature" section subsequently). There is a clear need to turn a critical eye onto ideas of masculinity in relation to literature and the canon.

"Men's literature"

As already noted, masculinity and manhood in Japanese literature have typically received less attention than femininity and women. Moreover, when masculinity is discussed, it is often within discourses of anxiety. There is a massive body of work on Japanese male authors' writing, yet it is rarely written from a consciously gendered standpoint. Thus, the shift towards marking the male author and masculinity is significant against this strong precedent.

Due to this limited history, there is not yet a clear narrative in English around masculinity in Japanese fiction. The contemporary international reception of Japanese literature has been strongly defined by big names such as Kawabata Yasunari, Ōe Kenzaburō, Mishima Yukio,

Murakami Haruki, and Murakami Ryū (1952–). Yet, although there has been some gendered analysis of their works, it is relatively limited.

Mishima made his name through his exploration of sexuality and death and his pushing of stylistic bounds. This invitation for a gendered analysis has been taken up to some extent, for example, Starr (1994) includes some discussion on masculinity as machismo and Mishima's uneasy relationship with homosexuality. Similarly, Otomo (2001) explored the relationship between imperialism and modernism and Mishima's interest in the male Japanese body. Napier's *Escape from the Wasteland: Romanticism and Realism in the Fiction of Mishima Yukio and Ōe Kenzaburō* (1991) directly compares Mishima and Ōe regarding their use of sex and violence and the deep misogyny she identifies in their works. Strikingly, Snyder (1999) also draws parallels between Murakami Ryū and Ōe's depictions of aberrant sexuality.

Despite Murakami Haruki's domestic and international popularity and his characteristic use of the masculine personal pronoun *boku* and other gendered innovations, and despite Japanese gender studies of his works (including *Danryū bungakuron*; see Ueno et al. 2006), it is only in the post-2000s that gendered reading of his works has emerged in English (e.g. Clark 2015; Flutsch 2010; Hansen 2016; Lo 2004; Nihei 2013; Szarota 2010). This suggests that a trend towards gendered readings of major male literary figures is taking place. One of the major Anglophone works to interrogate the idea of "men" in Japanese literature is Slaymaker's (2004). Slaymaker examines the immediate postwar works of so-called "flesh writers" who focused on carnality and the body—Tamura Taijirō (1911–1983), Noma Hiroshi (1915–1991), and Sakaguchi Ango (1906–1955). He identifies such male authors' anxiety in establishing an acceptable masculinity in the wake of the emasculating loss of the Pacific War. Yet these authors failed to acknowledge the structures of gender within Japanese society that they recreated. Meanwhile, a psychoanalytic lens has also been turned towards the Japanese canon in the post-2000s; of particular note is Cornyetz and Vincent's (2010) edited collection, which is a bid to promote Freudian readings of major authors, as well as more targeted works—e.g. Long's (2009) take on Tanizaki Jun'ichirō.

A key area for gendered discussions of male authors has been literary depictions of homosexuality (as opposed to popular culture depictions—see Ting in this volume) and exploring the narrowing space for male-male sexuality in the Meiji context especially. Few works explicitly identify homosexuality as their topic when focusing on women. This is not to say that homosexual women's voices are absent—notable authors include Yoshiya Nobuko (1896–1973), Miyamoto Yuriko (1899–1951), and Yuasa Yoshiko (1896–1990)—but fewer works collectively explore female-female sexuality and literature, with trends towards looking at Yoshiya Nobuko (e.g. Suzuki 2006; Robertson 2005), and *Seitō's* association with both feminism and lesbianism (e.g. Wu 2007)—McLelland, Suganuma, and Welker's edited collection (2007) highlights some of these issues.

The most sweeping historical work on literary engagements with male-male sexuality is Plugfelder's *Cartographies of Desire: Male-Male Sexuality in Japanese Discourse 1600–1950 (1999)*. Plugfelder highlights the genealogy of male-male sexuality in Japan and the distinctions between this history and European history. This work joins a significant body of discussion on sexuality in Japan more generally, as well as being a foundational text for *literary* depictions of male-male sexuality. In something of a trilogy, Reichert, Vincent, and Angles have all approached the issues surrounding male-male sexuality in the late nineteenth to early-mid twentieth centuries. Reichert's *In the Company of Men: Representations of Male-Male Sexuality in Meiji Literature* (2006) deals with the representation of male-male sexuality in fiction from that period. Reichert has a particular focus on the place of *nanshoku*, with the shift towards male-male sexuality becoming unspeakable, concluding with Natsume Sōseki and Mori Ōgai. Angles's *Writing the Love of Boys: Origins of Bishōnen Culture in Modernist Japanese Literature* (2011) argues that Murayama Kaita

(1896–1919), Edogawa Ranpo (1894–1965), and Inagaki Taruho (1900–1977) sought creative methods to depict male-male desire. In *Two-Timing Modernity: Homosocial Narrative in Modern Japanese Fiction* (2012), Vincent explores homosocial narratives mostly from the first half of the twentieth century, with homosexual desire delimited to the time of youth, or the perpetual past, separated from adult masculinity. These texts demonstrate a concentrated shift that is taking place in Japanese gendered literary studies, as men, masculinity, and desire are brought specifically into the discussion and canonical texts are re-examined through a range of new critical lenses.

Pivot points

Despite these topics, categories such as "female author" and "male author" continue to carry significant weight, often defining the construction and reception of texts. However, a number of contemporary authors seek to destabilise gender binaries as part of a greater destabilisation of the bounds between human, animal, and the self. For example, Matsu'ura Rieko (1958–) and Tawada Yōko (1960–) have consistently played with the physical self as changeable and permeable, detaching the taken-for-granted connections between sex and the gendered body. Hoshino Tomoyuki (1965–) explores gendered bodies together with national and ethnic identities. Chiya Fujino (1962–)—one of very few publicly acknowledged transgender authors—has repeatedly explored themes of otherness, permissible gendered boundaries, and social exclusion. As Campana (this volume) notes in relation to poetry, the literary contributions of transgender authors towards opening discussion of gender norms has yet to be deeply addressed in the research and is worth further pursuit.

An intersectional approach to ideas of gender is vital to developing the field. One avenue is the investigation of gender in literature by authors who identify and engage with minority groups in Japan: emerging research and translations make available in English, for example, Ainu stories (see Strong 2011), Okinawan literature (see Bhowmik and Rabson 2016), and work by Koreans living in Japan (see Wender 2011). Literature on *burakumin*, a socioculturally disadvantaged group of ethnically Japanese people, is famously represented in the work of Nakagami Kenji (1946–1992), which has been examined from gender and sexuality studies viewpoints (e.g. Cornyetz 1999).

Thematic analyses of literature also offer alternative entry points to the exploration of gender. For example, Aoyama's *Reading Food in Modern Japanese Literature* (2008) and Hansen's *Femininity, Self-Harm and Eating Disorders* (2016) reveal contradictory gendered engagements with food and the body. Yuki (2015) also lends an ecocritical perspective to the matter. As will become apparent in the discussion subsequently, genre fiction is another crucial area for the "undoing" of gender.

Gender in popular genres

Detective and crime novels

Japanese detective and crime fiction emerged in the Meiji period, with Edogawa Ranpo as one of its key literary forefathers. Sai Kawana's *Murder Most Modern: Detective Fiction and Japanese Culture* (2008) explores a marked shift from early detective fiction as largely the field of male authors, with a tendency to victimise women or demonise female killers through the concept of *dokufu* (poison women). However, with the turn of the millennium, many female authors are now using these violent genres to explore contemporary social issues. Since the early 2000s, there has been a marked increase in the availability of Japanese detective fiction in English, with many translated works from women such as Miyabe Miyuki (1960–), who has won many literary awards despite being relegated to "genre fiction"; Nonami Asa (1960–), known for her use of female detectives and horror elements; and Kirino Natsuo (1951–), who has faced controversy over her depiction of female violence and her exploration of women's difficulties in contemporary Japan.

Increasingly, genre works are being seen as challenging cultural norms and expressing social concerns, which often have a gendered element. In *Bodies of Evidence: Women, Society, and Detective Fiction in 1990s Japan* (2004), Seaman finds that the women authors challenge the norms and tropes of the detective genre, as well as placing the roots of violence in social problems. Similarly, Copeland (2004, 2018) and Hemmann (2017) have focused on Kirino Natsuo's use of violence and sex, while Mikals-Adachi (2004) sees Nonami Asa's fiction as revealing the disintegration of the Japanese family and traditional gender roles. Thus, critical engagements with detective fiction have taken a strongly gendered lens, particularly regarding the aims of female authors.

Science fiction and fantasy

In the postwar period, Japanese science fiction (SF) has undergone a significant boom, although its roots are as a subgenre of detective fiction (Tatsumi 2005). Much like its source, SF has consistently faced exclusion from "pure" literature, although SF and fantasy elements have been incorporated into mainstream writing for a number of years—Tatsumi points to Murakami Haruki, Murakami Ryū, and Ōe Kenzaburō, amongst others. Women writers' presence in SF is seen as starting with Suzuki Izumi (1949–1986), followed by pioneering authors who sought to critique femininity and target a female reading market (Kotani 2007). Key voices have included Hikawa Reiko (1958–), Matsuo Yumi (1960–), Arai Motoko (1960–), and Yamao Yūko (1955–).

The tropes within the genre itself lend it to play with gender and the body. For example, Kotani's chapter in *Robot Ghosts and Wired Dreams: Japanese Science Fiction from Origins to Anime* (2007) notes that the "freakish female body," the monstrous feminine in the family, and altered male bodies are all common themes. Nakamura's (2007) discussion of the body in Yumeno Kyūsaku's (1889–1936) work suggests that the uncanny relationship between machinery and the body has been a consistent focus since early-Shōwa SF works. Napier notes the presence of fantastic elements in Japanese fiction more broadly in *The Fantastic in Modern Japanese Literature: The Subversion of Modernity* (1996) while exploring SF and fantasy with deep recourse to desire, symbols, and the relations between men and women. Napier is particularly interested in establishing SF and fantasy as worthy of analysis. Genre fiction in general has long been subject to what Zähringer (2017) terms the "realism argument" in criticism: that is, that it hides from the grievances and challenges of the real world. However, SF creates space to imagine and articulate social fears and embody them in metaphor and technology, thus making it uniquely suited to revealing embodied and gendered anxieties that plague contemporary Japan.

Fairy tale and folklore retellings

In the realm of the fantastic, strong and innovative practices around parody, pastiche, and other types of conscious intertextuality in Japanese literature have meant that fairy tales, folklore, and other storytelling traditions have offered rich sources for a range of authors. Dazai Osamu; avant-garde filmmaker, poet, and author Terayama Shūji (1935–1983); and biting satirist Kurahashi Yumiko all reverse and subvert the gender roles of imported and local folk and fairy tales. Tsushima Yūko (1947–2016) and Ōba Minako have employed global mythic, folkloric, and indigenous peoples' stories in their explorations of female identity and empowerment, and Tanabe Seiko (1928–2019) retells classic volumes of mythology, literature, and Western fables. Folk and fairy tale elements also emerge in the works of more recent authors such as Tawada Yōko, Ogawa Yōko (1962–), and Kawakami Hiromi (1958–). In the 1990s, Japanese scholarship, popular essays, and fiction saw a boom in works claiming a kind of deep psychoanalytical explanation of the "true," "dark" nature of fairy tales such as the Grimms'. However, recent scholarship in the blossoming field of fairy tale studies takes an interest in the literary and gendered implications and effects of fairytale and folktale play (see Murai 2015; Fraser 2017).

Children's literature and young adult fiction

Folktale and fairy tale figures and plots also informed the influential early works of Japanese children's literature. Iwaya Sazanami's (1879–1933) engaging stories from the late nineteenth century are tied to imperialist and nationalist projects (Henry 2009). Ogawa Mimei (1882–1961), who developed a more "romantic" vision of the child in his tales in the 1910s–1930s, was vocal in promoting idealistic stories. The fantastical and charming work of Miyazawa Kenji (1896–1933), discovered posthumously, is known for its utopian vision and has been effectively re-read in the light of gender studies (e.g. Kilpatrick 2010). In the scholarship, Karatani Kōjin's (1980, trans. 1993) notion of the "discovery of the child" as occurring in tandem with the development of modern literature was deconstructed from a gender perspective by pioneers such as Honda Masuko (1992; see Aoyama 2010).

The translation and authorship of children's literature often offered women writers more freedom and opportunity than the more lauded literature for adults. Celebrated female translators of classic children's works include Wakamatsu Shizuko (1864–1896), known for translating Frances Hodgson Burnett's *Little Lord Fauntleroy*; Muraoka Hanako (1893–1963), whose translations of L. M. Montgomery's *Anne of Green Gables* books are widely loved; and Yagawa Sumiko (1930–2002), one of the best-regarded translators of Lewis Carroll's *Alice* books. Yoshiya Nobuko was influential in developing *shōjo* (girl) culture with her original work from the 1920s and also achieved great popular and financial success with adult readers for other works. Ishii Momoko (1907–2008) paved the way for more women writers in the postwar period with her original work and translations.

Translated children's classics, combined with Japanese girls' stories, formed a tradition of girls' fiction that in the 1980s and 1990s took the form of serialised novels for young female readers, famously represented by the Cobalt imprint published by Shūeisha—these series are routinely mentioned in chronologies of girls' literature and culture, but little research is available in English. Girls' culture is now very visible in the form of anime and manga (see Ting, Borggreen, and Taylor-Jones and Thomas-Parr in this volume). The role of Cobalt and other such imprints has now largely been replaced by *raito noberu* (light novels) which are targeted at young female *or* male readers, with anime-style characters featured on the covers. Doi (2017) characterises light novels as focussed on characters' actions and on immersing readers in a closed story world. In contrast, the popular, fantastical *Moribito* series (1996–2012) by Uehashi Nahoko (1962–), represents children's and young adult literature that has "psychological or descriptive depth" and political and social awareness and breaks down stereotyped gender roles; such works for children frequently explore other contemporary social issues such as family relationships, bullying, and *hikikomori* (social withdrawal).

Conclusion

Through a brief exploration of Japanese literary history from a gendered perspective, some key trends emerge. The first is that although gender issues permeate all areas of Japanese literature and its study, historically gender has been understood as "female," with male canonical authors left largely unmarked. However, a major shift is occurring both in terms of the respect and attention afforded to female authors, but also in gendered approaches and priorities in literary enquiry. These enquiries can and are being effectively pursued through thematic approaches, which often enable the freedom to compare works from vastly different times and contexts. A growing number of studies of popular and prolific genres such as detective novels, fantastical and science fiction genres, and children's and young adult literature are demonstrating that ideas of gender can and should be interrogated beyond those works that are traditionally deemed to have more literary "value". Nevertheless, there are many areas of interest that are still emergent or awaiting stronger engagement within the Anglophone Japanese literary studies sphere, as intersectionality, masculine norms, and post-binary gender issues still await us.

Related chapters

2   Gender in Pre-Modern Japan
29 Gender and Poetry
30 Gender, Manga, and Anime
32 Gender and Visual Culture
33 Gender, Media, and Misogyny in Japan
34 Representing Girls in Cinema

References

Angles, J. (2011) *Writing the Love of Boys: Origins of Bishōnen Culture in Modernist Japanese Literature*, Minneapolis: The University of Minnesota Press.
Aoyama, T. (1994) "The Love that Poisons: Japanese Parody and the New Literacy," *Japan Forum* 6 (1) 35–46.
Aoyama, T. (2006) "Embroidering Girls' Texts: Fashion and Feminism in the Fiction of Kanai Mieko," *U.S.-Japan Women's Journal* 29, 99–117.
Aoyama, T. (2008) *Reading Food in Modern Japanese Literature*, Honolulu: University of Hawai'i Press.
Aoyama, T. (2010) "The Genealogy of the 'Girl' Critic Reading Girl," in T. Aoyama and B. Hartley (eds) *Girl Reading Girl in Japan*, Oxon: Routledge, 38–49.
Bardsley, J. (2007) *The Bluestockings of Japan: New Woman Essays and Fiction from Seitō, 1911–16*, Ann Arbor, MI: University of Michigan Press.
Bargen, D. G. (1996) "Translation and Reproduction in Enchi Fumiko's 'A Bond for Two Lifetimes—Gleanings'," in P. G. Schalow and J. A. Walker (eds) *The Women's Hand: Gender and Theory in Japanese Women's Writing*, Stanford: Stanford University Press, 165–204.
Bhowmik, D. L. and Rabson, S. (eds) (2016) *Islands of Protest: Japanese Literature from Okinawa*, Honolulu: University of Hawai'i Press.
Birnbaum, P. (ed) (1982) *Rabbits, Crabs, etc. Stories by Japanese Women*, Honolulu: University of Hawai'i Press.
Brown, J. (2001) "De-Siring the Center: Hayashi Fumiko's Hungry Heroines and the Male Literary Canon," in R. L. Copeland and E. Ramirez-Christensen (eds) *The Father-Daughter Plot: Japanese Literary Women and the Law of the Father*, Honolulu: University of Hawai'i Press, 143–166.
Bullock, J. C. (2010) *The Other Women's Lib: Gender and Body in Japanese Women's Fiction*, Honolulu: University of Hawai'i Press.
Clark, L. (2015) "Negotiating the Salaryman's Hegemonic Masculinity in Murakami's *A Wild Sheep Chase*," *electronic journal of contemporary japanese studies* 15 (3) www.japanesestudies.org.uk/ejcjs/vol15/iss3/clark.html
Copeland, R. (2004) "Women Uncovered: Pornography and Power in the Detective Fiction of Kirino Natsuo," *Japan Forum* 16 (2) 249–269.

Copeland, R. (ed) (2006a) *Woman Critiqued: Translated Essays on Japanese Women's Writing*, Honolulu: University of Hawai'i Press.

Copeland, R. (2006b) "Women Critiquing Men: Watching the Ripples on the Pond," in R. Copeland (ed) *Woman Critiqued: Translated Essays on Japanese Women's Writing*, Honolulu: University of Hawai'i Press, 206–209.

Copeland, R. (2018) "Kirino Natsuo Meets Izanami: Angry Divas Talking Back," in L. Miller and R. Copeland (eds) *Diva Nation: Female Icons from Japanese Cultural History*, Oakland, CA: University of California Press, 13–33.

Copeland, R. and Ortabasi, M. (2006) *The Modern Murasaki: Writing by Women of Meiji Japan*, New York: Columbia University Press.

Copeland, R. and Ramirez-Christensen, E. (eds) (2001) *The Father-Daughter Plot: Japanese Literary Women and the Law of the Father*, Honolulu: University of Hawai'i Press.

Cornyetz, N. (1996) "Power and Gender in the Narratives of Yamada Eimi," in P. G. Schalow and J. A. Walker (eds) *The Woman's Hand: Gender and Theory in Japanese Women's Writing*, Stanford, CA: Stanford University Press, 425–460.

Cornyetz, N. (1999) *Dangerous Women, Deadly Words: Phallic Fantasy and Modernity in Three Japanese Writers*, Stanford, CA: Stanford University Press.

Cornyetz, N. and Vincent, K. J. (eds) (2010) *Perversion and Modern Japan: Psychoanalysis, Literature, Culture*, London: Routledge.

Doi, Y. (2017) "The *Moribito* Series and Its Relation to Trends in Japanese Children's Literature," in J. Stephens (ed) *The Routledge Companion to International Children's Literature*, London: Routledge, 399–409.

Ericson, J. (1997) *Be a Woman: Hayashi Fumiko and Modern Japanese Women's Literature*, Honolulu: University of Hawai'i Press.

Flutsch, M. (2010) "Murakami Haruki's Shōjo Kasahara Mei," in T. Aoyama and B. Hartley (eds) *Girl Reading Girl in Japan*, Oxon: Routledge, 119–129.

Fowler, E. (1992) "Rendering Words, Traversing Cultures: On the Art and Politics of Translating Modern Japanese Fiction," *The Journal of Japanese Studies* 18 (1) (Winter) 1–44.

Fraser, L. (2017) *The Pleasures of Metamorphosis: Japanese and English Fairy Tale Transformations of "The Little Mermaid,"* Detroit: Wayne State University Press.

Hansen, G. M. (2016) *Femininity, Self-Harm and Eating Disorders in Japan: Navigating Contradiction in Narrative and Visual Culture*, Oxon: Routledge.

Hartley, B. (2016) "Feminism and Japanese Literature," in R. Hutchinson and L. D. Morton (eds) *Routledge Handbook of Modern Japanese Literature*, London: Routledge, 82–94.

Hemmann, K. (2017) "Dangerous Women and Dangerous Stories: Gendered Narration in Kirino Natsuo's Grotesque and Real World," in J. C. Bullock, A. Kano and J. Welker (eds) *Rethinking Japanese Feminisms*, Honolulu: University of Hawai'i Press, 170–184.

Henry, D. (2009) "Japanese Children's Literature as an Allegory of Empire in Iwaya Sazanami's *Momotarō* (Peach Boy)," *Children's Literature Association Quarterly* 34 (3) 218–228.

Honda, M. (1992) *Ibunka to shite no kodomo*, Tokyo: Chikuma Shobō.

Karatani, K (1993) *Origins of Modern Japanese Literature*. Trans. Brett de Bary. Durham and London: Duke University Press.

Kawana, S. (2008) *Murder Most Modern: Detective Fiction and Japanese Culture*, Minneapolis: University of Minnesota Press.

Kawasaki, K. (2010) "The Climate of the Girl in Yoshimoto Banana: ♥?♥!♥!?" trans. T. Aoyama and B. Hartley, in T. Aoyama and B. Hartley (eds) *Girl Reading Girl in Japan*, Oxon: Routledge, 50–63.

Kilpatrick, H. (2010) "Transcending Gender in Pictorial Representations of Miyazawa Kenji's 'Marivuron and the Girl,'" in T. Aoyama and B. Hartley (eds) *Girl Reading Girl in Japan*, Oxon: Routledge, 145–159.

Kotani, M. (2007) "Alien Spaces and Alien Bodies in Japanese Women's Science Fiction," trans. M. Nakamura, in C. Bolton, I. Csicsery-Ronay Jr. and T. Tatsumi (eds) *Robot Ghosts and Wired Dreams: Japanese Science Fiction from Origins to Anime*, Minneapolis and London: University of Minnesota Press, 47–74.

Layne, C. (ed) (2006) *Inside and Other Short Fiction: Japanese Women by Japanese Women*, Tokyo, New York: Kodansha International.

Lippit, N. M. and Selden, K. I. (eds) (2015) *Japanese Women Writers: Twentieth Century Short Fiction*, Oxon and New York: Routledge.

Lo, K. C. (2004) "Return to What One Imagines to Be There: Masculinity and Racial Otherness in Haruki Murakami's Writing About China," *Novel: A Forum on Fiction* 36 (3) 258–277.

Long, M. (2009) *This Perversion Called Love: Reading Tanizaki, Feminist Theory, and Freud*, Stanford, CA: Stanford University Press.

Marran, C. L. (2007) *Poison Woman: Figuring Female Transgression in Modern Japanese Culture*, Minneapolis: University of Minnesota Press.

McLelland, M., Suganuma, K. and Welker, J. (eds) (2007) *Queer Voices from Japan: First Person Narratives from Japan's Sexual Minorities*, Lanham, MS: Lexington Books.

Mikals-Adachi, E. (2004) "Nonami Asa's Family Mysteries: The Novel as Social Commentary," *Japan Forum* 16 (2) 231–248.

Miller, L. and Bardsley, J. (eds) (2005) *Bad Girls of Japan*, New York: Palgrave Macmillan.

Miller, L. and Copeland, R. (eds) (2018) *Diva Nation: Female Icons from Japanese Cultural History*, Oakland, CA: University of California Press.

Mishima, Y. (2006) "On Narcissism," trans. T. Aoyama and B. Hartley, in R. Copeland (ed) *Woman Critiqued: Translated Essays on Japanese Women's Writing*, Honolulu: University of Hawai'i Press, 83–87.

Miyoshi, M. (1991) *Off Center: Power and Cultural Relations Between Japan and the United States*, Cambridge, MA: Harvard University Press.

Mostow, J. S. (2001) "Mother Tongue and Father Script: The Relationship of Sei Shonagon and Murasaki Shikibu to Their Fathers and Chinese Letters," in R. L. Copeland and E. Ramirez-Christensen (eds) *The Father-Daughter Plot: Japanese Literary Women and the Law of the Father*, Honolulu: University of Hawai'i Press, 115–142.

Murai, M. (2015) *From Dog Bridegroom to Wolf Girl: Contemporary Japanese Fairy-Tale Adaptations in Conversation with the West*, Detroit: Wayne State University Press.

Nakamura, M. (2007) "Horror and Machines in Prewar Japan: The Mechanical Uncanny in Yumeno Kyūsaku's *Dogura magura*," in C. Bolton, I. Csicsery-Ronay Jr. and T. Tatsumi (eds) *Robot Ghosts and Wired Dreams: Japanese Science Fiction from Origins to Anime*, Minneapolis and London: University of Minnesota Press, 3–26.

Napier, S. J. (1991) *Escape from the Wasteland: Romanticism and Realism in the Fiction of Mishima Yukio and Ōe Kenzaburō*, Cambridge: Harvard University Press.

Napier, S. J. (1996) *The Fantastic in Modern Japanese Literature: The Subversion of Modernity*, London: Routledge.

Nihei, C. (2013) "Resistance and Negotiation: 'Herbivorous Men' and Murakami Haruki's Gender and Political Ambiguity," *Asian Studies Review* 37 (1) 62–79.

Orbaugh, S. (1999) "Arguing with the Real: Kanai Mieko," in S. Snyder and P. Gabriel (eds) *Ōe and Beyond: Fiction in Contemporary Japan*, Honolulu: University of Hawai'i Press, 245–277.

Otomo, R. (2001) "'The Way of the Samurai': Ghost Dog, Mishima, and Modernity's Other," *Japanese Studies* 21 (1) 31–43.

Plugfelder, G. M. (1999) *Cartographies of Desire: Male-Male Sexuality in Japanese Discourse 1600–1950*, Berkeley and Los Angeles, CA: University of California Press.

Reichert, J. (2006) *In the Company of Men: Representations of Male-Male Sexuality in Meiji Literature*, Stanford, CA: Stanford University Press.

Robertson, J. (2005) "Yoshiya Nobuko: Out and Outspoken in Practice and Prose," in J. Robertson (ed) *Same-Sex Cultures and Sexualities: An Anthropological Reader*, Malden, MA: Blackwell Publishing, 196–211.

Saitō, M. (2006) "Yoshimoto Banana and Girl Culture," trans. E. Sekine, in R. Copeland (ed) *Woman Critiqued: Translated Essays on Japanese Women's Writing*, Honolulu: University of Hawai'i Press, 167–185.

Sakaki, A. (2001) "Kurahashi Yumiko's Negotiations with the Fathers," in R. L. Copeland and E. Ramirez-Christensen (eds) *The Father-Daughter Plot: Japanese Literary Women and the Law of the Father*, Honolulu: University of Hawai'i Press, 292–326.

Schalow, P. G. and Walker, J. A. (eds) (1996) *The Woman's Hand: Gender and Theory in Japanese Women's Writing*, Stanford, CA: Stanford University Press.

Seaman, A. C. (2004) *Bodies of Evidence: Women, Society, and Detective Fiction in 1990s Japan*, Honolulu: University of Hawai'i Press.

Sherif, A. (1999) "Japanese Without Apology: Yoshimoto Banana and Healing," in S. Snyder and P. Gabriel (eds) *Ōe and Beyond: Fiction in Contemporary Japan*, Honolulu: University of Hawai'i Press, 278–301.

Slaymaker, D. N. (2004) *The Body in Postwar Japanese Fiction*, London and New York: RoutledgeCurzon.

Snyder, S. (1999) "Extreme Imagination: The Fiction of Murakami Ryū," in S. Snyder and P. Gabriel (eds) *Ōe and Beyond: Fiction in Contemporary Japan*, Honolulu: University of Hawai'i Press, 199–218.

Starr, R. (1994) *Deadly Dialectics: Sex, Violence, and Nihilism in the World of Yukio Mishima*, Honolulu: University of Hawai'i Press.

Strong, S. (2011) *Ainu Spirits Singing: The Living World of Chiri Yukie's Ainu Shin'yōshū*, Honolulu: University of Hawai'i Press.

Suzuki, M. (2006) "Writing Same-Sex Love: Sexology and Literary Representations in Yoshiya Nobuko's Early Fiction," *The Journal of Asian Studies* 65 (3) 575–599.

Szarota, P. (2010) "Masculinity in Haruki Murakami's Early Novels," in A. Kwiatkowska and A. Chybicka (eds) *Culture & Gender: An Intimate Relation*, Gdansk: Gdanskie Wydawnictwo Psychologiczne, 268–279.

Tanaka, Y. and Hanson, E. (eds) (1982) *This Kind of Woman: Ten Stories by Japanese Women Writers*, Stanford, CA: Stanford University Press.

Tatsumi, T. (2005) "Japanese and Asian Science Fiction," in D. Seed (ed) *A Companion to Science Fiction*, Malden, MA, Oxford and Australia: Blackwell Publishing, 323–336.

Treat, J. (1993) "Yoshimoto Banana Writes Home: 'Shōjo' Culture and the Nostalgic Subject," *The Journal of Japanese Studies* 19 (2) 353–387.

Ueno, C., Ogura, C. and Tomioka, T. (2006) "On Men's Literature," trans. M.T. Mori, in Rebecca Copeland (ed) *Woman Critiqued: Translated Essays on Japanese Women's Writing*, Honolulu: University of Hawai'i Press, 210–234.

Vernon, V. V. (1987) *Daughters of the Moon: Wish, Will, and Social Constraint in Fiction by Modern Japanese Women*, Berkley: University of California Press.

Vincent, K. (2012) *Two-Timing Modernity: Homosocial Narrative in Modern Japanese Fiction*, Cambridge, MA: Harvard University Asia Centre.

Wender, M. L. (ed) (2011) *Into the Light: An Anthology of Literature by Koreans in Japan*, Honolulu: University of Hawai'i Press.

Wilson, M. N. (2013) *Gender Is Fair Game: (Re)Thinking the (Fe)Male in the Works of Ōba Minako*, New York: M.E. Sharpe.

Wu, P. (2007) "Performing Gender Along the Lesbian Continuum: The Politics of Sexual Identity in the Seitō Society," in S. E. Wieringa, E. Blackwood and A. Bhaiya (eds) *Women's Sexualities and Masculinities in a Globalising Asia*, New York and Hampshire, England: Palgrave MacMillan, 77–99.

Yuki, M. (2015) *Foodscape of Contemporary Japanese Women Writers: An Ecocritical Journey Around the Hearth of Modernity*, trans. M. Berman, New York: Palgrave Macmillan.

Zähringer, R. (2017) *Hidden Topographies: Traces of Urban Reality in Dystopian Fiction*, Boston: De Gruyter.

29
GENDER AND POETRY

Andrew Campana

What do we gain from looking at gender and poetry in concert, both within the context of Japanese studies and more broadly speaking? The matter cannot be reduced to a simple drawing of distinctions between "male poets" and "female poets," as has historically so often been the case. Considerations of gender can enhance our understanding of every stage of poetic production, circulation, and reception. How do poets identify, for example, and how does that identity relate, or not, to the voices used in their poems? How do we understand the poet's body and its expression through written text and live poetic performance? What are the gendered divisions within poetry audiences, journal readerships, and poetry societies? What are the gendered aspects of languages in Japan and how are they used in poetry? What are the discourses around what "women's poetry" might look like, or what kind of poems a "woman poet" should write? All of these questions represent collisions between these two concepts, and all are and have been potential sites of analysis, disruption, and play, taken up by poets, critics, and audiences alike.

Moving beyond what gender can tell us about poetry, equally if not more important is what poetry can tell us about gender, which will be the focus of this chapter. Poetry, due to its tendency to be at the cutting edge of experimentation with language, has a special capacity for taking conventional media and modes of expression and remaking them *otherwise*, and also for actively engaging with new developments in the rethinking of sex and gender. Poets and their work have the potential to shape our understanding of gender identity and expression, gendered norms and life experiences, and the distinctions between genders. Masculinities, femininities, and concepts of gender that lie between or beyond these binaries might not only be described, but constructed or challenged through poetic text. Whatever one's operative definition of poetry—as a concentrated form of literature or language art, perhaps, or more broadly as a stance towards composition across multiple media forms—poetry actively aims to do what other art forms do *not*, and that includes the kinds of questions it asks about gender. In this chapter, I will focus on poetry and femininity in contemporary Japan, as a particularly effective lens through which to discuss the complex relationship between poetry and gender more broadly. There is an almost overwhelming abundance of materials that explore this connection in the postwar era, allowing us a way into some of the most pressing and recurring questions about how poetry and gender relate to the body, to literature, to the technologies of reading, to audiences, and to one another. My focus will be on poets from the last few decades who identify as women, whose work is available in English translation, and whose poetry innovatively engages with some of the multiple questions raised previously.

"Women's poetry"?

To think about contemporary poetry and femininity together does not simply mean to look at "poems by women," or to take a category like "women's poetry" as a given, but rather to look at the ways in which the categories of "poem" and "woman" have historically inflected one another and what particular works and figures have done to create and diverge from these norms within a given place and time—in the case of this chapter, at several moments over the last five decades in Japan. As Sara Ahmed points out, when considering the relationship between "woman" and "writing," the "who" of "who is writing" matters not in the sense that the identity of the author (and their gender) fully determines the text's meaning, but in that it "opens out a broader social context which is neither inside or outside of the text itself" (1998, 122).

The pioneering feminist performance poet Shiraishi Kazuko firmly believed this as well. In her much-referenced 1991 article "The 1980s and Women's Poetry [*80 nendai to joseishi*]," Shiraishi traces the conventional genealogy of the modern idea of the "woman poet [*josei shijin*]," starting with Yosano Akiko and her wild, romantic *tanka* in the early twentieth century and Sagawa Chika's sharp-eyed surrealism in the 1920s and 1930s; next are the postwar "women poets" like Ishigaki Rin, Ibaragi Noriko, and Shinkawa Kazue, who explored themes such as motherhood and domesticity in their work through what we might now call a feminist lens, though Shiraishi insists that that term had not yet gained purchase in Japan (1991, 64–65). After that came her own generation, including the cerebral Tada Chimako, the restless and experimental Tomioka Taeko, and the queer poet and community-builder Yoshihara Sachiko; finally, in the 1980s, according to the conventional genealogies, came a "boom" in popularity for "women's poetry" in Japan, with a surge of publication and readership of poetry books and anthologies by women. But Shiraishi expresses her distrust not only for this ostensible "boom" and what led up to it, but also for the category "women's poetry [*joseishi*]" itself. While lauding the emergence of a new generation of women poets influenced by feminist movements in Japan and abroad, she rejects "women's poetry" as a genre outright, seeing it as a discriminatory term that renders women poets into a minority, while dominant groups are able to remain unmarked as, say, "male poets" or "white poets" (1991, 64).

The imaginary poems of Yoko Ono

Yoko Ono is one poet who does not fit into the aforementioned neat, conventional history of postwar "women poets" that Shiraishi sketched out and pushed back against. Her poetic work across media over the last six decades, however, has consistently engaged with questions of femininity, the body, and power, and has been deeply influential in wide-ranging fields of practice. Being equally active in the United States and Japan (hence my rendering her name in the "Western" naming order), and using the English language just as much in her work as Japanese, or more so, has led to Ono being elided in accounts of "Japanese literature." However, it is precisely her troubling of boundaries of nation, language, and media which make her a crucial figure through which to consider poetry and gender in Japan and beyond.

As a pioneering experimental artist in multiple disciplines, poetry, to Ono, is a form in which words—whether spoken or printed on the page—are neither the material nor the boundary of what constitutes a "poem," but rather a catalyst for all manner of creative and poetic acts both on and off the page. Her "Touch Poem #5" from around 1960, for example, eschewed words entirely, taking the form of a notebook into which small blank squares of paper and locks of hair—hers, and others'—are glued onto the page in lieu of written text, making "poetry" into something visceral and concrete, literally consisting of parts of her own body. Writing here has become an act of assemblage of things not normally considered textual, but texture has replaced text; reading has changed too, becoming something tied not solely to visuality but also tactility, scent, and movement.

Perhaps her most significant work in relation to poetry is her seminal 1964 collection of instructional poems, *Grapefruit*, a bilingual art book in English and Japanese in which short poetic texts entreat readers to perform all manner of unusual acts, either actualised or imagined. "Touch poem no. 3" is said to take place in "Nigeria, Africa" on the impossible date of "March 33rd, 1964," the description only telling readers to "wash your hair well before attending" (perhaps in preparation to make poems out of that hair?); "City Piece" asks one to "Walk all over the city with an empty baby carriage"; "Number Piece I" to "Count all the words in the book instead of reading them"; another "Touch Poem" says to "Give birth to a child/See the world through its eye/Let it touch everything possible/and leave its fingermark there/in place of a signature" (Ono 1964). *Grapefruit*'s follow-up, *Acorn*, was written and published about 50 years later. It is a book in much the same vein, but released in the context of a global art and literature scene in which its predecessor left an undeniable impact; indeed, Ono's work in the 1960s was directly responsible for much of what is now called "conceptual art" (Ono 2013).

Within the context of the male-dominated global experimental art scenes of the 1960s—especially those of Tokyo and New York—Ono was a singular figure, using her elite status and cultural capital to create shocking works of feminist visual and performance art, poetry, and music. Perhaps most famous is her 1964 "Cut Piece," performed in Japan and the United States, in which audience members were encouraged to take scissors and cut pieces off the dress Yoko was wearing while she sat on stage, creating a charged scene spectacularizing the interplay between gender, the body, vulnerability, and power. But her explicitly poetic works—including her "Touch Poems," instructional poems, and even her many non-existent poems whose titles she compiled into lists—have just as much to say on the topic of gender. A keyword to link together much of her wildly diverse output might be "imaginary": not necessarily as in make-believe or just daydreaming, but rather an artistic focus on what it means to imagine something—an object, a situation, an activity, a body, a collectivity—into being. Ono takes the basic act of reading—looking at text and conceptualizing or imagining things based on that text—and uses the "poem" as a tool to expand what that act can do, where not only words and letters can be played with, rearranged, and extrapolated upon, but also the body, societal conventions, habits, and gendered expectations and expression.

Put another way, her poems became a launching pad for a kind of wide-ranging imaginative power that aims to directly reshape the world both in thought and action, including the misogyny of which she was a constant target. Over and over, Yoko Ono used her work to ask what it would look like if women had the kind of agency and access that was regularly denied to them even within the ostensibly utopian spaces of unfettered creativity promised in global experimental art scenes. If blank paper and hair can be "read" as a literary text, then the hierarchy of meaning-making with certain kinds of (men's) literary language placed at the top is upended, opened up to alternative forms of poetic practice in which women's bodies are centred—not as fetishised objects or muses, but as both the agents of and literal materials for creation. "Giv[ing] birth to a child"—something that virtually all women were pressured to do at the time of *Grapefruit*'s release—is portrayed as a radical artistic act, through which one can reach out to "everything possible" in the world and leave "fingermark[s]" (Ono 1964). Alternatively, an "empty baby carriage" can be put to use, pushed around the city in "City Piece" in order to generate absurd encounters, the carriage shedding its conventional associations with motherhood, transformed into a receptacle or tool at play in a poem that emerges at the intersection of body, place, and performance.

Itō Hiromi's poems as bodily functions

Itō Hiromi is perhaps the most critically lauded and discussed contemporary "woman poet" in Japan, and it is hard to think of a poet in Japan more strongly associated with issues of gender. Indeed, a prominent workshop on Itō's work held at a university in Japan in 2017 was entitled "Poetry and Gender" (*Jendā to shi*), with the poet herself as the featured guest. Itō emerged onto the scene in the late 1970s with work filled with frank and explicit depictions of women's bodies, bodily processes, and pregnancy, to the extent that, as Jeffrey Angles notes, "many people, both inside and outside the literary world, began calling her by the sobriquet *shussan shijin*, or 'poet of childbirth'," though of course this nickname massively oversimplifies the wild diversity of approaches, themes, and media forms used in her poetry (Itō 2009, x). In Japan's poetry scene, says Shiraishi Kazuko, Itō appeared as a "radical shamaness" who "without using decorative language or metaphor . . . directly used sexual terms, and conveyed the details of sexual acts . . . pregnancy, childbirth, [and] excretion" in a "concrete and frank" way in which poets, especially "women poets" were not allowed or able to do before (1991, 66–67).

Itō is extremely prolific, having published over 40 solo-authored and 20 co-authored books in a variety of genres from 1978 to the present, including a book on sexuality in collaboration with a porn star, two self-illustrated guidebooks on pregnancy and child rearing, a poetry collection featuring intimate nude photographic self-portraits, a documentary film in which she tells stories about her obsession with plucking out her hair, and a huge array of video and audio recordings of her performing her poetic work live. Leith Morton stresses how "the splintering or diffusion of the female voice or female consciousness," somewhat characteristic of several poets in the 1970s and 1980s, reached its extreme in the works of Itō (2004, 102). Even within any given poem, one of the only reliable characteristics is how multi-faceted they are in diction, register, and tone—prayerful, rough, formal, casual, medical—with multiple narrators and sometimes even sizes of text, sometimes evoked by Itō accompanying herself with a tape recording of her own layered voices in live performances.

Centred in the vast majority of her work, however, is the body: women's bodies, in general, and her own body in particular, never stable or disciplined, always mutating, unruly, encroached and encroaching, porous, and fluid. This is in line with Margrit Shildrick's emphasis on the female body as something conceived as inherently "leaky," in many senses of the term—"especial[ly] immanent," fluid (and filled with/excreting fluids), boundary-breaching, threatening the distinctions between "mind/body, self/other, inner/outer"—which, in the "male cultural imaginary," becomes a sort of "unease, even horror" (1994, 12). In an infamous prose poem called "Peristalsis [*Zendō*]," Itō's description of pregnancy takes a clinical tone, as she explores the feeling of having an alien being inside of her. "I am still having the ongoing realization, however, that the thing in my center, behind my bellybutton and connected to my uterus by an umbilical cord, is a foreign object, and not a fetus"; the next few lines multiply the font size several times, however, a not infrequent example in her work of using the visuality of the text to convey an emotional intensity at odds with the detachedness of the words (1985, 95). In "Father's Uterus, or The Map," the first titular object appears, suspended in formaldehyde, seemingly at an exhibit of medical specimens: "And that is you/ The men pointed to a breast with cancer/ And that is my father's uterus/ The men pointed to a uterus that had grown teeth" (Itō 2009, 53). In "Moving," we see one of her signature motifs: the confluence of lactation and ejaculation, two acts of bodily secretion conventionally cordoned off to different sexes in cisnormative accounts of the body—"The reason my breasts leak each night/Is because they want to ejaculate each night" (Itō 2009, 6).

Most significantly, there is a repeated stress throughout her work, implicitly and explicitly, on *poetry as a form of bodily function*, often included in Itō's characteristic litanies of bodily secretions and acts: the narrators of her poems might talk about having diarrhoea, writing poetry, masturbating, giving birth, and lactating, all within one stanza. This has radical implications for how we think about the body, poetry, sex, and gender—poetry becomes corporealized, taken from the abstract realm of text, thought, and idea, and is rendered immanent, concrete, and irrevocably tied to the body from which it came. What is highlighted here is poetry not as a purified or concentrated form of thinking, but as a form of composition and reception emerging through the interaction of fingertips, nerves, and muscles holding the pen or typing on the keyboard; the lips, teeth, tongue, and larynx that produce words aloud; the listener's ear and its tiny vibrating bones, the vitreous and aqueous humours within a reader's eye, and so on. Gender, too, becomes one bodily production among many, something that emerges from the traffic of viscera and excretions across multiple bodies, but is not inherently tied to any of them, femininities and motherhoods and fatherhoods and masculinities rising up, mutated and mutable, from the murk. Itō delights in challenging overly sanitised conventional portrayals of motherhood, not to mention every other body-related taboo; she revels in recreating her own body in her poetry in a fluid, "leaky" way, changing wildly from work to work and medium to medium, across poetic text, illustrations, films, sound recordings, photographs, and live performances.

The artificial poems of Minashita Kiriu

"I/was/born/in the Precambrian Sea/My transparent body/wiggling raw," says the poet Minashita Kiriu in her poem "Life History"; "I/was/born remote/controlled,/fiber optic/Test Quality- Inner- Alive Within" (Minashita 2017, 9–11). A feminist sociologist and critic who has published widely on women's labour, the poverty of single mothers, and marriage, Minashita gained widespread acclaim in the 2000s with her two poetry collections, *Sonic Peace* (2005; English translation 2017) and *Border Z* (2008; selections appear in English translation in Nakayasu 2006; Minashita 2012). Much of Minashita's poetic work deals with electric, electronic, and digital technologies: how they shape subjectivity, how they produce and hinder expression and communication, and the interplay between technology and identity.

Her poetry also differs from many other so-called "women poets" in that it is consistently genderless in its diction, its narrators or main characters, and even in its imagery. On the most obvious level, Japanese, unlike many languages, has several common options for the first-person pronoun, most of which are gendered masculine or feminine. Many male-identified poets, for example, favour "*boku*," while many female-identified poets opt for "*atashi*." The narrators within Minashita's poetry, however, never stray from the relatively neutral "*watashi*"; her *nom-de-plume* is gender ambiguous as well, with "Minashita" meaning field with no water, and "Kiriu" meaning a flow of energy or air.

This neutral "*watashi*" is usually paired in her work with a "*kimi* [you]," also of unspecified gender, with a recurring motif about the possibilities of communication between them and beings in general—helped, hindered, or just made otherwise by electronic technologies. "Taking me connected to you/by vision and audio/On a picnic today as well," states the narrator in "*A Nettai* [Tropic A]" (Minashita 2012). This is not, however, an "I" that is uncomplicatedly equivalent to a single person's perspective; rather, it is a multiplied "I" that coexists, program-like, across many "versions"—"Taking all the versions of me/Now, I'm going to meet you" (Minashita 2012). In "Border Z/Delete, and Rewrite," the narrator asks "Is it possible to melt by communication/Beforehand already constantly"; the title of this section, "raundo • fou [PASSWORD IS INCORRECT]," however, gives a hint to the negative answer, with small "ruby" characters in the katakana script (a syllabary that evokes digitality, among other phenomena) floating next to the main text and announcing computer-like errors and malfunctions embedded in the poem itself (Nakayasu 2006, 15).

More generally speaking, Minashita plays with and rejects the expectations—formed by critics, publishers, audiences, and other poets—that have weighed on "women's poetry" over the last several decades. There are expectations that poems written by women, for example, should be intensely emotional; that they should be concerned with women's bodies, families, and households; that they should be in a "confessional" mode in which the "I" of the poem's speakers are equivalent to the poet herself, writing about her own "real" experiences. In lieu of these, we find in Minashita's work an array of unconventional poetic tropes, metaphors, and bodily descriptions—lightbulbs, coelacanths, cables, iron, organs, and frozen sunlight and thermoexpansion—that are repeatedly deployed, seemingly broadcast from some alternate universe, on a channel to which only she has access. The overarching motif is one of intense *artificiality*: a "made-ness" that is not necessary a "manmade-ness," where building materials and bits of technology take the place of more conventional natural landscapes, and the sun, wind, and rain gain colours, angles, and shapes. This extends to the characters that populate the poems, including the narrators and narratees; they seem not quite human, not quite machine, with transparent skin, lightbulb bodies, wiring, and audio-visual capacities. As a sociologist focused on issues relating to the body and women's labour, however, Minashita is taking a far from neutral stance in her characters' ostensible gender neutrality. Her use of artificiality in her language and imagery swings freely between utopian and dystopian modes, but never fails to take things that are commonly thought of as inherent to what it means to be human—love, relationships, names, life stories, memories, bodies, gender—and create a kind of techno-feminist poetics by portraying them as not just constructed, but *modifiable*.

ni_ka's poetry as augmented reality

One of the figures at the very cutting edge of poetry in the 2010s is the Tokyo-based artist and poet ni_ka. Where Minashita often thematises digitality in her poetic texts, ni_ka favours creating new kinds of poems only made possible through digital media. Most of her works can be categorised as either "monitor poems [*monita-shi*]" or "AR poems [*AR-shi*]." "Monitor poems" are explicitly designed for the computer screen: taking the form of blog posts, the reader scrolls down through forests of emoji, animated GIFs, and constantly moving Japanese text, as hearts, stars, bubbles, flowers, panda bears, and Hello Kitties unfurl, firework-like, across the reader's field of vision, layered over the poem underneath. Her AR, or Augmented Reality poems, use a specialised smartphone app that enables the user to look through one's phone camera at particular locations in Tokyo and beyond, with her poetry literally seeming to float in the air.

Her poetry draws from multiple inspirations, most importantly the experimental use of kanji and visuality by Japanese avant-garde concrete poets like Niikuni Seiichi and Kitazono Katsue and the cutting-edge use of communication technologies by teenage girls. In her monitor poems, there is not only text in a rainbow of colours and in all shapes and sizes, but text that runs across the page; text that bounces; text that hides, flows, and blinks into and out of existence; Japanese scripts are mixed with those of multiple other languages and hundreds or even thousands of images, ranging from the tiniest of emoji to large animations. The words themselves are fragmented and difficult to understand, but the tone is often manifesto-like, with her poems confidently laying out her vision for new forms of poetics. In one poem—with the characteristically complex title of "Ｗ Ｅ Ｂ　　ｈ ａ l l e l u j a h　　「a」 －blood／arch (WEB・Hemal Hallelu jah)" she entreats the reader to "scream through the Web through your heart/so you don't have to use your THROAT" (ni_ka 2014). In another—"'Floating Towards 2011 Monitor Poetry' 2011: A Space Odyssey"—she declares herself the "★★★ apollo of a SUPERFICIAL cute poetic vision ★★★," and that "the ni_ka poetry bloom ✿ has finished its enlightenment 更新 update" (ni_ka 2011).

Through internet-related technologies like blogs, animated images, and smartphone apps, she not only aims to remake how we compose and experience poetry, but also how, for example, poetry can relate to mourning. This is seen in her augmented reality works that fill spaces in Tokyo with candles, flowers, and notes to the victims of the triple disaster in the Tōhoku region of Japan on 11 March 2011. Augmented reality also proves to be an apt description, not just of some of the technologies that ni_ka uses, but of her view of poetry's capacity to affect the world. The majority of works of art and design that take advantage of cutting-edge technologies tends to aim for a "futuristic" masculine or gender-neutral aesthetic; ni_ka's work, on the other hand, is aggressively, garishly, exultantly feminine and cute, challenging the common view of girlish things as frivolous, unserious, or non-technical. Due to the ease of publishing and circulation of texts, especially those that take advantage of multiple media forms, the internet and its many platforms remain the space where one is most likely to encounter the most radical experiments within poetry, like ni_ka's digital work. In her vision, poetry itself becomes the augmentation to our experience of the world; she uses intensely "girly" aesthetics to create a radically intimate connection with digital media, mobilised in ways unintended by the corporate creators of given platforms and technologies.

Conclusion

In this chapter, I aimed to use diverse examples of contemporary Japanese poetry and femininity as a lens through which to show that, no matter the era or medium, a combined analysis of both poetry and gender can only augment the reality of our understanding of each. Other lenses could have been used—topics that have often been taken up by past scholarship include gender and traditional *waka* poetry in the Heian era and (less frequently) haiku and masculinity in the Edo period. A few examples of such work can be found in the "Further Reading" section subsequently. Masculinity remains a highly understudied topic—in relation to poetry, and in Japanese studies more generally—a state of affairs that often has the effect of recreating the masculine as neutral, unmarked, and central, with the feminine as the "other." It is vital to continue interventions in literary and media studies by focusing on and uncovering works that centre women—their stories, achievements, histories, and oppressions. But another side of this feminist project is work that explores the constructedness of masculinity—work that challenges conventional conceptions of maleness and masculinist hierarchies. The role of masculinity in male-dominated poetry scenes throughout Japan's history, modern and pre-modern, is a largely unexplored site of inquiry in the existing academic literature. At a time where conversations surrounding gender are so ubiquitous and fraught, it remains urgent for scholarship to look to poetry as a concentrated site in which both masculinities and femininities have always been evoked, contested, and rethought.

Another significant avenue for future research, and one that has not yet been explored in scholarship in any language, is poetry in relation to transgender experiences in Japan. This would include those of trans women, trans men, and "x-gender [*x-jendā*]" people—the lattermost being a term roughly equivalent to non-binary or genderqueer, an identity between or beyond "female" or "male" that is increasingly prominent within Japan's queer communities (Dale 2012; see also Dale in this volume). Inside and outside of Japan, gender identities and expressions that resist the conventions of masculinity and femininity—or aim to travel fluidly between them—will only gain in prevalence, as communities of gender non-conforming people grow in both on- and offline spaces. It is in these communities, perhaps, that we will find the next wave of poetic pioneers, experimenting with language and media to find new articulations of gender that reflect the reality of their experiences.

Further reading

Beichman, J. (2002) *Embracing the Firebird: Yosano Akiko and the Birth of the Female Voice in Modern Japanese Poetry*, Honolulu: University of Hawaii Press. A key study of how the figure of the "woman poet" formed around Yosano in the early twentieth century.

Vieillard-Baron, M. (2013) "Male? Female? Gender Confusion in Classical Poetry (Waka)," *Cipango—French Journal of Japanese Studies* 2. http://journals.openedition.org/cjs/270. This paper explores classical Japanese poetry and its often fluid relationship with voice and gender.

Schalow, P. G. (1998) "Theorizing Sex/Gender in Early Modern Japan: Kitamura Kigin's *Maidenflowers* and *Wild Azaleas*," *Japanese Studies* 18 (3) 247–263. This paper looks at two Edo-period collections of what might be categorised as women's poetry and queer male poetry respectively, while at the same time troubling those categories.

Sato, H. (2008) *Japanese Women Poets: An Anthology*, Armonk, NY: M. E. Sharp. A wonderful collection that brings together translations of works of over 100 "women poets" from more than a millennium ago to the present, along with biographical notes and commentary.

Yoda, T. (2004) *Gender and National Literature: Heian Texts in the Construction of Japanese Modernity*, Durham: Duke University Press. A deep consideration of not just gender and voice in classical literature but on the ideologies behind the gendering of literatures in different periods of criticism from the early modern to the contemporary era.

References

Ahmed, S. (1998) *Differences that Matter: Feminist Theory and Postmodernism*, Cambridge, UK: Cambridge University Press.

Dale, S. P. F. (2012) "An Introduction to *X-Jendā*: Examining a New Gender Identity in Japan," *Intersections: Gender and Sexuality in Asia and the Pacific* 31. http://intersections.anu.edu.au/issue31/dale.htm

Itō, H. (1985) *Teritori-ron 2* (On Territory 2), Tokyo: Shichōsha.

Itō, H. (2009) *Killing Kanoko: Selected Poems of Hiromi Itō*, trans. J. Angles, Notre Dame, IN: Action Books.

Minashita, K. (2005) *Onsoku Heiwa* (Sonic Peace), Tokyo: Shichōsha.

Minashita, K. (2008) *Zekkyō* (Border Z), Tokyo: Shichōsha.

Minashita, K. (2012) "Minashita Kiriu," trans. L. Morton, *Connotation Press*. www.connotationpress.com/featured-guest-editor/fge-2012/1422-minashita-kiriu-translated-by-leith-morton

Minashita, K. (2017) *Sonic Peace*, trans. E. E. Hyett and S. Thurlow, Los Angeles: Phoneme Media.

Morton, L. (2004) "Language as Feminist Discourse: Contemporary Women's Poetry," in *Modernism in Practice: An Introduction to Postwar Japanese Poetry*, Honolulu: University of Hawai'i Press, 84–112.

Nakayasu, S. (2006) *Four from Japan: Contemporary Poetry & Essays by Women*, Brooklyn: Litmus Press.

ni_ka (2011) "'2011-nen monita-shi e fuyū' 2011: A Space Odyssey ['Floating Towards 2011 Monitor Poetry' 2011: A Space Odyssey," *Nikanika Burogu!* [Nika Nika Blog!] https://web.archive.org/web/20120629121701/https://yaplog.jp/tipotipo/archive/237

ni_ka (2014) "ＷＥＢ ｈａｌｌｅｌｕｊａｈ 「a」 －blood／arch（WEB・Hemal Hallelujah）," trans. A. Campana, *CURA Magazine* 14. http://curamag.com/issues/2014/12/3/renderings-h-a-l-l-e-l-u-j-a-habloodarch

Ono, Y. (1964) *Grapefruit*, Tokyo: Wunternaum Press. Reprinted 2000, New York: Simon and Schuster.

Ono, Y. (2013) *Acorn*, Chapel Hill, NC: Algonquin Books.

Shildrick, M. (1994) *Leaky Bodies and Boundaries: Feminism, Deconstruction, and Bioethics*, PhD Diss., University of Warwick.

Shiraishi, K. (1991) "80 nendai to josei-shi—feminizumu undō to heikō shite" (The 1980s and Women's Poetry—Parallelling the Feminist Movement), *Gendaishi Techō* 34 (9) 64–69.

30
GENDER, MANGA, AND ANIME

Grace En-Yi Ting

Since the 1990s, experts in fields such as literary studies, anthropology, sociology, and film studies have been increasingly active in exploring the histories and politics of popular cultural texts, particularly *manga* (comics) and *anime* (animated works including television series and films). Of particular interest has been the depiction of unconventional forms of gender and sexuality, often within texts involving more ambitious thematic and visual elements than the "average" non-Japanese comic or cartoon. Accompanying the transnational flow of these images, not only have new fandoms sprung up around the globe, but accounts of the seemingly bizarre desires and practices of Japanese fans, or *otaku*, have also become common.

Anime and *manga* in Japan—and, increasingly, outside of Japan—are an inextricable part of daily life, not self-contained, but part of franchises including merchandise, live-action television and film adaptations, and fiction in a media mix permeating society. With genres categorised according to increasingly blurred boundaries of gender and age, *manga* and *anime* not only reflect existing models of gender and sexuality but also reproduce or subvert them. Arguably, one's understanding of social realities—particularly the continued problem of sexism—in contemporary Japan must involve awareness of forms of imagination at work in *anime* and *manga*. Moreover, feminist perspectives—and queer perspectives, focusing on non-normative gender and sexuality—generally encourage new attention to previously dismissed forms of "low" culture and personal experience, such as that of fans.

Subsequently, I provide an overview of trends that have defined the main trajectories thus far in scholarly attention to gender and sexuality in the context of *anime* and *manga*. While I emphasize work available in English, Japanese-language scholarship has been invaluable in informing work by Anglo-American scholars, demonstrated by the place of English-language translations within the narrative subsequently.

The *shōjo*

At the beginnings of English-language *anime* and *manga* research in the 1990s, the *shōjo*, or the girl, appears as a major starting point for discussions concerning the gender and sexual politics of Japanese popular culture. In 1993, literary scholar John Whittier Treat discusses the 1987 debut of young female author Yoshimoto Banana, construed within male-dominated discourses as a *shōjo* symptomatic of Japanese consumer culture who wrote fiction compared to *shōjo manga* (girls' comics). Noting the modern nature of the *shōjo*, who appeared as a figure between childhood and adulthood in the Meiji period (1868–1912), he points to her contemporary reconfiguration as unproductive young woman at the centre of playful *kawaii* (cute) consumer culture, who is "attractive, and thus valorized, but lacks libidinal agency of her own" (Treat 1993, 363). Treat's frequently cited work signals the ambivalence of the *shōjo*, which would figure in studies of *anime* and *manga* texts as well.

Earlier studies of *anime* and *manga* reflect growing awareness of Japanese popular culture as a global phenomenon. For example, Anne Allison examined Tōei's *anime* television series *Sailor Moon* (1992–1997) in the context of consumer culture and global capitalism. She describes the female heroines as simultaneously sexy, fashionable, and strong, observing that the show reflects dual desires: for girls and some boys and men to identify with the girl/heroine, but also, for both female and male fans, "lust for the Sailor Scouts as sex objects" (Allison 2006, 134). In her reading, the postmodern condition is reflected by *Sailor Moon's* global popularity, where we find that identity is "decentered from any one modality/body and is fragmented into multiple pieces that girls around the world can mix and match" (Allison 2006, 160).

Representations of *shōjo* as strong girls also surface in the work of literary scholar Susan J. Napier, which provides an overview of gender and sexuality across numerous genres in textual analyses of metamorphosis, pornography, *mecha* (robot), and gender-bending. Taking up films by *anime* director Miyazaki Hayao, Napier observes the potential for identity construction for Japanese viewers through the *shōjo*, who "exhibits strength *plus* vulnerability in a way that is intriguingly feminine" (Napier 2001, 120). She suggests that Miyazaki's courageous young female characters are inspirational as role models, particularly flying girls who "[send] a message of boundless possibility ... to offer hope of a potentially attainable alternative world that transcends our own" (Napier 2001, 138).

Otaku and *moe*

After initial interest in the *shōjo* in *manga* and *anime* culture, understandings of her role were enriched by perspectives going beyond textual analysis to grapple with problems concerning the roles of male fans. *Otaku*, or fans, often refers by default to heterosexual male fans of *anime*, *manga*, and games, a demographic catapulted to fame in 1989 by the notorious case of Miyazaki Tsutomu, arrested for the serial killings of young girls and labelled by the press as an *otaku*—specifically, a fan of *lolicon*, series featuring sexualised young girls. Responding to the subsequent negative portrayal of *otaku*, scholars have argued for the value and legitimacy of *otaku* and their practices (Galbraith et al. 2015, 2). A key concept in describing *otaku* experience, *moe* generally refers to affection and possibly sexual arousal felt for fictional characters, engendering a range of questions concerning desire seen through *anime* and *manga* culture.

Saitō Tamaki's *Beautiful Fighting Girl* (2011), published in 2000 in Japanese, has further extended the work of Allison, Napier, and others on images of strong *shōjo* in works such as *Sailor Moon*. Drawing upon Lacanian psychoanalysis, psychiatrist Saitō delineates a history of the "beautiful fighting girls" seen in numerous works from the 1960s to the 1990s to outline the characteristics of a phallic girl who is "unaware and uninterested in her own sexual attractiveness," "loved for her ability to fight," and exists as "an absolutely unattainable object of desire" (Saitō 2011, 163–164). Supported by male heterosexual *otaku*, these girls embody intense pleasure and release through the imagination as part of an adaptive strategy for living through the restrictions of contemporary Japanese everyday life.

In response to prejudice in mainstream society construing *otaku* as immature and perverted, Saitō suggests, "In the imaginary realm all human beings have the right to be perverts" (Saitō

2011, 31). In his introduction as translator, literary scholar Keith Vincent acknowledges the argument of media theorist Thomas Lamarre and others who criticize Saitō's assertions concerning the *otaku*'s "normal" heterosexual existence in society—based on a clear separation between fiction and reality—but points to the relevance of Saitō's perspective for scholars interested in non-normative sexualities, arguing, "his articulate defense of the otaku against those who insist that desire must be rooted in real bodies suggests the critically queer potential of otaku sexuality" (Vincent 2011, xxii).

Cultural critic Azuma Hiroki has taken a fundamentally different stance towards the problem of sexuality in *Otaku: Japan's Database Animals* (2009), published in Japanese in 2001. Azuma declares that sexuality is irrelevant for postmodern *otaku*—they are "database animals" interested in neither sexuality nor narrative, instead focused on fulfilling basic needs by consuming *chara-moe, moe* towards characters produced through "fragmentary illustrations or settings" (Azuma 2009, 36). *Moe*-elements are mostly visual but can involve "a particular way of speaking, settings, stereotypical narrative development, and the curves of a figurine" (Azuma 2009, 42), with examples including maid costumes, cat ears, angels, and glasses. Translators Jonathan Abel and Shion Kono explain that Azuma uses philosopher Alexandre Kojève's concept of "animalization" to describe humans who "use cultural products for the immediate satisfaction of needs without searching for or desiring profound underlying meaning from them" (Abel and Kono 2009, xvi). They suggest the potential of Azuma's rejection of an animal/human opposition in the postmodern condition, asking, "Yes, animals are lacking, but we are all animals ... What do animals offer that the human and snobbish alternatives deny?" (Abel and Kono 2009, xxviii).

Several less widely translated Japanese scholars have also contributed to this genealogy of discourses on girls, *otaku* culture, and societal issues. The foremost theorist of popular culture in the 1980s, cultural critic and writer Ōtsuka Eiji has theorized the relationship between the *shōjo*, girls' culture, and late capitalism in ways profoundly influencing Treat and others. Much of his work emphasizes the gendered nature of consumer culture, although he has reflected more generally upon the habits of *otaku* and even the average Japanese consumer heralding "the closing scene of the consumer society that saw the endless play of *things* as signs" (Ōtsuka 2010, 113).

Appearing slightly after Ōtsuka, Miyadai Shinji, a sociologist and cultural critic, is known for his work documenting the *enjo kōsai* (compensated dating) phenomenon of the 1990s and defending the agency of girls involved. He argues that these schoolgirls demonstrate an unprecedented ability to overcome the normative restrictions of society. Miyadai connects phenomena such as *enjo kōsai*, the Aum Shinrikyō gas attacks of 1995, *sekai-kei* (world-type) *anime*, and discrimination against *otaku* to illustrate a broader landscape of contemporary Japan (Miyadai 2011). And, finally, subcultural theorist Uno Tsunehiro represents a new generation of critics, rising to fame for his explanation of the zeitgeist of twenty-first century Japan through popular *anime* and *manga* texts. Reflecting upon changes in the cultural imaginary following the March 2011 tsunami and earthquake, Uno comments upon the gendered escapism of "everyday/atmosphere-type" (*nichijōkei* or *kūkikei*) series depicting the peaceful daily lives of girls in a school setting, excluding "not only a close observation of minimal interpersonal relations but also factors such as heterosexuality, family composition, and old age" (Uno 2015, 134).

These scholars as a group have offered provocative investigations of *otaku* and *moe* embedded in historical trends in contemporary Japan, using interdisciplinary methods including textual analysis, ethnography, and Western philosophy to theorize *anime* and *manga* culture's central role in the transforming nature of narrative and media in Japan. In moving past denigration of *otaku* desire, the imagination of *otaku* culture—seen at events such as Tokyo's Comic Market, which attracts about half a million attendees twice per year (Lam 2010, 232)—serves as a rich topic of analysis.

Shōjo manga

If studies of *otaku* and *moe* have emphasized male fans, work on *shōjo manga*—or girls' comics, referring to *manga* targeting young female readers—has shared a commitment to acknowledging the desires and agency of girls and women as well as theorizing a unique homosocial space for community and expression beginning with male artists but eventually dominated by "female artists who shared the same desires and dreams with girls" (Toku 2007, 23). Feminist perspectives have served as the driving force behind recent research delineating *shōjo manga* as a historically important genre. This work recognizes systemic sexism in modern Japan and views *shōjo manga*—and girls' culture more broadly—in terms of its potentially subversive role but also its complicity in reproducing gender and sexual norms.

Importantly, Takeuchi Kayo has charted a longer history of *shōjo manga* research in Japan compared with scholarly activity in English (Takeuchi 2010). Since the early 1990s, translations of short pieces by Fujimoto Yukari, a groundbreaking *shōjo manga* scholar, have appeared (Fujimoto 1991), but recently a surge in translation has offered additional resources on *shōjo manga* history, representation, and readership. Among major contributions are the *U.S.-Japan Women's Journal* 2010 special issue on *shōjo manga* in which Takeuchi's essay appears alongside work by other Japanese scholars (Aoyama et al., 2010); Tomoko Aoyama and Barbara Hartley's collection *Girl Reading Girl in Japan* (2012), which includes a 1982 essay by Honda Masuko, a pioneering scholar of girls' culture; and Masami Toku's *International Perspectives on Shojo and Shojo Manga: The Influence of Girl Culture* (2015), which features essays by both Japanese and non-Japanese scholars, as well as interviews with Japanese *manga* artists and critics.

Deborah Shamoon's *Passionate Friendship* (2012) has been the first full-length study in English to build on earlier work to provide an extensive history of *shōjo manga*, from its prewar origins to its dramatic transformation in the 1970s. First, Shamoon examines early representations of the *shōjo* as schoolgirl within novels by canonical male authors of the Meiji period, where the *shōjo* operates "as both the object of the desiring male gaze and the ultimate Other that threatens to disrupt the family unit and … the Japanese nation as a whole" (Shamoon 2012, 14) alongside the redefining of femininities in the rise of education for girls. Moving to the realm of mass culture in the Taishō (1912–1926) and early Shōwa (1926–1989) periods, she engages with the all-female theatre troupe Takarazuka and illustrated girls' magazines and fiction containing aesthetics of exaggerated eyes and decorative styles, reflecting "the ideals of girls' culture: innocence, purity, longing, and the beauty of the S relationship" (Shamoon 2012, 68), found in fleeting romantic relationships built on "spiritual" love between girls.

These prewar aesthetics influenced male artists in the immediate postwar period who were central to the development of *shōjo manga*, such as Tezuka Osamu and Takahashi Macoto, as well as the emergence of the subgenre of boys love and Ikeda Riyoko's classic gender-bending *manga Rose of Versailles* (1972–1973) in the 1970s. Importantly, the female "Year of '24" (*24-nen-gumi*) artists born around the year Shōwa 24 (1949)—including Ikeda, Hagio Moto, Takemiya Keiko, Ōshima Yumiko, and others—have been widely credited for the soaring popularity of *shōjo manga* in the 1970s, shaping not only the future of *shōjo manga* as a genre but influencing other genres and media as well. These artists disregarded existing convention to experiment with interior monologue, images spilling over panels, and layering to prioritize the depiction of emotions, creating "what Takemiya refers to as the 'lawlessness' of *shōjo manga*, that is, a world in which emotion is given free range" (Shamoon 2012, 116). This innovation allowed for a strong emphasis on emotions represented specifically through *manga* as a unique medium, suggesting one reason the focus of existing scholarship remains oriented more towards *shōjo manga* rather than *anime*.

Alongside the embrace of emotions and striking montage-style layouts, as well as decorative or literally flowery motifs, *shōjo manga* has been known for representations of gender-bending characters and homoerotic relationships—in short, what we might consider queer or non-normative forms of gender and sexuality. In her classic study of Takarazuka, Robertson discussed how the revue served as inspiration for *manga* artist and *anime* director Tezuka's *Princess Knight* (1953–1956), a precedent for *Rose of Versailles*, which in turn was adapted to become the revue's most successful postwar production in a history of mutual influence (Robertson 1998, 74). *Princess Knight* is a well-known early example of *dansō* ("female-to-male" cross-dressing), in which the heroine Sapphire is forced throughout much of the narrative to dress as a male prince in order to ensure her path to the throne. Fujimoto has commented on the status of *Princess Knight* as the first "story *manga*" (long serialized *manga*) in the history of *shōjo manga* and declared, "when Takarazuka was transplanted into *manga* at the hands of Tezuka Osamu, the direction of *shōjo manga* was determined" (Fujimoto 2004, 78).

Another case of *dansō* performed out of filial duty, the woman Oscar in *Rose of Versailles* serves Marie Antoinette as the leader of the Royal Guards before dying in the French Revolution. Critics have discussed the legendary status of this *manga*, with Nobuko Anan arguing that it represented the "contradictory desires" of women during the *ūman ribu* (woman's liberation) movement of the 1970s, so that "through her death, [Oscar] lives as an androgyne, an egalitarian, an aristocrat, a patriotic soldier, and a child of Mars" (Anan 2014, 60). A more recent work, the 1990s *manga* and *anime Revolutionary Girl Utena*—produced by artist Saitō Chiho and the collective Be-Papas—is frequently discussed alongside these two series and features the cross-dressing character Utena who aspires to be a "prince," dreams of meeting the "prince" from her childhood, and fights in fantastical duels to defend Anthy, the so-called "Rose Bride." Japanese feminist media scholar Kotani Mari points to Saitō's battling or fighting girl as a "mirror of boys' desires, for their liberation" (Kotani 2006, 166). For Kotani, the girl-prince Utena is such a figure, who nonetheless, along with Anthy, also contains the potential "to liberate femininity and female desire" (Kotani 2006, 168).

Such representations often have ambivalent gender and sexual politics, situated somewhere between performing in transgressive ways and reinforcing heteronormative standards. *Shōjo manga* shies away from depicting female sexual desire, although this is remedied to some extent by *shōjo manga*'s offshoot, ladies' comics (*redīsu komikkusu*) (Ogi 2003). Jennifer Prough, in her ethnographic study of the *shōjo manga* industry, has also argued that the affective labour of *shōjo manga* "at once creates relationships and community while reifying the salience of gender and the role of women as the consummate consumers" (Prough 2011, 136). Meanwhile, Sharalyn Orbaugh remarks upon how Sapphire in *Princess Knight* ultimately "learns to accept her feminine gender in a heterosexual romance" (Orbaugh 2003, 208) and circles back to problems of male-dominated *otaku* culture by linking this celebrated classic text to 1990s "*man*-made" female protagonists in *manga* and *anime*, with "their strong and talented bodies … not for maximizing their own pleasure or satisfaction but for serving the purposes of the state or their (always male) creator, or both" (Orbaugh 2003, 226). *Shōjo manga* continues to exist as an ambivalent gendered space, but one generally open to feminist and queer purposes, with artist Hagio Moto saying, "Although men may laugh and underestimate the value of shojo manga, I believe that all female power is hidden and untold in shojo manga" (Hagio 2015, 211).

Boys love

Some of the most challenging and provocative analysis concerning the subversion of gender and sexual norms has been raised by recent work on a subgenre of *shōjo manga* called boys love, also known as BL or *shōnen ai* in Japanese and English, referring to representations of male-male romance. The term *yaoi* has sometimes been used as an umbrella term for texts involving male-male romance but often refers to fiction and art by fans creating romantic pairings of male characters from popular *anime* and *manga* series. Today, boys love studies has flourished into an interdisciplinary area of research, seen in recent collections engaging with "diverse fields including anthropology, cultural studies, history, literature, and sociology" (McLelland et al. 2015, 3).

By the early 2000s, English-language scholarship noted that these *manga* allow for female readers to identify with male characters in order to experiment with gender and sexuality in a space of fantasy removed from the restrictive realities of Japanese society (McLelland 2000; Ogi 2001). The formation of boys love as a genre is widely acknowledged to be marked by the androgynous *bishōnen*, or beautiful boys, of Hagio Moto's *The Heart of Thomas* (1974) and Takemiya Keiko's *The Song of the Wind and the Trees* (1976–1984), two early boys love texts at the heart of the 1970s revolution in *shōjo manga*. These texts depend upon exoticised Western settings to create an atmosphere of fantasy, sharing a fascination with both androgyny and the West with Takarazuka and other series such as *Rose of Versailles*.

While research initially emphasized feminist perspectives, later arguments reflect the influence of Anglo-American queer theory, which seeks to question limitations of heteronormativity more broadly. James Welker argues for a perspective taking into account possibilities "of liberating readers not just from patriarchy but from gender dualism and heteronormativity" (Welker 2006, 843). Welker refers to reader responses to suggest the significance of boys love for members of the Japanese lesbian community. Along similar lines, lesbian scholar and activist Akiko Mizoguchi has declared, "I write from the subject position of a fan and a researcher who 'became' a lesbian via reception, in my adolescence, of the 'beautiful boy' comics of the 1970s" (Mizoguchi 2003, 49). Nevertheless, tension also exists between *fujoshi*—(often) heterosexual female fans of boys love—and LGBT individuals in Japan, seen early on in the 1992 "*yaoi* dispute" (*yaoi ronsō*) when "one gay man criticized *yaoi* stories as discriminatory against gay men" in a feminist zine (Hori 2013).

At the intersection of scholarship on *otaku* and *shōjo manga*, boys love has offered opportunities to investigate female *otaku* in the form of *fujoshi*. In addition to writing on *moe* and male *otaku*, Patrick Galbraith has conducted ethnographic studies of *fujoshi* arguing for the queer "transgressive intimacy" of *fujoshi* practices in which they "reinterpret touches, words, and glances in *shōnen* manga as indirect expressions of affection" (Galbraith 2011, 213) in playful misreadings of existing series. Yaoi culture, particularly *dōjinshi* (fan-created *manga*), represents some of the most creative aspects of *otaku* culture. Although scholarship on boys love began with an emphasis on textual analysis, anthropological and sociological studies of fandoms now make up a substantial portion of the field.

Work on boys love continues to expand along a range of trajectories. Recent collections have dealt with topics including transnational fandoms; depictions of female characters; alternate histories behind contemporary boys love; the shifting nature of terms and genres; intersections between boys love, feminism, and LGBT identities in recent *manga*; and the diversification of readership such as with *fudanshi*, or heterosexual male fans of boys love (Levi et al. 2010; Nagaike and Suganuma 2013; McLelland et al. 2015). It is important to note that boys love has also been shown by literary scholar Kazumi Nagaike and others to have close ties to fiction by modern Japanese women writers (Nagaike 2012).

Conclusion

Explorations of gender and sexuality in *anime* and *manga* studies in English began with the *shōjo* as a recurrent object of study in a period when the impact of *anime* and *manga* was beginning to be felt globally outside of Japan. The striking—young, beautiful, active, and sometimes androgynous—girls appearing in *manga* and *anime* texts, as well as reports of girls wielding consumer power in postmodern Japan, reflected much of what is still fascinating and difficult to evaluate about the gender and sexual politics of Japan. Attention to the *shōjo* was followed by the translation of Japanese theories concerning the reception of texts by male *otaku*. Key to these arguments was the emphasis on *moe* as a new form of narrative consumption and/or sexuality. At the same time, research on *shōjo manga* began to flourish, with emphasis placed on the agency of female readers and communities, as well as a history of gender-bending and other possibly transgressive depictions. Currently, the most active area of research is arguably boys love studies, which poses questions concerning queer aspects of boys love and *fujoshi* culture.

In summary, questions such as the following have defined much research up to this point: are depictions of powerful girls subversive or not? Along similar lines, how do we evaluate gender-bending or homoerotic characters? Are attachments to fictional characters—often young and female—perverse, sexist, and immature, or can we instead see them as transgressive or queer? Especially in recent years, scholars have tended towards arguing for the feminist or queer potential of these representations and relationships to texts, even while suggesting how *anime* and *manga* simultaneously reinforce certain gender and sexual norms. Intellectual exchange between Japanese and English scholarship has helped lead to richer, thought-provoking perspectives on these issues. Similarly, attention to the transnational, such as the recent emphasis on boys love culture within Asia, has helped promote issues of intersectionality.

What are future trajectories that would lend themselves towards expanding the breadth of analyses of gender and sexuality in *anime* and *manga*? First, attention should continue to be spent on the translation of Japanese-language scholarship or work in other languages, leading to better grasp of historical context, greater diversity in terms of perspectives, and increased creativity in developing interdisciplinary approaches. Crucially, seminal texts need to be translated and circulated with a critical eye concerning problems of sexism, even in the case of famed cultural critics. For example, despite powerful arguments for queer elements of *otaku* culture, feminist scholars such as Kotani have stated, with less enthusiasm, that *moe* does not represent a significant break in the male approach to fantasy, also seen with male fandoms of female idols (performers) (Kotani 2014).

Additionally, the *shōjo* and *shōjo manga* have long existed as focal points for discussions of gender and sexuality, and recent volumes such as *Shōjo Across Media: Exploring "Girl" Practices in Contemporary Japan* (Berndt et al. 2019) demonstrate that much room still exists for new insight. Nevertheless, critiques of other figures and genres are also needed. In part, this tendency may be explained by the projection of social anxieties onto female bodies in times of social transformation or—on the other hand—the feminist politics of promoting the value of girls' culture. In addition, we might note *shōjo manga*'s fascinating representation of unusual sexualities and gender-bending characters, or even the gender-bending practices of female readers experimenting with sexuality through depictions of male bodies. Nevertheless, feminist and queer approaches have valuable contributions to make in other areas, such as with increased analyses of masculinities or genres targeting boys or men, known as *shōnen* and *seinen manga/anime*, respectively. Angela Drummond-Mathews points to the enormous popularity of *shōnen manga* in Japan and on a global level as a genre consumed "by boys, men, girls, and women alike" (2010).

And although boys love studies in particular has become representative of queer work in *manga* and *anime* studies, varied frameworks and perspectives are needed in order to challenge limitations to how we understand gender and sexuality or—in other words—to keep alive the political significance of a concept such as "queer" in terms of non-normative or radical potential. Such work might involve turning scholarly attention to overlooked forms of representation that initially seem to possess less literary value or appear overly conventional. At present, with growing interest in Japanese popular culture within the academy, *anime* and *manga* contain numerous possibilities for research on gender and sexuality that have yet to be realised.

Related Chapters

27 Performing Gender: Cosplay and Otaku Cultures and Spaces
31 Cuteness Studies and Japan
33 Gender, Media, and Misogyny in Japan
34 Representing Girls in Cinema

References

Abel, J. E. and Kono, S. (2009) "Translators' Introduction," in H. Azuma (ed) *Otaku: Japan's Database Animals*, Minneapolis, MN: University of Minnesota Press.
Allison, A. (2006) *Millennial Monsters: Japanese Toys and the Global Imagination*, Berkeley, CA: University of California Press.
Anan, N. (2014) "*The Rose of Versailles*: Women and Revolution in Girls' Manga and the Socialist Movement in Japan," *The Journal of Popular Culture* 7 (1) 41–63.
Aoyama, T., Dollase, H. T. and Kan, S. (2010) *Shōjo Manga: Past, Present, and Future* (special issue). U.S.-Japan Women's Journal 38.
Aoyama, T. and Hartley, B. (eds) (2012) *Girl Reading Girl in Japan*, New York: Routledge.
Azuma, H. (2009) *Otaku: Japan's Database Animals*, trans. J. E. Abel and S. Kono, Minneapolis, MN: University of Minnesota Press.
Berndt, J., Nagaike, K. and Ogi, F. (2019) *Shōjo Across Media: Exploring "Girl" Practices in Contemporary Japan*, New York: Palgrave Macmillan.
Drummond-Mathews, A. (2010) "What Boys Will Be: A Study of Shōnen Manga," in T. Johnson-Woods (ed) *Manga: An Anthology of Global and Cultural Perspectives*, New York: Continuum.
Fujimoto, Y. (1991) "A Life-Size Mirror: Women's Self-Representation in Girls' Comics," trans. J. Dvorak, *Review of Japanese Culture and Society* 4 53–57.
Fujimoto, Y. (2004) "Transgender: Female Hermaphrodites and Male Androgynes," trans. L. Flores, K. Nagaike and S. Orbaugh, *US-Japan Women's Journal* 27 76–117.
Galbraith, P. W. (2011) "*Fujoshi*: Fantasy Play and Transgressive Intimacy Among 'Rotten Girls' in Contemporary Japan," *Signs* 37 (1) 219–240.
Galbraith, P. W., Kam, T. H. and Kamm, B. O. (2015) "Introduction," in P. W. Galbraith, T. H. Kam and B. O. Kamm (eds) *Debating Otaku in Contemporary Japan: Historical Perspectives and New Horizons*, London: Bloomsbury Publishing.
Hagio, M. (2015) "Profile and Interview with Moto Hagio," trans. M. Toku and J. Aull, in M. Toku (ed) *International Perspectives on Shojo and Shojo Manga: The Influence of Girl Culture*, London: Routledge.
Hori, A. (2013) "On the Response (or Lack Thereof) of Japanese Fans to Criticism That *Yaoi* Is Antigay Discrimination," trans. N. Noppe, *Transformative Works and Cultures* 12.
Kotani, M. (2006) "Metamorphosis of the Japanese Girl: The Girl, the Hyper-Girl, and the Battling Beauty," *Mechademia* 1 162–169.
Kotani, M. (2014) "Interview with Kotani Mari," trans. P. W. Galbraith, in P. W. Galbraith (ed) *The Moe Manifesto: An Insider's Look at the Worlds of Manga, Anime, and Gaming*, North Clarendon, VT: Tuttle Publishing.
Lam, F. Y. (2010) "Comic Market: How the World's Biggest Amateur Comic Fair Shaped Japanese *Dōjinshi* Culture," *Mechademia* 5 232–248.
Levi, A., McHarry, M. and Pagliassotti, D. (eds) (2010) *Boys' Love Manga: Essays on the Sexual Ambiguity and Cross-Cultural Fandom of the Genre*, London: McFarland.
McLelland, M. (2000) *Male Homosexuality in Modern Japan: Cultural Myths and Social Realities*, New York: Routledge.
McLelland, M., Nagaike, K., Suganuma, K. and Welker, J. (eds) (2015) *Boys Love Manga and Beyond: History, Culture, and Community in Japan*, Jackson, MS: University Press of Mississippi.

Miyadai, S. (2011) "Transformation of Semantics in the History of Japanese Subcultures Since 1992," trans. S. Kono, *Mechademia* 6 231–258.

Mizoguchi, A. (2003) "Male-Male Romance by and for Women in Japan: A History and the Subgenres of *Yaoi* Fictions," *US-Japan Women's Journal* 25 49–75.

Nagaike, K. (2012) *Fantasies of Cross-Dressing: Japanese Women Write Male-Male Erotica*, Boston, MA: Brill.

Nagaike, K. and Suganuma, K. (2013) "Transnational Boys' Love Fan Studies," (special issue) *Transformative Works and Cultures* 12. https://doi.org/10.3983/twc.2013.0504

Napier, S. (2001) *Anime from Akira to Princess Mononoke: Experiencing Contemporary Japanese Animation*, New York: Palgrave Macmillan.

Ogi, F. (2001) "Gender Insubordination in Japanese Comics (*Manga*) for Girls," in J. A. Lent (ed) *Illustrating Asia: Comics, Humor Magazines, and Picture Books*, Honolulu, HI: University of Hawai'i Press.

Ogi, F. (2003) "Female Subjectivity and *Shoujo* (Girls) *Manga* (Japanese Comics): *Shoujo* in Ladies' Comics and Young Ladies' Comics," *The Journal of Popular Culture* 36 (4) 780–803.

Orbaugh, S. (2003) "Busty Battlin' Babes: The Evolution of the *Shōjo* in 1990s Visual Culture," in J. S. Mostow, N. Bryson and M. Graybill (eds) *Gender and Power in the Japanese Visual Field*, Honolulu, HI: University of Hawai'i Press.

Ōtsuka, E. (2010) "World and Variation: The Reproduction and Consumption of Narrative," trans. M. Steinberg, *Mechademia* 5 99–116.

Prough, J. S. (2011) *Straight from the Heart: Gender, Intimacy, and the Cultural Production of Shōjo Manga*, Honolulu, HI: University of Hawai'i Press.

Robertson, J. (1998) *Takarazuka: Sexual Politics and Popular Culture in Modern Japan*, Berkeley, CA: University of California Press.

Saitō, T. (2011) *Beautiful Fighting Girl*, trans. K. Vincent, Minneapolis, MN: University of Minnesota Press.

Shamoon, D. (2012) *Passionate Friendship: The Aesthetics of Girls' Culture in Japan*, Honolulu, HI: University of Hawai'i Press.

Takeuchi, K. (2010) "The Genealogy of Japanese *Shōjo Manga* (Girls' Comics) Studies," *U.S.-Japan Women's Journal* 38 81–112.

Toku, M. (2007) "Shojo Manga! Girls' Comics! A Mirror of Girls' Dreams," *Mechademia* 2 19–32.

Toku, M. (ed) (2015) *International Perspectives on Shojo and Shojo Manga: The Influence of Girl Culture*, New York: Routledge.

Treat, J. W. (1993) "Yoshimoto Banana Writes Home: *Shōjo* Culture and the Nostalgic Subject," *Journal of Japanese Studies* 19 (2) 353–387.

Uno, T. (2015) "Imagination after the Earthquake: Japan's *Otaku* Culture in the 2010s," trans. J. C. Guarneri, *Verge* 1 114–136.

Vincent, J. K. (2011) "Translator's Introduction," in T. Saitō (ed) *Beautiful Fighting Girl*, Minneapolis, MN: University of Minnesota Press.

Welker, J. (2006) "Beautiful, Borrowed, and Bent: 'Boys' Love' as Girls' Love in *Shôjo Manga*," *Signs: Journal of Women in Culture and Society* 31 (3) 841–870.

31
CUTENESS STUDIES AND JAPAN

Joshua Paul Dale

Kawaii, cute, cuteness

Kawaii and cute are increasingly prominent aesthetics in contemporary global culture. While Japan's kawaii boom arguably began in the 1970s (Kinsella 1995, 220), it wasn't until the late twentieth/early twenty-first century that cuteness began to explode worldwide as the number of cute images, commodities, foods, fashions, and fandoms underwent rapid expansion (Dale 2017, 1). The new field of cuteness studies, formed to address this phenomenon, analyzes not only its history and development, but also the connection between cuteness and gender, race, ethnicity, age, nationality, politics, and interspecies affiliations. Its aim is to take seriously what is often dismissed as a facile commodity aesthetic because of its gendered association with femininity, childhood, and the domestic sphere (Dale 2017, 2; Ngai 2012, 3).

Until recently, the study of kawaii was primarily concerned with how this aesthetic emerged and propagated in Japan. Now, cuteness studies as a whole is taking on an expanding number of themes and concerns. Both the "Cute Studies" issue of the *East Asian Journal of Popular Culture* (2016) and the edited volume *The Aesthetics and Affects of Cuteness* (2017) place the kawaii and cute aesthetics within the framework of cuteness affect by considering cultures of emotion as well as commodity consumption. An issue of *M/C Journal* (2014) explores both aesthetics within the digital realm, while *The Retrofuturism of Cuteness* (2017) takes on the fascinating project of exploring the viability of reading cuteness into historical periods prior to the aesthetic's—and the word's—existence. Simon May's *The Power of Cute* (2019) makes the case that cute and kawaii are key aesthetics to explain the current Zeitgeist. My forthcoming book *Irresistible: How Cuteness Wired Our Brains and Conquered the World* explores the origins of this affective response deep in our evolutionary past and traces the development of both the cute and kawaii aesthetics up to the present day. Thus, cuteness studies challenges conventional ways of thinking about time and geographical space, as well as gendered subjectivities, by analyzing both the cute and kawaii aesthetics while also considering the common affect that underlies them.

The influence of Japanese kawaii on the global popularity of cuteness is growing rapidly. Scholarly works such as Christine Yano's *Pink Globalization: Hello Kitty's Trek Across the Pacific* attest to the importance of kawaii as a form of soft power that negotiates both within and beyond national and ethnic identities in a globalized consumer market. Yet scholars sometimes fail to see the differences between Japanese kawaii and other cute aesthetics (Ngai 2012, 78;

Plourde 2016, 7). In this chapter, I contend that the aesthetic of cute is rooted in the etymology of the English word in a way that positions it in opposition to kawaii. This fundamental difference makes it difficult for those steeped in cute to understand kawaii and vice versa. It also means that critical insights gained from the study of one aesthetic may become valuable tools for analyzing the other.

This chapter employs the word "cuteness" to indicate the affective reaction felt when a subject finds an object to be cute or kawaii. In addition to the scholarship in cultural and media studies outlined previously, there is a burgeoning amount of research in the physical and behavioural sciences on this affect. Empirical methods of data collection employed in over 50 years of scientific study range from simple surveys to increasingly sophisticated ways of tracking the body's physical reactions to cuteness. fMRI and MEG brain scan studies of subjects exposed to images of babies manipulated to show high levels of cuteness revealed significant activity in the reward centres of the brain (Glocker 2009; Kringelbach 2008). Taken as a whole, this body of scholarship indicates that the cuteness response has its origins in the evolution of *Homo sapiens*.

Our ability to feel cuteness may be based in an evolutionary mechanism brought about by natural selection, but there are important cultural components to the aesthetics that have developed around this affect. Starting in childhood, experience and learning drawn from family and friends as well as media representations become the foundations of the disparate aesthetics of cute and kawaii. Seen in this light, the evolutionary origin of the cuteness response provides a starting point: a common ground from which to elucidate the cultural differences at work in the way this emotion is stimulated, expressed, and communicated. The most fundamental of these differences lies in the etymology of "cute" and "kawaii," so this is where I begin.

According to the *Oxford English Dictionary*, "cute," a shortened form of "acute," may also mean "clever or cunning." Accordingly, native English speakers are apt to view cute objects or people as inherently manipulative (Ngai 2012, 86). On the other hand, though the dictionary definition of kawaii still includes "pitiable" among its meanings, in modern usage, the word has lost all negative associations: kawaii is an affective adjective that simply expresses the feeling of cuteness (Nittono 2016, 81; Yomota 2006, 73). Thus, while "Don't be cute!" is a common admonition in American English, there is no equivalent phrase in Japanese using the word kawaii. One may say, "don't be childish" in Japanese, but "don't be cute" has no direct translation.

This difference has profound effects. In this chapter, I outline the history and development of kawaii in Japan to ascertain why this gendered aesthetic originally associated with children, girls, and women has spread to so many areas of contemporary Japanese culture and investigate the social implications of its popularity on both women and men. Turning to the scholarship on the cute aesthetic, I examine how its secondary meaning of clever has caused many scholars to locate negative affects, from despair and abjection to sadism and violence, at the heart of this seemingly benign aesthetic. Finally, I propose that kawaii culture—still driven by, but no longer solely associated with, Japanese girls and women—may provide an alternative viewpoint that would benefit scholarship on the cute aesthetic.

History and development of the kawaii aesthetic

Like the English cute, the word kawaii did not enter common usage until the late nineteenth/early twentieth century. However, cuteness has been expressed in Japanese literature and art for almost a thousand years, and its deepest origins lie in Japanese women's culture. *The Pillow Book (Makura no Sōshi)*, completed by court attendant Sei Shonagon in 1002, includes objects and behaviours now called kawaii in her list of beautiful (*utsukushii*) things. These include young children in ceremonial costumes, dolls and small things in general, plus interactions with baby birds and children (Shirane 2007, 277).

The word kawaii derives from *kawahayushi*, which first appeared in the *Anthology of Tales from the Past (Konjaku Monogatarishū)* from the late Heian period (late twelfth century). Literally "face dazzled," it meant ashamed, describing the case when one's face flushes due to a guilty conscience; even today, characters in manga and anime are drawn with reddened cheeks to indicate they are feeling *kawaii*, and this blushing reaction occurs in people as well (Esposito 2014). This word evolved into *kawayui* over the next few hundred years, and the meaning shifted to pitiful or vulnerable. Yomota Inuhiko traces the first appearance of the (proto) word kawaii to 1603, when the word "*cauaij*" appeared in a Japanese-to-Portuguese dictionary compiled by the Society of Jesuits in Nagasaki (34). At that time the Japanese word was *kawairashii* (*kahayurashi*) (Yomota 2006, 29–36). The modern meaning of kawaii is expressed by this word as early as 1686 in the novel *The Life of an Amorous Woman (Kōshoku Ichidai Onna)* (Yomota 2006, 34). By the late Edo era, the connotation of pity had disappeared and kawaii attained its present meaning: a sense of love or affection, especially but not exclusively felt for small, vulnerable things such as children and animals (Nittono 2016, 81).

The explosion of printmaking (*ukiyoe*) in the Edo period (1603–1868) included many artists whose works are perceived as kawaii today. The mid-Edo period saw the publication of albums of comic pictures (*toba ehon*) by Ōka Shunboku, Hasegawa Mitsunobu, and others. Considered a forerunner of modern manga, many of the drawings they contain are cute as well as funny (Shimizu 2013, 16). Several recent exhibitions have collected works that showcase the development of kawaii in the visual arts throughout the Edo period. The exhibited works may be seen in several published catalogs (Fucho Art Museum 2013; Hinohara 2017; Takahashi 2014).

A two-part exhibit at the Fuchu Art Museum in 2013 divided kawaii artworks into several areas. These included works that evoke emotional qualities such as pitiable, *kenage* (admiration for something small trying its best despite its diminutive size); funny; pure/innocent and small/alone; general principles such as geometry of form, minimalist techniques, and reiteration; childlike forms; and qualities such as the charms of awkwardness and naivety. This exhibition was intended to define and display the precepts of kawaii as they gradually emerged in Japanese art. The exhibition was quite popular, and I found the visiting crowd engaged in continual discussion about whether particular works were or were not kawaii.

Going forward from the Edo period to the twentieth century requires consideration of the *shōjo* (adolescent girls), who would become the first mass market for kawaii goods and images. The category of *shōjo* emerged through late nineteenth and early twentieth century educational reforms. These focused on the education of boys who, in an increasingly militarized Japan, were being formed by the state to become future soldiers. Girls' education beyond elementary school was only available to the urban middle and upper classes and sought merely to turn them into mothers and wives (Takahashi 2013, 116). Thus *shōjo* emerged as a liminal category, indicating girls who were protected not only from sexual activity but also physical labour. Early twentieth-century magazines marketed to girls emphasized this status by featuring images of dreamy, fashionable girls indulging in a world of the imagination (Takahashi 2013, 116). Though this ideal was modelled on the upper classes and the nobility, it provided a popular aspirational model for girls of the middle classes (Kawamura 1994, 32).

In 1914, a key event in the history of kawaii occurred: the illustrator Takehisa Yumeji opened a shop in Nihonbashi, Tokyo, that sold his own line of products to schoolgirls such as embroidery, writing paper, umbrellas, dolls, and so on (Nakamura 2013, 13). Takehisa mixed traditional Japanese and contemporary Western themes into his designs, incorporating items such as musical scales and playing cards (Nakamura 2012, 10–13), and referred to his designs as kawaii, an

Figure 31.1 Nagasawa Rosetsu's late 18th c. depiction of a frolicking puppy.
Source: Courtesy of Homma Museum of Art.

early use of the word (Nakamura 2013, 13). He represents a pioneering example of artists who blurred the boundary between fictional worlds and reality by offering young girls the chance "to literally buy into the *shōjo* look" (Takahashi 2013, 117). Moving forward a few decades, Nakahara Junichi, who specialized in drawing dreamy girls with large eyes, was extremely popular among girls in the 1930s. A postwar revival of his style made him very influential in the development of the kawaii aesthetic further in the century (Takahashi 2013, 119–120).

Kawaii extends its reach

In postwar Japan, kawaii continued its rise as an aesthetic largely aimed at and consumed by girls and, increasingly, women. From the 1950s, the illustrator Naito Rune drew in the "large-headed" (*nitōshin*) style and popularized the word kawaii, expanding its meaning beyond the merely childish (Nakamura 2013, 14). This large-headed style, also embodied by Mickey Mouse and other Disney characters, mimics the proportions that tend to provoke a cuteness response, and it has an important place in the history of both the cute and kawaii aesthetics. A famous early example of crossover between the two is the Kewpie doll, invented as a character by Rose O'Neil in 1909 and produced as bisque figures starting in 1912. A worldwide hit, the Kewpie doll influenced the development of kawaii. The eponymous Kewpie Mayonnaise—a staple of the Japanese kitchen—began including an illustration of a Kewpie doll on its packaging in 1925. By that time, several Japanese companies were producing celluloid Kewpies for both domestic and overseas consumption.

In the 1950s, the large-headed phenomenon expanded when first banks, then other companies, began producing plastic mascot items to advertise their services. As Japan's postwar economic expansion gained force, more women became housewives and (unlike housewives in most Western countries) usually had control of the family finances. As salaries rose, banks began offering free goods as incentives to set up accounts, and plastic coin banks that depicted young children in the large-headed style proved to be a hit with these new consumers. Other

Figure 31.2 Nakahara Junichi's 1941 cover illustration for the magazine *The Shōjo's Friend*
Source: ©JUNICHI NAKAHARA/HIMAWARIYA

companies, such as pharmaceutical firms, soon followed suit with their own cute mascots. Sato-chan, a cute elephant advertising the Sato Company, appeared in 1955, while the twin frogs Kero and Koro-chan made their debut in 1958 advertising the Kowa Company. Kawaii mascots and characters were thus well established in Japanese mass culture well before the debut of Hello Kitty in 1975.

The oil and dollar crisis caused by the 1973 Arab oil embargo led more Japanese companies to focus on the domestic market rather than on exports to the United States. Thus, the success of Hello Kitty quickly spawned a host of imitators, and the kawaii boom was truly launched

Figure 31.3 The original Kewpie Mayonnaise jar from 1925
Source: The Kewpie Corporation.

(Nakamura 2013, 16). Countless new characters and designs found a willing audience not only in young girls, but also adult women who had spent their childhoods following the work and buying the "fancy goods" designed by illustrators such as Takehisa, Nakahara, and Naito.

The 1980s saw a shift in girls' (*shōjo*) manga away from exotic locales with fantastical storylines to everyday life in Japan in a new genre known as maiden's (*otomechikku*) manga (Prough 2011, 51). The heroines of these stories were drawn to appear cute rather than beautiful (Kan 2007, 200). Moreover, as Kan Satoko writes, they had "cute inner minds," meaning that the characters were appealing due to their ordinary imperfections, which helped foster self-affirmation in the girls who read this genre (Kan 2007, 201).

Kawaii has been expressed in the fine arts in Japan for almost a thousand years. It became associated with mass consumption gradually: first in magazines and fancy goods that marketed an image of upper class schoolgirls to the middle class and then, with the postwar economic expansion, to girls of all classes and ages. Many girls who had grown up with kawaii found themselves still drawn to this aesthetic when they became adults (Kinsella 1995, 245; Ōtsuka

Eiji quoted in Prough 2011, 51–52). As housewives in charge of family finances, their economic power grew in proportion to the national economy. Companies responded to this growing domestic market by producing more and more kawaii goods aimed predominantly at women and children, who made up over half the population.

Yet this does not explain the sheer size of the footprint that kawaii now occupies in Japanese culture overall. The key to understanding this ubiquity, many critics believe, lies in the extent to which the *shōjo* became a symbol of the archetypal Japanese consumer in the later stages of postwar economic development. As the postwar economic boom continued, the image of the *shōjo*—drifting, searching, dreaming of a rose-coloured future always on the horizon—became increasingly attractive to Japan's stressed-out students and salarymen trapped in the rat race of late-modern capitalism. Due to their youth, *shōjo* were detached from both the economy of production and reproduction. They faced no demand to inhabit a productive place in society, which represented an unattainable freedom to adults. The *shōjo* became a symbol, relegated to "pure play as pure sign" as John Treat puts it, and kawaii was the main signifier of this sign (1993, 362–363).

In the late 1980s and early 1990s, male Japanese critics such as Horikiri Naoto, Yamane Kazume, and Ōtsuka Eiji wrote about the conspicuous consumption that characterized the Japanese economy of the period as a feminizing and infantilizing process (Orbaugh 2003, 202). Asada Akira made the link explicit when he coined the phrase "infantile capitalism" to describe the childlike passion and play that characterized the frenzied consumerism arising in Japan's postwar economic recovery (1989, 275). Katō Norihiro, in his evocatively titled essay "Goodbye Godzilla, Hello Kitty," traces the current boom in kawaii to the contradictions, discomfort, and dislocation experienced in occupied Japan after the war. According to Katō, the wartime history that Japan did not want to confront was swept under the rug, and frantic postwar consumerism arose as a way to keep it there (2006, 77). As proof, he points not only to the rise of Hello Kitty but also the domestication of Godzilla, who has evolved from an uncanny monster to a kawaii character (2006, 78).

For Katō, the decline of the bellowing Godzilla and the rise of the mouthless Hello Kitty mark the disappearance of the authentic in Japanese culture. However, he closes on a note of ambivalence, writing that Hello Kitty also looms "as a symbol of the unknown powers of the voiceless" (2006, 79). Though aspects of Katō's historical analysis are compelling, his characterization of anyone who produces, consumes, or embodies kawaii as "voiceless" indicates a refusal to listen to the women and men drawn to this female-dominated aesthetic who are using it to redefine authenticity altogether.

The power of kawaii

In the late capitalist Japan of the 1980s and 1990s, more and more young people—men as well as women—began to see the position of the *shōjo* as desirable. The origin of this desire is often traced to the end of the student protest movement of the 1960s. From the 1970s on, university students turned inward, to fantasies in manga and magazines, and away from politics (Kinsella 1995, 251; Treat 1993, 365). In the 1990s, as new crossover manga and anime such as *Sailor Moon* began to combine the action and adventure of boys' manga with *shōjo* characters, more and more men found themselves occupying a position of both desire and identification vis-à-vis the *shōjo* and, as such, became consumers of kawaii. The paradoxical strength wielded by the heroines of girls' manga and anime is key to their appeal (Shiokawa 1999, 107). Their popularity stems from the fact that the *shōjo*'s unformed state of kawaisa (cuteness) allows for a seemingly infinite power for transformation while still retaining a liminal state of "relative freedom from socially prescribed rules, and an unmarked gender" (Orbaugh 2003, 217, 226).

Hasegawa Yuko, in her work on contemporary Japanese women artists, goes further when she writes that deliberately existing in a state of kawaisa, in which maturity is never reached, is an oppositional stance that "has the potential to perform a political function of undermining current ideologies of gender and power" (2002, 140). There are recent signs that some Japanese men seek not merely to consume but also to embody the position—and power—of the *shōjo*. The recent "genderless" fashion style is a case in point. Sharon Kinsella identified this as a nascent trend as far back as the late 1980s (1995, 243). Taking both genderless men and kawaii girls as his subject, Thorsten Botz-Bornstein offers an intricate analysis of the paradoxical "strength out of weakness" that allows kawaii to twist and distort existing structures of gender without overturning them (2016, 111, 120).

Masafumi Monden maintains that the kawaii aesthetic may function as a "soft revolt" in the way it presents an asexual cuteness as an authentic aspect of femininity. He writes: "Crafting and performing *shōjo* through gestures and particularly clothes, allows Japanese women to present themselves as being segregated from obvious sexualization" (2015, 85). This is part of a larger movement of women in older age brackets identifying with aspects of kawaii. The fashion magazine *JJ* coined the term *otona-kawaii* (adult kawaii) in 2004 to describe adult women who wished to extend the kawaii aesthetic into adulthood (Yomota 2006, 137–138). The term *joshi*, formerly indicating young women, became popular in the early 2000s as a word for these adult women to describe themselves as they forged a new identity focused on adult cuteness (Yonezawa 2014, 3, 4). Through their collective use of this term, some Japanese women partake in a communal feeling of identification that transcends age and social status, which allows them to see themselves as active subjects rather than passive recipients of a male gaze (Baba and Ikeda 2012, 11, 12).

Kawaii has now evolved into a standard aesthetic of contemporary Japanese culture (McVeigh 2000, 135). Even state agencies, from the post office to the police and self-defence forces, have kawaii mascots (McVeigh 2000, 150). Along with such official mascots, localities from cities to prefectures have created thousands of *yuru kyara*, or "wobbly characters" to represent their regions. Less polished than company products, *yuru kyara* are hugely popular with all ages, and the overwhelming majority of them are kawaii. *Yuru kyara* often appear in full-body costumes (*kigurumi*) that impede the movement of the person inside, making them more wobbly and increasing their kawaii appeal. In fact, when performing, the interaction of *yuru kyara* with their fans is limited to arms waved in greeting (Occhi 2012, 122–125).

When I attended my first *yuru kyara* parade in 2015, I was surprised by the number of adults who waved back at these kawaii characters, in spite of the fact that the people inside the *kigurumi* suits couldn't see them. Then I realized they were waving at a character, not a person. The act of waving is simply enjoyable even as an indirect act of communication. It enables a crowd to share kawaii affect and testifies to the power of this aesthetic to exert such a broad appeal to so many.

Cute vs. kawaii

There is a significant strand of scholarship on the cute aesthetic that claims negative affects as defining attributes of cuteness in general. Sianne Ngai, in her work on cuteness in the avant-garde, claims that the cute is inextricably tangled with a long list of adverse aspects: from violence to sadism, aggression to betrayal, despondency to abjection. Several of her examples are from Japanese kawaii, which she misreads as the same aesthetic as the cute (2012, 78). For example, when Ngai analyzes the artworks of Nara Yoshitomo, the Japanese avant-garde artist with an international reputation who is known for his depictions of creepily cute children, often holding knives or cigarettes, she concludes that Nara's work involves a self-conscious foregrounding of the violence that Ngai believes is constitutive of the cute aesthetic as a whole (2012, 78). Thus,

Figure 31.4 A small girl meets a yuru kyara at the 2018 Yuru Kyara Grand Prix in Osaka

when Ngai concludes that cute objects seem to call forth an "aggressive desire to master and overpower" them, she is including kawaii in this formulation (2012, 78).

I argue elsewhere that Ngai places too much importance on the English word's secondary meaning of cunning or clever in order to locate aggression and violence at the heart of the cuteness response (Dale 2017, 38, 39). Scholarship on kawaii as a separate aesthetic yields an alternative view. In her article "The Art of Cute Little Things: Nara Yoshitomo's Parapolitics," Marilyn Ivy takes Ngai's argument in a new direction when she argues that the cute objects within commodity culture "embody an extreme powerlessness that can turn over into its opposite: resistant testimony to the violence of domination" (2010, 14). Ivy's nuanced use of Ngai's argument allows her valuable insights into Nara's predominantly female fan community and their relationship to kawaii.

Ivy argues that by "cutifying" the raw impulse towards rebellion among youth in capitalist societies, Nara creates a movement of political resistance based on shared affects and attachments that "generates forms of association and communality difficult to establish in late capitalist Japan" (2010, 23). Ivy's reading differs from the other modes of kawaii as resistance outlined previously (see also Miller 2011). Rather than attempting to remain in a state of immaturity, Nara's fans transform the anomie of life in capitalized, commodified culture through their collective engagement in his art, thereby: "forming unexpected solidarities based on a grappling with the kawaii, the aesthetic marker for the most reified of objects and the most vulnerable of subjects" (Ivy 2010, 26).

Conclusion

The World Economic Forum's Global Gender Gap Report of 2017 lists Japan in 114th place out of 144 countries. Certainly some aspects of kawaii, such as "immature" and "childlike," further gender inequality to the extent that they inform the social expectations placing Japanese women into a position subordinate to that of men. Yet kawaii culture, driven by Japanese women's tastes and preferences, also pushes back against this sexist stereotyping. I close by considering the rapid expansion of new portmanteau categories generated by young Japanese women that combine kawaii with both allied and opposing affects. These new kawaii combinations not only include *kimokawa* (disgusting), *gurokawa* (grotesque), and *busukawa* (ugly), but also *tsuyokawa* (strong) (Aoyagi and Yuen 2016, 101; Miller 2011; MyNavi 2017). These new categories offer a fundamentally different approach than that taken by much scholarship on the cute aesthetic. Instead of locating negative qualities inside the concept of the cute, these portmanteau words emphasize the gap between kawaii and the added quality in order to create fresh opportunities to feel kawaii affect, expanding the field of cuteness aesthetics.

Related chapter

30   Gender, Manga, and Anime
31   Cuteness Studies and Japan
32   Gender and Visual Culture
33   Gender, Media, and Misogyny in Japan
34   Representing Girls in Cinema

References

Aoyagi, H. and Yuen, A. M. (2016) "When Erotic Meets Cute: Erokawa and the Public Expression of Female Sexuality in Contemporary Japan," *East Asian Journal of Popular Culture* 2 (1) 97–110.
Asada, A. (1989) "Infantile Capitalism and Japan's Postmodernism: A Fairy Tale," trans. K. Selden in M. Miyoshi and H. Harotoonian (eds) *Postmodernism and Japan*, Durham: Duke University Press, 273–278.
Baba, N. and Ikeda, T. (eds) (2012) *Joshi no Jidai!* (The Age of Joshi!) Tokyo: Seikyusha.
Botz-Bornstein, T. (2016) "Kawaii, Kenosis, Verwindung: A Reading of Kawaii Through Vattimo's Philosophy of 'Weak Thought,'" *East Asian Journal of Popular Culture* 2 (1) 111–123.
Boyle, J. and Kao, W. (eds) (2017) *The Retro-Futurism of Cuteness*, New York: Punctum.
Dale, J. P. (2017) "The Appeal of the Cute Object: Desire, Domestication, and Agency," in J.P Dale et al. (eds) *The Aesthetics and Affects of Cuteness*, London: Routledge, 35–55.
Esposito, G. et al. (2014) "Baby, You Light-up My Face: Culture-General Physiological Responses to Infants and Culture-Specific Cognitive Judgments of Adults," *PLOS ONE* 9 (10) 1–8.
Glocker, M. L. et al. (2009) "Baby Schema Modulates the Brain Reward System in Nulliparous Women," *PNAS* 106 (22) 9115–9119.
Hasegawa, Y. (2002) "Post-Identity Kawaii: Commerce, Gender and Contemporary Japanese Art," in F. Lloyd (ed) *Consuming Bodies: Sex and Contemporary Japanese Art*, London: Reaktion Books, 127–141.
Hinohara, K. (2017) *Kawaii! Ukiyo-e*, Tokyo: Tokyo Buutsu.
Ivy, M. (2010) "The Art of Cute Little Things: Nara Yoshitomo's Parapolitics," *Mechademia* 5 3–30.
Kan, S. (2007) "'Kawaii': The Keyword of Japanese Girls' Culture," in *Miryoku aru daigakuin Kyoika inishiatibu: <taiwa to shinka> no jisedai josei rīda no ikusei*, Tokyo: Ochanomizu Daigaku 'miryoku aru daikaguin kyoiku' inishiatubu jinshakei jimukyoiku 200–202.

Katō, N. (2006) "Goodbye Godzilla, Hello Kitty: The Origins and Meaning of Japanese Cuteness," *The American Interest* 2 (1) 72–79.

Kawamura, K. (1994) *Otome no shintai: Onna no gendai to sexuality* (The Body of the Maiden: The Modernity and Sexuality of Women) Tokyo: Kinokuniya Shoten.

Kinsella, S. (1995) "Cuties in Japan," in L. Skov and B. Moeran (eds) *Women, Media and Consumption in Japan*, Honolulu: University of Hawai'i Press, 220–254.

Kringelbach, M. L. et al. (2008) "A Specific and Rapid Neural Signature for Parental Instinct," *PLOS ONE* 3 (2) 1–7.

May, S. (2019) *The Power of Cute*, Princeton, NJ: Princeton University Press.

Meese, J. and Lobato, R. (eds) (2014) "Cute", special issue of *M/C Journal* (2014) 17 (2) http://journal.media-culture.org.au/index.php/mcjournal/issue/view/cute.

McVeigh, B. J. (2000) *Wearing Ideology: State, Schooling and Self-Presentation in Japan*, Oxford: Berg.

Miller, L. (2011) "Cute Masquerade and the Pimping of Japan," *International Journal of Japanese Sociology* 20 (1) 18–29.

Monden, M. (2015) *Japanese Fashion Cultures: Dress and Gender in Contemporary Japan*, London: Bloomsbury.

Museum of Fucho City (2013) *Cute Edo Paintings* (*Kawaii Edo Kaiga*), Tokyo: Yoruhito.

MyNavi Teens Lab (2017) *Fifteen Kawaii Words*. https://teenslab.mynavi.jp/column/15-kawaii-words.html.

Nakamura, K. (2012) *Nihon no Kawaii Zukan: Fancy Goods no 100 Nen* (Japanese Kawaii Illustrated: 100 Years of Fancy Goods), Tokyo: Kawaride Shobo Shinsha.

Nakamura, K. (2013) "Interview," in M. Ozaki and G. Johnson (eds) *Kawaii! Japan's Culture of Cute*, Munich: Prestel.

Ngai, S. (2012) *Our Aesthetic Categories: Zany, Cute, Interesting*, Cambridge, MA: Harvard University Press.

Nittono, H. (2016) "The Two-Layer Model of 'Kawaii': A Behavioural Science Framework for Understanding Kawaii and Cuteness," *East Asian Journal of Popular Culture* 2 (1) 79–95.

Occhi, D. (2012) "Wobbly Aesthetics, Performance, and Message: Comparing Japanese Kyara with Their Anthropomorphic Forebears," *Asian Ethnology* 71 (1) 109–132.

Orbaugh, S. (2003) "Busty Battlin' Babes: The Evolution of the Shōjo in 1990s Visual Culture," J. Mostow, N. Bryson and M. Graybill (eds) *Gender and Power in the Japanese Visual Field*, Hawai'i: University of Hawai'i Press, 201–228.

Plourde, L. (2016) "Babymetal and the Ambivalence of Cuteness," *International Journal of Cultural Studies* 21 (3) 293–307.

Prough, J. S. (2011) *Straight from the Heart: Gender, Intimacy and the Cultural Production of Shōjo Manga*, Honolulu: University of Hawai'i Press.

Shimizu, I. (2013) "A Brief History of Early-Modern and Modern Manga," in N. Hamada (ed) *Manga: The Pre-History of Japanese Comics*, Tokyo: PIE International, 16–19.

Shiokawa, K. (1999) "Cute but Deadly: Women and Violence in Japanese Comics," in J. A. Lent (ed) *Themes and Issues in Asian Cartooning: Cute, Cheap, Mad and Sexy*, Bowling Green, OH: Bowling Green State University Popular Press, 93–125.

Shirane, H. (ed) (2007) *Traditional Japanese Literature: An Anthology, Beginnings to 1600*, New York: Columbia University Press.

Takahashi, M. (2013) "Opening the Closed World of Shōjo Manga," in M. W. MacWilliams (ed) *Japanese Visual Culture: Explorations in the World of Manga and Anime*, New York: M.E. Sharpe, 114–136.

Takahashi, M., Mito, N. and Hanawa, M. (2014) *Jakūchu's Adorability and Shōen's Beauty: "Kawaii" in Japanese Art*, Tokyo: Yamatane Museum of Art.

Treat, J. W. (1993) "Yoshimoto Banana Writes Home: Shojo Culture and the Nostalgic Subject," *The Journal of Japanese Studies* 19 (2) 353–387.

Yano, C. R. (2013) *Pink Globalization: Hello Kitty's Trek Across the Pacific*, Durham: Duke University Press.

Yomota, I. (2006) *Kawaii Ron* (Essay on "Kawaii"), Tokyo: Chikuma Shobo.

Yonezawa, I. (2014) *Joshi no Tenjō* (The Birth of "Joshi"), Tokyo: Keiso Shobo.

32
GENDER AND VISUAL CULTURE

Gunhild Borggreen

Visual culture and gender

Visual culture is the name of both a cultural phenomenon and a field of research. In broad terms, "the visual" covers everything that can be "seen"—from visual artefacts such as conventional pictures and photographs to moving images in film and video; from visual appearances of human and non-human beings to landscapes, architecture, and images from outer space; from historical and contemporary visual arts to global media flows; from the visualization of concepts and ideas to virtual images that emerge in fantasy or memory. All such types of visual materials or phenomena are produced and shaped by the societies from which they derive. The visual is an intrinsic part of art and everyday life in any society.

Visual culture as a research field may be identified as "the study of the cultural construction of the visual in arts, media, and everyday life" (Dikovitskaya 2005, 1). Visual culture is an interdisciplinary field, which draws upon many other disciplines such as art history, media studies, cultural studies, and philosophy, as well as anthropology and social sciences. The key argument for identifying visual culture as a specific field of investigation is that contemporary societies appear to become increasingly "visual" by the continuous flow of images in everyday life through media, fashion, popular culture, and many other types of cultural production (Sturken and Cartwright 2001). At the same time, issues of identity formation and negotiation such as gender, race, and ethnicity have been at the core of scholarly inquiries into art and culture from the 1990s onward, and lead to a number of "new art history" approaches to historical as well contemporary visual arts, in which questions of representation became salient.

Gender in this chapter is understood as the social and cultural construction of the concepts of "femininity" and "masculinity." Gender is a performance of social norms ascribed to biological bodies, which in most cases are defined as "male" or "female" at birth. Every culture and historical era has a set of values and modes of behaviour that are associated with male and female bodies, and these norms change over time as the individuals in society challenge and change the normative practices of femininity and masculinity, for example, when women began wearing trousers. However, even if gender is seen as a performance and therefore something that in principle can be altered, social norms and discourses are so powerful that the ascribed gender identity of the individual subject is difficult to redefine. As philosopher and feminist scholar Judith Butler (1993) notes, the subject is formed by discourse and is not a free agent to "choose" his or her gender as a "garment" from a closet to be changed the next day. The gender of the subject is "performed" by the discourse, which is always already there. In the context of visual culture, images, as much as written or verbal texts, are a central part of the discourse that constitute the subject in the formation and negotiation of identity.

Visual culture and Japan

Some scholars argue that Japanese culture is more visually oriented compared to other cultures. Susan J. Napier (2005), for example, states that Japan traditionally has been more "pictocentric" than Western cultures due to the use of characters or ideograms since the introduction of Chinese writing system (*kanji*) in the fifth century. Leo Loveday and Satomi Chiba (1986) suggest that "certain social constraints on linguistic expressiveness" lead to a preference for non-verbal communication, and that in Japan, "iconicism is not inherently inferior to language." While such generalizations should be read with caution because they may be difficult to assert, they represent an attempt to create a historical continuity from the past to the present as a means to explain the proliferation of popular visual culture such as manga (Japanese-style narrative comics) and anime (animation television series and films) produced and consumed in contemporary Japan. During the 1990s, Japanese manga and anime became popular outside Japan, first through fan-based translations and distribution on the Internet and later commercialized to form a large export industry (Iwabuchi 2002; Kelts 2006; Napier 2007). Other forms of visual products have followed, many of which are related to each other by media convergence (that is, the production of adaptations and other associated texts in different media), including electronic games, visual novels, character goods, gadgets, fashion items, design products, food, and fan-based community activities such as *cosplay* (short for costume play), where fans produce costumes and accessories in order to dress up as their favourite manga character. These products form part of a global craze for "Cool Japan," a concept adapted by the Japanese government as a means to brand Japanese culture and enhance the nation's soft power potential (McGray 2002; Daliot-Bul 2009; Valaskivi 2013; Watanabe and McConnell 2008). Furthermore, digitalized images and visual representations of cultural practices are circulated and shared on social media such as Facebook and Instagram as well as domestic Japanese apps such as Line and Mixi. The many forms of visual cultures in (and from) Japan have provided the basis for new focus areas for scholars in and outside Japan. Numerous books and anthologies are published that focus on the visual elements of popular culture both in a contemporary and in a historical perspective (Brill 2018; Ishioka 2014; MacWilliams 2008; Schodt 1983, 1993; Napier 2005). Most references within the area of manga and anime are drawn from English-language publications.

Gender in manga and popular culture

Within the vast bulk of images and visual phenomena that makes up Japan's visual culture, a large part is already gendered at the stage of production and circulation. Since the birth of consumer culture of postwar Japan, mass media and commercial products from the entertainment industries such as manga and anime, the print media of fashion, food, and other lifestyle magazines, as well as television (to mention just a few) have specific groups of users that are often defined in terms of gender and age. The visual parts of mass media products are created to communicate with a specific target group by representing what the producers believe to be a shared field of interest in order to make the individuals in the target group identify with the product or concept and feel compelled to consume more. Manga was produced and marketed for gender and age groups such as *shōjo manga* (manga for young females) with an emphasis on romance and emotions, *shōnen manga* (manga for young males) with emphasis on adventure and action, *seinen manga* (manga for adult males), and others. However, in the manga market, some genres and formats lose readerships and disappear; for example, as manga scholar Jaqueline Berndt points out, *seinen* magazine titles have slumped in number in favour of *tankōbon* books, and the *seinen* genre is now, in part, becoming a "non-gendered" manga for mature readers (Berndt 2015, 234). Publications such as the anthology *Shōjo zasshiron* (*Theory on Girls' Magazines*, Ōtsuka 1991) trace the history of printed media for girls, while other research identifies the relationship between *shōjo* manga and other cultural formats, such as the stage productions of the all-female Takarazuka Revue Company (Yamanashi 2013).

Scholars in and outside Japan analyse specific *shōjo* manga or anime productions for their feminist potential, for example, in terms of cross-dressing and gender-bending in early works such as Tezuka Osamu's *Princess Knight* (*Ribon no kishi*, 1953–1956) and Ikeda Riyoko's *Rose of Versailles* (*Berusaiyu no bara*, 1972–73), and how the figure of the androgynous revolutionary Oscar in the latter may have influenced the development of women's liberation movements in the 1970s (Anan 2014). Other scholars discuss the potential empowerment of female viewers when reading manga about powerful women, especially around the mid-1990s where *shōjo anime* television series such as *Sailor Moon* (1992–1997) and *Revolutionary Girl Utena* (1997) featured *mahō shōjo*, girls with magical superpowers and heroic actions. The female protagonists are ordinary girls, who can change into powerful female warriors, albeit at the same time depicted as desirable sex icons with long legs, narrow waists, and miniskirts. Anthropologist Anne Allison, for example, notes that *Sailor Moon* defies "easy categorization as either (or simply) a feminist or sexist script," and she quotes Japanese feminist commentator Minomiya Kazuko's comment that the anime reflects a "positive shift in gender reality" and that it might encourage real girls to be both "comfortable as girls and inspired to seek out careers or missions as adults unrestricted by gender" (Allison 2006, 135–136). Film and TV studies scholar Akiko Sugawa-Shimada (2013), in her study of the specific *goth-loli shōjo* (gothic lolita girl) genre, argues that stereotypical representations that seem to cater to male fantasy also serve as representations of girls who have both strength and child-like cuteness and choose not to be consumed as sex objects. Japanese literature and popular culture scholar Sharalyn Orbaugh locates the potential power of the "battlin' babes" in the tension between their sexual potential and their refusal to activate it, but in the end she finds that the narratives in her study "ultimately reinscribe hegemonic and heterocentric sex/gender/sexuality ideologies, obviating much of the promise of resistance or social transformation" (Orbaugh 2003, 227).

Many scholars analysing the visual culture of *shōjo* manga and anime imply a mixed readership of not only female readers/viewers, but also male viewers, who focus on the eroticized image of *bishōjo*, beautiful female characters. Translated as "nerd" or "geek," the term *otaku* was used among amateur manga artists and fans in the 1980s, but transgressed its subcultural usage and became a mainstream word in media and entertainment industries in Japan. The word *otaku* was primarily used about male fans, although there are many female manga amateurs and fans (Kinsella 2000). Media scholars Okabe and Ishida (2012) have analysed a segment of *otaku* that consists mostly of women known as *fujoshi*, literally "rotten women", identified among other things for their interest in *yaoi* and BL ("boys' love") manga that feature sexual relationships between men.

Gender in visual mass media

Anthropological and sociological studies of representations in media focus on women. For example in the volume *Women, Media and Consumption in Japan* (1995), editors Lise Skov and

Brian Moeran argue that women are not only key figures in Japan's consumer culture, they also make up a large part of the visual representation in printed mainstream media and advertisement industry. Images in lifestyle magazines communicate fashion trends and new products, but they also visualize and promote certain ideologies or normative modes of appearance through complex layers of semiotic codes. Anthropologist Moeran (1995), for example, has analysed the visual representations of women in the monthly woman's magazine *Katei gahō* (Household Pictorial) in the early 1990s. Moeran extracts an image of "Japanese femininity" which is defined as "upperclass, sophisticated, upmarket, smooth-skinned, and immaculately groomed" and which represents middle-aged housewives and mothers and is not related to sexuality. The medium of photography often used for representations of female bodies in magazines and advertisements makes the images appear to be authentic and real because viewers believe that the camera has captured a true situation. The stereotypical representation of housewives and mothers create certain expectations for the viewer of what a housewife or a mother looks like while at the same time making invisible (or unthinkable) possible alternative versions. The reality effect of photography helps naturalize or make implicit the gendered ideologies at stake: for example, an advertisement may be promoting an elegant tableware set, but indirectly the image communicates an idealized notion of female homemaking activities and domestic bliss. Such images may contribute to a discourse that affirms a hegemonic social and cultural order, in this case conventional gender roles of women as homemakers and mothers.

Images of women may affect how real women act and behave, but at the same time, images of new ways of performing the role of womanhood or displaying "femininity" emerge in society and become new flows of images. Cultural studies scholar Stuart Hall (1980) questions the assumption that all viewers (or consumers) passively absorb the messages conveyed through media and entertainment, and he identifies the three different modes of "preferred," "negotiated," and "oppositional" readings among audiences. A number of anthropological studies from Japan show how traditional gender roles are constantly challenged by counter-images. One example is anthropologist Sharon Kinsella's (1995) research from the early 1990s, which shows how the concept of *kawaii* (cute) and its visual manifestation in fancy goods, clothes, food, and other *shōjo* cultural products was used by young females themselves to express a resistance towards growing up and having to become a responsible adult citizen. In later research, Kinsella (2014) analyses the media images (both textual and visual) of *kogyaru* (young school girls) in the late 1990s and argues that the visual appearance of young women with dark tanned faces and white make-up around the eyes and the mouth (dubbed *ganguro*, "black face") and wild hair dyed in different colours, as well as *kogyaru*'s unruly behaviour in urban public space created a "social panic" among the mainstream male-dominated news media. The anthology *Bad Girls of Japan* (Miller and Bardsley 2005) likewise presents studies of how Japanese girls and women defy the conventional image of women as demure and obedient, with several chapters that analyse how feminist disrupature takes place in the field of visual culture. A study by Japan studies scholar Gitte Marianne Hansen (2016) examines the relationship between normative femininity and women's self-directed violence by analysing how some manga address social and psychological issues such as self-harm and eating disorders.

Numerous research studies discuss gender-bending in popular culture, ranging from the *otoko-yaku* (male roles) played by female actors in the Takarazuka Revue (Robertson 1998; Nakamura and Matsuo 2003) to female-female desire in manga that may liberate readers/viewers from gender dualism and heteronormativity in sexual relations (Welker 2006; Suter 2013). Fashion studies scholar Masafumi Monden, writing on visual images in fashion magazines, music videos, and film, argues that, contrary to Euro-American cultures, in Japan not only young women but also young men can be the object of the gaze, and that "positive evaluation of their appearance can enhance these young men's self-assurance" (Monden 2015, 18). More importantly, analyses of men's fashion publications seem to suggest that there are increasingly more modes of masculinity available to compete with what Monden calls "the worn-out, dowdy 'salaryman'" (Monden 2015, 151). Philosopher Masahiro Morioka (2013) analyses the concept and visual appearance of the "herbivore man," a term that became trendy in 2008–2009 which connotes young men who are impassive in regard to sex and prefer to have romantic and equal relationships with women. These and many other research publications analyse mass media and popular culture images and visual cultural products with attention to how they challenge gender stereotypes and dichotomies.

Gender issues in "new art history"

Gender issues became a significant topic within visual culture studies in Japan in the early 1990s, and much of the discussion of gender began in the context of new art history research in parallel with other critical theories concerning identity politics, including colonialism, ethnicity, and nationalism. Some of the early scholarly activities were based on feminist art history from the United States and Great Britain, such as feminist art historians Wakakuwa Midori and Hagiwara Hiroko (1991), who reference international pioneers in the field of feminist art history such as Linda Nochlin and Griselda Pollock. The feminist approach aimed at creating more equal opportunities for female artists, both from an art historical perspective by crediting female artists whose artworks have been "forgotten" by the narratives of art history, as well as by revealing the structures of suppression of women that exist in institutions such as art academies, museum collections and displays, and art history education.

While a feminist approach focused on the suppression of women, other scholars used the term gender in order to broaden the poststructuralist scope and challenge the notion of a mutually exclusive binary system that categorizes bodies as either male or female. One of the leading scholars in the formation of a critical gender approach in art history and visual culture in Japan was the late art historian Chino Kaori, who in 1994 published an influential article entitled "Nihon bijutsu no jendā" (Gender in Japanese Art), which has since been translated into English in several publications (Chino 1996a, 2003). In the article, Chino applies the gendered concepts of *danseisei* (masculinity) and *joseisei* (femininity), but argues that rather than fixed binary categories, they should be understood as dynamic notions of values that are negotiated within specific cultural, political, and historical contexts. The important aspect of such a concept of gender is that the notion of "masculinity" and "femininity" can be challenged and transformed, and thus visual images and their context can provide a basis for social and cultural change. In her article, Chino calls for new ways of interpreting art history by changing conventional value systems.

Other art historians and visual culture scholars in Japan were engaged in the broad topic of gender issues and feminist art in the 1990s. Art historians such as Ikeda Shinobu (1998) provided overviews of female figures in Japanese art history from a gender perspective, and art historian Wakakuwa Midori (1997) published critical analyses of representations of female nude figures in pre-modern and modern art. Several edited anthologies both in Japanese and in English have taken up the topics of gender in art and visual culture in conjunction with critical perspectives such as nationhood and colonialism (Suzuki et al. 1997; Kumakura and Chino 1999; Bryson et al. 2003; Croissant et al. 2008). These volumes broaden the field of inquiry not only to cover art history but also to include visual material such as media images of the imperial family and contemporary manga, as well as contemporary visual art.

Gender in contemporary visual art

Gender issues entered discussions of contemporary art during the late 1980s and 1990s. A special issue of the leading art magazine *Bijutsu techō* (Art notes) in 1986 on "Bijutsu no chōshōjotachi" ("Supergirls in art") presented a number of female artists, most of them young and upcoming on the art scene. The focus on female artists in this case, however, was not explicitly feminist in nature, as it did not question some of the underlying structures of inequality in the art system or gendered lifestyle expectations that young generations of female artists were (still) facing (Borggreen 2003). Another strand of the study of gender issues in contemporary visual arts is related to the themes addressed by the artists in their artworks. The artist Shimada Yoshiko, for example, uses photographs and images drawn from wartime propaganda magazines from the early 1940s. In many of her graphic prints, Shimada juxtaposes contrasting images of women as subjects under Japanese Imperialism during the war time period, namely the figure of the patriotic housewife, with the figure of the so-called *ianfu* "comfort woman," women of mostly Korean descent who were forced into sexual labour by the Japanese army during the war (Bloom 1998). In a different vein, the artist Morimura Yasumasa stages his own body in photographic appropriation of female figures in famous Western artworks or Western movie starts, hereby pointing out how complex power structures across gender and ethnicity are closely linked to the visual (Chino 1996b).

Many artists of the 1990s explored the effects of everyday visual culture in terms of gender conformity by referring to and appropriating images from mass media and popular culture such as manga and popular magazines. The artists often exaggerate elements of social norms and values in order to point out what otherwise might be invisibly embedded in society. In a series of large paintings, the artist Fukuda Miran copied advertisements from lifestyle magazines featuring female models and exaggerated these images of the "happy housewife" by making the female figure very large and out of human proportion or by gluing kitschy ornaments on top of the canvas. Similar aesthetic strategies of exaggerating gendered stereotypes can be seen in installation works by Nishiyama Minako, who points out the ambiguous border line between cute and innocent *shōjo* culture of pink Rococo ribbons and lace and the eroticized *shōjo* consumed as image and body in the sex industry. Sawada Tomoko uses photography in her ironic paraphrases of group photography and *shōjo* identity to highlight the stereotypes of schoolgirl femininity represented in three "cute ambassadors" appointed by Japan's Ministry of Foreign Affairs in 2009 (Borggreen 2015). The line-up of numerous mannequin-like female service workers in identical uniforms (known also as "elevator girls") in the staged and manipulated photographs of Yanagi Miwa may be seen as commentary on the close relationship between gender and consumption and on the striking homogeneity of beauty ideals. As curator and art critic Hasegawa Yūko points out, female artists like Nishiyama, Yanagi, and others respond to the fantasy image of the powerful *shōjo* from the new types of manga narratives that developed in the 1990s. Hasegawa argues that the state of *kawaisa* (cuteness) formulated in the artworks by these female artists "has the potential to perform a political function of undermining current ideologies of gender and power" (Hasegawa 2002, 140).

The Neo-Pop art movement in the 1990s aligns with the boom in manga, anime, and popular culture in the same period. Male artists such as Murakami Takashi, Yanobe Kenji, and Nara Yoshitomo identified themselves as otaku and produced art that reflected their male cohort's consumption of and participation in popular culture. Neo-pop artists appropriated many of the visual elements of *kawaii* (cute) from the *shōjo* world, and the concept of *kawaii* was not only seen by some as an aesthetics native to Japan but was also used as a metaphor for an "immature" consumer culture (Koma 2013). Others saw *kawaii* as symbolizing the infantilization of Japanese cultural or national self-identity, as when Murakami Takashi describes the postwar Japanese population as "deeply pampered children" (Murakami 2005, 141). In his critical analyses of the period around the Shōwa emperor's illness and death in 1989, cultural critic Ōtsuka Eiji identifies congruence between *shōjo* culture and the nationalist tendencies of the Japanese imperial system (Ōtsuka 2003).

In the 2000s, a number of female artists such as Takano Aya and Aoshima Chiho became affiliated with Murakami's art production company Kaikai Kiki and pushed the notion of *shōjo* and *kawaii* in other directions. Art critic Matsui Midori draws upon the sociological analyses of *shōjo* culture by Ōtsuka but opposes his dismissal of *shōjo* culture. Instead, Matsui argues that the feminine reinvention of otaku genres by artists such as Takano and Aoshima in their use of erotic icons and science fiction vocabulary contribute to creating "subversively feminine visions of Utopia" (Matsui 2005, 211).

Conclusion

The amount of images and visual phenomena that make up the totality of visual cultures in Japan is overwhelming. Using a limited selection of examples from popular culture, mass media, and contemporary visual art in this chapter, I aim to contribute to an overview of how gender issues are present in the visual phenomena themselves and the way in which visual culture is consumed and appropriated by users. I have also emphasized how gender issues frame the perspectives of much of the research on the cultural practices that entail visual elements. The main point is that however much mainstream media representations of men and women promote certain normative modes of gendered appearance, behaviour, and social interaction, there are also images that contest and challenge such discourses. While critics and scholars may disagree on the social and political effects of counter-images, the visual cultures of Japan are nevertheless an important field in which to study the continuous negotiations and transformations of gender roles and perceptions in Japanese society.

Related chapters

Introduction
30 Gender, Manga, and Anime
31 Cuteness Studies and Japan
33 Gender, Media, and Misogyny in Japan
34 Representing Girls in Cinema

References

Allison, A. (2006) *Millennial Monsters. Japanese Toys and the Global Imagination*, Berkeley: University of California Press.
Anan, N. (2014) "*The Rose of Versailles*: Women and Revolution in Girls' Manga and the Socialist Movement in Japan," *Journal of Popular Culture* 7 (1) 41–63.
Berndt, J. (2015) *Manga: Medium, Kunst und Material/Manga: Medium, Art and Material*, Leipzig: Leipziger Universitätsverlag.
Bloom, L. (1998) "Gender, Race, and Nation in Japanese Contemporary Art and Criticism," in N. Mirzoeff (ed) *The Visual Culture Reader*, London: Routledge, 215–226.
Borggreen, G. (2003) "Gender in Contemporary Japanese Art," in N. Bryson, M. Graybill and J. Mostow (eds) *Gender and Power in the Japanese Visual Field*, Honolulu: University of Hawaii Press, 179–200.
Borggreen, G. (2015) "Cute and Cool in Contemporary Japanese Visual Arts," in A. Michelsen and F. Tygstrup (eds) *Social Aesthetics. Ambience—Imaginary*, Leiden: Brill, 129–151.

Brill (2018) *Japanese Visual Culture*. https://brill.com/view/serial/JVC?qt-qt_serial_details=1&quickt abs_brill_serial_tabs=0

Bryson, N., Graybill, M. and Mostow, J. (eds) (2003) *Gender and Power in the Japanese Visual Field*, Honolulu: University of Hawaii Press.

Butler, J. (1993) *Bodies That Matter: On the Discursive Limits of "Sex,"* New York: Routledge.

Chino, K. (1994) "Nihon bijutsu no jendaa" (Gender in Japanese Art), *Bijutsushi* 136 235–246.

Chino, K. (1996a) "Gender in Japanese Art," trans. J. S. Mostow, *Aesthetics* 7 49–68.

Chino, K. (1996b) "Onna o yosōu otoko: Morimura Yasumasa Joyū-ron" (A Man Pretending to Be a Woman: On Yasumasa Morimura's *Actresses*), in *Morimura Yasumasa: Bi ni itaru yamai—joyū ni natta watashi* (Morimura Yasumasa: The Sickness unto Beauty—Self-Portrait as Actress), Yokohama: Yokohama Bijutsukan, 131–162.

Chino, K. (2003) "Gender in Japanese Art," in N. Bryson, M. Graybill and J. Mostow (eds) *Gender and Power in the Japanese Visual Field*, Honolulu: University of Hawaii Press, 17–34.

Croissant, D., Yeh, C.V. and Mostow, J. S. (eds) (2008) *Performing "Nation": Gender Politics in Literature, Theater, and the Visual Arts of China and Japan, 1880–1940*, Leiden: Brill.

Daliot-Bul, M. (2009) "Japan Brand Strategy: The Taming of 'Cool Japan' and the Challenges of Cultural Planning in a Postmodern Age," *Social Science Japan Journal* 12 (2) 247–266.

Dikovitskaya, D. (2005) *Visual Culture: The Study of the Visual after the Cultural Turn*, Cambridge, MA: MIT Press.

Hall, S. (1980) "Encoding/Decoding," in Centre for Contemporary Cultural Studies (ed) *Media, Language: Working Papers in Cultural Studies*, London: Hutchinson, 128–138.

Hansen, G. M. (2016) *Femininity, Self-Harm and Eating Disorders in Japan: Navigating Contradictions in Narrative and Visual Culture*, London: Routledge.

Hasegawa, Y. (2002) "Post-Identity Kawaii: Commerce, Gender and Contemporary Japanese Art," in F. Lloyd (ed) *Consuming Bodies. Sex and Contemporary Japanese Art*, London: Reaktion Books, 127–141.

Ikeda, S. (1998) *Nihon kaiga no joseizō. Jendaa bijutsushi no shiten kara* (Images of Women in Japanese Painting. From a Gender Art Historical Viewpoint), Tokyo: Chikuma Shobō.

Ishioka, Y. (2014) *Shigakubunka 'chō' kōgi* (Lectures on "Super" Visual Culture), Tokyo: Film Art.

Iwabuchi, K. (2002) *Recentering Globalization. Popular Culture and Japanese Transnationalism*, Durham: Duke University Press.

Kelts, R. (2006) *Japanamerica. How Japanese Pop Culture Has Invaded the U.S.*, New York: Palgrave Macmillan.

Kinsella, S. (1995) "Cuties in Japan," in L. Skov and B. Moeran (eds) *Women, Media, and Consumption in Japan*, Honolulu: University of Hawai'i Press, 220–254.

Kinsella, S. (2000) *Adult Manga: Culture & Power in Contemporary Japanese Society*, Honolulu: University of Hawai'i Press.

Kinsella, S. (2014) *Schoolgirls, Money and Rebellion in Japan*, Abingdon: Routledge.

Koma, K. (2013) "*Kawaii* as Represented in Scientific Research: The Possibilities of *Kawaii* Cultural Studies," *Hemispheres* 28 103–115.

Kumakura, T. and Chino, K. (1999) *Onna? Nihon? Bi? Aratana gendaa hihyō ni mukete* (Woman? Japan? Beauty? Towards a New Gender Criticism), Tokyo: Keiō Gijuku Daigaku Shuppankai.

Loveday, L. and Chiba, S. (1986) "Aspects of the Development Toward a Visual Culture in Respect of Comics: Japan," in A. Silbermann and H. D. Dyroff (eds) *Comics and Visual Culture: Research Studies from 10 Countries*, München: K.G. Saur Verlag, 158–184.

MacWilliams, M. W. (ed) (2008) *Japanese Visual Culture: Explorations in the World of Manga and Anime*, Armonk: M.E. Sharpe.

McGray, D. (2002) "Japan's Gross National Cool," *Foreign Policy* (May–June) 44–54.

Matsui, M. (2005) "Beyond the Pleasure Room to a Chaotic Street: Transformations of Cute Subculture in the Art of the Japanese Nineties," in T. Murakami (ed) *Little Boy: The Arts of Japan's Exploding Subculture*, New York: Japan Society, 208–239.

Miller, L. and Bardsley, J. (eds) (2005) *Bad Girls of Japan*, New York: Palgrave Macmillan.

Moeran, B. (1995) "Reading Japanese in *Katei Gahō*: The Art of Being an Upperclass Woman," in L. Skov and B. Moeran (eds) *Women, Media, and Consumption in Japan*, Honolulu: University of Hawai'i Press, 111–142.

Monden, M. (2015) *Japanese Fashion Cultures: Dress and Gender in Contemporary Japan*, London: Bloomsbury.

Morioka, M. (2013) "A Phenomenological Study of 'Herbivore Men'," *The Review of Life Studies* 4 1–20.

Murakami, T. (2005) "Earth in My Window," in T. Murakami (ed) *Little Boy: The Arts of Japan's Exploding Subculture*, New York: Japan Society, 98–149.

Nakamura, K. and Matsuo, H. (2003) "Female Masculinity and Fantasy Spaces: Transcending Genders in the Takarazuka Theatre and Japanese Popular Culture," in J. E. Robertson and N. Suzuki (eds) *Men and Masculinities in Contemporary Japan: Dislocating the Salaryman Doxa*, London: RoutledgeCurzon, 59–76.

Napier, S. J. (2005) *Anime from Akira to Howl's Moving Castle: Experiencing Contemporary Japanese Animation*, Gordonsville, VA: Palgrave Macmillan.

Napier, S. J. (2007) *From Impressionism to Anime: Japan as Fantasy and Fan Cult in the Mind of the West*, New York: Palgrave Macmillan.

Okabe, D. and Ishida, K. (2012) "Making Fujoshi Identity Visible and Invisible," in M. Ito, D. Okabe and I. Tsuji (eds) *Fandom Unbound: Otaku Culture in a Connected World*, New Haven: Yale University Press, 207–224.

Orbaugh, S. (2003) "Busty Battlin' Babes: The Evolution of the *Shōjo* in the 1990s Visual Culture," in N. Bryson, M. Graybill and J. Mostow (eds) *Gender and Power in the Japanese Visual Field*, Honolulu: University of Hawaii Press, 201–228.

Ōtsuka, E. (ed) (1991) *Shōjo zasshiron* (Theory on Young Women's Magazines), Tokyo: Tokyo Shoseki.

Ōtsuka, E. (2003) *Shōjotachi no 'kawaii' tennō: Sabukaruchaa tennōron* (The Young Women's 'Cute' Emperor: Subcultural Theory of the Emperor), Tokyo: Kadokawa Shoten.

Robertson, J. (1998) *Takarazuka: Sexual Politics and Popular Culture in Modern Japan*, Berkeley: University of California Press.

Schodt, F. L. (1983) *Manga! Manga! The World of Japanese Comics*, Tokyo: Kodansha.

Schodt, F. L. (1993) *Dreamland Japan: Writings on Modern Manga*, Berkeley: Stone Bridge Press.

Skov, L. and Moeran, B. (eds) (1995) *Women, Media, and Consumption in Japan*, Honolulu: University of Hawai'i Press.

Sturken, M. and Cartwright, L. (2001) *Practices of Looking: An Introduction to Visual Culture*, Oxford: Oxford University Press.

Sugawa-Shimada, A. (2013) "Grotesque Cuteness of *Shōjo*. Representations of *Goth-Loli* in Japanese Contemporary TV *Anime*," in M. Yokota and T. G. Hu (eds) *Japanese Animation: East Asian Perspectives*, Jackson: University of Mississippi Press, 199–222.

Suter, R. (2013) "Gender Bending and Exoticism in Japanese Girls' Comics," *Asian Studies Review* 37 (4) 546–558.

Suzuki, T., Chino, K. and Mabuchi, A. (1997) *Bijutsu to jendā: Hitaishō no shisen* (Art and Gender: The Asymmetrical Regard), Tokyo: Brücke.

Valaskivi, K. (2013) "A Brand New Future? Cool Japan and the Social Imaginary of the Branded Nation," *Japan Forum* 25 (4) 485–504.

Wakakuwa, M. (1997) *Kakusareta shisen—Ukiyo-e, yōga no josei rataizō* (The Gaze That Was Concealed: The Nude Female Figure in Woodblock Prints and Western-Style Painting), Tokyo: Iwanami Shoten.

Wakakuwa, M. and Hagiwara, H. (1991) *Mō hitotsu no kaigaron: Feminizumu to geijutsu* (Another Painting Theory: Feminism and Art), Kyoto: Wuimenzu bukku sutoa.

Watanabe, Y. and McConnell, D. L. (eds) (2008) *Soft Power Superpowers: Cultural and National Assets of Japan and the United States*, New York: M.E. Sharpe.

Welker, J. (2006) "Beautiful, Borrowed, and Bent: 'Boys' Love' as Girls' Love in *Shōjo* Manga," *Signs: Journal of Women in Culture and Society* 31 (3) 841–870.

Yamanashi, M. (2013) "Tezuka and Takarazuka. Intertwined Roots of Japanese Popular Culture," in M. Yokota and T. G. Hu (eds) *Japanese Animation: East Asian Perspectives*, Jackson: University of Mississippi Press, 135–154.

33

GENDER, MEDIA, AND MISOGYNY IN JAPAN

Sally McLaren

Japan is a media-saturated society, and at its core are powerful and persistent images of what it means to be a woman or a man. Gendered media messages, which include stereotypical and highly stylised normative images of femininities and masculinities, are ingrained in daily life. The commute to school or work is a good example of this. From the train station platform to the train ride itself, commuters are bombarded with advertisements for cosmetics, diet products, education, travel and commercial media productions. Advertising for print magazines and television dramas, now commonly referred to as "traditional media," continues to be a ubiquitous part of the visual environment of train carriages in Japan. As an extension of this traditional media, many train companies also have small television screens in carriages showing a mix of news, sport, weather and entertainment, some pre-programmed but sometimes also including live broadcasting. In this environment, many commuters will also be engaged with "new media"—watching YouTube videos or anime, playing games or using social media on their smart phones or tablets. It's not uncommon to catch a glimpse of explicit content in this congested public space, such as *lolicon* (sexualized prepubescent girls) anime viewed on smartphones or the "soft porn" images of naked women in *shūkanshi* (weekly tabloid) magazines and sports newspapers. These media representations and messages are consumed during the daily commute in a sociocultural context in which there is a high incidence of *chikan* (train groping) and sexual harassment of women (Horii and Burgess 2012), leading to the introduction of women-only train carriages in major Japanese cities in 2000. This is not to assert a causal link but rather to establish that the characteristics of media-saturated Japan are intertwined in complex and often troubling ways with culturally accepted notions of gender and deeply rooted patriarchal norms (Suzuki 2005). In this chapter, I will examine the process of "mediated misogyny" in Japan and its associated patterns of marginalization, trivialization, and stereotyping (Vickery and Everbach 2018, 8), which impact not only women but also non-normative masculinities, as well as gender and sexual minorities. Since systemic gender inequality continues to be a major issue that is impeding social and economic progress in contemporary Japan (Ehara 2013), the role of media and the gendered nature of the media industry itself are pertinent topics.

This chapter will employ a critical feminist perspective to show how the structure and patterns of mediated misogyny permeate and perpetuate mainstream media culture and the male-dominated media industry in Japan and consider why these patterns persist and who benefits from them. I begin with a brief overview of the Japanese media environment and trace some of the past and present scholarship on gender and media issues in Japan. In order to demonstrate the processes of mediated misogyny, the chapter will focus on three short case studies related to news media in Japan—weekly magazine *Shūkan Bunshun*'s annual "Onna ga Kiraina Onna" (The Women Hated By Women) readers' poll, media panics surrounding the low birth and marriage rates in Japan as exemplified by *sōshokukei-danshi* (herbivore men) and *nikushokukei-joshi* (carnivore women) discourses, and the case of raped journalist Itō Shiori and the #MeToo movement in Japanese media instigated by women journalists. I will conclude by summarizing how media practices in Japan, though not solely responsible for persistent gender inequality and embedded misogyny, play an important cultural role in maintaining gendered hierarchies and preserving patriarchal norms.

The Japanese media environment

The contemporary Japanese media environment is highly concentrated, in terms of ownership, (McNeill 2014) and highly diffuse (Holden and Ergul 2006; Villi and Hayashi 2015), in terms of audience reach. Just six major media organizations (five commercial companies—*Yomiuri, Asahi, Mainichi, Nikkei* and *Sankei*—plus public broadcaster NHK) and their affiliates control the broadcast news and entertainment media landscape. These organizations also publish newspapers, magazines and books. To some extent, the media industry has resisted global media trends, and traditional media in Japan has endeavoured to remain dominant. Japan still has one of the highest newspaper circulation rates in the world, with home delivery of morning and evening editions still visible in daily life (Villi and Hayashi 2015). Television has also managed to retain large viewer rates whilst occupying "center stage in the government-initiated policy of digitalization of media, culture and the economy" (Yoshimoto 2010, 3).

Though the vast array of broadcast, digital and print media on offer can be characterized as "colourful and diverse," this description is deceptive (McNeill 2014, 64). News and entertainment media are essentially conservative, controlled, and constrained. There are three main reasons for this. First, just three major advertising agencies dominate in Japan—Dentsu, Hakuho and ADK—and their clients are not only corporate but also political. The largest agency, Dentsu, has a longstanding relationship with the ruling Liberal Democratic Party and also holds accounts with Japan's largest car manufacturers, such as Toyota and Honda. Similarly, just one large talent agency, Johnny's Jimusho, has managed and controlled the lives and careers of Japan's biggest *aidoru* and *tarento* for decades and organizes which commercials, variety shows and television dramas, for example, they will appear in (Marx 2012).

Second, the closed *kisha kurabu* (press club) system constricts news reporting because only journalists from mainstream media organizations are embedded on site and given direct access to information from government ministries and agencies, the police, corporations, religious organizations and universities. They, and typically only they, are also allowed to attend media conferences and do exclusive interviews with officials and representatives. This results in a conformity of views (Freeman 2000, 124), an aversion to investigative reporting (Kingston 2017, 3), collusion with official sources (McNeill 2016) and self-censorship (Kingston 2017, 4) that is reinforced by cross-media ownership and the symbiotic relationships with the advertising agencies.

Third, the Japanese media industry is a "male-dominated corporate society" (Ishiyama 2013, 404) with women making up only 14.8 percent of full-time regular employees in news companies, for example (Byerly 2011, 241). Media companies are overwhelmingly controlled by men, with just 1.4 percent of women in top-level management positions (Ishiyama 2013, 411). This situation is compounded by the "gender track" system (Shikata 2018, 133), where young female recruits are funnelled into particular roles in media organizations with the expectation that their careers will be curtailed when (rather than if) they leave to marry and have families. The television industry in particular exhibits a blatantly sexist division of labour, with young female announcers and journalists often appearing as mere "assistants" to older male colleagues (Takenobu 2017, 7). In general, both female and male broadcast media workers have lengthy working hours, and the necessity of demonstrating devotion and commitment to the organization has normalized this system (Hayashi and Tanioka 2013). This is reinforced further according to Hayashi and Kopper's finding that Japanese journalists prioritize "information based human relationships and communication rather than that which is harvested out of rational choices" (2014 1143). Since these information networks and decision-making processes are overwhelmingly male, the Japanese media system is able to reproduce and maintain its gendered hierarchy.

Gender and media research

Japanese scholars have been actively analysing contemporary Japanese media content and the industry in relation to gender since the 1970s, with several key texts published in the decades after that. Initially, the focus was mostly on textual analyses of the role and representation of women and men in conventional media genres such as magazines (Inoue et. al 1989), newspapers (Tanaka and Morohashi 1996) and television dramas (Muramatsu and Gössman 1998). These studies criticized the overwhelming majority of media representations of gender as being stereotypical and biased against women, relegating them to roles in the domestic sphere, whilst men were normatively represented in active and professional roles (Valaskivi 2015, 69). Due to the ubiquity of women's inequality, gender and media research during this time is generally seen to have been understood as predominantly analysing the relationship of women to media in Japan (Valaskivi 2015, 69). However, any assumption that "women" in Japan are a unified and homogenous category remains a contentious issue in research.

Suzuki's much-cited 1995 article has remained a key source in English. In it, she argues that "wide shows," morning television programs aimed at women that focus on celebrity scandals, sensationalized murder cases and tips for housewives, "offer nothing to a woman that would help her to manage her daily affairs independently" and leave her "estranged from information" (77). Suzuki was also concerned with the large amount of time that media audiences in Japan spent viewing television commercials, which in the mid-1980s amounted to 74 minutes a week based on daily viewing (78). According to her research, television commercials were more likely that any other media genre to "depict women in the role of housekeeper and child rearer" (79). She also criticized news broadcasting, where men have the main roles of newscasters and women are assistants, as reinforcing "the traditional discriminatory division of labour" (79), and women in dramas and anime are negatively represented as "materialistic, perverse and vain" (80). Suzuki cautioned that it would be naïve to assume that "if women are portrayed on television as having careers, the problems will disappear" (80). Writing a decade later, Suzuki (2005) was emphatic that in a media-saturated society such as Japan, "where democracy is still in the process of development," the continued coexistence of traditional patriarchal culture in the context of a hi-tech digital media environment was cause for alarm and could only be countered by increased media literacy (83).

Painter's contemporaneous ethnographic research at an Osaka television station (1996) noted an established hierarchical culture where women were inferior (50) and sexual harassment was both normalized and "a sort of rite of passage" (51). He also observed how gender was constructed in wide shows and dramas produced at the station, including the profiling of *shufu* (housewives) into six discrete types as "targets and markets" for advertisers (56). Although Painter determined that this dominant view of women as "domestic creatures" was already changing in mid-1990s Japan, "the continuing domination of television programming and production by older males has kept TV firmly on the conservative side in cultural struggles over gender" (57).

Painter (1996) and Valaskivi (2015) both note that research on media audiences has not been a strong focus in studies of Japanese media. Painter predicted that research with Japanese TV viewers would show how ideas of gender are rapidly changing in Japan (1996, 70). My own audience research in Japan (McLaren 2008, 2015) has shown that media audiences critically read gendered media representations but see them as interconnected with other types of inequality and discrimination in Japanese society. In particular, the exclusion of youth and minority perspectives in Japanese media was of concern to audiences I have done research with because they felt that it also excluded them from discourses on Japan's future (McLaren 2008, 104) and perpetuated exclusionary social norms about who "naturally" has power in society (105).

In general, work by the previously mentioned scholars set the focus and direction of much research on gender and media in Japan up until the 2010s. From this point, two interesting and pertinent research trends have emerged that help to inform our understanding of Japanese media culture and its relation to heteronormative configurations of gender as a contested and evolving space. First, research on LGBT and queer identities in mainstream media has shown that the "hyper-visibility" (Maree 2018, 200) of LGBT people in mainstream media is deceptive—greater visibility has not necessarily resulted in wider acceptance and full legal rights (Maree 2017). Suganuma (2018) notes that although mainstream media have promoted the visibility of sexual minorities in society, "they have simultaneously exploited queer representations" as a form of entertainment (169) and used these representations to "re-inscribe the heteronormative gender system" (171). However, Suganuma sees the crossdressing gender-queer *tarento* Matsuko Deluxe as an exception, arguing that her performance destabilizes gender categories and makes mainstream media attempts to exploit gender-queering people less effective (2018, 178).

Second, research on the intensification of idol culture in Japan following the 2011 Fukushima disaster has not only exposed the multiple ways that both young female and male performers are controlled by powerful *jimusho* agencies (Marx 2012) but also how the marketing of idols is intrinsically linked to the commercialization of highly gendered norms (Miller 2011). This is particularly the case with young female idols, who are expected to maintain a "squeaky clean, child-like *kawaii* image" whilst performing seductively for men in bikinis and schoolgirl uniforms (Luck 2017, 25). The gendered double standards in the idol industry are compounded by conservative political efforts to strengthen traditional values and national identity through idols such as all-male group Arashi (Mandujano-Salazar 2018). After being referred to by the Japanese media as *kokuminteki aidoru* (national idols), they came to represent the ideal of "Japanese male attractiveness and young masculinity" as well as promoting "the values of traditional Japanese manhood" (Mandujano-Salazar 2018, 159). The contradictions in the gender norms and ideals of idol culture thus have wider connotations. However, as writer and activist Kitahara Minori states in the documentary *Tokyo Idols* (2017), "this society will stop at nothing to protect male fantasies and provide comfort for men."

Misogyny in media culture

Expressions and practices of misogyny, the hatred of women, are the extreme outcome of a culture of gender discrimination, inequality and sexism. Unlike sexism, which justifies the patriarchal order, misogyny is "hostile" (Manne 2018, 78). Manne asserts, "misogyny's primary function and constitutive manifestation is the punishment of 'bad' women, and policing of women's behaviour," especially against those who challenge male domination (2018, 192). However, in this system of punishment and reward, it shouldn't be assumed that a totalising binary is solely at work. Manne argues that we should be concerned with the "valorising of women who conform to gendered norms and expectations," as well as the "policing of men who flout the norms of masculinity," because misogyny works in conjunction with these mechanisms to enforce and coerce gender conformity (2018, 193).

These patterns of domination and subordination are visible in media practices and representations, which are also sites for the policing and maintenance of gender norms. When misogyny is mediated, women are marginalized as social actors and their activities are represented as less important than men's (Byerly 2004, 225). Through repeatedly narrow and negative representations, the value of women in society is eroded and demeaned—something that Japanese scholars of media and gender, mentioned previously, have been arguing for decades. Mohanty (2003) says that "the interwoven processes of sexism, racism, misogyny, and heterosexism are an integral part of our social fabric, wherever in the world we happen to be" (3), and certainly this is the case in Japan. When women destabilize this social fabric by challenging "the hegemonic notions of masculinity that underpin misogyny" (Vickery 2018, 45), their very existence and their challenge to power creates fear and mistrust (Thumin 1998, 103). Muta (2016) refers to this phenomenon as "the deeply embedded bifurcation of women in Japanese society," which divides women into "good" and "bad" (621). The following case studies reveal recent examples of how this anxiety permeates Japanese media representations that punish women and men who do not conform to but rather destabilize gender norms.

Case studies

The three subsequent case studies reveal the process of "mediated misogyny" in Japan—whether it be blatant fear of women, the shaming of men who fail to conform in appearance and behaviour to the standards of hegemonic masculinity or the marginalization of gender and sexual minorities. These cases also demonstrate that mediated misogyny is evident both in media content and industry practices.

The Women Hated by Women readers' poll

Weekly magazines, known as *shūkanshi*, occupy both an unusual and controversial space in the Japanese media landscape. They are published by newspaper companies and other independent publishers and split into various subgenres based on audience (female or male, stratified by age) and whether they emphasize literary and journalistic coverage, gossip, "soft" pornography (in the case of male readership-targeted publications) or a combination of these (Gamble and Watanabe 2004, 74). On one hand, they fill the gap in mainstream news journalism by focusing on investigative articles that newspapers don't report for fear of offending government officials and being frozen out of the *kisha kurabu* system, of which *shūkanshi* journalists are not a part (Gamble and Watanabe 2004, 85). They also tend to deal with "taboo" topics that mainstream media avoid, such as the imperial family, for example. However, many of the articles they publish are "racist, sexist and xenophobic" and rely heavily on unsubstantiated, anonymous sources (McNeill 2014, 69), as well as the misrepresentation, exaggeration and fabrication of events (Gamble and Watanabe 2004, 97).

Given these characteristics, it is not surprising that the *shūkanshi* aimed at a male readership publish content that is blatantly misogynistic and degrading. *Shūkan Bunshun*'s annual readers' poll that ranks the women in Japan most hated by other women is one such case. This *shūkanshi* focuses on political and economic news, does not include pornography and is aimed at an elite readership (Gamble and Watanabe 2004, 76). According to the Japan Magazine Publishers Association's data from late 2018, *Shūkan Bunshun* has a weekly circulation of 595,646 (JMPA 2018). However, its sensational headlines are most probably seen by many more through advertising on trains and internet news sites who report on *shūkanshi* stories. The *Onna ga Kiraina Onna: Waasuto 50* (The Women Hated by Women: Worst 50) annual readers' poll is based on "more than" 2000 survey responses from female members of the *Bunshun Online* mailing list. Well-known women from the political and entertainment worlds are ranked from 1 (the worst) to 50, and the accompanying article quotes the reasons given by respondents. The 2018 poll was the 13th time the poll had been held and singer Kudo Shizuka, the wife of actor, singer and former SMAP member Kimura Takuya, was voted the most hated. Some respondents blamed Kudo for forcing Kimura to marry her and changing the future of SMAP and others noted that she has said things that hurt the feelings of SMAP fans. Kudo was ranked fourth in 2017 and fifth in 2016. In second place was actress Matsui Kazuyo, who outed her husband's affair in a dramatic video on YouTube in 2017; she was in first place in the 2017 poll. Television announcer Itō Ayako, who dated a member of idol group Arashi, took third place. In the 2016 poll, the top three rankings were women with complex identities—*enka* singer Wada Akiko, an ethnic Korean, was in first place; *hāfu talento* Bekky, whose mother is Japanese and father is white British, was ranked second and Japanese-Taiwanese politician Renho, then head of the Democratic Party of Japan, was in third place.

Shūkan Bunshun's poll not only provides a disturbing snapshot of mediated misogyny in weekly magazines, it also exposes the coercion and complicity of women in maintaining the patriarchal status quo in Japan as a form of entertainment and confirmation bias for male readers. Since the readers' poll is based on votes from women, it's implied that their evaluation carries weight, whilst simultaneously satisfying the assumption of *Shūkan Bunshun*'s target audience that it is legitimate to "hate" women who are "the worst." Furthermore, this kind of negative and trivializing representation both reinforces and sustains the exclusion of women from power in Japanese society.

Herbivore men and carnivore women

Media panics surrounding the low birth and marriage rates in Japan are exemplified by sensational reporting on the existence of *sōshokukei-danshi* (herbivore men) and, to a lesser extent, *nikushokukei-joshi* (carnivore women) in Japanese society. The term *sōshokukei-danshi* was coined by journalist Fukasawa Maki in a 2006 Nikkei Business article to describe young heterosexual men who don't actively pursue women (Saladin 2017). However, Saladin stresses that Fukasawa's intention to show a positive development was interpreted negatively, and "herbivore men are now seen as not being 'proper' men, because they are said to lack assertiveness and ambition" (2017). They are blamed for Japan's demographic woes and frequently derided in media discourse on Japan's shrinking population. Notably, there is far less media and academic attention towards *nikushokukei-joshi* (carnivore women), which appears to signify some kind of unknown female "other."

Ōta (2016) describes *sōshokukei-danshi* (literally, grass-eating men) as young Japanese men who are "tender and passive" (223) but also "indecisive and unreliable" (227). On the other hand, *nikushokukei-joshi* (literally, meat-eating women) are merely "predatory-like" (226) and Ota does not discuss them further. Charlebois (2017) has proposed a "working definition" of herbivore masculinity as being "under-pinned by non-aggressiveness in the areas of professional and academic success and romance," ostensibly rejecting "the practices of a work-centred lifestyle and aggressive heterosexual prowess" (177).

Media images of *sōshokukei-danshi* tend to depict men who are ineffective communicators, sexually passive and uninterested in sexual relationships. This type of non-hegemonic masculinity is constructed as problematic because it undermines the hegemonic ideals of stable employment (Dasgupta 2013) and disrupts the ways in which work and masculinity are heavily intertwined in Japan (see Cook in this volume). However, Saladin's (2017) analysis of the representation of herbivore men in the 2009 television drama *Ohitorisama* (*The Single Lady*, Han Choru and Ueda Hisashi) offers some useful insights into how media representations need not negatively reinforce gender conformity but instead "provides an idea of what a new form of masculinity might look like—one which is clearly different from hegemonic masculinity in terms of emotional capacity and in the ability to approach professional life and relationships" (Saladin 2017). At best, the drama "provides a more comprehensive idea of what herbivore men could actually be like" and, Saladin notes, illustrating "a positive example of how masculinity in contemporary Japan could evolve." Representations of this type in dramas are important because they could potentially help to counter fears of weak masculinity, women's empowerment and the "unreproductive" LBGT community in media discourses on Japan's demographic challenges.

Itō Shiori and the #MeToo movement of women journalists

In 2017 journalist Itō Shiori went public with allegations that she had been raped by a well-known television journalist, Yamaguchi Noriyuki, in 2015. Itō had met Yamaguchi, then the Washington Bureau Chief of Tokyo Broadcasting System, as well as friend and biographer of Prime Minister Abe Shinzo, to discuss an internship at a bar in Tokyo. She became unwell, passed out, and alleges that he raped her after dragging her back to his hotel room unconscious. Her fight to be taken seriously despite systematic obstruction, threats and a nasty online backlash have been well documented in Itō's book, *Black Box* (2017), and her BBC documentary *Japan's Secret Shame* (Jenkin 2018). Both these works emphasise the fact that rape is considered a taboo topic in Japanese society and media and rape victims are invisible. Itō says that because of this injustice she had no choice but to make herself the story and use her journalistic training to document her experience and fight for justice (Itō 2018).

Itō says that, "if the press in Japan was free from the shackles of social convention, then the problems with Japan's century old rape laws, the lack of rape crisis centres, and the re-enacting of alleged rapes with lifesize dolls [a common practice in police investigations of sexual violence in Japan] might have been raised many year ago" (Itō 2018). However, Itō's ordeal and the salient points she makes about Japan's patriarchal media system are part of what Muta (2016) has described as "the long history of systematic and deeply embedded bifurcation of women in Japanese society" (621). Muta traces this insensitivity towards sexual violence in Japanese society across time, drawing connections to the denial and negation of the experiences of victims of Japan's wartime military sexual slavery—the so-called "comfort women"; these are all, for Muta, rooted in misogyny. She also argues that because "male dominance has to be maintained in fantasy at least ... the more forcefully the surviving comfort women insist on an official apology, the more they are denigrated" (631). This pattern is evident in Itō's demand for justice, as she refused to be silenced once the police dropped her case. She held press conferences and gave interviews to international media organizations, whilst enduring an aggressive and traumatic backlash from the media, the public, and many politicians.

Itō's fight for justice in Japanese society and the media coincided with the slow emergence of the #MeToo movement in Japan, as other women journalists complained of sexual harassment and assault. When allegations by a TV Asahi woman journalist of sexual harassment against top Finance Ministry bureaucrat Fukuda Jun'ichi were published in the weekly *Shūkan Shincho* in early 2018, he resigned and many other women journalists came forward to tell their stories (Daimon and Aoki 2018). Itō says that the TV Asahi journalist told her she was inspired to speak out because of Itō's actions and the global #MeToo movement (Itō 2018). In a survey of women journalists after the Finance Ministry scandal, 35 respondents reported being victims of sexual harassment, a third of which involved "lawmakers, government officials and law enforcers" (Yamaguchi 2018). This momentum in breaking the silence over the prevalence sexual harassment led to the establishment of an industry group called Women in Media Network Japan, who immediately began to lobby the government for clearer guidelines and protections against sexual harassment, as well as publishing their own recommendations (Baird 2018). Ōta et al. (2017, 19) argue that bypassing mainstream media and using social media to disseminate information on rights and freedom of expression, as well as maintaining links between women working in media and social activists, are two of the ways they hope to help combat sexual harassment in Japanese media.

Conclusion

This chapter has examined how misogyny permeates mainstream Japanese media culture and sustains the male-dominated media industry. Discriminatory and marginalizing media practices are not solely responsible for persistent gender inequality and embedded misogyny in Japan, but it is clear that they play an important cultural role in attempting to maintain gendered hierarchies and preserving patriarchal norms. The chapter began with a description of the gendered visual messages that train passengers encounter on their media-saturated daily commute—a "hot mess" of normative femininities and masculinities, entertainment, detailed weather information, sophisticated product commercialisation and a wide array of hi-tech communication devices. What appears at first sight to be a colourful and eclectic media landscape is, however, deceptive in a number of ways. As the case studies presented previously show, mediated misogyny is a prevailing characteristic of twenty-first-century Japanese media culture. Therefore, in conclusion, it is important to consider the following questions: why is this culture persisting? Who benefits? And how will it change?

First, mainstream Japanese media culture is constrained by ingrained practices and relationships such as the *kisha kurabu* system and the powerful influence of advertising agencies. Media digitalization is yet to dislodge some of the cosy and unequal relationships that have maintained this system. Second, the media industry in Japan has normalized male dominance and tried to hide harmful practices and behaviours that discriminate against women and gender minorities. The beneficiaries of misogynistic practices are patriarchal elites, who might currently be intent on resisting any challenge to their authority but are also anxious about the destabilisation of gender norms. Finally, patriarchal ideologies collide daily in Japanese media culture with new and complex notions of gender that have the subversive potential to challenge the status quo. Continuing to study these representations, practices and interactions will help us to understand more fully the dynamics of the relationship between gender, media and misogyny in Japan.

Further reading

Darling-Wolf, F. (ed) (2018) *Routledge Handbook of Japanese Media*, Abingdon, Oxon: Routledge. (Interdisciplinary perspectives on contemporary issues in Japanese media)
Galbraith, P. and Carlin, J. (eds) (2012) *Idols and Celebrity in Japanese Media Culture*, Basingstoke: Palgrave Macmillan. (The production and consumption of idols and fandom)
Lukacs, G. (2010) *Scripted Affects, Branded Selves: Television, Subjectivity, and Capitalism in 1990s Japan*, Durham and London: Duke University Press. (The political economy of television dramas)

Miller, L. and Bardsley, J. (2005) *Bad Girls of Japan*, New York: Palgrave Macmillan. (Women's deviancy in art and performance)

Prough, J. (2011) *Straight from the Heart: Gender, Intimacy and the Cultural Production of Shōjo Manga*, Honolulu: University of Hawai'i Press. (Ethnographic account of the shōjo manga industry)

Related chapters

Introduction
5   Masculinity Studies in Japan
22 Gender and Musical Subcultures in Japan
23 Gender in Digital Technologies and Cultures
30 Gender, Manga, and Anime
31 Cuteness Studies and Japan
32 Gender and Visual Culture
34 Representing Girls in Cinema
35 Gendered Desires: Pornography and Consumption

References

Baird, C. (2018) "New Industry Group Slams Government's Response to Sexual Harassment in Media," *The Japan Times* 15 May. www.japantimes.co.jp/news/2018/05/15/national/new-industry-group-slams-governments-response-sexual-harassment-media.

Byerly, C. (2004) "Shifting Sites: Feminist, Gay, and Lesbian News Activism in the U.S. Context," in M. De Bruin and K. Ross (eds) *Gender and Newsroom Cultures: Identities At Work*, Creskill: Hampton Press.

Byerly, C. (2011) *Global Report on the Status of Women in the News Media*, Washington DC: International Women's Media Foundation.

Charlebois, J. (2017) "Herbivore Masculinities in Post-Millennial Japan," in X. Lin, C. Haywood and M. Mac an Ghaill (eds) *East Asian Men: Masculinity, Sexuality and Desire*, London: Palgrave Macmillan.

Daimon, S. and Aoki, M. (2018) "Me Too Rises in Japan as Sexually Harassed Journalists Speak Out," *The Japan Times* 22 April. www.japantimes.co.jp/news/2018/04/22/national/social-issues/sexual-harassment-scandal-highlights-a-larger-problem-in-japans-media.

Dasgupta, R. (2013) *Re-Reading the Salaryman in Japan: Crafting Masculinities*, London: Routledge.

Ehara, Y. (2013) "Japanese Feminist Social Theory and Gender Equality," in A. Elliot, M. Katagiri and A. Sawai (eds) *Routledge Companion to Contemporary Japanese Social Theory*, London: Routledge.

Freeman, L. A. (2000) *Closing the Shop: Information Cartels and Japan's Mass Media*, Princeton: Princeton University Press.

Gamble, A. and Watanabe, T. (2004) *A Public Betrayed: An Inside Look at Japanese Media Atrocities and their Warnings to the West*, Washington, DC: Regnery Publishing.

Hayashi, K. and Tanioka, R. (2013) *Terebi Hodo Shoku no Waaku Raifu Anbaransu: 13 Kyoku Danjo 30jin no Kikitorichoosa kara* (The Work Life Unbalance of Television Broadcasting Work: From 30 Interviews with Employees of 13 Broadcasters), Tokyo: Otsuki Shoten.

Hayashi, K. and Kopper, G. (2014) "Multi-Layer Research Design for Analyses of Journalism and Media Systems in the Global Age: Test Case Japan,' *Media, Culture & Society* 36 (8) 1134–1150.

Holden, T. J. M. and Ergul H. (2006) "Japan's Televisual Discourses: Infotainment, Intimacy and the Construction of a Global Uchi," in T. J. M. Holden and T. J. Scrase (eds) *Medi@sia: Global Media/tion in and Out of Context*, London: Routledge, 105–127.

Horii, M. and Burgess, A. (2012) "Constructing Sexual Risk: 'Chikan', Collapsing Male Authority and the Emergence of Women-Only Train Carriages in Japan," *Health, Risk and Society* 14 (1) 41–55.

Inoue, T. and Josei Zasshi Kenkyūkai (1989) *Josei zasshi o kaidoku suru: Comparepolitan – nichi-bei-mekishiko hikaku kenkyū* (Reading into Women's Magazines: Comparepolitan – Comparative study of Japanese, American and Mexican Magazines). Tokyo: Kakiuchi-shuppan.

Ishiyama, R. (2013) "Japan: Why So Few Women Journalists?" in C. Byerly (ed) *The Palgrave International Handbook of Women and Journalism*, Basingstoke, UK: Palgrave Macmillan.

Itō, S. (2017) *Black Box*, Tokyo: Bungeishunju.

Itō, S. (2018) "Japan's Attitudes Towards Sexual Violence Are Locked in the Past," *BBC Two*. www.bbc.co.uk/programmes/articles/3z44Njyr5wzm3wbVMGZ7tFr/shiori-ito-japan-s-attitudes-to-allegations-of-sexual-violence-are-locked-in-the-past.

Japan Magazine Publishers Association (2018) *Insatsu Busu Kōhyō* (Print Circulation Figures). www.j-magazine.or.jp.

Jenkin, E. (2018) Japan's Secret Shame. London: BBC.

Kingston, J. (2017) *Press Freedom in Contemporary Japan*, London: Routledge.

Kiyake, M. (2017) *Tokyo Idols* [DVD] New York: KimStim.

Luck, A. (2017) "Japan's Madonna Complex," *Index on Censorship* 46 (1) 22–25.

Mandujano-Salazar, Y. Y. (2018) "Media Idols and the Regime of Truth About National Identity in Post-3.11 Japan," in F. Darling-Wolf (ed) *Routledge Handbook of Japanese Media*, Abingdon, Oxon: Routledge.

Manne, K. (2018) *Down Girl: The Logic of Misogyny*, New York: Oxford University Press.

Maree, C. (2017) "Weddings and White Dresses: Media and Sexual Citizenship in Japan," *Sexualities* 20 (1–2) 212–233.

Maree, C. (2018) "Writing Sexual Identity onto the Small Screen: Seitekishosu-sha (Sexual Minorities) in Japan," in F. Darling-Wolf (ed) *Routledge Handbook of Japanese Media*, Abingdon, Oxon: Routledge.

Marx, W. D. (2012) "The Jimusho System: Understanding the Production Logic of the Japanese Entertainment Industry," in P. Galbraith and J. Carlin (eds) *Idols and Celebrity in Japanese Media Culture*, Basingstoke: Palgrave Macmillan.

McLaren, S. (2008) "Gender and Beyond: Audiences, Critical Perspectives and Media Literacy," *Ritsumeikan Social Sciences Review* 43 (4) 91–108.

McLaren, S. (2015) "Documenting 'Sexless' Japan: Audience Analysis of the BBC's 'No Sex Please, We're Japanese,'" paper presented at the *19th Biennial Conference of the Japanese Studies Association of Australia*, La Trobe University, Melbourne.

McNeill, D. (2014) "Japan's Contemporary Media," in J. Kingston (ed) *Critical Issues in Contemporary Japan*, Abingdon, Oxon: Routledge.

McNeill, D. (2016) "False Dawn: The Decline of Watchdog Journalism in Japan," *The Asia Pacific Journal Japan Focus* 14 (20–2). https://apjjf.org/2016/20/McNeill.html

Miller, L. (2011) "Cute Masquerade and the Pimping of Japan," *International Journal of Japanese Sociology* 20 18–29.

Mohanty, C. P. (2003) *Feminism Without Borders: Decolonizing Theory, Practicing Solidarity*, Durham and London: Duke University Press.

Muramatsu, Y. and Gossman, H. (1998) *Media ga tsukuru jendaa: Nichidoku no danjo, kazokuzō o yomitoku* (Gender Created by Media: Reading representations of men, women and the family in Japan and Germany), Tokyo: Shinyosha.

Muta, K. (2016) "The Comfort Women Issue and the Embedded Culture of Sexual Violence in Contemporary Japan," *Current Sociology* 64 (4) 620–636.

"Onna ga Kiraina Onna" (The Women Hated By Women) (2016) *Shūkan Bunshun*, 3 November.

"Onna ga Kiraina Onna" (The Women Hated By Women) (2017) *Shūkan Bunshun*, 17–24 August.

"Onna ga Kiraina Onna" (The Women Hated By Women) (2018) *Shūkan Bunshun*, 13 September.

Ōta, K., Kojima, K. and Takenobu, M. (2017) "Media Sekuhara ga Oko Suru Shakai no Haikei to Kore Kara" (The Background and Future of a Society Where Media Sexual Harassment Is Rampant), *Onnatachi no 21 Seiki* 91 8–20.

Ōta, S. (2016) "Herbivorous Boys and Predatory Girls: Gender, Consumerism, and Low Birthrate in Japan," in S. Nagy (ed) *Japan's Demographic Revival: Rethinking Migration, Identity and Sociocultural Norms*, Singapore: World Scientific Publishing.

Painter, A. (1996) "The Telerepresentation of Gender in Japan," in A. Imamura (ed) *Re-Imaging Japanese Women*, Berkeley: University of California Press.

Saladin, R. (2017) "Herbivore Masculinity in Media Discourse: The Japanese TV Drama Ohitorisama," *Intersections: Gender and Sexuality in Asia and the Pacific* 41. http://intersections.anu.edu.au/issue41/saladin.html#n8.

Shikata, Y. (2018) "Jendā to Media" (Gender and Media), in S. Oi, N. Tamura and Y. Suzuki (eds) *Gendai Jyānarizumu o Manabu Hito no Tame ni* (For Those Who Study Contemporary Journalism), Kyoto: Sekaishisosha.

Suganuma, K. (2018) "Queering Mainstream Media: Matsuko Deluxe as Modern-Day *Kuroko*," in F. Darling-Wolf (ed) *Routledge Handbook of Japanese Media*, Abingdon, Oxon: Routledge.

Suzuki, M. F. (1995) "Women and Television: Portrayal of Women in the Mass Media," in K. Fujimura-Fanselow and A. Kameda (eds) *Japanese Women: New Feminist Perspectives on the Past, Present, and Future*, New York: The Feminist Press.

Suzuki, M. F. (2005) "Media Literashi to Jendā" (Media Literacy and Gender), in Kita Kyushu Shiritsu Danjo Kyodo Sankaku Senta (ed) *Jendā Hakusho Vol 3: Josei to Media* (Gender White Paper Vol. 3: Women and Media), Tokyo: Akashi Shoten.

Takenobu, M. (2017) "Josei ga kagayaku: Seisaku no Futsugona Shinjitsu" (The Inconvenient Truth of the Women Can Shine Policy) *Onnatachi no 21 Seiki* 91 4–7.

Tanaka, K. and Morohashi T. (eds) (1996) *Jenda kara mita shinbun no ura omote: Shinbun joseigaku nyūmon* (Gender Analysis of Newspapers: Introduction to Women's Studies on Newspapers), Tokyo: Gendai Shokan.

Thumin, J. (1998) "Mrs Knight Must Be Balanced: Methodological Problems in Researching Early British Television," in C. Carter, G. Branston and S. Allen (eds) *News, Gender and Power*, London: Routledge.

Valaskivi, K. (2015) "Mass Media in Japan," in J. Babb (ed) *The Sage Handbook of Modern Japanese Studies*, London: Sage.

Vickery, J. R. (2018) "This Isn't New: Gender, Publics and the Internet," in J. R. Vickery and T. Everbach (eds) *Mediating Misogyny: Gender, Technology and Harassment*, New York: Palgrave Macmillan.

Vickery, J. R. and Everbach, T. (2018) "The Persistence of Misogyny: From the Streets, to Our Screens, to the White House," in J. R. Vickery and T. Everbach (eds) *Mediating Misogyny: Gender, Technology and Harassment*, New York: Palgrave Macmillan.

Villi, M. and Hayashi, K. (2015) "The Mission Is to Keep this Industry Intact," *Journalism Studies*, DOI: 10.1080/1461670X.2015.1110499.

Yamaguchi, M. (2018) "Female Journalists in Japan Report Being Victims of Sexual Misconduct: Poll," *The Japan Times* 22 May. www.japantimes.co.jp/news/2018/05/22/national/social-issues/japanese-female-journalists-report-victims-sexual-misconduct-poll.

Yoshimoto, M. (2010) "Why Japanese Television Now?" in M. Yoshimoto, E. Tsai and J. Choi (eds) *Television, Japan, and Globalization*, Ann Arbor: Center for Japanese Studies, University of Michigan.

34
REPRESENTING GIRLS IN CINEMA

Kate Taylor-Jones and Georgia Thomas-Parr

Picture this: a white-gowned girl with long black hair crawling out of your television, each bloodied, nail-less finger gripping the floor as she pulls herself towards you. With this image of Sadako, one of the most easily recognizable horror figures from the last two decades, the girl takes centre stage. From innocent virgins to figures of pure evil, from idols to anime characters, the girl proliferates as a moving image across Japanese popular media. Girls are victims and survivors, threat and saviour, sexual objects and sexualized subjects, figments of the male imagination and self-defining creators of their own cultures of girlhood.

This chapter will focus on how girls have been represented in live-action cinema even though images of the girl extend far beyond film, permeating screens and billboards, from endless anime visuals to virtual YouTubers to characters in "dating-sim" games. These depictions usually reflect not the lived experiences of actual girls but rather youthful femininity as an image that transcends actual girlhood itself (Yoda 2017). The representation of girlhood is therefore intimately and inexorably intertwined with the cultural and historical moment in which is created, circulated, and debated.

Constructing girlhood

Given the proliferation of girlhoods that are now present in the modern media-scape (Projansky 2014; Driscoll 2002; Harris 2004), it is hard to both define and draw the boundary around what constitutes "girl," "girlhood," "girl culture," or even the more media-specific "girl-scape" (Yoda 2017). There is a wide lexicon to describe girlhood in Japan, of which the term *shōjo* is the most utilized. *Shōjo-ron* ("girl theory") is a growing field of research but, as Laura Miller and Jan Bardsley (2005) note, problematically, the term has often come to be used as catch-all phrase to label and define wide-reaching and diverse experiences of femininity. More problematically, it has at times been dominated by male writings *about* girls (Yamane 1989, 1993; Kawamura 1994, 2003). Critical theorist Ōtsuka Eiji's *The Native Ethnology of Girls* (1989) is perhaps the best known of this literature and interlinks the girl with several of Ōtsuka's preoccupations with consumption, media, and crisis. His work posits *shōjo* culture as a potential threat to the Japanese nation (1989, 249) via an increasing infantilization of adulthood, which is something that needs to be intensely resisted for Japan to flourish. Ōtsuka's focus on the idea of the national body as under threat from the girl both articulates the girl as outsider in her oppositional status to masculine modes of expression whilst simultaneously denying girls their own subjective and interrogative stance towards their own culture and modes of expression (for example, fashion, film, and music) via a dismissal of their experiences as valuable or worthwhile.

This dismissal by scholars is illustrated by Ōtsuki Takahiro's study on *rabukome* (romantic comedy genres) in *shōjo* manga when he argues that *shōjo* and *shonen* can be conflated. In his view, the boundary-crossing nature of *shōjo* means that it no longer holds a specific market or audience need. As Kukhee Choo (2008) points out, this approach privileges the male experience over the female and reduces the *shōjo* to a lesser companion to her male counterpart rather than an important figure in her own right. This male-orientated reading of *shōjo* and her representations are in contrast to female writers such as Honda Masuko (1982, 1986, 1990, 2010), Takahara Eiri (2006), Miyasako Chizuru (1984), Kawasaki Kenko (1990, 2008), and Inoue Miyako (2006) who see *shōjo* culture as identifiable, valuable, and filled with potential. Scholars writing in English, including Tomoko Aoyama (2010), Hiromi Tsuchiya Dollase (2003, 2008), Sharon Kinsella (2014), Deborah Shamoon (2012, 2008), and Sharalyn Orbaugh (2003), have utilized this work in their own thinking on the subject and have explored the representation of the *shōjo* in a wide variety of cultural and media products and settings. Therefore, using the term *shōjo* incorporates a wide range of approaches and representations that, rather unhelpfully, do not always agree with each other.

Shōjo may be used to refer to a variety of different things, including a genre of manga and girls' culture, a symbol of the girl, and the liminal period between adolescent girlhood and womanhood. Defined by John Treat as an "[ambiguously] pubescent female with the physical traits of a woman, yet one who still has the sexual naiveté and innocence of a child" (1996, 280), *shōjo* was originally a pre-war term used in Japan to define a girl who deferred her marriage and, with this, (presumably) sex and pregnancy, by continuing her education (Takahashi 2008).

Being a *shōjo* in Japan also involves behavioural traits that are related to *kawaii* (cuteness) (Treat 1996; Mackie 2009; J. Dale in this issue). The *shōjo* has always had a complicated connection between good and bad. She is, in many ways, the hyper-ideal female figure that adheres to modes of emphasized femininity, often including a focus on dress and make-up and "girly" character traits such as a caring nature and a desire to please. Nevertheless, she also encapsulates power and the possibility of disrupting structural hegemonies since, as Honda notes, "*shōjo* is neither adult woman or girl child, neither man nor woman" (quoted in Treat 1996, 281). In her desire to remain in a state of adolescence rather than moving into the category of adult women, Treat notes that this liminal status allows the *shōjo* to "detach from the reproductive economy of heterosexual reproduction" (1996, 281).

Honda articulates the nature of *shōjo* via the term *hirahira*, used to denote the ephemeral fluttering of ribbons and the poetic "lyrical word chains" (2010, 20) seen in the popular fiction of writers such as Yoshiya Nobuko (particularly her series *Hana monogatari/Flower Tales*, 1916–24) and the illustrations of Nakahara Jun'ichi. The alternative and potentially subversive narrative of *shōjo* is painted by Honda as tapping into the "acute sensitivities of girls" (2010, 27), something "alogical and unworldly" (2010, 36) and off-limits to "non-girls," especially men. She notes that the concept of girls' culture always embodies fantasy and for Aoyama this is her "subversiveness against patriarchal norms" (2008, 208). Indeed, Honda's view of *shōjo* moved beyond regressive notions that reduce the girl to a set of polarities, instead working towards understanding the represented girl as being part of a paradoxical continuum: not "either/or" but "neither and both" (Honda quoted in Aoyama 2010, 40). Key in this process is the work of several scholars who have offered a vital historical focus on girlhood. Kawamura Kunimitsu's (1993) work on pre-war girls' culture, Watanabe Shūko's (2007) focus on Meiji and Taisho, and Imada Erika's (2007) exploration of the early Showa. All three studies explore the products produced by and for girls, moving the *shōjo* away from ideas of nationhood towards a vision of *shōjo* as girls themselves engaged with, and as, *shōjo*. These female-authored insights into the world of girlhood offered alternative perspectives to the previously male-dominated area of Japanese scholarship on the subject. Inoue Miyako (2006) speaks of *shōjo* culture in Japan as being a counter-public sphere, governed by girls only. As Honda states, girls constructed a "girls' imagined community" (Honda 1990 186), where they can explore and articulate their own desires and experiences. Nonetheless, this positive vision of girl-space coexists in a climate where the girl has been heavily commodified by visual media in an attempt to control and make sense of the girl (Dyhouse 2014; McRobbie 2009). With this in mind, it is important, as Shamoon notes, "to distinguish between those mainstream male authored texts aimed at male audiences and the image of the girl that emerged within girl's culture" (2012, 11). Defining girlhood is therefore a complicated arena, where we might consider, as Catherine Driscoll aptly asks, "How do the ambivalences of girlhood affect the definition of girl culture?" (2002, 267). Indeed, "What girl culture might name, or how it might be used, is difficult to strictly delimit because what seems most obvious about it—girls—is what makes it hardest to define" (2002, 267).

Screening girlhood

As discussed, the social and cultural dimensions that mark the status of girl as a category make her definition a complex topic. *What* the girl does is therefore perhaps more important than age as the defining marker of girlhood. As Jennifer Robertson (1998) notes, at its point of conception, the *shōjo* category itself was defined in the popular imagination in two Janus-facing figures of the early twentieth century: the "new working woman" (*shinshokugyō fujin*) and the *moga*, or "modern girl." Both these visions of femininity caused widespread social concern in the 1910s and 1920s because they were seen as refuting what was expected and esteemed as being ideal of womanhood: the dominant Meiji vision of *ryōsai kenbo*, the "good wife, wise mother" who was confined to the role of domestic housekeeper (see Uno 1993). However, as Barbara Sato notes, not all *moga* were working women (and vice versa) but both were defined in that moment of modernity and cosmopolitanism (2003, 119). On the shoulders of the modern girl, the uncertain future of Japan came to rest.

In cinema, early female stars such as Aizome Yumeko, Hara Komako, Mizukubo Sumiko, and the better-known Tanaka Kinyuo and Hara Setsuko, offered a wide range of "girlhoods," from the traditional to the nonconformist, for the cinematic audience to enjoy throughout the 1920s and 1930s. A popular example is Ozu Yasujirō's 1933 silent film *Dragnet Girl/ (Hijōsen no Onna)*, where two very different types of girl come into conflict. The hard-working law-abiding innocent Kazuko (Mizukubo Sumiko) is placed in opposition to the gangster's moll Tokiko (Tanaka Kinuyo). Whilst Tokiko sports sleek modern clothing, Kazuko's attire is traditional kimono—clearly setting up visual markers that defined girlhood as both old and new, both pure and deviant.

Girlhood would continue to be defined by its in-between status as Japan entered into the war. As Dollase notes, *shōjo* culture, as an experience of creative communality, often bypasses more negative (specifically wartime) girls' culture that girls' magazines such as *Shōjo no tomo* imparted to their young readers (2008). *Shōjo* may be a time of play, but wartime required a focus on a more military experience (*gunkoku shōjo*) in order to best serve the nation-state. This is evident in Kurosawa Akira's 1944 film *The Most Beautiful (Ichiban utsukushiku)*, which follows the experiences of a group of young women working in a lens factory. In a complete self-sacrificial subservience to the war effort, the drive for these girls to act like their male counterparts is shown in their desire to have the same production targets as the men. At the same time, the film stresses a patriarchal need for girls to remain dependent on male advice and leadership, shown in images of tear-stained faces and occasional lapses in judgment.

Following Japan's defeat in the Asia-Pacific War/s and the subsequent US-led occupation, the *shōjo* became an icon of victimization with whom the nation could identify (Coates 2016). The body of the girl became the locus of fears about miscegenation, Japan's failure as a nation, and concerns for what the postwar would bring. As Kinsella notes, anxieties "about the necessity to bodily reproduce a distinctive Japanese race" (2014, 126) are often visualized as female. Girls would play an important role in the immediate postwar cinematic focus on rebuilding Japan with films such as *No Regrets for Our Youth* (*Waga seishun ni kui nashi*, Kurosawa Akira, 1946) and *Drunken Angel* (*Yoidore tenshi*, Kurosawa Akira, 1948) visualizing the girl as the site of a new future and the affective means via which older society could come to terms with the new Japan (Horiguchi 2011; Coates 2016). Features such as *24 Eyes* (*Nijūshi no hitomi*, Kinoshita Keisuke, 1954), *Children of the Bomb* (*Genbaku no ko*, Shindō Kaneto, 1952), *Escape at Dawn* (*Akatsuki no dassō*, Taniguchi Senkichi, 1950), and the 1965 remake *Story of a Prostitute* (*Shunpuden*, Suzuki Seijun) and *The Tower of Lilies* (*Himeyuri no tō*, Imai Tadashi, 1953) feature the bloody, irradiated, and dying bodies of young girls as representations of Japan's status as "innocent" victim.

The image of the girl would also play a pivotal role in debates on Japan's future. Whilst the abused bodies of those who had lived through the war were still highly visible on screen, a new figure began to emerge: the girl growing up in the postwar moment. As Japanese democracy developed and postwar hardships began to fade, consumerism once again took hold and the girl would operate as the site to debate the changes Japan was undergoing. Film directors such as Naruse Mikio, Suzuki Seijun, Imamura Shōhei, Kinoshita Keisuke, and Ōshima Nagisa featured the girl as a site of social anxiety around postwar development. From the anarchic vision of girlhood seeking sex and violence in Ōshima's *Cruel Story of Youth* (*Seishun zankoku monogatari*, 1960) to the heartless Utako of Kinoshita Keisuke's *Tragedy of Japan* (*Nihon no higeki*, 1953), who rejects her loving lower-class mother in favour of the financial benefits her married lover appears to offer, girlhood operated as a site of both anxiety and desirability.

In Suzuki's *Gate of Flesh* (*Nikutai no Mon*, 1964), the young prostitute Maya idealizes the postwar moment as both a victim and a symbol of strength. After being raped by American GIs and left starving on the street to become prey to pimps, she falls in with a group of women who are happy to control their own sexuality for profit. The group live together and have only one rule: no sex without money. Their lives are disturbed when former soldier and convict Shintarō enters their hideout. Here, girlhood is not just narratively constructed but is also visually enhanced. The women wear bright dresses that make them stand out from the surroundings, and the over-the-top acting style the actresses were instructed to use includes "loud voices and broad gestures" (Vick 2015, 49) that move them away from the more nuanced and subtle acting styles of Japan's sweethearts such as Hara Setsuko. The image of the girl is superimposed with other patterns, colours, and shapes. When the girls torture one of the other prostitutes for sleeping with Shintarō, we see Maya's face superimposed onto her naked body as she internally contemplates her own desires for the forbidden male figure.

Girlhood in this way is marked both visually and spatially as the innocent girl of the pre-war features moves away from the safety of the home to the chaotic, lawless (often unidentifiable) ruins of the city and the prostitute's run-down hideout. Whilst she may be a victim, Maya is also capable of articulating, and acting upon, her own desires, and this new image of girlhood moves far away from the almost asexual girls of films such as *The Most Beautiful* whose desire was to serve the nation-state. Imamura's *Pigs and Battleships* (*Buta to gunkan*, 1961) ends on an image of the character of Haruko as she walks away from her arranged marriage with an American serviceman to a new life outside of the city of Yokosuka. In her experiences of abortion, rape, and being arrested, Haruko's trajectory marks a move away from the "innocent virgin" girlhood trope. Yet, when most of the male characters are dead, it is the girl who will walk away to a new life.

The endless potential space of resistance that girlhood offers would be enhanced by the low-budget, non-studio films of the later 1960s. Furthermore, the move in the 1970s and 1980s towards exploitation cinema as a means to try to maintain audience shares provided fertile ground for new female exploration in Japanese film, from the female yakuza (Coates 2017) to female revenge films such as *Lady Snowblood* (*Shurayuki-hime*, Fujita Toshiya, 1973). However, as Miller and Bardsley (2005) note, the tendency to trivialize and eroticize girls means that "Bad Girls' efforts at resisting do not always creative new alternative as much as new models and categories that are similarly conscripting" (2005, 5). In short, "even potentially disruptive images may be neutralized once they are incorporated into mainstream media" (2005, 5).

An ideal example of this is the *sukeban*. The term *sukeban* (used to denote a delinquent girl of middle or high school age, or the boss of a girl gang, the female equivalent of *banchō*) references both a horror and a fascination with teenage subcultures (Sato 1991). Pulp magazine stories titillated their readers with tales of girls carrying razors under long school skirts and participating in violent crime purely for pleasure. With Suzuki Norifumi's *Girl Boss Guerilla* (*Sukeban gerira*, 1972) and the *Terrifying Girls' High School* (*Kyofu Joshi Koko*) series as notable key examples, the *sukeban* films sought to present an alternative female subculture that defines itself by its own rules whilst offering a substantial dose of softcore pornography. The women are brave, strong, sexually liberated, and more than capable of dealing with their male gang counterparts, as Sharp (2008) and Kozma (2012) note. A potential privileging of female subjectivity in the film narrative means that many see these films as the ideal space to offer a new and empowered experience of girlhood. However, the countercultural or recuperative narrative of filmmaking that feminist textual analysis has brought to the mainstream (Kuhn 1982) must also be contextualized in light of the modes of production and reception that surround the products. The pinky violence genre that the *sukeban* films belonged to were created inside a male-dominated system that allowed women very little power, despite some high-profile exceptions such as Hamano Sachi and Yoshiyuki Yumi. Whilst the girl-boss films may feature girls, girls were not necessarily their target market in their initial conception, given the "intensely gendered theatre spaces" in which they were shown (Zahlten 2017b, 64) that privileged and catered to the male viewer over the female. It is true that women would still have attended and enjoyed the films (and the arrival of the VHS and other forms of media has opened up the films to wider audiences), but the endless visual engagement with the girl gangs was made at the expense of engaging with actual girls themselves. Therefore, the girl-boss often became a site of male fascination and eroticism rather than female empowerment, with a clear privileging of visual fantasy over an informed, self-created, and diverse lived experience of girlhood.

More recently, the spirit of the *sukeban* can be seen in another female teenage group, all-girl motorcycle gangs, or *bōsōzoku*. The feminine *bōsōzoku*—more typically gendered as male in media and popular culture—would be famously brought to the screen by Nakashima Tetsuya in the 2006 film *Kamikaze Girls* (*Shimotsuma monogatari*, 2008). Based on a novel by Takemoto Novala, *Kamikaze Girls* follows the friendship of Lolita-obsessive Momoko and Ichigo, a member of an all-girl biker gang. The film seeks to bring to the audience a vision of a girls' culture that is not defined solely by girls' images but rather by their active and self-aware interrogation of their individual experiences of girlhood. Girlhood here is established as a site of potential power, as female friendship, creativity, and strength become defining tropes. In short, the *sukeban* motif becomes a site of female play and development. However, as Kuraishi Takahiro's part-journalistic, part-folklorist work on subcultures in Shibuya notes (2002), the media frenzy that surrounded the rise of girls' subcultures like *bōsōzoku* or the *kogyaru* in the 1990s was a sign that girls were still considered a problem and a matter of national concern. Seized by the media in a cynical distraction from the failures of men following the collapse of the bubble economy (Kinsella 2014), the non-conforming girl once more provided an ideal scapegoat for societal issues.

This link between girlhood and the neo-liberal agenda would come to define the girlhood of the 1990s onwards. The role that the girl played in defining a new moment of play and consumerism had been seen in the literary field during the late 1980s and early 1990s, as the novels of author Yoshimoto Banana rose to both critical and popular acclaim on the international stage. As Treat (1993) notes, Yoshimoto was seen as both *shōjo* herself (despite being notably older) and a key author in the construction of *shōjo*, with the direct address of *shōjo* author Yoshimoto to her *shōjo* audience "suggestively narcissistic" (Treat 1993, 380). This public move towards self-love and selfishness spoke to a broad range of female experiences and desires. Similarly, the so-called "girly" photographers (*onnanoko shashinka*) of the 1990s, Ninagawa Mika, Hiromix, and Nagashima Yurie, despite their markedly different styles, allowed for girls to see themselves and their lives as worthy of display on the walls of galleries. Girls' experiences became notable enough to warrant acclaim and, of course, monetization. Whilst girlhood had always been intertwined with discourses of consumerism, the contemporary idol would take this connection to new levels of intensity.

The idol film era

Whilst idol studies go far beyond the scope of this chapter (see Aoyagi 2005; Galbraith and Karlin 2012), in terms of cinema, idol culture is nothing new. Throughout the 1970s and 1980s, young female stars such as Yakushimaru Hiroko, Harada Tomoyo, and Watanabe Noriko (the *Kadokawa sannin-musume*, or "three Kadokawa girls"), provided an ideal platform for both film sales and cross-over merchandising between film, magazine, and music. These women were key players in what has become known as the idol film era. Films such as *Four Sisters* (Shimaizaka, Ōbayashi Nobuhiko, 1985), *Memories of You* (*Rabu sutorii wo kimi ni*, Sawai Shinichiro, 1988), and *Tokyo Heaven* (*Tōkyō jōkū irasshaimase*, Sōmai Shinji, 1990) presented their young, attractive female stars in a variety of tales that range from crime drama (*The Tragedy of "W"/"W" no higeki*, Sawai Shinichiro, 1984) to romance (*Young Girls in Love/Koi suru onnatachi*, Ōmori Kazuki, 1986) all the way to science fiction (*The Girl Who Leapt Through Time/Toki o Kakeru Shōjo*, Ōbayashi Nobuhiko, 1983).

Contemporary girlhood is heavily entangled in both consumer culture and bodily surveillance. Aoyagi (2005) argues that, far from a liberating vision, female idols hold substantial capitalist value and contribute heavily to the creation of an endlessly consuming audience for media products. This is interesting in light of Alexander Zahlten's comment that in order "to remain semiotically flexible and mobile across media platforms, actresses had to remain as empty, and, in a sense, as unreal as possible" (2017a, 208). Idol cinema offered a space for female pleasure via characters they could both identify with and aspire towards, but, as Joanna Hollows notes, film also reproduces the female spectator as a consumer (2000, 53). In the current age, the girl idol (*shōjo aidoru*) is arguably now one of the most esteemed feminine positions in Japanese society. A ubiquitous figure on the contemporary Japanese cultural landscape, she has bought the teenage girl a level of visibility that is arguably unprecedented anywhere else. A cinematic vision of the phenomenon can be found in Miyake Kyoko's documentary *Tokyo Girls* (2017), which follows the pathway of teen pop star Rio. Rio is bright, articulate, and hard working, and, in her navigation of male fans under the shadow of her inescapable ageing, she shows a firm sense of business ability. She is an ideal example of the young woman who is aware of the limited (and limiting) power and validation made available to her in her state of girlhood and negotiates the reward system under the processes of neoliberal self-autonomy that, as Diane Negra writes "fetishises female power and desire while consistently placing these within firm limits" (2008, 4). In the case of the girl, her period of liminal power is constrained by social ideas around ageing and desirability. *Tokyo Girls* focuses on Rio's endless work to produce her body in the idealized format that appeals to her male fan base. Her bodily presentation, both online and offline, is a fantasy, not reality, that she is selling, and in world of the teen idol, this fantasy is based firmly on the transitory category of youth. Girlhood therefore is conceived of as a temporary state, marked by the endless passing of time.

For girls, as Judith Butler notes, adolescence exists in the state of flux. It is a temporal process that is (re)constituted via a competing process of reiteration and destabilization (Butler 1993). This can be seen in the 2016 film *Japanese Girls Never Die* aka *Haruko Azumi Is Missing* (*Azumi Haruko wa yukuefumei*, Matsui Daigo), where the image of the girl is both seen and unseen, reiterated and then destabilized. Haruko's missing-person poster is ignored, but when two teenage graffiti artists begin to use her image in Warhol-esque prints across their town, the local population take notice. In this film, the image of the girl and real girls are both in flux. Girlhood in this film is constructed on both the spatial, visual (the missing poster and the art work), and temporal plane (the film offers a non-linear timeline). Haruko is depressed, lonely, and endlessly told by the family and co-workers that time is running out as she approaches her early twenties. With the clock ticking on her "desirable" state of girlhood, Haruko is caught in a liminal space, an in-between moment that neither the "real" woman nor her image can escape from. Spatially, girlhood in the film exists in a variety of formal (work, home) and informal (parks, river banks, car parks) spaces. Haruko operates in what Augé calls non-places; "if a place can be defined as relational, historical and concerned with identity, then a place which cannot be defined as relational, historical and concerned with identity will be a non-place" (1995, 78). For Augé, spaces of transition such as airports, leisure parks, large retail outlets and shopping malls, and rail stations are designated non-spaces (1995, 79), yet, as we see in *Haruko Azuma is Missing* and in numerous other films such as *Our Little Sister* (*Umimachi Diary*, Koreeda Hirokazu, 2015), *Suicide Club* (*Jisatsu Sākuru*, Sono Sion, 2001), *Bounce Ko-Gals* (*Baunsu kōgarusu*, Harada Masato, 1997), and *Wolf Girl and Black Prince* (*Ōkami Shōjo to Kuro Ōji*, Hiroki Ryūichi, 2016), the spaces of girlhood are rarely formal ones. Girlhood and non-place are therefore closely interlinked. Haruko decides to "go missing" after she sees a group of violent teenage girls beat a man by the side of a river, and the film concludes as she and her female friends vanish on a road trip, destination unknown. For the cinematic girl, the non-place is the site where she flourishes, existing in a state of temporality and flux.

Conclusion

Metaphorically speaking, the girl, caught between a nostalgic past and uncanny future, may be seen as representing the fleetingness of time itself (Kawasaki 1990; Wilson 2017). If the *shōjo* condition is one that rejoices in and gains power from liminality, perhaps this is why her position as an image captivates in the way that it does. The photographic image freezes her in her liminal state, defying the passing of time and, with it, her inevitable womanhood. As Robertson contends, "controlling the *shōjo* was desirable because she was fascinating, attractive and weak, and it was necessary because she was powerful, threatening and different" (Robertson 1998, 158). As theories of the *shōjo* have argued, the *shōjo* as an icon has the potential for delivering progressive messages for girls, to enhance and develop her ability to be "liminal, transformative, liberatory and potentially resistant" (Orbaugh 2003, 206). However, on the other side of the coin, many *shōjo* protagonists and narratives also arguably conform to a postfeminist ideology that has significantly less positive connotations. These two sides once again illustrate the contradiction that is so inherent to the symbolic figure of the girl, which continues to intrigue the cinematic gaze in Japan and worldwide.

Related chapters

30   Gender, Manga, and Anime
31   Cuteness Studies and Japan
32   Gender and Visual Culture
33   Gender, Media, and Misogyny in Japan

References

Aoyagi, H. (2005) *Islands of Eight Million Smiles: Idol Performance and Symbolic Production in Contemporary Japan*, Cambridge: Harvard University Press.
Aoyama, T. (2010) "The Genealogy of the 'Girl' Critic Reading Girl," in T. Aoyama and B. Hartley (eds) *Girl Reading Girl in Japan*, London and New York: Routledge, 38–49.
Augé, M. (1995) *Non-Places: Introduction to An Anthropology of Supermodernity*, trans. J. Howe, London and New York: Verso.
Butler, J. (1993) *Bodies That Matter*, London and New York: Routledge.
Choo, K. (2008) "Girls Return Home: Portrayal of Femininity in Popular Japanese Girls' Manga and Anime Texts During the 1990s in Hana Yori Dango and Fruits Basket," *Women: A Cultural Review* 19 (3) 275–296.
Coates, J. (2016) *Making Icons: Repetition and the Female Image in Japanese Cinema, 1945–1964*, Hong Kong: Hong Kong University Press.
Coates, J. (2017) "Gambling with the Nation: Heroines of the Japanese Yakuza Film, 1955–1975," *Japanese Studies* 37 (3) 353–369.
Dollase, H.T. (2003) "Early Twentieth Century Japanese Girls' Magazine Stories: Examining Shōjo Voice in Hanamonogatari (Flower Tales)," *The Journal of Popular Culture* 36 (4) 724–755.
Dollase, H.T. (2008) "Girls on the Home Front: An Examination of Shōjo no tomo Magazine 1937–1945," *Asian Studies Association of Australia* 32 (3) 323–339.
Driscoll, C. (2002) *Girls: Feminine Adolescence in Popular Culture and Theory*, New York: Columbia University Press.
Dyhouse, C. (2014) *Girl Trouble: Panic and Progress in the History of Young Women*, London: Zed Books.
Galbraith, P. and Karlin, J. (2012) *Idols and Celebrity in Japanese Media Culture*, London and New York: Palgrave Macmillan.
Harris, A. (2004) *Future Girl: Young Women in the Twenty-First Century*, New York: Routledge.
Hollows, J. (2000) *Feminism, Femininity and Popular Culture*, Manchester: Manchester University Press.
Honda, M. (1982) *Ibunka to shite no kodomo* (The Child as Another Culture), Tokyo: Kinokuniya Shoten.
Honda, M. (1986) *Shōjo fuyu* (Floating Girls), Tokyo: Seidosha.
Honda, M. (1990) *Jogakusei no keifu: saishiki sareru Meiji* (The Genealogy of the Schoolgirl: The Enriched Meiji Period), Tokyo: Seidosha.
Honda, M. (2010) "The Genealogy of Hirahira: Liminality and the Girl," trans. T. Aoyama and B. Hartley, in T. Aoyama and B. Hartley (eds) *Girl Reading Girl in Japan*, Abingdon: Routledge, 92–104.
Horiguchi, N. J. (2011) *Women Adrift: The Literature of Japan's Imperial Body*, Minneapolis: University of Minnesota Press.
Imada, E. (2007) *Shōjo no shakaishi* (A Social History of the Shōjo), Tokyo: Keisō Shoin.
Inoue, M. (2006) *Vicarious Language: Gender and Linguistic Modernity in Japan*, Berkeley: University of California Press.
Kawamura, K. (1993) *Otome no inori: kindai josei ime ji no tanjō* (Prayer of the Maiden: The Birth of Modern Women's Image), Tokyo: Kinokuniya Shoten.

Kawamura, K. (1994) *Otome no shintai: onna no kindai to sekushuariti* (The Girls Body: Women's Modern Era and Sexuality), Tokyo: Kinokuniya Shoten.
Kawamura, K. (2003) *Otome no yukue: kindai josei no hyoshōto tatakai* (Where the Girl Went: The Image and Struggle of Modern Women), Tokyo: Kinokuniya Shoten.
Kawasaki, K. (1990) *Shōjo Biyori* (Fine Days for Girls), Tokyo: Seikyūsha.
Kawasaki, K. (2008) "Osaki Midori and the Role of the Girl in Shōwa Modernism," trans. L. Fraser and T. Aoyama, *Asian Studies Association of Australia* 32 (3) 293–306.
Kinsella, S. (2014) *Schoolgirls, Money and Rebellion in Japan*, London and New York: Routledge.
Kozma, A. (2012) "Pinky Violence: Shock, Awe and the Exploitation of Sexual Liberation," *Journal of Japanese and Korean Cinema* 3 (1) 37–44.
Kuhn, A. (1982) *Women's Pictures: Feminism and Cinema*, New York: Verso.
Kuraishi, T. (2002) "Shibuya kenkyu to yamamba no umareta" (Shibuya Study and the Birth of the Yamamba), *Shibuya Keizai Shinbun* 11 (15).
Mackie, V. (2009) *Feminism in Modern Japan*, Cambridge: Cambridge University Press.
McRobbie, A. (2009) *The Aftermath of Feminism: Gender, Culture and Social Change*, Los Angeles and London: SAGE Press.
Miller, L. and Bardsley, J. (2005) *Bad Girls of Japan*, London and New York: Palgrave Macmillan.
Miyasako, C. (1984) *Cho Shōjo* (Super Girl), Tokyo: Hokueisha.
Negra, D. (2008) *What a Girl Wants? Fantasizing the Reclamation of Self in Postfeminism*, London: Routledge.
Orbaugh, S. (2003) "Busty Battlin' Babes: The Evolution of the Shōjo in 1990s Visual Culture," in J. Mostow, N. Bryson and M. Graybill (eds) *Gender and Power in the Japanese Visual Field*, Honolulu: Hawai'i University Press, 200–228.
Orbaugh, S. (2009) "Girls Reading Harry Potter, Girls Writing Desire: Amateur Manga and Shōjo Reading Practices," in T. Aoyama and B. Hartley (eds) *Girls Reading Girls*, Abingdon: Routledge, 174–186.
Ōtsuka, E. (1989) *Shōjo minzokugaku* (Ethnography of the Shōjo), Tokyo: Kōbunsha.
Ōtsuki, T. (2003) "Omoikkiri Ōzappana 'Rabukome'/Shiron" (A Completely Tentative "Love-Comedy" Analysis) in S. Ōtsuki (ed) *Datsu Bungaku to Chō Bungaku* (Post Literature and Super Literature), Tokyo: Iwanami Shoten, 147–176.
Projansky, S. (2014) *Spectacular Girls: Media Fascination and Celebrity Culture*, New York: New York University Press.
Robertson, J. (1998) *Takarazuka Sexual Politics and Popular Culture in Modern Japan*, Berkeley: University of California Press.
Sato, B. (2003) *The New Japanese Woman: Modernity, Media, and Women in Interwar Japan*, Durham: Duke University Press.
Sato, I. (1991) *Kamikaze Biker: Parody and Anomy in Affluent Japan*, Chicago: University of Chicago Press.
Shamoon, D. (2008) "Situating the Shōjo in Shōjo Manga," in M. W. MacWilliams (ed) *Japanese Visual Culture: Explorations in the World of Manga and Anime*, New York: M.E. Sharpe, 137–154.
Shamoon, D. (2012) *Passionate Friendship: The Aesthetics of Girls' Culture in Japan*, University of Hawai'i Press.
Sharp, J. (2008) *Behind the Pink Curtain: The Complete History of Japanese Sex Cinema*, London: FAB.
Takahara, E. (2006) "The Consciousness of the Girl: Freedom and Arrogance," trans. T. Aoyama and B. Hartley in Rebecca L Copeland (ed) *Women Critiques: Translated Essays on Women's Writing*, Honolulu: University of Hawaii Press, 185–193.
Takahashi, M. (2008) "Opening the Closed World of Shōjo Manga," in M. W. MacWilliams (ed) *Japanese Visual Culture: Explorations in the World of Manga and Anime*, Abingdon: Routledge.
Treat, J. W. (1993) "Yoshimoto Banana Writes Home: Shōjo Culture and the Nostalgic Subject," *Journal of Japanese Studies* 19 (2) 353–387.
Treat, J. W. (1996) "Yoshimoto Banana Writes Home: The Shōjo in Japanese Popular Culture," in J. Treat (ed) *Contemporary Japan and Popular Culture*, Honolulu: University of Hawaii Press, 275–308.
Uno, K. (1993) "The Death of 'Good Wife, Wise Mother?'" in: A. Gordon (ed) *Postwar Japan as History*, Berkeley: University of California Press, 293–324.
Vick, T. (2015) *Time and Place and Nonsense: The Films of Seijun Suzuki*, Seattle and London: University of Washington Press.
Watanabe, S. (2007) *Shōjo zo no Tanjo: Kindainihon ni okeru "Shōjo" no Kihan no Keisei* (The Birth of the Girl: Formation of the "Girls" Code in Modern Japan), Tokyo: Shinsensha.
Wilson, E. (2017) "Scenes of Hurt and Rapture: Céline Sciamma's Girlhood," *Film Quarterly* 70 (3) 10–22.

Yamane, K. (1989) *Hentai shōjo mōji* (Morphology of Girls' Handwriting), Tokyo: Kōdansha.
Yamane, K. (1993) *Gyaru no kōzō* (The Structure of the Girl), Tokyo: Kōdansha.
Yoda, T. (2017) "Girlscape: The Marketing of Mediatic Ambience in Japan," in M. Steinberg and A. Zahltan (eds) *Media Theory in Japan*, Durham: Duke University Press, 173–200.
Zahltan, A. (2017a) "1980s Nyū Aka: (Non) Media Theory as Romantic Performance," in M. Steinberg and A. Zahltan (eds) *Media Theory in Japan*, Durham: Duke University Press, 200–221.
Zahlten, A. (2017b) *The End of Japanese Cinema: Industrial Genres, National Times and Media Ecologies*, Durham: Duke University Press.

35
GENDERED DESIRES
Pornography and consumption

Alexandra Hambleton

Japan has one of the largest pornography industries in the world. An estimated 50–60 billion yen worth of videos are sold annually (Nakamura 2017), and this figure does not include anime, manga, video games, "pink" movies, "gravure" photo books, erotic magazines, and other materials. Japanese pornography is also a large cultural export, particularly throughout east and southeast Asia (see Wong and Yau 2014, 2017). Despite the size of the industry, pornography has only recently become a central subject of academic enquiry. This chapter will introduce pornography in Japan, explain its history and the forms it has taken from the past to today, outline some of the debates surrounding pornography, introduce contemporary scholarship on the issue, discuss some of the issues scholars in the field face, and consider future directions for research. Porn studies is a growing academic field and provides a rich mode of inquiry into gender, desire, and consumption in Japan today.

Defining pornography is an ongoing difficulty for anyone grappling with the medium and a task that requires reassessing with every new form of porn that becomes available. Is something only pornographic if it features "real" sex? Do simulated sex scenes count as porn? Can cartoon sexual activity depicted in anime and manga be considered pornographic? This chapter takes pornography to mean any material that depicts erotic behaviour and is intended to cause sexual excitement. Under this definition, any number of film, manga, anime, and games found in Japan today, aimed at both heterosexual and LGBT audiences, can be described as pornographic.

Historical perspectives

Pornography in Japan, like global markets, has been greatly influenced by developments in media, technology, and censorship. In the Edo period (1603–1868), *shunga* woodblock prints (*ukiyo-e*) were a popular form of erotic art and depicted all manner of sexual material for both male and female consumers from a range of social classes until changes to censorship legislation in 1870 made their production increasingly difficult. Key provisions of censorship law enacted at this time remained in place until the end of the Pacific War in 1945 and gave the state the power to regulate what aspects of sexuality could be discussed openly and what was deemed obscene (Mitchell 1983; Buckland 2013, 268). Nevertheless, pornography could be found in the "erotic, grotesque, nonsense" (*ero-guro-nansensu*) periodicals which depicted all manner of "strange" and "unusual" sexual behaviour and thrived during the relative freedom of the interwar Taisho era

(1912–1926) as curiosity and demand for entertainment grew along with the development of metropolitan life (McLelland 2012a, 31–32). In the 1930s, as John Dower has argued, libertines, hedonists, and escapists attempted to revive the "erotic, grotesque, nonsense" in what Dower describes as a "thinly sublimated expression of protest against the rising tide of militarism" (2012, 254). The consumption of entertainment focused on non-reproductive sexuality could be a form of protest against a government strongly encouraging reproduction for the sake of the nation and later the war effort.

In the postwar period, a libertarian focus on sexual self-determination (Kinsella 2013, 35) and the increased production of the film industry meant new forms of sexual expression became possible and even deemed desirable. Kissing, banned since the 1920s as an obscene act, was lauded as a symbol of democracy in the early postwar years, with Supreme Commander for the Allied Powers (SCAP) censors encouraging its inclusion in films (McLelland 2010, 530). In the 1960s, before the development of the rental and sale adult video market, pink films (*pinku eiga*) were a popular form of pornographic titillation. Often shot on 35-mm film, the films often featured violence, S&M, action, scantily clothed actresses, and simulated sex scenes shot with as much creativity as possible so as to circumvent censorship regulations. Pink films also came to be known as Nikkatsu *roman-poruno* after studio Nikkatsu began to focus on the genre in the 1970s with prolific production of "narrative-based porn" as the studio attempted to counter falling cinema attendance (see Nornes 2014). These efforts were ultimately unsuccessful, and the industry shrank considerably in the wake of the introduction of adult videos in the 1980s, but still remains known for spawning many directors and independent filmmakers who got their start in the relative creative freedom of pink film production. Today a few pink film specialist cinemas remain (including the Ueno Ōkura Theater in Tokyo and the Senbon Nikkatsu in Kyoto), patronized almost entirely by men and die-hard fans of the genre.

The first adult video was released in 1981, with the industry peaking in the early 2000s (AV joyū no kyōkasho) with as many as 30,000 videos made every year (Morita 2004). Today adult video production companies struggle to compete with freely available, uncensored porn found on the Internet and the number of production companies has plummeted. Nevertheless, at video rental stores around the country, the adult video section can still be found curtained off towards the back of the store and filled with thousands of titles catering to a wide variety of tastes and fetishes. To survive in today's increasingly difficult market, pornography producers and performers must increasingly market themselves in creative ways as they attempt to court new audiences and loyal fans willing to pay for a product that is now freely available anytime, anywhere. To counter falling sales, porn production companies are increasingly turning to new audiences in an attempt to survive in the Internet era, but it must be noted that very few are succeeding (Hambleton 2016). The adult video industry in Japan is struggling and is increasingly competing with other forms of erotic content.

As defined previously, porn does not just refer to erotic films or adult videos. Instead it can also encompass erotic manga, anime, and video games, which have become increasingly popular in recent decades. Examples include dating and sex simulation games (see Galbraith 2017), hardcore *hentai* (pornographic) manga and animation (see Allison 2000; Ortega-Brena 2009), and boys love manga (see Mori 2010; McLelland et al. 2015). Ortega-Brena draws on the work of Anne Allison (2000) to explain how "a significant part of the appeal of the Japanese pleasure industry lies in its capacity to transport the spectators or participants, male as well as female, into an imaginary space that escapes the severe everyday constraints imposed by work and social and familial responsibility" (2009, 21). In manga, anime, and video game pornography, this imaginary space provides an arena for sexual titillation, along with escape from the stresses of everyday life. Expanding our understanding of what constitutes porn and considering what it means for those who consume it is therefore a herculean task and one which requires the cooperation of researchers from diverse fields.

Pro- and anti-porn debates

In her chapter "Can Sex Be Separated from Personhood? Porn Debates" (Sekkusu wa jinkaku to kirihanaseru ka: poruno ronsō), Miya Yoshiko (2009, 238) outlines the four positions feminists commonly take towards pornography.

1 From a conservative or religious perspective, a society overflowing with sex should not be permitted;
2 From a radical feminist perspective, all pornography is damaging to women and must be banned;
3 Pornography that is violent towards women should be banned; and
4 Regulation of pornography should not be permitted.

Japanese pro- and anti-porn activists span the range of these positions.

Patrick Galbraith argues that, "Japan did not experience as robust—or successful, in that feminists, led by lawyer Catharine MacKinnon, got ordinances passed—an anti-pornography movement as North America" (2017, 2). Nevertheless, recent years have seen a surge in focus on the perceived social impacts of pornography and accompanying anti-porn activism. Morita Seiya, representing the Anti-Pornography and Prostitution Research Group (*Poruno Higai to Seibōryoku o Kangaeru Kai*, literally "Group for Considering Sexual Violence and the Harms of Pornography," which has more recently become known as PAPS or People Against Pornography and Sexual Violence) argues that the final decade of the twentieth century was a paradoxical time for Japan (2004). Despite the introduction of a number of laws protecting the human rights of women and the success of a number of sexual harassment trials, sex work also grew and pro-sex feminist discourses proliferated, arguing that "nothing is wrong with pornography or prostitution because consent has been given by the persons concerned" (2004, 64). Morita (somewhat simplistically in my opinion) conflates increases in porn production and consumption with increases in sexual assault and explains that anti-porn activists in Japan struggle due to the position of porn within the law. Pornography falls under "obscenity" laws rather than being viewed as "conflicting with the human rights and equality of women," thereby resulting in a situation in which "a great deal of sexist and violent pornography is in the mass marketplace without any regulation" (2004, 78). Authors such as Nakamura Atsuhiko (2017) have similarly focused on the very real violence experienced by women who are coerced into performing in adult videos, criticizing the industry heavily for the way in which it irresponsibly exploits performers, ultimately destroying the lives of the women it relies upon to maintain its business model. According to Takeyama (2018), performers become nothing more than products that are most valuable in their first appearance and then continue to lose value with each subsequent adult video in which they perform. Their careers are therefore particularly short lived, yet they are often unable to find other work once it becomes clear to future employers that they have been involved in the adult industry. This exploitative practice is common throughout the adult video industry.

Anti-porn activists in Japan often focus on the concept of harm, although the definition of harm when it comes to anime or manga can be somewhat obscure. In his examination of controversial rape simulation game *RapeLay*, Galbraith outlines the difficulty of making an argument against an adult computer game as no women were physically harmed in the process of making the game. Instead, he explains how the argument shifts to "the more controversial claim that depictions of sexual violence normalize sexual violence" (2017, 3), in other words, the oft-cited argument that "pornography is the theory, and rape is the practice" (Robin Morgan quoted in Williams 1990, 16). Similarly, feminist activists have argued that pornographic images of women in public places constitute a form of sexual discrimination and even violence towards women, and must be stopped. For example, Nanae Sakamoto (2009) describes a successful campaign to have pornographic advertising posters and television commercials withdrawn, arguing that using images in which women look as though they have been attacked or raped to sell whiskey is both sexist and has the effect of making women feel deeply uncomfortable in the public spaces they inhabit. Harm-focused debates often move beyond the imaginary space of a specific media text to consider the impact of the presence of violent sexual depictions on those who must use the same physical spaces in their daily lives.

Anti-porn debates have also raged over depictions of underage characters in anime, manga, and video games. Until 2014, the possession of child pornography was not illegal in Japan, remaining unchallenged even after its production and distribution were banned in 1999 (see Amada 2016). Nevertheless, manga, anime, and games escaped regulation, as they were found to fall under "freedom of expression" and are therefore understood as "victimless." The United Nations special envoy on child protection has pushed for Japan to ban such images but so far has had little success (McCurry 2015). In contrast, supporters of erotic manga, anime, and games argue that the relation between fiction and reality is not straightforward, and that the reception of such images (particularly those of supposed "underage" characters) is more diverse than them merely being consumed for sexual titillation (see Galbraith 2011; McLelland 2015).

Unsurprisingly, many of those who are pro-porn come from the pornography industry itself. Pornography is viewed as an inevitable part of consumer culture, as an export product for Japan to be proud of, as a way for men and women to explore their sexuality, and as an important space through which to explore the right to freedom of expression. In his book *Everyone Becomes Naked* (*Hito wa mina, hadaka ni naru*, 2007), billed as an introduction to sociology for younger readers, adult video director and author Baksheesh Yamashita argues that sex is a natural part of the human experience and that the pornography industry is just like any other industry. Baksheesh Yamashita explains that using your body in sex work is just like any other labour, from building buildings to writing catch copy for advertising, or even selling shares. Producing, directing, and performing in adult videos is also just regular labour. This stance was heavily criticized by anti-porn activist Miyamoto Setsuko, who could not believe that respected publisher Rironsha would commission a porn director to write a book aimed at younger readers (2017). Miyamoto and supporters began a petition to have the book withdrawn from sale, gathering support from women's groups from around the country and eventually sending a petition with over 10,000 signatures to Rironsha in December of 2008, when they were invited to speak to the president of the company. Discussions concluded with Rironsha reiterating the importance of freedom of expression, and Miyamoto and supporters founding PAPS in 2009 with the hope that they could continue the anti-porn work that they had begun.

It should be noted that not only men view the porn industry as a positive space for the exploration of sexuality. Director Makino Eri, founder of the Silk Labo brand of female-friendly pornography for major production company Soft on Demand, views her product as potentially disruptive to traditional adult video sexual scripts which are damaging to women (see Hambleton 2016). Makino has even published a book (2012) in which she urges women to learn more about their own bodies and experience sexual pleasure in a way that is generally seen as taboo for women in contemporary Japan. While there is an irony in a producer employed by a mainstream porn production company criticizing the sexual scripts of adult videos and the way in which they teach men to have sex that is unsatisfying to women, Makino's efforts to create an alternative form of sex education in the porn she produces can be described as both sex positive and disruptive to the status quo. Similarly, Mori Naoko in her book *Women Read Porn* (*Onna wa poruno o yomu*, 2010) argues that hardcore boys' love manga provides a safe space for women to explore their sexual desires, away from potential social sanction (see also Suzuki 1998). Similarly, Thomas Baudinette outlines how online pornography allows young gay men to explore their desires, describing it as liberating, satisfying, and educational (2015). Pornography can be both liberating and exploitative, and as the debates outlined previously demonstrate, it remains deeply controversial.

Censorship

No discussion of pornography would be complete without examining the issue of censorship. As discussed previously, pornography falls under obscenity law, governed by Article 175 of the criminal code, which prohibits the sale or distribution of materials containing "obscenity" (*waisetsu*). Article 175 originated in 1907 during Japan's period of modernization, but just what is actually classified as "obscene" material has been a matter of diverse and conflicting interpretations. Currently the law operates "according to the concept of the infringement upon public morals of the (public) stimulation of sexual desire" (Allison 2000, 165). In practice, this means that publishers and producers face the threat of prosecution and bans for the depiction of genitalia and sexual penetration. As a result, policing by industry bodies, and self-surveillance on the part of artists, authors, and publishers means that such censoring is "incorporated into a popular aesthetic . . . evidenced by such staples in mass culture as voyeurism, where what is hidden does not prevent looking as much as inspire looking of a particular kind" (Allison 2000, 166). In other words, what cannot be shown becomes a greater fetish, a greater source of sexual excitement, for the very fact that it remains hidden.

The largest organization that exists to police porn is the Japan Contents Review Center (*Nihon Kontentsu Shinsa Sentā*), which ostensibly works to ensure that no genitalia is shown in either adult videos, manga, anime, or games. Instead, genitals are pixilated using digital mosaics (known as *bokashi*), although the rules have been relaxed in the past decade to allow the showing of some pubic hair (see Allison 2000; Cather 2012). What results is a situation in which there is little difference in the level of explicitness between pink films and hardcore pornography, although with uncensored pornography now readily available on the internet, including unmosaiced Japanese porn from overseas markets, there is debate as to whether there is much point to pixilation at all. Despite easy access to uncensored genitalia online, those who do not censor in Japan do fall foul of the law and risk prosecution. Most recently, artist and activist Rokudenashiko was arrested for distributing 3D scan data of her vulva to crowd funding supporters in her effort to make a "pussy canoe" to highlight the ridiculousness of Japanese obscenity law and celebrate her body (see McLelland 2018). The law may seem nonsensical in the internet era, but it remains a threat to those involved in creating erotica and porn.

This particular aspect of Japan's censorship laws has done far more than prevent the depiction of genitalia in Japanese pornography, animation, manga, and magazines. Instead, producers and artists substitute penises with objects such as vibrators, cameras, medical instruments, and even octopi tentacles (reminiscent of Hokusai's famous Edo period *shunga* "The Dream of the Fisherman's Wife"). The inability of pornography producers to show the penis—necessitated in pornography by what Williams calls the "erotic organization of visibility" (1990, 271)—has led to the proliferation of pornography that is often viewed as fetish, bizarre, or deviant outside Japan. Similarly, a lack of legislation surrounding erotic content has meant that extreme violence and rape remain free from censorship. Obscenity legislation has done much to colour the content of Japanese pornography, allowing for violence, rape, depictions of underage characters, and tentacle fetishes provided there are no actual human genitals visible.

Outside of national laws, a number of local ordinances have been drafted with the intention of protecting youth from the perceived dangers of pornography and other materials deemed "indecent." One notorious example is that of 2010 amendments to the Tokyo Metropolitan Ordinance Regarding the Healthy Development of Youth which proposed installing filtering devices on the mobile phones of young people and restricting the availability of "imaginary visual representations of sexualised youth," including what came to be known as "non-existent youth" in the form of fictional or imaginary characters who could be perceived as looking or sounding as though they were under the age of 18 (McLelland 2011). Widespread opposition to the bill, and to the idea of allowing a panel of bureaucrats to decide what might be "harmful" or "anti-social" for manga consumers, came from manga artists, publishers, and even the Japan Federation of Bar Associations, who believed that it was an "intrusion by government into issues that were better handled by parents who should have oversight of their children's reading matter" (McLelland 2011, 355–356). Nevertheless, a revised version of the bill passed in 2010, requiring works restricted under the ordinance to be labelled as "adult" (*seijin*), shelved separately to unrestricted works, and for age checks to be performed at the point of sale.

In 2019, a number of convenience stores announced that they would end the sale of pornographic magazines, citing an increase in the number of elderly, female, and young customers, as well as an expected flux of foreign tourists during the 2019 Rugby World Cup and 2020 Tokyo Olympics as reasons. As the previous examples detail, censorship of pornography is not only the realm of the national government but also of local governments, publishers, artists, and vendors.

Current research

In 2014 the journal *Porn Studies* was founded (edited by UK academics Feona Attwood and Clarissa Smith), marking the move of the study of pornography into mainstream academia. Nevertheless, there remain a number of ethical and methodological challenges for academics working in the field. The first surrounds the legal ramifications of researching media that may be legal in one jurisdiction whilst illegal in another. Mark McLelland, in his work on erotic manga, has critiqued Australian legislation that aligns the fantasy lives of young Australian fans with paedophile networks (2011). Similarly, Patrick Galbraith argues that the reception of lolicon (*rorikon*) manga, anime, and games that contain explicit depictions of (amongst other things) seemingly underage characters in sexual situations cannot be read in a singular manner and that no physical harm is done in the production of manga and anime images. As a result, they should not be subjected to legislation that criminalizes them as "thought censorship" (McLelland 2011). Nevertheless, accessing or exporting such materials outside of Japan puts researchers at risk of falling foul of the laws of the countries in which they work.

Another struggle faced by researchers is access to the pornography industry itself. As Akiko Takeyama outlined in her talk "Gender, Labor, and Justice in Japan's Adult Video Industry" (2018), gaining access to both the pro-porn production side of the pornography industry and the anti-porn activist side requires great delicacy on the part of researchers. Balancing between those in the industry who believe in freedom of expression above all and those who have been harmed by pornography is a challenge that researchers must approach with respect and care.

In recent years, the voices of current and former pornography actors and actresses are increasingly becoming a part of the academic discourse, as exemplified by Tristan Taormino's *The Feminist Porn Book* (2013). In Japan, this push was led by former porn performer and author

Iijima Ai. Recruited into the industry at the age of 20, Iijima was a rare example of a former adult video performer who was able to make the crossover into the mainstream media upon the completion of her adult video career. Iijima's book *Platonic Sex* (*Puratonikku sekkusu*, 2000) was a best seller and was turned into both a television series and a more explicit film. Iijima died in 2008 but right up until her death was a mainstay in the Japanese mainstream media, as well as a safe sex activist. More recently, journalist and author Suzuki Suzumi has written extensively on her life as an adult video performer in a number of books, including *The Sociology of Adult Video Actresses: Why Do They Have so Much to Say About Themselves?* ("*AV Joyū*" *no shakaigaku: Naze kanojotachi wa jōzetsu ni mizukara o kataru no ka*, 2013) and *Selling Your Body Is the End: Love and Happiness for Women Who Work at Night* (*Shintai o uttara sayōnara: Yoru no onēsan no ai to kōfuku ron*, 2016). Opening up academia to those involved in porn and sex work (examples include sex worker activist group SWASH and author, sex worker, and activist Mizushima Kaorin) allows for the *tōjisha* (involved parties) to bring their voices to the table (see McLelland 2009) and adds further depth to the study of pornography in Japan today.

Recommendations for future research

Debates surrounding the oppressive or emancipatory nature of porn have continued for as long as the medium has existed, propelled by the development of the second-wave women's movement in the 1970s, the rise of pro-porn discourses in the 1990s and 2000s, and increased scrutiny on the pornography industry as exploitative by organizations such as PAPS today. Despite the passion shown by those on both sides of the debate, I caution researchers against falling into the trap of pitting pro- and anti-pornography groups against each other. Rather, I hope that future research will provide a more nuanced examination without resorting to simplistic conclusions about the beneficial or harmful nature of erotic content. Pornography is not created in a vacuum and instead holds the power to both reflect and influence the sexual scripts and desires of consumers. Providing women access to means of production (see Juffer 1998) has meant great diversification in the erotic desires depicted in both adult videos and manga. Likewise, queer porn holds the ability to upset static notions of gender binaries and heteronormativity (see Baudinette 2015). Porn can even create communities or spaces for those who feel excluded from society or who have struggled to find a place to explore or express their desires, which may have been seen as taboo or socially undesirable (see Mori 2010; McLelland et al. 2015; Hambleton 2016).

Finally, I wish to encourage readers to avoid being entirely confined by their own cultural lens when viewing phenomena in Japan. Although Morita Seiya describes Japan as "backward in the field of sex equality" (2004, 64), it is unhelpful to view social development as a linear process when considering the impact of pornography in societies around the globe. Considering Japanese pornography—be it extremely violent adult videos or erotic depictions of ostensibly underage manga characters—through the lens of one's own cultural values and perspectives means that any results may be disingenuous at best, or fabricated at worst. Instead, I invite researchers to come to an understanding of Japan as a country with its own history, legislation, and debates and to do their best to understand how these have come together to create the environment we see today. For scholars of pornography, the challenge remains to do meaningful work in what can be inhospitable academic environments. Scholars can face direct hostility from universities, departments, and colleagues unwilling to be associated with what can be viewed an undesirable topic of inquiry. Similarly, researchers may experience indirect hostility in the form of ethics committees creating huge hurdles for those attempting to undertake projects into porn. Conservative standards imposed on sex research and the terms required by committees regarding talking to users and producers can be restrictive to the point of making projects impossible.

Finally, I hope for the expansion of porn research outside of European and American scholarly networks. Katrien Jacobs calls for the "internationalization of porn studies" (2014), arguing that non-Western pornographies are "not just a set of global and regional cultures to be mapped and studied, but are a tool for interrogating broader questions of technological innovation, internet politics, sexuality rights and obscenity legislation" (2014, 114). Expanding scholarship beyond the "harm" versus "emancipation" dichotomy, working to further research to explore more than just the "Euro-American controversies around pornography" (Jacobs 2014, 114), and drawing in voices from Japanese scholarship will allow for a broader, more in-depth understanding of Japanese pornography of all types, the environment in which it is produced, the impact it has on participants, and the diverse readings made by consumers.

Related chapters

3   Debates in Japanese Feminism
11 Intimacy in and Beyond the Family
17 Sex Work
23 Gender in Digital Technologies and Cultures
32 Gender and Visual Culture
33 Gender, Media, and Misogyny in Japan

References

Allison, A. (2000) *Permitted and Prohibited Desires: Mothers, Comics, and Censorship in Japan*, Berkeley: University of California Press.
Amada, Y. (2016) "Recent Legislation in Japan No.2 'Criminal Regulations Regarding Child Pornography in Japan: Revisions to the Child Pornography Act and Related Issues,'" *Institute of Comparative Law*, Waseda University. www.waseda.jp/folaw/icl/news-en/2016/07/05/5505.
Baudinette, T. (2015) "The Construction of Desire: Young Gay Men and Media in Japan" [Public lecture], Melbourne: Monash University.
Baksheesh, Y. (2007) *Hito wa mina, hadaka ni naru* (Everyone Becomes Naked), Tokyo: Rironsha.
Buckland, R. (2013) "'Shunga' in the Meiji Era: The End of a Tradition?" *Japan Review* 26 (January) 259–276.
Cather, K. (2012) *The Art of Censorship in Postwar Japan*, Honolulu: University of Hawaii Press.
Galbraith, P.W. (2011) "Lolicon: The Reality of 'Virtual Child Pornography' in Japan," *Image and Narrative: Online Magazine of the Visual Narrative* 12 (1) 83–119.
Galbraith, P.W. (2017) "RapeLay and the Return of the Sex Wars in Japan," *Porn Studies* 4 (1) 105–126.
Hambleton, A. (2016) "When Women Watch: The Subversive Potential of Female-Friendly Pornography in Japan," *Porn Studies* 3 (4) 227–442.
Iijima, A. (2000) *Puratonikku sekkusu* (Platonic Sex), Tokyo: Shogakukan.
Jacobs, K. (2014) "Internationalizing Porn Studies," *Porn Studies* 1 (1–2) 114–119.
Juffer, J. (1998) *At Home with Pornography: Women, Sex, and Everyday Life*, New York: New York University Press.
Kinsella, S. (2013) *Schoolgirls, Money and Rebellion in Japan*, London and New York: Routledge.
Makino, E. (2012) *Joshi no hoken taiiku* (Physical Education for the Protection of Women's Health), Tokyo: Takarajimasha.
McCurry, J. (2015) "Japan Urged to Ban Manga Child Abuse Images," *The Guardian* 27 October. www.theguardian.com/world/2015/oct/27/japan-urged-to-ban-manga-child-abuse-images.
McLelland, M. (2009) "The Role of the 'Tōjisha' in Current Debates About Sexual Minority Rights in Japan," *Japanese Studies* 29 (2) 193–207.
McLelland, M. (2010) "'Kissing Is a Symbol of Democracy!' Dating, Democracy and Romance in Occupied Japan, 1945–52," *Journal of the History of Sexuality* 19 (3) 508–535.
McLelland, M. (2011) "Thought Policing of the Protection of Youth? Debate in Japan over the 'Non-Existent Youth Bill'," *International Journal of Comic Art* 13 (2) 348–367.

McLelland, M. (2012a) *Love, Sex, and Democracy in Japan During the American Occupation*, London: Springer.

McLelland, M. (2012b) "Australia's 'Child-Abuse Material' Legislation, Internet Regulation and the Juridification of the Imagination," *International Journal of Cultural Studies* 15 (5) 467–483.

McLelland, M. (2015) "Sex, Censorship and Media Regulation in Japan: A Historical Overview," in V. Mackie and M. McLelland (eds) *Routledge Handbook of Sexuality Studies in East Asia*, New York: Routledge.

McLelland, M. (2018) "Art as Activism in Japan: The Case of a Good-for-Nothing Kid and Her Pussy," in G. Meikle (ed) *The Routledge Companion to Media and Activism*, New York: Routledge, 162–170.

McLelland, M., Nagaike, K., Suganuma, K. and Welker, J. (eds) (2015) *Boys Love Manga and Beyond: History, Culture, and Community in Japan*, Jackson: University Press of Mississippi.

Mitchell, R. H. (1983) *Censorship in Imperial Japan*, Princeton: Princeton University Press.

Miya, Y. (2009) "Sekkusu wa jinkaku to kirihanaseru ka: poruno ronsō," in *Nihon No Feminizumu 6: Sekushuaritī*, Tokyo: Iwanami Shoten, 237–250.

Miyamoto, S. (2017) "AV no naka no seibōryoku o kokuhatsu suru: poruno higai to seibōryoku o kangaeru kai (PAPS)" (Complaining About Sexual Violence in AV: Group for Considering Sexual Violence and the Harms of Pornography) *Nihon no Feminizumu* (Japanese Feminism), Tokyo: Kawade Shobō Shinsha, 74–81.

Mori, N. (2010) *Onna wa poruno o yomu: Josei no seiyoku to feminizmu* (Women Read Porn: Female Sexual Desire and Feminism), Tokyo: Seikyūsha.

Morita, S. (2004) "Pornography, Prostitution, and Women's Human Rights in Japan," in *Not for Sale: Feminists Resisting Prostitution and Pornography*, Melbourne: Spinifex Press, 64–84.

Nakamura, A. (2017) *AV joyū shōmetsu: sekkusu rōdō kara nigedasu onna tachi* (Vanishing AV Actresses: The Women Who Escape from Sex Work), Tokyo: Gentosha.

Nornes, M. (ed) (2014) *The Pink Book: The Japanese Eroduction and Its Contexts*, Kinema Club.

Ortega-Brena, M. (2009) "Peek-a-Boo, I See You: Watching Japanese Hard-Core Animation," *Sexuality & Culture* 13 (1) 17–31.

Sakamoto, N. (2009) "'Sanraku' reipu rensō posutā eki atama kara kieru," in *Nihon no feminizumu 6: Sekushuaritī*, Tokyo: Iwanami Shoten, 229–236.

Suzuki, K. (1998) "Pornography or Therapy? Japanese Girls Creating the Yaoi Phenomenon," in S. A. Inness (ed) *Millennium Girls: Today's Girls Around the World*, Lanham: Rowman and Littlefield Publishers, 243–268.

Suzuki, S. (2013) *"AV joyū" no shakaigaku: naze kanojotachi wa jōzetsu ni mizukara o kataru no ka* (The Sociology of Adult Video Actresses: Why Do They Have So Much to Say About Themselves?), Tokyo: Seidosha.

Takeyama, A. (2018) "Gender, Labor, and Justice in Japan's Adult Video Industry" [Public lecture] Sophia University, July 13.

Taormino, T., Parreñas Shimizu, C. Penley, C. and Miller-Young, M. (2013) *The Feminist Porn Book: The Politics of Producing Pleasure*, New York: Feminist Press at the City University of New York.

Williams, L. (1990) *Hard Core: Power, Pleasure, and the "Frenzy of the Visible,"* London: Pandora Press.

Wong, H. and Yau, H. (2014) *Japanese Adult Videos in Taiwan*, New York: Routledge.

Wong, H. and Yau, H. (2017) *The Japanese Adult Video Industry*, New York: Routledge.

PART VI

Texts and contexts

Case studies

36
GENDERED HIGH AND LOW CULTURE IN JAPAN

The transgressing flesh in Kawabata's dance writing

Fusako Innami

The distinction between high art and low art, or what might be considered popular culture, can be considered arbitrary, especially when set in the context of rapid urbanization and modernization in the early twentieth-century Japan. Urbanization, cosmopolitanism, and consumerism in the 1920s and 1930s were tied to venues such as department stores, theatres, dance halls, and cinemas. These were also key influences in the formation of autonomous consumer subjects; Miriam Silverberg suggests that the consumer subject in Japan around this time was both "a subject of the emperor and a subject with agency, acting as autonomously as the imperial system would allow" (2006, 4). While being interpolated into the body of the nation, consumer subjects in this period actively participated in consumption and various social and cultural activities.

Interwar cosmopolitan and intimate, hybrid, and sensual popular and erotic performance styles allowed wide participation and attracted audiences from various class backgrounds. Rishona Zimring, analyzing the interwar dance scene with its elements of Ballets Russes, jazz music, and folk song and dance in London's West End, writes that the shift toward liberating dance practices has been characterized as a move towards "highly-charged cosmopolitan and erotic sociability," allowing "an emancipatory openness to foreignness and racial alterity" (2014, 102). The Asakusa area of Tokyo at the time was like Montmartre in Paris, Alexanderplatz in Berlin, or the West End in London, introducing jazz and tango, Western opera and theatrical works, comic song with modern costumes mixed with indigenous Japanese elements, foreign performers dressed in kimono and using Japanese words, and with erotic feeling and a sense of humour.

Performances in Asakusa at this time offered popular pleasure to broad audiences that included authors and artists such as Tanizaki Jun'ichirō and Fujita Tsuguharu. These cultural producers depicted the area as home to a mixture of high and low cultures. For example, Tanizaki (1886–1965), in his 1920 novel The Mermaid (*Kōjin*) (*kōjin* being an imaginary mermaid-like figure in China), depicts various street scenes in Asakusa of the time, with theatre dancers and actresses wearing cheap-looking items, the young poor seeking financial support, and many other human beings in various situations. The mixture of those scenes prompts a "noble and miserable feeling," elevated by a flickering touch of poetry and painting that seemed too good for the place (Tanizaki 2017, 26, my translation unless otherwise indicated). Similarly, Kawabata Yasunari's (1899–1972) short story "Dancing Girl and Foreign Mother" (*Odoriko to ikokujin no haha*) from

1932 depicts an Asakusa revue house playing popular songs from the street, theme songs for films, and folk songs sung in a weird pitch. Kawabata notes that the exotic manner of a foreign performer's nervous singing was welcomed in Asakusa (1980d, 615). In "Asakusa Diary" (*Asakusa nikki*, 1931), Kawabata illuminates the transience of human relations in the first-person narrative account of a street girl. Different times of the day bring her different types of customers, which leads her to feel her experience of time itself to be strange, and herself along with it (1981a, 231). As Donald Richie writes, mercantile Asakusa "was also acceptingly human" (2005, x). Asakusa was a place of vitality and humanity where various types of audiences, as well as performers, shared the lived art forms that made supposedly high cultures popular and reachable by crossing the boundaries between them, even in the rising militarism of the interwar and wartime periods.

This chapter aims to develop an approach to the gendered cultures that may be hierarchically valued as "high" or "low" by mediators or receivers by focusing on the body as a medium of expression. In particular, I argue, through my literary analyses, for the possibility of the embodied experience (the lived experience or, particularly here, the incorporated bodily practice) being employed as a way to perform the "other" and transgress cultural, class, and hierarchical boundaries. Thomas J. Csordas writes of embodiment as "an indeterminate methodological field defined by perceptual experience and mode of presence and engagement in the world" (1994, 12). It is the embodied practice itself that affects one's relation to the world. When one employs certain instruments to create artwork, such as a brush, ink, pens, musical instruments, and photographic or filmic machines, those instruments themselves affect how the artwork is made, perceived, and consumed in society, along with the relationship between the subject and the creator. But what happens when nothing but the body is the medium of expression? How does this body affect the cultural evaluation of its art as high or low? How does it inform gender configuration, intersecting with the receiver's imagination? By addressing these questions, I approach gendered iterations of "high" and "low" culture, especially as related to performance and transgression, via literary depictions of the body. In particular, given Kawabata's argument for the placing of dance on the same level of importance as other genres of art such as music, fine art, and literature, I aim to balance out our visually and verbally centred manners of understanding cultures by focusing on dance as an effective scope to examine gender performativity and reconfiguration of the body. Given the ephemeral and transient nature of physical performance art, I rely on the literary records created by writers who inhabited these spaces where high and low culture merged.

It is not difficult to name examples demonstrating how male authors might have viewed various types of dance and respective, especially female, dancers. There is Mori Ōgai's "The Dancing Girl" (*Maihime*, 1890), Akutagawa Ryūnosuke's "Ball" (*Butōkai*, 1920), Tanizaki Jun'ichirō's *Naomi* (*Chijin no Ai*, 1924), and Nagai Kafū's "The Dancing Girl" (*Odoriko*, 1946), to name a few well-known examples, all illuminating some aspects of gender, class, and cultural differences. Among them, Kawabata, author of a number of stories about dancing figures, dance reviews, and criticism, writes in his essay "The Voice of Purity" (*Jun'sui no koe*, 1935), "The beauty of the female [*onna*] culminates in dance" (Kawabata 1982a, 109). His writing illuminates the often ambivalent relationship between Western and Japanese dance, an ambivalence marked in the sentiments of dancers themselves, as well as various forms of dancing in modern Japan, while it also attempts to rescue dance itself from social disregard. Given this background, I will first discuss the hierarchies of "high" and "low" in relation to cultural multiplicities observed in urban space, with a particular attention to dance, and then undertake a case study of Kawabata's dance-related writing (fiction and essays), examining the reception of cultural formats and practitioners' status. Kawabata's presentation of transient dancing bodies poses questions regarding the way in which the acquisition of bodily knowledge involves crossing the boundaries of such an embodied other. Since Kawabata's dance-related fictions combine a presentation of historical background with fictional characters lacking any living models, the discussions of dance in his works is a good way of analyzing common Japanese perceptions of the gendered character of culture at the time. The combination of factual background and fictional characters facilitates an imagination of uses of bodily knowledge that might be effective as well as creative. In the end, it may be the form of bodily practice that mobilizes its effective character more than its attributed sociological and political qualities, such as its belonging to "high" or "low."

From his early characterizations of dancing girls, including his script for the film *A Page of Madness* (*Kurutta ippēji*, 1926), to those in the postwar novel *Dancing Beauty* (*Maihime*, 1951), dancing figures in Kawabata's writing have elegiac, ephemeral, and phantasmatic features (Kawabata, 1980a; 1980b). Kawabata's dance writing on the one hand sharply illuminates the unattainable eternity he ascribes to female bodies—a key feature of his literary creations, corresponding to a fundamental ephemerality and unrepeatability of dance as an art form. On the other hand, it conflates gendered dancing bodies belonging to various social categories—mad women, dance hall girls, geishas, and strip girls—with the men who possess them and also conflates dancers trained in Japanese dance with those coming from ballet, in both cases acquiring the bodily knowledge sometimes used to cross social boundaries. Kawabata's support for children and adolescents writing *tsutzurikata* essays during the rise of nationalism (Wei 2014) and his involvement in girls' novels as well as his contribution to the discovery and support of various writers (Dollas 2003) have been discussed. Considering his involvement and work with dance, Komaki Masahide—who in the interwar period danced for Ballets Russes in Shanghai and worked with Kawabata on the film adaptation of *Dancing Beauty*—regards Kawabata as a hidden supporter of the movement promoting ballet (1975, 233). His literary contributions to dance and dance criticism have still not garnered sufficient academic attention, which could be employed as an effective analytical scope to examine hierarchically evaluated gendered culture.

Mobilizing high and low cultures in the urban space

Dance in modern Japan is an effective scope to illuminate hierarchical valuations of the gendered "high" and "low" as well as of different forms of art while reflecting both Western imagery and elements of indigenous performing arts such as Kabuki and Japanese dance. Western imagery of dance was typically conflated with modernization, including ballroom dancing at Rokumeikan, which was seen as a symbol of Westernization and used as an international socializing space, mainly for state guests and foreign diplomats. At Rokumeikan, Western dances in which men and women hold hands and intimately touch each other were considered a beneficial manner of communication between the sexes by some, while considered inappropriate and harmful by others (Nagai 1991, 26). These new bodily norms were historically particular even in Europe, as Marcel Mauss writes about dancing in a partner's arms as a product of European modernity (1973, 82–83). Touch-based dancing was a modern development for Europeans, as it was for the Japanese, despite the Japanese tendency at the time to conflate the Western with the modern or new. As Silverberg attends, various manners of addressing modern experience present complexities of Japanese modern, including modernization as an economic process; modernity as a philosophical inquiry referring to a post-traditional temporality; the Japanese terms of *kindai*, implying a presentist temporality in modernity; *modan*, indicating the dynamic post-traditional capitalistic world; and modernism, characterized by the Western "liberation by mores" (2006, 13–14). Western dance continued to be practiced among some in the upper class, while leaving many Japanese with impressions of sexual immorality, such that when introduced into women's physical education as an educational tool to enrich movement and as recreational exercise in

Osaka, it caused a public dispute, leading to a general discussion in Tokyo regarding social dance's status in Japanese society, instead of whether social dance is necessary for physical education (Nagai 1991, 29–35).

The Imperial Theatre (*Teikoku Gekijō*) was built in 1911 to replace some functions of Rokumeikan, and the Italian former ballet dancer, director, and choreographer Giovanni Vittorio Rosi was appointed as a ballet teacher there, introducing performances of operas such as Mozart's *Magic Flute*. Although its affiliates, such as dancer and choreographer Ishii Baku, would later contribute to the development of modern dance forms after the opera section's closure in 1916, ballet dancer and director Komaki would later lament the Imperial Theatre's inappropriateness as a national theatre, as it included strip dancing (1975, 42–43). This might be a form of lament against the high merging with the popular at a venue that was meant to represent the heights of national cultural power. The 1920s further witnessed the rapid development and popularity of Western dance practice, which also led to a ballet boom, especially in the postwar period via ballet figures like Eliana Pavlova who were involved in teaching social dance. Kuwahara Kazumi suggests a rather inclusive use by Kawabata of the term *buyō* (dance), adding jazz dance and dance theatre (*buyōgeki*) to the general understanding of the "Western dance" (*yōbu*) that came to the country after the opening of Japan and including ballet, modern dance, Spanish dance, tap dance, and social dance (1989, 16). Although ballroom dancing with formal Western dress was mostly limited to the upper class, "dance" itself allowed for much wider participation, corresponding to social changes that included more and more women working as waitresses at cafes and dancers employed at theatres, dance halls, and dance troupes. These were often depicted in Kawabata's works set in the Asakusa neighbourhood, as in *The Scarlet Gang of Asakusa* (1930), where the narrator says that in Asakusa, various desires dance naked together: "All races, all classes, all jumbled together forming a bottomless, endless current, flowing day and night, no beginning, no end. Asakusa is alive" (2005, 30).

The introduction of opera after WWI, the revue after the Great Kantō Earthquake and its further popularization through screenings of works of American and French cinema, and the strip show after WWII attracted many visitors to Asakusa. The hybridity of Asakusa culture manifested a vitality, which Kawabata conveys in terms of "both the sensory perceptions of rapidly modernizing Tokyo and the aspects of social relations and material culture that he believed best represented the allure and anxieties of early-twentieth-century urban life" (Freedman 2005, xxxiii). There was a multiplicity not only of performance styles and practices, but also of those who engaged with them, including performers, teachers and directors, and audiences. While female dancers embodying the modern, intimate, and transient culture reflected the audience's desire for it, some of the dance figures contributed cross-culturally to the later development of "art" forms of modern dance in Japan, including Ishii Baku, Eguchi Takaya, and Miya Misako, all of whom went abroad to study dance and later shaped their forms and impetus for modern dance, and professionals of ballet such as Rosi, Russian ballerina Elena Smirnova, and Anna Pavlova, as well as Eliana Pavlova, who contributed to teaching and performing ballet dance and social dance in Japan, and Choi Seung-hee (Sai Shōki), who achieved international recognition in Japanese overseas and mainland territories and in Europe and the United States.

Demonstrating the popularity of dance culture, not only did the number of dance halls in Tokyo around this time rise to 27 and dancers up to around 500, but also dancers were popularly recognized as one of top professionals who characterized the 1920s (Unno 1988, 39). Although Western dance culture in early to mid-twentieth-century Japan allowed for wide participation, it also faced ongoing condemnation. Nagai Yoshikazu finds that dancing in the cafes and bars that were under police control was banned, while dance halls were required to have a concealed storefront. Just as in the Meiji period, social dance had to be kept away from public eyes, and intimate interactions between the sexes were effectively confined in specific spaces (Nagai 1991, 67–72). Furthermore, in her analysis of dance-hall floors in the 1920s and 1930s, with reference to the dance-hall scenes in Tanizaki's fiction *Naomi*, Vera Mackie points out that although women's bodies and sexuality were commodified by male patrons, there also existed among them hierarchical differences in earnings between, on the one hand, the café waitresses, dance hall girls, factory workers, and domestic servants, and those with higher education who tended to work as teachers, shop assistants, or telephone operators (2013, 72). This low status of dancers at the time is also depicted in Nagai's "The Dancing Girl": "These girls were for the most part products of tenements. If they had not become dancers, they would have had to go to work as factory girls, waitresses, nursemaids, or bus conductors, to contribute to the family income" (1965, 338), relating the not-always-fortunate circumstances of dancing girls to the backstreet life. Dancing bodies, while incorporating cross-cultural bodily practices and accommodating some racial differences, were gendered and hierarchically differentiated. The more Kawabata viewed dance, the more he became critical of it in depicting not only gender differences but also the difference that existed among different types of dance and performers. While the performing arts in urban space, such as in Asakusa, functioned as a way to mingle people from various backgrounds, the ways in which performing arts practices are embodied, inhabit one's body, and are performed in relation to the external are complicated by the process of crossing the boundaries between "low" and "high" culture.

Unfixing the high and low through embodied practice

Following the previous discussion, I further examine how hierarchical judgments such as "high" and "low" are potentially mobilized through the body as a medium of expression, especially when the embodied experience lets the body move beyond the boundaries, using Kawabata's literary works as a case study. By analyzing how the embodied practice may affect one's relation to the world, I further pose the possibility of mobilizing the boundaries and potentially rewriting the body in the inhibited social space.

Kawabata only sometimes differentiates dance as a "high" art form, including both Japanese dance and ballet, from the dances in revue clubs, cafés and bars, and dance halls. And yet, when it comes to bodily training, certain distinctions are made. Kawabata writes in "My Views on the Dance World" (*Buyōkai shiken*, 1934) that girls from affluent backgrounds who engage in "artistic dance" seem to look down on dancing girls in revues due to a concern for art, even though those in the former group may not always be more skilled than the revue girls or able to cope with the physical demands of certain dance styles. Kawabata thought of the showgirls as lacking mastery of the techniques of classical ballet (1982b, 40). In "Hill Myna of Asakusa" (*Asakusa no kyūkanchō*, 1932), a girl describes a dance by revue girls at the inn as a fake geisha's dance (1981b, 319), associating the local geisha culture with the dazzling mixed dances of revues, while Kawabata notes the rigorous discipline required for dancers in ballet and Japanese dance, often affiliated with a particular school (1981b, 322). Also, the narrator of *The Scarlet Gang of Asakusa* presents revue dance as a strange, grotesque, or unpolished mixture of the Western and Japanese. Kawabata confesses in his essay "About *Scarlet Gang of Asakusa*" (*Asakusa kurenai dan ni tsuite*, 1951) that, when he found a talented dancing girl at Casino Follies during one of his frequent visits to Asakusa, he tried to persuade her to train as a ballet dancer (1970, 382). And in "The Diary of a Dancing Girl" (*Maihime no koyomi*, 1935), when the heroine Yumiko, a trained dancer, offers to work and financially support her partner Kunio during his study in Tokyo, he responds: "If I were to make you work as a waitress (*jokyū*) or dancer in Tokyo, I would much prefer throwing you into the basin of a waterfall" (1981c, 25), showing a pejorative view on dancers at the dance hall, café, and revues. Kawabata considered ballet dance essential training for dancers whose benefits should not be limited to girls of the middle and upper class, corresponding to his effort in *tsuzurigata* to encourage a wider participation in composition.

Kawabata lets his literary characters exchange hierarchical depictions of various dance styles, marking the transition from Asakusa opera and revue to "artistic dance" (*geijutsu buyō*). Komaki notes that, while postwar performances of *Swan Lake* by the Tokyo Ballet Company were not welcomed by commercial operators at the time, as they considered ballet a kind of finishing school for girls and the performance of full-scale ballet an unprecedented adventure (1977, 44), it was nevertheless a success, with stage design by Fujita Tsuguharu and accompaniment by the Tōhō Symphony Orchestra. Prompted by the first full-scale performance of *Swan Lake* in 1946 and the Bolshoi Ballet's first visit to Japan in 1957, ballet experienced a boom in postwar Japan, becoming a desired "education" for girls who would study dance as an art for their education alone and not as a profession.

Kawabata's well-known dance story *Dancing Beauty* (*Maihime*), when read along with his essays on dance, shows the different receptions of the various types of dance and the Japanese ambivalence toward Western dance, along with the larger theme of the corruption of the *ie* system (the Japanese patriarchal system meant to ensure the continuation of the family through organized succession) in postwar Japan. The heroine, Namiko, a former ballet dancer and teacher from a privileged background in her 40s, financially supports her family, including her husband Yagi, an unstable academic, with her parents' inheritance. Yet the postwar transformation diminishes their wealth to the extent that she needs to continue marketing the goods she sells and relying on her longtime lover Takehara. When her manager Numata suggests that Namiko teach ballet for a living, she hesitates, prompting Numata to comment, "You should do it [as a profession], not as part of the luxurious life of a well-educated lady" (1980b, 404). At the same time, Yūko, Namiko's assistant, shocks both Shinako (Namiko's daughter) and Namiko by deciding to make money through striptease dancing in Asakusa to support her lover's sick children.

While making contrasts among different types of dancing figures and depicting male dancers, including actual figures such as Ishii Baku, Kawabata's dancing bodies are gendered. Namiko's husband Yagi says to Shinako, "As female beauty culminates in dance, I didn't stop your mother's dance. But the women don't dance with the mind but just the body (*nikutai*)" (1980b, 470). Nozu, choosing Shinako as his practicing partner and wishing to have her as his life partner, supports her body during dance practice. Yet Shinako perceives of him as a noble, fashionable, and rather feminine man. Commenting on the gendering of bodies in ballet, Susan Leigh Foster observes:

> Even when costumed in the most unisex unitards, *she* wears point shoes, and *he* wears ballet slippers. *She* elaborates a vast range of intricate coordinations for legs, feet, arms, and head, while *he* launches into the air, defying gravity in a hundred different positions. *She* extends while *he* supports. *She* resides in front and *he* remains in back. *She* looks forward and *he* looks at her. *She* touches his arms, hands, and shoulders, whereas *he* touches her arms and hands and also her waist, thighs, buttocks, and armpits.
>
> (1996, 1)

The gendered bodies and movements in ballet were transported to Japan also in the adoption of the bodily vocabulary and grammar of ballet dance. Ballet was regarded as a matter of luxury education, as opposed to dancehall and revue dances performed for a living, with some ambivalence expressed toward the Japanese people practicing Western dance. This corresponds to how Namiko regards dance even in the postwar context, possibly reminding the reader of the prewar *ryōsai kenbo* (good wife and wise mother) ideology, wherein women were expected to serve the healthy development of their families and the education of their children to serve the nation.

Kawabata, along with his conflicting views of different types of dance, also thought about genres of art with an awareness that dance is an art conveyed through the body. In "The Day for Japanese Dance" (*Nihon buyō no hi*, 1937), he questions:

> In the case of music and painting, musical instruments and paints as well as clothing and accompaniments completely differ between Japan and the West, but I wonder about dance where the same medium of flesh expresses things. How about literature? The manner in which Japan and the West are opposed or together will be manifest variously, depending on the fields of art.
>
> *(1982c, 175)*

In the short story "Dance" (*Buyō*, 1931), comparing how a dancer husband and a painter relate to the heroine Suzuko's body, the narrator says, "It is the same thing that painter and dancer deal with females and flesh. Yet how differently they deal with it! How many days her new husband spent taking her hand, matching her foot step, and transferring his bodily music into her body! And he made it one body" (1980c, 506). While Kawabata depicts gendered dancing bodies with connotations of class and social status, it is through the body and embodied experiences that he shows the possibility of unfixing divisions.

As a case in point, Kawabata is attentive to bodily practices that affect reflectiveness and consciousness. For example, the heroine Yumiko in "The Diary of a Dancing Girl" has trained in Japanese dance since the age of five or six. She feels as if dance has permeated her mind and body, and she feels her body moving when learning songs in elementary school (1981c, 25). Also, Chikako, who studies ballet, talks about Isadora Duncan's dance school, which accepted homeless and beggar girls, and says that those girls, strangely, transformed into graceful young ladies (*ojōsan*) in just three weeks, with better posture and more beautiful faces, testifying to the power of the rhythm and music of dance (1981c, 68). The cases of the previously mentioned Yūko shifting from ballet training to strip dance and Shinako's perception of her practice partner Nozu as a rather feminine man in *Dancing Beauty* also illuminate the possibility of crossing class or even assumed gender divisions through bodily training. The knowledge that is lived in the body continually modifies, rather than merely "fixing," one's relationship to the world. Additionally, embodiment may even perform its relation to the "other." While gender performativity for Judith Butler is produced within a set of regulatory practices, its unfixed mutability is also what underlies an indeterminacy of gender and sexual identities as roles that are constituted through performances, as "doing" (2007, 34) or even acting toward the external aspects of one's body. Such embodied practices may function as a way to cross hierarchical differences.

Conclusion: rewriting the body

Dance critic Ashihara Eiryō comparatively analyzes ballet through the *pas* (step), a foot movement in relation to gravity, as the unit of one movement and Japanese dance through *geste* (gesture) considered unresolvable into smaller units (1986, 256–271). Mauss similarly illuminates techniques ingrained in everyday life in specific cultures (1973), arguing that one's daily bodily practice shapes how one moves, acts, and potentially thinks. And yet, one's bodily knowledge does not fix one to particular communities, but also can involve a rewriting of one's relationship to the outside world. Kawabata depicts characters who, amid social and historical turmoil, and even unconsciously, "rewrite" the body, making use of it as the very medium of expression. Reflecting on the semantic association between writing and choreography, Mark Franco writes, "dancing does not derive from writing or leave writing in its wake as a record. Instead, her dancing acquires the generative power of writing to produce images" (2011, 329). As this characterization of the human body as medium indicates, Kawabata's attention to dance suggests the possibility not only of writing about the gendered dancing body but also, potentially, rewriting the body—contrary to the general association of Kawabata with Japanese icons such as dancing geisha and hot springs.

In aiming to reach the pure flesh through dancing, Kawabata's works, instead of merely fixing gendered dancing subjects to certain social and cultural categories of "high" and "low," let them use their embodied knowledge to rewrite their bodies and re-perform their life. In this sense, although high-and-low hierarchical views of certain cultural practices and their types and forms exist, literary and cultural representations also imply rather a question of how embodied knowledge is used and reconfigures itself bodily. Such an approach indicates how the body is situated and mobilized in society, and how it engages with others, added to the particular historical context, such as in Asakusa in the interwar period, where the high and low have gathered together to create one urban space. As Kawabata tried to rescue dance from a generally pejorative views, cultural creation is an attempt to challenge and mobilize judgments and values.

Related chapters

28 Gender in Japanese Literature and Literary Studies
29 Gender and Poetry
32 Gender and Visual Culture
33 Gender, Media, and Misogyny in Japan
34 Representing Girls in Cinema

References

Ashihara, E. (1986) *Buyō to shintai* (Dance and the Body), Tokyo: Shinjuku shobō.
Butler, J. 2007 [1990]. *Gender Trouble*: Feminism and the Subversion of Identity. New York: Routledge.
Csordas, T. J. (1994) "Introduction," in T. J. Csordas (ed) *Embodiment and Experience: The Existential Ground of Culture and Self*, Cambridge: Cambridge University Press, 1–24.
Dollase, H. T. (2003) "Mad Girls in the Attic: Louisa May Alcott, Yoshiya Nobuko, and the Development of *Shōjo* Culture," PhD Diss., Purdue University.
Foster, S. L. (1996) "The Ballerina's Phallic Pointe," in S. L. Foster (ed) *Corporealities: Dancing Knowledge, Culture and Power*, London: Routledge, 1–24.
Franco, M. (2011) "Wiring for the Body: Notation, Reconstruction, and Reinvention in Dance," *Common Knowledge* 17 (2) 321–334.
Freedman, A. (2005) "Translator's Preface," trans. A Freedman in A. Freedman (ed) *The Scarlet Gang of Asakusa*, Berkeley and Los Angeles: University of California Press, xxxiii–xlviii.
Kawabata, Y. (1970) "Asakusa kurenai dan ni tsuite," in *Kawabata Yasunari Zenshū*, vol. 12, Tokyo: Shinchōsha, 375–384.
Kawabata, Y. (1980a) "Kurutta Ippēji," in *Kawabata Yasunari Zenshū*, vol. 2, Tokyo: Shinchōsha, 385–418.
Kawabata, Y. (1980b) "Maihime," in *Kawabata Yasunari Zenshū*, vol. 10, Tokyo: Shinchōsha, 257–500.
Kawabata, Y. (1980c) "Buyō," in *Kawabata Yasunari Zenshū*, vol. 21, Tokyo: Shinchōsha, 497–506.
Kawabata, Y. (1980d) "Odoriko to ikokujin no haha," in *Kawabata Yasunari Zenshū*, vol. 21, Tokyo: Shinchōsha, 613–624.
Kawabata, Y. (1981a) "Asakusa nikki," in *Kawabata Yasunari Zenshū*, vol. 4, Tokyo: Shinchōsha, 213–243.
Kawabata, Y. (1981b) "Asakusa no kyūkanchō," in *Kawabata Yasunari Zenshū*, vol. 4, Tokyo: Shinchōsha, 279–350.
Kawabata, Y. (1981c) "Maihime no Koyomi," in *Kawabata Yasunari Zenshū*, vol. 23, Tokyo: Shinchōsha, 7–192.

Kawabata, Y. (1982a) "Jun'sui no koe," in *Kawabata Yasunari Zenshū,* vol. 27, Tokyo: Shinchōsha, 105–110.
Kawabata, Y. (1982b) "Buyōkai shiken," in *Kawabata Yasunari Zenshū,* vol. 27, Tokyo: Shinchōsha, 38–41.
Kawabata, Y. (1982c) "Nihon buyō no hi," in *Kawabata Yasunari Zenshū,* vol. 27, Tokyo: Shinchōsha, 172–177.
Kawabata, Y. (2005) *The Scarlet Gang of Asakusa,* trans. A. Freedman, Berkeley: University of California Press.
Komaki, M. (1975) *Petorūsyuka no dokuhaku* (Confession of Petrushka), Tokyo: Sankei shoin.
Komaki, M. (1977) *Baree to watashi no sengo shi* (Postwar History of Ballet and Myself), Tokyo: Mainichi Shinbunsha.
Kuwahara, K. (1989) "Shōwa jidai shoki no buyō: Kawabata Yasunari o tōshite" (Dance in the Early Showa Period: Through Kawabata Yasunari), *Buyōgaku* 12 7–18.
Mackie, V. C. (2013) "Sweat, Perfume and Tobacco: The Ambivalent Labor of the Dancehall Girl," in A. Freedman, L. Miller and C. Yano (eds) *Modern Girls on the Go: Gender, Mobility and Labor in Japan,* Stanford: Stanford University Press, 67–82.
Mauss, M. (1973) "Techniques of the Body," *Economy and Society* 2 (1) 70–88.
Nagai, K. (1965) "The Dancing Girl: Chapter 10," trans. E. Seidensticker, in E. Seidensticker, *Kafū the Scribbler: The Life and Writing of Nagai Kafū, 1879–1959,* Stanford: Stanford University Press, 336–338.
Nagai, Y. (1991) *Shakō dansu to Nihonjin* (Social Dance and the Japanese), Tokyo: Shōbunsha.
Richie, D. (2005) "Foreword," in A. Freedman (ed) *The Scarlet Gang of Asakusa,* Berkeley: University of California Press, ix–xxxii.
Silverberg, M. (2006) *Erotic Grotesque Nonsense: The Mass Culture of Japanese Modern Times,* Berkeley and Los Angeles: University of California Press.
Tanizaki, J. (2017) *Tanizaki Jun'ichirō Zenshū,* vol. 8, Tokyo: Chūoh kōronsha.
Unno, H. (1988) *Modan toshi Tokyo: Nihon no 1920 nendai* (Modern City Tokyo: The 1920s in Japan), Tokyo: Chūoh kōronsha.
Wei, C. (2014) "Kawabata Yasunari to *tsudurikata*: Senjichū no teikokushugi to tsunagaru kairo" (Yasunari Kawabata and *Tsudurikata*: The Way That Is Connected to Japanese Imperialism), *Juncture: Chōikiteki nihon bunka kenkyū* 5 104–113.
Zimring, R. (2014) "Ballet, Folk Dance, and the Cultural History of Interwar Modernism: The Ballet *Job*," *Modernist Cultures* 9 (1) 99–114.

37
GENRE AND GENDER
Romantic friendships and the homosocial imperative in the ninkyō (chivalrous) genre film

Isolde Standish

In earlier works, I analysed the popular *yakuza* and its derivative *ninkyō* (chivalrous) genres in terms of socially established norms of gender and relationships between, on the one hand, men and men, and, on the other, between men and women in terms of the Neo-Confucian codes of *jingi* (morality) implicit within the narrative patterns (Standish 2000, 2005). I argued that the *yakuza* and *ninkyō* genres from the late 1950s, 1960s and 1970s ultimately supported a conservative ethos of loyalty to an organisation or institution (the family as the *ie* or the criminal organisation as the *kumi*) above personal emotional attachments. Despite the seeming anti-social, violent and rebellious nature of many of the plot lines, a conservative position is ultimately upheld in the narrative through the death or imprisonment of the "tragic hero" in the denouement, which is, as I have argued elsewhere, at the same time, a hubristic homosocial expression of the incorruptible subjectivity of the "tragic hero" as he goes to his fate accompanied by his brother-in-arms (*kyōdaibun*). Satō Tadao describes the significance of these scenes in terms of the *michiyuki* of the kabuki play when star-crossed lovers walk to the place in which they will carry out their suicide pact:

> These scenes in which the hero and his brother-in-arms walk in silence to their deaths are enacted according to a prescribed mode; these scenes represent a continuation of the michiyuki in the double suicide plays (shinjū) of the kabuki theatre. These scenes are a revival of the traditional aesthetic which depicts the beauty of the incomparable purity of the love and trust of two people who are resolved to die.
>
> (Satō 1996, 52)

That is, in its manifestations in the subtext of the *ninkyō* films, two people of the same-sex are linked in a homosocial "romantic friendship," the sexual consummation of which is deflected through violence and death.

Thus, the *yakuza* and *ninkyō* genres, while purporting to offer fantasies of rebellion through the depiction of the criminal underworld, in effect, support conservative gendered social and sexual roles within organisations and the extended family of the *ie*—the two institutions often being conflated in the narrative. In this chapter, I want to go beyond my earlier analysis and focus specifically on the question of "romantic friendship" as an expression of a sexually non-consummated, homosocial love and the more recent inclusion of female characters into this hitherto exclusive male tradition in the Tōei Studio series' *Gangster Women* (*Gokudō no onna*), which ran from 1986 to 2005. Furthermore, I shall argue that in Tōei Studio's formulaic *yakuza* and *ninkyō* genre series, characters transcend gender, whether biological males or females; through their portrayal in the narrative, they become symbolic representatives of social roles rather than individual men or women per se, and it is this that permits female characters a degree of gender fluidity. As Shiba and Aoyama, in their discussion of the 1960s female *yakuza* character played by Fuji Junko in the *Scarlet Peony Rose Gambler* (*Hibotan bakuto*) series state in reference to one of the series directors, "his concept was that even if you escaped from the status quo to the world of the outlaw (*autorō*), there were still laws (*okite*) that regulated outlaw life. And as this world was a completely male world Oryū [Fuji Junko] of the scarlet peony rose could not exist unless she became a man" (Shiba and Aoyama 1998, 53). This theme is borne out in the first film of the series in which Oryū, after the assassination of her father, a Kyushu *oyabun* (the patriarchal leader of the gang), states that from now until she can avenge her father, she is no longer a woman. The tattoo of the scarlet peony rose on her body bears testimony to her stoic intent. Therefore, it is important when considering the gender fluidity of female characters and the homosexual undertones of "romantic friendships" within these narratives not to fall into the easy temptation to frame the analysis solely within contemporary academic scholarship in terms of queer theory but to also focus on Neo-Confucian precepts that are institutionalised in the group and that bind the individual into relations of power.

In this chapter, I shall primarily focus on the last film in the Tōei Studio series *Gangster Women: Burning Desire* (*Gokudō no onna: jōen*, Hashimoto Hajime, 2005) while referring to earlier series discussed at greater length in my *New History of Japanese Cinema*. The *Gangster Women* series is significant, as it extends the hitherto predominantly masculine centred *jingi* ethic of the *yakuza* organisation to include "active" women and therefore on the surface appears to support aspects of women's inclusion and empowerment. However, as with the depiction of male heroes in the earlier series, I shall argue that a conservative ethic is ultimately upheld by the plot lines and that the inclusion of a female hero was in effect a further twist to the genre's negotiation between convention and novelty. I also suggest that this inclusion of the female in this series into the male world of the *yakuza* on equal terms does, in certain respects, mirror changes in social attitudes to women's place in Japanese society at the turn of the twenty-first century. Furthermore, following the genre's conventions, the series provided a star vehicle for popular, but ageing, actresses. Just as Arashi Kanjūrō, a star of the pre-war *jidaigeki* films and their postwar reiteration in the late-1950s, made a comeback in the 1960s as the benevolent leader/father (*oyabun*) figure in the long-running *Abashiri Prison* (*Abashiri bangaichi*) series, so too, Iwashita Shima (1941–), in the twilight of her acting career, appears in seven films of the *Yakuza Women* series. Takashima Reiko (1964–) appeared in a further five films of the series, including the last one, which forms the main example of this chapter. Genealogically, Fuji Junko (1945–), as the star of the *Scarlet Peony Rose Gambler* series (1968–1972), set the precedent to be developed in this later series (see Coates 2020).

The social context

As Bachnick and Quinn have argued in their edited book *Situated Meanings: Inside and Outside in Japanese Self, Society and Language*, within Neo-Confucian gender norms, men's and women's place within the social has traditionally been defined indexically through situationally defined social orders. In their study, they focus on the topographical terms of *uchi* and *soto*: *uchi* being the inside, the private world symbolised by the home, the family unit, whereas *soto* represented the outside, the public sphere.

> Although usually unnoticed, these distinctions are crucially important: uchi/soto is a major organizational focus for Japanese self, social life, and language. In uchi/soto, the inside/outside orientations are also specifically linked with another set of meanings, denoting "self" and "society". Thus the organizing of both self and society can be viewed as situating meaning, through the indexing of inside and outside orientations.
> (Bachnick and Quinn, eds. 1994, 3)

These often gendered dichotomies of place are further reinforced through their linguistic adaptation into the familial through the use of "*uchi*" as a personal pronoun used by women, the husband's reference to his wife as "*kanai*," which can be translated literally through the colloquial English expression "her indoors," or the more polite term *okusan*, literally inside person, used as a more formal address to denote someone else's wife. Despite the traditional acknowledgement of the complementary nature of this division, these concepts combined to keep women, in status terms and in discourse, in a secondary position as supporters of their men and carers of children and elderly relatives. With the advent of rapid industrialisation following defeat in World War II, this model was adapted to the needs of Japanese enterprise as economic migration from the countryside, and concomitant urbanisation, led to the rise of the nuclear family, which had the effect of undermining the traditional extended family. It should also be pointed out that within the traditional family, the *ie*, sons as well as women are ranked hierarchically according to their importance for the continuance and prosperity of the family as an institution. The first-born son, as potential inheritor of the family property and future head of the household under a rigid system of primogeniture, held the top position, and subsequent sons' secondary positions were only slightly removed from their sisters, who occupy the lowest rank, as they are expected to marry outside their natal home and transfer their loyalty to their husband's family (*yome ni iku*). This hierarchical ranking of family members is prescribed in language, as the first-born son is known as the *chōnan* and second-born son *jinan* and so forth. Thus, these institutional arrangements set the scene for the inherent conflict between the individual and the social—if an individual's desires are not in accord with the perceived needs of the family as an institution, the classic *giri* (obligation) versus *ninjō* (human emotion) scenario arises.

In the long post-war period of high economic growth, despite women's increased autonomy granted as a legal right under the terms of the 1947 "peace" Constitution, the centrality of marriage for women was maintained, as women were often forced out of the workplace and into marriage in their mid- to late twenties, often marrying men from within the company where they were employed. The company acted as a marriage broker through the *nakōdo* system. The wife was thought to have inculcated the company ethos during her training and employment with the company and would, therefore, be a strong support for her husband in his work. Furthermore, in the example of high-status companies, it was thought she would easily fit into the community of the company-sponsored *shataku* (apartment block). Thus, the company, not only through the prospect of lifetime employment, but also through arranged marriages, took over many of the functions of the traditional extended family. It was only women employed in government institutions (for example, the Post Office) who could consider continuing in the workplace with the slim possibility of promotion through internal government examination systems. Yet this option was not seen as a lifestyle choice but as a failure to secure a husband through some fault on the part of the woman—for example, an inability to bear children. After all, it was a generally accepted social myth that a woman's happiness/fulfilment in life (*shiawase*) was through children and home. It should also be pointed out that men were similarly under a compulsion to marry and produce offspring. Failure to do so would result in not being considered for promotion at work and would risk alienating parents and family members. While "romance" was promoted as a basis for marriage and a key theme in the cinema in the immediate post-defeat period—David Conde of the Civil Information and Education Section (CIE), the propaganda arm of the Supreme Command for the Allied Powers (SCAP), insisted on kissing scenes being included in Japanese films—in reality, in many instances, company policies and social norms impacted this major life decision. Statistics quoted by Takeda Tomohiro (2013, 79) demonstrate the lag behind the implementation of policy, that is, women's autonomy in decisions of marriage as sanctioned in the post-war Constitution and the realisation of the policy in the life cycle of women. Between 1955 and 1959, only 36.2 percent of marriages were listed as "love marriages" (*ren'ai kekkon*) as opposed to "arranged marriages" (*miai kekkon*); between 1960 and 1964, the number of "love marriages" increased slightly to 41.7 percent, rising substantially between 2005 and 2009 to 88 percent. I would suggest that this element of social compulsion in marriage for both men and women is one of the key factors in the significance of the "romantic friendship" for an individual, as one is free to choose one's friend in a way that one could not necessarily choose one's marriage partner. Therefore, I would suggest that one of the reasons for the great popularity of the post-war *yakuza* and *ninkyō* genres resided in its portrayal of this conflict between the individual as an emotional being and the social and economic institutions which would impose order by controlling an individual's life choices. Furthermore, the slow breakdown of the social ethos around the extended family in the long post-war period combined with more recent changes in population demographics (a declining birth-rate and an ageing population) increasingly required the emergence of women into the *soto*, the public sphere. It is this period of transition that the series *Gangster Women* mediates, presenting a conservative re-working of an "active" femininity through the Neo-Confucian ethos of the *yakuza* and *ninkyō* genres for the modern age.

In these films, the *onēsan*, literally "elder sister," as de facto head of the *yakuza* organization, must bear the burden of "obligation" (*giri*) in much the same way as defined in the classic line uttered by male *ninkyō* stars in numerous films: "When forced to weigh the balance between duty (*giri*) and human emotions (*ninjō*), duty weighs most heavily in a man's world." The female leads in the *Gangster Women* films, as surrogate leaders of their organisations and honorary males, adhered to this ethos throughout the series. In many cases, as I have argued in *A New History of Japanese Cinema* (2005), this conflict is played out between her obligations to the gang and a conflicted loyalty to a blood-related family member or a lover. However, in the case of *Gangster Women: Burning Desire*, the Onēsan played by Takashima Reiko enters into a "romantic friendship" with a Korean female *yakuza*. The relationship is framed within the male *ninkyō* narrative conventions established by stalwarts such as Takakura Ken and Ikebe Ryū in that in the denouement, they go to the rival gang's headquarters. With Takashima wielding a sword and her Korean allay a pistol with a knife fitted as a bayonet, they decimate the opposition, leading to the death of the Korean woman, cradled in Takashima's arms. Both in terms of plot and visual style, the earlier episodes building up to these final scenes define the relationship as just one step removed from the sexual.

Romantic friendships

In linguistic terms, "romantic friendships" are sealed with the verb *horeru*, which in a very literal sense may be translated as "to fall in love" but also carries connotations associated with the word *shinsui* to be "fascinated by," or "infatuated with" someone and is employed in cinematic narratives in same-sex "friendships." In contrast, in heterosexual relationships *suki*, "to become fond of," or *ai suru* literally "to love" are the usual words of endearment (see Alexy in this volume). Thus, in film narratives, linguistically the distinctions between types of "love" and emotional attachments are clearly delineated with different verbs of endearment available to same-sex "romantic friendships" and others to heterosexual couples. For example, in the 1983 version of *The Theatre of Life* (*Jinsei gekijō*, Fukusaku Kinji, Satō Jun'ya, and Nakashima Sadao), an old retainer/*yakuza* (Wakayama Tomisaburō) visits a younger *yakuza*, Kaku (Matsukata Hiroki), in prison. In response to Kaku's question, "Why are you being so kind (*shinsetsu*)?" Wakayama states, "it is simple," and that he is "infatuated" with Kaku (*Horetan desu. Omae tada sore dake*). According to genre conventions, this does not in any way appear subversive or odd. In terms of visual style, the relationship is further reinforced as the two gaze meaningfully into each other's eyes through the prison grille in a series of close-up facial reverse shots. The exchange of "looks," in the sense used by Laura Mulvey in terms of desire, is a common motif of the genre. However, it is not men looking at women, but men looking at other men and, in the example of the *Gangster Women* series, women looking at other women. Takakura Ken, in earlier series, made a feature of the "gaze," as he has a series of expressive looks, which thanks to the voice-over songs denote his "true" feelings, while maintaining the outwardly stoic persona of the silent male hero. In a *The Theatre of Life* scene, the prison setting ensures that the love between the two men remains platonic, as a physical barrier, the wire grille of the prison visiting room, is placed between them and we know that Kaku is going to be incarcerated for many years, as he is in prison for murder.

A similar scene appears in the 1990 film *Gangster Women: the Last Battle* (*Gokudō no onna: saigo no tatakai*), but this time it is enacted between two women, Iwashita Shima as the substitute *oyabun* and Katasei Rin as a younger acolyte. Iwashita's husband is in prison and she goes to visit him accompanied by Katasei. During the course of the visit, Katasei discloses that she has brought with her a small bottle of *sake* and a *sake* cup, as she wants to become a blood-sister to Iwashita in the time-honoured *yakuza*-style of *sakazuki* or the exchange of cups. When asked why, she states because "I am infatuated with you sister" (*Nēsan horetan desu*). "Together until death, I want to walk one road" (*Issho shinu made, hitotsu no michi o arukitain desu*). Iwashita turns to look at her husband and asks; "Can women become sisters-in-arms?" (*Kyōdaibun nara onna dōshi sakazuki ga dekiru*). After this, they perform the ceremony, each pricking her finger and drinking the other's blood mixed with the *sake*. The camera holds on a series of reverse cuts in close-up of their eyes as they gaze in silent communication. Ultimately, Onēsan (Iwashita) is betrayed by her husband, and as a result Natsumi (Katasei) is killed in an assassination attempt. In the final scenes, Onēsan takes her revenge, killing the rival *oyabun* in the full knowledge that she will be imprisoned. After shooting him, a close-up of her face as tears well up is followed by short flashback to Natsumi at the point when they exchanged *sake* cups. This flashback reinforces Onēsan's motives; she acted out of loyalty and love for her dead sister-in-arms rather than for her duplicitous husband, thus expressing the "purity" of their love per Satō Tadao's observation quoted previously. This narrative marks a shift from the earlier *Scarlet Peony Rose Gambler* series in which in the denouement of the first film in the series Fuji Junko sets out on the *michiyuki* with a male colleague and is saved by Takakura Ken, who subsequently dies in her arms, confounding any possible romantic attachment hinted at earlier in the film. However, the most radical depiction of a "romantic friendship" between women is the last film of the *Gangster Women* series.

Onēsan's husband is assassinated at the beginning of the film, and Onēsan is attempting to defend their faction's position in the organisational hierarchy at a time when the senior *oyabun* is on his deathbed. She becomes acquainted with a Korean woman who is looking for her husband, now a successful *yakuza* in Japan remarried to the (Japanese) daughter of the dying *oyabun*. She has been in prison in South Korea, where she had a tiger tattooed onto her back, affirming her *yakuza* credentials and her national identity as a Korean (the Asian tiger is symbolic of Korea). There are two significant scenes that establish the relationship between the two women through the "gaze." In the first, the Korean woman comes to the Saigo gang office seeking information about her husband. The two women exchange looks, fetishized through a series of reverse-cut close-ups. Later, Onēsan is on the dance floor with a rival faction leader who is threatening her when the Korean woman intervenes and asks to change partners. Naturally the male partner assumes she wishes to dance with him, but the Korean woman whisks Onēsan off on the dance floor. The act of dancing together offers many opportunities for shots of the two women looking at each other and the exchange of knowing smiles interspersed with shots of the angry and humiliated *oyabun* scowling in the corner.

The relationship between the women thus established, after the death of a young girl closely associated with both, they go together to take revenge. After laying waste to the rival gang, the Korean woman dies in Onēsan's arms, professing her love. In this denouement, while Onēsan wears a kimono in keeping with genre conventions, the Korean woman wears a black leather jacket and military-style fatigue trousers. During the course of the action, she takes her jacket off to reveal not a singlet-style T-shirt as might be expected, but a white breast bodice constraining her ample bosom but also allowing her tattoo to be clearly visible. Thus, she is clearly following the convention established in earlier series by Takakura Ken of having his tattoo and white cumber band (*haramaki*) visible in these scenes. Through this convention we, the spectator, are permitted to "look" at and admire his/her body as it is being punished.

A discourse of interpellation and the homosocial imperative

> [*Ninkyō*] films portray all that has been lost in the modern age. (A statement made by a designer working on the *Tales of Japanese Chivalry* series, quoted in Shiba and Aoyama 1998, 42)

Judith Butler, in her study on *The Psychic Life of Power: Theories in Subjection*, attempts to reconcile Althusser's explication of the individual's "interpellation" into the social and Foucault's incorporation of this theory in his understanding of "power" with the psychoanalytic theories of Freud. In simple terms, if we accept the view that "power," as understood by Foucault, has a "double valence" in that it not only presses on the subject from outside but also forms the subject, "providing the very conditions of its existence and the trajectory of its desire, then power is not simply what we oppose but also [...] what we depend on for our existence and what we harbour and preserve in being what we are" (Butler 1997, 2). This brings us back to Althusser and "interpellation" in the sense that we recognise our existence and acquiesce to given roles in the social, which then provides the ideological framework through which one defines one's identity, sexual and otherwise. Traditional Neo-Confucian institutional structures locate the individual in pre-prescribed roles through, amongst other things, linguistic codes designating social functions—first son (*chōnan*), second son (*jinan*), wife/inside person (*okusan*)—that are underpinned by the economic imperative of primogeniture, which, in turn, is based on the biological need for heterosexual reproduction. Butler, in the Western example, takes the theoretical argument forward into questions of the "psychic" to explain the consequent social prohibition on homosexuality.

> If we accept the notion that the prohibition on homosexuality operates throughout a largely heterosexual culture as one of its defining operations, then the loss of

homosexual objects and aims [...] would appear to be foreclosed from the start. I say, "foreclosed" to suggest that this is a preemptive [sic] loss, a mourning for unlived possibilities. If this love is from the start out of the question, then it cannot happen, and if it does, it certainly did not. If it does, it happens only under the official signs of its prohibition and disavowal.

(1997, 139)

And this, I would argue, is the narrative subtext of the "romantic friendship" of the *ninkyō* film: the ritualised playing out of this loss, the "mourning" of the possibility of a homosexual love sublimated onto a sanctioned but fated homosocial love (*horeru*) of brothers/sisters-in-arms. The narrative schematic trajectory is simple—affirmation and then disavowal through a formulaic prohibition which carries the ultimate juridical sanction, the death of one of the lovers and incarceration of the other. As Butler explains,

When the prohibition against homosexuality is culturally pervasive, then the "loss" of homosexual love is precipitated through a prohibition which is repeated and ritualized throughout the culture.

(Butler 1997, 140)

In the Japanese historical context, the "loss" of homosexual love should be considered against the concept of *shudō* as applied to the samurai class; "far from being condemned [homosexuality] was considered a passion more gracious than heterosexuality [...] The rapid decline of *shudō* started with westernization" (Watanabe and Iwate 1989, 11). As the epigraph that opens this section states: [*Ninkyō*] "films portray all that has been lost in the modern age."

Women and power

While these few examples (with the emphasis on few) from the *Gangster Women* series appear (through the generic visual motif of the fetishized gaze and the death or incarceration of the heroine in the narrative) to admit female characters into the hitherto masculine traditions of the "tragic hero" and "romantic friendship," one still has to ask whether this is in fact a progressive image in terms of women's relationship to power. Certainly, in terms of the "gaze" and women looking at women within the diegesis (issues of the spectator and "looking" are beyond the scope of this chapter), these films do indicate a shift in the genre. In the few mainstream films depicting same-sex desire between women, the women are all portrayed as emotionally unstable; for example, the 1965 adaptation of Kawabata Yasunari's novel *The Beauty and the Pity* (*Utsukushisa to kanashimi to*) directed by Shinoda Masahiro centres on female revenge, while the two adaptations of Tanizaki Jun'ichirō's novel *Manji* depict either a narcissistic "gaze" as in Masumura Yasuzō's 1964 version or sadomasochistic rituals of desire as in the 1983 version directed by Yokoyama Hiroto. In all these literary adaptations, the women's relationship is invariably structured around a man and is reduced to a common discourse of competition between the women rather than a "mourning" for a lost homosexuality, as I have argued is the case with the "romantic friendship" of the *ninkyō* narrative.

There is a further aspect to be considered which Mary Beard has highlighted in the European context in her recent book *Women and Power: a Manifesto*. In this book, she sets out an historical trajectory to demonstrate her thesis that powerful women are "packaged into a male template." "[M]y basic premise is that our mental, cultural templates for a powerful person remains resolutely male" (2017, 53). This is significant in light of Cordelia Fine's recent study

Testosterone Rex: Unmaking the Myths of Our Gendered Minds, in which she argues there is no biological foundation for concepts of "difference" as historically attributed to "masculine" and "feminine" gender distinctions in patriarchal societies. In the example of Iwashita Shima as Onēsan of the *Gangster Women* series, while she is literally cloaked in tradition, wearing elaborate kimono, she also takes on masculine traits in that she lowers the timbre of her voice. This is evident when compared to her "normal" speaking voice when being interviewed in television documentaries about the series. Furthermore, she smokes and is depicted as a heavy drinker. However, the most obvious example is her use of what is often defined as "masculine" language forms as opposed to "feminine" forms in her conversations with both underlings (*chinpira*) and senior members of the gang and other faction leaders. Thus, I would argue that the language structures are not divided along gender roles so much as reflections of hierarchical positions of power, as junior males will defer to Onēsan using formal language structures normally associated with the female. Gender becomes a factor in the sense that most women would, due to interpellation in the sense developed by Althusser and expanded upon by Butler, automatically accept their status as secondary when addressing a male, a position not adopted by Iwashita in the role of Onēsan in which, as a powerful woman, she is "packaged into a male template."

The last film of the series, *Gangster Women: Burning Desire*, visually locates Takashima Reiko as the Onēsan and surrogate leader of her *yakuza* faction within the *ninkyō* genre. In an early scene in the gang's headquarters, she is shot sitting at her desk with the Chinese ideographs for "the way of chivalry" (*ninkyōdo*) written in elaborate calligraphy behind her. While she is depicted as wielding power, she is also depicted as the surrogate, a symbolic male who is protecting the interests of her husband's gang (*kumi*). The structure of the *ninkyō* narrative remains dominant, the female characters as the Onēsan do the same job as their male counterparts. Thus, they do not bring an alternative discourse that could challenge the patriarchal authority of the *yakuza* organisations, which, as I have argued elsewhere, is founded on Neo-Confucian hierarchical precepts of "morality" (*jingi*). This series therefore reinforces the position first articulated by Fuji Junko in *The Scarlet Peony Rose*. In order to achieve an acceptable goal—revenge or the safeguarding of the institution of the family and/or gang—a female may take on this role in the *soto*, assuming there is no suitable male available, but she must temporarily assume a masculine position. This fluidity of gender roles is symbolised through sartorial choices. When assuming the authoritative role of the surrogate leader, the Onēsan invariably wears a formal kimono. On occasions when she is no longer occupying this role, she is depicted in Western attire. While, in a few films in the series, the homosocial relationship between women offers positive images of female solidarity, these plot lines are in the minority and often overshadowed by the more common themes of jealousy and treachery. Although providing a vehicle for female "activity," this activity is still structured around a dominant heterosexual sexuality. While the Onēsan characters are not overtly sexualised (being tightly confined within constricting kimono), other female characters are clearly displayed for their "to-be-looked-at-ness." Katasei Rin is objectified in many of the films in the series with her ample breasts being exposed. The women are "powerful," but they are substitutes for their men, as the Japanese title of the series indicates *Gokudō no onna*, the "*no*" being the possessive pronoun binding the women to both the organisation and their men. Through the (*furigana*) reading of the Chinese ideograph for "wife" (*tsuma*) as "women" (*onna*), we are directed to a conflation between the two meanings. Thus, the Japanese title of the film clearly directs the spectator to a narrow understanding of the women's authority as not having achieved "power" in their own right.

Although the Onēsan are "women of the gangster organisation" per the Japanese title of the series, they do, in some of the films, have a certain autonomy which finds expression in the "romantic friendship" for which they are willing to sacrifice their lives—literally in death or through the prospect of a long period of incarceration. These relationships are subversive, in that they transcend their affiliations to their husband's organizations, yet they are also denied the "mourning" of a lost homosexuality. Unlike male homosexuality amongst the warrior class in Japan in the Tokugawa period (*shudō*), which is well documented, as with much social history pertaining to women, there seems to be little in the record regarding same-sex relations between women. Where it occurs, the films' inclusion of women into the male homosocial tradition of "romantic friendship" has by necessity been "packaged into a male template." Therefore, just as in the male example exemplified by Takakura Ken and Ikebe Ryū, the "romantic friendship" must, in the denouement, be disavowed and social mores upheld. In the conflict between *giri* (obligations) and *ninjō* (emotions), *giri* must prevail regardless of whether one is male or female for the good of the social order. This series depicts women caught between a traditional destiny imposed on them by a patriarchal organisational structure reminiscent of the *ie* and its non-viability for the women themselves; their emotional inclinations pull them in other directions. The narratives frequently expose these contradictions, which can only be resolved in death or incarceration. The genre's refusal of a "happy ending" ensures the contradictions raised are solved in terms of a conservative social ethos. In concluding, I would suggest that what is distinctive about the Onēsan characters in this series is that through the inclusion of female characters into the "tragic hero" and "romantic friendship" narrative traditions, these characters highlight these contradictions for women in ways that the earlier male-centred series did not.

Related chapters

4 Gender and Language
5 Masculinity Studies in Japan
6 Transgender, Non-Binary Genders, and Intersex in Japan
7 Gender and Ethnicity in Urban Japan
21 Lesbians and Queer Women in Japan
33 Gender, Media, and Misogyny in Japan

References

Bachnick, J. M. and Quinn, C. (eds) (1994) *Situated Meaning: Inside and Outside in Japanese Self, Society and Language*, Chichester: Princeton University Press.
Beard, M. (2017) *Women and Power: A Manifesto*, London: Profile Books.
Butler, J. (1997) *The Psychic Life of Power: Theories in Subjection*, Stanford, CA: Stanford University Press.
Coates, J. (2020) "A Genre Endorsed by the People: Addressing the Appeal of the Yakuza Genre," in H. Fujiki, Hideaki and A. Phillips (eds) *The Japanese Cinema Book*, London: BFI Publishing.
Fine, C. (2017) *Testosterone Rex: Unmaking the Myths of Our Gendered Minds*, London: Icon Books.
Satō, T. (1996) *Nihon Eigashi 1960–1990* (Japanese Film History) vol. 3. Tokyo: Iwanami Shoten.
Shiba, T. and Aoyama, S. (1998) *Yakuza eiga to sono jidai* (Gangster Films and Their Era), Tokyo: Chikuma Shinsho.
Standish, I. (2000) *Myth and Masculinity in the Japanese Cinema: Towards a Political Reading of the Tragic Hero*, Richmond, Surrey: Curzon/Routledge.
Standish, I. (2005) *A New History of Japanese Cinema: a Century of Narrative Film*, New York and London: Continuum.
Takeda, T. (2013) *Shōwa 30 Nendai no (Igai)na Shinjitsu*, Tokyo: Daiwa Bunko.
Watanabe, T. and Iwata, J. (1989) *The Love of the Samurai: A Thousand Years of Japanese Homosexuality*, trans. D. R Roberts, London: GMP Publishers.

38
GIRLS WITH ARMS AND GIRLS AS ARMS IN ANIME
The use of girls for "soft" militarism

Akiko Sugawa-Shimada

In films featuring male leads, battles with robots and high-tech machines are often used to construct the protagonist's masculinity and coolness. In contrast, women and children are often situated as victims to be protected by these central male characters. However, in Japanese animation (*anime*), the machine-wielding fighting girl is one of the most popular motifs. These girls are used as metaphors for conventional adolescent troubles—conflicts of love, identity crises, struggles with gendered self-image, questioning the meaning of life, and so on. However, since the 2000s, several Japanese TV anime programs targeted primarily at young male audiences have featured cute and vulnerable girls, closely associated with World War II weaponry and the Japanese Self-Defense Forces (JSDF).

The year 2015 was a particular high point in the production of such anime, coinciding with the seventieth anniversary of the end of the Second World War. Anime around this time included:

- the Strike Witches series (Sutoraiku uicchiizu, 2008, 2010, 2016), based on a Fumikane Shimada and Projekt kagonish media mix project produced by Kadokawa and released as two Original Animation Videos, three TV anime series, and one movie as of 2018;
- Girls und Panzer (Gāruzu ando pantsā 2012–2013; hereafter Garupan), an original anime produced by Bandai Visual, Lantis, Hakuhodo DY Media Partners, Show Gate, and Movic, QTec (Sudō 2016, 141);
- Arpeggio of Blue Steel: Ars Nova (Aokihagane no arupejio 2013, hereafter Arpeggio), based on Ark Performance's manga (2009-ongoing) of the same title; and
- Kantai Collection (Kantai korekushon, 2015; hereafter KanColle), based on Kadokawa Games and DMM.com's browser game (2013–ongoing) of the same title;
- High School Fleet (Haisukūru furīto 2016; hereafter HSF), an original TV anime adapted into manga in 2015 and 2016.

In the same year, the Japanese government led by Prime Minister Abe Shinzō attempted to pass a bill expanding the role of the JSDF, which caused nationwide anti-war demonstrations. Despite civic protest, new national security laws came into effect later in 2015. These enable the JSDF to fight overseas. In 2018, the Abe Cabinet made a proposal to change the Constitution to include a clause to give legal standing to the JSDF.

Despite the revisionist political context, anime based on World War II scenarios and the JSDF are superficially presented as fantasy. The *Strike Witches* series features girls in miniskirts with flying machines attached to their bodies; *Arpeggio* sees submarines and warships personified as cute girls, as does *KanColle*, in which the characters represent personality traits associated with the histories of various war apparatus. Although there are no explicit war-related depictions in *Garupan*, high school girls in sailor school uniforms operate tanks as part of a school club activity—a form of wargaming as sport—and in *HSF*, young girls enter a Marine High School to become cadets by practicing on battleships inspired by real ships used in the Second World War.

Girl protagonists in these anime are characterized by *moe* ("characterological empathy" (Nozawa 2016, 181)) traits—huge eyes, large busts, and high-pitched voices—that is, childish or *kawaii* (childlike cuteness) qualities (see Joshua Dale in this volume). Each world in which the story operates is shared across several media platforms—TV series, movies, manga, and games. This is generally called a "media mix," a serial of franchises across multi-media platforms that work to create a certain *sekaikan* (story world) (Steinberg 2012, viii). Within this "media mix," the *sekaikan* is maintained even when anime-related events are transplanted to "real life." However, in this chapter, I argue that while this may work in many contexts, there is something particularly problematic when anime-related *sekaikan* are grounded in active collaborations with the JSDF. This is not because they directly trigger nationalistic sensitivities among young fans—audience study research shows that many fans are astute consumers of complex media (Shohat and Stam 1994; Ang 2006). Nevertheless, underlying nationalist militarism is masked through the fantastic *sekaikan* in which these stories operate. These media outputs prompt feelings of intimacy with militarism through links between fiction and reality. Although the anime mentioned previously are directly or indirectly based on militarized contexts, their fans are not particularly patriotic and conservative. However, as Sudō suggests, through fan participation, "a nationalistic sentiment is *consequently* constructed [among fans] favourable to authority due to obedient and enthusiastic totalitarian tendencies *unintentionally* being shared" (original emphasis; translation mine; Sudō 2016, 140).

In discussing how young people's unintentional nationalism is constructed by popular culture such as manga, Sakamoto suggests that "'[p]op' nationalism is about ordinary people's modes of relating to the nation-state and is often mediated by the dynamics of mass/popular culture. It relies heavily on images and icons that are cut-off from their historical meanings" (Sakamoto 2008, 10). Psychoanalyst and critic Kayama has criticized this pop nationalism among young people by identifying it as a syndrome of "petit [or soft] nationalism" (Kayama 2002, 27–28). She later expanded on this idea by analyzing growing hate speech by young people against Chinese and Korean people in public and online, arguing that these anonymous forms of communication are driving a more serious "*gachi* (hardcore) nationalism" among young people who use these methods to shore up a national identity perceived as threatened by socioeconomic change and by the challenge immigration has made to perceptions of Japan as racially and culturally homogenous over the last two decades (Kayama 2015, 166–167, 185).

This chapter explores how girls are associated with war imagery and militarism in anime, and how tie-up or collaborative events between anime and the JSDF serve to promote the JSDF's public image. I will analyze *Garupan* and *High School Fleet*, both of which depict human girls associated with JSDF, and then *Arpeggio* and *KanColle*, both of which feature anthropomorphized girls based on WWII warships. I argue that representations of girls are used to connect young audiences to "soft" nationalistic ideology by alleviating antipathy against extreme and obvious militarism. This has profound implications for contemporary Japan at a time of increased revisionism in mainstream politics and is, in my view, as important a problem to focus on as the *gachi* nationalism that Kayama identifies.

JSDF and representations of girls in *Garupan* and *HSF*

The Japanese Self-Defense Force was set up in 1954, consisting of the Ground SDF (GSDF), the Maritime SDF (MSDF), and the Air SDF (ASDF). Because Article 9 of the 1947 Japanese Constitution renounces war as a sovereign right of the nation and the threat or use of force to settle international disputes, the political standing of the JSDF has been always controversial. Due to its ambiguous constitutional position, Japanese people had largely negative impressions of the JSDF at least until the 1990s. This began to shift as the JSDF took more prominent roles in international peacekeeping and, most dramatically, because of positive media coverage of its work in disaster relief operation in the aftermath of the Great East Japan Earthquake in 2011. Since then, the image of the JSDF has improved among Japanese youth and more generally the Japanese public (Cabinet Office 2015).

In order to recruit young people and improve its image, the JSDF's Provincial Cooperation Office (PCO) began to use anime-style characters in promotional materials. The setting of *High School Fleet* (HSF) in Yokosuka, Kanagawa Prefecture, led to the Kanagawa PCO, for instance, pursuing a tie-up promotional poster with anime producers, with both sides seeing mutual benefit in the campaign (High School Fleet Homepage 2016; Yamamura 2017) Since real Second World War battleships and a fictional women's school based on the Maritime Self Defense Force appear in *HSF*, audiences could easily connect girl characters to the current MSDF.

A similar connection between anime featuring girls and the JSDF can be also observed in *Garupan*. *Garupan* is an original TV anime program mainly produced by Sugiyama Kiyoshi of Bandai Visual Co. Ltd. It was later released as a movie, making 2.1 billion yen at the box office (Matsumoto 2016). The story of *Garupan* takes place in a girls' high school located in Oarai town, Ibaraki Prefecture, with the protagonist, Nishizumi Miho, unwilling to register for the *senshadō* (way of tanks) club. The suffix *dō* (literally, "way") is associated in Japan with sets of traditional practices that require training and structure, including martial arts like *jūdō* and *kendō*, as well as things like flower arrangement (*kadō*) and tea ceremony (*sadō*) (see also Benesch and Ikeda in this volume). In the *sekaikan* of this anime, and in contrast to historical aversions to associating femininity with violence, *senshadō* is an important female cultural activity, alongside *kadō* and *sadō*. In the club, girls are divided into small teams that operate Second World War–era weaponry in a realistic townscape with scenery from Oarai town used as background setting for the anime. Teams are named after animals, including Team Bunny (Usagi-san) and Team Turtle (Kame-san); for Japanese viewers, these names would be reminiscent of those assigned to kindergarten classrooms (Holloway 2013). This infantilizing language sits awkwardly alongside both the apparatus under the girls' control and the competitiveness of the club's activities; Miho and her teammates eventually win the National High School Tank Tournament.

Realistic illustrations of Second World War tanks placed alongside cute girls with *moe* traits and the kindergarten associations of the tank team names immediately drew much attention from male audiences. Due to this combination of *moe* girls with tanks, the phrase, "*Garupan* wa iizo!" [*Garupan* is awesome!] has become a catchphrase among fans (see, for example, Garupan ojisan, n.d.). Producer Sugiyama remarked on the reasons for the use of such realistic settings by explicitly contrasting the setting with the fantastic elements of the story itself: "the story is unrealistic because girls compete in tank tournaments in Japan, and for this reason, the setting has to be real in order to make the story look realistic" (Matsumoto 2016). The pursuit of reality through the use of the real setting of Oarai Town induced "contents tourism," or tourism created by the depiction of a place within a media text (Kamaishi and Okamoto 2015; Seaton et al. 2017). By participating in the tourist culture of Oarai, fans could readily overlap the images of fictional scenes with the real townscape.

Along the main local shopping street in Oarai town, life-sized cardboard cut-outs of female characters in *Garupan* stand in front of stores. Representations of the girls serve as a means for local people and fans visiting this town to communicate with each other through staging of photographic opportunities and the facilitation of conversations, for example, around settings, scenes, or activities represented in *Garupan*. Because Oarai town was damaged by a tsunami in the East Japan Great Earthquake in 2011, such collaborations between the anime and the local authority also aim to revitalize the town. The Monkfish Festival (*Ankō Matsuri*), Oarai town's traditional annual festival held each November, collaborated with the GSDF in 2012 as part of a promotion for earthquake recovery. In the Spring Kairaku Festival in Oarai town in 2013, a real 74-type tank used by the GSDF was displayed at the festival site. There were public speeches by the tank's driver (a GSDF member) and a video message sent from the then–secretary general of the ruling Liberal Democratic Party, Ishiba Shigeru (Sakimura 2013). Although fans acknowledged that the *Garupan* world is a fantasy and JSDF's collaboration was part of public support from earthquake recovery, fiction and reality were intermingled in fans' imagination, creating a sense of intimacy with the military and the JSDF (Sudō 2018, 185).

Voice actors also serve an important role in sustaining the "reality" of the fiction. Popular voice actress and singer Fuchigami Mai, who voiced Nishizumi, also played the female lead, Iona the submarine, in *Arpeggio*. Her fans could connect *Garupan* to *Arpeggio* due to the same voice and similar war-related settings.

Arpeggio and *KanColle*—anthropomorphized girls in Second World War scenarios

Ships are often represented as women and/or mothers in Japanese culture, as well as in Western culture, since the ship crews have historically been most often men. This problematic gendering has additional issues when it comes to the common representation in anime of warships as girls. The story of *Arpeggio* starts in 2039, when much land has been lost to or damaged by global warming. The world is in chaos and serious damage is being caused by civil wars in the aftermath of environmental disaster. Against this backdrop, a mysterious group of unmanned warships called the "Fleet of Fog" begins attacking humans. Seventeen years later, the protagonist, Chihaya Gunzō, a young male cadet, encounters a girl called Iona. She is a humanoid life form called a *mentaru moderu* (mental model), an anthropomorphized I-401 submarine, who has betrayed the Fleet of Fog and now follows human orders.

The I-401 was the largest submarine in the Japanese Imperial Navy during the Pacific War. Other figures in The Fleet of Fog are also modelled on actual warships of the Imperial Japanese Navy and are all personified as young women: for example, the heavy cruiser Takao, the battleships Haruna and Kirishima, and the flagship Kongō. In *Arpeggio*, although they act like humans, these girl-ships often conduct their conversations in a "cyber tearoom" by sending signals during battle. The anthropomorphized warships acknowledge that they are just machines; however, as the battles with Iona intensify, the Fleet of Fog ships begin to struggle with the awakening of their emotions. As such, the sentimentality and emotions of girls are often emphasized in the story, especially when Iona attempts to persuade Kongō to cease an attack. Embracing Kongō in imaginary cyberspace, Iona tells her that, "You are not alone. I'm here with you."

KanColle features a similar story, based on Kadokawa Games' online browser game *Kantai Collection*, in which players called the Admiral (*teitoku*) customise their favourite warship, the avatar for which is always a girl. In the TV anime spinoff, the story is depicted from the perspective of the teenage-like girl, Fubuki, a Second World War destroyer who enters the Guardian

Office (*chinjufu*). The personified warships as young women fight against a mysterious fleet, The Abyssal, which has devastated the ocean. Other senior warships with *moe* traits in *chinjufu* include the standard carrier, Akagi, and the destroyers, Kisaragi and Mutsuki. The story primarily depicts these girls' daily life, focusing on how the newcomer Fubuki gets along with other girls and trains herself to become a fully-fledged battleship. However, one emotional moment comes when her colleague and friend, Kisaragi, is seriously damaged and sinks into the ocean after a sudden attack by the Abyssal. Despite their initial shock and sorrow, Fubuki and Mutsuki bravely fight the enemy again.

The motifs taken from Second World War warships are similar to those found in *Arpeggio*. However, the iconography is very different. Girls in *KanColle* are called *kanmusu* (ship maidens) and are represented as girl-ship hybrids with ship-like appendages and *moe* traits in their fighting. The body and weaponry of the *kanmusu* are merged, which has led to some fans seeing battleship girls as sexual objects, with fan sites often discussing explicitly fans' sexual attraction to the characters. The extended anthropomorphized bodies of *kan musu* as weapons often receive serious damage, which is highlighted through the girls' screams.

Images of girl-ship hybrids inspired by the Second World War probably first appeared in the illustrated story, *Heat Haze Girl, Tan'yan* (2009), by Zeco, a Taiwanese illustrator and comic artist, based around the real history of a former Japanese Imperial Navy destroyer, the Yukikaze (Snowy Wind). Yukikaze was a Kagerō-class destroyer (Kagerō literally means "heat haze"), a group of 19 destroyers that were known as some of the most effective naval weaponry at Japan's wartime disposal. After the war, Yukikaze was sent to Taiwan, renamed as Tan'yan, and remained in service in the Republic of China's navy until 1966. As in the later *KanColle*, Zeco depicted Tan'yan as a cute girl with *moe* traits. A manga featuring similar motifs, *Battleship Girl*, started to be serialized in *Web Comic Gum*, a Japanese manga website, in 2011. Thus, by the time of the launch of the *KanColle* browser game in 2013, a ready audience existed across both Japan and Taiwan. Although Taiwan was occupied by the Japanese Imperial Army during the Second World War and there remain unresolved issues around war legacy, *KanColle* fans tend to detach the wartime context from the setting of *KanColle*. An example of this can be seen in the fan association of President Tsai Ing-wen with the *KanColle* character Kirishima (Baseel 2016). Images of *moe* girls can serve to alleviate any antipathy towards the dark history of the war, with war memory reduced simply to entertainment as the products are popularized. This is not an accidental byproduct, with fans induced to connect fantasy in *Arpeggio* and *KanColle* to reality through active collaboration between *Arpeggio* and the MSDF and through the MSDF's unofficial activities regarding *KanColle*.

Fans' cultural practices—connecting to MSDF without war memories

Contents tourism induced by *Arpeggio* and *KanColle* has gained much popularity since 2013. According to a list of "the 88 anime sacred sites" designated by the Anime Tourism Association, there are five sites based on *KanColle* in Japan: Mutsu (Aomori Prefecture), Yokosuka (Kanagawa Prefecture), Maizuru (Kyoto), Kure (Hiroshima Prefecture), and Sasebo (Nagasaki Prefecture) (Anime Tourism Association 2018). Unexpectedly, no sites from *Arpeggio* appear on this list, but fans of both series have also generated their own maps and/or uploaded photos taken at sacred sites on social media (see Sugawa-Shimada 2019).

Some of this contents tourism is a result of direct collaboration between the MSDF and producers. The JSDF has been utilizing popular culture for its public relations since the 1990s. The JSDF's "softening" strategy using popular culture—such as manga, rock concerts, and calendars of female JSDF members in swimming suits—encouraged young people to feel connected with the JSDF (Oizumi cited by Sudō 2013, 84). Responding to the rise in anime contents tourism, the MSDF released a DVD, *Weapon Front-Line JMSDF: Aegis Combat System* (2015) with special footage in which Numakura Manami (a voice actress who dubbed the heavy cruiser Takao in *Arpeggio*) visits an Aegis ship, Kirishima. The MSDF's promotional DVD/BD *Shitte okitai, kaijō jieitai* (I Want to Know: MSDF) series is narrated by *Arpeggio* voice actors Fuchigami Mai and Okitsu Kazuyuki, who describe MSDF submarines and the life of its crews, with reference to *Arpeggio* episodes.

Further, in bonus footage on *Arpeggio*'s Blu-Ray releases, Numakura, Fuchigami, Okitsu, and Yamamura Hibiku (as the battleship Haruna) introduce MSDF-related venues such as MSDF ships, submarine training centres, the MSDF museum in Kure, and the Naval Academy in Etajima. Tours are facilitated by a member of the MSDF's public relations office in each venue and often refer to *Arpeggio*'s story and characters' lines. Frequent reference to the story of *Arpeggio* and characters' lines spoken in the characters' voices draws a direct connection for fans between the fictional characters and the real MSDF ships and submarines.

Despite no explicit collaboration, fans of *KanColle* among MSDF members have unofficially utilized *kanmusu* characters in public relations activities. During Fleet Week in Yokohama in 2015, for example, a *KanColle* tapestry featuring Atago (the personified character of the heavy cruiser) was displayed on the MSDF escort vessel of the same name, which was anchored in Maizuru port. This was relayed by many civilian fans on social media. At the same Fleet Week, Fuchigami, Numakura, and Yamamura, who also work together as a music band called Trident, held a talk show and a mini concert. The interplay between fiction and reality occurred in official and unofficial collaboration between the JSDF and *Arpeggio* and *KanColle*; fans' online activities around contents tourism; and, most importantly, fans' active visitation to "sacred" sites and events. Throughout those public relations and collaborative events, the wartime context is completely void or ignored.

Conclusion

In the context of emerging neo-conservatism symbolized by the Abe Cabinet's introduction of new national security laws in 2015 and the following proposal for a change to Article 9, anime based on or related to WWII scenarios and weaponry have been consumed as fantasy. However, this fantasy regularly slips into reality in dangerous ways. Fans of *Garupan* were reportedly excited to see a real JSDF tank at the Kairaku Festival. On visiting a shopping street in Oarai town, visitors can see panels featuring the *Garupan* protagonists and have an entry point into conversation with local people. Fans of *HSF*, *Arpeggio*, and *KanColle* feel intimacy with their favourite characters when visiting sacred sites and seeing the battleships of MSDF which characters are modelled on. The use of anthropomorphized girls with *moe* traits can serve to appeal to (male) fans, alleviating negative images of war, war memory, and militarism.

Such wartime-context-void consumption of popular culture is possible in Japan, as the country has not been actively involved in war since 1945, and Article 9 legally prohibits the JSDF from physically participating in actual battles. However, the shifting attitudes towards the JSDF are at least partially a response to gendered public relations. This occurs in several ways. Fans are attracted to images of *moe* girls along with the voice actresses who dub them, and contents tourism to sacred sites and related events drive feelings of intimacy towards the JSDF. The danger in this moment of rising nationalism is that these fans remain unaware of how this nurtures a "soft" militarism and its extremely dangerous possible consequences.

Acknowledgements

This work was supported by Japan Society for the Promotion of Science KAKENHI Grant Number 26243007.

Further reading

Jaworowicz-Zimny, A. (2018) "Nazi Cosplay in Japan," *Journal of War & Culture Studies* 11 (1) 1–18. About military cosplay in Japan.
Seaton, P. (2018) "War, Popular Culture, and Contents Tourism in East Asia," *Journal of War & Culture Studies* 11 (1) 1–18. An overview about war and popular culture in East Asia.
Sugawa-Shimada, A. (2018) "Playing with Militarism in/with *Arpeggio* and *KanColle*: Effects of *Shōjo* Images in War-related Contents Tourism in Japan," *Journal of War and Culture Studies* 11 (1) 1–14. About representations of girls in military-related anime.

Related chapters

30 Gender, Manga, and Anime
31 Cuteness Studies and Japan
32 Gender and Visual Culture
33 Gender, Media, and Misogyny in Japan
34 Representing Girls in Cinema

References

Ang, I. (2006) *Desperately Seeking the Audience*, London and New York: Routledge.
Anime Tourism Association. (2018) "Anime Seichi 88 [88 Anime Sacred Sites]." https://animetourism88.com/ja/sanctuary.
Baseel, C. (2016) "Taiwanese President-Elect's Resemblance to Anime Character Reportedly Affecting Comic Sales," *Sora News* 2 February 2016. https://soranews24.com/2016/02/02/taiwanese-president-elects-resemblance-to-anime-character-reportedly-affecting-comic-sales/
Cabinet Office, Government of Japan (2015) "Public Opinion Survey on SDF and Defense in 2014." https://survey.gov-online.go.jp/h26/h26-bouei/zh/z07.html.
Garupan ojisan (n.d.) "Garupan ojisan no memochô." www.garupan-wa-iizo.net/.
High School Fleet homepage. (2016) "Jieitai Kanagawa chiho kyoryoku honbu to TV anime 'Haifuri' no korabo posuta kansei!" (Collaborative Poster Between SDF Kanagawa PCO and TV Anime 'High School Fleet' Is Out!) *News*. www.hai-furi.com/?article_id=38085.
Holloway, S. (2013) *Contested Childhood: Diversity and Change in Japanese Preschools*, New York: Routledge.
Kamaishi, N. and Okamoto, T. (2015) "Garuzu ando panzha: taiappu gata kontentsu tsurizumu no tenkai" (Girls and Panzer: Development of Tie-Up Style Contents Tourism), in T. Okamoto (ed) *Kontentsu turism kenkyu: johoshakai no kanko kodo to chiho shinko*, Kyoto: Fukumura shoten, 160–161.
Kayama, R. (2002) *Puchi nashonarizumu shokogun: wakamonotachi no nippon shugi* (Petit Nationalism Syndrome: Japanism of the Youth), Tokyo: Chuokoronsha.
Kayama, R. (2015) *Gachi nashonarizumu: "aikokusha" tachi no fuan no shōtai* (Serious Nationalism: The True Identity of Fear for "Patriots") Tokyo: Chikuma.
Matsumoto, A. (2016) "*Garupan* Sugiyama P, 'Anime niwa machiokoshi no chikara nante nai'" (Sugiyama, the Producer of *Girls und Panzer*, Says 'Anime Has No Power to Revitalise Towns.'" http://ascii.jp/elem/000/001/173/1173185/.
Nozawa, S. (2016) "Ensoulment and Effacement in Japanese Voice Acting," in P. Galbraith and J. P. Karlin (eds) *Media Convergence in Japan*, Kinema Club, 169–199. https://kinemaclub.org/media-convergence-japan.
Sakamoto, R. (2008) "Will You Go to War? Or Will You Stop Being Japanese? Nationalism and History in Kobayashi Yoshinori's *Sensoron*," in M. Heazle and N. Knight (eds) *China-Japan Relations in the Twenty-First Century: Creating a Future Past?* Cheltenham: Edward Elgar.

Sakimura, T. (2013) "Oarai ni sensha ga yattekita! 'Kairaku festa' *Girls & Panzer* repoto," *Otakuma Keizai Shinbun* 25 March. http://otakei.otakuma.net/archives/2013032504.html.

Seaton, P., Yamamura, T., Sugawa-Shimada, A. and Jang, K. (2017) *Contents Tourism in Japan: Pilgrimages to "Sacred Sites" of Popular Culture*, Amherst, NY: Cambria Press.

Shohat, E. and Stam, R. (1994) "The Politics of Multiculturalism in the Postmodern Age," in E. Shohat and R. Stam (eds) *Unthinking Eurocentrism: Multiculturalism and the Media*, London and New York: Routledge, 338–362.

Steinberg, M. (2012) *Anime's Media Mix: Franchising Toys and Characters in Japan*, Minneapolis: University of Minnesota Press.

Sudō, N. (2013) *Jieitai kyōroku eiga: "Kyō mo ware ōzora ni ari" kara "Meitantei Konan" made* (SDF's Collaborative Films: From "I'm in the Blue Sky as Usual" to "Detective Conan"), Tokyo: Ōtsuki Shoten.

Sudō, N. (2016) "'Bunkaken' toshite no *Girls und Panzer*: Sabukarucha o meguru sankanmin no 'nashonaru' na yago" (*Girls und Panzer* as "Cultural Sphere:" "Nationalistic" Illicit Relationships Among Private and Public Sectors and Industry in Subculture) in S. Park, T. Tanigawa and S. Yamada (eds) *Taishubunka to nashionarizumu [Popular Culture and Nationalism]*, Tokyo: Shinwasha, 139–167.

Sudō, N. (2018) "Bunka seisaku ron: Girls und panzer ni miru hiseijiteki na seijisei [A Study of Cultural Policy: Apolitical Politics in Girls und Panzer], in M. Koyama and A. Sugawa (eds) *Anime kenkyū nyūmon ōyōhen: Anime o kiwameru 11 no kotsu* (Introduction of Anime Studies II: 11 Keys to Studying Anime), Tokyo: Gendai Shokan, 174–196.

Sugawa-Shimada, A. (2019) "Playing with Militarism in/with *Arpeggio* and *Kantai Collection*: Effects of *shōjo* Images in War-Related Contents Tourism in Japan," *Journal of War and Culture Studies* 12 (1) 53–66.

Yamamura, T. (2017) "Cooperation Between Anime Producers and the Japan Self-Defense Force: Creating Fantasy and/or Propaganda?" *Journal of War & Culture Studies* 10 1–16.

39

BEYOND THE "PARASITE SINGLE"

Lynne Nakano

Never-married women in Japan are given disparaging names in the media such as "parasite singles" (*parasaito shinguru*) and "loser dogs" (*makeinu*) and are criticized in Internet forums as selfish, overly choosy, and consumer-oriented or for having personality problems. Single women have become a lightning rod for criticism from the state, media, and conservative commentators. The average age of first marriage for women is currently 29.4 (Ministry of Health, Labor and Welfare 2017), and the numbers of single women have been rising (13.9 percent of women aged 30 to 34 were single in 1990 compared to 34.6 percent in 2015) (Statistics Bureau 2010, 2015), but these are not the only demographic changes occurring in Japan. In the past few decades, Japanese families have increasingly diversified. Three-generational households and nuclear families have been on the decline, while the number of single-person households has risen. Fewer people enter into marriage, and they tend to have fewer children. Men marry later than women, and single men outnumber single women—in 2015, 47.1 percent of men aged 30–34 were single compared to 34.6 percent of women in the same age range (Statistics Bureau 2015). In spite of these significant and complex trends, single women are targeted for criticism.

Media and public fascination with single women is due in part to gender discrimination, as women are seen as responsible for marriage, fertility, and reproduction and, by extension, broader demographic issues. Single women are expected to marry in heterosexual unions (as same-sex marriage is not legalized in Japan, despite a small number of local relationship registration schemes [see Murai 2015]) and raise the country's birth rate in an aging society. Single women are targeted because few births occur outside of marriage, married couples have few children, and the government is reluctant to adopt an open immigration policy to address the nation's population and labour needs.

In this chapter, I address how single women in Japan are viewed by experts, the media, and in popular culture. I suggest that we should be wary of attempts to explain the rising age of marriage using single-factor explanations such as single women's selfishness or choosiness. These explanations are based on one-dimensional characterizations of single women and are contradicted by studies that show significant variation in single women's views and life experiences. It is also important to be wary of discussing single women as symbolic of women's empowerment or liberation from the family system. In fact, most women report that they wish to marry and care for a family while working in some capacity. A recent national survey found, for example, that 34.6 percent of never-married women would like to marry, stop work temporarily while having children, and return to the workforce later. Another 32.3 percent of respondents wish to marry and continue to work while caring for a family (Ministry of Health, Labor and Welfare 2015).

I suggest that we may consider singlehood in Japan as part of a larger social trend in which participation in social institutions that were once considered mandatory has now become optional. As a result of this "optionalization" of marriage, single women who may support the normative division of labour in marriage may nonetheless remain single for a variety of reasons. In this sense, single women may not intend to challenge the institution of marriage, yet by building their lives outside of marriage, they are developing new pathways for women outside of motherhood and wifehood.

Explaining the rise of singlehood in Japan

Most women and men say that they want to marry. In 2015, 89.3 percent of single women and 85.7 percent of single men said that they would like to marry at some point in their lives (National Institute of Population and Social Security Research 2015). This is not surprising because gender and family ideals remain tied to the housewife-salaryman pairing (Aoyama et al. 2017, 1; White 2002, 11). Dasgupta maintains that the pairing of domestic femininity and salaryman masculinity continues to be "ideologically hegemonic" (2013, 8) in contemporary Japan. His salaryman informants unanimously intended to marry and saw marriage as "natural" (*atarimae*) (2013, 106).

If most women and men wish to marry, why is the age of marriage rising? One common argument is that women have more opportunities for education and work, while the conventions and expectations of marriage for women have not changed; women are still expected to adopt a highly domesticated and subordinated position in the home. Women are thus said to be postponing marriage and extending their enjoyment of single life (see Ogura 2003; Tsuya and Mason 1995; Yamada 1999). Other arguments consider men's declining employment security (see Cook 2016) and ability to support a full-time housewife. Yamada (1999) argues that women continue to desire marriage with a man who would earn a sufficient salary to allow them to live as fulltime housewives, yet such men have become increasingly scarce due to the depressed economy since the 1990s. Thus according to Yamada, women delay marriage because they are unable to find men who meet their expectations.

Scholars have also noted the role of Japan's employment structures in delaying marriage. Rosenbluth (2007) contends that gender discrimination at work leads women to devote more time to success at work, thus delaying marriage and childbirth. Yoshida outlined structural obstacles to marriage such as gender segregation at workplaces, lack of support from companies that previously provided opportunities for mingling between genders, overwork for men, long working hours for career-track women, and discrimination against successful women (2017, 47–52).

These theories are helpful in understanding the various situations in which single women find themselves in Japan. That being said, it is also important to consider that the age of marriage is rising around the world. Other developed societies in East Asia, such as South Korea, Singapore, Taiwan, and Hong Kong, and cities in mainland China have experienced similar trends of later marriage. Gavin Jones argues that later marriage among women in East and Southeast Asia is generally associated with higher education and urban areas, and the rise in the ages of marriages are partly the result of greater urbanization in the region accompanying rapid economic growth (2003, 18).

Demographers note that in developed societies in the West, later marriage occurs alongside a number of other demographic changes including sustained low fertility, alternatives to marriage, more single persons living alone, higher rates of cohabitation among partners, and higher fertility outside of marriage (Lesthaeghe 2014). Labelled "the Second Demographic Transition," these changes have been explained in two major ways. One argument holds that marriage has become less attractive as women's economic opportunities have risen (see Becker 1996). A second approach contends that family change is grounded in changing values such as growing desire for individual fulfilment and self-realization (Maslow 1954). Sociologists of late modernity have argued that expectations about relationships are changing; Giddens argues that partnerships based on mutual satisfaction and equality in a "pure relationship" for its own sake have become central in the postmodern world (1992). Beck and Beck-Gernsheim have argued that demographic changes are grounded in the rise of individualism and personal choice along with the decline of social norms (2002).

The changes described in these theories apply to Japan to some degree. Japan has seen levels of education for women rise and greater employment opportunities, as well as rising discourses of self-fulfilment. But it would be incorrect to conclude that delayed marriage and family change is entirely the result of increasing opportunities for women, as inequality and gender discrimination are also prominent across institutions of work and family, and women have fewer economic opportunities than men and greater domestic responsibilities. The notion that Japanese women are motivated by greater individualism is also problematic. On the one hand, neoliberal market reforms of the Japanese economy have meant that the protections of the corporate system have deteriorated for women and men. Both women and men feel that they need to make their own way in the economy by improving their skills and market position. But women are not turning away from marriage because they are calculating that it does not benefit them. Nor are they rejecting marriage out of clear values of individualism over self-sacrifice. Rather, they are open to marriage if the right person appears and are not marrying because it is no longer imperative to do so both financially and socially. While they may choose not to marry, unlike many Western societies, women do not feel they may easily choose to have children outside of wedlock (see Hertog 2009) or other alternative marital and family relationships. In other words, many single women find the path to marriage and children to be narrow and difficult to navigate.

Media portrayals of single women

A wealth of media buzzwords have emerged to describe women and later marriage. In the 1970s and 1980s, women who were single beyond the age of 25 were called "Christmas Cakes" because just like Christmas cakes, usually eaten on 25 December, they were supposedly unwanted after the age of 25. The term "*bankonka*" was used in the 1990s to describe later marriage, along with the term for later ages of birth (*bansanka*) (Coulmas 2007, 10). In the late 1990s, the phrase "unmarried aristocracy" (*dokushin kizoku*) was used to describe young people who delayed marriage to enjoy consumption and leisure. Yamada Masahiro's book, *The Age of Parasite Singles* (*Parasaito shinguru no jidai*, 1999), introduced the term "parasite single," which the media used to describe single women who enjoyed a comfortable lifestyle while living with their parents. The term "loser dog" (*makeinu*) emerged following the publication of the book *Distant Cry of the Loser Dog* (*Makeinu no tōboe* 2003) by Sakai Junko, a single woman herself who wanted to emphasize the difficulties faced by single women. Although Sakai used the term ironically, the media used the term to reference single women as losers in contrast to married women.

Yamada Masahiro, the same sociologist who launched the term "parasite single," also introduced the word "*konkatsu*" (marriage hunting, in reference to the word "*shūkatsu*" or job hunting in Japanese) in the best seller *The Age of Marriage Hunting* (*Konkatsu no jidai*) (2008) written with journalist Shirakawa Tōko. Goldstein-Gidoni points out that the term *konkatsu* "reinforces the idea and significance of marriage" (2012, 200) and strengthens views of marriage as a practical and contractual institution (2012, 200). *Konkatsu* and much of the popular media terminology for single women often start out as neutral or even positive terms but are used by the media to negatively label single women and urge their conformity to normative marriage expectations.

Terms that convey positive qualities of women's singlehood have also emerged, many from women writers. Iwashita Kumiko (2001) introduced the word "*hitorisama*" to refer to women, both married and single, who enjoy themselves alone at nice restaurants and on vacations. The term was further popularized by Ueno Chizuko's book *Aging Alone* (*Ohitorisama no rōgo*, 2007) that argued that, regardless of their current marital status, women are likely to spend a number of years single and that they should start to prepare for such an eventuality.

TV serial dramas have been important in introducing and reflecting new perspectives on single women and have generally viewed single women sympathetically. Freedman and Iwata-Weickgenannt argue that the TV drama, *Around 40: Demanding Women* (*Araundo 40: Chūmon no ōi onnatachi*) broadcast in 2008 emphasizes the importance of individual happiness rather than service to the family even as the drama reproduces stereotypes of single women as insatiable in wanting to have their various desires fulfilled (2011, 297). Mandjujano-Salazar argues that the dramas, *I Won't Marry* (*Kekkon shinai*) broadcast in 2012 and *It Is Not That I Can't Marry, I Won't* (*Watakushi kekkon dekinainjanakute shinain desu*) broadcast in 2016, represent a counter-narrative to earlier dramas in that they portray single women as not rejecting femininity or men but asserting their "right to choose diverse patterns of femininity and personal fulfilment" (2017, 540).

TV dramas focusing on single men such as *The Man Who Cannot Marry* (*Kekkon dekinai otoko*, 2006) depict middle-aged single men as having problems such as poor communication and social skills. Internet forums and articles describe men in negative terms such as being overly independent or only interested in much younger women. Some mention that men may remain single because they are financially unable to support a family due to working in non-regular jobs (*furītā*). In general, however, single women are viewed more harshly than single men. This being said, a growing body of social science literature questions the one-dimensional portraits of single women.

Diversity of single women's experiences

Studies based on interviews or ethnography point out the importance of examining the diversity of women's experience. Sociologist Ogura Chikako interviewed unmarried women living in urban areas and found that educational level strongly influenced their marital strategies (2003). Okano also suggests the importance of socioeconomic class in understanding women's experiences. Her working-class informants had no desire for social mobility and made decisions according to their preferences which were shaped by "a sense of comfort" (*igokochi no yosa*) (2009, 9). They felt that media terms such as "parasite single" or concern with *omiai* (arranged meetings for marriage) did not apply to them. One suspects that they would also find the media's current emphasis on "*konkatsu*" and the push to marry similarly alien.

In a recent study, Yoshida emphasized generational differences as central to interpreting single women's difficulties in getting married. She argues that "boom cohort" women born between 1962 and 1984 who experienced Japan's economic growth period believed that they should marry by age 25 but continued working because they were welcomed in the labour market and could enjoy previously inaccessible luxuries and leisure activities (2017, 25). Recession cohort women, born between 1972 and 1984, on the other hand, did not feel bound by a marital age norm and "drifted into singlehood, due in part to the absence of clear normative guidance" (2017, 39).

An important source of diversity that has not been fully investigated are differences that arise for women living in urban and rural areas. Most studies have taken place in mega-cities such as Tokyo where opportunities for career advancement for women are concentrated and where women may have greater anonymity and freedom from pressures of family, friends, and neighbours. Rosenberger interviewed single women in Tokyo and in rural Tohoku and found that the majority of women who are financially and socially successful are living in Tokyo, while the majority of those who are "struggling and crashing" due to financial problems and inability to manage social and institutional expectations are living in rural Tohoku (2013, 55). More research is needed on the institutional pressures faced by women outside of Japan's major urban areas.

There are signs that the media is beginning to recognize that many single women are struggling financially. Drawing on recent reports that up to 40 percent of single women are engaged in irregular employment (Ministry of Health, Labor, and Welfare 2015), newspapers have carried stories showing that large numbers of single women are financially vulnerable and that their situation may worsen as they age, especially if they need to care for ailing parents. I hope that "struggling singles" will not become another stereotype and that recognition of recent employment statistics will contribute to developing a more nuanced discussion of single women.

Interpreting delayed marriage

Should later or non-marriage be interpreted as women's resistance against gender and family norms? Or are women victims of social structures and discrimination that prevent them from marrying? My view is that single women's choices are structured by institutions such as marriage and employment markets (see Nakano 2014), yet women choose not to marry particular persons at particular times, thus delaying their marriages, sometimes indefinitely. However, as Dales has pointed out (2014, 28), the focus on women's agency only in regard to marriage may overlook women's experiences in other equally if not more important areas of life such as work, friendships, and relationships with parents and siblings.

A related issue is whether the rising age of marriage represents a major shift in value orientations. Studies suggest that in the 1980s and 1990s, women delayed marriage to enjoy the benefits of single life (Tsuya and Mason 1995) and not because they rejected basic domestic ideals for women. After the 2000s, many studies, including my own, found that most women hoped to marry and care for families. The majority of women I met did not consciously reject or resist the marital ideal; many wish to marry even as they enter late middle age. But there is an overall shift, as others such as Dales (2014) and Yoshida (2017) have noted, that marriage today is understood to be one lifestyle choice among many.

In what follows, I describe one person's experience, a single woman who first arrived in Tokyo from the regional city of Fukuoka in the mid-1980s. I met her for the first time in 2004 when she was 42 years old and again in 2014 when she was 52 years old. She wanted to marry and thought she would become a fulltime housewife if she had children, but did not feel compelled to marry unless the right person came along. I introduce her story to show how conservative views of marriage coincide with indefinite marriage delay.

Yasuda Junko

Junko was born in 1962 in the Western city of Fukuoka in Kyushu. After completing high school, she convinced her parents to let her move to Tokyo to pursue her dream of becoming a flight attendant, one of the few jobs that offered women something of a career. She was unable to obtain a position in the competitive field, however, and instead obtained a travel agent license.

After five years of short-term contract work, she obtained a job as a regular employee with full benefits at a travel agency that served employees of a large Japanese firm.

Junko enjoyed her work and was valued for the knowledge and skills she had acquired. She understood her customers and was well travelled herself, so she was able to provide useful advice and services. She said:

> I like my job and I am responsible for my own work. I don't have a superior looking over my shoulder telling me what to do. Of course there are some crazy customers who yell but on the whole it's a satisfying job. I've been doing the job for a long time so there are customers who keep coming back because they trust me. Recently a couple went on a 200,000 yen trip to Europe for two weeks and when they came back they brought me a special kind of Belgian chocolate. When that kind of thing happens I feel satisfied with my job.

When I met her in 2004, although already 43 years old, she still hoped to marry and even have children. She explained that she had opportunities to marry in the past:

> When I was in my twenties I was seeing someone and we talked about it [marriage]. But I just couldn't make that final decision. In the end I decided against marriage with that person. I was 28 and I just wasn't sure whether he was the right person. Now I think that at 28 you don't really know yourself well enough to make that kind of decision. At about 35 you start to know yourself but as you get older you start to lose chances to meet people. Most of the men [I know] now are married. Those who want to get married have already married.

In her thirties, she played tennis on weekends but stopped when she broke up with a boyfriend from the tennis club. She now spends most weekends resting at home. Although she claims to want to marry, one gets the impression that marriage is not her most pressing priority. If she marries, for example, she is only half joking when she says that she would like the man to live in a separate residence and only visit her on weekends. And she feels that she would have to give up her work so that she could cook for him and take care of children.

When I met her ten years later, in 2014, she worked at the same travel agency and had yet to marry although she still was open to it. The first thing she told me was that she had bought a small condominium and "will somehow be OK in old age." Also, she was no longer living alone; her niece who came to Tokyo to attend university has been living with her for three years. In a few years when she receives her twenty-year employment bonus, Junko is planning to take her niece with her on vacation to France.

Recently she has had to think seriously about her own mortality. In the past years, two travelling companions of about her same age suddenly passed away. Her mother has had a stroke and is being cared for by her father. She is thinking about her own retirement, perhaps in Yokohama, which may be cheaper than Tokyo, and says that she is prepared to live on a budget under 150,000 yen per month.

Interpreting Junko's experience

The voice of one single woman or even one hundred cannot represent the voices of all single women. Junko represents only herself. We can see that her experience is shaped by her middle-class upbringing, ability to find permanent stable work as a regular staff member (*seishain*), her optimistic personality, and the relatively good health of herself and her family members. My point here is not to explain why she remained single. Rather, I suggest that Junko's experience provides an example of how someone with conservative beliefs—she thought that a married woman should quit her job and care for her family fulltime—can nonetheless remain single. Statistically we know most women report a wish to marry and that women and men express the belief that women should prioritize family. Junko wanted to be sure that the man she married would be an appropriate person who made this sacrifice of her career worthwhile. As she believed that marriage was optional, she preferred to continue as a single person rather than marry inappropriately.

Junko defies media stereotypes in a number of ways. In contrast to media reports that single women are selfish, she is a devoted aunt who took in her niece. She enjoys her work, but she is not particularly ambitious and does not see herself as career oriented. While singlehood is assigned second-class status by the media, Junko does not see herself as living a second-class life. Singlehood enables her to create a life based on her enjoyment of her work, building of relationships with other women, and as a caring aunt. She has created her life on her own terms even as her lifestyle was made possible because she was fortunate to have held onto a secure position that provided financial stability.

Conclusions

In this chapter, I have suggested how the rise of singlehood may occur without a major change in social values. Many single women support a gendered division of labour in the family as previous generations did and may even want to quit their jobs to marry and start a family. Yet as marriage has become optional, women and men feel that they do not need to force themselves to marry if the timing and the partner are not right.

Optionalization of marriage allows marriage to retain its current form as those who desire marriage in its current state will marry, while those with doubts about the institution or their fit for it stay away altogether. How long this situation will continue remains to be seen; there may be a future tipping point if the current two choices—marriage in its current form or non-marriage—become unsatisfactory to women and men who desire alternative formats of intimacy and reproduction.

Single women tell me that their lives are mundane and the images of single women in the media are far from their own experiences: they are not living the high life as professional women as shown in TV dramas. Nor are they distraught "leftovers" unable to marry. Rather, they are quietly building their lives. The sum of their choices, however, has the unintended consequence of challenging core assumptions about marriage and family in Japan.

Acknowledgements

Substantial portions of the work described in this chapter were supported by a grant from the Research Grants Council of the Hong Kong Special Administrative Region, China (Project No. CUHK4018/02H). The research was also made possible by a 2001 Summer Grant for Research and a 2001–2002 Direct Grant awarded by the Chinese University of Hong Kong. I thank Moeko Wagatsuma, Chan Yim Ting, and Candy Lam for their assistance in conducting research.

Related chapters

9 Attitudes to Marriage and Childbearing
10 Family, Inequality, and the Work-Family Balance in Contemporary Japan
11 Intimacy in and Beyond the Family
33 Gender, Media, and Misogyny in Japan

References

Aoyama, T., Dales, L. and Dasgupta, R. (2017) "Introduction," in T. Aoyama, L. Dales and R. Dasgupta (eds) *Configurations of Family in Contemporary Japan*, London and New York: Routledge.
Beck, U. and Beck-Gernsheim, E. (2002) *Individualization: Institutionalized Individualism and Its Social and Political Consequences*, London: Sage Publications.
Becker, G. (1996) *A Treatise on the Family*, Cambridge, MA: Harvard University Press.
Cook, E. (2016) *Reconstructing Adult Masculinities: Part-Time Work in Contemporary Japan*, Abingdon, Oxon and New York: Routledge.
Coulmas, F. (2007) *Population Decline and Ageing in Japan: The Social Consequences*, London and New York: Routledge.
Dales, L. (2014) "Ohitorisama, Singlehood and Agency in Japan," *Asian Studies Review* 38 (2) 224–242.
Dasgupta, R. (2013) *Re-Reading the Salaryman in Japan: Crafting Masculinities*, New York: Routledge.
Freedman, A. and Iwata-Weickgenannt, K. (2011) "Count What You Have Now. Don't Count What You Don't Have:" The Japanese Television Drama Around 40 and the Politics of Women's Happiness," *Asian Studies Review* 35 (3) 295–313.
Giddens, A. (1992) *Transformation of Intimacy: Sexuality, Love and Eroticism in Modern Societies*, Cambridge: Polity Press.
Goldstein-Gidoni, O. (2012) *Housewives of Japan: An Ethnography of Real Lives and Consumerized Domesticity*, New York: Palgrave Macmillan.
Hertog, E. (2009) *Tough Choices: Bearing an Illegitimate Child in Japan*, Stanford: Stanford University Press.
Iwashita, K. (2001) *Ohitorisama* (Singlehood), Tokyo: Chuokoron-Shinsha.
Jones, G. W. (2003) "The 'Flight from Marriage' in South-East and East Asia," *Asian Metacentre Research Paper Series No. 11*, Headquarters at Asia Research Institute, National University of Singapore. www.populationasia.org/Publications/RP/AMCRP11.pdf
Lesthaeghe, R. (2014) "The Second Demographic Transition: A Concise Overview of its Development," *Proceedings of the National Academy of Sciences of the United States of America* 111 (41) 18112–18115.
Mandujano-Salazer, Y.Y. (2017) "It Is Not That I Can't, It Is That I Won't: The Struggle of Japanese Women to Redefine Female Singlehood through Television," *Asian Studies Review* 41 (4) 526–543.
Maslow, A. (1954) *Motivation and Personality*, New York: Harper and Row.
Ministry of Health, Labour and Welfare. (2015) "Population of 15 Years Old and Over in Agricultural and Non-Agricultural Industries by Labour Force Status, Status in Employment, Type of Employment, Age and Marital Status," *Labour Force Survey 2015*. www.stat.go.jp/data/roudou/report/2015/ft/zuhyou/a00400.xls.
Ministry of Health, Labour and Welfare. (2017) "Marriages," *Vital Statistics in Japan*. www.mhlw.go.jp/toukei/list/dl/81-1a2.pdf.
Murai, S. (2015) "Tokyo's Shibuya and Setagaya Wards Issue First Same-Sex Partnership Papers," *The Japan Times* 5 November. www.japantimes.co.jp/news/2015/11/05/national/social-issues/shibuya-set-issue-first-certificates-recognizing-sex-couples/#.WoEHakxuKU1
Nakano, L. (2014) "Single Women in Marriage and Employment Markets in Japan," in S. Kawano, G. S. Roberts and S. O. Long (eds) *Capturing Contemporary Japan: Differentiation and Uncertainty*, Honolulu: University of Hawaii Press.
National Institute of Population and Social Security Research. (2015) "Never-Married Persons' Intention to Marry, by Survey," *The Fifteenth Japanese National Fertility Survey in 2015: Marriage Process and Fertility of Married Couples Attitudes toward Marriage and Family among Japanese Singles*. www.ipss.go.jp/ps-doukou/e/doukou15/Nfs15R_points_eng.pdf.
Ogura, C. (2003) *Kekkon no Jōken* (Conditions for Marriage), Tokyo: Asahi Shinbunsha.
Okano, K. (2009) *Young Women in Japan: Transitions to Adulthood*, London and New York: Routledge.

Rosenberger, N. (2013) *Dilemmas of Adulthood: Japanese Women and the Nuances of Long-Term Resistance*, Honolulu: University of Hawaii Press.
Rosenbluth, F. M. (2007) *The Political Economy of Japan's Low Fertility*, Stanford: Stanford University Press.
Sakai, J. (2003) *Makeinu no tôboe* (Distant Cry of the Loser Dog), Tokyo: Kodansha.
Statistics Bureau. (2010) "Population Aged 15 and over by Marital Status, Age Group (5-Year) and Sex: National (1990, 2000 and 2010)" *Population Census 2010*. www.stat.go.jp/data/kokusei/2010/kihon1/pdf/gaiyou1.pdf.
Statistics Bureau. (2015) "Population Aged 15 and over by Marital Status, Age Group (5-Year) and Sex: National," *Population Census 2015*. www.stat.go.jp/data/kokusei/2015/kekka/kihon1/pdf/gaiyou1.pdf.
Tsuya, N. O. and Oppenheim Mason, K. (1995) "Changing Gender Roles and Below-Replacement Fertility in Japan," in K. Oppenheim Mason and A. Jensen (eds) *Gender and Family Change in Industrialized Countries*, Oxford: Clarendon Press, 139–167.
Ueno, C. (2007) *Ohitorisama no rôgo* (Aging Alone), Tokyo: Hôkyû.
White, M. (2002) *Perfectly Japanese: Making Families in an Era of Upheaval*, Berkeley: University of California Press.
Yamada, M. (1999) *Parasaito shinguru no jidai* (The Age of Parasite Singles), Tokyo: Chikuma Shobō.
Yamada, M. and Shirakawa, T. (2008) *Konkatsu jidai* (Era of Marriage Hunting), Tokyo: Deisukabuā touenteiwan.
Yoshida, A. (2017) *Unmarried Women in Japan: The Drift into Singlehood*, Abingdon and New York: Routledge.

40
JAPANESE GAY MEN'S EXPERIENCES OF GENDER
Negotiating the hetero system

Thomas Baudinette

Throughout much of Japanese history, questions of gender identity have proven central to the lived experiences of same-sex-desiring Japanese men. Particularly in the postwar period, when sexual mores changed rapidly via the democratisation of Japanese society and the concomitant opening of spaces for the exploration of so-called "perverse desires" (*hentai seiyoku*) such as homosexuality (McLelland 2012a), many public intellectuals, activists, and academics have debated the relationships between gender and sexual desire (see, for example, Fushimi 1991, 2002; Kabiya 1955; Ōta 1957; Ōtsuka 1995; Takahashi 1954). From the US-led Occupation (1945–1952) until the present day, same-sex-desiring Japanese men have found themselves figuratively pulled between mainstream society's positioning of them as "effeminate" (*onnappoi*) on the one hand and the "gay" (*gei*, defined fully subsequently) sub-cultural media's promotion of "masculine" (*otokorashii*) identities as normatively desirable on the other hand (Baudinette 2017a, 2017b; Mackintosh 2010; Maekawa 2017; Moriyama 2012). These tensions also play out across a number of media platforms targeting same-sex-desiring men—including dating sites, signage in gay districts, pornographic films, and within the pages of manga comics—with the performance of a normatively masculine and "straight-acting" (*nonkeppoi*) identity typically promoted as desirable in comparison to a less desirable "cute" (*kawaii*) and/or "camp" (*onēppoi*) identity. Like much of the rest of the world, Japanese same-sex-desiring men's experiences of gender are thus complex and shifting, dependent upon the social contexts within which they are operating at any given time.

In this chapter I explore the complexities surrounding the gendered experiences of those Japanese men who identify as "gay" (*gei*) across several different social contexts. Within Japan, "gay" represents a specific identity category with its own particular history that I define more fully subsequently (for references to broader discussions of "queer" identity, see Dale, Standish, and Wallace in this volume). Within this chapter, I particularly tease out the differences and similarities between the gendered ideologies attached to gay male experience within mainstream society and within Japan's burgeoning gay sub-cultural spaces. I couple a survey of both activist and academic sources with the reported experiences of young gay men who have participated within my previous studies of media consumption in Japan to paint a broad introductory picture of the various gendered ideologies with which Japanese gay men engage in their everyday lives. Through this discussion, I introduce the key issues surrounding the study of gender and Japanese gay male experience, focusing on how the heteronormative nature of Japanese society—or what noted gay activist and public intellectual Fushimi Noriaki (1991, 2007) refers to as the "hetero system" (*hetero shisutemu*)—positions same-sex-desiring men as "trans-gendered." By "trans-gender," I signify a gendered identity that "crosses" the gender binary, with the use of the hyphen representing my attempt to render via translation how the term is deployed within many of the theoretical Japanese works I cite within this chapter. "Transgender," without the use of a hyphen, in turn signifies the identity category that has emerged out of LGBT identity politics (see Dale in this volume). I also provide a brief survey of representations of masculinity within Japanese gay media to elucidate how normative expectations concerning the desirability of certain gay identities are intimately tied to gendered knowledge. In so doing, I investigate young Japanese gay men's understandings of the gender ideologies circulating throughout what I term the "Japanese gay media landscape" and briefly explore how gender may act as disciplinary knowledge that conditions how Japanese gay men understand their sexual identities.

Before commencing this discussion, however, some brief comments on scope and terminology are necessary. As noted previously, this chapter focuses on the experiences of "gay" Japanese men rather than a broader collective of "queer" Japanese men, where queer represents "an umbrella term to refer both to ideas and groups of people that are gender and sexually nonnormative in a broad sense" (Suganuma 2011, 345). "Queer" as it is understood within the context of English-language academic discourse—that is, sexual identities tied to "whatever is at odds with the normal, the legitimate, the dominant" (Halperin 1997, 62)—does not have wide currency amongst Japanese same-sex-desiring men (McLelland 2005, 2). This is despite the attempts of academics such as Shimizu Akiko (2017) and activists such as Fushimi Noriaki (2003, 2007) to raise awareness of the term queer (*kuia*) in mainstream Japanese society and amongst Japanese sexual minority communities respectively (see also Maree and Shimizu in this volume). Instead, use of terms such as *gei* (gay) to refer to same-sex-desiring cis-gendered men and *x-jendā*, *nyūhāfu*, and *toransujendā* to refer to transgender men are much more common in contemporary Japan, having gained popularity in the early 1990s. This was due to extended media reporting of the early gay rights movement coupled with widespread use of the term "gay" (*gei*) on the Japanese internet at this time (McLelland 2005, 184). It is important to note that these terms still continue to be understood in multiple ways by different people and thus definitions are in a constant state of flux (Dale 2012; Label X 2016; McLelland 2005, 177; Suganuma 2011).

In recent years, due to the so-called "LGBT boom" that swept through Japanese society in 2015, mainstream awareness of the term "gay" has increased (see Sunagawa 2015). Many same-sex-desiring men—whether cis-gendered or otherwise—have now come to adopt "gay" (*gei*) as an identity label because of this wider mainstream recognition (Sunagawa 2015). Whilst I recognise that there is a broad range of queer male experiences possible in Japan, it is certainly the case that the experiences of Japanese cis-gendered men identifying as "gay" (*gei*) have dominated much of the previous literature. For reasons of scope, this chapter will thus largely focus on such men's experiences, with other chapters in this collection focussing on the experiences of other "queer" groups (see Dale and Wallace in this volume).

Negotiating gender within the "hetero system"

To fully understand how Japanese gay men experience gender, it is instructive to think through how gender and sexuality are understood within Japanese society. As discussed throughout many of the chapters in this volume, contemporary mainstream Japanese society is strongly heteronormative. "Heteronormativity" is a key concept within sexuality studies more broadly—and within queer theory in particular—which refers to the construction of heterosexuality as both "compulsory" and "default" for all social subjects (see Rich 1980). As an ideological system that conditions knowledge concerning sexuality and gender, heteronormativity represents a "regulatory order" (Warner 1991, 8) that constructs heterosexuality as "normal" through the marginalisation of same-sex-desiring people as possessors of "deviant" and "abnormal" desires (Suganuma 2011, 353). Writing in an American context, Chambers (2003) has argued that societal heteronormativity especially emphasises the extent to which everyone, whether they are attracted to the same or opposite sex, is evaluated from the perspective of the default construction of the social subject as heterosexual. As such, heteronormativity represents a form of "interpellation" (Althusser 1971), the process through which a social subject's identities are positioned and constructed via ideological systems circulating throughout a given society. That is to say, social structures condition individuals to read others as heterosexual, rendering same-sex attraction as "marked," "different," and "exceptional" (Bucholtz and Hall 2004).

Reflecting upon Japanese mainstream understandings of same-sex-desiring individuals, Fushimi (1991, 2007) has persuasively argued that Japanese society is dominated by a "hetero system" (*hetero shisutemu*) that promotes heterosexual, cis-gendered men as the default Japanese social subject. Under this system, same-sex-desiring men (and women) are conceptualised not only as possessors of "perverted desires" (*hentai seiyoku*) but also as potentially problematic or even dangerous elements due to the non-reproductive nature of their sexual practices (2007, 21). An example of this attitude are remarks made in 2018 by LDP lawmaker Sugita Mio, who suggested in an article published in the conservative magazine *Weekly Shinchō* (*Shūkan Shinchō*) that LGBT individuals are not deserving of state welfare due to their perceived inability to have children, which Sugita argues renders this group "unproductive" (*seisansei ga nai*) (*Japan Times* 2018). Simply put, due to the association of gay men with a supposed inability to participate in reproductive sexuality, they are often positioned as "failed" or "problematic" men by mainstream society.

Integral to the hetero system as envisioned by Fushimi is the notion that sexual desire and biological sex are intimately linked (2007, 68). This heteronormative logic underpins Japanese mainstream conceptualisations of sexuality more broadly. Nakamura Mia (2008, 19) notes in her "queer sexological" studies that contemporary Japanese attitudes towards sexuality are firmly situated within a highly essentialist paradigm that constructs an individual's gendered and sexual identities as equivalent to their biological sex. Fushimi (2007, 71–72) further notes that the hetero system purports that there are only two static genders—the "male role" (*dansei*) and the "female role" (*josei*)—and that this sexual ideology promotes a rigid, heteronormative "system of gender/sexual duality" (*seibetsu nigensei*) where men actively desire women and women are rendered passive objects of men's desires. Here, drawing on the earlier work of activist and social critic Tōgō Ken, Fushimi engages with wordplay to stress the constructed nature of these sexual roles. Rather than employing the standard Japanese orthography for the terms man (*dansei*) and woman (*josei*), Fushimi replaces the typical character *sei* meaning "nature," "essence," or "gender/sex" with the homophonous character *sei* meaning "regulation," "law," or "rule" to create a neologism.

According to Mark McLelland (2005), such understandings emerged within Japan because of the importation of Western (particularly German) sexological literature during the nineteenth century and were strongly enforced during the wartime years as the Japanese militaristic government adopted increasingly pro-natalist views. As Frühstück insightfully notes within her history of sexual knowledge in modern Japan, this sexological knowledge was deployed by Meiji-Era leaders to manage the population and thus develop a modern state based in a "normative sexuality . . . viewed as existing between women and men" (2003, 2). Whilst McLelland (2005) and Frühstück (2003) carefully historicise the development of heteronormative understandings of sexuality, charting how Western science was domesticated to form a particularly

Japanese conceptualisation of sexual modernity, Fushimi takes a somewhat problematic ahistorical approach. For Fushimi, the hetero system is universal, can be traced back to pre-history, and is thus neither simply "Japanese" nor "Western" (1991, 167–168). It is instead integral to all human cultures, and Fushimi therefore ahistorically stresses that the hetero system must be considered "natural" to human socialisation (Fushimi 1991, 168).

Within the hetero system, "passive desire" for other men is implicitly coded as feminine and is "naturally" attached to those bodies understood to be biologically female (Fushimi 2007, 72). As such, the hetero system equates (or perhaps conflates) gay men's desires with the desires of heterosexual women, and both gay men and women are thus understood as passive in their desires for heterosexual men, whose desires are consequently positioned as active (Fushimi 2007, 68). The "system of gender/sexual duality" promoted by the hetero system ultimately constructs gay men as inherently possessing "womanly" attributes, with same-sex-desiring men subsequently being understood as effeminate (*joseiteki*) (Fushimi 2007, 69). Fushimi refers to this process as "androgynification" (*chūseika*), another neologism that refers to the way that gay men are ideologically positioned as somehow "in the middle" (*chū*) of the male role (*dansei*) and the female role (*josei*) (2007, 77). Fushimi's notion of "androgynification" echoes the work of Murakami and Ishida (2006), who argue that same-sex-attracted men were typically presented as "feminised men" (*joseika shita otoko*) in postwar Japanese magazines until at least the late 1990s. Due to the "androgynification" of same-sex-desiring men inherent to the hetero system, the common image most Japanese people have had of gay men until very recently is a "trans-gendered" one of women "trapped" in men's bodies (Nakamura 2008, 101; Yoshinaga 2000). In this sense, Japanese gay men are understood to be "trans-gendered" in that they figuratively "cross" between the two gender roles identified as forming part of the hetero system (Fushimi 2007, 72).

Wim Lunsing's (2001) sociological study of 1990s Japanese gay and lesbian organisations indicated that many Japanese gay men accepted the validity of such heteronormative conceptualisations of gender and sexuality as "common-sense" (*jōshiki*). The lingering acceptance of the "common-sense" nature of the hetero system throughout the 1990s is perhaps why early radical activists for the rights of sexual minorities such as Tōgō Ken called for same-sex-desiring men to "overcome common-sense" (*jōshiki o koete*) and embrace perversity, androgyny, and "faggotry" (*okama de aru koto*) in his memoir (Tōgō 2002; translated in McLelland 2012b). In fact, in his earlier work, Fushimi (1991, 127) went to great lengths to explain that the hetero system is more than just "hetero-sexualism" or heteronormativity. Instead, the hetero system represents both a "system of gender/sexual duality" (Fushimi 2007, 71) and a "theory of eros" (Fushimi 1991, 167) that also ideologically conditions how sexuality and sexual roles are understood within queer male and female cultures themselves. Fushimi's "theory of eros" suggests that individuals—whether heterosexual or homosexual—require the use of the terms "male" and "female" to make sense of their desires due to social conditioning (1991, 168). It is therefore not surprising to writers such as Fushimi that gay men continue to draw upon such gendered knowledge as "common-sense" when articulating their desires (2007, 72). As I will discuss more thoroughly subsequently, the lingering ideological power of the hetero system is so strong that most Japanese gay media promote heteronormative masculinity as desirable.

The same-sex-desiring male as "trans-gendered"

The default positioning of same-sex-desiring men as "womanly" and "trans-gendered" is particularly apparent within Japan's mainstream media. This is especially true within the so-called "world of show business" (*geinōkai*), where a number of celebrities known as *onē tarento* (literally, "older sister talents") have become increasingly popular over the last decade (Maree 2013, 15).

The term *onē tarento* conventionally refers to cross-dressing and/or effeminate men who utilise a stereotypically-feminine linguistic register known as *onēkotoba* ("queen's language" or "camp language"), who perform a highly parodic style of feminine body language, and who are typically understood as possessing same-sex desire (even if they do not necessarily explicitly identify as such) (Maree 2013, 15). Famous *onē tarento* in Japan at the time of writing include Matsuko Deluxe, IKKO, and Mitsu Mangrove. *Onē tarento* commonly serve a comedic function within variety shows, with their inability to "pass" as women consistently portrayed as a source of humour. Recently, *onē tarento* have also come to use their so-called "poisonous tongues" (*dokuzetsu*) on variety shows to sassily critique social norms in ways analogous to drag queens in the West (Maree 2013, 59). The role of *onē tarento* has been gradually changing within Japan's contemporary mediascape, with many *onē tarento* starting to appear as fashion and romance gurus in infomercials, touristic guidebooks, and self-help magazines particularly aimed at young women (Maree 2013, 22).

Ideologically speaking, *onē tarento* strongly conform to—and thus bolster—the norms of the hetero system because the supposed possession of same-sex desire renders *onē* as somehow "trans-gendered," their feminine performances subsequently linked to their status as sexual beings situated between "real" men and women. For Fushimi (2007, 70–74), *onē tarento* thus represent an example of the "female role" (*josei*) that is inherently "passive" within the "system of gender/sexual duality," with the widespread conflation between *onē* and all same-sex-desiring men thus contributing to the "androgynification" of Japanese gay men within the mainstream imaginary. Whilst the "*onē* boom" is a relatively recent media phenomenon, which Maree (2013, 17) suggests began with the broadcast of the popular talk show *Onēmanzu* on NTV between 2006 and 2009, "trans-gendered" depictions of same-sex-desiring men in mainstream media that conform to the ideologies underpinning the hetero system have been commonplace throughout Japan's postwar history. As Murakami and Ishida (2006, 530) note, mainstream media in the late 1950s presented many lurid exposés of bars for "men who love men" which focussed on "feminised" bar staff known as *gei bōi* (gay boys), and these representations did much to cement the mainstream notion that same-sex-desiring men were "trans-gendered."

The 1960s saw two seminal events that further consolidated the mainstream media's focus on "feminised" *gei bōi*. These were the 1963 and 1964 visits to Japan of Le Carrousel, a French dance troupe composed of transsexual "blue boy" dancers (McLelland 2005, 111) and the 1965 prosecution of a doctor for removing the testicles of three cross-dressing male prostitutes (all of whom had been taking a regular course of oestrogen hormonal supplements) in what became known as the "Blue Boy Trial" (McLelland 2005, 115–116). Such "trans-gendered" representations show the genesis of what has eventually become *onē tarento* in contemporary Japan. Some famous *gei bōi* performers from the 1950s and 1960s such as Miwa Akihiro and Peter are now even presented and understood as *onē tarento* in contemporary Japanese media.

Whilst research has suggested that overtly antagonistic and derisory attitudes towards *onē tarento* are relatively scarce amongst heterosexual television viewers (Maree 2013, 11–12), the *onē tarento*'s role in bolstering and perpetuating the hetero system has been critiqued by some Japanese gay men. Indeed, according to a report published by the non-profit LGBT advocacy group Reach, 45 percent of the 11,301 gay men surveyed by the organisation reported a belief that stereotypical representations of same-sex-desiring men in Japanese mainstream media were strongly discriminatory (Reach Online 2014). Japanese gay men's ambivalent attitudes towards *onē tarento* could perhaps be due to the implicit links between such celebrity performers and another stereotypical image of same-sex-desiring men in Japan's heteronormative culture: the *okama*. A slang term literally referring to the pot within which one traditionally cooks rice, *okama* has a similar connotation to the English term faggot, evoking the image of the buttocks (which apparently appear similar to the traditional Japanese rice pot). The term *okama* typically conjures the image of a "mincing" (*memeshii*) and "effeminate" (*onnappoi*) gay man who engages in passive anal sex and cross-dresses. In other words, mainstream society understands an *okama* to be a woman trapped within the body of a man, even more so than *onē tarento* (see Fushimi 2007, 47). As is evident, the *okama* and the *onē* both represent the "female role" within the hetero system, with the primary difference between the two being that the *onē* is performative and lacks the derogatory connotations of *okama*. Also, an *onē tarento* may cease their performance when not on television, whereas the *okama* is often understood as more of a lifestyle choice.

Tensions surrounding the term *okama* came to a head in June 2001 because of the so-called "*Weekly Friday* Discriminatory Expression Case" (*Shūkan Kin'yōbi Sabetsu Hyōgen Jiken*). These tensions specifically related to concerns over the gendered ideologies attached to use of the term *okama*. Simply put, the 6 June 2001 issue of the national magazine *Weekly Friday* (*Shūkan Kin'yōbi*) contained a profile of early activist Tōgō Ken entitled "The Legendary *Okama*" (*densetsu no okama*), written by a heterosexual male journalist named Oikawa Kenji, that certain gay activist groups such as Sukotan Project found to be discriminatory. Founded in 1994 by Itō Satoru (who contacted the publishers of *Weekly Friday* to personally protest their use of the term *okama*), Sukotan Project was a gay rights activist and support group at the time of the incident that had developed a certain notoriety for calling out media firms for "negative" depictions of gay men. Because of the controversy surrounding the use of the term *okama* in a national magazine, Fushimi Noriaki convened a symposium of many different activists, public intellectuals, and publishers to discuss whether *okama* truly is a discriminatory phrase, although both Itō and Tōgō declined to attend (Fushimi et al. 2002, 35).

The broad positions which emerged out of the debate were explicitly gendered. Those who argued that *okama* is a discriminatory term, such as members of Sukotan Project, highlighted that use of *okama* reinforced the problematic notion that same-sex-desiring men were inherently effeminate (Fushimi et al. 2002, 148). Others such as Fushimi Noriaki himself stressed that Tōgō Ken preferred to refer to himself as an *okama* to destabilise the "common-sense" notions which structure Japanese society. Fushimi further suggested that Sukotan Project's stance was heteronormative, implying that the only legitimate form of gay male identification was based in "normative" notions of masculinity (Fushimi et al. 2002, 145). Overall, a survey conducted by Fushimi before the symposium suggested that whilst many same-sex-desiring men found *okama* to be a discriminatory term, there was also considerable discomfort amongst those surveyed about activist organisations' policing of gender performances (Fushimi 2007, 8–10).

These debates reveal that tensions concerning gender identity and the ideological power of the hetero system were very real issues for same-sex-desiring Japanese men, especially those who may not align with the cis-gendered men who identified as "gay" (*gei*). Furthermore, Fushimi's symposium revealed a lack of unified understandings about which gendered performances are considered "appropriate" for same-sex-desiring Japanese men, although there was a tendency for cis-gendered "gay" (*gei*) activists to strategically embrace heteronormativity as a platform to challenge mainstream positionings of same-sex-desiring men as "trans-gendered" (Fushimi et al. 2002, 145). Contemporary Japanese gay media, on the other hand, do indeed appear to promote a unified notion of what forms of masculine gendered performance should be considered normatively desirable.

Desirable genders in Japan's gay media landscape

Fushimi (2007, 72) argues that the hetero system's focus on locating identity and desire within a gender binary is just as influential to the formation of gendered knowledge within queer communities as it is outside those communities. Nowhere is this more apparent than within the media produced for and by gay Japanese men. The Japanese gay media landscape comprises several interrelated media platforms awash with ideologies that construct heteronormative masculinity as desirable for these media's target demographic of young Japanese gay men in their late teens and early twenties. Subsequently, I explore two examples of this: the discourses appearing on a Japanese gay dating site and on the signage in a Japanese gay district. I note here that the privileging of hyper-masculinity has a long history in Japan's gay media, with Mackintosh's (2010) historic study of 1970s magazines for same-sex-desiring Japanese men revealing that magazines such as *Barazoku* and *Adon* both prioritised "masculine" (*otokorashii*) imagery within their pages as an explicit response to the popularity of "trans-gendered" *gei bōi* in the mainstream media. The legacies of the hyper-masculine identity tied to these magazines can be seen in contemporary Japanese gay media, where similarly "masculine" images of gay men tend to dominate in response to mainstream media's privileging of *onē tarento*.

Through discursive analysis of 200 posts to a gay dating bulletin board system which I have given the pseudonym JP Men's Club, I encountered tensions surrounding being "hunky" (*sawayaka*) and "straight-acting" (*nonkeppoi*) on the one hand and being "cute" (*kawaii*) and "effeminate" (*onnappoi*) on the other hand (Baudinette 2017a). My analysis of the linguistic strategies deployed by users of the site revealed that the vast majority of those men who posted to JP Men's Club understood "hunkiness" to index a form of masculinity that was both highly desirable and similar to that of a fetishised straight man (Baudinette 2017a, 255). Concurrently, whilst a minority of users of the dating site expressed a desire for "cute" partners, many men who self-identified as "cute" strategically did so in such a way as to mitigate the threat of potentially appearing "effeminate" (Baudinette 2017a, 256–257). Such strategies imply that to be effeminate was somehow problematic, and it was clear that it was also undesirable (Baudinette 2017a, 258). The users of JP Men's Club whose posts I analysed thus appeared to construct a continuum of desirability that conforms to the logics laid out in Fushimi's theory of the hetero system. Desirability was often explicitly linked to what Fushimi terms the "male role," drawing upon heteronormative logics attached to the heterosexual male as "active," whereas undesirability was linked to passivity and what Fushimi terms the "female role."

My ethnographic analysis of the signage appearing within Shinjuku Ni-chōme, Tokyo's most prominent gay district, also revealed similar tensions. Examining how men's bodies were utilised as semiotic tools within the district's signage, I uncovered that most signs privileged heavily muscular bodies that many informants explained were desirable specifically due to their explicit "manliness" (Baudinette 2017b, 513–514). Indeed, speaking to the owners of gay bars revealed that many strategically and knowingly deployed such "masculine" imagery on their signage (particularly on impermanent signage referred to as *kanban* and on event pamphlets) because to do so was to meet a demand amongst their clientele for young, masculine, and, importantly, "straight-acting" men (Baudinette 2017b, 510). Due to the prominence of these impermanent signs throughout the centre of the district, I argued that desires for "masculinity" became normative and noted that bars catering to a "cute" (*kawaii*) clientele were often only to be found outside the centre of Ni-chōme, indexing the lack of privilege desire for cuteness has within this space (Baudinette 2017b, 522). As these two brief case studies of the Japanese gay media landscape reveal, what is referred to as a "hunky" and "straight-acting" form of masculinity is privileged within Japan's gay male culture. This trend is particularly interesting considering the fact that recent young women's media has tended to privilege a "cute" form of masculinity typified by male idols such as Arashi and Hey!Say!Jump.

Desirability within the Japanese gay media landscape thus also appears to be anchored to the two roles which underpin Fushimi's theory of the hetero system. That is, to be desirable relied upon adopting the "male role" in the hetero system. This seems to suggest that Fushimi's so-called "theory of eros," wherein individuals require binary categories to make sense of their desires and identities (1991, 168), holds true within the Japanese gay male culture. These heteronormative logics, however, have been damaging to those men who are either unwilling or unable to live up to the gendered expectations of the Japanese gay media landscape. One of my informants, a 24-year-old man named Haruma who explicitly identified as "cute," explained to me that, "many gay men will tell you that being cute is effeminate ... and that others may say that [being cute] is androgynous." Furthermore, Haruma suggested that being cute is a "problematic" identity since it ultimately positions one as a "failed" gay man. More importantly, Haruma explained that the pressure to perform a "straight-acting" masculinity was mentally, emotionally, and even physically exhausting and had led him to develop numerous self-esteem issues. Haruma ultimately described Japanese gay media as "poisonous" due to its promotion of identity categories tied to heteronormative masculinity and stated that he was personally more drawn to the "positive lifestyles" lived by *onē tarento*. Indeed, he viewed *onē* as influential role models for his life as a young gay Japanese man. Haruma's experiences are important because they destabilise a common assumption within the literature on Japanese gay men's lived experiences of gender that mainstream media are disempowering, whereas gay media addresses this disempowerment by providing positive discourses that affirm gay masculinity (Fushimi 2007; Moriyama 2012; Suganuma 2011).

Concluding remarks

Whilst the discussion presented within this chapter is brief, Haruma's experiences reported previously reveal that there is still much investigation to be done when it comes to understanding the complex relationships between Japanese gender ideologies, the hetero system, and Japanese gay men's lived experiences and understandings of their identities and desires. Overall, it is certainly the case that problematic heteronormative logics strongly influence both mainstream and gay media in Japan and that a "system of gender/sexual duality" composed of a "male role" and "female role" maintain strong ideological force within contemporary Japan. It is the role of future scholarship and activism to further tease out the implications of this for contemporary Japan, particularly as LGBT rights politics and new subject positions such as "x-gender" and "asexual" are becoming increasingly prevalent amongst Japanese people (Label X 2016, 31). Only time will tell just how ideologically persuasive the hetero system will remain as both public intellectuals like Fushimi Noriaki and regular men like Haruma continue to critique such heteronormative ideological systems.

Related chapters

- 4 Gender and Language
- 5 Masculinity Studies in Japan
- 6 Transgender, Non-Binary Genders, and Intersex in Japan
- 21 Lesbians and Queer Women in Japan
- 37 Genre and Gender: Romantic Friendships and the Homosocial Imperative in the *Ninkyō* (Chivalrous) Genre Film

References

Althusser, L. (1971) "Ideology and Ideological State Apparatuses," in L. Althusser (ed) *Lenin and Philosophy and Other Essays*, New York: Monthly Review Press.

Baudinette, T. (2017a) "Constructing Identities on a Japanese Gay Dating Site: Hunkiness, Cuteness and the Desire for Heteronormative Masculinity," *Journal of Language and Sexuality* 6 (2) 232–261.

Baudinette, T. (2017b) "Stratifying Space in Shinjuku Ni-chōme Through Queer Semiotics," *ACME: An International Journal for Critical Geographies* 16 (3) 500–527. www.acme-journal.org/index.php/acme/article/view/1357.

Bucholtz, M. and Hall, K. (2004) "Theorizing Identity in Language and Sexuality Research," *Language and Society* 33 (4) 469–515.

Chambers, S. A. (2003) "Telepistology of the Closet; or, the Queer Politics of *Six Feet Under*," *The Journal of American Culture* 26 (1) 24–41.

Dale, S. P. F. (2012) "An Introduction to X-Jendā: Examining a New Gender Identity in Japan," *Intersections: Gender and Sexuality in the Asia Pacific* 31. http://intersections.anu.edu.au/issue31/dale.html

Frühstück, S. (2003) *Colonizing Sex: Sexology and Social Control in Modern Japan*, Berkeley: University of California Press.

Fushimi, N. (1991) *Puraibēto gei raifu* (Private Gay Life), Tokyo: Gakuyō shobō.

Fushimi, N. (2002) *Gei to iu keiken* (The Experience Called Being Gay), Tokyo: Potto Shuppan.

Fushimi, N. (2003) *Hentai (kuia) nyūmon* (An Introduction to Perversity [Queer]), Tokyo: Chikuma Bunko.

Fushimi, N. (2007) *Seiyoku mondai: hito wa sabetsu o nakusu tame dake ni ikiru no de wa nai* (Sexual Desire: People Don't Just Live in Order to Remove Discrimination), Tokyo: Potto Shuppan.

Fushimi, N., Oikawa, K., Noguchi, K., Matsuzawa, K., Kurokawa, N. and Yamanaka, T. (eds) (2002) *"Okama" wa sabetsu ka: Shūkan kin'yōbi no sabetsu hyōgen jiken* (Is the Word "Fag" Discriminatory?: The *Weekly Friday* Discriminatory Expression Incident), Tokyo: Potto Shuppan.

Halperin, D. M. (1997) *Saint Foucault: Towards a Gay Hagiography*, Oxford and New York: Oxford University Press.

Japan Times. (2018) "LDP Lawmaker Mio Sugita Faces Backlash after Describing LGBT People as 'Unproductive'," *Japan Times* 24 July. www.japantimes.co.jp/news/2018/07/24/national/politics-diplomacy/ldp-lawmaker-mio-sugita-faces-backlash-describing-lgbt-people-unproductive/#.W3OR_rh9hPY

Kabiya, K. (1955) "*Gei bā no seitai*" (Lifestyles in the Gay Bars), *Amatoria*, (July) 38–46.

Label X (ed) (2016) *X-jendā tte nani? Nihon ni okeru tayō na sei no arikata* (What Is X-Gender? The Current State of Gender Diversity in Japan), Tokyo: Ryokufu Shuppan.

Lunsing, W. (2001) *Beyond Common Sense: Sexuality and Gender in Contemporary Japan*, London: Kegan Paul.

Mackintosh, J. D. (2010) *Homosexuality and Manliness in Postwar Japan*, London: Routledge.

Maekawa, N. (2017) *Dansei dōseiaisha no shakaishi: Aidentiti no juyō, kurōzetto e no kaihō* (A Social History of Male Homosexuality: Reception of Identity and Liberation from the Closet), Tokyo: Sakuhinsha.

Maree, C. (2013) *Onēkotoba-ron* (On the Language of Queens), Tokyo: Seidōsha.

McLelland, M. (2005) *Queer Japan from the Pacific Age to the Internet Age*, Lanham, MD: Rowman and Littlefield.

McLelland, M. (2012a) *Love, Sex and Democracy in Japan During the American Occupation*, New York: Palgrave Macmillan.

McLelland, M. (2012b) "Death of the "Legendary Okama" Tōgō Ken: Challenging Commonsense Lifestyles in Postwar Japan," *The Asia-Pacific Journal: Japan Focus* 10 (25) http://apjjf.org/2012/10/25/Mark-McLelland/3775/article.html.

Moriyama, N. (2012) *"Gei komyuniti" no shakaigaku* (Sociology of the "Gay Community"), Tokyo: Keiso shobō.

Murakami, T. and Ishida, H. (2006) *Sengo Nihon no zasshi media ni okeru "otoko o ai suru otoko" to "joseika shita otoko" no hyōshō-shi* (A Representational History of "Men Who Love Men" and "Feminised Men" in Postwar Japanese Magazine Media), in M. Yajima (ed) *Sengo Nihon josō dōseiai kenkyū* (Research on Postwar Japanese Cross-Dressing Men and Homosexuality), Hachiōji: Chūō Daigaku Shuppanbu, 519–547.

Nakamura, M. (2008) *Kuia sekusorojī: sei no omoikomi o tokihogusu* (Queer Sexology: Unravelling Misconceptions Concerning Sex), Tokyo: Inpakuto Shuppankai.

Ōta, T. (1957) *Daisan no sei* (The 3rd Sex), Tokyo: Myogisha.

Ōtsuka, T. (1995) *Ni-chōme kara urokō: Shinjuku gei sutorīto zakkichō* (Tales from Ni-chōme: Shinjuku Gay Street Notebook), Tokyo: Shōeisha.

Reach Online. (2014) "Reach Online 2013 chōsa kekka no go-hōkoku (Announcement of the Results of the Reach Online 2013 Survey)." www.gay-report.jp/2013/index.html

Rich, A. (1980) "Compulsory Heterosexuality and Lesbian Existence," *Signs: Journal of Women in Culture and Society* 5 (4) 631–660.

Shimizu, A. (2017) "*Daibāshiti kara kenri hoshō e: Toranpu ikō no beikoku to 'LGBT būmu' no nihon* (From Diversity to Safeguarding Rights: America After Trump and Japan's 'LGBT Boom,'" *Sekai* (May) 134–143.

Suganuma, K. (2011) "Ways of Speaking About Queer Space in Tokyo: Disorientated Knowledge and Counter-Public Space," *Japanese Studies* 31 (3) 345–358.

Sunagawa, H. (2015) "Tayō na shihai, tayō na teikō" (Diverse Domination, Diverse Resistance), *Gendai Shisō* 43 (16) 100–106.

Takahashi, T. (1954) "Kitai dōseiai-dan (Discussing Weird Homosexuality)," *Fūzoku zōshi*, (January) 74–82.

Tōgō, K. (2002) *Jōshiki o koete: okama no michi 70 nen* (Overcoming Common-Sense: 70 Years Travelling the Okama Road), Tokyo: Potto Shuppan.

Warner, M. (1991) "Introduction: Fear of a Queer Planet," *Social Text* 29 3–17.

Yoshinaga, M. (2000) *Seidōitsusei shōgai: Seitenkan no ashita* (Gender Identity Disorder: The Day After the Sex Change), Tokyo: Shūeisha.

INDEX

abortion 23, 33–5, 62, 108, 116, 138–9
activism: artistic 242; Korean 74, 216; *koseki* 83, 85; LGBTQ 62–4, 66, 409–11, 413; mothers 213–14, 244; pornography 363–4, 367; religious practices 148; women's political activism 31–2, 34–5, 70, 21–6, 221; *see also* feminism
adulthood 121, 130, 327; manhood 53, 100, 176, 234–6, 343; mature masculinity 295, 270–6; womanhood 200, 234–5, 334, 351–2, 383–5; *see also* girl; youthhood
adult videos 362–4; *see also* pornography
advertisements 270–2, 274–5, 334–5, 340, 345, 364, 414
affective labour 75, 120, 245, 247, 315
affirmative action 159–60, 163, 201, 205–6
agency 27–8, 43–4, 89, 150; female 192, 233–5, 304; girls 312–14, 317, 327; *see also* empowerment
aging population 115, 118, 225, 240; caregiving 129–30, 132, 193, 247; workforce 161, 162, 385
aidoru see idols
Ainu 70, 72–73, 295; *see also* minorities
anarchism 212
anime 312, 326, 332, 391–6
Arashi 53, 272, 343, 345, 414; *see also* idols; Jpop
Arpeggio 391–2, 394–6
arranged marriage 96, 180, 384–5, 402
art: digital 241–2; high *vs.* low 373–5, 377, 380; history 241, 303–4, 335–6, 361; *kawaii* 322, 325, 327–8; *see also* woodblock prints

ballet 375–9; *see also* dance
Basic Act for a Gender Equal Society 36, 157, 160
beautiful boys 271–2, 274–5, 280, 283, 294–5, 316, 333; *see also* male beauty; boys' love

beauty: crossdressing 283, 285–6; female 235, 333, 336, 378; girls 312; *kawaii* 321; male 270–6; *see also* beautiful boys
birth rate 34, 36, 54, 118, 135, 345, 399; *see also* fertility rate
bishōjo 284; *see also* beauty; *shōjo*; girl
bishōnen see beautiful boys
BL 314–16, 333, 362, 365; *see also* beautiful boys; desire; manga; *shōnen*
body: cosplay 282–5; ethnicity 70–1, 75; female 242, 303–7, 317; hybridity 393–4; literary depictions 23–5, 294, 296, 374–5, 377–9; male 53–4, 270–6, 414; nationalism 252, 254–5, 373; rights 33; taboo 305–6; transgendered 61–5
bōsōzoku 232, 355–6
boy 271–2, 274–6, 294–5, 312, 315, 317, 322; *see also* boys' love; girl
boys' love 314–16, 333, 362, 365; *see also* beautiful boys; desire; manga; *shōnen*
Brazil 74, 190; *see also* minorities
budō see martial arts
burakumin 70, 72–73, 295; *see also* minorities
burial customs 138–9, 141–3; *see also* death
bushido 71–2, 262–3, 265–7; *see also* military; soldiers

capitalism 35–6, 127, 236–7, 326, 328, 356; global 15, 312–13
carnivore woman 341, 345; *see also* herbivore man
censorship 266, 341, 361–3, 365–6; *see also* obscenity laws; pornography
childbirth 115, 135–42, 147, 303, 305–6; *see also* birth rate; children; pregnancy
childcare 94, 100–1, 107–9, 157, 160–1, 175
child pornography 312, 340, 364, 366; *see also* obscenity laws; pornography

Index

children: attitudes to 94, 96, 101, 203; *kawaii* 321–322; legal concerns 85–6, 88; *see also* childbirth; childcare; fatherhood; motherhood; parental leave
children's literature 297; *see also* literature
China: fan practices 280–1, 392; historical relationship 70–1, 181, 263, 265; influence 84, 262, 271; migrants 73–5, 190–2, 194–5; tensions 392; *see also* minorities; nationalism; war history
Christianity 14, 151, 265; *see also* religion
cinema *see* film
citizenship 73–4, 86, 88–9, 116, 121, 213
Civil Code 84–6, 88–9, 211
class 52, 232, 253–4, 264, 266–7: language 42–3, 45
clothing 24, 235, 378, 389; fashion 334–5; girls 232, 252–4, 392; regulation 70–1, 281–4; *see also* cosplay
clubs 121, 182–3, 185, 191; *see also* human trafficking; sex industry; sex work
comfort women 13, 73, 181, 216, 336, 346; *see also* human trafficking; war history
commercials 270–2, 274–5, 334–5, 340, 345, 364
Communism 212
community groups 140, 220–2, 224–5
Confucian values 127, 211, 252, 262; *see also ie* system; religion
consumer culture 320, 364, 373; girls 311–13, 317, 336, 356; women 200, 213, 323, 325–6, 334, 356
contents tourism 126, 393–6; *see also* fan practices
contraceptive pill 33; *see also* abortion
conventions (cosplay) 279–84
cosplay 279–86
crisis discourses 267, 273, 293–4, 296
crossplay 282–6; *see also* crossdressing; gender-bending
cuteness 320–1, 327–8; *see also kawaii*

dance: film depiction 387; literary depiction 373–7; physical education 252, 256; sex work 179–80, 191; subcultures 234–6
death 135, 138–43, 294
desire: body 24, 273; girls and women 314–15, 354; intersectionality 75, 270; passive 410–14; sanctioned 53–4, 312–13; *see also* same-sex desire; sexual desire; sexual fantasy
digital communication 245–8; *see also* online communities; social media
digital kinship 245–8; *see also* friendship; online communities; social media
digital technologies 241–8, 332; media 306–8, 362, 365; *see also* online communities; social media
divorce 86, 96, 108, 118
domestic labour 36, 169–70, 175

domestic violence 86, 204–5
drag 283–5

education: attainment 110, 128, 162, 174, 213, 400–2; gender segregation 253; girls 250–6, 314, 322, 352, 375; international students 190; university 95, 100, 194, 215, 252, 254, 256; women 35, 107, 127, 252–4, 292
embodied practice 374, 377, 379; *see also* body; dance
empowerment 333, 355, 357, 383, 385, 388–9
enjo-kōsai 184, 313; *see also* girl; sex work
Equal Employment Opportunity Law 36, 94, 108, 157–9, 165, 169–70
eroticism 24, 272–4, 314–16, 333, 335–6, 355; *see also* objectification; sexualization
ethnic identity 74–5; *see also* ethno-racial discourses; nationalism
ethno-racial discourses 70–3; *see also* nationalism
Eugenic Protection Law 62, 138; *see also* abortion; eugenics
eugenics 33–5, 62, 138; *see also* abortion

fairy tales 296–7
family formation 92–4, 96, 102, 173, 399, 401; *see also* family
family: caregiving 129–30, 168, 170, 247; depictions of 296, 303, 307; diversity 109–11; ideal 115–18, 127; legal definition 83–4; patriarchal structure 211–12; *see also* family formation; multi-generational households; nuclear family; same-sex marriage
fascism 254–6; *see also* nationalism
fatherhood 44, 51–2, 120, 174; *see also* motherhood; parental leave
femininity: alternatives 235, 312, 314–15, 327, 334, 402; girlish 307–8, hyperfemininity 284, 352; hyper-sexualisation 75; language 40–1, 44–5; male 271–2, 275; media representations 204, 342–3; writing 292, 302, 308; *see also* womanhood
feminised labour migration 191–4
feminism: activism 31–2, 34–5, 72, 200, 215; arts 292, 294, 303–4, 307–8, 335; backlash 33, 36; branches 14–15, 24, 28, 35, 219, 221, 253–6; debates 31–6, 212, 221, 363–5; girl 315, 317; #MeToo 1–3, 341, 346–7; pornography 363, 365; religion 23, 27–8; *see also* activism; women's liberation movement
fertility rate 92, 94, 118, 128, 172, 189, 399–401; *see also* birth rate
fighting girl 391–5
film: digital cinema 244–5; *Gangster Women* 382–3, 385–8; pornography 362–4; representation of girl 353–7
folk cultures 135–42

419

folklore 135, 141–2, 148–9, 296–7; *see also* folk cultures
folktales 135, 141–2, 148–9, 296–7; *see also* folk cultures
forced prostitution 180–181; *see also* sexual slavery
friendship 245, 247–8, 274–6, 355; *see also* homosociality; romantic friendship
fujoshi 316–17, 333
Fukushima Daiichi nuclear disaster *see* 3.11; triple disaster
furusato 126

games 240, 243–4, 312, 351, 362–6, 295
Garupan 391–4, 396
gaze 143, 220, 222, 335; female 271–272, 276; male 314, 327; shared 386–8
gender binary: fluidity 383, 389; LGBT 64–5, 215, 221–2, 367, 409–10, 413
gender equality: backlash 33, 36, 216; policy 159–60, 168, 175, 201, 205–6; political empowerment 158, 200–5, 257–8; *see also* affirmative action; Basic Act for a Gender Equal Society; Equal Employment Opportunity Law; suffrage
gender fluidity 26, 383, 389; *see also* performativity of gender
gender identity 63–5, 84, 281, 286, 408, 413; *see also* gender identity disorder; transgender individuals
gender identity disorder 60, 62–5, 67, 88
gender play 25–6; *see also* crossdressing; cross-play; gender-bending
gender queering 343; *see also* crossdressing; cross-play; gender-bending
gender reassignment surgery 61–3, 65
gender-bending 314–15, 317, 333–4; *see also* crossdressing; cross-play; gender play
Genji Monogatari 22–4, 26, 28, 292; *see also* literature
genre fiction 295–6; *see also* literature
girl: clothing 232, 252–3, 352–54, 392; consumer 311–13, 317, 336, 356; desire 314–15, 354; feminism 315, 317; girlhood 280, 351–7; nation state 351–4; representation 293, 311–12, 353–7; sexualization 312, 327, 333, 336, 340, 355, 393; *see also* kawaii; *shōjo*
globalization 15, 165, 189, 191, 320
good wife, wise mother *see ryōsai kenbo*
Great East Japan Earthquake *see* 3.11 triple disaster
grief 139–41
gymnastics 252, 256

harassment in the workforce: marital discrimination 170; maternal 159, 165; racial harassment 194–5; sexual harassment 159, 340, 343, 346–347; *see also* misogyny
hegemonic femininity 71–2, 235

herbivore man 53, 244, 335, 341, 345–6
hetero system 410–15
heteronormativity: *koseki* 83–5, 119; language 44; masculinity 53, 236; religion 151; romance 333–4; *see also* heterosexism; homosexuality; *koseki*; marriage
heterosexism 222–4, 236
hip-hop 233–3, 237
homoeroticism 314–16; *see also* boys' love
homogeneity discourses 42–3, 45–6, 69, 73
homophobia 224, 236, 282, 412–13
homosexuality: depictions 294–5, 314–16, 333, 411–15; female 215, 219–25, 294, 383; male 54, 294–5, 408–12, 415; "mourning" 387–8; pornography 365, 367; social tensions 115–16, 118–19; *see also* boys' love; same-sex marriage; sexualities
homosociality 117, 120, 295, 314, 382–3, 387–90; *see also* friendship
host clubs 121, 183, 185; *see also* sex industry; sex work
hostess clubs 182–3, 185, 191; *see also* sex industry; sex work
housewife: activism 213–14; consumers 323, 326; professional 93, 95, 98, 108, 118, 400, 403; representation 334, 336, 342–3; *see also* family; *ryōsai kenbo*
human trafficking 13, 121, 180, 184–5, 191; *see also* comfort women; sex work
hyperfemininity 284; *see also* femininity
hypermasculinity 274, 276, 284, 294, 414; *see also* masculinity

ianfu 13, 73, 181, 216, 336, 346
idols: femininity 232–3, 235, 317, 343, 351, 356–7; industry 341; masculinity 53, 272, 274, 343, 414
ie system: contemporary impact 118, 128–9, 132, 382; history 70, 84, 116, 127–8, 180, 211, 378, 384; *see also* family; *koseki*; marriage
ikumen 52–3, 120, 175
imagined community 69, 353
immigration 121; labour 72–4, 157, 161, 163, 165, 170; sex work 185–6; types 189, 191–2, 194
immigration policy 72–4, 190–5
Imperial Japan 73, 236, 251, 265–6, 336; *see also* nationalism
Indonesia 191, 193
industrialization 70, 128, 199–200, 384
infant mortality 135, 138–9; *see also* death; maternal mortality
infantilization 326, 336–7, 351, 393; *see also* girl
interpellation 387, 389, 410
intersectionality: class 23, 26, 107–8, 110–11; feminism 215; race 16, 69, 72–5, 232–4, 286, 295
inter-sex individuals 66, 87

intimacy 52–3, 115–19, 245; paid 183, 120–1; *see also* affective labour; love; marriage; sex work
Itō Hiromi 305–6

Japanese Family Register 83–8, 116, 119, 224; *see also* family; *ie* system; marriage
Japanese-ness 70–3, 76, 129, 236–7, 266, 279; *see also* homogeneity discourses; nationalism; patriotism
Japanese Self-Defense Forces 391–6; *see also* military
Japarege 234–5, 237
journalism 204, 342–7
Jpop 231–3, 235, 272; *see also* idols; music
jun bungaku 292–3, 298; *see also* art; literature

KanColle 391–2, 394–6
Kawabata Yasunari 373–80, 388
kawaii 320–9; aesthetic 232–4, 333, 336–7, 343, 352; anime characters 392; consumer culture 312, 322–4, 334; male 270, 408, 414–15; rebellious 327–8, 334; technology 243, 245; *see also* girl; *shōjo*
kegare 137, 141, 148–9
Korea: comfort women 216, 336; depiction in film 385–7; tensions 392; *Zainichi* Koreans 70, 73–5, 224, 295; *see also* comfort women; minorities; nationalism; war history
koseki 83–9, 116, 119, 224; *see also* family; *ie* system; marriage

labour policy 72–4, 117
language 40–2, 44–7, 247, 306; LGBTQ terminology 215, 219–20, 223, 411–13
legal sex 83–5, 87–8
lesbian 219–25; discrimination 63, 118–19; community 220–4, 316; feminism 215, 219, 221; film representation 383, 386–90; literature and manga 284, 294, 314, 334; marriage 224–5; *see also* homosexuality; same-sex marriage; sexual desire; sexuality
LGBTQ in Japan 118–19, 340; activism 409–11, 413; language 215, 219–23, 409, 411–15; media presence 61–3, 66, 224, 343; narrativizing 219–223; religion 151–2, 224; *see also* homosexuality; same-sex marriage; transgender individuals
liminal: spaces 280–1, 283, 286; state 131, 148, 322, 326, 352, 357–8; *see also* girl
literature: classical texts 23–8; contemporary 291–8, 373–80; *see also* Yoshimoto Banana
lolicon 312, 340, 364, 366; *see also* moe; obscenity laws; *otaku*; pornography
love 24, 116, 118–119, 180, 183, 192, 244, 385; homosocial 382–3, 385–6; *see also* intimacy; romance

magazine: debates 2, 31–2, 410; gender constructions 234, 332, 342, 272; girls 314, 322, 325, 353, 355; female representation 184, 256, 334, 336, 340–1; queer 54, 220–1, 411, 413–14; *shūkanshi* 344–5; *see also Seitō*
male beauty 270–6
male-dominated spaces: arts 292, 304, 308, 311, 335–6; media 334, 341–2, 346; politics 202–4; society 143, 253, 258, 355; subcultures 233–7, 315; *see also* misogyny
male productivity 50–4, 168, 175–6, 346
management practices 159, 161–3, 195; promotion 159, 174; recruitment procedures 159, 162, 169–70, 174; two-track system 162, 169, 174, 341–2; *see also* workers' rights
Manchuria 73–4
manga 66, 74–5, 334, 336; *see also shōjo* manga; *shōnen* manga
manhood 53, 100, 176, 234–6, 343; *see also* adulthood; mature masculinity
marriage: attitudes to 93–9, 100–2, 211; Buddhism 149–50; legal basis 34, 83–7, 224; "love marriage" 385; migration 191–2, 195; rate 341, 345; *see also* arranged marriage; marriage delay; same-sex marriage
marriage delay 94, 118, 121, 399–403, 405; *see also* family formation; marriage rate
marriage rate 341, 345
martial arts 255–6, 261–8; *see also* sport
mascots 323–4, 327
masculinity: alternative 51–2, 237–8, 335, 340, 344–6; body 53–4, 270–6; depictions 293–4, 308; elite 263–4, 267; language 42, 44–5; martial masculinity 263–6; nation state 70, 76, 261; *see also* crisis discourses; effeminate masculinity; herbivore men; hypermasculinity; *ikumen*; male beauty; male productivity; *otaku*
maternal mortality 135, 138, 141–2
mature masculinity 295, 270–6; *see also* adulthood; manhood; womanhood
media panics 341, 345
media practices 341, 344, 346
media representation: language 45; LGBTQ individuals 61–3, 66, 224, 343, 409–11, 413; misogyny 204, 342–3
mediated misogyny 340–5; *see also* misogyny
medicine 61–6, 135–40, 240, 305; *see also* modernization
metal music 236–7
#MeToo movement 1–3, 341, 346–7; *see also* feminism; sexual harassment
midwives 135–7, 141; *see also* childbirth; medicalization
migrant flows 13, 74
militarism 31, 245, 261, 266, 362, 392–6
military 322; conscription 255–6; discourses 254–6, 261–2, 264; Japanese Self-Defense

Forces 391–6; martial masculinity 263–6; *see also* comfort women; soldiers; war history
Minashita Kiriu 306–7
minorities 70, 72–6, 190–3, 195, 295; *see also* ethnic identity; racism
misogyny 3, 232, 294, 304, 326, 364; mediated misogyny 340–1, 343–5; religion 23, 27–8, 149–50; *see also* male-dominated spaces; sexual harassment; violence
mizuko kuyō 138–9, 141
modern girl 353; *see also* girl
modernization 11–13; class structures 261, 264–6, 210–11; countryside 125–8; family structure 106–8, 116, 180; folk cultures 141; high *vs.* low culture 374–5; *see also* nation state
moe 313–14, 316–17, 392–3, 395; *see also* otaku; sexual fantasy
monstrous women 143, 296
motherhood: activism 213–14, 244; depictions 303, 305–6, 342–3; discourses 107, 120, 203, 252–4, 334, 384–5; protection 34–6; quitting work 95, 98, 109, 111, 172–4; returning to work 247–8; sacrifice 100–1, 130, 136–7; *see also* children; maternal mortality; *ryōsai kenbo*
music 232–7

national identity 69–72, 76, 267, 343; countryside 125–6, 129; immigration 189, 392; *see also* Japanese-ness; nationalism
nationalism 236–7, 251, 255, 261, 263, 392; *see also* Imperial Japan
nation state 70–2, 76, 210–11, 261, 297, 410; as body 373; as family 115–16; as girl 351–4; women 106–7, 199–200, 251, 256; *see also* modernization; national identity
Neo-Confucianism 382–3, 385, 387, 389; *see also* Confucian values; religion
neoliberalism 121, 131, 165, 233–4, 357, 401
Nepal 74, 195
new religions 150–1; *see also* religion
news broadcasting 341–2
ni_ka 307–8
ninkyō films 382–3, 385–9; *see also* film
noise music 236–7
non-regular employment 99–100, 109, 158, 173, 176; *see also* workers' rights
nostalgia discourses 125, 128, 131–2, 262, 264

objectification 193, 275, 312, 333, 389, 395; *see also* eroticism; sexualization
obscenity laws 242, 362–3, 365–8; *see also* censorship; pornography
okama 61, 411–13
Okinawa 70, 72–3, 149, 181, 295; *see also* minorities
Olympic Games 186, 255–8
onē tarento 411–15

online communities: blogs 1–2, 248–9; feminist debates 33; subculture spaces 279–80, 283, 286, 392, 396; *x-jendā* 64, 66, 216, 409; *see also* digital communication; social media
otaku 279, 282, 311–17, 333, 336–7; sexuality 53

"parasite single" 399, 401–2; *see also* marriage delay; singlehood
parental leave 35, 109, 157, 160–1, 172, 174; *see also* fatherhood; motherhood
participation rate 169, 175, 256
part-time work 163–5, 170
patriotism 236–7
Philippines 74–5, 185, 191–3; *see also* human trafficking
physical education 251–7, 375–6; *see also* education; martial arts; sport
poetry 23, 26, 35, 292, 302–9
politics 200–6, 213
pollution 146–9; *see also* kegare; purity
pornography 184, 222, 242, 344, 355, 361–8; child/*lolicon* 312, 340, 364, 366; *see also* obscenity laws; pornography industry; sex work
pornography industry 361–4, 366–7; *see also* obscenity laws; pornography; sex work
poverty 110–11
precarity 109, 125, 173, 175, 400–2; legislation 158, 163–5; *see also* workers' rights
Pretty Soldier Sailor Moon 284, 312, 326, 333
production of knowledge 410–11
productive labour 50–4, 95–6, 99, 168, 175–6, 191–2
punk 235–6
pure literature 292–3, 298; *see also* art
purity 71–2, 147–9, 314, 382, 386; *see also* kegare; pollution; religion

racism 194–5, 234–5, 237–8, 344, 392
religion 15, 265; women 146–8, 150–1; LGBTQ issues 224; religious rites 138–9; sacred spaces 146–8
reproductive labour 36, 41, 169, 191–2, 200
reproductive technologies 33–4; *see also* abortion; eugenics
Rokudenashiko 242, 365; *see also* art; feminism
romance 25–6, 116, 180, 192, 314–15, 332–3, 385; *see also* boys' love; intimacy; love
romantic friendship 382–3, 385–90; *see also* friendship; homosociality
rural decline 128–9, 131–2, 191–2, 225; *see also* rural Japan; rural revitalization
rural Japan 125–6, 128–32, 248, 265, 403
rural revitalization 125–6, 131–2
ryōsai kenbo: contemporary housewives 36, 384–5; education 251–2; language 41; nationalism 71–2, 107, 254; resistance 35, 353, 378–9; *see also* housewife

Index

Sailor Moon see Pretty Soldier Sailor Moon
same-sex desire 221, 294, 334, 408–12, 415; *see also* desire; sexual desire; sexual fantasy; sexuality
same-sex marriage: adult adoption 87, 224–5; legal measures 66–7, 87–8, 118–19, 399; social tensions 115–16; *see also* homosexuality; lesbian; marriage
Seitō 31–3, 35, 212, 254, 292, 294; *see also* feminism; magazines
sex education 365; *see also* education
sex/gender binary 25–7, 87, 410–12
sex industry 180–3, 186; *see also* human trafficking; pornography; sex work; sex workers
sexual assault 13–14, 204, 341, 346, 354, 363–366; *see also* violence
sexual desire 116, 221, 243, 272–3, 315, 364–5; *see also* desire; same-sex desire; sexuality
sexual fantasy 243, 273, 316, 317, 333, 336, 355; *see also* sexual desire
sexual harassment 159, 203–4, 258, 340, 342, 346–7, 363; *see also* #MeToo movement; sexual assault
sexualities *see* homosexuality; sexual fantasy
sexualization: girl 312, 327, 333, 336, 340, 355, 393; *vs.* eroticism 273; lesbians 220–2; migrant 75; *see also* eroticism; homoeroticism; objectification; sexual fantasy
sexual pleasure 364; *see also* desire
sexual scripts 317, 366–7
sexual slavery 13, 73, 181, 216, 336, 346; *see also* comfort women; forced prostitution; human trafficking
sex work: attitudes 180, 184, 192, 212, 412; history 61, 75, 120–1, 179–83; legality/illegality 184–6, 191; sex tourism 192; *see also* human trafficking; pornography
sex workers 179–85, 354, 363, 367; *see also* human trafficking
Shintoism 148–9, 265; *see also* religion
shōjo 311–17; 271–2; aesthetics 322–3, 327, 336–7; consumer 322–3, 325–6; culture 280, 293, 297, 352–3; cultural anxieties 332–4, 351–2, 354, 356–7; *see also* girl; *shōjo* manga
shōjo manga: beautiful boys 270–2; girl 311–12, 325, 332–4; history 314–17, 352; *see also* girl; *shōjo*
shōnen 271, 316–17, 333, 352; *see also* bishōnen
shōnen ai 314–16, 333, 362, 365; *see also* beautiful boys; desire; manga; *shōnen*
shōnen manga 333, 352, 316–17; *see also* manga; *shōjo* manga
singlehood 118, 121, 203, 399–405
single parenting 109–11; *see also* childcare; divorce; family formation; singlehood
skinship 120; *see also* intimacy
smart phones 245–8; *see also* online communities; social media

socialism 35, 200, 211–13
social media: activism 1–2, 347; fan practices 279–80, 395–6; sex work 182; visual culture 332, 340; *see also* digital communication; digital technologies; online communities
social policy 36, 107–10, 115–16, 118, 125
soft power 320, 332
soldiers 71–2, 182, 254, 265, 322, 354; *see also* military; war history
sōshokukei danshi 53, 244, 335, 341, 345–6
sport 251–8; martial arts 261–3, 265–8; *see also* martial arts; physical education
spousal tax system 93, 108, 161–2, 169, 173
suffrage 15, 32, 107, 200, 212–13; *see also* activism; politics
sukeban 355–6; *see also* girl

Taiwan 73–74, 395
Takarazuka Revue 314–16, 333–4; *see also* cosplay; cross-dressing; gender-bending
Tale of Genji, The 22–4, 26, 28, 292; *see also* literature
Tanizaki Jun'ichirō 373–4, 377; *see also* literature
Thailand 185
tōjisha narratives 222–3
totalitarianism 254–5
tradition 148, 251–2, 255, 261, 343; conservative ethos 382–3; rural 125–32
transgender individuals: cosplay 281; legal gender change 62–3, 88; representation 61–4; rights 67, 87, 215, 223, 282; *see also* inter-sex individuals; LGBTQ in Japan; *x-jendā*
translation 46, 62, 116, 291, 297, 317, 321, 332, 409
transnational flow 311, 317
3.11 triple disaster: aftermath 12, 139, 240, 248, 308, 313; activism 214, 244; disaster relief 393–4; institutional responses 132, 205, 343

ukiyoe 141–2, 186, 273, 322, 361; *see also* art
ūman ribu 32, 36, 214–215, 219, 315
university education 95, 100, 194, 215, 252, 254, 256
urbanization 70, 72, 125–7, 248, 373, 400; *see also* urban spaces
urban spaces 374, 376–8, 380, 403; *see also* urbanization

Victorian ideals 252–3, 265; *see also* Westernization
Vietnam 74, 191, 193, 195; *see also* minorities
violence 243, 296, 334; against women 13, 204, 216, 236, 243, 295, 312; depictions 295, 354, 363–6; female violence 296; *kawaii* 327–8; self-directed 334; sex 294, 296, 354, 382; *see also* sexual assault; sexual harassment

war history 13, 73, 181, 216, 326, 346, 396; *see also* comfort women; Imperial Japan; soldiers

Index

weaponry 262–4, 391–5
Westernization 126; influence 252–4, 375–6, 388
womanhood 200, 234–5, 334, 351–2, 383–5; *see also* adulthood; manhood
womenomics 109, 157, 160, 165, 169
women's liberation movement 32, 36, 214–215, 219, 315; *see also* activism; feminism
woodblock prints 141–2, 186, 273, 322, 361
workers' rights 158–61, 163–5, 175, 182, 211–13, 215, 401
work-life balance 51, 101, 160, 174, 273, 276

x-gender *see x-jendā*
x-jendā 61, 63–67, 215, 409, 415; *see also* LGBTQ in Japan; transgender individuals

yakuza films 382–3, 385–6, 389; *see also* film
yōkai 135, 141–3; *see also* folk culture; folklore
Yoko Ono 303–4
Yoshimoto Banana 293, 311–12, 356; *see also* girl; *shōjo*
Yoshiwara district 179–80; *see also* sex work
youthhood 270–1, 273–6, 294–5, 317, 322; desires 312, 315; girlhood 280, 351–7; *see also* boy; girl